PLATO AND THE CREATION
OF THE HEBREW BIBLE

Plato and the Creation of the Hebrew Bible for the first time compares the ancient law collections of the Ancient Near East, the Greeks and the Pentateuch to determine the legal antecedents for the biblical laws. Following his 2006 work, *Berossus and Genesis, Manetho and Exodus*, Gmirkin takes up his theory that the Pentateuch was written around 270 BCE using Greek sources found at the Great Library of Alexandria and applies this to an examination of the biblical law codes.

A striking number of legal parallels are found between the Pentateuch and Athenian laws, specifically with those found in Plato's *Laws* of ca. 350 BCE. Constitutional features in biblical law, Athenian law and Plato's *Laws* also contain close correspondences. Several genres of biblical law, including the Decalogue, are shown to have striking parallels to Greek legal collections, and the synthesis of narrative and legal content is shown to be compatible with Greek literature. This evidence points to direct influence of Greek writings, especially Plato's *Laws,* on the biblical legal tradition. Finally, it is argued that the creation of the Hebrew Bible took place according to the program found in Plato's *Laws* for creating a legally authorized national ethical literature, reinforcing the importance of this specific Greek text to the authors of the Torah and Hebrew Bible in the early Hellenistic Era.

This study offers a fascinating analysis of the background to the Pentateuch and will be of interest not only to biblical scholars but also to students of Plato, ancient law and Hellenistic literary traditions.

Russell E. Gmirkin is a writer, researcher, and Dead Sea Scrolls scholar living in Portland, Oregon. He is the author of *Berossus and Genesis, Manetho and Exodus: Hellenistic Histories and the Date of the Pentateuch* (2006).

COPENHAGEN INTERNATIONAL SEMINAR

General Editors: Ingrid Hjelm and Thomas L. Thompson
both at the University of Copenhagen

Editors: Niels Peter Lemche and Mogens Müller,
both at the University of Copenhagen

Language Revision Editor: James West at the Quartz
Hill School of Theology

Available:

REPRESENTING ZION
Frederik Poulsen

MYTHS OF EXILE
Edited by Anne Katrine De Hemmer Gudme and Ingrid Hjelm

REWRITING PETER AS AN INTERTEXTUAL
CHARACTER IN THE CANONICAL GOSPELS
Finn Damgaard

SYRIA-PALESTINE IN THE LATE BRONZE AGE
Emanuel Pfoh

BIBLICAL INTERPRETATION BEYOND HISTORICITY
Edited by Ingrid Hjelm and Thomas L. Thompson

HISTORY, ARCHAEOLOGY AND THE BIBLE
FORTY YEARS AFTER "HISTORICITY"
Edited by Ingrid Hjelm and Thomas L. Thompson

Forthcoming:

THE JUDAEO-KARAITE RECEPTION
OF THE HEBREW BIBLE
Joshua A. Sabih

PLATO AND THE CREATION OF THE HEBREW BIBLE

Russell E. Gmirkin

Routledge
Taylor & Francis Group

LONDON AND NEW YORK

First published 2017
by Routledge

2 Park Square, Milton Park, Abingdon, Oxfordshire OX14 4RN
52 Vanderbilt Avenue, New York, NY 10017

Routledge is an imprint of the Taylor & Francis Group, an informa business

First issued in paperback 2019

British Library Cataloguing-in-Publication Data
A catalogue record for this book is available from the British Library

Library of Congress Cataloging-in-Publication Data
Names: Gmirkin, Russell E., 1954– author.
Title: Plato and the Creation of the Hebrew Bible / Russell E. Gmirkin.
Description: First edition. | New York : Routledge, [2016] | "2016 | Series: Copenhagen international seminar | Includes bibliographical references and index.
Identifiers: LCCN 2016002737 | ISBN 9781138684980 (hardback : alk. paper) | ISBN 9781315543581 (ebook)
Subjects: LCSH: Middle Eastern literature—Relation to the Old Testament. | Bible. Old Testament—Comparative studies. | Bible. Old Testament—Criticism, interpretation, etc. | Plato. | Philosophy and religion.
Classification: LCC BS1184 .G55 2016 | DDC 221.6—dc23
LC record available at http://lccn.loc.gov/2016002737

ISBN: 978-1-138-68498-0 (hbk)
ISBN: 978-0-367-87836-8 (pbk)

Typeset in Times New Roman
by Apex CoVantage, LLC

CONTENTS

ACKNOWLEDGMENTS

Many thanks to all those who helped at every stage in the writing of this book: to Thomas L. Thompson, who suggested that I look into the biblical parallels with Plato and other Greek writers cataloged by Philippe Wajdenbaum; to Joann Patty of the Beaverton Public Library for chasing down my never-ending interlibrary loan requests for exotic sources not found in Portland university holdings during the investigative phase; to my lovely wife Carolyn Tracy, the brilliant daughter of local detective Edward "Skip" Tracy, for her many penetrating insights into Plato's dark psychology; to both Carolyn and my son Michael for encouragement during the intensive research and writing phases; to all the friendly employees of Starbucks for allowing me to write major portions of this book in a pleasant and highly caffeinated environment; to both Greg Doudna and Philippe Wajdenbaum for their valuable critical insights and editorial suggestions during the proofing of this manuscript; to both Greg Doudna and Daniel Samson for convincing me of the need to disseminate the results of my research outside of academia proper and laying out strategies to do so; and once again to my editor, Thomas L. Thompson, for accepting this long-awaited study as part of the Copenhagen International Series and for helping to streamline the manuscript with his keen editorial suggestions, bringing the project full circle.

ABBREVIATIONS

AB	Anchor Bible
AJA	*American Journal of Archaeology*
AJP	*American Journal of Philology*
*ANET*³	*Ancient Near Eastern Texts Relating to the Old Testament*. Edited by James Bennett Pritchard. 3rd ed. Princeton, NJ: Princeton University Press, 1969.
ANF	Ante-Nicene Fathers
AOAT	*Alter Orient und Altes Testament*
ARAB	*Ancient Records of Assyria and Babylonia*. D. Luckenbill. 2 vols. Chicago: University of Chicago Press.
ASORB	American Schools of Oriental Research Books
BA	*Biblical Archaeologist*
BASOR	*Bulletin of the American Schools of Oriental Society*
BZAW	*Beihefte zur Zeitschrift für die alttestamentliche Wissenschaft*
ca.	*circa*
CQ	*Classical Quarterly*
FGrH	Felix Jacoby, *Fragmente der Griechischen Historiker*. 15 vols. Berlin: Wiedmannsche Buchhandlung, 1923–1969.
GR	*Greece and Rome*
GRBS	*Greek, Roman and Byzantine Studies*
Historia	*Historia: Zeitschrift für Alte Geschichte*
HL	Hittite Laws
HSCP	*Harvard Studies in Classical Philology*
HTR	*Harvard Theological Review*
HUCA	*Hebrew Union College Annual*
IEJ	*Israel Exploration Journal*
JAOS	*Journal of the American Oriental Society*
JBL	*Journal of Biblical Literature*
JCS	*Journal of Cuneiform Studies*
JEA	*Journal of Egyptian Archaeology*
JHS	*Journal of Hellenic Studies*
JNES	*Journal of Near Eastern Studies*

JQR	*Jewish Quarterly Review*
JSOTSup	*Journal for the Study of the Old Testament,* Supplement Series
JTS	*Journal of Theological Studies*
LCL	Loeb Classic Library
LE	Laws of Eshnunna
LH	Laws of Hammurabi
LL	Laws of Lipit-Ishtar
LNB	Neo-Babylonian Laws
LOx	Laws about Rented Oxen
LU	Laws of Ur-Nammu
LX	Laws of X
MAL	Middle Assyrian Laws
MAPD	Middle Assyrian Palace Decrees
NRSV	New Revised Standard Version
OTP	*The Old Testament Pseudepigrapha.* Edited by J. Charlesworth. 2 vols. New York: Doubleday, 1983.
PAAJR	*Proceedings of the American Academy for Jewish Research*
SAA	State Archives of Assyria
SBL	Society of Biblical Literature
SBLDS	SBL Dissertation Series
SBLSymp	SBL Symposium Series
SJOT	*Scandinavian Journal of the Old Testament*
SLEx	Sumerian Laws Exercise Tablet
SLHF	Sumerian Laws Handbook of Forms
ST	*Studia Theologica*
TAD	*Textbook of Aramaic Documents from Ancient Egypt: Newly Copied, Edited and Translated into Hebrew and English.* Edited by B. Porten and A. Yardeni. 4 vols. (A–D). Jerusalem: Hebrew University, 1986–1999.
TAPA	*Transactions of the American Philological Association*
TAPhA	*Transactions and Proceedings of the American Philological Association*
TAPhS	*Transactions of the American Philosophical Society*
VT	*Vetus Testamentum*
VTE	Vassal Treaty of Esarhaddon
VTSup	*Vetus Testamentum,* Supplement Series
WAWSBL	Writings from the Ancient World
ZA	*Zeitschrift für Assyriologie*
ZAW	*Zeitschrift für die Alttestamentliche Wissenschaft*

1

INTRODUCTION

This book is a sequel to *Berossus and Genesis, Manetho and Exodus: Hellenistic Histories and the Date of the Pentateuch,* in which literary source-critical methods were brought to bear on the timeworn questions of date, provenance and authorship of the Pentateuch (Gmirkin 2006). I there argued an extensive use of the Babylonian historian Berossus (278 BCE) by the authors of Gen. 1–11 and the use of the Egyptian historian Manetho (ca. 285–280 BCE) by the authors of the Exodus story. Using this and similar data, I inferred that the Pentateuch was written ca. 270 BCE,[1] drawing on a variety of sources written in Greek and housed in the Great Library of Alexandria. This in turn led to the conclusion that the authors of the Pentateuch were the same group of seventy aristocratic, Greek-educated Jewish scholars that ancient tradition credited with having translated the Pentateuch into Greek at Alexandria at almost exactly the same time (ca. 273–269 BCE). *Berossus and Genesis* thus laid out a methodological and historical framework in which the Pentateuch could be understood as an early Hellenistic Era composition that drew on earlier sources written in Greek.

The current study deals with similar themes, considering the possibility that both the Pentateuch and the Hebrew Bible as a whole drew on the writings of Plato found at the Great Library of Alexandria. This hypothesis is explored via two lines of argument: that the Pentateuch's law collections, despite containing a few laws of Ancient Near Eastern origin, are in large part based on Athenian law and on Plato's *Laws* (Chapters 2–5), and that the Hebrew Bible as a literary collection was based on instructions found in Plato's *Laws* for creating a national literature (Chapter 6).

1. Greek comparative studies

External evidence does not exclude either a Hellenistic Era date or substantial Greek influence on the biblical text. This indicates that comparative studies with biblical literature may legitimately include the Greek world and that there is no compelling reason to exclude either Hellenistic Era cultural features or literature from such studies.

1

Various studies from the early twentieth century to the present explored evidence for ancient cultural contacts between the Greek world and Ancient Near East, including the Jews. The existence of some sort of cultural interchange between east and west in the Greek Archaic Era or earlier seems beyond dispute. The penetration of Near Eastern culture in the Greek world is demonstrated through eastern material remains found in Mediterranean archaeological sites,[2] similar institutions and customs[3] and numerous eastern traditions that were adopted in Greek mythology and literature.[4] Phoenician trade in the west is thought to have been a key mechanism by which eastern wares and ideas spread across the Mediterranean.[5] Similarly, there is archaeological evidence for the penetration of Greek material culture into the east in sites along the Levantine coast from Cilicia to the Egyptian delta from the Mycenaean era to the fourth centuries BCE, and direct Greek contacts with traders living at Dor, Akko and other coastal locations may have provided opportunity for the exposure of Phoenicians and others to Greek influences.[6] Literary, inscriptional and archaeological evidence suggests Greek mercenaries were employed in Cilicia, Ashdod, Egypt and in the Judean Negev in pre-Hellenistic times.[7] Literary and inscriptional sources also document military clashes and diplomatic contacts between Greeks and Persians leading up to Alexander's conquests.[8] However, there is little evidence that these contacts led to the flow of Greek ideas into the Ancient Near East. After the conquests of Alexander the Great, however, Greek influences in the east are well documented and uncontroversial.

Contacts between Greek and biblical laws have been commented on from Graeco-Roman antiquity to modern times.[9] Such legal parallels have raised questions regarding the direction of influence, the relative chronology of Greek and biblical legislation and the circumstances under which Greek and Jewish cultural exchanges could have taken place (Gmirkin 2014: 56–60). In classical antiquity, such points of comparison were explained as evidence of Greek plagiarism of Mosaic law,[10] a theory still advocated in some circles as late as the mid-nineteenth century (see Gmirkin 2014: 57 and literature cited there). This model became increasingly difficult to reconcile with chronological schemes proposed under higher criticism, in which the emergence of biblical law took place contemporary with similar developments in Archaic and Classical Greece, not centuries earlier as in a pre-critical reading of the biblical text. Twentieth-century comparisons between Greek and biblical laws no longer suggested direct Greek exposure to biblical literature, a simplistic model that failed to meet modern critical standards. Finding a satisfactory alternative explanation for Greek and biblical legal parallels posed a considerable ongoing problem.

Greek comparative studies, once a favorite topic of research among biblical scholars versed in Classical literature, were largely eclipsed in the early twentieth century in favor of Ancient Near Eastern literary and cultural comparisons, where the relative chronological priority of biblical and extra-biblical traditions was easily established. In Ancient Near Eastern comparative studies in the aftermath of the 1902 publication of the Hammurabi Law Code, biblical influence from antecedent cultures and legal traditions were fully acknowledged. Theories that posited Ancient Near Eastern influence on the biblical law collections posed no chronological difficulties, because the Old Babylonian collections such as LE and LH predated the biblical monarchy and the first biblical law codes by hundreds of years. Theories regarding possible Greek influence on the biblical law collections were more problematic under higher criticism, because comparable Greek legislation was a phenomenon of the seventh to the fourth centuries BCE, contemporary with or later than the biblical laws codes under either the older documentary theories of higher criticism or recent redaction critical models.

Nevertheless, modern scholars of ancient legal systems kept noting contacts between Greek and biblical legal traditions. The existence of shared Greek and Jewish legal traditions was difficult to accommodate under a view in which the biblical law collections were believed to have been created prior to the arrival of the Greeks in the east. Points of comparison between Greek and Jewish historiography, prophetism and other cultural and literary institutions were similarly problematic. As a result, various strategies were employed to explain Greek legal and literary features in biblical literature in pre-Hellenistic times. Purely typological parallels came under increasing disparagement in comparative studies, and properly so.[11] Instead, comparative studies came to be viewed as methodologically valid only if the cultures or literatures being compared were within the same "historical stream," that is, if the societies under comparison were in geographical proximity and sufficiently close in time to allow for a direct or mediated flow of ideas.[12] A major difficulty in applying this approach to Greek comparative studies was that possible influences were artificially restricted to the historical period when Samaria and Judah were kingdoms or provinces within the Ancient Near East, prior to Alexander's conquests of the east and the first major contacts between Greeks and Jews.[13]

The problem of apparent Greek legal and literary influences on biblical writings prior to arrival of the Greeks in the east met with a variety of explanations.[14] One solution commonly posed by authors of comparative studies was to posit an intermediary group who communicated Greek ideas to the east. Such proposals included Greek and Cretan troops allegedly employed by the biblical King David (Weinfeld 1993),[15] Greek mercenaries stationed in the Negev during the late Judean monarchy (West 1997: 617, among other modes of transmission), Phoenicians (Van Seters 1983: 53–4; Israel was characterized as an "inland Phoenician culture" in Brown 1995, 2000, 2001) or Philistines (Garbini 1988: 85–6). Direct contacts between the educated elites of the Greek and Jewish worlds in archaic times prior to the conquests of Alexander the Great, or the conveyance of Greek writings to Jewish readers and thinkers, even by way of intermediaries, has never been seriously proposed. The idea that complex legal notions and sophisticated literary traditions were communicated from the Greek world into the hinterlands of Judah or Samaria[16] by way of mercenaries stationed in desert border fortresses or merchants engaged in trading Greek pottery and other wares also appears unlikely.[17] It is difficult to visualize these hypothetical intermediaries serving as a channel for the required flow of ideas in the historical stream.

An alternative method for accommodating Greek influences on biblical literature in archaic times was proposed by the great legal scholar Raymond Westbrook. Taking for granted that some communication between east and west must have anciently existed, based on inferences from similar laws found among the Greeks, Romans, Hittites, Babylonians, Assyrians and in biblical legal writings, Westbrook hypothesized a shared Eastern Mediterranean legal culture that embraced all these legal traditions.[18] In effect, Westbrook claimed that Archaic and Classical Greece and the Ancient Near East were within the same historical stream, despite the lack of geographical proximity and without specifying a mechanism for the communication of ideas. Although Westbrook's idea of a shared legal culture met with a variety of criticisms by his contemporaries, it served to legitimize ongoing research into shared legal traditions and has been adopted in recent years by several biblical researchers engaged in productive comparative studies using Greek legal materials (Hagedorn 2004: 43–53, 60–2; Knoppers and Harvey 2007: 105–41). A major methodological flaw in Westbrook's theory is that to a significant degree it rested on shared Greek and biblical legal traditions that were assumed, but not proven, to have existed deep in archaic times, but which may in fact have first appeared in biblical literature of the Hellenistic Era, a possibility never envisioned by Westbrook. This circularity in Westbrook's reasoning both relied upon and was used to support a dating of biblical legal tradition contemporary with Archaic and Classical Greece. Although an intersection of Greek and biblical legislation can scarcely be doubted today, it may be questioned whether the mechanism for this shared legal tradition was the common East Mediterranean culture hypothesized by Westbrook and whether the communication of Greek legal values, institutions and laws to the biblical authors took place prior to Alexander's conquests and the Hellenization of the east as Westbrook assumed.

2. The current volume

The first reliable external evidence for the composition of the Pentateuch is the Septuagint translation at Alexandria ca. 270 BCE (Gmirkin 2006: 34–88; Gmirkin 2014), well into the Hellenistic Era. The current volume therefore adopts the position that comparative methods used to illuminate the biblical text should include Greek literature and cultural institutions from the Classical and early Hellenistic Eras alongside those of the Ancient Near East. In Chapters 2–5, a systematic comparison will be made among biblical, Greek and Ancient Near Eastern legal traditions.[19] Striking parallels will be shown to exist between biblical and Greek constitutional and social institutions (Chapter 2), laws (Chapter 3), law collections (Chapter 4) and legal narratives (Chapter 5) that are for the most part absent from Ancient Near Eastern legal tradition. Many of these points of comparison show a special relationship between biblical and Athenian laws and institutions as well as those described in Plato's *Laws*. Such parallels are exceedingly difficult to explain under the hypothesis that biblical legal traditions developed in the Persian Era or earlier, when direct Athenian influence on Jewish legal writings can be ruled out, even under the theory of an Eastern Mediterranean cultural sphere. However, Jewish access to the legal collections found in the Great Library of Alexandria provides a direct mechanism whereby the biblical authors could have become familiar with both Athenian laws and with Plato's *Laws*. In Chapter 6, it is further argued that the Hebrew Bible as a whole was created in the third century BCE under the influence of Plato's *Laws,* which featured instructions for creating a national library of approved texts with ethical content (§§ 1–2), and that the Jewish theocracy historically established in the early Hellenistic Era was directly patterned on the novel form of government under divine laws also laid out in Plato's *Laws* (§§ 4–6). A picture emerges in which Plato's *Laws,* which described how to establish a new government with its constitution, laws and other institutions, had a decisive influence on the refounding of the Jewish nation and the creation of its national literature ca. 270 BCE.

Notes

1 More accurately, the Pentateuchal dating arguments from *Berossus and Genesis* point to a definite date of 278–269 BCE and a likely date of 273–272 BCE. See chart at Gmirkin 2006: 245. For convenience of reference, this book will abbreviate the date of composition to ca. 270 BCE.

2 See especially Burkert 1992; cf. Astour 1967: 323–57.

3 Points of commonality include similar conceptions of divine kingship, common elements in oaths and treaties and common sacrificial and divinatory practices. See Burkert 1992: 41–87; West 1997, especially 14–23, 41–2; Launderville 2003.

4 See discussions in the sources from the preceding footnote. Specialized discussions of eastern influences on Hesiod and Homer include Gordon 1955: 43–108; Walcot 1966; Penglase 1994; Morris 1997; Louden 2011.

5 West 1997: 606–24. Greek contacts with eastern craftsmen located in Crete played a hypothesized role in the spread of Ancient Near Eastern legal traditions to the Greeks and Romans in Mühl 1933. Evidence Mühl cited for his theory of early legal contacts between east and west included the existence of written law collections in Greece and Rome; the existence of an early Roman law of *lex talionis* that later sources attributed to either Zaleucus of Locri in ca. 660 BCE (Demosthenes, *Against Timocrates* 140–1) or Charondas of Catana in ca. 675 BCE (Diodorus Siculus, *Library* 12.17.4–5); and certain other laws shared by Greeks, Romans and the biblical authors. For a critique of Mühl's theories, and especially of the hypothesized role of Cretan craftsmen in propagating written law collections to the Greek world, see Gagarin 1986: 62.

6 See Waldbaum 1997; Niemeier 2001. Evidence for a Greek settlement at Al Mina in northern Syria is no longer considered supported by archaeological evidence. Unambiguous Greek remains in Syria appear to be limited to pottery: Greek temples (except perhaps at Tall Sukas) or other architectural remains or Greek burial sites have not been discovered. Greek lettering on pottery appears the best evidence for Greek presence in the Levant. The establishment of a Greek trading post at Naucratis in the Egyptian delta in ca. 620 BCE is well known from historical sources.

7 Niemeier 2001: 16–24. See Herodotus, *Histories* 2.152–54; Diodorus Siculus, *Library* 1.66–67 for the employment of Carian and Ionian mercenaries by Psammetichus I.

8　See Kuhrt 2007: 1–417 for Greek political and military contacts with the Persians. In Kuhrt's exhaustive survey of the primary sources, the lack of detectable Greek influences on Persian literature, culture or notions of legislation is striking.

9　Legal parallels were noted in passing in Josephus, Apion 2.151–286 and systematically at Eusebius, *Preparation for the Gospel* 12.35–47.

10　Jewish and Christian claims for the priority of Moses and biblical literature were discussed in Droge 1989. Such claims were made by the Jewish writers Eupolemus, Aristobulus, Philo and Josephus; the Church Fathers Justin Martyr, Tatian, Clement of Alexandria, Origen, Eusebius and Augustine; and "pagan" authors such as Numenius of Apamea.

11　The iconic example of broad, typological comparisons between cultures with no geographical or historical contact was Frazer 1911–15. Such erudite but uncritical comparative studies came under criticism in various influential discussions on comparative methodology, including Sandmel 1962; Malul 1990; Talmon 1991. Noth's theory of an Israelite amphictyonic league during the Judges period (Noth 1966) was eventually rejected, among other reasons, for its unsound typological comparisons with much later Greek institutions.

12　Malul 1990: 13–18, 89–91, 99–101; Talmon 1991: 386. Malul contrasted the "historical comparative approach," in which an effort is made to demonstrate a shared historical stream and inter-cultural flow of ideas, with the "typological comparative approach," which is satisfied with cataloging parallels.

13　This bias is illustrated in Malul 1990: 19–85, where an Ancient Near Eastern background to biblical laws was assumed throughout.

14　See Kuhn 1996: 77–91, on coping strategies employed by those who have inherited a research paradigm to eliminate apparent contradictions posed by conflicting or anomalous data.

15　Weinfeld 1993: 1–2 argued that the genre of foundation story independently arose among the Greeks and Israelites because both were "based on colonization and founding of new sites," unlike the "autochthonous cultures" of the great Ancient Near Eastern empires, where this genre was entirely unknown. Weinfeld dubiously sought to bolster this model by arguing for a historical basis for the Exodus and Conquest traditions (1993: 41–51). Weinfeld believed that the foundation stories "crystallized in the Davidic period, when there were contacts with elements originating in the Greek sphere, such as Krethi and Plethi" (1993: 2). This thesis appears to involve anachronisms, because the Greek colonization movement and the genre of foundation story are to be dated in the eighth century BCE (Malkin 1987: 262–6). A better explanation for the literary parallels is the direct influence of Greek literature on the formation of the biblical text in the Hellenistic period.

16　Josephus, seeking to explain the fact that Greek literature took no notice of the Jews and Jewish literature took no notice of the Greeks, noted that the Greeks knew mainly about coastal people with whom they had trade contacts, whereas the ancestral lands of the Jews were located inland from the sea and isolated from international commerce (Apion 1.60–68). His observations still appear valid and relevant.

17　A key problem unaddressed in proposals of Phoenician or Philistine intermediaries between Greeks and Jews is that neither group produced literature or legal traditions of the type they are hypothesized to have communicated to the Jews. Nor are such traditions associated with Greek soldiers or merchants anciently residing in the east. The social networks in which legal traditions were discussed and shared in the Greek world are known to have consisted of highly educated, ruling class elites, as documented in Classical Greek sources, not tradesmen or military. Osborne (2009) argued from archaeological data that neither the creation of new social networks nor a dissemination of Greek culture, practices and learning accompanied the trade in Greek pottery in the Mediterranean world.

18 Westbrook's arguments appeared in a series of articles conveniently assembled in Wells and Magdalene 2009. In the present volume, I will cite Westbrook's articles with the original titles, but with page numbers taken from Wells and Magdalene 2009. Westbrook's theory was critiqued in Greengus 1994: 60–87.

19 Literary dependence of some Pentateuchal laws on Plato's *Laws* was first argued by Kupitz 1997. My own study of Plato's writings was largely stimulated by the impressive collection of biblical parallels assembled at Wajdenbaum 2011: 158–205. Biblical parallels to other Greek writers found in Kupitz 1997 and Wajdenbaum 2011 are often less convincing.

Bibliography

Astour, Michael C., *Hellenosemitica: An Ethnic and Cultural Study in West Semitic Impact on Mycenaean Greece*. Leiden: E. J. Brill, 1967.

Brown, John Pairman, *Israel and Hellas*. 3 vols. *BZAW* 231, 276, 299. Berlin: De Gruyter, 1995, 2000, 2001.

Burkert, Walter, *The Orientalizing Revolution: Near Eastern Influence on Greek Culture in the Early Archaic Age*. Revealing Antiquity 5. Cambridge: Harvard University Press, 1992.

Droge, Arthur J., *Homer or Moses?: Early Christian Interpretations of the History of Culture*. Hermeneutische Untersuchungen zur Theologie 26. Tübingen: Mohr, 1989.

Frazer, James, *The Golden Bough: A Study in Magic and Religion*. 12 vols. London: MacMillan, 1911–15.

Gagarin, Michael, *Early Greek Law*. Berkeley: University of California Press, 1986.

Garbini, Giovanni, *History and Ideology in Ancient Israel*. New York: Crossroad, 1988.

Gmirkin, Russell E., *Berossus and Genesis, Manetho and Exodus: Hellenistic Histories and the Date of the Pentateuch*. Library of the Hebrew Bible/Old Testament Studies 433. Copenhagen International Series 15. New York: T & T Clark, 2006.

———, "Greek Evidence for the Hebrew Bible." Pages 56–88 in Thomas L. Thompson and Philippe Wajdenbaum (eds.), *The Bible and Hellenism: Greek Influence on Jewish and Early Christian Literature*. Durham, UK: Acumen Publishing, 2014.

Gordon, Cyrus, "Homer and the Bible: The Origin and Character of East Mediterranean Literature," *HUCA* 26 (1955): 43–108.

Greengus, Samuel, "Some Issues Relating to the Comparability of Laws and the Coherence of the Legal Tradition." Pages 60–87 in Bernard M. Levinson (ed.), *Theory and Method in Biblical and Cuneiform Law*. JSOTSup 181. Sheffield: Sheffield Academic Press, 1994.

Hagedorn, Anselm C., *Between Moses and Plato: Individual and Society in Deuteronomy and Ancient Greek Law*. Göttingen: Vandenhoeck & Ruprecht, 2004.

Knoppers, Gary N. and Paul B. Harvey Jr., "The Pentateuch in Ancient Mediterranean Context: The Publication of Local Lawcodes." Pages 105–41 in Gary N. Knoppers and Bernard M. Levinson (eds.), *Pentateuch as Torah: New Models for Understanding Its Promulgation and Acceptance*. Winona Lake, IN: Eisenbrauns, 2007.

Kuhn, Thomas S., *The Structure of Scientific Revolutions*. Chicago: University of Chicago Press, 1996.

Kuhrt, Amelie, *The Persian Empire: A Corpus of Sources from the Achaemenid Period*. New York: Routledge, 2007.

Kupitz, Yaakov S., "La Bible est-elle un Plagiat?" *Science et Avenir* 86 (1997): 85–8.

Launderville, Dale Francis, *Piety and Politics: The Dynamics of Royal Authority in Homeric Greece, Biblical Israel, and Old Babylonian Mesopotamia.* Grand Rapids, MI: W.B. Eerdmans, 2003.

Louden, Bruce, *Homer's Odyssey and the Near East.* Cambridge: Cambridge University Press, 2011.

Malkin, Irad, *Religion and Colonization in Ancient Greece.* Leiden: E.J. Brill, 1987.

Malul, Meir, *The Comparative Method in Ancient Near Eastern and Biblical Legal Studies. AOAT* 227. Neukirchener: Verlag Butzon & Bercker Kevelaer, 1990.

Morris, I., "Homer and the Near East." Pages 599–623 in I. Morris and B. Powell (eds.), *A New Companion to Homer.* Leiden: Brill, 1997.

Mühl, Max, *Untersuchungen zue Altorientalischen und Althellischen Gesetzebung.* Leipzig: Dieterich'sche Verlagsbuchhandlung, 1933.

Niemeier, W.-D., "Archaic Greeks in the Orient: Textual and Archaeological Evidence," *BASOR* 322 (2001): 11–31.

Noth, Martin, *Das System der zwölf Stämme Israels.* Darmstadt: Wissenschaftliche Buchgesellschaft, 1966.

Osborne, Robin, "What Travelled with Greek Pottery?" Pages 83–93 in Irad Malkin, Christy Constantakopoulou and Katerina Panagopoulou (eds.), *Greek and Roman Networks in the Mediterranean.* London: Routledge, 2009.

Penglase, Charles, *Greek Myths and Mesopotamia, Parallels and Influences in the Homeric Hymns and Hesiod.* London: Routledge, 1994.

Sandmel, S., "Parallelomania," *JBL* 81 (1962): 1–13.

Talmon, Shemaryahu, "The 'Comparative Method' in Biblical Interpretation – Principles and Problems." Pages 381–419 in Frederick C. Greenspahn (ed.), *Essential Papers on Israel and the Ancient Near East.* New York: New York University, 1991.

Van Seters, John, *In Search of History: Historiography in the Ancient World and the Origins of Biblical History.* New Haven, CT: Yale University Press, 1983.

Wajdenbaum, Philippe, *Argonauts of the Desert: Structural Analysis of the Hebrew Bible.* London: Equinox Publishing, 2011.

Walcot, Peter, *Hesiod and the Near East.* Cardiff: University of Wales, 1966.

Waldbaum, J., "Greeks in the East or Greeks and the East? Problems in the Recognition and Definition of Presence," *BASOR* 305 (1997): 1–17.

Weinfeld, Moshe, *The Promise of the Land: The Inheritance of the Land of Canaan by the Israelites.* Berkeley: University of California Press, 1993.

Wells, Bruce and F. Rachel Magdalene (eds.), *Law from the Tigris to the Tiber: The Writings of Raymond Westbrook.* Winona Lake, IN: Eisenbrauns, 2009.

West, M.L., *The East Face of Helicon: West Asiatic Elements in Greek Poetry and Myth.* Oxford: Oxford University Press, 1997.

2

ATHENIAN AND PENTATEUCHAL LEGAL INSTITUTIONS

The *ktisis* or foundation story was one of the most popular literary genres among the ancient Greeks. In a typical Greek foundation story, negative circumstances led to sending forth an expedition under the divinely sanctioned leadership of a founder-figure who led his forces to establish a colony in a new land. The founder-figure acted as commander, religious guide and lawgiver, conquering territory for settlement, apportioning land, setting up altars and writing a constitution and laws for the infant nation. The biblical story about the Israelite Exodus and wilderness Sojourn under the leadership of Moses and the Conquest under his successor Joshua closely conforms to this Greek literary genre.[1] The presentation of Mosaic law codes within a recognizably Greek narrative framework raises the possibility that the formulation of the law codes themselves may display influences from Greek legal genres and content.

The notion of the Pentateuch as having been composed in the early Hellenistic Era is suggested by the existence of constitutional elements within the Pentateuch. Certainly many authors in Hellenistic and Roman antiquity viewed the Torah as the authoritative constitutional document of the Jews. They included ancient Jewish writers[2] and the Church Fathers[3] as well as Ptolemaic,[4] Seleucid,[5] Jewish[6] and Roman[7] regimes that all interpreted the Torah as the foundational document that recorded the ancestral laws and constitution of the Jews. This ancient interpretation of the Torah as possessing constitutional elements is supported by biblical scholarship of recent decades that also detects constitutional content in the Pentateuch, especially in Deuteronomy.[8]

The last ten years have seen several studies that have illuminated Deuteronomistic constitutional elements by comparison with Greek legal materials and institutions. Such studies as a rule have been predicated on a hypothetical shared East Mediterranean culture in a pre-Hellenistic context rather than contemplating the possibility of direct Jewish knowledge of Greek – and especially Athenian – legal institutions (e.g. Hagedorn 2004: 43–53, 60–2; Knoppers and Harvey 2007: 105–6, 139–41). Although no literary or historical evidence exists to support direct diplomatic or cultural contacts between Athens and Judea in pre-Roman times, the extensive corpus of Greek legal writings at the Great Library of Alexandria in the early Hellenistic Era raises the possibility that Jewish knowledge of Athenian legal institutions was mediated by Jewish access to Greek legal writings.

Direct Greek influences on biblical legal content can be tested only by a systematic comparative study of Greek and Jewish constitutional legal content and institutions. The current chapter explores parallels between Pentateuchal legal institutions and those found in the Greek world, especially in Greek constitutional literature. The next chapter explores parallels between Pentateuchal, Ancient Near Eastern and Greek laws, including those found in Plato's *Nomoi* or *Laws* of ca. 350 BCE.

1. Greek constitutions and the Pentateuch

The constitution, an important Greek legal innovation essential for citizen self-rule, defined the arrangement of offices in the government, especially the highest offices, outlining their duties and the manner in which the officials were to be appointed.[9] The framing of a constitution was considered distinct from the enacting of legislation:[10] the constitution *(politeia)* defined the form of government,[11] whereas laws *(nomoi, thesmoi)* defined the rights, responsibilities and rules of conduct for both magistrates and for those governed.[12] Edicts or decrees *(psephemata)* were a separate category of enactment that addressed the day-to-day business of government.[13]

The importance of constitutional matters in Greek life is summed up by famous statements by the Athenian orator Isocrates ("the constitution is the soul of the state" [Isocrates, *Areopagitus* 14; Isocrates, *Panathenaicus* 138]) and the philosopher Aristotle ("the constitution *is* the state" [Aristotle, *Politics* 3.1279a]). Constitutions could and did define a variety of types of government found in the Greek world, which included not only the six basic forms of government listed by Aristotle (monarchy, tyranny, aristocracy, oligarchy, the *polis* or constitutional city-state and democracy), but also other forms of "mixed constitutions" that included elements from two or more of these types.[14]

An idea of what the Greeks understood by the term constitution and of the topics dealt with under Hellenistic constitutional law may be gleaned by such works as Aristotle's *Politics,* which dealt with political science; Aristotle's *Athenian Constitution,* which dealt with the history of constitutional change at Athens and the features of the Athenian constitution in Aristotle's time;[15] Plato's *Republic,* which outlined Plato's ideal state; Plato's *Laws (Nomoi),* which dealt with Plato's ideas of how to frame an ideal constitution and laws;[16] Xenophon's *Lacedemonian Constitution* and Pseudo-Xenophon's *Athenian Constitution;*[17] fragments of other ancient books on constitutions that have survived in later quotations;[18] and excerpts from various Greek constitutions quoted by Athenian orators[19] or preserved on surviving inscriptions (Meiggs and Lewis 1969; Rhodes and Osborne 2003). Typical elements that appeared in ancient Greek constitutions or related topics discussed in constitutional literary sources included the following (with Athenian institutes discussed in the footnotes):

- The basic form of government, whether monarchy, tyranny, aristocracy, oligarchy, constitutional democracy or pure democracy.[20]
- The geographical boundaries of the nation.[21]
- Requirements for citizenship,[22] procedures for the enrollment of citizens[23] and the legal status of foreigners, slaves and other non-citizens.[24]
- Citizen rights and responsibilities, including military service (Aristotle, *Athenian Constitution* 42.2–5) and participation in judicial and democratic assemblies (Aristotle, *Athenian Constitution* 7.3; 19.1; 41.2).
- Definition of special deliberative bodies entrusted with legislative, judicial and executive functions.[25]
- Magistrates:[26] their qualifications, procedures for appointment, administrative duties and mechanisms for their oversight and review.[27]
- Judicial structures and procedures.[28]
- Military organization (Aristotle, *Athenian Constitution* 4.2; 22.2; 31.2–3; 45; 61.1–7; 62.3; Plato, *Laws* 6.755b-756b), education and military training (Aristotle, *Athenian Constitution* 42.2–4; Plato, *Laws* 7.804c-e).
- Religious matters, including the appointment of religious personnel, the supervision of temple precincts, and oversight of religious festivals (Aristotle, *Athenian Constitution* 54.6–8 [which listed commissioners of sacrifices and national festivals]; Plato, *Laws* 8.828a-829c).

A constitutional definition of legal institutions and their functioning was essential to the citizen self-rule of the *polis,* in which the citizens themselves held the reins of government. It was for this reason that the constitution arose as a distinct genre among the Greeks, but was unknown in the Ancient Near East.[29] Under the absolute rule that characterized both the great empires and the lesser city-states of the Ancient Near East, the exercise of governmental power did not require a formal constitution, because the state was essentially an extension of the power of the king and those under his command. Aristotle correctly understood the characteristic form of government among the "barbarians" (non-Greeks) of the east to be the monarchy, in which the king ruled subject peoples who did not directly participate or own a share in their government (Aristotle, *Politics* 3.1285a). A similar negative view of government in the Ancient Near East was seen at Deut. 17.14 and 1 Sam. 8.5, 19–20; 10.19, where the Israelites expressed a desire to be ruled by a king "like the nations around us."[30] In 1 Samuel, the change of government to monarchy patterned on the neighboring kingdoms was interpreted as a full rebellion against Yahweh (1 Sam. 8.7–9; 10.18–19) that would result in a new enslavement of Israel to its own kings (1 Sam. 8.10–18; cf. 10.18–19), something that soon took place under Solomon (1 Kgs 12.1–14). According to Aristotle, the barbarian peoples of the east were by nature servile, and therefore required a king to both rule and take care of them, whereas in 1 Samuel the predicted enslavement under the monarchy was a result of the Israelites having chosen that form of government: other than the reversal of the direction of cause and effect, the biblical and Aristotelian views of the enslaved state of the population under the kings of the east was the same.[31]

Both the anti-slavery traditions found throughout Exodus–Deuteronomy and the anti-monarchic tradition found in Deuteronomy, 1 Samuel and 1 Kings constitute a rejection of the Ancient Near Eastern institution of kingship, in which society was divided into the tribute-imposing ruling class and tribute-bearing subjects.[32] Deuteronomy–Judges instead envisioned a different, more egalitarian form of government in which the Israelites would rule themselves under a system of national assemblies, councils of elders and magistrates with civil and military powers (as circumstances required), along with priests and prophets to guide them in sacred matters. This biblical concern over choosing the proper form of government, unprecedented in texts from the Ancient Near East, finds its closest parallel in the Greek world, where constitutional issues were debated and discussed in both political and philosophical circles. Explicit constitutional content has been detected by biblical critics in the constitutional sub-document Deut. 16.18–18.22, which detailed the selection and responsibilities of the magistrates who would rule Israel in the Promised Land.[33] Some scholars have argued for the existence of a larger constitutional program to be found in Deuteronomy as a whole.[34] Constitutional content is sometimes attributed to other Pentateuchal legal materials, notably those associated with the Sinai theophany of Ex. 19–24.[35] Many topics characteristic of Greek constitutions and constitutional literature but absent from Ancient Near Eastern law collections appear prominently in Pentateuchal law codes and narratives with legal content:

- National and tribal geographical boundaries.
- Requirements for citizenship, procedures for the enrollment of citizens and the legal status of foreigners, slaves and other non-citizens.
- Citizen rights and responsibilities, including military service and participation in judicial and democratic assemblies.
- Definition of special deliberative bodies entrusted with legislative, judicial and executive functions.
- Magistrates: their qualifications, procedures for appointment, administrative duties and mechanisms for their oversight and review.
- Judicial structures and procedures.[36]
- Military organization, including conscription and command structure.
- Religious matters, including the appointment of religious personnel, the supervision of temple precincts and oversight of religious festivals.

These various topics, discussed in greater detail in the following sections, point to the constitutional concerns of Pentateuchal legal content. The overlap of Pentateuchal legal topics with Greek constitutional issues suggests the possibility that the Pentateuch's authors were acquainted with Greek literature on laws and constitutions. In light of this, the interpretation of the Mosaic law code as a national charter on a par with Greek constitutions as found in Josephus (cf. Rodgers 2008: 129–48) and other authors of antiquity cannot be dismissed as a late, anachronistic Hellenistic Era interpretation of earlier Ancient Near Eastern legal content, but may in fact be correct.[37]

A systematic comparison between Pentateuchal and Greek legal institutions, as carried out in the remainder of this chapter, suggests a specific acquaintance with the Athenian city-state. The following constitutional comparisons will take into account both actual Athenian legal institutions and the theoretical recommendations found in Plato's *Laws*, which discussed the imagined drafting of a constitution and laws for a new colony to be found in the Cretan district of Magnesia. Although the city-state envisioned in Plato's *Laws* was a philosophical and literary construct that contained various idiosyncratic features, it was largely based on Athenian institutions.[38] Significantly, many features of the Pentateuchal legal institutions conform more closely with the system described in Plato's *Laws* than with historical Athenian institutions, leading to the conclusion that the biblical authors were acquainted with this specific text of ca. 350 BCE, Plato's last work.

2. Citizenship and enrollment

True citizenship was a characteristically Greek notion that went beyond national or ethnic identity.[39] Unlike the Ancient Near East, where a sharp divide existed between the ruling and subject classes,[40] in Athens and most of the Greek world the citizenry owned a share in their own government and participated in it through public assemblies, jury duty and the elective process whereby they could choose their own magistrates from among the citizen body.[41] All members of the Athenian *polis* were expected to participate in its government: it was deemed shameful not to. As share-holders in the *polis*, Athenian citizens also actively participated in its defense through military service in the Athenian cavalry, hoplite army or navy, according to their assessed financial ability.

Full citizenship at Athens was restricted to adult males who were officially enrolled into the citizen registry at age twenty, when they also became subject to military duty.[42] As citizens they had the right to speak and vote at national assemblies, held four times a year, and to participate on juries. The lowest economic strata of Athenians – those too poor to possess their own armor – had once been excluded from Athenian political life (Aristotle, *Athenian Constitution* 4), but under Solon's constitutional reforms of ca. 594 BCE obtained citizenship rights, including rights to be admitted both to the Assembly and to juries.[43] Participation in the franchise was considered both an honor and an advantage, because citizens were accorded important legal rights, including that of land ownership. Disenfranchisement or exclusion from citizenship *(atimia)* was an extremely serious matter.[44]

Athenian citizenship was conferred on legitimate offspring. After the citizenship law of Perikles in 451/450 BCE, a requirement for citizenship was Athenian parentage on both sides, father and mother.[45] Subsequently it became illegal for an Athenian, man or woman, to marry a non-Athenian.[46] The question of whether bastard children of a man and his concubine were excluded from Athenian citizenship is a matter of continuing debate.[47]

Although full participation in Athenian political life was restricted to the males, both Athenian women and children possessed indirect citizen rights and legal protections. The protection of family members was the legal obligation of the *kurios* or head of household, namely the husband, father or (for widows and orphans) appointed male guardian. Lesser legal rights were also accorded to *metics,* the special class of resident foreigners – welcomed at Athens mainly as merchants and craftsmen[48] – who were subject to a special tax of twelve drachma per year for the privilege of living in Athens and who were also subject to military duty.[49] Strangers *(xenoi)* who arrived in Athens were expected within a certain number of days – probably a month – to find a sponsor,[50] enroll as a *metic* at the village of their residence and begin paying the *metoikos* or *metic*-tax.[51] As non-citizens, *metics* could not participate in the assembly or on juries, own land or fill priesthoods (Whitehead 1977: 69–70), but had recourse to a court in Athens dedicated to cases involving foreigners.[52] Slaves, who were mostly non-Greeks, were considered the property of their owners. As such they possessed no citizen rights, and few legal rights, mostly exercised through their owner. If freed, they did not thereby attain citizenship, but only the status of *metic*.[53]

Pentateuchal regulations regarding citizenship in Israel closely corresponded to the Athenian legal model. For both Greeks and Israelites, participation in the military was an important aspect of citizenship.[54] The children of Israel who constituted the citizen body of the Mosaic *polity* were described as an army in Pentateuchal narratives.[55] The book of Numbers treated at length the enrollment of the adult males into the army from all the tribes of Israel at age twenty and their assignment to military duties in the citizen army.[56] Like the citizens of Athens, the children of Israel appeared in a national assembly – the *edah* – and (once settled in the land) in lesser local assemblies that possessed judicial functions, as in the Athenian model. The children of Israel were also assigned the responsibility of appointing magistrates from among the citizen body to serve in various positions, including as judges and, strikingly, as king (Deut. 16.18–18.22, especially 17.5). As in Athens, land ownership was restricted to citizens,[57] and disenfranchisement or exclusion from citizenship was an extremely serious matter.[58]

The status of women, children and slaves in Israel was the same as in Athens. Under both biblical and Athenian political and legal systems, full participation was restricted to adult males. Women and children possessed citizen rights and legal protections through the male head of household or (at Athens) appointed guardian in the case of widows and orphans. Slaves were considered household property and possessed no citizen rights and few legal protections.

Although Athens had a reputation of *xenophilia* and the Jews of the later Hellenistic Era acquired an undeserved reputation of xenophobia, the legal status of foreigners was virtually identical under Athenian and biblical law. Both distinguished between the foreigner *(xenos, nokri)* – visitors not yet accorded resident status[59] – and the resident alien *(metoikos, ger)*.[60] As a class, the *gerim* or resident aliens closely corresponded to the *metics* of Athens. Like the *metics* of Athens, the resident aliens in Israel were presumed to reside in a specific village and perhaps to have a family as a sponsor.[61] The legal rights of both foreign visitors and resident aliens were protected in both biblical Israel and Athens.[62]

Citizen status of offspring was an issue common to Athenian and Pentateuchal legislation. Athenian law restricted citizenship to legitimate offspring of a wife: children engendered by concubines, slaves or mistresses were not considered heirs (unless adopted) or potential citizens. The citizenship law of Perikles in 451/450 BCE further stipulated that both father and mother must be Athenian citizens, denying legitimacy of marriage and offspring to a foreign mother, except as allowed in individual cases and by legislative decree.[63] Along similar lines, Deut. 23.2 legislated that the offspring of illegitimate unions could not be admitted into the assembly (that is, were denied citizenship status). Although Deut. 23.3–8 allowed for the possibility of Moabites and Ammonites being admitted into the assembly in the third generation – that is, the grandchildren of the offspring of a marriage between an Israelite man and a Moabite or an Ammonite wife – citizenship requirements were made more severe in Ezra–Nehemiah by the disallowing of foreign wives, as in the law of Perikles.[64]

3. Tribal organization and the military

Athens possessed a citizen army that consisted of adult males of age twenty and older. There was no need to finance it through taxes, except in extraordinary times of war,[65] because the citizens themselves provided their own weaponry, according to their economic class. Citizens were divided into classes according to an economic assessment.[66] The richest class under Solon's reforms was the *pentacosiomedimni,* who held positions of greatest financial responsibility such as treasurers and generals (Aristotle, *Politics* 3.1282a; cf. Ostwald 2000: 51, 70). The next richest class, the *hippeis* or knights, served at their own expense as cavalry in the army[67] and were periodically called upon to underwrite the cost of festival sacrifices and other expenses. The third class, the *zeugitae,* consisting of poor tenant farmers, served as hoplites and provided their own armor and weaponry. The fourth and poorest class, the *thetes,* consisted of those who owned no land and could not afford armor, who served as light infantry or as sailors in the Athenian fleet.[68]

Military training – the *ephebate* – began at age eighteen. The early history of the *ephebate* in Athens is a matter of some debate. It appears to have been an educational institution in Athens available to the sons of the elite since the fifth century BCE but became a compulsory part of Athenian education as a result of the law introduced by Epicrates ca. 335 BCE (Aristotle, *Athenian Constitution* 42.1, 4; cf. Rhodes 1993: 494–5). The three branches of education at Athens consisted of letters *(grammata)*, music *(mousike)* and gymnastics *(gymnastike)*.[69] Letters included early training in the alphabet and later readings in Homer and other Greek classics. Music included training in both lyre and voice. Gymnastics included dance, which was thought to promote coordination and agility in battle.[70] The *ephebate* included training in basic hoplite warfare[71] – such as the use of javelin, sword and other weapons – and rigorous exercise to promote strength, endurance and agility. All military and athletic training took place in the public gymnasia, of which there were three in Athens.[72] The first year of military training, starting at age eighteen, was devoted to training, which included contests with real weaponry to promote courage in battle.[73] Athenian festivals such as the Panathenaia were occasions for military, athletic and artistic contests, as well as martial displays such as parades, mock battles and military dance such as the *hoplomachia* (Wheeler 1982), which stressed the agility of the armed participants. The *epheboi* participated in such public military displays and contests. At age nineteen, the *epheboi* were assigned guard duties in the fortresses and border posts of Attica. At age twenty, the *epheboi* were inducted as citizens and soldiers.[74]

Enrollment into the citizen army was by tribe *(phyle)*, brotherhood *(phratry)*, clan *(genos)* and household *(oikos)*. The primary purpose for the tribal divisions was military.[75] The troops enrolled under each tribe formed their own company under the command of a tribal general or *phylarchos*.[76] The overall command of the military forces was traditionally invested in the *polemarchos;* after ca. 510 BCE command was given to one of the ten tribal *phylarchoi* on a rotating basis.[77] The brotherhood or *phratry*, a kinship group intermediate in size between the clan and tribe, was also a primarily military associate, although its exact nature and origin is somewhat uncertain.[78] Conscription and military service by kinship group presumably contributed to ease of marshaling forces for war and to greater loyalty to fellow-soldiers, a matter of considerable importance in battle. Deployment in battle took place in units or arrays of fixed size, the largest being the *chiliarchy* or thousand.

The stories about the rise of David provide special insights into the weaponry and training of the Israelite pre-monarchic army, as envisioned by the biblical writers. As is well known, the battle of David and Goliath, which has close literary parallels to battles between opposing champions in Homer's *Iliad,* had Goliath dressed in the full traditional armor of the *hoplite* warrior, and even assigned the Philistine a shield-carrier.[79] David rejected similar armaments, preferring the agile fighting style of the Greek light infantry (which included slingers).[80] The youthful David appeared in the guise of an *ephebe* or youthful warrior-in-training. David was described as young, bronzed and good-looking (1 Sam. 16.12, 16; 17.42), in accordance with Archaic and Classical Greek aesthetic ideals.[81] Not only was David a courageous warrior, but he was proficient with the lyre (1 Sam. 16.14–23; 18.10–11; 19.9–10; 2 Sam. 6.5),[82] an agile dancer (2 Sam. 6.14–16)[83] and a talented songwriter (2 Sam. 23.1–2), qualities strikingly out of place for a military figure of the Ancient Near East, but thoroughly consistent with a young man undergoing Greek instruction in the *gymnasium*. Military tales in 1 and 2 Samuel featured target practice (1 Sam. 20.20–22, 35–42; cf. 2 Sam. 1.18), races (2 Sam. 2.18–23) and "play" contests at arms (2 Sam. 2.12–17), all familiar aspects of Greek military training.[84] The gift of armor as an expression of friendship (1 Sam. 18.3–4) was a well-known Homeric literary motif.[85] Public honors for military valor (2 Sam. 21.17–22; 23.8–23) also reflected Greek military values.[86] One gains the impression that the author of the tales of military exploits in Samuel was well acquainted with the Greek *gymnasium, ephebate* and *hoplite* army; the recurrent themes taken from Homer's *Iliad* also suggest a basic background in Greek literature.[87]

It is significant that the biblical tribal enrollment in Numbers was for the purpose of military organization. Like the Athenians, the biblical army was grouped into tribal divisions (Num. 1–3, 10, 26), each having a tribal general corresponding to the Athenian *phylarch* (Num. 1.4–16; 7.1–2),[88] these twelve generals under the command of the overall military leader.[89] In Numbers, the twelve tribes were grouped into four larger military units of three tribes each, much like the archaic Athenian division into four tribes of three *trittyes* each (Num. 2.1–32). The travels of the children of Israel in the wilderness were in forced marches in military formation, arrayed by tribal units (Num. 10.14–28). Although in the biblical account three tribes elected to reside in the choice lands of Transjordan, their military participation in the conquest of the Promised Land was required. In all subsequent appearances of the twelve tribes in the Judges period, they came together for military purposes (Judg. 7.23–24; 20.1–11; cf. 1 Sam. 4–7). The twelve tribes of Israel were thus portrayed primarily as military divisions in biblical narratives about the pre-monarchic period as in Athens. Within the twelve tribes, the citizens of Israel were enlisted by kinship groups, clans and finally by household, a system also integral to Athenian military and social organization (Num. 1–3). The biblical account even anachronistically referred to secretaries or scribes who enrolled the soldiers into the citizen army, in conformity with Athenian practices (Num. 1.5–16). As at Athens, military service began at age twenty in the Pentateuchal regulations (Num. 1.2–4). The wilderness army was without cavalry, but was composed exclusively of foot soldiers.[90] It is perhaps for this reason that enrollment in the citizen army and assignment of military duties did not involve an economic assessment, as at Athens. The enlisted troops were assigned into divisions of thousands, hundreds, fifties and tens (Ex. 18.25; Num. 1.16; 7.85; 10.4; 31.48, 52, 54; Deut. 1.15; Josh. 22.21, 30). This system is not attested for ancient Israel in extra-biblical sources, and in the Persian period only units of thousands and hundreds are documented as military units for troops stationed in Egypt.[91] But Greek and Hellenistic armies were also organized on the decimal system, and units of 1,000 *(chiliarchia)*, 100 *(hekatontarchia)*, 50 *(pentekostys)* and 10 *(dekas* or *dekania)* are all attested (although units of hundreds and fifties were first introduced in the 160s BCE, under Roman influence).[92] It thus appears that the biblical military units displayed some awareness of Hellenistic military organization.

The biblical organization into twelve tribes was once thought to have been modeled on the Greek institution of the *amphictyony,* a tribal or city alliance for the purpose of financing and (as necessary) defending a common sacred sanctuary. According to Martin Noth's proposal, the biblical organization into twelve tribes in the "judges" period was based on a common worship of Yahweh and could be considered as a historical expression of a wider contemporary "Mediterranean" phenomenon of twelve tribe *amphictyonae* or religious alliances centered on a central cult (Noth 1966). But such alliances are first documented in the twelve tribe Delphic *amphictyony* of the Archaic Era (700–480 BCE) and in various *amphictyonic* city alliances of the Classical Era (480–323 BCE), so their projection back into the biblical Judges period is distinctly anachronistic. Furthermore, such alliances were only rarely composed of twelve members, and only in the Delphic league of the Archaic Era were these members tribes.[93] Additionally, the books of Joshua and Judges contained no traditions regarding tribal participation in a centralized cult that would form an analogy to the *amphictyonae* (de Geus 1976: 69–119; Gottwald 1999: 345–57). Rather than a religious confederacy centered on a cult site, the twelve tribes of Israel were instead portrayed as military, judicial and civic units within the national and societal organization (Gottwald 1999: 376–82). As a result of these various objections, the Nothian theory of the twelve tribes as an ancient historical *amphictyony* in pre-monarchic times is no longer considered tenable.[94] However, the objections that Gottwald and other critics raised against the twelve tribes as an *amphictyonic* league do not carry over to the twelve tribes as having been modeled on Athenian tribal organization: unlike the religious *amphictyonae,* but exactly like the twelve tribes of Israel, the Athenians were organized into tribes for military, judicial and political purposes.

The Athenian system of ten or twelve tribes corresponds closely to the biblical tribal divisions. The biblical tribes each claimed descent from an eponymous ancestral figure, the twelve sons of Israel forming an analog to the four sons of Ion, or to the later ten or twelve ancestral heroes of later Athenian tribal organizations. The lists of ten or twelve eponymous tribes of the Israelites vary in the names listed, suggesting that the number of tribes was more important than the tribal figures.[95] There is no inscriptional evidence to support the organization of the northern kingdom of Bit-Omri (Samaria or Israel) into ten tribal districts, and the provincial districts created by the Assyrians fail to correspond in name or geographical extent to biblical tribal divisions.[96] This tribal division may be considered (like the Athenian tribal divisions) a legal fiction. The invention or selection of twelve eponymous ancestors for the tribes of Israel was likely not too dissimilar from the selection of eponymous ancestors of the Attic tribes under Kleisthenes in 508/507 BCE.[97]

Tribal military and political organization was a feature in many Greek city-states, but a system of twelve tribes was best known from Athens.[98] The citizens of Athens were subdivided into several tribes (or *phylae*) whose number changed several times in the course of Athenian history. Legend had it that Ion divided the people of Attica into four tribes named after Ion's four sons. Each of these tribes was in turn divided into thirds, or *"trittyes,"* presumably so that obligations could rotate among the twelve *trittyes* on a monthly basis (Aristotle, *Athenian Constitution* 7–8; cf. Stanton 1990: 68–73). This system persisted into the start of the Classical Era of Athens. In 508/507 BCE Kleisthenes, whom later generations considered the founder of Athenian democracy, redistributed the population of Athens and Attica into ten new tribes for political purposes, each with its own eponymous hero, which the Delphic Oracle selected out of a list of 100 candidates.[99] The system of twelve *trittyes* was still retained for religious purposes, however, and appeared in the Athenian sacred calendar published in 403/402 BCE.[100] Plato's ideal system of twelve tribes in his *Laws* (ca. 350 BCE) is thought to have been modeled on the old system of twelve *trittyes* (Oliver 1950: 53–4; cf. Plato, *Laws* 5.745b-e, 746d; 6.758e, 760d, 771a-d; 8.828b, 848c-e; Aristotle, *Athenian Constitution* 8 3). In 307/306 BCE, Athens formally adopted a system of twelve tribes by the addition of two new tribes named the Demetriad and the Antigonid, after Demetrius Poliorketes and Antigonus Monophthalmus (Plutarch, *Demetrius* 8–10; Diodorus Siculus, *Library* 20.45.1–46.4; cf. Pritchett 1940; Rhodes 1993: 304; Harding 2008: 170–1), the two Macedonian generals who overthrew the tyrant Demetrius of Phalerum in 307 BCE and returned Athens to a democratic form of government. (For the reign and eventual downfall of Demetrius, see O'Sullivan 2009.) The Athenians thus basically alternated between an organization of twelve or ten tribal subdivisions, like biblical Israel, until 224/223 BCE, when Athens added a thirteenth tribe Ptolemais, after Ptolemy III Euergetes of Egypt.[101] In 201/200 BCE two tribes were removed and a new one added, Attalis, resulting in a return to twelve tribes.[102]

The biblical system of ten or twelve tribal divisions[103] corresponds numerically to the ten tribes of the Kleisthenes reforms that lasted from 508 to 307 BCE and the twelve tribes of the reorganized Athenian state from 307 to 223 BCE. The major Pentateuchal division into twelve tribes may have been modeled on the historical Athenian system of 307–223 BCE. However, the biblical system may have been based on Plato's *Laws* of ca. 350 BCE, which also advocated a twelve tribe system (Kupitz 1997: 86–7; Wajdenbaum 2011: 55, 57, 73, 189–90). Alternatively, the biblical system may have drawn on the foundation story of Judea found in the *Aegyptiaca* of Hecataeus of Abdera in ca. 315 BCE in which Moses was said to have created a system of twelve civic tribes.[104] The visit of Jewish scholars to Alexandria to create a copy of Jewish "legislation" for the Great Library in ca. 270 BCE provides an opportune occasion in which Jewish legal scholars could have become acquainted with Athenian legal institutions, with the Jewish foundation story in Hecataeus of Abdera's *Aegyptiaca,* and with Plato's *Laws,* and adopted the notion of political and military organization into twelve tribes found in all three.

4. Tribal allotments and land distribution

In both archaic and early classical Athens, the fundamental social division was the tribe *(phyle),* and under that the brotherhood *(phratry),* clan *(genos)* and household *(oikos).* This organization by tribal and familial grouping was the basis for military organization and took precedence over geographical location: members of a single kinship group (especially powerful landed families) might be distributed across Attica. The prominence of certain rich, powerful kinship groups who possessed excessive representation and control of Athenian government was considered undesirable by the less wealthy masses. In order to break up and curtail oligarchic influences in the Athenian *polis,* in 508/507 BCE Kleisthenes initiated certain democratic reforms in the constitution that created a new system of ten tribes, each allotted its own geographical district (Aristotle, *Athenian Constitution* 21 [in the archonship of Isagoras]; cf. Rhodes 1993: 245). This tribal reorganization and territorial (re)districting cut across old kinship lines. Although the old kinship categories of brotherhood, clan and household were retained, another parallel social organization was created in which citizens were also enrolled by tribe and district township *(deme),* where each contiguous tribal district possessed the villages within its fixed boundaries (cf. Lacey 1968: 90–1; Rhodes 1993: 251). For the first time in the Athenian *polis,* a tribe was associated with a district and villages as well as its own (fictional) ancestral associations. In 307/306 BCE, two additional tribes were created and Attica underwent a new districting of tribal territories and associated *demes.* Reorganization of *demes* took place again during the tribal reorganizations of 224/223 and 201/200 BCE.[105]

The establishment of a new colony typically involved the creation of tribal divisions, commonly ten or twelve in number.[106] A partitioning of the land into tribal territories was presumably accomplished with relative ease, because it did not supersede earlier territorial or kinship divisions. The founder's first acts after the acquisition of land for the colony – typically by conquest – and the setting aside of land for the city and sacred buildings was to assign each colonist his own individual plot of land (Morrow 1993: 103). This took place in two distinct phases. First the land was surveyed by *geonomoi,* one from each tribe, who would partition the land into plots of equal value.[107] After the land was so divided, individual plots were assigned among the colonists by lot or *kleros* (hence the name cleruchy, signifying a landholding). Despite the impracticality of implementing land equality in city-states with existing economic stratification, the Greeks considered land equality an ideal, closely associated with allied notions of democracy and *isonomia* or equality under the law.[108] Attempts to impose land equality in existing city-states were strongly resisted by the wealthy oligarchs, and could be accomplished only by revolution and a change in constitution.[109] Such changes were sometimes promised by demagogues attempting to gain support from among the impoverished under-class (e.g. Plutarch, *Dion* 37.5, discussed at Weinfeld 1995: 15). On occasion an anti-oligarchic revolution succeeded, accompanied by land redistribution with equal allotments for all citizens.[110] But calls for land redistribution historically led to political strife and were accordingly condemned by most political theorists.[111] Equal land distribution was most practical at the foundation of a new colony (Aristotle, *Politics* 2.1266b; 6.1319a; Plato, *Laws* 3.684e; 5.736c), and several Greek colonies were set up with such democratic initial landholdings.[112] The prospect of achieving both political and land equality was, indeed, a powerful inducement to participate in a colonizing expedition, and was consequently a prominent feature found in several foundation decrees, guaranteeing that the colonists would all start out on an equal footing (Graham 1964: 58–9). Some foundation decrees and political constitutions made landholdings inalienable, ensuring that those initially granted an equal allotment could not later be deprived of their property and have their rights diminished through the rise of a new oligarchy.[113]

Plato's *Laws* (ca. 350 BCE), which contained a fictional dialogue about the foundation of a new colony in Crete, illustrates many of the notions just discussed. Plato's *Laws* envisioned that the initial set of colonists in a new foundation should be divided by lot into twelve tribes, each with its own name and tribal god (*Laws* 5.745d). A key task of the founders was to allot the land among the new colonists. The first task was to identify a suitable site for the main city and to set aside a sacred *temenos* in the acropolis for the temples and to ring it around with solid walls (5.745b). Next the land was surveyed and marked off into equal allotments for division among the colonists (5.737e, 745c).[114] Both the city (or *astu*) and the surrounding country (or *chora*) were divided into twelve districts of equal size, making suitable compensations for the quality of the land (5.745d-e). In Plato's system, each tribal district possessed twelve villages; the main marketplace or *agora* and the temples were located at the district's centrally located chief village, which possessed a walled stronghold built on the highest ground, manned by a garrison, with the temples located within these fortifications (8.848d-e).[115] After having assigned the colonists to tribes and having divided up the land by tribe, village and individual allotment, the colonists were organized by *phratry* (brotherhood) and *deme* (district) for military and civic purposes (5.746d). An important feature in Plato's system was that land was to be inalienable (5.741c). The equality and inalienability of land ownership in Plato's ideal colony was intended to eliminate both poverty and luxury.[116]

A system of dual enrollment of citizens by both kinship group and by geographical district thus characterized the political organization of Athens after the reforms of Kleisthenes, various Greek colonies and the ideal political system envisioned in Plato's *Laws*. Kinship organization by tribe *(phyle)*, brotherhood *(phratry)*, clan *(genos)* and household *(oikos)* was central to military conscriptions and organization. Geographical organization by tribe *(phyle)* and district *(deme)* was important for territorial administrative purposes, featuring in elections, judicial organization and military defense. Crucial to both systems of citizen enrollment was the tribe, perhaps once grounded in kinship relationships, but since the time of Kleisthenes a convenient legal fiction retained for the purposes of social, military and civic organization. What is remarkable in this tribal system was the strict correlation between tribal "kinship" and tribal geography, an exact correspondence artificially created in Athens by the creation of tribal districts by Kleisthenes and seen elsewhere in the Greek world in other political systems patterned on the Athenian model. Such a system is unknown in the Ancient Near

East, where tribal designations reflected either real kinship groups or in some cases perhaps social classes, but did not typically correspond to bounded geographical areas or form the formal basis for provincial organization.

A system of dual enrollment remarkably similar to that at Athens is also seen in the Hexateuch, where the twelve tribes of Israel reflected both kinship groups and geographical districts. Genesis contained stories regarding the eponymous ancestors of the twelve tribes. In Exodus–Numbers, where the twelve tribes are seen almost exclusively in their military aspects, kinship relationships were emphasized.[117] The military enrollment of the nation of Israel *(bene Israel)* there took place by tribe *(shevet, matteh),* brotherhood or clan *(mishpachah,* sometimes *eleph)* and household *(beth ab).*[118] The occupation of the land and geographical districting was mentioned in Num. 26.52–56; 33.54; 34.1–18; 36.2–3 in connection with the assignment of tribal territories east of the Jordan. In Deuteronomy both kinship and geography were treated with a new emphasis on life in the land. The "laws for the land" in Deuteronomy[119] were intended for application within a carefully defined geographical or territorial setting, within the national boundaries of the Promised Land. Because Deuteronomy anticipated a time when the children of Israel had taken full possession of the land, topics of military conscription and organization were mostly neglected in Deuteronomy in favor of town life and domestic political institutions such as city elders.[120] The book of Joshua narrated the conquest of the land, the creation of tribal territories and the allotment of land to the colonists. Joshua 13, 15–19, 21 presumed kinship relations among the tribal conquerors but also included extensive boundary descriptions and lists of walled cities and villages for the twelve tribes of Israel. The identification of the children of Israel by tribe and village closely parallels the Athenian enrollment of citizens by tribe and district *(deme)* under the reforms of Kleisthenes and thereafter. One thus sees the body of citizens known as the children of Israel defined both in terms of kinship relationships for military purposes and in terms of geography in both Numbers and Joshua. The dual biblical conception of tribes as representing both a kinship group and a geographical district with villages appears to reflect awareness of the democratic reorganization of Athens by Kleisthenes in 508/507 BCE.

The system whereby the children of Israel were allotted land also closely corresponds to the Greek practices discussed earlier. The scribes charged with allotting land divisions and recording ownership of allotted parcels at Num. 34.1–29, one from each tribe, have an exact analogy in the tribal *geonomoi* who supervised identical activities at the foundation of Greek colonies (cf. Weinfeld 1993: 35–6). The procedures by which individual estates were to be assigned apportioned among the children of Israel within each tribal district by random lot (Num. 26.52–56; 33.53–54; 34.16–19; Josh. 13.6–7; 14.2; 15.1; 16.1; 17.1–2, 14–18; 18.1–19.51) also exactly corresponds to Greek practices. The land allotted to the children of Israel was to be inalienable, like that in several Greek colonies, in order to prevent citizen landowners from succumbing to a state of permanent impoverishment or debt slavery.[121]

5. Kinship groups

Each Athenian citizen belonged to a specific *oikos* (household), *genos* (clan), *phratry* (brotherhood) and *phyle* (tribe). Although the *phyle* or tribe no longer constituted an actual kinship group after the Athenian reforms under Kleisthenes, the *oikos, genos* and *phratry* in most cases designated actual kinship groups.[122]

Kinship groups served various purposes under Athenian law. One important function of the kinship group was the prosecution or avenging of murder. According to old Greek religious traditions, when a man was slain by violence (whether the homicide was intentional or unintentional), his blood cried out for vengeance and his disembodied spirit, angered and disquieted at his violent end, haunted the places he once frequented and became troubled at the presence of his murderer at these same places (see especially Plato, *Laws* 9.872d-e). The Furies were thus aroused to vengeance by bloodshed; the duty to avenge the slain fell specifically to the next of kin, who would arouse the wrath of the dead if he did not fulfill this duty (Plato, *Laws* 9.866b, 870e-871b). In archaic Athens, justice for homicide is thought to have been left completely in the hands of the kinship group.[123] Under the homicide law of Drakon, the oldest preserved Athenian law, judicial self-help by the kinship group was curtailed and the responsibility for avenging homicide was partially taken over by the courts, who had the duty for making a determination that a homicide had in fact taken place.[124] The kinsmen of the victim still had the duty of prosecution at trial, because Athens had neither police nor professional prosecutors.[125] Homicide suspects had the legal option of voluntarily going into exile. If an accused suspect remained in Attica and appeared in any public place such as a temple or the Athenian *agora* prior to trial, the kinsmen of the victim had the right to slay him with impunity.

Kinship groups such as the *bet ab* and the *mishpachah*[126] played a virtually identical role in biblical traditions dealing with the prosecution and avenging of homicide. The mythology attached to shed blood in biblical texts closely resembles that found in the Greek world:[127] innocent blood "cried out" to Yahweh for vengeance (Gen. 4.10; Isa. 26.21; Ezek. 24.7–8; Job 16.18) and stained the land with pollution (Num. 35.33; cf. Deut. 19.10, 13; 21.7–9). Unavenged innocent blood put a curse on the land (Parker 1983: 257–80). The nearest kinsman, the *go'el ha-dam* or blood avenger,[128] was charged with hunting down and slaying the perpetrator. Several biblical examples exist of murderers who fled into exile (Gen. 4.14 [Cain]; Ex. 2.15 [Moses]; 2 Sam. 13.37–38 [Absalom]). For unintentional homicide, provision was made for cities of refuge where the slayer could seek asylum (Num. 35.6–34; Deut. 19.1–13; Josh. 20.1–9). If the slayer was caught before he reached asylum, he could be slain with impunity (Num. 35.19). Once reaching a city of refuge, however, he could appeal to the city elders as a supplicant; if the elders accepted his plea, the supplicant would be admitted into the city with guarantees of safety until a proper trial was held (Num. 35.12; Josh. 20.3–6, 9). In biblical as in Athenian law, the kinsmen of the homicide victim acted as prosecutors at trial (Num. 35.24). If asylum was rejected or if the accused was convicted of intentional homicide, he would be turned over to the blood avenger for execution in biblical texts (Num. 35.24–25; Deut. 19.11–13). If the homicide was found to be unintentional, he would be allowed to live in exile at the city of refuge (Num. 35.24–28, 32; Josh. 20.3–4). The exiled individual presumably still had an income from the estates in his home village.[129] The Mosaic and Athenian legal provisions were virtually identical except that in the biblical system self-exile was allowed in the six designated cities of refuge and that the exile ended, not after the lapse of a fixed number of years, but (in passages critics have traditionally assigned to the priestly source P) at the death of the high priest.

A second function of the kinship group in Athens was to ensure the perpetuation of a family line that was threatened with extinction by the death of the head of household without a male heir to succeed him. Athenian law contemplated several solutions to address such a situation.[130] Sometimes the head of household would adopt a son during his lifetime or appoint one in his will. This adopted son would serve as *kurios* of the estate but would not inherit it: his obligation was instead to marry and have a son who could later inherit and perpetuate the family name of the deceased. If the head of household died with neither biological nor adopted son nor one designated by will, his eldest daughter was designated heiress and required to marry within the kinship group and generate offspring to inherit the family estate. Failing this, the deceased man's nearest male relative within the kinship group was required to marry the widow (divorcing his own wife, if he was already married) and raise up offspring in the name of the deceased, "that his name should not perish."[131] This process guaranteed the perpetuation of the family, inheritance within the family and the continuation of the household cult, an important aspect of the Athenian family.[132] Similar laws also appear in the Greek world outside Athens.[133]

The biblical institution of levirate marriage, whereby a near kinsman was charged with marrying the widow of a landed man who died without an heir (Num. 27.1–11; 36.1–12; Deut. 25.5–10; Josh. 17.3–6), was virtually identical to the system in Athens. Both legal systems explicitly defined near kinsmen as the circle of brothers, cousins and second cousins.[134] Both legal provisions even contained identical language: "that his name should not perish."[135] In both legal systems, if there was no male heir, but a daughter existed as heiress, she was to marry within the kinship group, or if no near kinsman was available, within the tribe, so that the estate would not pass into the possession of another tribe or to a stranger (Num. 36.8).

The biblical system also assigned a third function to the near kinship group: to act as redeemers, either to purchase a relative out of captivity or debt slavery or to purchase (redeem) their ancestral land if it was sold to an outsider.[136] Redemption from debt slavery was not required in Athens, which outlawed debt slavery altogether.

6. The household

The fundamental political and economical unit in the Greek world and in Athens was the *oikos* or household.[137] The household was a broader concept than family, but included parents, children, servants, servants, slaves, livestock and even *xenoi* or guest-friends (Lacey 1968: 15, 31, 72, 237 n. 4; cf. Aristotle, *Politics* 1.1252b). The family patriarch was the *kurios* or lord of the household (comparable to the Roman *paterfamilias* [Lacey 1968: 21]) and as such was the guardian and legal representative of his wife, his children and his slaves. The *kurios* of a household was always male, except for widows and divorcees who chose to maintain their own household.

The patriarch of a household also had legal responsibilities within the wider kinship group. He was obligated to act as caretaker for parents advanced in age who resided within his house under his supervision. On marriage, a daughter became part of her husband's household, but on widowhood or divorce might return to the household of her father. A patriarch might also be appointed guardian over a male relative's widow and her minor children, if the widow's father was deceased, but the widow could choose to reside in the house of her deceased husband as *kurios* of that household until her eldest male child became an adult. A patriarch might also be appointed guardian over orphans (typically within his kinship group) and administer their estate until they reached adulthood.

The appointment of guardianships was normally decided by the kinship group. The Eponymous Archon of Athens was charged with the legal oversight of guardianships and other family-related matters and might intervene if guardianships were badly administered. Widows, orphans and aged parents thus constituted special protected classes whose care was extensively addressed under Athenian law.

A patriarch might also act as host to a stranger residing in his house or as a sponsor to a foreign resident who maintained a separate residence within his village. Patriarchs were also legally responsible for the actions of their slaves. The *kurios* of a household thus presided over an extended social group, and every person residing in Attica was legally attached to a specific household, in some sense protected and accountable to the *kurios* of that household.

The Hebrew term *beth* signified either "house,"[138] "household" or "family" (especially in the phrase *beth ab*),[139] closely corresponding to the Greek *oikos*. The term *beth,* like the Greek *oikos,* could refer either literally to a house or domicile or to the people living there (Gottwald 1999: 248; cf. MacDowell 1989: 10). The head of the biblical household was called its *baal* or lord, which corresponded to the Greek *kurios*.[140] The sabbath law is illustrative of the biblical household: the command to rest on the seventh day included husband, wife, children, slaves, servants, guests and even livestock – that is, all members of the household (Ex. 20.8–11; 23.12; Deut. 5.12–15).

The family head was *baal* over both his wife and children and acted as their legal representative in all matters. As in Athens, a wife or daughter could not enter into binding legal contracts on her own, but required the approval of the head of the household (Num. 30.3–6, 10–13; cf. Lacey 1968: 229); an exception was made for widows with minor children and divorcees who elected not to return to their father's house but to remain independent and to support themselves by their dowry or by trade (Num. 30.9).

Pentateuchal legislation expressed concern for the protection of parents, widows and orphans, as well as both resident aliens and strangers. Mistreatment of widows, orphans and strangers was strongly condemned, the main difference from the Athenian system being the lack of a specific magistrate appointed for the oversight of these protected classes or a specific recognition of the formal legal concept of appointed guardian. Instead, biblical texts appear to envision the care of protected classes as an internal family matter to be handled within the kinship group.

It appears to have been assumed, for instance, that an aged parent would continue to reside in the same household, obviating the need for the appointment of a guardian. Parental "blessings" on their children, as expressed in patriarchal stories in Genesis, took place on the occasion of the patriarch's retirement, when he passed on the role of head of household to his favored child (usually the eldest) and came under his protection.[141] The penalty for mistreating parents was severe (one might say "Draconian") (Ex. 21.15, 17). The Pentateuch generally assumed that impoverishment issues and other family matters would be handled at the local village level[142] or within the kinship group (Lev. 25.25, 35–43; Deut. 15.7–8, 11), but did not explicitly address guardianship over widows and orphans. The biblical threat that God would severely punish those who mistreated widows and orphans (Ex. 22.22–24, 27) seems to acknowledge the lack of a formal legal institution (such as Athenian family court) to enforce their protection and care.

7. Deliberative bodies

In Athens, the two main deliberative bodies were the *Boule* or Council and the *Ekklesia* or Assembly.[143] The Council, instituted by Solon in ca. 594 BCE, was first known as the Four Hundred, with 100 members elected from each of the four archaic tribes (Aristotle, *Athenian Constitution* 4.3; 8.4; Aristotle, *Politics* 6.1319b; Plutarch, *Solon* 19.1; cf. Stanton 1990: 68–73, no. 42; Rhodes 1993: 153); then, starting in 508/507 BCE, as the Five Hundred, with 50 members chosen by lot from each tribe of the ten newly created tribes;[144] this system effectively remained in place in Athens throughout the Classical period, except when briefly interrupted by the Oligarchy of Four Hundred in 411 BCE,[145] and later again by the Thirty Tyrants of 404 BCE.[146] The Council's duties included drafting laws and decrees for consideration by the Assembly, scheduling both regular and extraordinary sessions of the Assembly and setting the agenda for each such session.[147] The Assembly, which all adult male citizens could attend, with rights to speak and vote, approved or rejected the proposed laws and decrees after suitable discussion.[148] During the oligarchic revolution of 411 BCE, when citizen rolls were restricted in number, the Assembly was known as the Five Thousand. In addition to their legislative duties, the Council and Assembly also exercised judicial functions for extraordinary cases, including accusations of treason. A third deliberative body in Athens, the Council of the Areopagus, a body consisting of all previously elected Archons, served as a court for auditing and hearing cases regarding magistrates, meting out punishments as appropriate.[149] Other Greek city-states also typically included an Assembly and some sort of Council[150] (in some cases a council of elders or *gerousia*);[151] sometimes there was also a king or panel of kings *(basileis)*.[152]

The executive, legislative and judicial powers of Athenian deliberative bodies were subject to important limits, except during those dark periods in Athenian history when the city was under the sway of tyrannical political forces. In the course of the fifth century BCE, the judicial process became increasingly democratic, with most non-trivial cases adjudged by citizen juries *(dikasteria)* whose sizes varied according to the seriousness of the crime. Additionally, judicial decisions were subject to appeal. By the end of the fifth century BCE, Athens also fully developed the important idea of rule by written law.[153] Judges were forbidden from enforcing laws not committed to writing,[154] and it became a punishable offense to propose a new law or decree that conflicted with the existing constitution and laws (Aristotle, *Athenian Constitution* 59.2; Demosthenes, *Against Aristocrates* 87; Demosthenes, *Against Timocrates* 33). Fixed laws *(nomoi)* were terminologically distinguished from edicts or decrees *(psephemata)* dealing with transitory matters of state; laws were also enacted under a different procedure than decrees.[155] The immutability of Athenian law and laws of other Greek states was to some extent a fiction, because legislative bodies in practice could and did pass new laws that modified existing institutions to a lesser or greater degree, but the respect accorded to written laws, especially those promulgated by revered lawgivers of the past, gave the legal systems and the governments they underpinned an aura of respect and stability that counteracted revolutionary forces (Szegedy-Maszak 1978).

Rather than an Assembly and two Councils, as found in Athens, the biblical deliberative bodies consisted of an Assembly and a single Council. The Assembly was designated by the terms *qahal* or *edah* and consisted of the entire citizen body. The Council was described as a body of "seventy elders" in Exodus and Numbers. In Exodus–Joshua, both the Assembly and Elders appeared as national democratic institutions that operated subordinate to the leadership of Moses and Joshua. During the Sojourn they typically gathered at the Tent of Meeting or Tabernacle. In Deuteronomy–Samuel, the institutions of Assembly and Elders also appeared at the local level, administering town affairs. In Deuteronomy, the "elders at the gate" often acted in a judicial capacity. Tribal elders (such as the "elders of Judah") were sometimes mentioned. The Assembly and Elders also sporadically appeared in Judges as national ruling bodies convened in times of crisis, and both featured in the anointing of Saul and David as kings in 1 and 2 Samuel.[156] Both Assembly and Council were also historically known as governing institutions in Hellenistic Judea, when the Council was called the *gerousia* in Jewish sources written in Greek; in the Roman period the preferred designation was *Sanhedrin*.

The biblical "seventy elders" appear to reflect the seventy(-two) elders of the Hellenistic Era Jewish *gerousia* and Roman Era Sanhedrin.[157] In *The Letter of*

Aristeas 32, 39, 46–50, the seventy-two elders were composed of six representatives from each of the twelve tribes. Here the *gerousia* was clearly modeled on a Greek constitutional prototype (cf. Honigman 2003: 57–8). The Greek version of the Pentateuch housed in the Great Library of Alexandria was called the Septuagint, or Seventy, after this same deliberative body. Various Jewish traditions numbered the *gerousia* at seventy (Ginzberg 1937: 3.123, 250–1; 6.27 n. 163),[158] seventy-one (Ginzberg 1937: 6.344 n. 6) or seventy-two (Ginzberg 1937: 6.87 n. 477).[159] Conversely, the number of translators of the Septuagint were also numbered at seventy (Josephus, Ant. 12.57, 86), seventy-one[160] or seventy-two.[161] The name of this Jewish legislative body, "the Seventy," appears to reflect Athenian conventions: the Athenians had a predilection for naming governing public institutions after the number of members.[162] Although their deliberative bodies often had an odd number to prevent a tie in voting, their designation was typically a round number.[163]

One noteworthy discrepancy between the biblical and Athenian system of deliberative bodies was the makeup of the Council. In the biblical texts, council members on either the national or local (city) level were designated "elders," suggesting an age requirement. Many Greek city-states had a *gerousia* or council of elders,[164] but Athens did not. Instead, members of the main Athenian Council were democratically selected by lot from among all the citizens. But a second Athenian deliberative body resembled a *gerousia* in some respects, namely the Council of the Areopagus, which consisted of senior statesmen who had formerly served as Athenian Archons or chief magistrates. At Num. 11.16, qualifications for special membership among the "seventy elders of Israel" included their already having served as elders and magistrates. In this respect it more closely resembles the Athenian Council of the Areopagus.

The business of the biblical Assembly and Council, like that of their Athenian counterparts, included judicial, executive and legislative matters (Wolf 1947: 108). Both Pentateuchal elders and assemblies, like their Athenian counterparts, heard a variety of judicial cases, including homicide cases.[165] The entire assembly was involved in passing special executive decrees that addressed immediate questions of national policy, such as declarations of war or the establishment of treaties.[166] The assembly was also responsible for the nomination and appointment of magistrates.[167] As at Athens, any interested citizen could address the assembly.[168] Neither the council nor the assembly had the responsibility or authority to draft legislation, which was – as at Athens – the special prerogative of the legislator(s). The laws were not enacted, however, until the assembly of Israel reviewed and approved the laws submitted to them.[169]

8. The judiciary

The Athenians had a number of different courts for conducting investigations and considering different classes of crimes and lawsuits:[170] one for scrutiny of magistrates before entering office and audits after leaving office; others for minor infractions against state laws, high treason, major torts and various classes of voluntary and involuntary homicide;[171] disputes involving resident aliens;[172] small claims court and family court.[173] After the reforms of Kleisthenes in 508 BCE, Athens had a standing court or *dikasteria* with paid jurors selected by lot for hearing routine cases (Harrison 1968: 2.43–49).

In general, smaller civil lawsuits were resolved at a local level, whereas the courts at Athens were reserved for criminal cases, appeals and lawsuits involving large amounts. Small claims (up to five drachmas) were typically settled by arbitration by judges selected by the two parties (Plato, *Laws* 12.956b-d); judicial arbitration was considered a key civic duty of elders above the age of sixty (MacDowell 1978: 207; see Harrison 1968: 2.61–68 on public and private arbitration). Provisions were made for appealing a verdict to higher courts, with increased fines for failed appeals. Local villages had their own small claims courts, in which the *demarch* played a role (Rhodes 1993: 256–57; MacDowell 1978: 206). Appealed cases were heard by tribal courts and second appeals were heard at Athens. Under the tyrant Pisistratus, a roving panel of judges, known as the Thirty, toured the villages to administer justice, alleviating the need to travel to Athens for appeals or for larger torts (Aristotle, *Athenian Constitution* 16.5; cf. Rhodes 1993: 255); this circuit court was reinstituted in 404 BCE as the Forty.[174]

Criminal trials and major lawsuits received jury trials with jurors selected by lot from the citizens. Such jury trials were seen as a significant democratic advance. Juries often had 200, 300 or 500 members who voted on their verdict after hearing arguments from both sides. The term *dikastes* meant either judge or juror. Athens had no professional judges, prosecutors, professional lawyers or police force: self-help played a large role in both arrest and prosecution.[175] Any citizen could initiate a legal action on his or her own behalf (the *dike*). An important element in Solon's reform of ca. 594 BCE was that any citizen could initiate a legal action on behalf any other citizen (the *graphe*),[176] such as when they observed a child or an aged parent being mistreated by a guardian. Athenian citizens who brought charges in law court either acted as prosecutor (often with the help of a paid speech-writer trained in rhetoric) or could solicit the help of an unpaid public advocate to play this role; similar arrangements held for the defense. Cases of murder were presented by relatives of the victim;[177] failure of relatives to prosecute was itself considered a crime.[178] Litigants on both sides were expected to provide their own witnesses. Witnesses would be named at a preliminary hearing and summons issued, although the court had no enforceable powers of subpoena.[179] Normally both plaintiff and defendant were each allowed two speeches of fixed duration, timed by an hourglass; in cases of homicide or attempted homicide, the defendant had the option to go into voluntary exile as late as the conclusion of the first round of speeches.[180] Evidence was mainly testimonial, although documents were admitted as records of past transactions.[181] Hearsay evidence was not allowed,[182] unless the witness was deceased or unavailable. Defendants had the right not to incriminate themselves, although voluntary confessions of imprisoned wrongdoers, such as thieves caught in the act, were admitted as evidence, subject to appeal and could lead to immediate executions in capital cases (Aristotle, *Athenian Constitution* 52). Witnesses were examined at trial but not cross-examined, although their testimony could be impeached in the prosecutor or defendant's speech. Uncorroborated facts could be bolstered by formal oath.[183] Perjury was considered a serious crime, punishable by disenfranchisement after the third offense.[184] Bribery of either a judge (that is, juror) or senator was deemed a serious matter that undermined the foundations of democracy and justice. Criminal penalties at Athens included execution, disenfranchisement, exile, prison, stripes (a humiliating punishment reserved for slaves) and fines, depending on the severity of the charges (criminal penalties were examined in Hall 1996: 73–89; Allen 2000). The threefold purpose of punishment was to execute vengeance, to purify the land of pollution and serve as an example to teach others to obey the law (MacDowell 1963: 141–50).

Acts that posed a threat to Athenian democracy, such as impiety, treason, conspiracy, bribery or misleading the Assembly, constituted a special class of crime with special procedures.[185] Under the judicial procedure called *eisangelia*, a private citizen could raise an accusation of such a crime either before the magistrates, who were obligated to conduct a special investigation, or before the general Assembly. Such accusations were first referred to the Archons, the Council of the Areopagus or the Council – depending on the nature of the crime – for investigation in a special preliminary hearing. In the late fourth century BCE, this type of special investigation was known as *apophasis*, which involved a report to the Assembly. In the case of a serious conspiracy, informers were sometimes granted immunity by the Council or Assembly to testify against their accomplices.[186] After a preliminary investigation, the magistrates assigned the case to the appropriate court for a full trial with public prosecutors appointed by the Assembly. Political cases generally required trial before the full Assembly, with a quorum of 6,000 citizen jurors.[187] Although the magistrates investigated the facts, a democratic citizen court decided the punishment, even in the most serious cases.

The Pentateuch envisioned judicial hearings for most classes of crimes and lawsuits considered under Athenian law. Venues for trials included villages,[188] tribal court[189] and, for the most serious cases and those most difficult to adjudicate, the high courts located at "the place Yahweh would place his name" (Deut. 17.8 – perhaps Jerusalem or Mount Gerizim). 1 Sam. 7.15–17 had Samuel act as a roving circuit judge, like the traveling judges instituted in Attica under Perikles. The Pentateuch envisioned a hierarchical system of courts, organized according to both kinship and geography. In the wilderness period, most cases brought by the people were heard by tribal officers appointed over thousands, hundreds, fifties and tens, with only the "greatest" or "hardest" cases coming to Moses himself.[190] These lesser courts were seemingly envisioned as standing courts – like those at Athens – that could hear cases "in every season" (Ex. 18.22, 26). The Pentateuchal contrast between "small" and "great" cases (Ex. 18.22, 26) may be understood to distinguish between small claims courts and higher level courts for civil cases above a certain damages amount. On the other hand, the description of the "hardest" cases being brought to Moses may reflect a contrast between less serious and more serious (that is, criminal) cases (cf. Deut. 17.8–13) or, more likely, an estimation of the legal difficulties involved (cf. Num. 27.1–5). In Deuteronomy, the distribution of courts was geographical, in anticipation of conquering the Promised Land, with the people appointing judges and officials in all the tribes and towns (Deut. 16.18–20).[191] Deuteronomy recorded both trials by elders at the city gates and by city assemblies. The "elders in the gate" constituted a standing court that could hear cases brought by local residents at any time. In some instances elders or judicial magistrates appear to have conducted a preliminary inquiry before referring a case to full trial before the full assembly.[192] The "hardest" cases were referred to the levitical priests and the judges serving at that time (Deut. 17.9–13; cf. 19.17) in the place God would designate. One important difference in the biblical system was that homicide and other capital cases could be heard at the local level, whereas in Attica such cases were handled only at Athens.

Judicial procedures and rules of evidence in the Pentateuch are compatible with legal practices in Athens.[193] Under the biblical system, judges were appointed from the citizens[194] and served for a limited term of office (Deut. 17.9; 19.17). Private citizens had powers of arrest[195] and acted as prosecutors[196] or spoke in their own defense (Jer. 26.12–15; Job 31.37; cf. Wells 2004: 48). Litigants brought defendants to trial (Deut. 21.18–21; cf. Hagedorn 2004: 135) and summoned their own witnesses.[197] In some cases offenders were put in custody while they awaited trial (Lev. 24.12; Num. 15.34; cf. Westbrook 1991: 10). Homicide cases were brought by kinsmen of the victim and the payment of "blood money" was not allowed.[198] Evidence was primarily testimonial[199] and hearsay evidence was not allowed.[200] Uncorroborated testimony could be bolstered by oaths, as in both the Ancient Near Eastern and Greek worlds (Ex. 22.7, 10; cf. Wells 2004: 20–1). Trial by ordeal, found in both Pentateuchal and Ancient Near Eastern legal texts, was rare in the Greek world although not entirely unknown.[201] Pentateuchal law required two or three witnesses in capital cases (Num. 35.30; Deut. 17.6; 19.15), which does not agree with Athenian homicide law, but has precedents elsewhere in the Greek world.[202] Perjury was considered a serious matter, as in both the Greek and Ancient Near Eastern worlds.[203] Biblical jurors, like their Greek counterparts, were instructed not to receive payments or gifts.[204] The biblical text exhibited concern that judicial procedure not to be perverted (Ex. 23.8; Deut. 16.19; Prov. 17.23; Mic. 3.11; 7.3) either by a rich and powerful minority (Isa. 1.23; Job 6.22) or, strikingly, by the poor majority (Ex. 23.2–3; Lev. 19.15): the latter has its closest parallel to Athenian concerns about judicial corruption after juries began to be democratically selected from the less wealthy citizen populace, which led to the first recorded instances of judicial bribery.[205] Serious cases such as homicide, impiety or treason might be tried by the full town assembly (Num. 35.24–25; Deut. 17.5–7; cf. Wolf 1947: 103) or national assembly.[206] The range of available judicial penalties was similar under biblical and Greek law.[207] The aims of judicial penalties were also similar, including retaliation for criminal acts, the removal of pollution from the land and crime prevention.[208]

The Pentateuch also recorded a procedure whereby private citizens acted as informers to denounce offenders (Deut. 17.4, 7; 1 Kgs 21.9–13; cf. Westbrook 1991: 10) and bring public cases to the attention of the magistrates for investigation of serious state crimes (Deut. 13.8, 12–14; 17.4, 7; cf. Westbrook 1991: 10), a process analogous to that of *eisangelia* at Athens. Pentateuchal political crimes appear to have included conspiracy to introduce foreign cults (Deut. 13.1–18; 17.2–7), cursing the rulers (Ex. 22.28), misleading the people (Ex. 23.1) and overturning the decision of a higher court (Deut. 17.8–13).

9. Civil magistrates

In addition to its deliberative bodies, Athens was administered by a number of magistrates, elected officials who typically held office for a single year (see generally Aristotle, *Politics* 4.1299a-1300b; 6.1321b; Harrison 1968: 2.4–36; Morrow 1993: 178–95). Appointment to office by lot was considered a defining characteristic of democracy; wealth as a prerequisite for office defined oligarchy; whereas aristocracy featured educational and other qualifications for office.[209] Athens was governed under a mixed constitution that combined elements of both democracy and aristocracy.[210] Elections took place in assemblies at the local, tribal or national level. Some positions were democratically filled on a rotating basis among the citizens by lot, that is, by random chance.[211] Citizens of age thirty could serve in any magistracy, including the Council (Phillips 2013: 26). Other offices of exceptional importance (such as general) or having special educational requirements were elected by popular vote. Magistrates were subjected to scrutiny *(dokomasia)* with respect to their age, citizenship and (as required by the position) educational qualifications prior to assuming office.[212] At the end of their term of service, their performance in office was subject to audit *(euthyna)*.[213]

The most important magistrates of Classical Athens were the ten Archons:[214] the *Basileus* or King, who assigned cases of homicide – including arson and poisoning – to the proper court, and otherwise mainly presided over ceremonial matters;[215] the Polemarch or Warlord, who served as chief commander in times of war until the early fifth century BCE and presided over Athenian trials involving resident aliens in times of peace;[216] the Eponymous Archon, who presided over family court and oversaw the appointment of guardians over widows and orphans; six *thesmothetae,* who scheduled trials, recorded cases and reviewed Athenian laws on a yearly basis for internal consistency;[217] and a seventh *thesmothetae* who served as recorder for the archons.[218] After serving as Archon in one of these capacities, elder statesmen became life members of the Council of the Areopagus. Other state officials included judges, priests and city and local officials appointed over the treasuries, marketplaces, roads, the port and so forth. Some positions required special expertise and had educational requisites that candidates were required to prove at their scrutiny.

In biblical texts, magistrates or officers were referred to generically as *shotrim,* a term which included the "judges" who were said to have succeeded Joshua as local leaders in the pre-monarchic biblical era. Deut. 16.18–20 called for judges and magistrates to be appointed at both the tribal and village level throughout Israel to administer justice for all the people. The constitutional sub-document at Deut. 16.18–18.22 appears to have been addressed to the citizens of the Assembly (Hagedorn 2004: 113–18; Berman 2006: 539); if so, this indicates that the appointment was by popular election in Pentateuchal law as at Athens. An alternate method, appointment by random lots, appeared in the selection of Saul as king in 1 Sam. 10.20–21, suggesting that this procedure was also known to the biblical authors.[219] A limited term of office is alluded to in the recurring Deuteronomic phrase, "the levitical priest and the judge who is in office *in those days*" (Deut. 17.9; 19.17). Indications of a scrutiny process are implicit at Ex. 18.13–26 and Deut. 1.13–15, where judicial qualifications were listed;[220] similar qualifications for judges and condemnation of judicial bribery were found at Plato, *Laws* 6.767d-e. Biblical evidence for magisterial audits is explicit at 1 Sam. 12.1–5, which recorded the public hearing at which Samuel gave an accounting of his term as judge,[221] and which displays a remarkable similarity to Athenian procedure, with which the passage appears to display acquaintance.[222] Although various biblical passages recognized serious crimes such as bribery and judicial murder, and the Pentateuch repeatedly enjoined judges to judge fairly and refuse payments,[223] Pentateuchal law did not specify a legal procedure comparable to the Athenian *apophasis* for trying corrupt magistrates.

Civil magistrates envisioned under Pentateuchal law included military officers,[224] judges (Deut. 1.16; 16.18; 17.9, 12; 19.17–18; 21.2; cf. Josh. 8.33; 23.2; 24.1), scribes or secretaries[225] who may perhaps have acted as recorders of case law,[226] supervisors of citizen rolls (Num. 1.1–46; 26.2–51) and perhaps of property allotments (Num. 34.14–29; cf. 26.52–56; 33.54), and the generic *shotrim* or officers presumed at the local, tribal and national levels (Num. 11.16; Deut. 1.15; 16.18; 20.5, 8–9; 29.10; 31.28; Josh. 1.10; 3.2; 8.33; 23.2; 24.1). Certain laws regarding weights and measures and about market pricing suggest awareness of the Athenian office of market supervisor or *agoranomos*.[227] An informal position found in the Pentateuch was the leader "set over the congregation" like Moses or Joshua, who directed the affairs of the nation in important times (Num. 27.16–23; cf. Gordis 1950: 383). This roughly corresponds to the notion of political leadership in Athens, where the nation turned to a notable figure like Solon or Kleisthenes as *hegemon* in important times of change or crisis. Financial and temple treasurers only appeared later in Ezra–Nehemiah (Ezra 8.24–30, 33–34; Neh. 11.9–11, 15–16, 22–23; 12.44; 13.10–14).

The system of government outlined in the Pentateuchal legislation did not require a king. Supreme judicial and executive powers were invested in the national assembly and perhaps in the representative council of "seventy elders" and were mirrored on the tribal and local level by lesser councils and citizen assemblies. None of the activities envisioned for these constitutional entities, including the election of magistrates to higher or lower offices in the state, required a king[228] or the maintenance of a costly, top-heavy apparatus of state. The system as a whole may be described as a mixed constitution (cf. Berman 2008: 66), a political system with inherent checks and balances[229] that combined the elements of democracy (the Assembly) and aristocracy (as illustrated by the qualifications specified for tribal magistrates[230] and the council of elders[231]). The execution of all offices was strictly subject to the constitutional limitations and the procedures laid out in the written laws recorded in the Pentateuch.[232] This system is impossible to understand as a primitive precursor to the historical monarchies of Judah and Israel.[233] It is preferable instead to interpret this system of government as a reflection of Hellenistic Era Jewish political institutions.[234]

Pentateuchal legislation did, however, envision a day when the children of Israel would ask for a king, and the Torah of the King (Deut. 17.14–20) specified the qualifications required of that office. The description of the office of king contains many problematic elements inconsistent with the biblical monarchy in Samuel–Kings or indeed with kingship as practiced in the Ancient Near East.[235] The king of the Ancient Near East was a ruler over subjects, with authority passed down within a dynastic royal line, and whose dominion was an expression of raw power.[236] Ancient Near Eastern kings exercised supreme military, judicial, economic, executive and (as patrons of temples) cultic powers. Although these features of Ancient Near Eastern kingship generally cohere with the picture of kingship in Samuel–Kings,[237] they do not correspond to implicit and explicit features of kingship in Deuteronomy.[238] For instance, the Deuteronomic king appears to have been appointed by his fellow-citizens, that is, by the citizen assembly;[239] the king's rule was to be subject to written laws, from a copy prepared under priestly supervision;[240] the king was assigned no military,[241] judicial,[242] cultic[243] or executive responsibilities, and indeed the duties of his office are entirely unclear in the Torah of the King.[244] Although the title is that of king, in actuality the envisioned office of kingship appears to resemble that of other Ancient Near Eastern kings in name only. Nor did the Deuteronomic kingship resemble the Judean monarchy of biblical historiography.[245] The commands against accumulating horses, wealth and wives – especially foreign wives – were a conscious contrast to king Solomon's reign.[246] The famous speech of Samuel against the kingship at 1 Sam. 8.11–18 also implicitly contrasted the Deuteronomic ideal with the actual monarchy of Judah, which Samuel pictured as quickly descending into a tyranny[247] in which the creation of a standing professional army (8.11–12) and the indulgences of oligarchic luxury of a ruling class (8.13–17) were predicted to result in oppressive taxation and the creation of a poverty-stricken underclass (8.15–18).[248] It is thus difficult to understand the office of king in Deut. 17 as describing any biblical Judean or Israelite king[249] or even as broadly compatible with the institution of kingship as known in the Ancient Near East.[250]

Rather, the office of king as described in the Torah of the King appears to have been conceived along democratic Greek lines. Kingship, when it existed among the Greeks, was often an elected position.[251] Dynastic royal lines were mainly a feature of the legendary past (Aristotle, *Politics* 3.1285a), with a few exceptions in the historical period, such as at Sparta and Cyrene.[252] The evidence that Athens was ever ruled by a true king is inconclusive.[253] In those city-states that possessed an office of king, the idea of kingship varied from *polis* to *polis*. At Sparta there were two kings from different royal houses who presided over the *gerousia*, and whose equal power provided a check against each other.[254] By Spartan law, their kings functioned as generals and religious leaders only (Aristotle, *Politics* 3.1285b). At Cyrene, a reform of the kingship deprived the royal line of Battus of most powers, including military command, leaving them with only the priesthood (Herodotus, *Histories* 4.161; cf. Hagedorn 2004: 152; Berman 2008: 190 n. 23). At Mytilene and at Chios there was a panel of kings.[255] At Athens there was a single elected king, the *Archon Basileus* (described earlier) whose duties, other than supervision of homicide cases, belonged mainly in the ceremonial and religious realm.[256] The Athenian offices of king and military commander (Polemarch) were distinct since at least the Archaic Era (seventh century BCE). According to Aristotle, the most stable monarchic governments were those in which the functions of the king were most limited.[257] The absence of military duties for the office of king in Deut. 17 is highly reminiscent of elected kingship as practiced in Athens (Hagedorn 2004: 152; Berman 2008: 190 n. 23).

A striking feature of kingship as described in the Torah of the King was its subordination to written law. The book of the law was entrusted to the levitical priests (Deut. 17.18). The king was directed to make a copy of this law under priestly supervision (Deut. 17.18), to refer to it constantly and obey its every precept, in order that his tenure as king be long and happy (Deut. 17.19–20). The requirement that the duties of the king should be performed in strict conformity to written law is a characteristically Greek notion.[258] The creation of a copy of the law for royal reference is strikingly reminiscent of the publication of Athenian laws at the Royal Stoa. The subordination of royal rule to either written law or priestly supervision, as in the Torah of the King, ran contrary to Ancient Near Eastern notions of kingship, but had at least three parallels in early Hellenistic literature. In the *Aegyptiaca* by Hecataeus of Abdera, it was claimed that the ancient pharaohs of Egypt were directed in their royal activities by priests who ensured their obedience to the strictures of Egyptian law (Diodorus Siculus, *Library* 1.70–71). In the same text, it was claimed that Darius the Persian not only made a copy of all the ancient laws of Egypt, but studied Egyptian laws with the priests (Diodorus Siculus, *Library* 1.95.4–5). Finally, in the foundation story of the Jews also written by Hecataeus of Abdera, it was claimed that Moses selected the most capable men of the nation, appointed them as priests and judges, "and entrusted to them the guardianship of the laws and customs" (Diodorus Siculus, *Library* 40.3.4–5). None of these three Hecataean traditions can be credited as ancient or factual, but instead reflected Greek political notions foreign to both Egyptians and Jews of pre-Hellenistic times. In all three, the priests functioned as *nomophylakes* or Guardians of the Laws, and in the first two they additionally acted as supervisors and legal advisors to the kings of Egypt. The office of *nomophylakes* was found in many Greek city-states, including Athens (Aristotle, *Athenian Constitution* 4.4; 8.4; cf. Stanton 1990: 30–3, 68–73). Their primary responsibility was to ensure the magistrates obeyed the written laws of the *polis*.[259] Secondarily, the *nomophylakes* supervised public behavior, ensuring that those violating public decorum were reported to the proper authorities for prosecution.[260] In the Torah of the King, the requirement that the king, as an elected magistrate, should become knowledgeable in the written laws and perform his office in strict accordance with those laws (Deut. 17.18–20) was unequivocally a reflection of Greek political notions. The explicit role of the levitical priests as guardians and public advocates of the written laws that were to be obeyed by the magistrates and people alike,[261] and implicit responsibility for educating the king in his duties of office via these writings and enforcing the written statutes upon the king, casts the levitical priests in the distinctively Greek office of *nomophylakes,* the same office given the priestly successors to Moses in the Jewish foundation story by Hecataeus.[262]

10. Religious magistrates

In addition to civil magistrates, Athens had a number of officers of a religious or quasi-religious character. These included temple administrators,[263] priests and priestesses, experts in sacred law, prophets and prophetesses.

Priestly positions in Athens were partly filled by election and partly by lot (Aristotle, *Athenian Constitution* 57; Plato, *Laws* 6.759a-c; cf. Morrow 1993: 413–14). Priests were required to be physically perfect and pure in parentage (Plato, *Laws* 6.759c; cf. Morrow 1993: 415). The priestly office, which mainly involved the oversight of sacrificial slaughtering of animals, required no special education or training (Morrow 1993: 418). Some priestly positions were open to all citizens. Other prominent priestly offices in Athens and nearby Eleusis were held by certain priestly families such as the Eumolpidae and the Kerykes, comparable to the priestly lines of the Aaronids of the Pentateuch and the Zadokites of Ezekiel. Plato's *Laws* contemplated both hereditary and elected priests and legislated the annual election of three citizens regarded as possessing the highest virtue in the *polis* to serve in lifelong positions as priests of Apollo and Helios, of whom one would serve as "high priest" *(archheireon)* for that year.[264] Outside of Plato's *Laws,* the honorary position of "high priest" was unknown elsewhere in Greece until ca. 250 BCE.[265] The college of priests of Apollo and Helios in Plato's *Laws* had important civic duties as auditors of all the magistrates and as leading members of the Nocturnal Council, the supreme ruling body in the *polis*.[266] Plato was unique both in investing the office of priest with an aura of virtue and in assigning priests civic duties. The high priest and college of priests associated with him correspond strikingly to the Jewish high priest and chief priests who presided over the *gerousia* (Great Sanhedrin) and the nation.[267]

Not all priests officiated at a temple. Greek Comedy described a class of priestly freelance religious entrepreneurs as itinerant beggars dependant on the public for their income and willing to do a variety of religious rites if the price was right.[268] This category of second class, itinerant priests is roughly comparable to the Levites, not only in their landlessness (Deut. 12.11–19; 14.22–27; 26.11–13), but also in their dependence on charity for income (Num. 18.23–30; Deut. 12.17–19; 14.22–27; 26.11–13) and in their social mobility.[269]

Although priests officiated in the temple and performed sacred sacrifices and other religious rites, they were not considered religious experts and were not consulted on matters of sacred law. In the Greek world, religious practices were grounded in ancient, typically unwritten religious lore that the Greeks called "sacred law."[270] The experts in sacred law constituted a special class of officials, the Exegetes or expounders of sacred law.[271] In the Eleusian Mysteries, an important Attic cult, the Exegetes belonged to a single priestly family *(genos)*, the Eumolpidae.[272] The Exegetes of Classical Athens are primarily known through literary references, mostly found in Plato's *Laws,*[273] in the speeches of fourth century orators,[274] in fragments of *Exegetica*[275] and in a handful of inscriptions. From these references, it emerges that the Exegetes were most often questioned on the proper manner in which to handle various categories of religious pollution, most especially the pollution associated with voluntary and involuntary homicide.[275] In this respect the Exegetes of Classical Athens are closely analogous to the Levitical priests of Deuteronomy.[277] Levites were also given an explicit exegetical role in Nehemiah (Neh. 8.1–18). Levitical priests were brought onto the scene alongside judges and occasionally city elders wherever a homicide was committed (Deut. 21.1–9). They did not appear in a judicial capacity – judges were always mentioned separately – but instead seem to have been consulted on the proper rites to cure the pollution associated with acts of bloodshed.[278] Much as a rural homicide might require the consultation of an Exegete located in Athens (Plato, *Euthyphro* 4c, 9a; cf. Demosthenes, *Against Evergus and Mnesibulus* 67–9), so the authors of Deuteronomy presumed that Levitical priests could always be found in the place Yahweh would put his name.[279] It may have been in their capacity as much-needed religious experts that the itinerant Levites were characterized as dwelling in every village (Deut. 12.12, 18; 14.24, 27; 16.11, 14; 18.1–2, 6; 26.12).

Another category of religious official in Athens was the *mantis* or prophet.[280] Some Greek prophets and (more famously) prophetesses – such as the Pythian prophetess at Delphi – were associated with temple oracles, where they responded to inquiries, in some cases with a simple yes or no answer, and in other instances in obscure riddles composed in verse (for oracular riddles from Delphi, see Fontenrose 1978: 79–83). Other prophets were available for consultation outside a temple setting. Prophetic visions and spontaneous speeches outside a temple setting, although known in Classical Greece, especially in literary contexts such as the Homeric epics and in Greek tragic plays, appear with relative infrequency in Greek non-literary sources.[281] The *mantis* encountered in historical narratives was more typically skilled in technical divination[282] and in interpreting signs and omens such as the flight of birds and celestial phenomena.[283] Athens had a prophet specially charged with interpreting sacrificial omens (Aristotle, *Athenian Constitution* 54.7). The *mantis* was especially important in guiding military decisions and often accompanied the army at war to be consulted by the general.[284] It was in this semi-official capacity that the *mantis* received the most direct recognition as a figure important to the functioning of the Greek *polis*. However, disastrous military decisions based on prophetic consultations made during the Sicilian war in 413 BCE are thought to have resulted in a major setback in the prestige of the *mantis* in Athens.[285]

The Pentateuch displayed a high regard for the legendary prophetic figures in Israel's past, including Abraham, Joseph (in his capacity as an interpreter of dreams)[286] and Moses. The biblical text also mentioned prophetesses.[287] Technical divination was rejected, although the use of lots was sanctioned as a divine method of oracular divination. The consultation of the *Urim* and *Thummim* – perhaps a magical form of dice in the possession of the high priest[288] – was mandated in matters of war.[289] Although the Pentateuch allowed for the periodic appearance of legitimate prophets, the specter of false prophets was also raised, especially in Deut. 13 and 17. There those who claimed the office of prophet were to be carefully scrutinized according to various criteria:[290] their citizenship (Deut. 18.15, 18; cf. Hagedorn 2004: 159; Berman 2006: 541–2; Berman 2008: 70–3); speaking the words of Yahweh, not some other deity; the religious content of their message; and the accuracy of their predictions (Deut. 13.2–5; 18.19–22). Claiming prophetic inspiration for the institution of any religious practices contrary to the cult of Yahweh was a capital offense. Execution was also legislated for failed predictions, a grave matter that could prove disastrous to the state in times of war or crisis. The profound skepticism with which the authors of Deuteronomy viewed the state consultation of prophets mirrored attitudes in the Greek world of the late Classical and Hellenistic Eras (Hagedorn 2004: 157, 164–8).

11. Conclusions

This chapter surveyed constitutional features found in the biblical laws and narratives of Exodus–Joshua as compared with those found in the Greek world, especially at Athens.[291] Points of comparison included similar citizenship requirements and enrollment procedures; a dual social organization by kinship (tribe, brotherhood, clan and household) and geography (tribe and district); the dual definition of tribes as both a geographical and kinship group; the tribe as civil, judicial, military and political entity; the organization of a citizen army under tribal generals; similar procedures for land survey and equal allotment in new colonies; citizen self-rule by an assembly and council; deliberative bodies with a similar range of executive and judicial responsibilities; similar procedures for the citizen selection, scrutiny and audit of magistrates (including king); similar classes of government officials; and the striking subordination of governmental powers, including those exercised by the king, to written law.

These parallels indicate a systematic indebtedness of the constitutional features of the nation founded by Moses and Joshua in the biblical account to Greek political and legal institutions.[292] Some aspects of the biblical accounts point to a particular influence from Athenian legal institutions: the system of ten or twelve tribes, also found at Athens; command of the army under tribal generals; the dual kinship and geographical functions of the fictitious tribes, a feature of Athenian political organization dating to the reforms of Kleisthenes; the role of the kinship group in homicide prosecutions and in levirate marriage; the similar extended conception of the household that encompassed land, family, servants, animals and guests; comparable judicial procedures and rules of evidence; broadly similar classes of officials, including priests, exegetes, prophets, civic magistrates, judges and king; and an elective kingship that lacked the usual powers and trappings of rulership in the Ancient Near East.

The absence of direct contact between Athens and Judea in either pre-Hellenistic or Hellenistic times suggests that the influence of Athenian constitutional features on the biblical legal system was mediated by exposure to Greek literature on political topics during the Hellenistic Era. This possibility is reinforced by consti-tutional features in Mosaic writings that appear to display influence from Plato's dialogues. Many of the constitutional features common to the Mosaic and Athe-nian political systems mentioned earlier also appear in Plato's *Laws,* in which the proposed charter for the Cretan colony of Magnesia was modeled in large part on Athenian legal and constitutional traditions. Other aspects of the Mosaic system appear to draw on Platonic political ideas. These include the organization of the nation in twelve tribes, which is more easily explained by literary dependence on Plato's *Laws* or on the *Aegyptiaca* of Hecataeus of Abdera than awareness of the historical reorganization of the Athenian state from ten to twelve tribes in 307 BCE; the modeling of the Levitical expertise on sacred law on the Exegetes, a relatively obscure body of Athenian religious experts who are unlikely to have been directly known to the Pentateuchal authors, but who feature prominently in Plato's *Laws;* the supreme civic powers given to the Jewish high priest, a Hel-lenistic Era development that appears to have drawn on the office of high priest in Plato's *Laws;* and the supervision of the king of Deut. 17.14–20 by priestly Levites entrusted with preserving and promulgating the biblical laws, a role best understood as modeled on the Guardians of the Laws who have a preeminent role in the administration of government in Plato's *Laws.*

The Great Library of Alexandria housed an extensive section on laws that prominently included books on constitutions, laws and politics by Plato, Aristotle and other notable Athenian philosophers.[293] Jewish access to the Great Library with its comprehensive collection of legal writings is attested in *The Letter of Aristeas* in connection with the Septuagint translation at Alexandria, an occasion at which the biblical authors could have conducted legal research into Athenian and other political systems as they were devising the system of constitution and laws found in the Pentateuch.[294]

Notes

1 See especially Weinfeld 1993. The genre of foundation story and its biblical parallels is discussed in detail in Chapter 5 §2.

2 *The Letter of Aristeas* 10, 38 described Jewish legislation as authoritative in the time of Ptolemy II Philadelphus. Pseudo-Hecataeus claimed that the scroll the high priest Ezekias read at Alexandria contained the Jewish "story of their settlement and their

political constitution" (Josephus, Apion 1.189). According to Josephus, Moses was a lawgiver *(nomothetes)* who gave the Israelites both a constitution *(politeia)* and laws *(nomoi)*. He suggested that the idea of a constitution originated among the Jews, not the Greeks. See Josephus, Ant. 1.5; 2.180; 4.194, 196, 198, 302; 20.229, 251, 261; cf. Feldman 1993: 313, 320–1; Rodgers 2008: 129–34. His description of the Jewish constitution is taken from Deuteronomy; cf. Berman 2008: 52.

3 According to Eusebius, *Preparation for the Gospel* 7.6.1–2; 8.1.1–3, Moses created a constitution and legislation for the Jews that was intended to have force only for the land of Judea.

4 See LeFebvre 2006: 151–73 on evidence for the use of the Torah as a code of local Jewish law used in Ptolemaic courts after ca. 275 BCE based on a consideration of papyrological evidence.

5 An edict of Antiochus III in 198 BCE (Josephus, Ant. 12.138–44) allowed the Jews to have a form of government according to "ancestral laws." According to LeFebvre 2006: 173–82, Antiochus III recognized the same Jewish legal code and civic rights that existed earlier under Ptolemaic rule. The Torah continued to function as the constitution for the Jews until the Hellenistic Crisis (2 Macc. 4.7–9; 6.1; Josephus, Ant. 12.240–41).

6 A return to Jewish ancestral laws was effected in 164 BCE (2 Macc. 11.22–38). Conflicts between Pharisees and Sadducees on the interpretation of Jewish laws as affecting Hasmonean rule contributed to civil disturbances from the time of John Hyrcanus to the conquest of Jerusalem by Pompey (cf. Josephus, Ant. 13.293–98).

7 Roman historians portrayed Pompey's abolition of the Jewish monarchy and restoration of a rule by a *gerousia* and high priest in 63 BCE as a return to Jewish ancestral laws and institutions (Josephus, Ant. 14.41; Diodorus Siculus, *Library* 40.2; cf. Gmirkin 2006: 259–63). Traditional Jewish forms of government in accordance with their laws and customs were later affirmed by Julius Caesar and various other Roman officials in documents Josephus quoted in Ant. 14.190–267.

8 See note 33.

9 Aristotle, *Politics* 3.1278b. Plutarch, *Solon* 16.5, gives a good description of Solon as framer of the Athenian constitution: "[The Athenians] appointed Solon to reform the constitution and make new laws, laying no restrictions whatever upon him, but putting everything into his hands, magistracies, assemblies, courts-of-law, and councils. He was to fix the property qualification for each of these, their numbers, and their times of meeting, abrogating and maintaining existing institutions at his pleasure." All quotations from classical literature are taken from LCL.

10 See Aristotle, *Politics* 4.1289a on the difference between a constitution and laws. Aristotle, *Nicomachian Ethics* 10.1181b referred to usefulness of collections of laws and collections of constitutions for the study of political science. Aristotle, *Politics* 1.1247b discussed famous lawmakers of the past, some who created constitutions, some who made laws and others – including Solon of Athens and Lycurgus of Sparta – who did both. Aristotle's *Constitutions* collected and analyzed 158 constitutions; only his *Athenian Constitution* has survived mostly intact. Aristotle systematically compared features of actual and theoretical (proposed) constitutions at *Politics* 2.1260b–1274b.

11 The term *politeia* could be used to refer to a constitution, a form of government, those possessed of citizenship or a particular regime, depending of context. See discussions at Rhodes 1993: 89, 116. Plato's *Republic* or *Politeia,* for instance, discussed the ideal form of government but did not discuss the constitution *per se*. In Aristotle's classification of types of government, he used the term *politeia* to refer to a constitutional democracy or democracy subject to law, which he distinguished from a pure democracy that placed no limits on the will of the majority.

12 Plato, *Laws* 5.735a; 6.751a-b spoke of assigning laws to the various offices of the state. The *nomophylakes* or Guardians of the Laws were responsible for seeing that magistrates complied with the regulations that governed their duties and conduct.

13 Inscriptions with *psephemata* were comprehensively cataloged and summarized in Rhodes and Lewis 1997.

14 Both Plato and Aristotle held that the best laws did not benefit a single class, but were aimed at the common good. Plato (*Laws* 3.693d-e; 6.756e) and Aristotle (*Politics* 2.1265b-1266a; 4.1294b, 1297a) therefore recommended a mixed constitution as the most stable, because it was capable of balancing the interests of the wealthy few and the masses. Lycurgus, the legendary legislator of Sparta, was credited with having invented the mixed constitution, which featured both an oligarchic senate *(gerousia)* and an assembly (Aristotle, *Politics* 2.1265b; Polybius, *Histories* 6.3).

15 The constitution established in 403/402 BCE was still in effect, with minor changes, in ca. 325 BCE when the *Athenian Constitution* was written.

16 Aristotle described both Plato's *Republic* and *Laws* as essentially theoretical or utopian (*Politics* 2.1266a; cf. 1267b).

17 The authorship of the *Athenian Constitution* by Xenophon is now doubted; the unknown author is conventionally referred to as Pseudo-Xenophon or The Old Oligarch. According to Strabo, *Geography* 8.5.5, King Pausanias also wrote a pamphlet on the Lacedemonian Constitution after his exile from Sparta in 395 BCE.

18 See especially Fortenbaugh and Schütrumpf 2000 and vol. 2 of Fortenbaugh et al. 1992. Heraklides of Lesbos wrote essays *On Constitutions* and *On Lawgivers* in the second century BCE that have survived only in fragments quoted by later authors; cf. Stanton 1990: 11.

19 See Arnaoutoglou 1998: 74–95 for significant speeches and inscriptions with constitutional content. Useful source material is also found in Fornara 1983; Dillon and Garland 2010.

20 Plato's *Republic* (8.543a-569c) distinguished five forms of government, which he ranked as follows, from best to worst: monarchy or aristocracy (the rule of the "best"), which Plato considered equivalent; timarchy (a Platonic neologism signifying the rule of those with the greatest honors, mainly represented by the militant governments of Sparta and Crete); oligarchy (the rule of the wealthy); democracy (the unrestricted rule of the people); and tyranny (lawless one-man rule). Plato's *Laws* favored what we would call today a constitutional democracy, subject to written laws, but guided by aristocratic "Guardians of the Laws." Aristotle's *Politics* (3.1279a-b) distinguished six forms of government: three positive forms (monarchy, aristocracy and the *polis* or constitutional democracy) and their three perversions (tyranny, oligarchy and democracy). The last three negative forms were marked by arbitrary rule that favored only the interests of the ruling class, namely the tyrant, the wealthy or the masses respectively. Aristotle defined a dynasty as a hereditary oligarchy. Aristotle's *Athenian Constitution* chronicled eleven changes in the form of Athenian government, including the tribal kings of legendary times, the democratic reforms under Solon, the tyranny of Pisistratus, the constitutional democracy under Kleisthenes, the oligarchy of the Four Hundred, the tyranny of the Thirty and the restoration of constitutional democracy in Aristotle's day.

21 In the Greek world, a *polis* consisted of a city *(astu)* and its surrounding territory *(chora);* hence the common translation of *polis* as "city-state." The city-state of Athens was also known as Attica *(Attike ge),* "the land of the Athenians." Territorial boundaries were not a formal constitutional element. The ideal size and geographical situation of a city-state were nevertheless matters commonly discussed in constitutional literature: cf. Aristotle, *Politics* 7.1326b-1327a; Plato, *Republic* 4.423b-c; Plato, *Laws* 4.704a-705c. See also Aristotle, *Politics* 4.1299b, which discussed constitutional elements in distributing governmental power between central and local authorities.

22 Citizen qualifications differed according to the type of government. In an oligarchy, citizenship was effectively restricted to the wealthy, whereas in a democracy or mixed government, participation in the administration of the state typically extended to all males who were not foreigners or slaves.

23 Aristotle, *Athenian Constitution* 7.3; 13.5; 29.5 (list of 5000 in 411/410 BCE); 36.1–2 (list of 3000 in 404/403 BCE); 42.1–2 (residents within each *deme* or political district); Plato, *Laws* 6.785a-b. In Athens, foreigners were classified as either *xenoi* (guest-friends) or *metics* (resident aliens); the latter paid a special tax for living in Athens and could be subject to conscription. Women and children possessed citizen rights through the master of the household.

24 Aristotle, *Athenian Constitution* 58.2–3; Plato, *Laws* 8.849b, 850a; 12.949b-c. Plato, *Laws* 9.866b-c, 869d, 879d, 880c, contained special criminal laws for strangers and resident aliens.

25 Aristotle, *Athenian Constitution* 43–7. In the Athens of ca. 400 BCE, the Assembly *(Ekklesia)*, consisting of all citizens, was invested with the final authority over legislative, judicial and executive matters. The Council *(Boule)* had elected members who conducted pre-trial investigations of major cases, scheduled both regular and emergency sessions of the Assembly and set the Assembly's legislative and judicial agendas (Aristotle, *Athenian Constitution* 43.2–3; Plato, *Laws* 6.758d). The Council of the Areopagus, composed of ex-archons, was charged with oversight of Athenian magistrates by administering scrutinies and audits and conducting preliminary investigations into charges against public officials made by private citizens.

26 Aristotle, *Politics* 3.1278b. Athenian magistrates of ca. 325 BCE were discussed in Aristotle, *Athenian Constitution* 43–62. The arrangement of offices in Plato's *Laws* was largely modeled on those of Athens. The officers of Plato's ideal *polis* listed in Plato's *Laws* 6 included generals, elected council members, priests, expounders of the sacred law, treasurers, territorial guardians, rural judges, city wardens, market wardens, superintendents of education and the Guardians of the Laws charged with the oversight of the conduct of officials and citizens; cf. Morrow 1993: 191–5. Athens also possessed other distinctive magistries not found in Plato's *Laws,* notably the ten *archons* (the *basileus,* the *polemarch,* the *archon* and the seven *thesmothetae*) who had oversight of court cases, religious festivals and other administrative matters. These functions were taken over by the Guardians of the Laws in Plato's idealized legal system (Morrow 1993: 202).

27 The scrutiny of magistrates before taking office, their oversight by the *nomophylakes* or Guardians of the Laws, and the audit of magistrates after leaving office were all weighty constitutional matters in the Greek world; cf. Aristotle, *Politics* 4.1298a-b; 6.1322b; Aristotle, *Athenian Constitution* 8.4; 25.2; 26.1; 48.3–5; 59.2; Plato, *Laws* 6.751a-767e, *passim* (scrutiny); 6.774b; 12.945b-948b (audit); cf. Chase 1933: 138–9.

28 Aristotle, *Athenian Constitution* 52–3, 63–9; Plato, *Laws* 6.766d-768c; 12.948e-949c, 956b-958c. Smaller cases were handled by arbitration or by jury trials conducted in the villages of Attica. Certain types of cases were handled by tribal courts or by military tribunals. Major cases and appeal cases were referred to Athens. Athens had a prison for holding individuals awaiting trial, administered by the Eleven, gaolers who also possessed limited police and judicial powers.

29 The genre of constitutional law, which described the various offices of government, their qualifications, responsibilities and means of selection, was well represented in literature and inscriptions throughout the Greek world, but was entirely unknown in the Ancient Near East. Ancient Near Eastern law collections mentioned certain government offices, such as king (LE 48, 58; LH 129; MAL A 15, 47; MAL B 3; MAL C 8; MAL E 1; MAPD 2–3, 6–7, 9, 11, 15, 18, 21), governor (LH 24; MAPD 1), mayor

(MAL A 45; MAL B 6, 18) and judge (numerous). But these governmental officials were mentioned in connection with case law, sometimes as pertaining to jurisdictional issues, but never in a remotely constitutional setting. In 338 BCE, the oligarchic land-owners who ruled Xanthus in Lycia – then part of the Persian satrapy of Caria – issued a decree that established a local altar and priesthood for the cult for the Carian god Basileus Kaunios, an initiative approved by the central Persian government and pub-lished in a trilingual inscription recovered by archaeologists. See Teixidor 1978; Fried 2004: 140–54. The Xanthian Trilingual figures prominently in Frei's theory of Persian authorization of local constitutions, by which he argued a Persian Era date for the creation and authorization of the Torah in Frei 2001: 5–40. In this single Persian Era inscription, the central government seemingly accommodated a decree authorized by a non-monarchical form of governmental institution within one of its satrapies, which Frei took to indicate Persian interest in constitutional issues (Frei 2001: 40). However, because the Trilingual Inscription is an informal decree with no constitutional content, it supports neither Frei's thesis nor the existence of constitutional law as a genre in the Ancient Near Eastern world.

30 See Levinson 2001: 512–18, for a comparison of literary and historical portrait of Jewish monarchy with Ancient Near East kingship.

31 Herodotus, *Histories* 2.124 claimed that Cheops built the Great Pyramids using slave labor. Aristotle noted the pyramids of Egypt as a prime example of extensive building programs used to keep enslaved populations occupied and to prevent their rebellion (*Politics* 5.1313b; cf. 7.1327b). Biblical authors associated the enslavement of the Israelites with building programs under Pharaoh (Ex. 1.8–14) and under Solomon (in the anti-monarchic tradition represented by 1 Kgs 9.15; 12.4–14, 18). For the com-mon use of the term *missîm* or taskmasters to describe the officers of Pharaoh and Solomon, see Friedman 1987: 20.

32 See the contrast between "the dominant tribute-imposing class and the dominated tribute-bearing class" in the Ancient Near East, as discussed in Berman 2008: 4–5, and its tell-ing reflection in similar class divisions within the Mesopotamian pantheon (Berman 2008: 18–26). Berman was basically correct in his description of the egalitarian thrust of biblical law, although he exaggerated the absence of caste and wealth distinctions in Pentateuchal legislation; see the criticisms in the review article, Levinson 2010: 685–94.

33 Overtly constitutional content found at Deut. 16.18–18.22 has been extensively dis-cussed at Lohfink 1993; Hagedorn 2004: 108–71; Levinson 2006: 1853–88.

34 Discussions of the constitutional content of Deuteronomy as a whole are found in McBride 1987, 1993; Berman 2006; Berman 2008; Levinson 2008: 52–88. The influ-ence of Pentateuchal constitutional and political ideas on western civilization is explored in Berman 2008, and in rabbinic and later legal writings in Elazar 1995: 1.367–460.

35 The Covenant Code was interpreted as a foundational national charter in Paul 1970: 29–33; Elazar 1995: 1.19–466. Levinson 2008: 48–51 vastly overstated the constitu-tional content in biblical covenants starting with early Genesis (as criticized at Berman 2008: 28–9).

36 Ancient Near Eastern law collections, which dealt exclusively with case law, inciden-tally touched on judicial jurisdictions or on special procedures for determining fact or guilt, but neither judicial structures or procedures were discussed in a systematic manner comparable to Greek constitutional literature.

37 The interpretation of Deuteronomy as the constitution of the ancient Jews in Josephus is generally upheld by McBride (cf. 1993: 62).

38 Chase 1933: 131–92; Morrow 1993. A chart at Chase 1933: 189–90, listed sixty-three instances where Plato's institutions were based on Athenian models. A second chart at Chase 1933: 191, listed ten instances of special affinity with older institutions estab-lished by Solon.

39 "The Greek polis was universally grounded in a law-based system of mixed govern-ment. But what made the system cohesive was the notion of *citizenry:* the strong sense of fraternity, order, and responsibility shared by members of a common polity and their sense of striving for virtue, variously defined." Berman 2008: 54.

40 Parpola 2004: 12–15 argued that the Assyrians had a notion of citizenship reflected in national identity as the "people of Assyria" or "sons of Assyria"; obligations to pay taxes and perform military and corvée service; and rights to appeal to the judicial system or to the king, who was responsible for their protection, prosperity and justice. However, it may be questioned whether the subjects of a king may be considered citizens, except in an informal sense. Aristotle, who considered at length the question of what constitutes citizenship (*Politics* 3.1275a-1278b), concluded that "he who has the power to take part in the deliberative or judicial administration in any state is said by us to be a citizen of that state" (3.1275b). Aristotle (*Politics* 3.1285a) described the voluntary subjects of Near Eastern monarchies as falling somewhere between invol-untary slaves (as those ruled by a tyrant) and "citizens in the fullest sense" (3.1278a) who possessed a full share in the government.

41 Athenian laws on children and citizenship were collected at Phillips 2013: 174–215. In Athens, where membership in the Council was assigned each year by lot from all qualifying members of the *polis,* the ideal citizen was held to be one who could both rule and be ruled; cf. Aristotle, *Politics* 1.1252a; 3.1277a-b, 1279a, 1283b, 1287a; 7.1332b-1333a; Plato, *Laws* 1.643e.

42 Aristotle, *Athenian Constitution* 42.1–5. For citizen registries, see Rhodes 1993: 188. There were several registers: by *phyle* (tribe), *phratry* (brotherhood), *deme* (village) and perhaps *genos* (clan). Literary and inscriptional documentation for the implemen-tation of these registries varies. Athenian generals utilized published lists *(katalogoi)* of named conscripts when making war preparations (cf. Thucydides, *Peloponnesian War* 6.43.1; 7.16.1; 7.20.2; 8.24.2). Records of citizens by tribes were used for enroll-ment into the military in other Greek city-states (cf. Plutarch, *Nicias* 14.5). The loca-tion of some of these registries – whether at Athens or in local villages – is subject to debate. According to Plato, *Laws* 6.785a-b, children were to be enrolled into their phratry at birth: this probably reflects Athenian practices (cf. Chase 1933: 144). See Morrow 1993: 112–31 on citizenry in Plato's *Laws.*

43 Plutarch, *Solon* 18–19; Crawford and Whitehead 1983: 275; Stanton 1990: 35, 66–7, 73–4. Democratic participation in juries was encouraged in Classical Greece by pay for jury duty for the lowest classes.

44 "Loss of civil rights, *atimia,* was a serious penalty since it laid a person open to harm or even death inflicted by members of a community with impunity." Stanton 1990: 72; cf. MacDowell 1978: 73–5. A punishment of *atimia* could be imposed for trea-son, impiety, murder, adultery, male prostitution, mistreatment of parents or failure to repay a public debt; cf. Allen 2000: 142.

45 Aristotle, *Athenian Constitution* 20.4; Aristotle, *Politics* 3.1278a; Demosthenes, *Against Neaera* 16; cf. Davies 1978: 73, 104. The policy of *philoxenia* instituted by Solon induced foreigners to live at Athens – in part by the offer of citizenship – as members of a valued merchant class essential to Athenian economic life (Plutarch, *Solon* 24.1–2; 24.4; cf. Stanton 1990: 65–6), a policy later also extended under Kleisthenes (Aristotle, *Politics* 3.1275b; cf. Stanton 1990: 165–6). But the exercise of a craft was considered unworthy for an Athenian, and craftsmen were generally despised (Herodotus, *Histories* 2.164–67). As a result, craftsmen were excluded as citizens from the best city-states, according to Aristotle, *Politics* 3.1278a.

46 Demosthenes, *Against Neaera* 16, 52; cf. Lacey 1968: 112; MacDowell 1978: 67, 87; Arnaoutoglou 1998: 17–8. The citizenship law of Perikles was aimed at removing for-eigners added under the laws of Solon and Kleisthenes from the citizen roles, as well

as to prevent dangerous marriage-alliances with non-Athenians that might undermine Athenian political integrity.

47 The exclusion of bastards *(nothoi)* from Athenian citizen rolls was argued at Harrison 1968: 1.63–65; MacDowell 1976: 88–91; the conclusiveness of the evidence was questioned at Rhodes 1978. See also Walters 1983; Sealey 1984; Patterson 1990. Part of the debate hinged on whether *anchisteia* (the family relationship allowing inheritance) and *politeia* (the right of citizenship) were equivalent under Athenian law. It appears certain that a contract could stipulate that the offspring of a concubine would be free (that is, not owned by the father as slaves), but this falls short of guaranteeing citizenship.

48 According to Pseudo-Xenophon, *Athenian Constitution* 1.12, "The *polis* needs *metoikoi* because of the multiplicity of crafts and because of the fleet." Athenian *philoxenia* was famous since the days of Solon; cf. Crawford and Whitehead 1983: 288–91.

49 The most thorough treatment is Whitehead 1977; see also Harrison 1968: 1.187–99. For *metics* in the Athenian army (as hoplites or light-armed soldiers, but not as cavalry) and navy, see Whitehead 1977: 82–6; MacDowell 1978: 77.

50 The *metic* registered at a *deme* as a member of that village, where he presumably maintained his legal residence (although he could not own a house or land). The *prostates* presided over the enrollment of a *metic* in his deme or village and acted in some capacity as his representative in court. The inscriptional and literary evidence on *metics* and *demes* is discussed at Whitehead 1977: 72–5, 89–92; cf. Harrison 1968: 1.189–93.

51 The length of time before a visitor at Athens was required to register and become a *metic* is not fully established in our sources. Aristophanes of Byzantium stated, "For so many days he is called a *parapidemos* and is free from tax, but if he outstays the specified time he becomes a *metoikos* and liable to tax." A fifth century BCE treaty between Chaleum and Oeanthea in Locria specified one month. See Whitehead 1977: 7–10.

52 The *polemarch,* one of the ten archons of Athens, oversaw cases that involved foreigners, including crimes against *metics* or other *xenoi* and legal disputes between Athenian citizens and *metics*.

53 "Slaves freed by their masters also paid *metoikion*. Citizenship could not be acquired by a private act." Whitehead 1977: 16–17.

54 Aristotle, *Politics* 7.1329a-b; cf. Berman 2008: 61–2. In ancient Greece, only soldiers had political rights in early times; cf. Lacey 1968: 75, 267 n. 140.

55 The children of Israel who departed the land of Egypt were described as a host or army at Ex. 6.26; 7.4; 12.17, 41, 51. In the wilderness narratives they were described as a mobile army (Num. 1.3, 18–46; 26.2–51; 32.16–32) that marched in ranks (Num. 10.14–28). The "generation" who perished in the wilderness was specified as the members of the citizen army (Num. 15.29; 32.11; Josh. 5.4, 6). The Israelites who entered the Promised Land were similarly described as an army who incidentally possessed wives, children and herds (Num. 32.16, 24, 26). The conception of the Israelites of the Exodus as an army was central to the foundation story in Exodus–Joshua.

56 Num. 1–3, 26 described enrollments into the citizen army arrayed according to tribe, brotherhood and clan. Num. 15–16 listed the (fictitious) names or the secretaries or registrars who enrolled the troops. The presumption of literacy and public records among the wilderness Israelites is striking. Registrars also recorded and maintained citizen rolls in Attica. These rolls served the double function of defining the citizen body and facilitating military matters such as conscription, assignment to military units and wartime mobilization.

57 Foreigners could lease land for a limited period but were not allowed to permanently acquire land (Lev. 25.25, 47–54; Deut. 15.1–6).

58 Disenfranchisement appeared as a punishment at Lev. 20.3–6; Ezra 7.26; 10.8; cf. Ex. 12.15; Lev. 17.10; Num. 9.13.

59 The Greek term for foreigner *(xenos)* had many possible connotations, one of the most common being that of guest-friend (e.g. Thucydides, *Peloponnesian War* 2.13.1; Lysias, *On the Property of Aristophanes* 19; Isocrates, *Trapeziticus* 38, 43; Demosthenes, *On the Liberty of the Rhodians* 15.15; cf. Whitehead 1977: 10). Official sponsorship by an Athenian host, the establishment of a legal residence and formal enrollment changed the official status of a visiting foreigner from guest to *metic*.

60 See Berman 2008: 14 on the distinction between stranger (Lev. 25.1) and resident alien (Ex. 23.9). Benevolent treatment of both visiting foreigners and resident aliens was enjoined by Moses (Ex. 20.10; 22.21; 23.9, 12; Lev. 19.10, 33–34; 23.22; 25.35; Deut. 5.14; 10.19; 14.29; 16.11, 14; 26.11).

61 References to charity distributed to "the stranger within your gates" (Deut. 14.29; 16.11; 26.11–12) suggest that resident aliens in Israel were recognized as living in a specific village and lived under the protection of either some sponsoring household there or the village as a whole. Plato, *Laws* 8.846d-e foresaw aliens residing in every village, for a maximum of twenty years (8.850a-b), to act as craftsmen.

62 Foreigners who resided among the Israelites were to be afforded the same legal protections under civil law as the Israelites themselves (Lev. 24.22; Num. 35.15; Deut. 1.16; 24.17; cf. Deut. 31.12; Josh. 8.32–35, where the intended audience for the periodic reading of the Deuteronomic law included Israel's resident aliens).

63 See note 45. For a limited period after the disastrous war losses of the Peloponnesian War, citizen status was accorded to the children of concubines in order to replenish numbers in the Athenian armed forces (Diogenes Laertius, *Lives of Eminent Philosophers* 2.26).

64 Ezra 9–10; Neh. 9–10; 13.23–30. The penalty for those with foreign wives was disenfranchisement (Ezra 10.8). Comparison with the law of Perikles was made at Fitzpatrick-McKinley 2003: 17–48.

65 See Crawford and Whitehead 1983: 572 on the extraordinary war-tax or *eisphora*.

66 See Aristotle, *Athenian Constitution* 4, 7–8 on economic classes as determined by assessment under Drakon and Solon. See Ostwald 2000: 50–2 on property valuation and the oligarchic monopoly on political participation and office-holding prior to Solon's reforms. Plato's *Laws* 5.744c retained the Athenian system of four classes established by property assessment; cf. Chase 1933: 133–4; Morrow 1993: 131–8.

67 The *hippeis* were expected to own and maintain a horse. Athens periodically sent out horse-inspectors to make sure the horses were healthy and fit for use in battle.

68 In what follows, Athens' naval forces will be ignored, because these provide no parallel to biblical materials.

69 A discussion of the primary sources on Athenian education may be found at Carr 2005: 92–7. In some sources, letters and music were combined as one area of instruction, or letters was omitted altogether. Gymnastics or physical training was considered an essential aspect of education as preparation for the rigors of military service.

70 Plato's *Laws* is considered an important source on Athenian education. He indicated that training began in letters and then in playing the lyre. Pipes and flutes were not mentioned as part of the educational program, although Plato mentioned flute contests at festivals. Plato emphasized the importance of training in the military arts with realistic contests simulating circumstances of battle to promote courage. See generally Plato, *Laws* 7.794c, 804c, 813d-e; 8.829b-c, 833a-834d; cf. Morrow 1993: 334–5, 340–2, 381–2.

71 Because the *thetes* were not able to afford armor, Rhodes 1993: 503 doubts whether they participated in the *ephebate,* despite the silence of the sources on this question.

72 The establishment of three public gymnasia, which were to possess nearby race courses and fields for archery and javelin practice, was also found at Plato, *Laws* 6.764c, 779d; 7.804c-d; cf. Chase 1933: 138.

73 Cf. Aristotle, *Athenian Constitution* 42.3; Plato, *Laws* 8.829b; Morrow 1993: 180.

74 For the ephebic oath, sworn by all citizens at age twenty at acquiring citizenship and formal enrollment in the army, see Rhodes and Osborne 2003: 440–9; cf. Rhodes 2007: 12. Note that in Plato's *Laws,* the education of *epheboi* took place between the ages of twenty-five and thirty, in preparation for public office, instead of between ages eighteen and twenty in preparation for military service as at Athens; cf. Morrow 1993: 190 n. 87.

75 Rhodes 1993: 253. The tribes also formed the basis for election of members of the Council as well as other Athenian offices. Organization into tribes was common in Greek city-states.

76 Prior to the reforms of Kleisthenes, Athens had four tribal kings *(phylobasileis),* corresponding to the four tribes descended from Ion, the eponymous ancestor of the Ionians (Aristotle, *Athenian Constitution* 8.3; cf. Rhodes 1993: 150–1). By 501/500 BCE, Kleisthenes had fully implemented a new system of ten tribes, each of which elected its own tribal leader *(phylarchoi)* to act as general *(strategoi)* in the Athenian army (Herodotus, *Histories* 5.66, 69–73; Aristotle, *Athenian Constitution* 22.1–3; cf. Rhodes 1993: 244, 250, 676–7). For the relationship between the *polemarch* and the *strategoi,* see Hamel 1998: 79–83. At the battle of Marathon in 490 BCE, decisions were made by a vote among the ten generals, with an additional vote given to Kallimachos the *polemarchos* in case of a tie (Herodotus, *Histories* 6.94–117, especially 109). Plato's proposed system of government, patterned on that of Athens, had twelve tribes and generals (*Laws* 5.746d-e; 6.755c-e; cf. Chase 1933: 134–5; Morrow 1993: 122, 124).

77 Plutarch, *Aristides* 5.2; Herodotus, *Histories* 6.110; cf. Hamel 1998: 94. Somewhere between ca. 350 and ca. 230 BCE, generals ceased to be selected on a tribal basis (Rhodes 1993: 52).

78 The evidence is extensively discussed in Lambert 1993. The *phratry* was a military subdivision of the tribe at Plato, *Laws* 5.746d.

79 Literary parallels between the confrontation between champions in Homer, *Iliad* 3 and 7 and in the story of David and Goliath in 1 Sam. 17 have often been noted (cf. West 1997: 214–17; Yadin 2004 and the literature cited there). Significantly, Goliath's armaments were that of a Greek hoplite, with helmet, greaves, broad sword, long spear (the *sarissa*) and shield carried by a shield-carrier (1 Sam. 17.4–7; cf. Finkelstein and Silberman 2006: 196–9; and 1 Sam. 14.1, 13 for Jonathan's armor-bearer): Goliath's huge spear appears to show awareness of the transition from the shorter *dora* to the longer *sarissa* that took place in the Macedonian army around 350 BCE.

80 1 Sam. 17.34–39, 49–50. A division into armored infantry and light infantry is seen in narratives associated with David. David's crack units of Cherethites and Pelethites (1 Sam. 30.14; 2 Sam. 8.18; 15.18) are best interpreted to signify Cretans and *peltasts.* Crete was famous for its archers, who often served in mercenary military units. The *peltasts* were a new class of light armored Greek soldier, spear-throwers, who were first depicted in vase art of the sixth century BCE and were mentioned as having participated in the Peloponnesian War in the fifth century BCE at Thucydides, *Peloponnesian War* 1.60; 2.29; 4.93. In Homer, *Iliad* 13.716, Locrian slingers hurled stones at the enemy. Among the later Greeks, both Rhodians and Arcanians were noted for their expertise as slingers, although they typically used lead projectiles. See Plato, *Laws* 8.834a on military competitions with events for throwing and slinging stones.

81 The Greek physical ideal was the lean, athletic male warrior, tanned from exercise in the gymnasium. By contrast, the aesthetic ideal for women in Greek statuary and art depicted them as modestly covered. For a contrast between Greek and Ancient Near Eastern (including biblical) aesthetic ideals, especially with respect to nakedness, see Bonfante 1989. The description of the physique of the warrior hero is mostly absent from Ancient Near Eastern literature, except for the Gilgamesh Epic, which

emphasized the gigantic stature of its hero. The so-called Master of the Animals was also depicted as naked or wearing only a belt.

82 Athenian education included training on the lyre (cf. Plato, *Laws* 7.809e, 812 d-e; Morrow 1993: 340–2). The calming effect of David's music on Saul reflects Greek notions of music therapy, first seen in Homer, *Iliad* 1.472–74 and *Odyssey* 19.456–58 and later more fully developed by Pythagoreans and other philosophers. See Provenza 2012. See Morrow 1993: 303 for the beneficial mood-altering effects of music in Plato's *Laws*.

83 Agility was a key component of Greek dance. Michal criticized David for his immodest semi-nude attire, girded only in a linen ephod. Because the verb *chagar* ("gird") is biblically applied only to articles worn about the loins, it appears that David wore only a loin-cloth, like barbarian athletes were commonly depicted as wearing in Greek art, and like Greek athletes wore before they adopted the custom of exercising naked.

84 Plato, *Laws* 7.804c (gymnasia, horse tracks and training grounds for archery, javelins and slings); 8.829c-d (contests), 833a-d (foot-races), 833d-834d (contests for sword fighting, archery, javelins, slinging and horsemanship); cf. Morrow 1993: 381–2. Greek education was highly agonistic (competitive), with public festivals that sponsored literary and musical competitions for cultural purposes along with athletic competitions aimed at encouraging physical fitness and military training.

85 Homer, *Iliad* 6.215–34 (Glaucus and Diomedes); 7.301–5 (Hector and Ajax). The gods gave gifts of armor to their favored heroes at Homer, 18.462–617 (the Shield of Achilles).

86 For the awarding of *aristeia* or prizes for valor, see Hamel 1998: 64–70; cf. Plato, *Laws* 12.943b-c.

87 Homer was a staple of Greek education (cf. Plato, *Laws* 3.680c; Carr 2005: 100–1, 182–3).

88 The parallel between the biblical system of twelve tribal commanders and Plato, *Laws* 6.755d was noted at Eusebius, *Preparation for the Gospel* 12.47.

89 In Athens, the commander of the army was anciently termed the *polemarchos;* biblically this office was filled first by Moses (Ex. 17.6–16; Num. 21.31–35) and then by Joshua (Num. 27.15–23). In the list of David's chief magistrates, Joab acted as overall commander of the host (2 Sam. 20.23).

90 Biblical military narratives contained references to infantry and cavalry, but not navy, because the Israelites lacked a coast or harbor for deployment of warships. Chariotry and cavalry were disvalued as an unnecessary and expensive extravagance Deut. 17.16 and 1 Sam. 8.11–12. Mounted forces and chariotry appeared only in biblical historiography dealing with the monarchy (2 Sam. 8.3–4; 15.1; 1 Kgs 1.5; 4.26, 28; 9.19, 22; 10.25–26, 28–29; 12.18; 16.9, 25, 33; 22.4, 34–35, 38; 2 Kgs 3.7; 7.6, 14; 8.21; 9.16–21, 24, 27–28, 33; 10.2, 15–16; 13.7, 14; 14.20; 18.23–24; 23.30).

91 Only the *degel* (thousand) and century appeared in documents from Elephantine. See Porten 1968: 29–30.

92 Tarn 1930 is still useful in its analysis of the primary literary evidence. Note, however, that Lycurgus was credited with organizing the Spartan cavalry into units of fifty; cf. Feldman 2006: 533.

93 Rahtgen 1965. The amphictyonic league at Delphi had twelve members; at Helike and Samion, six; at Caularia, seven; the Boeotian league, at various times, ten, eleven and twelve members; the Achaean league grew from two to ten members; the Lykian league, twenty-three.

94 See Lemche 1984: 1–28 and the literature cited there, as well as Lemche 1985: 290–305, which critiqued Gottwald's theory of a twelve tribe confederation having arisen under the Davidic monarchy.

95 Tribal lists appear at Gen. 35.22–26; 46.8–27; 49.1–27; Ex. 1.1–15; Num. 1.5–15, 20–54; 2.3–29; 7.1–88; 10.11–28; 13.4–15; 26.5–50; 34.19–29; Deut. 33.1–29; Josh.

13–19; 21.4–8; Judg. 5.12–22; 12.24–38; 27.16–22; Ezek. 48.1–34. The order of the tribes varies in all these lists, and in the lists found in Numbers, Joshua and Judges, the two tribes of Ephraim and Manasseh substituted for Joseph and the tribe of Levi was omitted. The song of Deborah (Judg. 5) was notable for listing only ten tribes, omitting Judah, Simeon and Levi, and roughly corresponding to the ten tribes of Israel at 1 Kgs 11.31, 35.

96 Of the twelve biblical tribes, Judah is attested as a kingdom whose capital was Jerusalem from the time of Hezekiah (*LAR*, II, §§ 240, 311, which mentioned Jerusalem as the royal residence of Hezekiah the Judahite) until the fall of Jerusalem ("the city of Judah") to Nebuchadnezzar (*Babylonian Chronicle* no. 5 *[Fall of Nineveh Chronicle]* r. 12–13); Gad was mentioned in the Mesha Stele lines 10–11 as a group whose presence in Transjordan predated Omri's recent incursions; and "the wide land of [Naphta]li" has been suggested as a possible reconstruction in an inscription from the time of Tiglath-pileser III (*LAR*, I, §§ 815–16). Neo-Assyrian provinces included Samaria (Samerinu), Megiddo (Magidu), Gilead, Qarnaim (Qarnini), Dor (Du'ru), Tyre (Surro), Ashdod and Ekron. As a rule, these provinces preserved earlier political districts, but none of them correspond to biblical tribes of Israel. See Na'aman 2005: 1.220–29, on the Neo-Assyrian province system in the southern Levant.

97 According to Aristotle, *Athenian Constitution* 21.6, the ten tribal heroes were selected out of 100 candidates submitted to the oracle of Delphi.

98 A system of twelve tribes was considered ideal, since it conveniently allowed the monthly rotation of tribal responsibilities (cf. Plato, *Laws* 6.758b, 770b; Diodorus Siculus, *Library* 40.3.3), but systems with six tribes were also found, and among the Dorians a division into three tribes seems to have been preferred (Homer, *Odyssey* 19.177; Pindar, *Pythian Odes* 5.69–70; Plato, *Laws* 3.683d, 684a-b, 685a; cf. Tigerstadt 1965: 1.29–32). Athenian colonies divided into ten tribes included Thurii (Diodorus Siculus, *Library* 12.11) and Brea (Graham 1964: 10, 228; Meiggs and Lewis 1969: 128–33).

99 Herodotus, *Histories* 5.66.2–67.1; 69.1–2; Aristotle, *Athenian Constitution* 21.6; cf. Stanton 1990: 146–8. A monument in the Agora of Athens contained a bronze statue and inscription for each of the ten (later twelve) eponymous tribal heroes. On the correlations between historical references to these statues and their archaeological remains, first identified during excavations of 1931–32, see Shear 1970.

100 According to Aristotle, *Athenian Constitution* 21.6, the tribal reforms of Kleisthenes did not disturb religious institutions. For the sacred calendar of 403/402 BCE, see Oliver 1950: 31–2, 45.

101 On the date, see Pritchett 1942b. Literary sources do not record the circumstances surrounding the addition of this tribe.

102 Polybius, *Histories,* 16.25; Livy, *History of Rome* 31.15; cf. Shear 1970: 200. For a comprehensive history of changes in the Athenian tribes, including the addition of a thirteenth tribe in the time of Hadrian, see Pritchett 1942a.

103 From the Exodus through the reign of Solomon, Israel consisted of twelve tribes, although the song of Deborah at Judg. 5 featured only ten tribes. After the death of Solomon, ten tribes broke away to form the northern kingdom of Israel, leaving only the single tribe of Judah to the south (1 Kgs 10.11–13, 30–32, 36; 12.19–20). The combined number of tribes, north and south, famously do not add up to twelve, suggesting that the idea of a ten tribe political system for the northern kingdom did not have its origin in the narrative found at 1 Kgs 10–12.

104 "He [Moses] also divided up the people into twelve tribes, since this is regarded as the most perfect number and corresponds to the number of months that make up a year" (Diodorus Siculus, *Library* 40.3.3). See Gmirkin 2006: 49–50 on the Greek background of this statement, which, like other aspects of this foundation story, appears to

have drawn on Plato's *Laws*. Note the similar claim in a fictional work by Xenophon that "the Persians are divided into twelve tribes" (*The Education of Cyrus* 1.2.5).

105 For a definitive study of *demes* associated with Athenian tribes, based on inscriptional evidence and taking into account the reorganization of the tribal systems in 307/306, 224/223 and 201/200 BCE, see Traill 1975.

106 See note 98.

107 This process is most explicitly documented in the *Brea Foundation Decree*, lines 6–8: "Ten distributors of the land shall be chosen, one from each tribe. These shall allot the land." (See Graham 1964: 10, 228.)

108 Cf. Plato, *Laws* 3.684d-e. According to Aristotle, *Politics* 2.1266a, equal land allotments were considered essential under the political system advocated by Phileas of Chalcedon; cf. Morrow 1993: 101.

109 A redistribution of land was voted into law by the Assembly at Syracuse in 356 BCE after the overthrow of the tyranny of Dion, but the bill was quickly rescinded. See Fuks 1968: 207–23.

110 Lycurgus, the legendary author of Sparta's constitution, was said to have redistributed land equally among the citizens of Sparta (Plutarch, *Lycurgus* 8.1–4). However, this aspect of the legend of Lycurgus is only attested in later sources starting with Ephoros: Plato claimed the Spartan land allotment took place earlier, at the conquest of the land during the Return of the Heraklids (Plato, *Laws* 3.684d-e; 5.736c-e), and Isocrates also denied a Lycurgus land redistribution (cf. Tigerstadt 1965: 1.259).

111 Plato, *Laws* 3.684d-e. The decree of Black Corcyra contained a provision in which the rulers swore never to redistribute the land (Graham 1964: 59). See Lacey 1968: 74, 267 n. 133 on land division and political upheaval.

112 Equal land division was featured in foundation decrees for Brea, Cyrene and Black Corcyra (Graham 1964: 59). See Thucydides, *Peloponnesian War* 1.27.1 on the equality of status guaranteed for colonists to Epidamnus.

113 Aristotle, *Politics* 2.1266b; 6.1319a; cf. Lacey 1968: 22, 238 n. 7, 240 n. 25. Inalienability of land was a feature of the laws established by Moses in the foundation story of Judea found in Hecataeus of Abdera's *Aegyptiaca*. "The common people were forbidden to sell their individual plots, lest there be some who for their own advantage should buy them up, and by oppressing the poorer classes bring on a scarcity of manpower" (Diodorus Siculus, *Library* 40.3.7).

114 Each citizen was also to be allotted a place for his dwelling adjoining the main city in Plato's system, but this impractical scheme is not thought to have reflected arrangements in any historical city-state. See Morrow 1993: 103–11 for a comparison of Plato's system of land allotment with Athenian practices.

115 Greek temple complexes built on fortified hilltops such as Plato described have an obvious comparison to the *bamoth* or high places in the biblical text.

116 Morrow 1993: 531. The inalienability of land was a feature of several colonies' foundation decrees; cf. Lacey 1968: 19, 238 n. 7.

117 At Josephus, Ant. 2.312; 3.248, Moses arranged the children of Israel in "phratries" (brotherhoods or fraternities); cf. Feldman 1993: 320; Feldman 2006: 541.

118 See Wolf 1946. Conscription and wilderness military organization was extensively treated in the narratives of Num. 1–2, 26, 31. The *eleph* or thousand was roughly synonymous with *mishpachah* or clan in some passages, illustrating the kinship organization of the army pictured in biblical narratives; cf. Gottwald 1999: 270–82 (who described the *elephim* as "*mishpahim* in arms"). 1 Sam. 10.19–21 shows that the thousands retained their clan affiliation.

119 Deut. 4.5, 14; 5.31; 6.1; 12.1; cf. 11.24, which contained a brief description of the territorial boundaries of the land.

120 Berman saw a diachronic development between the prominent mention of tribal military commanders in Num. 2.1–31; 3.24, 30, 32; 10.14–28 and less prominent references

to tribal officials in Deuteronomy (Berman 2008: 74–6). He interpreted Deuteronomy as reflecting a program of change in which clan structure and tribal authority was being rejected in favor of city elders and a collective, national identity that transcended older tribal loyalties and power structure (*Created Equal*, 10, 55–6, 73–8; "Constitution, Class, and the Book of Deuteronomy," 542–5). Berman attempted to minimize the significance of the reference to tribal generals and judges at Deut. 1.9–18, which was inconsistent with this thesis. He noted the Greek reforms under Kleisthenes as an analogous effort to "dissolve entrenched kinship structures in an effort to forge a larger collective body" (Berman 2008: 73). Berman failed to properly appreciate the coexistence of kinship and village affiliations both under the Athenians under Kleisthenes and in Deuteronomy. Athenian military organization by tribe and *phratry* persisted alongside the civil organization by tribe and village *(deme)* throughout the Classical Era. Athens also had tribal courts throughout much of this same period (see §8).

121 Weinfeld 1993: 23–4 compared provisions for land inalienability at Lev. 25.23 and Num. 36 with Plato's *Laws* 5.741c.

122 The *oikos* designated the basic family unit under the *kurios* or head of household. The *genos* included related households who had a common ancestor. The exact nature of the *phratry* or brotherhood is debated, but it stood intermediate between *genos* and *phyle* and was primarily significant within the military structure. Both *genos* and *phratry* are thought to have conserved older aristocratic kinship relationships. See Lacey 1968: 8–13, 16, 19–20, 26, 63, 85; Rhodes 1993: 69.

123 See generally MacDowell 1963: 8–32; Lacey 1968: 48, 254 n. 94; MacDowell 1978: 59, 111. Plato, *Laws* 9.878d-879a treated the special case in which someone killed or injured someone of their own household.

124 Drakon's homicide law of ca. 620 BCE was revised and republished in 409/408 BCE in a public inscription discovered at Athens. See Gagarin 1981.

125 The primary duty of prosecution fell to members of the household of the victim. After the *oikos*, vengeance duty fell, not to the *genos*, but to the *phratry;* cf. Lacey 1968: 27, 243 n. 61.

126 For the *mishpachah*, see Westbrook 1991: 20–3; Gottwald 1999: 257–67. The *mishpachah* or brotherhood appears to signify the same degree of relatedness in biblical texts as the *phratry* does in Greek literature and inscriptions. 1 Sam. 20.6, 28–29 referred to an annual sacrifice and feast for the *mishpachah* group (cf. Westbrook 1991: 20; Gottwald 1999: 282–4; Willis 2001: 14) that appears closely analogous to Greek rites related to *phratries*. For inscriptions regarding the cult of Zeus of the *Phratries,* see Stanton 1990: 191–4; Rhodes and Osborne 2003: 2–11, 27–37.

127 Ghostly vengeance for unavenged homicide is found at Plato, *Laws* 9.865d-e, 872e and appeared in several homicide cases argued by Antiphon; cf. Johnston 1999: 127–60. This mythology was not cited in Drakon's homicide law or other Athenian laws; cf. Parker 1983: 134. The close affinities between the biblical traditions about spilled blood and Plato's *Laws* suggest a literary dependence.

128 Num. 35.12; Deut. 19.4–6, 10, 12–13; Josh. 20.3, 5, 9; cf. Plato, *Laws* 9.872e, "Justice [Dike], the avenger of kindred blood." See Westbrook 1991: 21 on kinship groups involved in biblical blood vengeance.

129 Josh. 20.6 indicated that an exiled murderer retained ownership of his ancestral lands; cf. Num. 35.32. According to Plato, *Laws* 9.877a-b, even those exiled for life still maintained an income from their holdings in the colony.

130 Plato, *Laws* 9.877c-878b addressed remedies for a related legal predicament in which a head of household went into exile for homicide or some other serious crime. Kinship groups were involved in the appointment of an heir or guardian for the family estate in this situation just as when the head of household died intestate.

131 The orator Demosthenes was assigned to marry the widowed daughter of a near relative and adopt her son and sire other offspring to prevent the family name of Hagnias

from becoming extinct (Demosthenes, *Against Macartatus* 11–13, 51, 54, 72–84). Demosthenes, *Against Macartatus* 75 quoted a law that commanded the "archon [to] take charge of orphans and of heiresses and of families that are becoming extinct." See Lacey 1968: 15, 23–4, 97, 99 on the importance for preserving households for the proper functioning of Greek political institutions. Both Corinth and Thebes had laws preventing the number of households from decreasing (Aristotle, *Politics* 2.1265b, 1274a-b).

132 Virtually every Greek social group, including private associations and households, had a religious aspect that involved a deity and cult. See Lacey 1968: 218 for Greek devotion to land, hearth and home.

133 Cf. Hagedorn 2004: 216–24. The laws specifying the order of inheritance within the kinship group at Gortyn resemble Athenian and biblical laws.

134 The sequence of relatives is found at Isaeus, *Aristarchus* 4–5; Isaeus, *Pyrrhus* 71–4; Isaeus, *Hagnias* 1–2; Andocides, *On the Mysteries* 117–19; Demosthenes, *Against Macartatus* 51; Plato, *Laws* 11.924c-926d; cf. Lacey 1968: 29–30.

135 See note 131.

136 The right of redemption was limited to the *mishpachah* at Lev. 25.48.

137 The term *oikos* could signify a family, a house or family property. See generally Crawford and Whitehead 1983: 40; MacDowell 1989: 10–21. Greek city-states were essentially associations of citizen-owned agrarian estates joined together for common political purposes such as self-defense. The *polis* or city-state was considered to be a union of such landed households (Plato, *Laws* 3.680a-681d; Aristotle, *Politics* 1.1252b; cf. Morrow 1993: 113–14, 118). All Greek states had laws about land and many regulated the number of *oikoi* (Lacey 1968: 221).

138 Gottwald 1999: 248. The temple or sanctuary was referred to as Yahweh's "house" at Ex. 23.19; 34.26; Lev. 19.30.

139 Westbrook 1991: 12; Gottwald 1999: 248, 285–92. The phrase *beth ab* could refer to either a household or a larger kinship group.

140 In the Septuagint, the phrase *baal ha-beth,* "master of the household," was translated as *kurios* at Ex. 22.7, Judg. 19.22–23, and in the feminine at 1 Kgs 17.17.

141 Gen. 27.1–40; 48.1–49.28. The parental blessing was irrevocable in Gen. 27.30–37. The parental blessing appears to have been envisioned as having carried legal force, and effectively corresponded in function to the Athenian will.

142 Festival and tithing laws take into account impoverished widows, orphans, poor, Levites and strangers "within the gates," suggesting distributions to the needy took place at the community level (Deut. 12.12, 18–19; 14.26–29; 16.11; 26.11–12). Judicial matters regarding families were handled by village elders (Deut. 21.18–21; 22.13–21).

143 For the Council, see especially Rhodes 1972. Both Council and Assembly were discussed in connection with Plato's *Laws* in Morrow 1993: 157–78.

144 Aristotle, *Athenian Constitution* 21.3; 43.2; 62.1–3. The latter passage may indicate that council members were selected from not only every tribe but also every district *(deme)*. Membership was limited to citizens of age thirty or older (Xenophon, *Memorabilia* 1.2.35), with a maximum of two terms per citizen. The Council of Five Hundred was divided into ten prytanes or presidencies, each tribe serving its course as standing council available for public business, except during certain festivals.

145 The oligarchic revolution of 411 BCE took place in reaction to the perceived failure of Athenian democracy in handling the expedition against Sicily in 413 BCE (Thucydides, *Peloponnesian War* 8.1.3–4). The Council of Four Hundred set up under the oligarchic revolution claimed to restore the ancestral laws in force under Solon (Aristotle, *Athenian Constitution* 29.5; 31.1, 3; 32.1). Two drafts of their constitution, preserved at Aristotle, *Athenian Constitution* 30–1, called for restricting Athenian citizenry to a body of Five Thousand, perhaps by excluding the *thetes* class (cf. Thucydides,

Peloponnesian War 8.65.3). Athenian democracy was restored in 410 BCE (Andocides, *On the Mysteries* 96).

146 The Thirty Tyrants ruled for a year after the Spartan victory over Athens in 404 BCE; cf. Aristotle, *Athenian Constitution* 35–7.

147 Aristotle, *Athenian Constitution* 43.3; 45.5; cf. Rhodes 1993: 154. There were forty regularly scheduled meetings of the Assembly each year. Extraordinary meetings were often called during wartime. The council discussed and drafted resolutions *(probouleumata)* that were publicly posted, then discussed and voted on as decrees *(psephemata)* in the Assembly and inscribed in stone if ratified. Voting could be by either show of hands or secret ballot.

148 Prior to Solon's reforms, the *thetes* or poor were excluded from the Assembly as courts; cf. Aristotle, *Politics* 2.1274a; 3.1281b; Rhodes 1993: 140. In later times, citizens received payment for attending the Assembly, allowing the poor to participate; cf. Aristotle, *Politics* 4.1293a; Aristotle, *Athenian Constitution* 41.3.

149 The Council of the Areopagus was among the oldest of Athenian political institutions. Both under Drakon and under the reforms of Solon in ca. 590 BCE, the Council of the Areopagus served primarily as *nomophylakes* or Guardians of the Laws, scrutinizing the qualifications and conduct of magistrates (Aristotle, *Athenian Constitution* 3.6; 4.4; 8.4; 60.3; Plutarch, *Solon* 19.1–4). Around 462 BCE, Ephialtes reduced its powers, reassigning some of its key functions to the Assembly, the Council, and the jury-courts (Aristotle, *Athenian Constitution* 25.1–4). Its primary duty in the fourth century BCE was trying cases involving intentional homicide or assault (Aristotle, *Athenian Constitution* 57.3; Demosthenes, *Against Aristocrates* 67–9).

150 The constitution of Chios had a *Boule* of 50 members per tribe; cf. Meiggs and Lewis 1969: no. 8. Erythrae had a *Boule* of 120 members; cf. Fornara 1983: 70–3. Cyrenaica had a *Boule* of 500 members; cf. Rhodes and Lewis 1997: 470–1.

151 Sparta had a *gerousia* of 30 members that included the two kings. Cyrenaica had a *gerousia* of 101 members.

152 Sparta had two kings whose duties were primarily military and religious (Herodotus, *Histories* 6.56–57; Xenophon, *Lacedemonian Constitution* 13.2–3; 15.2; Aristotle, *Politics* 3.1285a). Chios had a college of kings; cf. Crawford and Whitehead 1983: 38.

153 This practice may have originated with Solon's publication of laws on wooden tablets on public display (Plutarch, *Solon* 25.1). Public display made laws accessible to all Athenian citizens (Demosthenes, *Against Leptines* 93; Andocides, *On the Mysteries* 83–4). For a comparison of written law in Athens and in Plato's *Laws*, see Nightingale 1999.

154 Andocides, *On the Mysteries* 85, 87. This passage also emphasized Athenian *isonomia,* the equal application of laws and decrees for all citizens; cf. Demosthenes, *Against Timocrates* 17–18.

155 Aristotle, *Politics* 4.1292a. Each year the six Thesmothetae Archons conducted a review of existing laws, to identify contradictions requiring new, definitive legislation (Aeschines, *Against Ctesiphon* 38–9). Changes in laws could also be proposed in the Assembly or by a private citizen. The proposed changes were posted near the Statues of the Eponymous Heroes for public viewing. A board of citizen *nomothetae* ("lawgivers" or legislators) appointed by the Council and subject to the juror's oath, up to 1,001 in number, was convened to hear arguments in favor and against the proposed revisions and render their verdict on the new laws by show of hands. The laws were then published and read at the Assembly (Demosthenes, *Against Timocrates* 20–1, 23, 27, 33, 36; Aristotle, *Athenian Constitution* 54.4).

156 Assembly and Elders were discussed in Wolf 1947; Gordis 1950. Recent monographs on the Elders include Reviv 1989; Willis 2001.

157 Secondary literature has often attempted to detect diachronic developments in biblical governing institutions using biblical historiography as a guide. The most common

reconstruction has been to correlate an early phase of the tribal authorities seen in Exodus–Joshua with nomadic precursors to the Israelite settlements, followed by a middle phase of the city elders seen in Deuteronomy–Samuel, followed by a phase of attenuation of local democracy during the monarchic period of Samuel–Kings, followed by a post-monarchic phase of utopian or theoretical speculation after the fall of Jerusalem. The "seventy elders" of Exodus and Numbers, along with the pan-Israelite assemblies in Joshua–Judges are often considered fictitious artifacts of this last phase, when such national but non-monarchic or even anti-monarchic institutions were envisioned within a newly reconstituted Israel or Judah. See Gordis 1950: 384–8; Reviv 1989: 22–50, 187–8; Willis 2001: 1–4, 37–48, 308–12 and earlier literature cited throughout. But such theories are undermined by the Hellenistic Era dating of the entirety of Genesis–Kings argued here. The existence of Hellenistic and Roman Era references to the Seventy suggests a correlation between this historical delibera-tive body and the "seventy elders" of biblical tradition. Too little is known of town government in Hellenistic Era Judea to suggest historical correlations with the biblical accounts.

158 With the high priest and sagan, who acted as the leaders of the Sanhedrin, the number totaled 72.

159 Ginzberg 1937: 4.158 referred to the seventy golden chairs of the Sanhedrin under Solomon, plus two for the high priest and the sagan. This last appears to be the same scheme of seventy plus two envisioned at Ginzberg 1937: 3.250, where the seventy consisted of six elders from each tribe except for Levi, who had only four.

160 *The Letter of Aristeas* 47–51 listed only seventy-one names. One name evidently dropped out of the text at *The Letter of Aristeas* 48, because the fourth tribe has only five names, while *The Letter of Aristeas* 39, 46 specified that six elders were appointed from each tribe, and *The Letter of Aristeas* 50 referred to seventy-two elders.

161 *The Letter of Aristeas* 50. The philosophers' banquet at *The Letter of Aristeas* 187–294 had the seventy-two elders successively answer questions posed by the king.

162 Athenian deliberative bodies at various times included the Five Hundred (the Assem-bly of ca. 508 BCE), the Five Thousand (the proposed Assembly of 412 BCE), the Four Hundred (the Council of ca. 594 BCE), the Thirty (the oligarchic Council of 404 BCE; also a roving tribal circuit court of ca. 550 BCE), the Forty (a circuit court instituted in 404 BCE) and the Eleven (the Athenian prison officials, who also rendered an immedi-ate verdict on criminals who confessed their crimes).

163 The Four Hundred actually numbered 401 under Drakon (Aristotle, *Athenian Con-stitution* 4.3). The *Ephetai*, a homicide court of ca. 620 BCE reliably composed of fifty-one jurors (Drakon's law line 19; Demosthenes, *Against Macartatus* 57; Pollux, *Onomasticon* 8.125), had fifty members in Scholiast on Demosthenes, *Against Aristo-crates* 37.

164 Several Greek city-states were governed by a *gerousia*, typically in conjunction with a popular assembly; cf. Rhodes and Lewis 1997: 538. Sparta possessed the most famous *gerousia*, with thirty members of age sixty or greater, including the two *archagetai*, Spartan kings (Plutarch, *Lycurgus* 1.1–3; 26.1–3; Xenophon, *Lacedemonian Constitu-tion* 15.1–8). Legend said the Spartan *gerousia* was founded by the lawgiver Lycurgus (Plutarch, *Lycurgus* 6.1; Herodotus, *Histories* 1.65–66).

165 The seventy elders had an implied judicial role sharing the burden of government with Moses at Num. 11.14–17. City elders frequently appeared in a judicial capacity in Deuteronomy (listed in Willis 2001: 36). Homicide cases came before both the elders (Deut. 19.11–13) and the assembly (Num. 35.9–34). Non-capital cases were heard and decided by the city elders alone (Deut. 22.13–19; 25.1–10), but if preliminary investi-gation by the judges determined the case was a capital matter, the case came before the entire assembly (Deut. 22.20–21). The full assembly was involved in executing the

verdict in homicide cases (Num. 14.10; 15.35–36; cf. Wolf 1947: 103–4). It appears possible that the elders held a preliminary hearing while the entire assembly rendered the verdict. (This procedure appears to be reflected in Deut. 21.18–21, where parents declared their son rebellious before the city elders, but the execution was to be carried out by "all the men of his city"; and similarly in Deut. 22.13–21.) In Athens, the Council often conducted preliminary investigations for cases to be later decided either by jury trial or, in the most serious cases, by the entire assembly.

166 Wolf 1947: 103; Gordis 1950: 383. See Judg. 20.1–8 for the declaration of war against the tribe of Benjamin by the assembly of Israel. See Josh. 9.3–19 for the treaty established between ambassadors sent by the elders and assembly of Gibeon to Israel (9.11); the ambassadors' speech before Joshua and the assembly of Israel (9.6–14) and the ratification of the treaty by Joshua and the leaders of the assembly (9.15–19) is reminiscent of procedures at Athens, where foreign delegations were allowed to address the assembly on national matters. At Athens, major military decisions, such as sending expeditions or accepting terms of surrender, were decided by the vote of the entire Assembly, not by the generals. Although the elected generals were empowered to convene extraordinary sessions of the Assembly, they had to argue as normal citizens to convince the people to approve a particular course of action. See Hamel 1998: 5–14 on relations between the generals and the Assembly.

167 In Ex. 18.13–26; Deut. 1.16–18 the officers and judges over the thousands, hundreds, fifties and tens were men of reputation and ability nominated from all the tribes, but the selection was made by Moses; the same procedure was also seen for the seventy elders at Num. 11.14–17. In the constitutional sub-document at Deut. 16.18–18.22, the assembly of Israel (addressed as "you" by Moses throughout Deuteronomy) was to select both judges and king from among their own number; cf. Hagedorn 2004: 113–14, 116, 119–21, 279–81; Berman 2006: 530; Berman 2008: 60–1. In 1 Sam. 8.4–5, the elders of Israel requested a king, but the people as a whole acclaimed the kingship of Saul (1 Sam. 8.7, 10, 19, 21; 10.17–25), David (2 Sam. 5.1–3), Rehoboam (1 Kgs 12.1–15, had all gone well) and Jeroboam (1 Kgs 12.16, 20). Appointment to many Athenian offices was made by lot, a procedure that was anciently thought to both be democratic and to contain an element of divine providence (Plato, *Laws* 6.759b–c; cf. Morrow 1993: 162–3). Election by lot from the assembly was also seen at 1 Sam. 10.17–25, the appointment of Saul as king. Alternately, Athenian offices with special qualifications took place by citizen vote, either by show of hands or by secret ballot. Biblical elections appear to have been recorded either by clapping (perhaps), as at 2 Kgs 11.12, or by audible assent ("amen") as at Neh. 5.13.

168 This appears to be the implication of Judg. 20.7, where all the gathered children of Israel were asked to give their advice and counsel; cf. Wolf 1947: 102. After the Assembly at Athens opened with prayer and sacrifices, the herald *(korax)* first called down curses on anyone who misled the Assembly, then asked, "Who wishes to speak?" (See Demosthenes, *On the Crown* 191; Aeschines, *Against Timarchus* 23, 26; Aristophanes, *Acharnians* 46.) Those desiring to speak were first scrutinized to ensure that they were a citizen in good legal standing (Aeschines, 1 *Against Timarchus* 28–30). Otherwise, any Athenian citizen could address the Assembly, regardless of class or wealth (Plato, *Protagoras* 319d; cf. Plato, *Gorgias* 461e). See Monoson 2000: 51–63 on *isegoria* (the right to address the Assembly) and *parrhesiastes* (free speech) as expressions of Athenian democracy.

169 Foundational Athenian legislation was drafted by the lawgivers Solon (ca. 594 BCE) and by Kleisthenes (ca. 508 BCE) and approved by the Assembly. After 404 BCE, a panel of legislators *(nomothetes)* proposed new laws, as required, on a yearly basis. These were read at a special session of the Assembly, which voted on their approval or rejection. The same procedure is seen in Deuteronomy, where legislator Moses read

the foundational laws to the assembly of the children of Israel, who gave the laws their formal, binding assent. This corresponds to normal Greek legislative procedure, but lacks an Ancient Near Eastern parallel (as discussed in Chapter 4 §4).

170 Eight Athenian law courts, each with its own special jurisdiction, were enumerated at Aristotle, *Politics* 4.1300b. For the judicial machine at Athens, see Harrison 1968: 2.1–68; Morrow 1993: 251–73.

171 According to Aristotle, *Athenian Constitution* 57, trials for deliberate homicide, assault, poisoning and arson came under the jurisdiction of the Council of the Areopagus; trials for involuntary homicide or the murder of a slave or foreigner were held at the Palladium; trials for justified homicide at the Delphinium; trials of those appealing exile for homicide or assault at the Phreatus, with the defense delivered from onboard a ship; the *Archon Basileus* presided over trials for unknown murderers, animals and inanimate objects that took place at the Prytany. The various homicide courts, their jurisdictions and procedures, were discussed in detail in MacDowell 1963.

172 Aristotle (*Athenian Constitution* 57) subdivided these trials, over which the Polemarch of Athens presided, into disputes among resident aliens and disputes between Athenians and aliens.

173 Aristotle omitted family court from his list of law courts at *Politics* 4.1300b. The Archon presided over family court, whose purpose was to assign guardians to unprotected widows, orphans and aged parents, and to investigate charges of family abuse, whether physical or (in the case of guardianships) financial.

174 Harrison 1968: 2.18–21; Crawford and Whitehead 1983: 572; Stanton 1990: 108. The Forty were tribal judges, with four per tribe. Tribal judges also featured at Plato, *Laws* 12.956c.

175 A citizen was at liberty to kill an adulterer, traitor, highwayman, night-thief or temple robber caught in the act. Alternately, the citizen could arrest the perpetrator and deliver the person over to the Eleven who presided over the Athenian jail. Summary arrest and prosecution by a citizen was called *apagoge;* if by a magistrate, it was called *ephegesis.*

176 Aristotle, *Athenian Constitution* 9.1; Plutarch, *Solon* 18.6; cf. Gagarin 1986: 69. See Phillips 2013: 29–33, for the types of procedures for filing lawsuits in Athens, and Phillips 2013: 33–43, for the stages in judicial procedures.

177 Aristotle, *Athenian Constitution* 57.2–4; cf. Chase 1933: 173–4; MacDowell 1963: 34. Prosecution was undertaken by legal representatives in the cases of guardianships and by the Athenian sponsor of resident aliens.

178 Gagarin 1986: 111–16. Compulsory homicide prosecution in the Classical Era rendered unacceptable the Archaic Era option of paying blood money to kinsmen to avoid prosecution for homicide.

179 If a witness was summoned by a citizen prosecutor and refused to appear or submit written testimony, the witness was subject to a separate lawsuit; but Athens maintained no police force for executing either arrest warrants or bench warrants. They did, however, have a prison in Athens that was presided over by the Eleven; accused persons and witnesses in important cases could be delivered to prison to be held over for trial (or released if guarantee against flight was provided in the form of bail or hostages). See discussion at Morrow 1993: 285; cf. Plato, *Laws* 11.936e–937a. Athens maintained a force of 1,000 Scythian Archers to act as guards in the city, but their police functions were limited to crowd control at public gatherings such as sessions of the Assembly and Council.

180 Optional self-exile was a characteristic feature of Athenian homicide law since Drakon's law of ca. 620 BCE; cf. Gagarin 1981: 58–62, 164–8.

181 After ca. 390 BCE, witness testimony began to be routinely recorded in writing, either during a preliminary hearing or a separate deposition, for use at trial.

182 Isaeus, *Philoctemon* 53; Demosthenes, *Against Eubulides* 4; cf. Harrison 1968: 2.145. Women, slaves and children were excluded as witnesses except in homicide cases, although in practice their testimony often entered in anyway through statements by the *kurios* of the household in which they lived.

183 Harrison 1968: 2.150–53; Gagarin 2007. Plato forbade the use of oaths in lawsuits because of abuses of this practice; cf. Chase 1933: 139.

184 For perjury prosecutions and penalties, see Chase 1933:188; Harrison 1968: 2.143–47; Lacey 1968: 217; Gagarin 1986: 79; cf. Plato, *Laws* 11.937c.

185 See Aristotle, *Athenian Constitution* 59.1; Demosthenes, *On the False Embassy* 134; Demosthenes, *Against Meidias* 113; Demosthenes, *Against Timotheus* 10; Aeschines, *Against Timarchus* 86; Aeschines, *On the Embassy* 72; Dinarchus, *Against Demosthenes* 1, 50, 58.

186 Andocides, *On the Mysteries* 15, 27, 34, 40, 42; Lysias, *Against Andocides* 23; Thucydides, *Peloponnesian War* 6.27.2; cf. the use of informers at Plato, *Laws* 5.730d; 7.808e–809a.

187 Stanton 1990: 66. In the early mid-fifth century BCE, jurisdiction over political cases was taken away from the Council of the Areopagus, which was considered too oligarchic, and given instead to the *dikasteria*, the Council and the Assembly; cf. Ostwald 1986: 47–50. The Assembly in its judicial capacity called the *Heliaia* (Demosthenes, *Against Aristocrates* 28).

188 Num. 35.24–25; Deut. 16.18–20; 21.5, 18–21; 22.21; 25.5–10. The hearing of cases by village elders corresponds somewhat to local courts in each *deme* in Attica, except that only small civil cases came under the jurisdiction of the *demarchs*, whereas larger civil cases and criminal cases were referred to the courts in Athens.

189 Deut. 1.13, 16. This referred back to the judges in the wilderness, who were assigned according to the tribal military structure of the Israelites under Moses. Berman 2008: 74–6 saw a diachronic development from the tribal courts of Deut. 1 to the village courts in Deut. 21–25, but Deuteronomy appears to have pictured the two types of courts coexisting, as they were known to in Attica.

190 Three origin myths were given for the judicial hierarchy of the wilderness period. In Ex. 18.13–18, a system of justice was created at Jethro's recommendation, prior to the Sinai theophany. For Berman 2008: 64, this episode illustrated the Pentateuchal ideal of consultative government in which a ruler (Moses) listened to an initiative brought to him by the people (Jethro). The same judicial hierarchy appeared in Deut. 1.9–15, but the system there was instituted by Moses, without Jethro's advice, after the events of Sinai (Horeb). In Num. 11.16–17, the role of the tribal officers was taken over by the "seventy elders of Israel" who assisted Moses in the (judicial) administration of government.

191 See Willis 2001: 36 for a discussion of judicial personnel that variously appear in Deuteronomy, which included elders, judges, officers and priests. According to Levinson 2008: 71–6, Deuteronomy reflects a historical evolution in Israel's judicial institutions in which the tribal judges seen in Exodus–Numbers and Deut. 1 were replaced by city elders. Levinson minimized the significance of the system of tribal judicial authorities acknowledged in Deut. 1.9–15. In Attica, village courts, tribal courts, military courts and the various courts found at Athens all coexisted with distinct jurisdictions, similar to the multiplicity of courts found in the Pentateuch.

192 Judicial inquiries were referred to at Deut. 13.14; 17.2–4; 19.18. See Wells 2004: 94–102, on judicial investigations (and Wells 2004: 108–32 for Neo-Babylonian parallels). Wells 2004: 1–15 assumed biblical legal procedures had an exclusively Ancient Near Eastern background.

193 Due process and citizen participation in the judicial process in Deuteronomic and Athenian law were compared at Berman 2008: 68–70.

194 As noted at Berman 2008: 68, in his discussion of Deut. 16.18–19.
195 See Num. 13.24 for an instance of summary arrest. A defendant delivered over to the
     authorities on a serious matter remained in custody until a verdict was rendered (Lev.
     24.12; Num. 15.34; cf. Westbrook 1991: 10). Num. 25.6–11 appears to indicate that
     execution of a serious wrongdoer caught *in flagrante* was considered justified and for
     some categories of crime was encouraged, as at Athens.
196 See Wells 2004: 18, 44–6 on the accuser presenting testimony against a defendant.
197 Compliance to a court summons is featured in Lev. 5.1; Deut. 25.8; 1 Sam. 22.11; cf.
     Westbrook 1991: 9. See Wells 2004: 19, on judicial interrogation of witnesses at trial.
     The biblical text provides no example of cross-examination of witness testimony.
198 See Num. 35.24 on the blood avenger as prosecutor; Num. 35.31–32 on blood
     payments.
199 Although there are biblical references to both deeds (Jer. 32.9–14) and writs of divorce
     (Deut. 24.1, 3; Isa. 50.1; Jer. 3.8), biblical evidence mainly took the form of oral tes-
     timony (e.g. Num. 35.30; Deut. 17.6; 19.15). Wells 2004: 22–9 noted that economic
     and legal transactions in biblical narratives were often officially recorded by "observ-
     ing witnesses," such as city elders, rather than recorded in writing. Wells 2004: 40–2
     discussed the relatively rare biblical appearance of "impersonal witnesses," that
     is, evidence of a tangible rather than testimonial nature. After ca. 400 BCE, Athens
     came to require written legal documents for most matters. These were housed in the
     archives at the Metroön; cf. Posner 1972: 102–11; Sickinger 1999: 114–38.
200 Num. 35.20–21 (implicitly), 30; Deut. 17.6; 19.15 on eyewitness testimony; cf. Hage-
     dorn 2004: 135.
201 Num. 5.12–31; LU 13–14; LH 2; MAL A 17, 22, 24–25; Achilles Tatius, *Cleitophon
     and Leucippe* 8.11–13. Biblical trial by ordeal appears to have been a holdover from
     ancient local practices rather than an innovation taken from Greek law. Instructions
     for the high priest to wear the "breastplate of justice" that contained a pouch for the
     Urim and Thummim (Ex. 27.15–30) has led to speculations that the Urim and Thum-
     mim (apparently dice representing the twelve tribes of Israel) were used in oracular
     judicial decisions for particularly baffling cases (cf. Berman 2008: 68), but the Urim
     and Thummim were not used in any biblical judicial procedure, whereas Ex. 28.30
     assigned the breastplate a purely symbolic significance, comparable to that attached
     to the mitre (Ex. 28.38).
202 Several provisions of the Gortyn law code required two or three witnesses on various
     matters (*Gortyn Law Code* 1.39–46; 2.28–33; 5.51–54; cf. Hagedorn 2004: 132–3).
     Two witnesses were required for admission to phratries in Cycladic island of Tenos
     (Rhodes and Osborne 2003: 296–8). Perhaps most directly relevant to the biblical
     statutes, Cumae required more than one witness to convict a defendant of homicide
     (Aristotle, *Politics* 2.1269a; cf. Gagarin 1986: 64).
203 Ex. 20.16; 22.6–8; 23.1–3; Lev. 5.20–26; Deut. 5.20; 19.16–21; LH 1–4; Plato, *Laws*
     11.937b-d. At Deut. 19.16–21, perjurers were punished according to the principle of
     lex talionis, as at LH 3–4.
204 Deut. 16.19 instructed citizen judges not to take gifts. Athenian jurors in the Dikastic
     courts were sworn in with an oath containing closely comparable language; cf. Hage-
     dorn 2004: 118; Mirhady 2007: 54. See also Plato, *Laws* 12.955c.
205 See Aristotle, *Athenian Constitution* 27.4–5; cf. Noonan 1984: 713 n. 2. Appeal to the
     interests of the poorer classes, or outright judicial bribery, were especially emphasized
     by oligarchian critics of the democratization of the Athenian court system.
206 Deut. 13.9, 11, 14–16 (implied). Berman 2006: 539 understood Deut. 16.19 to refer
     to trials before the assembly, because Moses consistently addressed the assembled
     people as "you" throughout Deuteronomy.
207 Pentateuchal penalties included execution in capital cases (typically by stoning),
     exile (Num. 35.25; Deut. 19.3; Josh. 20.4; Ezra 7.26; 10.8), disenfranchisement (Lev.

20.3–6; Ezra 7.26; 10.8; cf. Ex. 12.15; Lev. 17.10; Num. 9.13), fines (Ex. 22.1, 9, 22, 30, 32; 22.7, 9; Lev. 5.16; 6.5) and corporal punishment (Ex. 22.24–25; Lev. 24.20; Deut. 25.1–3). In Ezra, a post-Pentateuchal text, the range of judicial penalties for serious crimes – especially crimes against the political order – closely conformed to available penalties found in the Greek world. Ezra 7.25–26 envisioned penalties of "death, banishment, confiscation of goods or imprisonment"; Ezra 10.8 prescribed a penalty of expulsion and confiscation of goods, comparable to Greek *atimia,* as noted in Blidstein 1974; the third century CE Lucianic version of Ezra renders banishment as *atimia.*

208 For retaliation, see Ex. 21.12, 14–17, 20; Num. 35.21, 31; Deut. 19.19; 24.7; for the removal of pollution, see Num. 35.33; Deut. 13.5; 17.12; 19.10, 13, 19; 24.7; cf. 21.7–8; 22.8; for judicial decisions as a means of instilling fear on evildoers, see Deut. 13.11; 17.13; 19.20; 21.21; cf. MacDowell 1963: 141–50 for the Greeks.

209 Aristotle, *Politics* 4.1299a. Aristotle considered the achievement of excellence *(arete)* as the proper aim of individual life, philosophy and politics (3.1288a; 4.1293b; 7.1324a) as well as a requisite for holding high office in the ideal *polis.*

210 A mixed constitution that combined aristocracy – the rule of the most excellent – and democracy was considered the most stable according to Aristotle, *Politics* 2.1265b-1266a; 4.1294b, 1297a; cf. Thucydides, *Peloponnesian War* 8.97.2 (the first mention of a mixed constitution); Plato, *Laws* 3.693d-e; 6.756e; Morrow 1993: 521–43. The Athenian mixture of aristocracy and democracy was described as "aristocracy with the approval of the people" at Plato, *Menexenus* 238d; cf. Morrow 1993: 88.

211 Offices filled by lot included membership in the Council and some priestly positions. Lots were also used for selection of citizens for jury duty.

212 See Ostwald 1986: 43–7, on the scrutiny at Athens. Scrutinies were held for archons and members of the Council (Aristotle, *Athenian Constitution* 55.1–4) and the Council of the Areopagus (Lysias, *On the Scrutiny of Evandros* 11–12), priests, advocates, heralds and ambassadors (Aeschines, *Against Timarchus* 19–20), public speakers at the Assembly (Aeschines, *Against Timarchus* 28–30), those enrolling as citizens at the *deme* or political district (Demosthenes, *Against Leochares* 41; Lysias, *On the Scrutiny of Evandros* 21) and at the Scrutiny of the Helpless, which examined the qualifications of the incapacitated poor, who received a pension from the state (Aristotle, *Athenian Constitution* 49.4). At all these public inquiries, the applicant was questioned about his qualifications, and a herald asked those present, "Does anybody wish to bring a charge against this man?" (Lysias, *For Mantitheus* 9; Lysias, *Against Philon* 1–2; Aristotle, *Athenian Constitution* 55.4; cf. Morrow 1993: 216). Although generals and treasurers were drawn from the wealthiest assessed classes in Athens because of the financial responsibilities of these magistracies, lesser Athenian offices had no wealth requirements (Aristotle, *Athenian Constitution* 7.4; 47.1). In Plato's *Laws,* there were no property qualifications for holding any office (3.696a-b), but instead qualifications of character and education (5.735a; 6.751c-d); cf. Chase 1933: 135.

213 For the audit at Athens, see Aristotle, *Athenian Constitution* 48.3–5; 59.2; cf. Ostwald 1986: 55–62; Morrow 1993: 219–20; Rhodes 1993: 115 (with an emphasis on parallels in Plato's *Laws*); Hamel 1998: 127–30 (on audits of returning generals). An audit generally first involved a review of financial ledgers by ten or twenty auditors called *logistai,* followed by a public review of general conduct overseen by a panel of ten *euthenoi.* Charges of misconduct in office were prosecuted, as required, by the ten *synergoi.* In the fifth century BCE, several Athenian generals were charged, and some executed, for mistakes made in their command. At Plato, *Laws* 12.945b-946e, the audit of magistrates was to be entrusted to a panel of the priests of Apollo and Helios who had been elected to that office as those possessing the greatest virtue of all the citizens. Plato was unique in having assigned such civic responsibility to a priestly body.

214 For Athenian traditions about the origin of the Archons and for their oath of office, see Aristotle, *Athenian Constitution* 7–8; Stanton 1990: 68–73, no. 42.

215 Harrison 1968: 2.8–9. In Drakon's homicide law of Archaic Era Athens, homicide cases were supervised by the *basileis* or kings (plural), perhaps a reference to the *Archon Basileus* and the four *phylobasileis* or tribal kings; cf. Gagarin 1981: 46.

216 See Harrison 1968: 1.193–96; 2.9. The office of *strategos* or general received increasing respect in Classical Athens as a position of great importance that required extensive training and experience.

217 "The Thesmothetai were appointed for the task of recording statutes and preserving them for judgments between litigants" (Aristotle, *Athenian Constitution* 3.4). Gagarin 1986: 56 was of the opinion that some early Athenian laws *(thesmia)* were the result of particular court cases.

218 The Archons do not appear in Plato's *Laws,* where their functions were taken over by the *nomophylakes* or Guardians of the Laws; cf. Morrow 1993: 202.

219 The divine element in selection of magistrates by lot was also a method found in texts of Classical Greece, such as Plato, *Laws* 3.690c: "Heaven's favor and good luck mark the seventh form of rule, where we bring a man forward for a casting of lots, and declare that if he gains the lot he will most justly be ruler, but if he fails he shall take his place among the ruled." Lots were a well-known device used at the oracle at Delphi.

220 Deut. 1.13, 15 emphasized that the wisdom and understanding of the tribal leaders to be appointed as judges and officers must be ascertained. This suggests that nomination and public scrutiny of candidates was performed on a tribal level.

221 Cf. Wolf 1947: 105. At Athenian audits, citizens were invited to step forward with complaints against the magistrate whose term of office had concluded (see note 213). Accusations of bribery had been raised against Samuel's sons (1 Sam. 8.3), but no such claims were made against Samuel at his audit.

222 The main procedural difference between the audit of Samuel's tenure as judge and Athenian audits of magistrates is that the process in 1 Sam. 12.1–5 was supervised by elders rather than a special panel of auditors.

223 For prospective judges, their qualifications and their instructions, see Ex. 18.21; Deut. 1.15–18; 16.18–20; for bribery in general, see Deut. 10.17–18; 1 Sam. 8.3; 12.3; Ps. 15.5; Prov. 17.23; Job 36.17–19; Amos 5.12; Isa. 1.23; 33.15; for judicial murder, see Ex. 23.6–8; 1 Kgs 21.8–14; Ps. 26.6–10; Ezek. 22.12 and perhaps Deut. 27.25. For more on bribery in biblical texts, see Chapter 3 note 284.

224 *Sarim* were mentioned at Num. 31.14, 48, 52, 54; Deut. 1.15; 20.9; Josh. 5.14–15; *roshim* or heads of thousands at Num. 1.16; 7.85; 10.4; Josh. 22.21, 30; *shaphatim* who served primarily as military leaders in the judges period (cf. Judg. 2.16–19) included Ehud of Benjamin (Judg. 3.12–30), Deborah of Ephraim and Barak of Naphtali (Judg. 4), Gideon of Manasseh (Judg. 6–8) and Jephthah of Gilead (Judg. 10.17–12.6).

225 The function is implicit in the enrollment of the citizen armies in Num. 1, 26. The offices of scribe and recorder are explicit in 2 Sam. 8.16–17; 20.24–25; 1 Kgs 4.3 and later in Kings. Athenian secretaries were important magistrates and officials, not mere clerks like the scribes of the Ancient Near East; cf. Thomas 1996: 24–5.

226 Two difficult cases regarding and allotment and inheritance involving the seven orphaned daughters of Zelophehad were recorded at Num. 27.1–11 and 36.1–12, where the judicial rulings were said to have become statutes for Israel for all time. On the surface, this appears to suggest the use of judicial precedent, what we today call "case law"; cf. Westbrook 2009: 18–19. But judicial precedent was used neither in the Ancient Near East nor in the Greek world. However, one duty of the seven *thesmothetae* who served as Archons at Athens was the recording of judicial cases. It has been suggested that these records could have functioned as case law (cf. Gagarin

1986: 561), but there is no example of any appeal to judicial precedent in the substantial body of preserved Athenian legal speeches. However, a key responsibility of the *thesmothetae* was to conduct a yearly review of Athenian law, looking for contradictions or legal points that needed clarification through a revised statute (Aristotle, *Athenian Constitution* 3.4). This was, indeed, their only legislative role, and seemingly the basis for their title as *thesmothetae* (or "lawgivers"). In my opinion, the judicial case records they created as court secretaries were used as notes for difficult legal points from hard cases that required legislative clarification. The same process appears indicated in the cases involving Zelophehad's daughters, in which a particular situation not envisioned in the original laws was highlighted in a court case, and its judicial resolution resulted in a new statute.

227 Accurate weights and measures (Lev. 19.35–36; Deut. 25.13–16); price regulations on barley (Lev. 27.16; Num. 18.16); cf. Simon the temple captain and *agoranomos* of 2 Macc. 3.4. See further Chapter 3 §11.

228 Not even the constitutional subdocument that included the Torah of the King assigned a role for appointment of judges or other magistrates by the king; cf. Berman 2006: 539.

229 Berman 2008: 78–80 viewed shared rule and the separation of powers in the Pentateuch – and especially in Deuteronomy – as checks against concentrated power in a king or tyrant. Berman claimed that the system of checks and balances found in biblical constitutional passages was not encountered again until the American constitution (2008: 10), but overlooked the same checks and balances found in the earlier political institutions at Athens (see note 231).

230 Qualifications at Ex. 18.21, 25 included capability, piety, love of truth and hate of greed; Plato, *Laws* 6.767d also mentioned capability and holiness as judicial qualifications. Deut. 1.13, 15 emphasized wisdom and an established reputation. In his book on qualifications for public office, Theophrastus included financial resources (for generals), a sense of justice, personal excellence, experience, practical wisdom and trustworthiness as qualities to be examined during the official scrutiny of candidates for magistracies; cf. Crawford and Whitehead 1983: 577–9.

231 The specifications for membership among the "seventy elders" included an established reputation and past service as officers in a lower capacity (Num. 11.16). Theophrastus also discussed the requirement for generals and other high offices to have gained experience from earlier posts.

232 As noted at Levinson 2006: 1884, all institutions of government in Deuteronomy were subordinated to the Torah.

233 Contra Reviv 1989: 22–50, 187–8, who postulated a hypothetical development from clan to tribal entities and rejected the seventy elders as a late anachronism.

234 An Elephantine Papyri of 407 BCE referred to Johanan the high priest *(rab cohen)* at Jerusalem and his priestly colleagues along Ostanes and the nobles of Judah (*TAD* A4.7.17–19). It is doubtful that the nobles represented a council of elders (as suggested at Albertz 1994: 2.443–50). Nobles *(chorim)* and elders *(zaqenim)* were not synonymous; cf. 1 Kgs 21.8, 11, where the two were distinguished. The nobles of *TAD* A4.7.19 suggest instead an oligarchic body of powerful or influential family leaders. In any case, a body of "seventy" (actually, seventy-two) elders appear to reflect later Hellenistic naming conventions (cf. note 162) and are first attested in the Septuagint tradition in *The Letter of Aristeas* in conjunction with events of ca. 270 BCE. To the extent that it may be credited, *The Letter of Aristeas* lends support to the existence of both an aristocratic Jewish *gerousia* of seventy-two elders (46, 121, 310) and a Jewish assembly (46, 310) in the time of Ptolemy II Philadelphus. References to the Jewish *gerousia* appeared in correspondence from Antiochus III in ca. 198 BCE quoted at Josephus, Ant. 12.138–44 (esp. 138, 142). A national assembly was later referred to at 1 Macc. 13.1–9; 14.28, 41–46 (the coronation of Simon).

235 See especially Levinson 2001: 511–34. Levinson noted the descriptions of royal rule in biblical historiography (that is, Samuel–Kings) conformed to Ancient Near Eastern kingship, but that the routine military and judicial activities and oversight associated with such rule are entirely absent in the Torah of the King; cf. Hagedorn 2004: 140–56; Berman 2008: 10, 53, 57–9; Berman 2008: 525. Berman also noted that the king in Deuteronomy, unlike typical kings in the Ancient Near East, was not pictured as an author of laws, lacked any cultic role and did not play a role in debt relief as benefactor of the people.

236 For Ancient Near East kingship, see note 32. At Aristotle, *Politics* 3.1285a, barbarian kingship was classified as hereditary and tyrannical, unlike kingship among the Greeks, in which the exercise of kingship was subject to the limitations of law. Plato, *Republic* 8.544d said that hereditary kingship was much more common among the barbarians – that is, the kingdoms of the east – than among the Greeks.

237 The biblical authors appear to have been aware of the similarities of the royal powers of the kings of Judah and Samaria with those of other Ancient Near Eastern kings, as illustrated by the elders' request to Samuel for a king like all the other nations (1 Sam. 8.5, 19–20; cf. Deut. 17.14).

238 Explicit features for a proposed office of king are found in the Torah of the King at Deut. 17.14–20. Implicit features are found throughout the rest of Deuteronomy, where the absence of a role for the king speaks volumes, especially in the constitutional sub-document of Deut. 16.18–18.22. It is important to consider both what Deuteronomy said about kingship and what it omitted, as noted at Levinson 2001: 521–4, 528–9; Berman 2008: 53.

239 The Torah of the King prescribed that the king was to be selected from the citizen body, the only qualification being that he should be "one of your own brethren"; the absence of the notion of dynastic succession was noted at Hagedorn 2004: 141, 156, 170; Berman 2008: 60–1, 63.

240 Levinson 2001: 511–12, 521–3. As noted at Levinson 2006: 1881–2; Levinson 2008: 79, in the Ancient Near East the king was usually credited with having promulgated law, but in the Torah of the King (Deut. 17.14–20) the king was instead made subject to law. Berman (2006: 532–3; 2008: 63) noted that the royal knowledge of the law was also mandated for all Israelite citizens and carried an identical reward: long life.

241 Hagedorn 2004: 148, 154; ; Berman 2006: 528–9; Berman 2008: 57–8. At Deut. 20.1–20, priests and officers regulated battles, not the king.

242 Levinson 2001: 518–20; Hagedorn 2004: 145–6; Levinson 2006: 1881; Berman 2008: 68. The description of the judiciary in Deut. 16.18–20; 17.2–13 made no mention of the king.

243 Berman 2008: 58–9 noted that Deut. 12 had no role for the king as founder or patron of the temple. Kings possessed prominent religious functions in Samuel–Kings, as noted at Grabbe 1995: 38–40.

244 Besides the absence of military, judicial, cultic and executive roles, the Torah of the King gave the monarch no role in economic relief; cf. Levinson 2001: 530. According to Hagedorn, the Torah of the King was more concerned with protecting the rights of the citizenry from royal abuses than with "actually setting up a law for kingship" (2004: 156; cf. 170).

245 The palace was associated with the administration of justice at 1 Sam. 8.5–6; 1 Kgs 3.9, 16–28. Military command and executive control of the nation, "like the other nations around us," were emphasized at 1 Sam. 8.20; cf. Levinson 2001: 518. The king had a prominent cultic role at 1 Kgs 8.12–64.

246 The harem, royal chariotry and ostentatious display of wealth proscribed by the Torah of the King were typical expressions of royal power under Ancient Near Eastern kingship, as noted at Hagedorn 2004: 142–4; Berman 2008: 62. Horses were also viewed

as an oligarchic excess at Aristotle, *Politics* 4.1289b. For Solomon, see 1 Kgs 5.6; 10.26, 28 (horses); 11.1–4 (harem); 10.21–23 (wealth).

247 Aristotle carefully distinguished monarchy, the lawful rule of a single, exceptionally qualified individual, whose aim was protecting the interests of both rich and poor, from tyranny, the rule of an individual bent on self-enrichment and absolute power (*Politics*, 3.1279a-b; 4.1295a; 5.1310b). Aristotle considered monarchy as identical with aristocracy (the rule of the *arete* or best), except that aristocratic rule involved rule by a council of several exceptional citizens instead of a single extraordinary individual (*Politics* 3.1279a). Aristotle considered tyranny a perversion of monarchy (as at 1 Sam. 8.11–18), much as oligarchy was a perversion of aristocracy.

248 Cf. 1 Kgs 12.4, 10–11, 14 on excessive taxation creating an economic underclass under Solomon.

249 In particular, the whole tenor of Deuteronomy, which systematically omitted any significant role for the king in the administration of government, appears inconsistent with its promulgation under Josiah; cf. Levinson 2001: 524 n. 37.

250 Secondary literature, lacking an Ancient Near Eastern comparison for the attenuated royal rule described in the Torah of the King, typically characterized the Deuteronomic conception of kingship as either utopian (e.g. Levinson 2001: 511–12, 533–34) or revolutionary (e.g. Berman 2008).

251 States with elected kings included Athens (Aristotle, *Politics* 3.1285a; Aristotle, Athenian *Constitution* 8.1) and Chios (Drews 1983: 25–6; Hagedorn 2004: 151).

252 Aristotle, *Politics* 3.1285a listed the four types of kingship as the lawful kings of the heroic era, barbaric hereditary monarchy, kingship as a special type of bureaucratic functionary and the kingship regulated by law at Sparta. Greek Cyrene also had a hereditary kingship descended from the founder Battus (Herodotus, *Histories* 4.153, 155, 159–62).

253 It was once thought that the largely ceremonial office of *basileus* found at Athens and recorded in the traditions of several other Greek *poleis* was a vestige of the Mycenaean (Bronze Age) era of hereditary kings; cf. Starr 1961. This view was challenged in Drews 1983, where it was argued that traditions about Archaic Era Greek kings were mostly late and legendary, and noted that the Linear B term *pa-si-re-u,* from which *basileus* derived, referred to a lower class of bureaucrat. He argued that monarchic kingship was a Dark Age feature of only such states as Sparta and Achaia where the *ethnos,* not the *polis,* was the dominant form.

254 See note 152.

255 Drews 1983: 25; Hagedorn 2004: 151. Plato's *Republic* envisioned the ideal state as ruled by a group of philosopher-kings.

256 See Aristotle, *Athenian Constitution* 57.1–2 on the religious duties of the king at Athens. For inscriptions elsewhere in the Greek world that mentioned a *basileus* or college of *basileis* with religious functions, see Lupu 2005: 312. The Homeric king also functioned as a priest (Homer, *Iliad* 2.400–19; *Odyssey* 13.181), and presided over sacrifices that did not belong to specific priesthoods (Aristotle, *Politics* 3.1285b; cf. 1 Kgs 8.62–64). Athenian archons and archon kings often presided over festivals (Aristotle, *Athenian Constitution* 56.3–5; 57.1).

257 "The more restricted the functions of kings, the longer their power will last unimpaired" (Aristotle, *Politics* 5.1313a). Of several types of monarchy, including the despotic rule of eastern kings, Aristotle favored "the so-called limited monarchy, or kingship according to law" (Aristotle, *Politics* 3.1285a).

258 Cf. Hagedorn 2004: 154–5. Aristotle described kingship in the heroic age as lawful and considered the Spartan monarchy a notable example of "monarchy regulated by law" (*Politics* 3.1285a). See also Aristotle, *Politics* 3.1286b, 1287a-b; 4.1292a on the importance of kingship being subject to written law. According to Plato,

Laws 4.715d, the state was safe only where "the law is master over the rulers and they are its subjects."

259 Aristotle, *Athenian Constitution* 4.4. The Guardians of the Laws scrutinized magistrates and listened to any citizen complaints against any magistrate who violated the law. Prior to the constitutional reform of Ephialtes in 462 BCE, the Council of the Areopagus functioned as Athenian Guardians of the Laws (4.4; 8.4). Prosecutorial power was taken away from the Council of the Areopagus and given to jury courts and to the Assembly under the change in constitution effected by Ephialtes (25.2–4), removing power from the oligarchs of the Areopagus and democratically investing it in the people, to whom the magistrates became directly accountable.

260 O'Sullivan 2009: 72–89. The Guardians of the Laws "used to observe the deeds of men and recall to them the laws" (Cicero, *On Laws* 3.46). According to Xenophon, *On Household Management* 9.14, "well ordered cities are not content only to pass good laws, but also appoint *nomophylakes* as overseers to commend the law-abiding and chastise the law-breakers."

261 The levitical priests were entrusted with the book of the law at Deut. 17.18; 31.9, 24–26; they exhorted the populace to obey these laws at 27.9–10; 31.9–13; 33.8–10.

262 It is interesting that in Plato's *Republic,* where the *phylakes* or Guardians constituted a special tribe of philosopher-kings, the *phylakes* were to possess neither land nor houses (*Republic* 3.416d-417e), much like the biblical tribe of Levites in Deut. 12.12, 18–19; 14.22–27; 18.1–2; Josh. 13.14, 33; 18.7 (but unlike the Levites who possessed cities and houses at Lev. 25.32–34; Josh. 21.1–42). See Morrow 1993: 195–215 on the Guardians of the Laws in Plato's *Laws*.

263 Aristotle, *Politics* 6.1322b; Aristotle, *Athenian Constitution* 54.6–7. Supervisory positions over sacrifices and matters of religion were often filled by non-priests.

264 Plato, *Laws* 12.945e-946c, 947a-b. The priests were to be between fifty and seventy-five years old, at which point they would retire from the priesthood.

265 Morrow 1993: 417–18. But Herodotus, *Histories* 2.37 mentioned an office of high priest among the Egyptians.

266 For the priests as *Euthynoi* (auditors), see Plato, *Laws* 12.945b-e. For the priests in the Nocturnal Council, see Plato, *Laws* 12.951d-e. Plato did not assign the priests religious or cultic duties.

267 The civic authority vested in the office of high priest at Jerusalem was a prominent, even distinctive feature of the Jewish nation, as documented in credible sources for the third century BCE on (cf. Josephus, Ant. 12.156–60). A figure called Johanan the high priest *(rab cohen)* was mentioned in the Elephantine Papyri of ca. 400 BCE *(TAD* A4.7.17–18), but he was subservient to the Persian governor. A survey evidence from Babylonia, Asia Minor, Egypt and Judea at Fried 2004: 6–233 demonstrated that the autonomy of temples and the authority of temple personnel diminished across the empire in the Persian Era, leading to the conclusion that hierocratic rule of the Jewish nation under a high priest was not instituted until sometime in after the end of the Persian Era (Fried 2004: 6–7, 233). Plato's *Laws* appears to have been instrumental in the invention of a hierocratic form of government in Judea in the early Hellenistic Era.

268 These *agurteis* or itinerant beggar priests were criticized at Plato, *Republic* 2.364b-e and ridiculed in the comedies of Aristophanes; cf. Lateiner 1993: 186; Flower 2008: 28, 66–7. One notable class of itinerant priests was those associated with the Orphic mysteries.

269 The Levites lacked an inheritance in Israel and were found in every village (Deut. 12.12, 18; 14.27–29; 16.11, 14; 18.6; 26.12). The Aaronid priesthood associated with P and H sacred legislation considered Levites second class priests and denied them a right to a portion of sacrifices in Jerusalem. Judges associated the Levites with questionable cults (Judg. 17–18).

270 Lysias, *Against Andocides* 10 referred to "the unwritten laws that the Eumolpidae expound."

271 Major discussions of the Exegetes in literary and inscriptional sources are found in Jacoby 1949: 8–51; Nilsson 1950; Oliver 1950, 1952, 1954, 1957; Bloch 1953; Clinton 1974: 89–93, 116; Morrow 1993: 419–27. Literary references to Exegetes were cataloged at Jacoby 1949: 11–16; Oliver 1950: 122–38; inscriptional reference were cataloged at Jacoby 1949: 8–11; Oliver 1950: 139–65. Secondary literature, including the reviews cited earlier, almost unanimously rejected both Oliver's theory that the board of Exegetes arose only in the fourth century BCE as successors to the Eumolpidae *chresmologoi* or oracle collectors of earlier times and Oliver's equation of the *chresmologoi* with the *manteis* or Greek prophets. The Exegetes diminished in importance after Plato's time, perhaps in part because of the publication of exegetical traditions starting with an *Exegetica* by Kleidemos in ca. 350 BCE (Athenaeus, *The Philosophers' Banquet* 9.409f) and did not receive mention in Aristotle's writings. Timotheus, an Eumolpid Exegete from Athens, was consulted by Ptolemy I Soter regarding the foundation of the Alexandrian cult of Serapis (Tacitus, *Histories* 4.83.2; Plutarch, *On Isis and Osiris* 28.362a; Oliver 1950: 135–6; Clinton 1974: 1–2). In later centuries, an archaizing revival of the Exegetes is documented in inscriptional sources.

272 Andocides, *On the Mysteries* 115–16; Jacoby 1949: 26; Oliver 1950: 19–20; Clinton 1974: 1. Some question whether the Exegetes were priests. A decree of 128 BCE referred to "the priest of Pythian Apollo, the exegetes, (and) the other priests," suggesting that Exegetes were a class of priests, but Plato, *Laws* 8.828b distinguished "exegetes, priests and priestesses, and prophets." See the discussion at Jacoby 1949: 47; Clinton 1974: 90.

273 Plato's *Laws* 6.759c-e; 6.774e–775a; 8.828a-b; 9.865b-d, 871a-d, 873d; 11.916c; 12.958d; cf. Morrow 1993: 424. See also Plato, *Euthyphro* 4b-e, which related an episode in which Euthyphro sent to Athens to consult the Exegetes on what to do about the death of a slave.

274 Isaeus, *Ciron* 38–9 (before 363 BCE); Demosthenes, *Against Evergus and Mnesibulus* 68–70 (ca. 350 BCE); *Andokides* 1.115–16; Lysias, *Against Andocides* 10. Other literary references to Exegetes appear at Theophrastus, *Characters* 16.6; Plutarch, *Theseus* 25.

275 The formerly unwritten laws of the Exegetes were finally put into written form starting in ca. 350 BCE. These collections of sacred laws that dealt with rituals and rules used on various occasions were known as either *Exegetica* or *Patria* (that is, "Ancestral Laws"), including one text called the *Eumolpidon Patria*. See especially Jacoby 1949: 16, 41, 44, 49–50.

276 Exegetes facilitated purifications related to homicide at Plato, *Euthyphro* 4c, 9a; Plato, *Laws* 9.865c-d; 11.916c; Demosthenes, *Against Evergus and Mnesibulus* 68–73; cf. Plato, *Laws* 9.873d on purifications after a suicide. Exegetes were involved in homicide cases because of the religious aspects of murder (Jacoby 1949: 22–3; MacDowell 1963: 11–16). Other matters on which they were consulted in an advisory capacity included purifications of polluted waters and streams, marriage and funeral rites, sacrifices, festivals and the sanctification of cult sites (cf. Jacoby 1949: 41–51).

277 Deut. 17.8–12; 21.1–9; at 24.8 the Levites were consulted on removing the plague of leprosy. Like the Levites, the Exegetes of Athens were members of a kinship group, the *genos* of the Eumolpidae, who had exclusive rights over matters of interpretation of sacred law (Andocides, *On the Mysteries* 116; cf. Jacoby 1949: 26; Oliver 1950: 19–20). Josephus claimed that the Pharisees were the most accurate *exegetes* of ancestral law at Wars 2.162; 1.110; cf. Ant. 13.297; 17.41. Mandel 2006: 26–7 compared Jewish religious experts and Athenian exegetes.

278 For a comparison of biblical and Greek procedures and personnel for the removal of pollution, especially from homicides, see Hagedorn 2003.

279 The appointment of the three *Exegetai Pythochrestoi* at Athens, perhaps comparable in authority to the Levites referred to at Deut. 17.8–9, required the consultation of the oracle at Delphi; cf. Parke and Wormell 1956: 1.110–12.

280 A full comparison of Ancient Near Eastern, Greek and biblical prophets and prophecy, although clearly indicative of substantial Greek influence on the biblical literary portraits of prophets and prophetic activities, is outside the scope of the present study. The present discussion focuses exclusively on constitutional issues relating to the office of prophet.

281 Prophetic visions were mentioned at Plato, *Laws* 5.738c. Consultation of prophets was mentioned at Plato, *Laws* 8.828b; 9.871c-d. Prophets in Plato's *Laws* were discussed at Morrow 1993: 427–30, 433–4. The figure of Socrates in Plato's dialogues as a *mantis* on a divine mission to educate and save Athens was that of an inspired prophet rather than one who relied on technical divination. The biblical literary stereotype of prophet as persecuted anti-establishment social critic, although comparable to prophets in Greek literature such as Teiresias and others, appears to have drawn most directly on the figure of Socrates.

282 Technical divination was also known in the Ancient Near East. It is thought that divination spread from the Ancient Near East across the Mediterranean in antiquity, perhaps facilitated by Phoenician trade (see Burkert 1992: 41–87 on the common culture of magic, medicine and divination in the Mediterranean and Ancient Near East).

283 Roth 1982: 98–101, 115–18, 238–42; See Johnston 2008: 4–32 for a survey of books on Greek divination from antiquity to the present. Plato referred to technical divination at *Charmides* 174a, *Theaetetus* 179a, *Laches* 195e, *Philebus* 67b, *Ion* 538e; cf. *Laws* 11.933e.

284 See Flower 2008: 153–87. Prophets who accompanied generals into war are attested in ca. 400 BCE in Xenophon's *Anabasis* and in accounts of Alexander the Great's conquests in ca. 325 BCE.

285 Herodotus, *Histories* 7.142–43; 8.96; Thucydides, *Peloponnesian War* 8.1; Plutarch, *Nicias* 13; cf. Oliver 1950: 25, 123, 134; Powell 1979; Crawford and Whitehead 1983: 422–5; .

286 Gen. 40.5–13; 41.1–36. Dream interpretation also appeared in Dan. 2, 4, 7–8, 10. Dream interpretation was a prominent feature in the *Genesis Apocryphon* (1QapGen 19.14–19), where Abraham was depicted as an interpreter of dreams.

287 Biblical narratives characterized both Miriam and Deborah as prophetesses (Ex. 15.20; Judg. 5), apparently in their capacity as songwriters. 2 Kgs 22.14 mentioned Huldah the prophetess.

288 Sir. 45.6–14; *The Letter of Aristeas* 96–9. Discussion of references to the Urim and Thummim in the Dead Sea Scrolls appeared in Fried 2007.

289 Exodus–Joshua assumed the consultation of the Urim and Thummim on important matters, especially relating to actions in war; cf. Num. 27.21–23; 1 Sam. 14.38–42; 28.6. Battle oracles appeared at Judg. 20.18–28; 1 Sam. 23.2, 4; 28.5–7; 30.8; 2 Sam. 2.1; 5.19, 23. Joshua's consultation of Eleazar, Aaron's successor, during military field operations during the Conquest (Num. 27.21) was fully analogous to Greek prophetic consultations before battle. Prophetic consultations during war were common throughout the ancient world and are well documented in Assyrian sources.

290 For constitutional issues regarding the office of prophet as illuminated by Greek comparisons, see especially the discussion of prophets in Deut. 18.9–22 at Hagedorn 2004: 156–69.

291 As discussed in note 29, the Ancient Near East lacked any form of constitutional literature.

292 The direct indebtedness of biblical constitutional features to Greek and especially Athenian political forms undermines the thesis that the Pentateuch represents a significant innovation in constitutional law, contemporary with or predating comparable features of Greek constitutions, as claimed at Berman 2008: 6–7, 52; Levinson 2008: 52–88.

293 See Chapter 3 §1.

294 See further Chapter 3 §1 on legislative research conducted by lawmakers in Greek antiquity. Many Greek states in antiquity – as well as ancient Rome – modeled their legal and political systems on that of Athens (Thucydides, *Peloponnesian War*. 2.37.1–40.2; Demosthenes, *Against Timocrates* 210; cf. Crawford and Whitehead 1983: 275). If the constitutional parallels presented earlier are accepted as valid, it appears that the authors of the Books of Moses did the same.

Bibliography

Albertz, Rainer, *History of Israelite Religion in the Old Testament Period*. 2 vols. Louisville, KY: Westminster/John Knox Press, 1994.

Allen, Danielle S., *The World of Prometheus: The Politics of Punishing in Democratic Athens*. Princeton, NJ: Princeton University Press, 2000.

Arnaoutoglou, Ilias, *Ancient Greek Laws: A Sourcebook*. New York: Routledge, 1998.

Berman, Joshua A., "Constitution, Class, and the Book of Deuteronomy," *Hebraic Political Studies* 1 (2006): 523–48.

———, *Created Equal: How the Bible Broke with Ancient Political Thought*. Oxford: Oxford University Press, 2008.

Blidstein, Gerald J., "Atimia: A Greek Parallel to Ezra X 8 and to Post-Biblical Exclusion from the Community," *VT* 24 (1974): 357–60.

Bloch, Herbert, "The Exegetes of Athens and the Prytaneion Decree," *AJP* 74 (1953): 407–18.

Bonfante, Larissa, "Nudity as a Costume in Classical Art," *AJA* 93 (1989): 543–70.

Burkert, Walter, *The Orientalizing Revolution: Near Eastern Influence on Greek Culture in the Early Archaic Age*. Revealing Antiquity 5. Cambridge: Harvard University Press, 1992.

Carr, David, *Writing on the Tablets of the Heart: Origins of Scripture and Literature*. New York: Oxford, 2005.

Chase, Alston Hurd, "The Influence of Athenian Institutions on the Laws of Plato," *HSCP* 44 (1933): 131–92.

Clinton, Kevin, "The Sacred Officials of the Eleusinian Mysteries," *TAPhS* 64 (1974): 1–143.

Crawford, Michael H. and David Whitehead, *Archaic and Classical Greece: A Selection of Ancient Sources in Translation*. Cambridge: Cambridge University Press, 1983.

Davies, J. K., *Democracy and Classical Greece*. Stanford, CA: Stanford University Press, 1978.

de Geus, C.H.J. *The Tribes of Israel: An Investigation into Some of the Presuppositions of Martin Noth's Amphictyony Hypothesis*. Studia Semitica Nederlandia 18. Amsterdam: Van Gorcum, 1976.

Dillon, Matthew and Lynda Garland, *Ancient Greece: Social and Historical Documents from Ancient Times to the Death of Alexander the Great*. New York: Routledge, 2010.

Drews, Robert, *Basileus: The Evidence for Kingship in Geometric Greece*. Yale Classical Monographs 4. New Haven, CT: Yale University Press, 1983.

Elazar, Daniel J., *Covenant and Polity in Biblical Israel: Biblical Foundations and Jewish Expressions*. 3 vols. New Brunswick, NJ: Transaction Publishers, 1995.

Feldman, Louis H., "Josephus' Portrait of Moses: Part Three," *JQR* 83 (1993): 301–33.

———, *Judaism and Hellenism Reconsidered*. Leiden: E. J. Brill, 2006.

Finkelstein, Israel and Neil Asher Silberman, *David and Solomon: In Search of the Bible's Sacred Kings and the Roots of the Western Tradition*. New York: Free Press, 2006.

Fitzpatrick-McKinley, Anne, "Ezra, Nehemiah, and Some Early Greek Lawgivers." Pages 17–48 in C. Hezser (ed.), *Rabbinic Law in Its Roman and Near Eastern Context*. Tübingen: Mohr Siebeck, 2003.

Flower, Michael Attyah, *The Seer in Ancient Greece*. Berkeley: University of California Press, 2008.

Fontenrose, Joseph, *The Delphic Oracle: Its Responses and Operations with a Catalog of Responses*. Berkeley: University of California Press, 1978.

Fornara, Charles W. (ed.), *Archaic Times to the End of the Peloponnesian War*. Cambridge: Cambridge University Press, 1983.

Fortenbaugh, William W., Pamela M. Huby, Robert W. Sharples and Dimitri Gutas (eds.), *Theophrastus of Eresus: Sources for His Life, Writings, Thought and Influence*. 2 vols. Leiden: E. J. Brill, 1992.

Fortenbaugh, William W. and Eckart Schütrumpf (eds.), *Demetrius of Phalerum: Text, Translation, and Discussion*. New Brunswick, NJ: Transaction Publishers, 2000.

Frei, Peter, "Persian Imperial Authorization: A Summary." Pages 5–40 in James W. Watts (ed.), *Persia and Torah: The Theory of Imperial Authorization of the Pentateuch*. SBLSymp 17. Atlanta, GA: Society of Biblical Literature, 2001.

Fried, Lisbeth S., *The Priest and the Great King: Temple-Palace Relations in the Persian Empire*. Biblical and Judaic Studies 10. San Diego: Biblical and Judaic Studies from the University of California, 2004.

———, "Did Second Temple High Priests Possess the *Urim* and *Thummim*?" *Journal of Hebrew Scriptures* 7.3 (2007): 1–5.

Friedman, Richard Elliott, *Who Wrote the Bible?* New York: Harper & Row, 1987.

Fuks, Alexander, "Redistribution of Land and Houses in Syracuse in 356 BC, and Its Ideological Aspects," *CQ* 18 (1968): 207–23.

Gagarin, Michael, *Drakon and Early Athenian Homicide Law*. New Haven, CT: Yale University Press, 1981.

———, *Early Greek Law*. Berkeley: University of California Press, 1986.

———, "Litigants' Oaths in Athenian Law." Pages 39–47 in Alan H. Sommerstein and J. Fletcher (eds.), *Horkos: The Oath in Greek Society*. Exeter: Bristol Phoenix Press, 2007.

Ginzberg, Louis, *The Legends of the Jews*. 7 vols. Philadelphia: The Jewish Publication Society of America, 1937.

Gmirkin, Russell E., *Berossus and Genesis, Manetho and Exodus: Hellenistic Histories and the Date of the Pentateuch*. Library of the Hebrew Bible/Old Testament Studies 433. Copenhagen International Series 15. New York: T & T Clark, 2006.

Gordis, Robert, "Democratic Origins in Ancient Israel – the Biblical Edah." Pages 369–88 in Saul Lieberman (ed.), *The Alexander Marx: Jubilee Volume on the Occasion of His Seventieth Birthday*. New York: Jewish Theological Seminary, 1950.

Gottwald, Norman K., *The Tribes of Israel: A Sociology of the Religion of Liberated Israel, 1250–1050 BCE*. Sheffield: Sheffield Academic Press, 1999.

Grabbe, Lester L., *Priests, Prophets, Diviners and Sages: A Socio-Historical Study of Religious Specialists in Ancient Israel*. Valley Forge, PA: Trinity Press International, 1995.

Graham, A. J., *Colony and Mother City in Ancient Greece*. New York: Barnes and Noble, 1964.

Hagedorn, Anselm C., "Deut. 17, 8–13: Procedure for Cases of Pollution?" *ZAW* 115 (2003): 538–56.

———, *Between Moses and Plato: Individual and Society in Deuteronomy and Ancient Greek Law*. Göttingen: Vandenhoeck & Ruprecht, 2004.

Hall, Margaretha Debrunner, "Even Dogs Have Erinyes: Sanctions in Athenian Practice and Thinking." Pages 73–89 in L. Foxhall and A.D.E. Lewis (eds.), *Greek Law in Its Political Setting: Justifications Not Justice*. Oxford: Clarendon Press, 1996.

Hamel, Debra, *Athenian Generals: Military Authority in the Classical Period*. Leiden: E. J. Brill, 1998.

Harding, Philip, *The Story of Athens: The Fragments of the Local Chronicles of Athens*. London: Routledge, 2008.

Harrison, A.R.W., *The Law of Athens*. 2 vols. Oxford: Clarendon Press, 1968.

Honigman, Sylvie, *The Septuagint and Homeric Scholarship in Alexandria: A Study in the Narrative of the Letter of Aristeas*. London: Routledge, 2003.

Jacoby, Felix, *Atthis: The Local Chronicles of Ancient Athens*. Oxford: Clarendon Press, 1949.

Johnston, Sarah Iles, *Restless Dead: Encounters between the Living and the Dead in Ancient Greece*. Berkeley: University of California Press, 1999.

———, *Ancient Greek Divination*. Oxford: John Wiley & Sons, 2008.

Knoppers, Gary N. and Paul B. Harvey Jr., "The Pentateuch in Ancient Mediterranean Context: The Publication of Local Lawcodes." Pages 105–41 in Gary N. Knoppers and Bernard M. Levinson (eds.), *Pentateuch as Torah: New Models for Understanding Its Promulgation and Acceptance*. Winona Lake, IN: Eisenbrauns, 2007.

Kupitz, Yaakov S., "La Bible est-elle un Plagiat?" *Science et Avenir* 86 (1997): 85–8.

Lacey, W.K., *The Family in Classical Greece*. Ithaca, NY: Cornell University Press, 1968.

Lambert, S.D., *The Phratries of Attica*. Ann Arbor, MI: University of Michigan Press, 1993.

Lateiner, Donald, "The Perception of Deception and Gullibility in Specialists of the Supernatural (Primarily) in Athenian Literature." Pages 179–86 in R. M. Rosen and J. Farrell (eds.), *Nomodeiktes: Greek Studies in Honor of Martin Ostwald*. Ann Arbor, MI: University of Michigan Press, 1993.

LeFebvre, Michael, *Collections, Codes and Torah: The Re-Characterization of Israel's Written Laws*. New York: T & T Clark, 2006.

Lemche, Niels Peter, "'Israel in the Period of the Judges' – The Tribal League in Recent Research," *ST* 38 (1984): 1–28.

———, *Early Israel: Anthropological and Historical Studies on the Israelite Society Before the Monarchy*. Leiden: E. J. Brill, 1985.

Levinson, Bernard M., "The Reconceptualization of Kingship in Deuteronomy and the Deuteronomic History's Transformation of Torah," *VT* 51 (2001): 511–34.

———, "The First Constitution: Rethinking the Origins of Rule of Law and Separation of Powers in Light of Deuteronomy," *Cardazo Law Review* 27 (2006): 1853–88.

———, *'The Right Chorale': Studies in Biblical Law and Interpretation*. Tübingen: Mohr Siebeck, 2008.

———, "The Bible's Break with Ancient Political Thought to Promote Equality – 'It Ain't Necessarily So'," *JTS* 61 (2010): 685–94.

Lohfink, Norbert, "Distribution of the Functions of Power: The Laws Concerning Public Offices in Deuteronomy 16:18–18:22." Pages 336–55 in Duane L. Christenson (ed.),

A Song of Power and the Power of Song: Essays on the Book of Deuteronomy. Winona Lake, IN: Eisenbrauns, 1993.

Lupu, Eran, *Greek Sacred Law: A Collection of New Documents.* Religions in the Graeco-Roman World 152. Leiden: E. J. Brill, 2005.

MacDowell, Douglas Maurice, *Athenian Homicide Law in the Age of the Orators.* Manchester: Manchester University Press, 1963.

———, "Bastards as Athenian Citizens," *CQ* 26 (1976): 88–91.

———, *The Law in Classical Athens.* Ithaca, NY: Cornell University Press, 1978.

———, "The Oikos in Athenian Law," *CQ* 39 (1989): 10–21.

Mandel, Paul, "The Origins of *Midrash* in the Second Temple Period." Pages 9–34 in Carol Bakhos (ed.), *Current Trends in the Study of Midrash.* Leiden: E. J. Brill, 2006.

McBride, Jr., S. Dean, "The Polity of the Covenant People: The Book of Deuteronomy," *Interpretation* 41 (1987): 229–44.

———, "The Polity of the Covenant People: The Book of Deuteronomy," Pages 62–77 in Duane L. Christenson (ed.), *A Song of Power and the Power of Song: Essays on the Book of Deuteronomy.* Winona Lake, IN: Eisenbrauns, 1993.

Meiggs, Russell and David Lewis (eds.), *A Selection of Greek Historical Inscriptions to the End of the Fifth Century* BC. Oxford: Clarendon Press, 1969.

Mirhady, David C., "The Dikasts' Oath and the Question of Fact." Pages 48–59 in Alan H. Sommerstein and J. Fletcher (eds.), *Horkos: The Oath in Greek Society.* Exeter: Bristol Phoenix Press, 2007.

Monoson, S. Sara, *Plato's Democratic Entanglements: Athenian Politics and the Practice of Philosophy.* Princeton: Princeton University Press, 2000.

Morrow, Glenn Raymond, *Plato's Cretan City: A Historical Interpretation of the Laws.* Princeton: Princeton University Press, 1993.

Na'aman, Nadav, *Ancient Israel and Its Neighbors: Interaction and Counteraction.* 2 vols. Winona Lake, IN: Eisenbrauns, 2005.

Nightingale, Andrea Wilson, "Plato's Lawcode in Context: Rule by Written Law in Athens and Magnesia," *CQ* 49 (1999): 100–22.

Nilsson, Martin P., "Review: Oliver, The Athenian Expounder of the Sacred and Ancestral Laws," *AJP* 5 (1950): 420–5.

Noonan, Jr., John T., *Bribes: The Intellectual History of a Moral Idea.* Berkeley: University of California Press, 1984.

Noth, Martin, *Das System der zwölf Stämme Israels.* Darmstadt: Wissenschaftliche Buchgesellschaft, 1966.

Oliver, James H., *The Athenian Expounders of the Sacred and Ancestral Law.* Baltimore: Johns Hopkins Press, 1950.

———, "On the Exegetes and the Mantic or Manic Chresmologians," *AJP* 73 (1952): 406–13.

———, "Jacoby's Treatment of the Exegetes," *AJP* 75 (1954): 160–74.

———, "The Exegetes of Athens: A Reply," *Harvard Studies in Classical Philology* 62 (1957): 37–49.

Ostwald, Martin, *From Popular Sovereignty to Sovereignty of Law: Law, Society, and Politics in Fifth Century Athens.* Berkeley: University of California Press, 1986.

———, *Oligarchia: The Development of a Constitutional Form in Ancient Greece.* Stuttgart: Franz Steiner Verlag, 2000.

O'Sullivan, Lara, *The Regime of Demetrius of Phalerum in Athens, 317–307* BCE: *A Philosopher in Politics.* Leiden: E. J. Brill, 2009.

Parke, H. W. and D.E.W. Wormell, *The Delphic Oracle*. 2 vols. Oxford: Blackwell, 1956.

Parker, Robert, *Miasma: Pollution and Purification in Early Greek Religion*. Oxford: Clarendon Press, 1983.

Parpola, Simo, "National and Ethnic Identity in the Neo-Assyrian Empire and Assyrian Identity in Post-Empire Times," *Journal of Assyrian Academic Studies* 18 (2004): 5–22.

Patterson, Cynthia B., "Those Athenian Bastards," *Classical Antiquity* 9 (1990): 40–73.

Paul, Shalom M., *Studies in the Book of the Covenant in the Light of Cuneiform and Biblical Law*. VTSup 18. Leiden: E. J. Brill, 1970.

Phillips, David, *The Law of Ancient Athens*. Ann Arbor, MI: University of Michigan Press, 2013.

Porten, Bezalel, *Archives from Elephantine: The Life of an Ancient Jewish Military Colony*. Berkeley: University of California Press, 1968.

Posner, Ernst, *Archives in the Ancient World*. Cambridge: Harvard University Press, 1972.

Powell, C.A., "Religion and the Sicilian Expedition," *Historia* 28 (1979): 15–31.

Pritchett, Kendrick W., "The Composition of the Tribes Antigonis and Demetrias," *AJP* 61 (1940): 186–93.

———, *The Five Attic Tribes after Kleisthenes*. Dissertation. Baltimore: Johns Hopkins University, 1942a.

———, "The Tribe Ptolemais," *AJP* 63 (1942b): 413–32.

Provenza, Antonietta, "Aristoxenus and Music Therapy: Fr. 26 Wehrli within the Tradition on Music and Catharsis." Pages 91–128 in Carl A. Huffman (ed.), *Aristoxenus of Tarentum Discussion*. Rutgers University Studies in Classical Humanities 17. New Brunswick, NJ: Transaction Publishers, 2012.

Rahtgen, Bruce Donald, "Philistine and Hebrew Amphictyonies," *JNES* 24 (1965): 100–4.

Reviv, Hanoch, *The Elders in Ancient Israel: A Study of a Biblical Institution*. Jerusalem: Magnes Press, 1989.

Rhodes, Peter John, *The Athenian Boule*. Oxford: Clarendon Press, 1972.

———, "Bastards as Athenian Citizens," *CQ* 28 (1978): 89–92.

———, *A Commentary on the Aristotelian Athenaeion Politeia*. Oxford: Clarendon Press, 1993.

———, "Oaths in Political Life." Pages 11–25 in Alan H. Sommerstein and J. Fletcher (eds.), *Horkos: The Oath in Greek Society*. Exeter: Bristol Phoenix Press, 2007.

Rhodes, Peter John, and David M. Lewis, *The Decrees of the Greek States*. Oxford: Clarendon Press, 1997.

Rhodes, Peter John, and Robin Osborne, *Greek Historical Inscriptions 404–323 BC*. Oxford: Oxford University Press, 2003.

Rodgers, Zuleika, "Josephus' 'Theokratia' and Mosaic Discourse: The Actualization of the Revelation at Sinai." Pages 129–48 in George John Brooke, Hindy Najman and Loren T. Stuckenbruck (eds.), *The Significance of Sinai: Traditions about Divine Revelation in Judaism and Christianity*. Leiden: E. J. Brill, 2008.

Roth, Paul, *Mantis: The Nature, Function and Status of a Greek Prophetic Type*. Dissertation. Bryn Mawr: Bryn Mawr College, 1982.

Sealey, R., "On Lawful Concubinage in Athens," *Classical Antiquity* 3 (1984): 111–33.

Shear, T. Leslie, "The Monument of the Eponymous Heroes in the Athenian Agora," *Hesperia* 39 (1970): 145–222.

Sickinger, James P., *Public Records and Archives in Classical Athens*. Chapel Hill: University of North Carolina Press, 1999.

Stanton, G. R., *Athenian Politics: c. 800–500 BC: A Sourcebook*. London: Routledge, 1990.

Starr, Chester G., "The Decline of the Early Greek Kings," *Historia* 10 (1961): 129–38.

Szegedy-Maszak, Andrew, "Legends of Greek Lawgivers," *GRBS* 19 (1978): 199–209.

Tarn, William Woodthorpe, *Hellenistic Military and Naval Developments*. Cambridge: Cambridge University Press, 1930.

Teixidor, Javier, "The Aramaic Text in the Trilingual Stele from Xanthus," *JNES* 37 (1978): 181–5.

Thomas, Rosalind, "Written in Stone? Liberty, Equality, Orality, and the Codification of Law." Pages 9–31 in L. Foxhall and A.D.E. Lewis (eds.), *Greek Law in Its Political Setting: Justifications Not Justice*. Oxford: Clarendon Press, 1996.

Tigerstadt, E. N., *The Legend of Sparta in Classical Antiquity*. 3 vols. Stockholm: Almquist & Wiksell, 1965, 1974, 1978.

Traill, John S., "The Political Organization of Attica: A Study of the Demes, Trittyes, and Phylai, and Their Representation in the Athenian Council," *Hesperia, Supplements* 14 (1975): 1–169.

Wajdenbaum, Philippe, *Argonauts of the Desert: Structural Analysis of the Hebrew Bible*. London: Equinox Publishing, 2011.

Walters, K. R., "Perikles' Citizenship Law," *Classical Antiquity* 2 (1983): 314–36.

Weinfeld, Moshe, *Deuteronomy and the Deuteronomistic School. The Promise of the Land: The Inheritance of the Land of Canaan by the Israelites*. Berkeley: University of California Press, 1993.

———, *Social Justice in Ancient Israel and in the Ancient Near East*. Minneapolis: Fortress Press, 1995.

Wells, Bruce, *The Law of Testimony in the Pentateuchal Codes*. Beiheft zur Zeitschrift für Altorientalische und Biblische Rechtsgeschichte 4. Wiesbaden: Harrassowitz Verlag, 2004.

West, M. L., *The East Face of Helicon: West Asiatic Elements in Greek Poetry and Myth*. Oxford: Oxford University Press, 1997.

Westbrook, Raymond, *Property and the Family in Biblical Law*. JSOTSup 113. Sheffield: Sheffield Academic Press, 1991.

———, "Biblical and Cuneiform Law Codes." Pages 3–20 in Bruce Wells and F. Rachel Magdalene (eds.), *Law from the Tigris to the Tiber: The Writings of Raymond Westbrook*. Winona Lake, IN: Eisenbrauns, 2009.

Wheeler, E. L., "Hoplomachia and Greek Dances in Arms," *GRBS* 23 (1982): 223–33.

Whitehead, David, *The Ideology of the Athenian Metic*. Cambridge: Cambridge University Library, 1977.

Willis, T. M., *The Elders of the City: A Study of the Elders-Laws in Deuteronomy*. Atlanta, GA: Society of Biblical Literature, 2001.

Wolf, C. Umhau, "Terminology of Israel's Tribal Organization," *JBL* 65 (1946): 45–9.

———, "Traces of Primitive Democracy in Ancient Israel," *JNES* 6 (1947): 98–108.

Yadin, A., "Goliath's Armor and Israelite Collective Memory," *VT* 54 (2004): 373–95.

3

BIBLICAL, ANCIENT NEAR EASTERN AND GREEK LAWS

In the preceding chapter, a wide-ranging comparison of biblical and Greek constitutional and social institutions led to the conclusion that Mosaic legal institutions were modeled on those of Athens. The current chapter will shift from constitutional concerns to specific laws covering different areas of social relations. Since the publication of the Hammurabi Law Code in 1902, parallels between cuneiform and Mosaic law have been thoroughly explored by both biblical scholars and experts on Ancient Near Eastern laws. The purpose of the current investigation is to determine whether there also exist valid parallels between Greek and Mosaic laws and in instances where both Greek and Ancient Near Eastern parallels exist, to evaluate which are the most compelling.

1. Greek legal literature

The use of comparative methods to study the Pentateuchal law collections appears entirely appropriate in light of the international setting given the Mosaic law code at Deut. 4.6–8, which claimed that the statutes and judgments he taught the Israelites were the most righteous of any nation and would demonstrate their wisdom in the sight of all the nations who would hear about them. This appears to indicate that the Deuteronomist(s) possessed a wide-ranging familiarity with other legal systems[1] and anticipated that the Deuteronomic law collection would be of interest to an international reading audience, pointing to an intellectual environment in which comparisons of the relative virtues of various legal systems was a topic of widespread interest. Although international comparisons of law collections are not documented in the Ancient Near East, in the Classical Greek world such comparative studies were considered a valuable preliminary for those engaged in crafting laws and constitutions. Research into legislation from other nations was often conducted by lawgivers in Greek antiquity prior to enacting new legal systems, such as at the foundation of a new colony or at the revision of an existing constitution and laws in conjunction with a *metastasis* or change in government. Legal experts from other lands were often consulted prior to creating or revising a law collection. Thus, for instance, Roman tradition claimed that the authors of their ancestral legal and political system of ca. 450 BCE first sent out a delegation to study Greek constitutions and laws;[2] the *Twelve Tablets* display definite influences from the laws of Solon in Athens, supporting the notion of Greek influences on early Roman law.[3] International law was an important topic of study at Plato's Academy.[4] Plato recommended that legislators charged with creating a new law code should first thoroughly acquaint themselves with constitutions and laws from other lands.[5] Plato's *Laws* of ca. 350 BCE contained provisions allowing senior officials to travel to foreign lands for up to ten years for the purpose of observing the laws and practices of other nations, and on their return to report back their findings to a panel of legal experts that Plato envisioned as providing continuing advice to the Cretan colony.[6] Aristotle recommended that political science be grounded in a thorough study of constitutions and laws of other nations (Aristotle, *Nicomachian Ethics* 10.1181a-b; Aristotle, *Politics* 2.1260b-1274b; Aristotle, *Rhetoric* 1.1360a), and by ca. 325 BCE had assembled for that purpose, with the assistance of his students at the Lyceum, the constitutions of 158 states from around the Mediterranean. His distinguished student and successor Theophrastus later completed a similar international study of laws.[7] Comparative legal studies thus flourished in the late Classical and early Hellenistic eras, especially in the study of political science at Athens, where a broad knowledge of legal systems and their historical effectiveness was considered essential to good governance. It appears likely that the request for a copy of the Jewish laws for the Great Library of Alexandria was made to further such international study of legal systems (see van der Kooij 2007: 289–300, especially 298–9).

If it is accepted that the Pentateuch was authored at the Great Library of Alexandria, as evidenced by the various Greek sources the Pentateuch drew on, then this would provide an economical explanation for the international setting implicit in Deut. 4.6–8. Legislative research conducted at Alexandria's library by the Jewish jurists who authored the Pentateuchal law collections could have exposed them to constitutions and laws found in city-states elsewhere in the Greek world, including Athens, providing the Deuteronomists with a tangible basis for the comparison of Israelite law to those of other nations. Furthermore, the addition of the Pentateuch (in Greek translation) to the Great Library's holdings made the Mosaic laws immediately available to a wider international reading audience, much as Deut. 4.6–8 envisioned. The laws of Moses were thus arguably composed and published in conversation with the legal traditions of the wider Mediterranean world.

It is thus entirely legitimate to view Mosaic and Greek legal traditions, including those at Athens, as part of the same historical stream during the early Hellenistic Era, justifying a direct comparison of biblical and Greek laws. Sources for the study of Greek laws are abundant and varied.[8] The most important sources are legal inscriptions from Classical Greece, especially Athens, where there was a strong tradition of posting written laws for public display.[9] Much of the original wording of Drakon's famous homicide law of ca. 620 BCE, for instance, has been preserved in an inscription discovered during nineteenth century excavations in the Agora at Athens. A large number of Athenian laws are known from the forensic speeches of the classical Greek orators, which often quoted or summarized statutes relevant to the cases being argued. Many references to Greek laws appeared in historical works, poetry and even Greek tragedies and comedies,[10] because of the important role written law played in the daily life of the *polis*. The Greek world also produced a substantial body of prose literature devoted to legal topics. Ideal government was a common topic of the Classical Greek philosophers, with books that dealt with various aspects of politics that were authored by Plato,[11] Aristotle,[12] Theophrastus,[13] Demetrius of Phalerum[14] and others.[15] Some of these books dealt specifically with the constitution and laws of Greek city-states, most prominently Athens. Unfortunately, most of this literature has perished and is known to us only by author and title. In a few other cases, some fragments have survived in quotations from later authors. A handful of texts authored by the philosophers Plato and Aristotle have come down to us substantially intact.

The indebtedness of Pentateuchal legislation to the Athenian constitution and laws, as indicated by the evidence presented in Chapter 2 and in the current chapter, does not require direct contacts between Athens and Jerusalem in the early Hellenistic period. Rather, Jewish knowledge of Athenian legal traditions appears to have been mediated by the extensive writings by Athenian philosophers on law and politics, books easily available to scholars with access to the Museum and Great Library of Alexandria. The Great Library is thought to have been founded around 300–290 BCE by Ptolemy I Soter, one of Alexander the Great's "companions" who had studied alongside Alexander under the philosopher Aristotle, had served as one of Alexander's generals in his conquest of the east, and after Alexander's death became the first king of Ptolemaic Egypt. Ptolemy I was assisted in the acquisition of books for the library by Demetrius of Phalerum, the former tyrant of Athens and a notable Peripatetic (that is, Aristotelian) philosopher. The ambitious aim for the Great Library was nothing less than to collect all the writings of the known world, and according to one credible tradition the core of the collection was Aristotle's library that had likely been acquired by Demetrius from his former teacher Theophrastus (Athenaeus, *The Philosophers' Banquet* 1.3a-b; cf. Strabo, *Geography* 13.1.54). Significantly, the *Pinakes* of Callimachus (ca. 275–240 BCE), a catalog of the texts housed at the Great Library, included one major division entitled *Nomoi* or Laws (Blum 1991: 154). It cannot be doubted that the Great Library sported a significant collection of Greek legal texts at an early date, including political treatises by the Athenian philosophers Plato, Aristotle, Theophrastus and Demetrius.[16] These legal texts would have been available to the Septuagint scholars whom Ptolemy II Philadelphus summoned to Alexandria to reside under the patronage of the Museum at Alexandria so that they could create an authoritative version of the Jewish law code to be placed in the Great Library. The authors of the Pentateuch thus had access to the legal texts of the Great Library: indeed, the books of Jewish legislation that they created at the initiative of Ptolemy II Philadelphus would have been housed in the same section of *Nomoi* or Laws that contained the texts the Pentateuchal authors consulted.

Although the Alexandrian library appears to have provided the Pentateuchal authors with the literature on Greek constitutions and laws on which Pentateuchal legislation was arguably modeled, the specific literary antecedents to the laws of Moses for the most part cannot now be identified. Neither the few surviving fragments of Theophrastus or Demetrius nor the more extensively preserved texts of Aristotle, such as *Politics* or *The Constitution of Athens,* provide convincing evidence of direct literary borrowing by the Pentateuchal authors. The same can be said for most of Plato's surviving political dialogues, including *The Republic* and *The Statesman.*[17] In only one surviving Hellenistic text does substantial borrowing by the Pentateuchal authors on legal or political topics appear indicated: Plato's *Nomoi* or *Laws.* This text, Plato's last known work, written ca. 350 BCE, contained a fictional dialogue in twelve books between Klinias of Crete, Megillus of Sparta, and an Athenian stranger (a stand-in for Plato) on how to best construct a system of government for a new colony to be established in Magnesia, a district in Crete. In effect, it presented a handbook or guide for the framing of a constitution and laws. Although it put forward a model for an ideal state and contained features unique to Plato's writings, for the most part it was based on the Athenian legal system (and to a lesser extent on those of Crete and Sparta) (Chase 1933; Morrow 1993: 17–94). Interestingly, the Pentateuch (it will be shown) borrowed some of these elements that are otherwise unique to Plato's *Laws,* showing a literary dependence on this specific text. One cannot exclude the possibility that the Pentateuchal authors also utilized other legal writings once found in the Great Library, by Theophrastus, Demetrius or others. Indeed, evidence for Pentateuchal influence by features of Greek and Athenian law that are not found in Plato's *Laws* appear to positively point to the use of other, unknown sources.

In the current chapter, comparative materials will be discussed for the different legal topics addressed under Mosaic law. The comparison will first summarize the biblical laws,[18] then Ancient Near East comparative materials (if any),[19] then Greek comparative materials (if any). Next discussed will be evidence (if any) for direct literary dependence of Pentateuchal law on earlier written sources, whether on Greek sources such as Plato's *Laws* or Ancient Near Eastern law collections or both. Finally conclusions will be drawn, where possible, on whether Greek or Ancient Near Eastern legal traditions provide the most compelling parallels to the biblical laws being considered. In several instances, it is possible to detect both archaic legal traditions and more recent influences from Greek sources. At the chapter's end, conclusions will be drawn regarding the relative contributions of Ancient Near Eastern and Greek legal traditions to Mosaic law.

2. Homicide laws

Biblical law

Biblical law recognized several categories of homicide:

- The most serious was premeditated homicide, which carried a death sentence (Ex. 21.12; 24.17; Lev. 24.17, 21; Num. 35.16–18, 31; Deut. 19.11–13; cf. Gen. 9.5–6; Deut. 27.24–25). Elements in this crime included malice (Num. 35.20–21; Deut. 19.11), lawlessness (Ex. 21.14),[20] forethought (Ex. 21.14),[21] laying an ambush (Num. 35.20; Deut. 19.11)[22] or the use of a weapon, whether an iron weapon, a rock or a wooden weapon (Num. 35.16–18). This category appears to have included conspiracy or murder-for-hire (Deut. 27.25, unless this referred to judicial homicide). The penalty was to be carried out only on the perpetrator, not on his family (Deut. 24.16; 2 Kgs 14.6). The method for executing the murderer is never specified. The body could be hung on a tree for an example (Deut. 21.22) – whether pre-mortem or post-mortem is debated – but must be taken down and buried the same day (Deut. 21.22–23; Josh. 8.29). Although homicide carried a death penalty, biblical narratives indicate that flight into voluntary exile was always an option (Gen. 4.14; Ex. 2.15; 2 Sam. 13.37–38; 14.13, 32).
- A second category was unpremeditated homicide. Malice might be an element in this crime – that is, the killer and victim might be enemies – but if forethought was absent, this category of murderer might seek asylum in a place of refuge God would appoint (Ex. 21.13).[23] Spontaneous quarrels and fistfights that resulted in a fatality are probably examples of unpremeditated homicide (cf. Ex. 21.18–19, 22–23, which also considered such fights). If a murderer sought asylum, but had laid in wait for his victim, he was to be taken from the altar to be slain (Ex. 21.14; Deut. 19.11–13).
- A third category was unintentional or accidental homicide,[24] in which the perpetrator was allowed to seek asylum in a city of refuge (Num. 35.9–15, 22–25; Deut. 19.4–6) until the death of the high priest (Num. 35.25). Elements of this crime included a lack of forethought (Num. 35.11, 15, 22; Deut. 4.42; 19.4; Josh. 20.3, 5), no history of animosity with the victim (Num. 35.22; Deut. 4.42; 19.4–5) and circumstances that pointed to an accident, such as an axe head that slipped off the shaft and struck the victim (Deut. 19.5).[25]
- A fourth category was justified homicide, such as killing a burglar who broke into a house by night (Ex. 22.2–3; if the burglary was by day, killing the intruder was not permitted). The killing of a murderer who sought asylum at a city of refuge, but was caught by the blood avenger outside the city bounds, was considered justified (Num. 35.26–28). Pentateuchal examples of mandated or virtuous homicide (Num. 25.5–11; Deut. 13.8–9) may be considered instances of justified homicide.

- A fifth category of homicide was animal homicide, in which a dangerous animal – a goring ox – slew a man and was subjected to death by stoning (Ex. 21.28–29).[26]
- A sixth category was negligent homicide, such as the owner's culpability for an accidental fall from a roof that lacked a parapet (Deut. 22.8, with no penalty specified) or contributory negligence by the owner of a goring ox, which carried a monetary penalty (Ex. 21.28).
- A seventh category was judicial homicide, in which false testimony led to the execution of an innocent man. This type of homicide was subsumed by the law on false witness (Deut. 19.16–21), in which the penalty was applied on the ancient principle of *lex talionis;* for judicial homicide this would have meant the execution of the false witness. The possibility of bribery or judicial corruption leading to wrongful executions was acknowledged in several passages without a comment on the appropriate penalty (Deut. 16.18–19), although one would presume this would have been death.
- An eighth category was fatally striking a slave of either sex with a stick (Ex. 21.20–21). Harsh treatment of foreign slaves was not illegal, and even a fatal beating of a slave was punished, probably with a monetary fine, only if the slave died the first day (Ex. 21.20).

For any kind of homicide, the close kinsmen of the victim appointed a *go'el ha-dam* or blood avenger to hunt down and slay the perpetrator (Num. 35.19, 21; Deut. 19.6; Josh. 20.5; cf. 2 Sam. 14.7).[27] Designated cities of refuge – the list varies[28] – were intended to provide a temporary asylum for murderers from the blood avenger until they could stand trial (Num. 35.12; Josh. 20.3–6, 9).[29] Any slayer could seek temporary asylum at a sanctuary altar (Ex. 21.13–14)[30] or in a city of refuge (Deut. 19.3; Josh. 20.3–4).[31] He would first declare his case to the elders at the city gate, and if they found his case sufficiently persuasive, he would be admitted into the city as a supplicant under their temporary protection (Josh. 20.4). Later, the slayer could be tried *in absentia* and fetched from asylum by his city's elders for punishment (Deut. 19.11–12) or handed over to stand trial before the congregation of the slayer's city (Num. 35.12; Josh. 20.6).[32] The blood avenger acted as prosecutor and the slayer acted as his own defense at the trial (Num. 35.24). At least two witnesses were required to convict him of intentional homicide (Num. 35.20; Deut. 19.15), in which case the city elders would turn him over to the blood avenger to be executed, presumably by sword or any other available weapon (Deut. 19.11–13). The cities of refuge had characteristics of both an asylum and a prison (Barmash 2005: 9, 101, 204). If the congregation deemed the homicide unintentional and the slayer was acquitted of premeditated murder, he was restored to the city of refuge for semi-permanent asylum, where he was required to reside in voluntary self-exile until the death of the high priest, on penalty of death at the hands of the blood avenger (Num. 35.24–28, 32). He retained ownership of his possessions, which presumably provided him an income during his exile, and returned to his house and possessions after the end of his exile on the death of the high priest (Josh. 20.6; cf. Num. 35.32).[33] The voluntary exile of the perpetrator of unintentional homicide preserved his life while also removing the temptation of the kinship group to pollute the land by shedding innocent blood (Num. 35.33–34; Deut. 19.10).

The prosecution of homicides was, like other prosecutions, for purposes of vengeance,[34] to rid the land of evil,[35] as a deterrent measure to strike fear into other potential wrongdoers,[36] and – uniquely for homicides – to avert the pollution of blood guilt on the city or land in which the crime took place.[37] In the case where a dead body was found in the countryside, but the slayer was unknown, responsibility was assigned to the nearest city, whose elders were required to sacrifice a red heifer and declare under oath that the slayer was unknown (Deut. 21.1–9). This procedure had both judicial and purificatory purposes.[38]

The method for executing a murderer is never specified (except perhaps at Ex. 21.29), although biblical executions typically took the form of stoning by the community;[39] mob or community anger directed at an individual typically took the form of stoning (Ex. 8.26; 17.4; Num. 14.10; Deut. 13.9–10; 17.5; 21.21; 22.21, 24; Josh. 7.25). If the execution was performed by the blood avenger, it was presumably with a sword or whatever weapon was on hand. The body of an executed offender could be hung on a tree for an example (Deut. 21.22), but was taken down and buried the same day (Deut. 21.22–23; Josh. 8.29).

Ancient Near Eastern law

Several categories of homicide appear in Ancient Near Eastern law collections (see generally Barmash 2005: 125–42).

- Intentional homicide carried a death sentence (LU 1); Hittite and Assyrian law allowed for the relatives to choose either blood money or execution as penalty (MAL A 10; MAL B 2; *Telepinu Edict* 49; cf. Barmash 2005: 31, 49), but there is no evidence that the kinship group played a role in either initiating or prosecuting a homicide.[40] One law specified breaking into a house as an element of the crime (MAL A 10). The method of execution for a murderer was not specified, with one exception: if a woman and her lover had their mates killed so they could be together, both were impaled (LH 153). If the killer was unknown there was no possibility for executing the perpetrator, but the kinship group was awarded a parcel of land from the village nearest to the crime, compensating them for their economic loss from the murder of their relative (HL 6; cf. LH 23–4, where similar fees were levied on the nearest village for the crimes of robbery and kidnap, discussed at Willis 2001: 147–8).
- Unintentional homicide or manslaughter carried a monetary penalty in the form of either silver (LH 116, 206–8; HL 5), slaves (HL 1–4) or real estate (HL 6). Instances of unintentional homicide included deaths that resulted from a quarrel (LH 207–8; LE 47; HL 1–4; cf. the discussion at Barmash

2005: 127–8), a beating in custody (LH 116), fatally beating a slave (MAPD 18; HL 4), causing a drowning during a river crossing with an ox (HL 43) or accidently pushing someone into the fire (HL 44). If a victim died in custody from maltreatment after having been seized for a loan that was not in default, this was considered an aggravating factor that warranted a death penalty (LH 116). Striking an upper class pregnant woman and accidentally causing her death was a capital crime (LH 210; LL e; MAL A 50).[41] A death resulting from excessive beating of one palace slave by another superior palace slave was in turn punished by a beating (MAPD 18).[42]

- Justified homicide was recognized by the Hittites for a husband who discovered his wife and her lover in the act (HL 197), for those engaged in rescuing a woman from her abductors (HL 37) or for a quarrel that turned physical between parties in a lawsuit (HL 38). Those caught trespassing in a field or burglarizing a house at night were to be slain (LE 12–13), but whether this referred to justified homicide by the owners or a later conviction and execution is uncertain.

- Instances of negligent homicide (discussed at Barmash 2005: 129–31) included deaths resulting from building a house that subsequently collapsed (LH 229–31), from failing to properly reinforce a wall (LE 58) or from surgical malpractice (LH 219). Deaths that resulted from a dangerous animal that was not properly controlled, such as a goring ox (LH 250–1; LE 54–5) or a vicious dog (LE 56–7), were treated as instances of negligent homicide. Penalties could include either death (LH 229–30), the payment of a slave (LH 219, 231) or of silver (LE 54–7). The animals were not punished (Katz 1993: 163–9). A common element of the crime necessary for prosecution was that the culpable party had received warnings from neighbors or the authorities about the dangerous structure or animal (LH 228–30; LE 54–8; cf. Barmash 2005: 139–40), but no such warning was required for deaths caused by incompetence of professionals such as builders and physicians.

- Judicial homicide could take the form of either a false accusation in a capital case (LH 1) or false testimony (LH 3). Neither Ancient Near Eastern law collections nor other cuneiform texts mention bribing a judge as a form of judicial homicide (cf. Noonan 1984: 9–10).

The purpose of prosecuting homicides was not stated in connection with the homicide laws themselves, but prologues to the law collections mention establishing justice in the land and freeing the land from violence.[43] The brutal implementation of *lex talionis* appears to have aimed at both satisfying community impulses for vengeance and as a deterrent to other potential wrongdoers. The higher levels of punishment for crimes against the upper class also sought to induce all classes – but especially the lower classes – to respect the rights of the nobility, whose interests largely coincided with the palace.

Cuneiform law collections document various forms of execution: burning alive (LH 25, 110, 157), drowning (LH 129, 133, 155), river ordeal (LH 2, 132, 143), impalement (MAL A 53; LH 153) and beheading (HL 173). Another form of execution that appeared as a penalty for adultery in private contracts was being killed with an iron dagger (Roth 1988; cf. Hermann and Johns 1904: 118).

Greek law

Athenian law recognized several categories of homicide, each with its own law court:[44]

- Cases that involved intentional homicide, attempted homicide, poisoning and arson were heard by the Council of the Areopagus.[45] A conviction for intentional homicide was punished by death, although the accused was allowed the option of avoiding a trial by entering self-imposed exile.[46] Those who planned a homicide were considered equally guilty (Gagarin 1981: 37–45). Elements of voluntary homicide included premeditation (Lysias, *Against Simon* 41–3); malice or harmful intent *(pronoia)* (Aristotle, *Athenian Constitution* 57.3; cf. MacDowell 1963: 59–60; Loomis 1972: 93–4; Gagarin 1981: 34; Phillips 2013: 45); and the use of a weapon such as a spear – as opposed to a blow with a stick or a fist (Lysias, *Against Simon* 42–3; cf. Lacey 1968: 52). Although madness was not addressed in Athenian law, it was considered an exculpatory factor in Plato's *Laws,* because it affected the ability to form intent (Plato, *Laws* 9.864d-e; 11.934c-d; cf. Chase 1933: 183). Trials for attempted murder were seemingly treated like homicide cases, except that the penalty was exile rather than execution (Plato, *Laws* 9.876e-877b).
- Plato's *Laws* contained an innovation on the Athenian laws for intentional homicide by distinguishing premeditated and unpremeditated homicide. Plato held that those murders committed with cold premeditation received a greater punishment in the form of a longer term of exile than those committed on impulse with no forethought, despite an equal degree of malice (Plato, *Laws* 9.866d-869e; cf. Chase 1933: 168–9, 171–2; Loomis 1972: 93–4; MacDowell 1978: 115; Gagarin 1981: 35).
- Trials of those appealing exile from Attica for homicide were held at the Phreatus. This allowed those accused of homicide who chose to flee the kinsmen avengers before trial to have a hearing and a chance for clearing their name and returning to Attica. The defendant was required to remain onboard ship while delivering his defense in order not to violate his exile.
- Trials for involuntary or unintentional homicide were held at the Palladium. The penalty for unintentional homicide was exile, but the term of exile could be foreshortened by pardon from the family of the victim.[47]
- Trials for the murder of slaves and foreigners were also held at the Palladium. Injuring or killing another man's slave involved only a financial penalty (cf. Plato, *Laws* 9.865c-d, 868a). If a master accidentally slew his own slave, he was required only to undergo the same rites of purification as for involuntary homicide (Antiphon, *On the Choreutes* 4; Plato, *Laws* 9.868a; cf. Chase

1933: 170, 176), unless the motive was to hide a crime of which the slave had knowledge (Plato, *Laws* 9.872c, which may reflect Athenian law).

- Cases of justified homicide were heard at the Delphinium (MacDowell 1963: 70–81). These included killing an adulterer caught *in flagrante* with a man's wife (Aristotle, *Athenian Constitution* 57.4; Lysias, *On the Murder of Eratosthenes* 30–1; cf. Phillips 2013: 67–8), accidentally killing a fellow-soldier in battle or during an athletic context (Demosthenes, *Against Aristocrates* 53; Aristotle, *Athenian Constitution* 57.3; Plato, *Laws* 9.865a-b), protecting a close relative from sexual assault (Demosthenes, *Against Aristocrates* 53; Plato, *Laws* 9.874c-d), killing a burglar who entered one's residence at night (Demosthenes, *Against Aristocrates* 60, citing a law of Solon; Plato, *Laws* 9.874b; cf. Chase 1933: 167–8; MacDowell 1963: 76) or acting in self-defense against an armed robber (Demosthenes, *Against Aristocrates* 53; Plato, *Laws* 9.874c; cf. Chase 1933: 177–8). Slaying a traitor involved in establishing tyranny or overthrowing the constitution was considered not only justified, but also a citizen's duty (Andocides, *On the Mysteries* 96–7; see discussion in §13). Instances of justified homicide might require religious rites of purification, but entailed no civil penalties (Plato, *Laws* 9.865a).
- The *Archon Basileus* and the four tribal kings *(phylobasileis)* presided over trials at the Prytany (Aristotle, *Athenian Constitution* 57.4; cf. Pollux, *Onomasticon* 8.90, 120; cf. MacDowell 1963: 86) for unknown murderers,[48] animals[49] and inanimate objects.[50] Reasons for such trials included the necessity for placating the ghosts and spilled blood of the murder victims,[51] purification of the city from the pollution of spilled blood (Parker 1983: 117–18), the removal of dangerous objects and animals (see MacDowell 1978: 117–18, although this reason was not mentioned in any ancient source) and an assignment of judicial blame to objects or animals in order to officially exonerate others from the death, which might otherwise be considered a prosecutable case of involuntary (negligent) homicide.
- Judicial homicide, either through malicious prosecution or through false testimony, was referred to in literary sources (Andocides, *On the Mysteries* 7, 51, 53, 60, 68; Xenophon, *Apology* 4, 21, 24–25; cf. Plato, *Apology* 30d-e, 39c-d) but did not constitute a separate category of homicide. Various Greek laws recognized the possibility of judicial corruption through bribes *(dora)*. Corruption cases that involved a magistrate were typically handled through audits, through accusations brought before the Council of the Areopagus (in the early Classical period) and sometimes through the application of treason laws. The establishment of a jury system with juries that numbered in the hundreds limited the possibility of judicial homicide by bribery.

The purpose of homicide law at Athens was threefold. The first aim was vengeance. A curse attached to homicides until they were avenged (MacDowell 1978: 1–7). The souls of the slain victims cried out for retribution (Aeschylus, *Choephorae* 286–7), and the Erinyes or Furies, underworld gods of vengeance, relentlessly pursued the wrongdoers (Hesiod, *Theogony* 219–24; Plato, *Laws* 9.880e; cf. Parker 1983: 191–206; Fletcher 2007: 105, 107–12; McLoughlin 2007: 97). The payment of blood money to the relatives of the murder victim in order to avoid homicide prosecution was not allowed at Athens.[52] The second aim of homicide prosecution was to cleanse the city of blood guilt.[53] The failure to prosecute and avenge a murder was an act of impiety that could bring drought or plague on the land (Parker 1983: 257–80; West 1997: 53). Even cases of accidental homicide that carried no criminal penalties, such as the beating death of a slave, required purification rituals carried out under the guidance of the Exegetes (Demosthenes, *Against Aristocrates* 72; cf. Greenburg 1959: 128). The third and final aim of homicide prosecution was as an example and deterrence against wrongdoing.[54]

At Athens, the kinsmen of the victim were responsible for bringing charges, prosecuting and avenging cases of homicide (Demosthenes, *Against Macariatus* 57; cf. Chase 1933: 173–4). A citizen's closest relatives were known as the *anchisteia*. This same circle of close relatives took over his family obligations at his death: if he did not have any heir, the closest relative stood to inherit his estate; or if he had only a daughter as heiress, the closest relative was required to marry his daughter to keep the estate within the family; and if he was the victim of murder, was required to prosecute or avenge his death.[55] Members of the kinship group were required to bring charges of homicide against the murderer before the *Archon Basileus* and to announce in the market, the temple and other sacred places of public assembly their intention to prosecute the named perpetrator (MacDowell 1963: 23–5). If, after this proclamation, the accused appeared in any such public place prior to formal trial, the kinsmen had the freedom and obligation to arrest or to slay him (see Plato, *Laws* 9.866b, 868b-c, 871d, 872e on the avenger of kindred blood).

If an accused person was caught in public by his avengers, he might escape summary execution by fleeing to a sacred altar, statue or temple and seeking temporary refuge or *hiketeia* as a supplicant.[56] After the supplicant entered the sacred place and made his plea, the religious authorities would either accept or reject his request for asylum and protection.[57] Several places in Athens served as places of refuge, including the old Temple of Athena in the Acropolis; the Altar of Eleos, the personification of Mercy, in the agora; the Altar of the Twelve Gods and others; various temples outside Athens and throughout Greece also provided temporary protection for those in imminent danger. In most cases, seeking *hiketeia* was unnecessary, because if the accused remained in his private residence, avoiding sacred or public places until his trial was held, his safety was guaranteed by Athenian law. Alternately, one accused of homicide could voluntarily flee into exile, although by this action he thereby legally conceded his guilt.[58] If the accused was tried and convicted of intentional homicide he could be executed. If it was adjudged that he did not hate his victim, that no weapon was used, and that the homicide was unintentional, the penalty was exile for at least a year, or until the victim's nearest circle of relatives unanimously pardoned him (Plato, *Laws* 9.864e, 865e; 869d-e). The absence of the slayer (whether the homicide was intentional or unintentional) would cleanse the land from the pollution of blood-shed (Plato, *Laws* 9.871b, 872e-873a), and in the case of unintentional homicide the perpetrator's absence allowed the wrath of the victim's spirit to quiet during the period of exile (Plato, *Laws* 9.865d-e). If the perpetrator returned from exile before the end of his term of punishment, the victim's kinsmen had the right to slay him. In the case of a murder conviction, the kinsman accuser was allowed, and possibly required, to be present at his execution (Chase 1933: 174; cf. Plato, *Laws* 9.871c).

Forms of execution in capital cases included being "hung" or "fastened to the wood" (probably by iron collars around the neck, wrists and ankles), drinking poison (hemlock) and being thrust through with a sword (in military executions).[59] Stoning was another form of execution, but as a spontaneous and extra-judicial expression of community outrage.[60] Athenian law generally required burial the same day for purification purposes by the nearest relative, not merely for homicides, but for deaths in general.[61] For some crimes the body was thrown out, unburied *(ataphia),* beyond the boundaries of Attica.[62]

Comparisons and conclusions

Biblical laws on homicide have almost nothing in common with the Ancient Near East. In Ancient Near Eastern law collections, homicide was treated as an offense of one class against another[63] or as a property crime (Paul 1970: 62). Penalties were intended as justice solely in the form of retaliatory vengeance and as terroristic deterrence. There was nothing of inculpatory or exculpatory factors or psychological factors that indicated degrees of culpability and punishment. There were no notions of blood pollution,[64] blood vengeance[65] or a role of the kinship group in prosecuting cases.[66] Although the Ancient Near East had many temple cities (Weinfeld 1995: 97–110), there is no evidence that these functioned as asylums for those accused of crimes. Unintentional homicide was remedied by monetary compensation, not the exile of the murderer. Ancient Near Eastern modes of execution included burning, drowning, the river ordeal, impalement, beheading and slaying with an iron dagger. Among all these gruesome forms of execution, death by stoning is notably absent, and in all cases it was state officials, not the community as a whole, who carried out the punishment.

There is some demonstrable literary dependence on Mesopotamian law collections for the biblical laws on the goring ox (Mühl 1933: 25; Paul 1970: 78–85, 104; Finkelstein 1981: 20; Van Seters 2003: 119–21; Barmash 2005: 140–1; Wright 2009: 7–8), for laws on penalties for assaults on pregnant women (Van Seters 2003: 113–14; Barmash 2005: 140, 142, 204) and for biblical passages that invoked the principle of *lex talionis* (Mühl 1933: 12, 25), but biblical homicide laws otherwise diverged in fundamental ways from the cuneiform legal tradition (so Barmash 2005: 50, 204–6). The Law of the Goring Ox in Ex. 21.28–32 shows evidence of both Mesopotamian and Greek elements. Literary dependence on LE 54–5 and LH 250–2 appears to be demonstrated in the biblical consideration of the degree of negligence of the owner and in the awarding of monetary damages in the death of a slave if the dangerousness of the animal could have been anticipated. In other details, the biblical law contains striking departures from the cuneiform legal tradition, such as in the separate determination of guilt for the owner and for his ox, the animal's punishment by stoning, the execution of its owner if it was determined that he knew his animal to be dangerous and the taboo status of the executed animal's carcass as unfit for human consumption, presumably to be consumed by wild animals at the stoning site outside the city.[67] These specific details have striking parallels in Athenian laws and in the *Laws* of Plato regarding cases of deaths caused by animals.[68]

The biblical mythology of spilled blood calling out for vengeance, the defilement of a city or region caused by innocent blood, the need for ritual purification for bloodshed of any sort,[69] the prominent role of the kinsman avenger in both judicial accusation and prosecution of murderers and in state-sanctioned extrajudicial vengeance, all fully comport with Athenian culture, custom and law. The categories of homicide and their penalties were also very similar in biblical and Athenian law. The prosecution of animals in the Covenant Code and at the Athenian court of the Prytany is striking: only biblical and Athenian law provide examples in antiquity of judicial proceedings against animals (Finkelstein 1981: 5, 58–60). The division of intentional homicide into premeditated and unpremeditated murder in the Covenant Code was not found in Athenian law, but first appeared as a legal innovation in Plato's *Laws* and is one of several indications of biblical literary dependence on Plato's writings.[70] Although biblical, Greek and Ancient Near Eastern law collections all recognized a category of justified homicide, the permissibility of slaying a night thief appeared only in biblical, Athenian and Roman law.[71]

The biblical prosecution and disposition of homicide cases also comport with Athenian procedures. The role of the kinship group and blood avenger has already been noted. The flight to a sacred altar or temple as a suppliant requesting sanctuary was also found in both the Greek and biblical worlds. In the biblical statute, as in Athenian law, refuge at an altar was only temporary and was contingent on the merits of the case: if it was determined that the suppliant was a lawbreaker, sanctuary could be revoked and the offender turned over for justice.[72] Under both systems of law, murderers could escape the blood avenger by fleeing into exile, either outside the territory of Attica or, in the biblical statutes, to a city of refuge. Under both Athenian and biblical law, a life in exile was required even in cases of unintentional homicide: the law allowed the blood avenger to execute the slayer if he returned before the allotted term of exile, even when the death was entirely accidental.[73] The biblical forms of execution by stoning and (possibly) hanging are consistent with Greek customs.

Many of the features common to biblical and Greek homicide laws point specifically to literary dependence on Plato's *Laws*.[74] This text, which contained the only complete system in Greek literature of a proposed constitution and law code, included a comprehensive categorization of types of homicide, procedures for prosecution and rules of evidence and specifications of punishments; discussions of unpremeditated homicide, homicide by dangerous animals and justified homicide of night thieves that correlate with unique legal features in the Covenant Code; the mythologies of spilled blood, of the vengeful spirit of the murder victim and of the Furies; and the role of the kinship group in homicide accusations, prosecutions and extra-judicial vengeance. Plato's *Laws* also specially addressed psychological issues such as passion, fear, impulse and premeditation – what we today refer to as "state of mind" – as exculpatory or aggravating factors in the crime of homicide.

Finally, the biblical preoccupation with stoning as a preferred method of execution of offenders by the community seems to reflect Plato's *Laws*. Although stoning was well known in the Greek world, it appears exclusively in extant sources as an extra-legal expression of community outrage with the sole exception of Plato's *Laws* 9.872c-873c, where the extraordinary crime of parricide was to be punished by stoning.[75] The Pentateuch's near-exclusive legal specification of execution by stoning is thus best explained by literary dependence on Plato's *Laws*.

3. Assault

Biblical law

The Pentateuch has a number of provisions on assault, mostly found in the Covenant Code. In the case of a brawl in which one party was laid up with injuries from being struck by a rock or fists, the injured party was entitled to physician costs and compensation for loss of income (Ex. 21.18–19). Disfigurement of a fellow-citizen was to be punished according to the principle of *lex talionis,* "Eye for eye, tooth for tooth, hand for hand, foot for foot, burning for burning, wound for wound, stripe for stripe" (Ex. 21.23–25; Lev. 24.19–20). If a fight broke out between two men and one opponent's wife intervened by grabbing the privates of the other man, her hand was to be cut off (Deut. 25.11–12). If a pregnant bystander was injured during a fight and suffered a miscarriage, her husband was to be financially compensated whatever he proposed, as approved by the judges; or, if the mother died, the man who struck her was liable for execution (Ex. 21.22–23).[76] A master who beat his slave so that he or she died was not liable to prosecution if the slave lingered a day or two (Ex. 21.20–21). A slave was awarded his or her freedom if they suffered disfiguring injuries from being beaten, losing either a tooth or an eye (Ex. 21.26–27). Assault on a parent was a capital crime (Ex. 21.15).

Ancient Near Eastern law

Types of criminal assault were mostly the same in Ancient Near Eastern and biblical law collections: brawls or quarrels, for which an injured party was entitled to physician costs (LH 206; HL 10) and a replacement worker while he was incapacitated (HL 10); disfiguring injuries, which were punished either by the same injuries inflicted on the assailant's person (LH 196–201, 206–14) or by set monetary fines (LU 18–22; LE 43–7; HL 7–9, 11–16); financial penalties for striking a pregnant woman and causing her to miscarry (LH 209, 211, 213–14; LL d, f; SLEx 1'-2'; MAL A 21, 50–52; HL 17–18);[77] and special penalties for a woman who touches a man's privates in a fight (MAL A 7–8); severe penalties – severing of the hands – for assault on a natural parent (LH 195) or the termination of adoption for assault on an adoptive parent (LH 186). Under Assyrian law, it was not considered criminal assault to beat one's debt slave or one's wife "when they deserved it" (MAL A 44, 59).

Greek law

Greek laws dealing with assault took into account whether the injuries were curable or incurable, whether the injured party suffered shame and disgrace and whether the injuries inflicted was deliberate or malicious. Athenian laws recognized three distinct classes of assault:[78] simple battery *(aikeia),* or starting a fight, with no use of weapons (see examples collected and discussed at Phillips 2013: 96); intentional wounding *(trauma ek pronoias),* which required evidence of premeditation *(pronoia)* (Lysias, *Against Simon* 41–3; Lysias, *On an Intentional Wounding* 6–7) such as the use of a weapon brought by the perpetrator to the scene of the attack[79] and which may in some instances have included attempted murder; and *hubris* or aggravated assault, in which the attack was intended aggrandize the perpetrator or humiliate the victim.[80] Examples of *hubris* included the intentionally demeaning assault by an aristocrat on someone of lower class or wealth, such as was sometimes carried out by a party of drunken revelers returning home from a symposium or drinking party;[81] insulting a magistrate engaged in the business of government, which was punished by loss of civic rights and exile or death (Demosthenes, *Against Timocrates* 32, 49–50; Demosthenes, *Against Conon* 23; Demosthenes, *Against Meidias* 31–3; cf. Chase 1933: 179, n. 4); false imprisonment and beating, in which a citizen was treated like a slave (see examples collected and discussed at Phillips 2013: 93–6); committing adultery with a married woman, which was considered an assault on the dignity of the husband and carried a death penalty under *hubris* laws (Lysias, *On the Murder of Eratosthenes* 24–5); and parental assault, which was also a capital crime, because it disrespected the person who above all others should be honored (Plato, *Laws* 9.878e, 881d-e; 11.932a-d).

Athenian laws took into account mental aspects of the crime, including premeditation and the intent to humiliate the victim. In Plato's *Laws,* malicious intent and premeditation were considered aggravating circumstances in assault cases, whereas mitigating factors included lack of premeditation and action under the influence of fear or passion.[82]

Penalties in assault cases ranged from monetary fines for simple battery to death for aggravated assault. Although the law of "an eye for an eye" was known at Locri in Italy, the principle of *lex talionis* was not applied for assault cases at Athens.[83] Financial compensation for assault was simple damages if unintentional or twice that amount if willful (Demosthenes, *Against Meidias* 43). Under Athenian laws, it appears the plaintiff simply submitted a proposed amount of compensation for the injuries he sustained.[84] If the injured party was incapacitated for military duty the perpetrator may have had to serve in his place.[85] Intentional wounding also carried the penalty of exile from the victim's city (Lysias, *Against Andocides* 15). The most serious form of assault was *hubris,* which was an injury not only to the person of the victim but to his dignity, and accordingly potentially carried a penalty of death.

Comparisons and conclusions

Some literary influence of Ancient Near Eastern law collections may be detected in the biblical laws of assault. Both prominently treated the case of a pregnant woman injured in the course of a street brawl (cf. Van Seters 2003: 113). Both applied the principle of *lex talionis* to establish penalties in assault cases,[86] although the biblical use of *lex talionis* was extremely perfunctory (Ex. 21.23–25; Lev. 24.19–20). The biblical liability of the guilty party for physician costs and loss of income during the period of recuperation in the case of assault appears to be another instance of literary dependence on Ancient Near Eastern law (Paul 1970: 68–9; Van Seters 2003: 109; Westbrook 2009a: 43–5). A significant difference appears in the penalty applied in the case of assault on a parent, which was the amputation in the son's hand at LH 195, but warranted death in biblical law, Athenian law and Plato's *Laws*.[87] The granting of freedom to a manservant or maidservant disfigured by loss of an eye or tooth by punishment from their master does not have a specific parallel in either Ancient Near Eastern or Greek laws. Lesser punishments for the crime of assault against a member of the slave class are a feature of Hebrew, Mesopotamian and Greek laws.

4. Theft

Biblical law

Instances of theft received different punishments according to the nature of the crime. A burglar caught at night could be killed with impunity; if during the day, he would suffer a financial penalty, or if penniless could be sold for his theft (Ex. 22.2–3). If an ox was stolen and killed, the penalty was fivefold compensation; if a sheep, fourfold (Ex. 22.1). If the animals were recovered alive, the penalty was double (Ex. 22.4). Goods deposited with a neighbor for safekeeping came under special laws. A standard twofold penalty was awarded if items deposited with a neighbor were stolen and the thief was discovered (Ex. 22.7). If the thief was not found, the judges would investigate whether the master of the house stole the goods (Ex. 22.8). If one neighbor accused another of theft, the judges were to investigate, and whoever was found at fault was required to pay double (Ex. 22.9).

Ancient Near Eastern law

Criminal laws dealing with theft comprise one of the largest categories of Ancient Near Eastern law. Stealing was punished with death (MAL A 3), corporal punishment (MAL A 4–5; MAL N 1–2), forced labor (MAL N 2) or punitive fines (LH 8, 112, 114), depending on the manner of theft and the social status of perpetrator and victim. Receiving stolen goods carried the same penalty as stealing (MAL A 3, 6). Lost articles that had been found but not returned were considered stolen (LE 50; HL 45). The inability to verify a claim to have purchased an item (including a slave) by witnesses or a receipt was considered proof that the item in question was stolen (LH 7, 9–13; LE 40). The most serious forms of theft were burglary and highway robbery. An aggravating factor in trespass and burglary was operating under cover of darkness, which warranted death; otherwise trespassers were only fined (LE 12–13; HL 93–5). Making a hole in a wall to enter a domicile also resulted in execution, with burial to take place at the site of the break-in (LH 21). A highwayman was executed (LH 22), and if he was not caught then the nearest village would compensate the victims (LH 23–4), likely on the suspicion that they knew the perpetrators, but in any case for failing to maintain local law and order. Temple theft and man-theft or kidnapping were capital crimes (LH 6–7; MAL A 1). Anyone who assisted in putting out a house fire who used the opportunity to steal items from the house was forthwith cast into the fire (LH 25). Thefts were punished with a multiple of the items stolen (or their value), from thirtyfold for property belonging to the temple or palace (LH 8), tenfold for property of a palace servant (LH 8), fivefold for items placed in safekeeping (LH 112), all the way down to simple reimbursement (LH 120). Goods deposited with a neighbor, either for safekeeping while traveling[88] or as pledges for a loan,[89] which the neighbor claimed to have been stolen out his house, required a special judicial inquiry. The house-owner's claim was accepted and he was not considered a thief if there was physical evidence of a break-in (LE 36), if he had also lost goods in the robbery (LE 37), or if he swore an oath (LH 126; LE 37). Items placed there for safekeeping were nevertheless replaced or reimbursed (LH 125), as agreed to in the contract. Items on pledge that were sold without notifying the owner were considered stolen (MAL C 9). Livestock or other items that were placed in a house as loan security and were subsequently sold – presumably with owner notification – had to be replaced or their value in silver forfeited (MAL C 4). Garments given to the cleaner while their owner was on a journey could not be sold and if lost had to be replaced (MAL M 3). Commercial embezzlement required the repayment of the corn or silver stolen and a forfeit of the commission (LH 113). Other forms of fraud included using a boat without permission (LE 6) and not showing up to harvest as promised (LE 9).

Greek law

Under Athenian law, the act of thievery could incur either civil or criminal penalties, depending on the severity of the crime.[90] Highwaymen, kidnappers, temple thieves and those who stole from public places like the *agora* were all liable to the death penalty as evildoers *(kakourgous)* (Chase 1933: 166–7; Rhodes 1993: 581; Hall 1996: 80–3; Phillips 2013: 334–5: Aristotle, *Athenian Constitution* 52.1). Armed robbers or thieves caught in the act of breaking into a house at night could legally be slain.[91] Daylight theft from a private residence and receiving stolen property incurred a standard twofold civil penalty[92] and might also incur punishment by confinement in stocks for five or ten days (Demosthenes, *Against Timocrates* 103, 114; Lysias, *Against Theomnestus* 1.16). A citizen had the right to inspect a suspected thief's residence for stolen goods, but had to do so naked or lightly dressed with no outer garment.[93] Magistrates accused during their audit of temple robbery *(hierosylia)* for stealing from sacred funds entrusted to them, or accused of other forms of embezzlement *(aposterein),* were penalized ten times the amount stolen (Demosthenes, *Against Timocrates* 111–12, 120; Aristotle, *Athenian Constitution* 54.2), in addition to possible criminal penalties (Philochorus, *FGrH* 328 F121 [execution for *hierosylia*]).

Comparisons and conclusions

Biblical laws significantly diverge from Ancient Near Eastern laws on theft. Property crimes such as simple theft did not warrant a death sentence in biblical law.[94] As noted in §2 earlier, if a burglar was surprised and slain at night, this was considered justifiable homicide in biblical, Greek and Roman statutes. There is no parallel for the laws of justifiable homicide and burglary in the Hammurabi Law Code, which held that theft should always be punishable by death. Both Athenian law and Plato's *Laws* applied a twofold penalty for theft, which was also the general case in biblical statutes (Ex. 22.4, 7, 9), except that the Covenant Code decreed a fivefold penalty for theft of cattle and a fourfold penalty for sheep, if the livestock was slain or sold (Ex. 21.1);[95] this law might broadly reflect Ancient Near Eastern laws, which had different multiples of financial penalties for different categories of theft.

5. Marriage and inheritance

Biblical law

In the biblical world, marriage came about as a result of negotiations between either the groom or the father of the groom and the father of the bride.[96] In the majority of narrative, legal and prophetic passages, the result of the negotiations was the payment of a bride-price *(mohar)* to the father of the prospective bride.

This could take the form of either a money transaction or its equivalent (Gen. 31.15; 34.12; Ex. 22.17; Ruth 4.10; Hos. 3.2) or (in fictional narratives with military content) a heroic deed (Josh. 15.16–17; 1 Sam. 18.25). The payment of a bride-price formally established a betrothal of the bride to her promised husband that had the legal force of marriage, although the father remained the *baal* of his daughter while she remained in his house. The marriage took full effect when the bride entered the house of the groom (cf. Gen. 2.24), at which point the husband became the *baal* of the wife. The bride brought into the marriage her own wealth in the form of a dowry provided from the father of the bride.[97] The purpose of the dowry was to support the wife in case of the husband's death. This dowry could take the form of money, which typically came out of the bride-price (cf. Gen. 31.15–16); maidservants (Gen. 24.59, 61; 29.24, 29); income-producing land (Judg. 1.15); or even cities (1 Kgs 9.16). The dowry became part of the husband's property, which he was expected to administer faithfully for his wife's benefit (Westbrook 1991: 152–4).

The aim of marriage was to produce male offspring to inherit the estate of the husband. The necessity to produce an heir of undisputed legitimacy created a high value on the virginity of the bride, an avoidance of circumstances that could lead to any suspicion of adultery and capital penalties attached to the proven act of adultery. The birth of a male heir was an occasion for rejoicing. Failure to produce an heir could be remedied by several measures. The wife could give one of her maidservants as a concubine to produce male offspring for the husband (Gen. 16.3; 30.1–14); if the wife subsequently gave birth to a son, the concubine could be demoted to servant or even expelled from the house (Gen. 21.9–21). A second option was for the husband to take a second wife (Gen. 25.1; 29.23–30; Deut. 21.15–17).[98] An option of last resort – and one inconsistent with Mosaic law, which kept inheritance strictly within families – was the designation of an unrelated male as heir (Gen. 15.2–4).

The biblical text allowed for the possibility of marriages being dissolved through a written bill of divorce (Deut. 24.1, 3; Isa. 50.1; Jer. 3.8). The divorced woman could either return to her father's household or live on her own; in the latter instance she could enter into contracts without the permission of either her father or her former husband (Num. 30.1–16). Remarriage was permitted, except to her former husband (Deut. 24.1–4; cf. Jer. 3.1). If a war-captive taken as a wife proved unpleasing, she could be divorced and freed, but could not be sold into slavery (Deut. 21.10–14). If a husband divorced his wife and she subsequently remarried and her second husband divorced her or died, the first husband could not remarry her (Deut. 24.1–4).[99]

Under biblical inheritance laws, sons may have shared equally in the inheritance except for the "firstborn" son, who received a double portion (Deut. 21.17). If there were two wives who both had sons, the second wife's child was prohibited from receiving the firstborn's share on the basis of preference (Deut. 21.15–17).[100] An abusive, rebellious son was liable not only to disinheritance, after a hearing by the elders of the city, but also execution by stoning (Deut. 21.18–21).[101]

Under normal circumstances, after the father's death the eldest son, if he was of age, became the new head of household. The widow might live in the house of her son, return to her father's house (with a return of the dowry to the father [Westbrook 1991: 154–6]), remarry, or, supported by her dowry, live on her own. If the eldest son was not of age, the widow temporarily became the head of the household and trustholder of the estate until the sons became old enough to inherit.[102] At this point the widow would become part of the son's household.

If the patriarch died without a son, his estate passed to his daughters or closest kinsman (Num. 27.1–11). If a daughter inherited, it was required that she marry within the kinship group (Num. 36.1–13). A severe crisis was posed if the head of household died without either sons to pass on his name or any daughters. In that instance, the brother of the deceased was required to marry the widow and have offspring to perpetuate his name[103] and to inherit his estate (Gen. 38.6–10; Deut. 25.5; Ruth 3.10–13; 4.5–10), an arrangement designated "levirate marriage."[104] If the closest relative declined to marry a widow or heiress, the responsibility fell to the next kinsman in succession (Ruth 4.5, 10). Refusing to marry the widow or to have sexual relations with her to perpetuate the name of the deceased was considered a serious shame (Gen. 38.8–10; Deut. 25.5–10).

The status of widows and fatherless children was precarious. There was no provision for a widow with sons to remarry. A widow living on her own and raising minor children had to live off her dowry, perhaps supplemented by a trade, and by gleaning others' fields after the harvest (a form of community charity for the destitute). Once a son was grown, he would become his widowed mother's guardian. An aged widow without sons or hope of marriage (Naomi's situation in the book of Ruth) was particularly vulnerable. The status of orphans with neither parent alive was not addressed in Pentateuchal law, but presumably a near kinsman took them in and became their guardian. In the case of a widow or orphan under the care of a guardian, a lack of maintenance by the guardian was the feared abuse. The absence of any guardian left widows and orphans even more vulnerable. The Pentateuch lacked specific provisions for the appointment of guardians or for legal penalties against an abusive guardian, but only promised divine protection for widows and the fatherless (Deut. 10.18; Jer. 49.11; Ps. 68.5; 146.9), promised blessings on those who helped them (Deut. 14.29) and threatened divine punishment for mistreating them (Ex. 22.22–24; Deut. 10.18; 24.15; 27.19; cf. Ps. 68.5; Isa. 10.1–2; Mal. 3.5).

Ancient Near Eastern law

The institutions relating to betrothal and marriage were virtually the same in biblical texts and the Ancient Near Eastern law collections:[105] marriage negotiations between the fathers of the groom and bride (LH 159–61; LU 15; LL 29, 32; LE 25, 27; MAL A 30–1; HL 28–30);[106] the payment of a monetary bride-price that formally established the marriage relationship (LH 138–9, 159–61, 163–4, 166; LU 15; LL 29, 32; LE 17–18, 25–6; MAL A 27, 30–2, 38, 43; HL 28–30,

36; cf. Willis 2001: 194, 245);[107] the dowry (LH 137–8, 142, 149, 162–4, 167, 171–4, 176, 178–84; LL 24; LNB 8–13; MAL A 29; cf. Westbrook 1991: 142–5) that the bride brought into the marriage to support the wife if her husband died (LH 171–4, 176; LNB 11–13) or divorced her (LH 137–8, 142, 149),[108] and which her sons inherited on her death (LH 162–4, 167, 171–4, 176; LL 24; LNB 13; MAL A 29; HL 27).[109] It was expected that the purchased bride would be a virgin, and various laws addressed issues of rape, seduction and infidelity as serious violations of the marital contract.[110] The main purpose of marriage was to have sons (LH 144, 163),[111] and if the primary wife (LH 138, 158, 170–1; LU 9; LL 24, 26–8) did not bear children the husband was allowed to take a second wife (LH 144–5, 148; LL 24, 28; LNB 8).[112] Ancient Near Eastern law collections addressed the rights of both wives with respect to upkeep (LH 148; LL 28), inheritance (LH 167; LNB 8, 15) and the status of their offspring (LH 167; LL 24; LNB 8). A wife who bore no children could give her handmaiden to her husband to be a second wife and give him offspring (LH 146–7, 170–1).[113] Ancient Near Eastern law also allowed for adoption and foster-care (LH 185–93; LL 20; SLHF 4.25–30; LE 32–35; MAL A 28).[114]

Ancient Near Eastern laws allowed for the possibility of divorce by either the husband (which involved a divorce payment under Babylonian law LH 137–40, 149; LU 9–11; SLHF 4.12–14; HL 26)[115] or wife (although the latter was rare and carried substantial risks [LH 141–3, 149]),[116] with the caveat that the husband could not divorce a wife who had given him children (LE 59) or in order to marry a prostitute against a judge's orders (LL 30). A man who divorced a wife with children had to both return her dowry and provide her with child support. After she had raised the children to adulthood, she was free to remarry (LH 137), or earlier with a judge's approval (LH 177). If a husband was absent for a long time – for instance, if he was taken prisoner of war during a campaign – and the wife lacked means of support, she was free to remarry, but on his return her husband had the right to take her back if he was unavoidably detained (LH 133–6; LE 29–30; MAL A 36, 45). If she deserted her husband or if she had the means to support herself but went to live with another in her husband's absence, she could be severely punished (MAL A 24).

On reaching adulthood the sons inherited their deceased father's estate or their deceased mother's dowry.[117] If the male head of household died without having a son, an unmarried daughter was designated his heir (LL b), or a son by a concubine (MAL A 41) or by a prostitute (LL 27). Certain categories of daughters devoted to temple duties also inherited a share of the estate (LH 181–2). Ancient Near Eastern law allowed for a preferred son to receive a double inheritance (MAL B 1; MAL O 3)[118] and required that the children of a primary wife should receive a greater inheritance share than those of a secondary wife, maidservant or concubine (LNB 15).[119] A father could disinherit a son, subject to judicial review (LH 158, 168–9, 191; SLEx 5'-6'; HL 171 recorded a procedure for a mother disinheriting a son), but a son who repudiated his real or adoptive parents was liable to severe punishment (LH 192–3 [mutilation]; SLEx 4' [slavery]). A widow would normally live within her deceased husband's house with her minor or grown children (LH 171; MAL A 33, 46), supporting the household with her dowry and income from her husband's estate (LH 29), but could leave the household in order to remarry (LH 172). If she had grown sons she lived with one of them (MAL A 33, 46). If adult sons attempted to throw her out, a judge would decide whether there was just cause, and if not she would be allowed to remain (LH 172). If she had no husband, father-in-law or sons she was legally a "widow indeed" (MAL A 33; cf. Willis 2001: 247). Ancient Near Eastern law collections lacked provisions comparable to the biblical institution of levirate or kinship marriage of a childless widow.[120] Although the prologues and epilogues of Ancient Near Eastern law collections described the king as protector of widows and orphans (LU prologue [A 4.162–68; C 2.30–39]; LH epilogue [47.59–78]), the collections contained no provisions for their relief other than the inheritance laws mentioned earlier.

Greek law

Marriage practices reflected in Greek law differ from those seen in literary texts about the Greek mythical and legendary past. Greek myths contain several examples of brides won by means of a heroic, often dangerous competition.[121] Obtaining a bride by kidnap or by capture in war is a common motif in both Greek myths and Homeric epic. Homeric literature contained many references to an earlier Greek custom of purchasing a bride by paying her father a bride-price (Homer, *Iliad* 11.243–45; 13.384; 16.190; 22.472; *Odyssey* 1.278; 2.196; 8.317–20; 11.117, 282, 287–92; 15.231–38, 367; cf. Harrison 1968: 1.5 n. 3; Aristotle, *Politics* 2.1268b). Although winning a bride by performing some extraordinary deed is likely an artifact of story and imagination, comparable to the fictional Labors of Herakles, there may be some basis to kidnap, war, and bride-prices as ancient paths to marriage in archaic times. By Classical times, these methods of obtaining a bride appear to have been become obsolete.

In Classical Athens, the objective of marriage *(gamos)* was to produce a legitimate male offspring to inherit the family estate and perpetuate the family name.[122] Athenian law allowed for a man to have only one wife.[123] In most cases the parent or guardian of the prospective bride negotiated and arranged a suitable marriage;[124] widows and divorcees not living under a guardian had greater personal latitude in choosing a prospective groom. The first stage in a marriage was the "pledge" or engagement *(engyesis)* (see Harrison 1968: 1.3–9), when the marriage was legally contracted before witnesses and a suitable dowry agreed upon.[125] Although the betrothed remained in the household of the father or guardian, at betrothal she was considered legally married. Because the aim of marriage was to engender a legitimate heir, the virginity of the bride was highly valued in Athens; daughters were married at a young age and a daughter often lived in virtual seclusion as a child until the day of her marriage. At a later date, at the "handing over" *(ekdosis)* of the betrothed, the betrothed entered into the house of the groom, and the marriage was consummated (MacDowell 1989). The *ekdosis* typically coincided with the transfer of the dowry. Although it was considered the wife's possession, the husband took control of the dowry, often investing it on his wife's behalf. It was considered an act of virtue to provide a dowry for a daughter of a father too poor to provide one himself[126] or to marry a daughter whose father could not afford a dowry.[127] Plato went against contemporary Athenian practices by advocating abolishing dowries altogether.[128]

The continuation of the family line was important not only for the clan, but also for the state: a legitimate heir was a citizen, soldier, taxpayer and juror. Athenian law therefore contained a number of provisions to guarantee the succession of an heir within the family. The birth of a son was a happy occasion, formally celebrated in a naming ceremony on the *decate,* the tenth day (MacDowell 1978: 91). Husbands were legally obligated to cohabit with their wives (Plutarch, *Solon* 20.2–3; cf. Harrison 1968: 1.32 n. 5; Stanton 1990: 82–3, no. 49). In 413 BCE, after the loss of a significant proportion of Athenian menfolk in war, the Assembly passed a decree that permitted citizens to marry one Athenian but have legitimate children by another (a concubine),[129] the closest approach Athens had to polygamy. In instances where a man did not have offspring to inherit his estate.[130] Athenian law allowed for the adoption of a son either during a man's lifetime or at his death through the instrument of a will.[131] Under the laws of Solon, sons had equal shares, except that a will might provide for a greater estate for one son.[132] Under Athenian law, an unruly son could be disinherited, but this severe act rarely took place.[133]

A husband who divorced his wife had to return the dowry unless it was shown in court that the wife had squandered the household funds. The filing of a written bill of divorce was required for legal purposes. If a wife became a widow, she could either remarry, return to the house of her father or guardian, along with her dowry, or continue to live off her dowry in her late husband's house.[134] In the latter case, when her eldest minor son came of age he would replace her as *kurios* of the household and she would come under his guardianship and the dowry would pass into his hands to be administered for her benefit. It was generally assumed that a young widow would remarry and that an older widow would have a son to care for her. If she had no son, invariably she would return to her kin's house.

The male *kurios* of the household was expected to act as provider and protector of all those within the household; his death left them legally and economically vulnerable. Under Athenian law, both widows and orphans were usually put under the legal guardianship of their next of kin. A widow's dowry was intended to provide subsistence if her husband died and she did not remarry, but because this was often administered by a male kinsman, this arrangement was subject to abuse, because the one who managed her funds could neglect her and use her assets for his own benefit instead. Similar comments applied to the guardianship of orphans whose parents were both deceased and were not competent to manage the estate to which they were heirs. The Athenian constitution and laws carefully attended to the special needs and difficulties of those who required legal guardianship owing to the death of the *kurios* of the household or other circumstances.[135] One of the three most important magistrates of Athens, alongside the *Archon Basileus* and *Polemarchos,* was the Eponymous Archon (or simply Archon) who presided over what we would today call family court. His central responsibility was the protection of households and their most vulnerable members: widows, orphans, elderly parents and those with infirmities such as insanity, senility or injury that required a legal guardian or care provider.[136] He saw to it that such individuals were appointed a guardian and that the guardian faithfully discharged his or her duties, although the Archon relied on an active citizenry to bring problems with guardianships to his attention. A key feature of Solon's legal reforms at Athens in ca. 594 BCE was that any citizen could file a lawsuit on behalf of any other citizen. Perhaps the most important application of this legal reform was the filing of lawsuits with the Archon in the case of a guardian who was seen to be abusing or neglecting a widow, orphan or elderly parent or mismanaging their finances and estate.[137] As a result of a case brought before his court, the Archon might arrange the appointment of a new guardian, financial penalties against the old guardian or criminal penalties in some cases: the abuse of the parents who gave one life was considered one of the most serious crimes, tantamount to sacrilege against the gods, and subject to severe penalties up to expulsion (Xenophon, *Memorabilia* 2.2.13; Diogenes Laertius, *Lives of Eminent Philosophers* 1.55) or death (Lysias, *Against Agoratus* 91; Lycurgus, *Against Leocrates* 147).

When the *kurios* of a household died, his children became *orphanoi,* fatherless "orphans," whether their mother was still alive. If there were no male orphans, but only daughters, these were designated *epikleroi* or "heiresses" because the estate would eventually devolve upon them (or, more precisely, the husbands they married).[138] This posed a potential problem, because the ancestral estate could pass out of the family's hands and the family name be extinguished through marriage outside the kinship group. The rules of inheritance for a man who lacked a male heir – whether a natural-born and legitimate son or an adoptive son – were as follows: first, if there was no *epikleros,* inheritance rights would pass to the closest male relative on the father's side, starting with brothers, then nephews, then male cousins; or else the closest female relative on the father's side, starting with sisters, then nieces, then female cousins; or if the father lacked close relatives, inheritance rights followed a similar sequence on the mother's side.[139] This group of relatives eligible for inheritance was known as the *anchisteia.* If there were no relatives within the kinship group, the inheritance passed to the closest relative on the father's side.[140] If there was an *epikleros,* when she became of a marriageable age she was required to marry among her kinsmen following the same sequence of relatedness so that the estate would not pass outside the immediate family.[141] This form of marriage was called *epidikasia* or marriage by adjudication.[142] A kinsman might decline to marry an *epikleros,* in which case the right would pass to the next in line (Isaeus, *Pyrrhus* 74; Isaeus, *Aristarchus* 4–5; cf. Phillips 2013: 239–40). A kinsman who declined to marry an *epikleros* of the impoverished *thetes* class was required to provide a dowry for her marriage. Marriage to an *epikleros* required the prospective husband to divorce his current wife, and for the *epikleros,* if married to someone other than her nearest kinsman, to divorce her husband (Isaeus, *Pyrrhus* 64; Demosthenes *Against Eubulides* 41). If the groom-elect refused to marry an *epikleros,* she was to marry the next in succession (Demosthenes, *Against Macartatus* 54); and if there was no available groom within the kinship group, the heiress inherited the entire estate and was free to marry whoever she chose, with the approval of her guardians.[143] A husband married to an *epikleros* was required to cohabit with her three times a month, and if he proved impotent she was permitted to consort with one of his kinsmen, presumably selected following the same sequence among the *anchisteia.*[144] The *epiklerate* laws at Plato, *Laws* 11.924e-925c closely resembled Athenian law, but differed slightly in the sequence of relatives eligible to marry the *epikleros* and inherit her estate (Chase 1933: 143–4).

Comparisons and conclusions

Laws and customs regarding marriage, divorce, widowhood and inheritance in the biblical, Ancient Near Eastern and Greek worlds shared many features. Negotiations for a bride followed a similar pattern, although in Ancient Near Eastern law it was always the father (if alive) or brothers (if not) who arranged a marriage, while in biblical narratives the groom often made direct negotiations with the father of the prospective bride. Sporadic biblical references to a bride-price, paid by the father of the groom to the father of the betrothed, have stronger parallels in the Ancient Near East than in the Greek world.[145] Although most brides in the Greek world were given dowries by their fathers – except brides from poor households whose father could not afford one – some influential thinkers at Athens sought to discourage or abolish the giving of dowries, which turned marriage into a type of business transaction.[146]

Biblical narratives and legal materials allowed for the possibility of polygamy, which does not appear to have been practiced in Athens. Polygamy was also presumed in Ancient Near Eastern law codes. Biblical polygamy thus appears to be an authentic survival of ancient Jewish practices.[147] It thus appears that in marriage matters the biblical laws conservatively preserved local customs inherited from earlier times, including polygamy, bride-prices and dowries, rather than adopting an Athenian model of monogamy with dowries. The laws regarding dowries, widowhood and inheritance were common to all three cultures.

Biblical law did not provide for an Archon for widows and orphans, as in Athens, nor did it put them under the control of the king as in the Ancient Near East. The Pentateuch left the question of guardianship and protection unaddressed, but assumed that it would be handled within the kinship group and invoked divine curses if relatives were oppressed.

Biblical, Ancient Near Eastern and Greek law collections all envisioned the problem of the rebellious son but proposed different solutions. The cuneiform tradition allowed for the rebellious (adopted) son to be sold into slavery. Both Athenian Law and Plato's *Laws* allowed a legal remedy whereby a rebellious son could be disinherited after a judicial hearing that included representatives from the extended family of near kinsmen. The Deuteronomic provision for stoning the rebellious son is closest in spirit to the law that called for the execution of a son who struck his parent in Plato's *Laws,* although Deut. 21.18–21 described the offense only as general unruliness, not physical assault.

Biblical indebtedness to Greek law seems incontrovertible in the statutes on heiresses, inheritance and levirate marriage, which corresponded in extraordinary detail with Greek *epiklerate* laws (Westbrook 1991: 164; Wajdenbaum 2011: 190–2, 205). The Greek laws addressed precisely the same legal issues that arose when the head of a household died without a male heir: the preservation of the family name, the role of the heiresses in disposition of the ancestral estates and the potential loss of such estates to the kinship group and the tribe. The solutions adopted for these problems within the biblical and Greek legal systems were virtually identical. The kinship group, which consisted of close relatives as far as second cousins,[148] played a prominent role in inheritance laws, the law of the levirate or *epiklerate* marriage, and in blood vengeance of homicides (as discussed in §2). If there was no heir whatever, the ancestral estate fell to the closest relative in succession within the kinship group. If there was a daughter, designated the *epikleros* in Athenian law, the closest relative within the group was required to marry the heiress.[149] The husband of the heiress was expected to raise up children in the name of the deceased, "so his name should not perish."[150] If there was no kinsman available to marry an heiress, she was free to marry the man of her choice, although the biblical statute added the restriction that the marriage must take place within the tribe.[151] Biblical law differed from Athenian law in one other slight respect, in that the widow of a deceased head of household who died without offspring played the same legal role as an heiress or *epikleros*.[152] There is no evidence for levirate marriage in the Ancient Near East (Barmash 2005: 49), so the dependence of biblical law on that of Athens appears certain.

6. Sexual offenses

Biblical law

Sexual relations sanctioned in the Pentateuch included those between a man and his first and second wives (Gen. 25.1; 29.23–30; Deut. 21.15–17; 1 Sam. 1.2), most important for the purpose of siring male heirs, although a romantic element also appeared in some narratives (Gen. 29.16–18); and between a man and a concubine (Gen. 22.24; 25.6; 35.22; 36.12; Judg. 19) or maidservant (Gen. 16.3; 25.6; 30.1–14; cf. 2 Sam. 3.7) for the purpose of having male offspring in the eventuality that his wife was barren. Frequenting a prostitute was tolerated,[153] but prostitution was formally restricted to resident aliens.[154] Some biblical passages may have referred to a special category of (Canaanite) sacred prostitution, although this is debated.[155]

Categorically prohibited sexual acts, prominently cataloged in Lev. 18 and 20, where they were described as unnatural, included male homosexuality (Lev. 18.22; 20.13), bestiality (Ex. 22.19; Lev. 18.23; 20.15–16; Deut. 27.21), cross-dressing (Deut. 22.5), and incest or other intra-familial relations (Lev. 18.1–18; 20.11–12, 14, 17–21; Deut. 22.30; 27.20, 22–23),[156] which were forbidden except in the case of levirate marriage, where such relations were required for the purpose of creating offspring for a deceased kinsman (Deut. 25.5–10). The penalty for all categorically forbidden sexual acts was death (Ex. 22.19; Lev. 18.29; 20.10–14) or disenfranchisement (Lev. 18.29; 20.17–18, "cut off from among their people," unless this referred to execution).

Other sexual acts were prohibited which were natural but which violated the terms of marriage.[157] As noted earlier, a husband could legally have two wives, concubines and frequent prostitutes, but a wife could have sexual relations only with her husband because of the possibility of having a child of doubtful parentage. The crime of adultery, which was specified to mean a sexual act with a woman married to a husband, carried a mandatory capital penalty for both if they were caught in the act (Lev. 18.20; 20.10; Deut. 22.22).[158] If a jealous husband suspected that his wife had been seduced, but could not prove it, she was made to undergo the jealousy ordeal to prove her innocence (Num. 5.12–31). A virgin who was betrothed was considered married in terms of the law, despite still living under the guardianship of her father. Sexual relations with a betrothed virgin thus carried a death penalty for both parties if consensual. The location of the crime played a decisive role in distinguishing seduction from rape. If the crime took place in the city and the girl did not cry out, it was assumed that the girl consented and both were to be stoned; but if in the countryside, it was an assumed case of rape, because it was possible no one heard the cries for help, and only the man was to be stoned (Deut. 22.23–27). If the virgin was unbetrothed and a free citizen, it was no longer a criminal case that carried the death penalty. Instead of being executed, the man who either raped or seduced the virgin was required to marry her and pay the father fifty shekels of silver and was not free to divorce her later (Ex. 22.16–17; Deut. 22.28–29).[159] In the case of sex with a betrothed maiden who was a slave girl, she was to be scourged, but the man would be forgiven after offering a ram as trespass offering (Lev. 19.20–22). A parent seemingly had discretion to slay a pregnant daughter whose seducer was unknown (Gen. 38.24; cf. Westbrook 2009d: 249). Adulteresses were subject to public shaming (Ezek. 16.38–39; Hos. 2.2–3). A false accusation that a bride was not a virgin carried a penalty of one hundred silver shekels to be paid to the father, but if her virginity could not be proven she was to be stoned for prostituting herself in her father's house (Deut. 22.13–21).[160]

Ancient Near Eastern law

The categories of permitted sexual relations in the Ancient Near Eastern law collections were essentially the same as in the biblical text: first and second wives, handmaidens, concubines and prostitutes.[161] However, Ancient Near Eastern prostitution was not limited to foreigners, and the acknowledged son of a prostitute might become the heir to an estate in the absence of other sons. Sacred prostitution does not appear to have existed in the Ancient Near East, as was once believed.[162] Hittite laws permitted any consensual sex between men and women that did not violate marriage contracts or sexual taboos (HL 190–1, 199).

Ancient Near Eastern laws touched on various forbidden sexual acts, but not as systematically as Leviticus. Unsubstantiated accusations of homosexuality were severely punished (MAL A 19) and homosexual rape carried an Assyrian penalty of castration (MAL A 20). One class of Assyrian prophets, the *assinnu* ("cult singers"), appears to have engaged in cross-dressing, suggesting that androgyny or gender ambiguity had an elevated status in the cult of Ishtar (Parpola 1997: xxxiv; Huffmon 2000: 52). The Hittites treated sexual acts with some animals as a capital crime. Sexual acts with other animals were permitted but disqualified the man from the priesthood or from palace service. An attempted sexual assault of a human by an animal merited punishment for the animal only (HL 187, 199–200).

Violating familial sexual taboos carried various punishments in Ancient Near Eastern law collections. The penalty for incest with a daughter was exile (LH 154); with a daughter-in-law death by drowning (LH 155);[163] with a mother death for the son (HL 189) or both mother and son (LH 157); with a father's chief wife (that is, a step-mother) expulsion from the household (LH 158) or death (HL 190, if the father was still living). It was permitted for a man to have sex with more than one female slave at the same time, or for two brothers or a father and son to successively or simultaneously have sex with a female slave or prostitute (HL 194). It was a capital crime for a man to sleep with his brother's wife while he was alive, or to sleep with both a daughter and her mother (HL 195), unless she was a war-bride (HL 200). If slaves engaged in unpermitted relations, they were sold into different cities and sheep sacrificed in their places (HL 196).

The act of adultery violated the husband's marital privileges (M. Roth 1988: 196–206; Westbrook 2009d: 245–87). If a man was caught in a sexual act with a married woman, both man and woman could be put to death, mutilated or released, at the husband's discretion (LH 129; MAL A 15–16, 22–3; the king could pardon both according to HL 198).[164] An exception was made if the man's wife initiated sexual relations, in which case she was to be executed, but the man exonerated (LU 7; MAL A 14, 16). If a man and woman were caught together and the wife admitted to sex but the man denied it under oath, he would pay a fine and undergo the River Ordeal (MAL A 22). Wives accused of infidelity by either a jealous husband or a neighbor underwent the River Ordeal: if she survived she was cleared of suspicion, and the accuser, if not the husband, paid a fine (LH 131–2; LU 13–14; MAL A 17–19; cf. LH 127).[165] A wife who unsuccessfully defended herself against forcible rape on the street was exonerated (MAL A 12), and a woman was also deemed innocent if a rape took place in the countryside, where her cries could not be heard (HL 197). But the woman's guilt was presumed if a rape took place indoors (HL 197) or in the man's residence (MAL A 13), unless she was lured there by the man's wife (MAL A 23). A runaway wife was punished along with the householders who harbored her (MAL A 24).

A betrothed maiden still living in her father's house was expected to retain her virginity for her husband. A man who violated another man's rights by raping his betrothed was to be executed (LH 130; LU 6; LE 26, 28), unless the perpetrator was the groom's father, in which case there was monetary compensation and the girl was free to marry who she pleased (LH 156). Another exception was if the betrothed virgin was a slave girl, in which case the penalty was only financial (LU 8; cf. LE 31). Slandering a virgin – perhaps by the groom after the wedding night – carried a financial penalty (LL 33).[166]

The rape or seduction of a virgin who had not yet been betrothed was not a capital crime.[167] The usual remedy was for the seducer or rapist to marry the maiden (SLEx 7'; MAL A 55) without subsequent divorce rights (MAL A 55). Under Assyrian law, the rapist's wife was also to be raped (by whom is not specified). If he either had no wife or swore the relation was consensual, a financial penalty was given to the maiden's father instead (MAL A 55–6). The maiden's father also had the option of letting his daughter marry someone else (MAL A 55).

Greek law

Besides a wife *(gynaekes)*, an Athenian man might also have a concubine *(pallakide)* residing in the house,[168] typically a slave or servant girl who served his recreational sexual needs, although some men brought a free woman into his household as a concubine. As a possession of the *kurios* of the house, an unmarried servant girl did not have the right to refuse the sexual advances of her master. The offspring of a master and servant girl were neither heirs nor citizens, but were themselves slaves; the offspring of a man and a concubine who was a free woman were free but not heirs or citizens. In 413 BCE, however, an exception was made, and the offspring of concubines were admitted as Athenian citizens, because of the depletion of manpower from military defeats in the preceding years.

In addition to a wife and concubine, an Athenian man might also have a girlfriend *(hetaira)* who did not live in his house.[169] The relationship between a man and his *hetaira* was not necessarily sexual in nature. *Hetairai* were considered women of class: educated, cultured and good conversationalists. Many *hetairai* were foreign women of independent means with whom marriage to an Athenian was forbidden as illegal (although some exceptions to this rule were granted by special legislative decree).

Finally, prostitution was a legally tolerated though not respected profession in Athens.[170] It was simply taken for granted that some women, mainly foreigners, survived in Athens by selling sexual favors and that they were frequented by Athenian men.[171] Athenian laws against prostitution were aimed at protecting Athenian women and children who possessed citizen rights.[172] It was forbidden for an Athenian citizen to sell his child or a minor under his guardianship into prostitution.[173] Further, Athenian males were forbidden to enter prostitution, with the penalty of forfeiting their citizenship.[174] The existence of sacred prostitution in the Greek world, mainly associated with the cult of Aphrodite, appears to be demonstrated by abundant literary references.[175]

Although Greek laws regarding incestuous relations have not been preserved, and likely existed only in the form of unwritten or sacred law,[176] the Greeks viewed incest with a direct descendant or ascendant with horror, and such forbidden relations unwittingly entered into and subsequently punished by the gods were the topic of several Greek tragedies.[177] Marriage with a half-sister was allowed, however, and marriage with a niece required under *epiklerate* law (Demosthenes, *Against Eubulides* 20–1; Aristophanes, *Clouds* 1371–3 with scholion; cf. Harrison 1968: 1.22). Although homosexuality was tolerated, various protections were afforded to the students of the *gymnasia* to ensure they were not subjected to sexual advances by adults.[178] Male prostitutes were excluded from public office, priesthood and assemblies, on pain of death.[179] Plato's *Laws* contained an extensive section with polemics against any sexual relations not potentially productive of offspring. He held that perpetrators of all unnatural acts, if detected, should be disqualified from all civic honors and treated like an alien.[180]

In Athens, engaged and married women were forbidden to have sexual relations with any man but their husband;[181] the same rule did not apply to married men, who were allowed to have sex with unattached women,[182] including their concubine, unbetrothed slave girls, girlfriends or prostitutes.[183] If a man was caught *in flagrante* in consensual relations with a married woman, his death at the hands of the husband was considered justifiable homicide;[184] alternately, an adulterer could be held hostage by the husband and subjected to unrestricted physical humiliations until ransomed by his family.[185] If not caught in the act by the husband, the adulterer could still be prosecuted in a special court presided over by certain Athenian Archons, the *thesmothetae* (Aristotle, *Athenian Constitution* 59.3; cf. Harrison 1968: 1.34). There exists some literary evidence that the adulteress could be tried and stoned by the community – at least in former times[186] – but the usual punishment was divorce. The convicted adulteress suffered a form of female *atimia,* forbidden to appear in temples or at public festivals at the risk of being stripped, beaten and humiliated by anyone who recognized her.[187] A husband could not continue to live with a convicted adulteress on penalty of losing his civic rights (Demosthenes, *Against Neaera* 87; cf. Harrison 1968: 1.35–36; Arnaoutoglou 1998: 22–3; Phillips 2013: 104).

The crime of adultery carried a more severe penalty than that of rape,[188] because the latter only violated a woman's body, whereas seduction also corrupted her soul (so Lysias, *On the Murder of Eratosthenes* 32–3). It seems likely that cases of seduction were distinguished from rape by location, because literary references situate adulterous encounters within the home and forcible rape outside the home.[189] Although the seduction or rape of a married woman or betrothed maiden were considered criminal matters under Athenian law,[190] the seduction or rape of an unbetrothed *parthenos* (virgin or maiden) carried only civil penalties. It was usually resolved, after negotiations between the fathers of the maiden and her seducer,[191] with the seducer or rapist agreeing either to wed the girl or to provide her with a dowry.[192] If a maiden was discovered to have lost her virginity, but her seducer was unknown, she became unmarriageable and her father or brothers could sell her into a life of prostitution.[193] Although the loss of a maiden's virginity was an extremely serious matter, no Greek laws have been discovered regarding false accusations against a maiden or new bride (Hagedorn 2004: 268).

Comparisons and conclusions

Pentateuchal case law for sexual crimes appears to reflect a legal understanding of the institution of marriage almost identical to that of Athens. Sexual exclusivity was required only for a married or betrothed woman. Sexual abstinence was required only of an unbetrothed maiden, in order to preserve her marriageability as a virgin. Adulteresses were subject to public shaming, as were maidens who failed to preserve their virginity. A man was allowed to have sexual relations with his wife (or biblical wives), his concubine(s), as well as with prostitutes. At Athens, a man might additionally have a girlfriend or mistress *(hetaira)* as a witty and educated social companion, but this figure does not have a biblical counterpart, unless one considers the depiction of wisdom as a woman in Prov. 8.1–36 to be based on a portrait of a *hetaira*.

The closest literary affinity of biblical legislation on categorically prohibited sexual acts was to Plato's *Laws* (so Wajdenbaum 2011: 172–5), but the connections are not sufficiently striking to demonstrate a direct literary dependence.

Laws with respect to sexual relations that were not categorically forbidden but violated norms with respect to betrothal and marriage were similar in the Ancient Near East, the Greek world and the biblical law collections. Sexual relations with a married or betrothed woman was a serious infraction, because it violated the contractual rights of the husband or groom-elect and called the paternity of the offspring of this union into question.[194] The violation of a slave girl, even one betrothed to another, was not a criminal matter, however, because she was the property of her master. The seduction or rape of an unbetrothed free maiden was typically resolved by the marriage of the girl to her violator or a fine to go to the maiden's bride-price (Paul 1970: 96–8).

7. Slavery laws

Most slavery in antiquity resulted from taking captives in war. These might either be distributed among the troops as war booty or might be taken as royal possessions and some perhaps subsequently sold or auctioned off into private ownership. A second source of slaves was debt slavery, whereby impoverished persons might put up their personal possessions, their land and ultimately their family or themselves as security for loans; if unable to make repayment, they might forfeit their family estates or their own freedoms. Other sources of slaves included piracy (mainly a Mediterranean phenomenon), kidnap and famine slavery (an Ancient

Near Eastern phenomenon). The three major types of slaves were public slaves (owned by either temples or the state), chattel slaves (owned by private individuals) and freeborn slaves (typically debt slaves).

Biblical law

Biblical narratives referred to several classes of public slaves employed in the temple. One class of temple slaves, drawers of water and hewers of wood, was given a fictional etiology as men of Gibeon who submitted to Israelite slavery during Joshua's conquest (Josh. 9.22–27). Ezra–Nehemiah referred to other classes of temple slaves, the Nethinim and the descendants of Solomon's servants (Ezra 2.43, 58, 70, etc.). All these categories of public slaves are otherwise unknown.

Chattel slaves were exclusively of foreign origin (Lev. 25.46), originating either as war-captives (Deut. 21.10–14) or in the local slave markets (Lev. 25.44–46). According to the laws of war, if a city afar off surrendered, its residents could be spared as tributaries (Deut. 20.10–11); otherwise all the males of conquered nations were to be utterly exterminated, including the children, and all women except for virgins, who could be taken as slaves or brides (Num. 31.9–11, 15–18; Deut. 20.12–15). With all the male lines terminated, this effectively constituted the extermination of the conquered people.

Israelite freeborn slaves constituted a different class of slaves with different rights under the laws of the Pentateuch.[195] Although both Pentateuchal narratives and laws envisioned a system in which all the children of Israel were landowners, it was recognized that Israelites could fall on hard times that might leave them temporarily destitute. In the biblical system, a direct relationship between landlessness, destitution and debt slavery was presumed. The impoverished Israelite was pictured as successively taking subsistence loans, first offering his family as security, then his land, and then his own person (Berman 2008: 87). At the end of this process, after having defaulted on these loans, the family lost the ancestral landholding that provided them with a source of income and entered into debt slavery. The kinship group was expected to halt this slide into destitution and slavery to the best of their ability, providing relatives with non-interest loans (Lev. 25.35–37) or redeeming them from debt slavery to foreigners (Lev. 25.47–49; cf. Chirichigno 1993: 342–3). Although chattel slaves could be treated harshly, Israelite slaves were to be treated mildly as hired servants, even by foreign masters (Lev. 25.43, 46, 50, 53); only their capacity for work had been purchased, not their persons (cf. Matthews 1994: 124–9).

Although foreign chattel slaves could be held in perpetual servitude, provisions in Pentateuchal laws stated that a freeborn Israelite ("Hebrew") servant should go out free after six years of servitude (Ex. 21.2–4; Deut. 15.12–15) and their ancestral lands returned either every seven years in the "year of release" that coincided with the land sabbath (Deut. 15.1–3; cf. Lev. 25.1–7), or the fiftieth year in the jubilee that was also called a "year of release" (Lev. 25.8–34, 50–54; cf. Jer. 34.8–14).[196] Under these legal provisions, Israelite debt slavery, in contrast to chattel slavery, was in actuality work-for-hire for a maximum period of seven years, whereas land forfeiture was in actuality land lease for a maximum of seven or forty-nine years.

Although these laws were aimed at guaranteeing in perpetuity the freedom of Israelite citizens and the inalienability of their ancestral lands, certain provisions appear to have undermined these ideals. First, the laws of manumission for men and women differed in several respects. If a Hebrew manservant entered into slavery with his wife, he and his wife (and presumably their offspring) would be freed together, but if a master gave the manservant a wife and the servant was freed, the wife and offspring would remain the possessions of the master (Ex. 21.3–4). The provisions in the Covenant Code appear to presume that a daughter sold to another man as a maidservant would serve either as a concubine or – if agreed upon by the father – as a wife to the purchaser. In the latter case the sale was understood as a bride-price.[197] An ordinary maidservant or concubine had no rights of redemption or release after six years, but the payment of a bride-price put the purchaser under contractual obligation to marry the daughter. If the master took a second wife, he could not reduce the first wife's provisions. If the daughter proved entirely unpleasing, the master had to allow her to be redeemed, betroth her to a son or release her without money. In no case was she to be resold (Ex. 21.8–11).

Furthermore, the basic intent of the law of manumission – to prevent Israelite citizens from ever falling into a state of chattel slavery – was undermined by some of its provisions. In the Covenant Code a maidservant did not possess the same rights of release after six years as a manservant (Ex. 21.7; *contra* Deut. 15.17). Additionally, in both the Covenant Code and Deuteronomy the manumission law allowed a Hebrew slave to waive his freedom at the expiration of six years and voluntarily enter perpetual servitude, having his ear pierced with an awl to mark him as a slave (Ex. 21.2, 5–6; Deut. 15.16–18). This provision, which appears subject to abuses to the benefit of the slave owners and at the expense of the slaves, seems contrary to the theme of escape from slavery that runs throughout the Pentateuch narratives as a central feature of Israelite heritage enshrined in their law codes. The status of the ancestral landholdings of the freeborn Israelite slave who voluntarily entered perpetual servitude was not addressed in this law.

Although freeborn slaves had fewer rights than free citizens, they were still accorded certain basic legal protections. Kidnap for the slave trade was a capital offense (Ex. 21.16; Deut. 24.7). Slaves who escaped a harsh master were to be given asylum (Deut. 23.15–16). Menservants and maidservants partook in the leisure of the sabbath (Ex. 20.10; Deut. 5.14), as well as the rejoicings that accompanied offerings (Deut. 12.12, 18) and feasts (Deut. 16.11, 14). On the other hand, fatally striking a slave was not a capital offense, and merited no punishment if he survived a day or two, "for he is his money" (Ex. 21.20–21).[198] As noted earlier, the punishment for sex with a betrothed slave girl consisted of a scourging for the girl and a trespass offering for the man (Lev. 19.20–22).

Ancient Near Eastern law

Types of slavery known from the Ancient Near East included slaves taken as war booty, by kidnapping, house-born slaves, famine slaves, debt slaves and slavery from contractual penalty or judicial punishment.[199] A significant portion of these slaves worked for temples or the palace.[200] Chattel slaves were considered property, and their only hope of freedom was escape or – if they were first-generation war prisoners – ransom by relatives from their land of origin. Debt slaves and famine slaves were individuals temporarily reduced to slavery because of economic distress. The slide into debt slavery was much the same as depicted in the biblical text, except that interest loans hastened the process: the impoverished Ancient Near Eastern head of household took loans for seed for planting or for subsistence, pledging as security first his own slaves, then family members, then his land and finally his own person. The end result was commonly a descent in social status from freedom via debt slavery into full chattel slavery.[201] This process could be arrested – at least temporarily – by release from debt slavery by redemption (the payment of the debt), by manumission (the unilateral freeing of a slave) or by debt release (the forgiveness of a debt).[202] These last two often took place as the result of a royal edict intended to effect social and economic relief.

Ancient Near Eastern law collections placed no restrictions on enslaving a fellow native or selling a man held as collateral for debt into a foreign land, as long as the debt value exceeded his value as a person (MAL C 2–3). One provision in the Hammurabi Law Code is often compared with the biblical freedom for debt slaves after six years (Ex. 21.2–4; Deut. 15.12–15). LH 117 set a limit of three years servitude for those who failed to repay a debt and thereby sold themselves into forced labor. LH 118 explicitly limited the earlier provision to debt slaves: chattel slaves were not subject to this measure of social relief. The Hammurabi Law Code does not reflect prescriptive law, nor does this provision appear to reflect a widespread legal principle in the Ancient Near East, because it is not reflected in any other Ancient Near Eastern law code or recorded case.[203] It likely represents the contents of a *misarum* edict issued by Hammurabi, perhaps at or near the start of his reign, as a measure of social relief.[204] Like other features of *misarum* edict by rulers in the Ancient Near East, it was likely a one-time measure rather than a recurring or perpetual social remedy.[205] The quoting of this provision from a *misarum* edict of Hammurabi was in line with the propagandistic purposes of the Hammurabi Law Code, which was intended to demonstrate Hammurabi's righteousness as the divinely appointed ruler and shepherd of his people (LH prologue [1.1–62]).

In the Hammurabi Law Code, kidnapping a minor son of the *awīlum* class was a capital offense (LH 14; cf. Paul 1970: 65), as was harboring or attempting to exit the city with a palace or free man's slave (LH 15–16, 19). In other law collections, kidnap could incur imprisonment and a fine (LU 3) and harboring a slave was penalized with either a slave exchange or the payment of a slave price (LL 12–14). A slave purchase without witnesses or a contract was considered man-theft and incurred the death penalty (LH 7). Kidnap by unknown persons resulted in a financial penalty paid to the relatives by the nearest community to the crime site (LH 22–3). Forcibly seizing a free person or another's slave because of a loan incurred a monetary penalty if the loan was not in default (LE 22). If a person seized and imprisoned for a debt died in custody, the penalty for the merchant holding the debt was either death or a monetary fine or was waived, depending on whether the loan was actually in default, the status of the victim, and whether death was from natural causes or from maltreatment (LH 115–16; LE 23–4).

Slaves were marked in various ways for easy recognition (LH 226–7; LE 51–2), most commonly by distinctive haircut or tattoos; slave girls were not to wear a veil in public (MAL A 40). Slave insignia discouraged runaways, because an escaped slave was easily recognized. Various laws dealt with prompt return of captured fugitive slaves and statutory rewards for returning them to their owners (LH 17–20, gap s; LU 17; LE 50; HL 19–24, 71). A slave purchased abroad, brought back into the country and subsequently recognized as a fugitive slave would be returned to his original owner if a native, but if a foreign slave and if a receipt could be produced, would be kept by the new owner (LH 280–1). A slave who denied his slave status was mutilated (LH 282). Slave girls who attempted to free their children by giving them away into adoption were not punished, but the children were returned to the slave owner or another child in their place (LE 33–5).

Lesser penalties were always incurred for crimes such as inflicting bodily injury if the victim was a slave (LH 199, 213–14, 217; LE 31, 55, 57).[206] This included the case in which a betrothed virgin was raped or seduced, normally a capital crime, but which incurred only a financial penalty if the betrothed was a slave girl (LU 8; cf. LE 31). Assyrian law permitted beating an Assyrian debt slave (MAL A 44). The murder of a slave was not considered in the Ancient Near Eastern law collections, but palace law called for corporal punishment of a palace servant who beat a palace slave woman in excess such that she died (MAPD 18). For crimes in which the perpetrator was a slave, the penalty usually took the form of corporal punishment, because slaves seldom had their own financial resources (LH 205; MAL A 4).

Ancient Near Eastern laws did not recognize any criminality in the master of the house or his sons having sexual relations with the slave girls in a household unless the maiden was betrothed or married. A master's legal claim to sexual exclusivity with a slave girl appears to have raised her legal status to that of concubine. Male children who resulted from sexual relations with either a slave girl or concubine might optionally be recognized as legal sons and have a share in the inheritance (LH 170–1) – indeed, a wife might give her handmaiden to her husband for just such a purpose (LH 146–7). A slave girl might also become a second wife, which would guarantee her offspring inheritance rights. If a wife had already given her husband children, it may have been more usual for the master to give the slave girl and their children freedom in lieu of an inheritance (LL 25). However, having children did not guarantee a rise in rank for either the slave girl or her offspring, who could remain slaves. If a man was forced to sell a slave girl by whom he had children, he had the right to redeem her once he raised the money (LH 119).

Alternately, slaves could enter into marriage (presumably with their master's permission), either to another slave within the household or outside the household to a free man or woman. If a slave married either a free man or woman, with the usual payment of a bride-price, the person appears to have forfeited his or her freedom under Hittite law (HL 34–6). But according to LH 175–6, if a male slave married the daughter of a free man, the children of such a union would remain free. If two slaves married and one was set free, the other slave along with the children would remain in slavery (LU 4–5).

Greek law

Athenian slaves came from various sources, including slaves captured in war or their descendants (house-born slaves), and those imported from abroad and purchased in the slave market.[207] Slaves were owned by individuals or by temples. A common practice in war was to dedicate a tenth of the war-captives to serve as slaves in the temple out of thanks to the deity, the so-called human tithe (Parke and Wormell 1956: 1.51–2). In Athens, Solon famously created a permanent legal solution to debt slavery by making it illegal for a citizen's person to be taken as security for a loan.

Prior to the reforms of Solon in 594 BCE, small landholders in Attica whose family estates barely provided a subsistence living often had to go to the larger landholders for loans to seed their crops or to survive as a family until harvest season and were liable to fall into debt slavery. If they could not repay these loans, such small landholders forfeited their land and often their persons to wealthy landowners, and were reduced to servitude, farming the same land they had formerly owned.[208] In Solon's time, "the poor were in slavery to the rich" (Aristotle, *Athenian Constitution* 2; Plutarch, *Solon* 13.2; cf. Stanton 1990: 34–6) and Athens was witness to its own citizens in chains being sold abroad by creditors into the international slave markets (Plutarch, *Solon* 13.2–3; Demosthenes, *On the False Embassy* 254–5, quoting Solon's poetry; cf. Stanton 1990: 41–2). Under the constitutional and legal reforms instituted by Solon, existing debts were lifted[209] and it became illegal for any Athenian to secure a loan to a fellow-Athenian with the person of the debtor (Aristotle, *Athenian Constitution* 9; cf. Stanton 1990: 78–9), thereby permanently abolishing debt slavery in Athens. The principle was established that Athenians could not enslave fellow-Athenians.[210] A wider ideal held that Greeks should not take fellow-Greeks as slaves, but enslave only barbarians,[211] although the definition of what constituted a Greek was not entirely unambiguous,[212] and although Greek residents of cities that fell in war to other Greeks often in fact were enslaved.[213]

Under Athenian law, kidnapping carried a death penalty.[214] Various legal remedies existed for unlawful enslavement: a third party could rescue an acquaintance from slavery by self-help *(apagoge),* first providing a surety to the slave owner and then proving in court the unlawfully enslaved individual's status as a free citizen. Alternately, a public or private lawsuit *(graphe* or *dike)* could be brought against the slave owner to compel the liberation of a slave.[215]

As property of their owner, slaves did not possess the legal rights of citizens. There was no penalty for sexual relations of a master with a slave (MacDowell 1978: 80); the crimes of rape and adultery only applied to a free woman (Demosthenes, *Against Neaera* 67). Athenian law since the time of Perikles restricted citizenship to the offspring of parents who were free Athenian citizens on both sides: the offspring of both slaves and concubines were considered bastards *(nothoi)* and excluded from citizenship. According to Plato, *Laws* 11.930d, the offspring of slave-women, whether mated with a slave, a free man or a freed slave, remained the possession of the master.[216] Severe corporal punishment of slaves was allowed under Attic law (cf. Plato, *Laws* 6.777a-e). As noted in §2, killing a slave involved only financial recompense to the owner and certain rites of purification. A mistreated slave had no avenues for legal redress, but could seek asylum at the Theseion and request a new master.[217]

Comparisons and conclusions

The enslavement of foreigners and especially war-captives was common to all the law collections under consideration. The biblical statute that an Israelite could not be enslaved by a fellow-Israelite or by a resident alien, however, has parallels with Attic laws against enslaving fellow-Athenians and Greek compunctions against enslaving fellow-Greeks,[218] but has no Ancient Near Eastern legal counterpart. No ethnic or national restrictions to enslavement appear in Ancient Near Eastern law collections; as discussed earlier, Assyrian laws explicitly permitted selling Assyrian debt slaves into servitude in foreign lands. Biblical statutes regarding the offspring of slaves appears to most closely conform to Athenian law and to Plato's *Laws,* in which the freedom (and citizenship) of a parent did not extend to his or her offspring (cf. Wajdenbaum 2011: 159). The Hammurabi Law Code expressed an opposite tendency in which the freedom of a parent guaranteed the freedom of his or her children and custody followed the free parent of either gender.

Pentateuchal laws regarding debt slavery appear to draw primarily on Ancient Near Eastern – not Greek – literary antecedents. In the Athenian laws authored by Solon, which no longer allowed loans to be secured by the person of the debtor and which removed mortgages on ancestral landholdings, debt slavery was outright abolished (Aristotle, *Athenian Constitution* 6.1; Plutarch, *Solon* 15.5). Although the Pentateuchal legislation shared some of the spirit of Solon's laws by providing prescriptive measures to alleviate both the severity and permanence of debt slavery and debt property forfeiture among the Israelites, the basic institution of debt slavery remained intact, in contrast to the situation in Athens after Solon's reforms. Athenian laws outlawing debt slavery contained no feature allowing a limited term of servitude. This feature of the biblical law appears to draw on the Hammurabi Law Code, which called for a release of debt slaves after three years of service (LH 117–18). The release of debt slaves after three years servitude at LH 117–18 was not intended as a universal law, but as a one-time measure of relief for those in debt slavery at the time the *misarum* edict was proclaimed. However, it seems unlikely that the biblical authors grasped this, because LH 117–18 reads as though it was a prescriptive statute in its present context. One may therefore accept LH 117–18 as the immediate literary prototype for the biblical statute limiting debt slavery of impoverished Jews to a temporary servitude of six years, with the caveat that the biblical authors misunderstood the antiquarian Old Babylonian legal tradition.[219]

Another aspect of the biblical laws regarding the manumission of slaves also appears to depend on Ancient Near Eastern legal traditions, namely, the creation of a slave insignia by piercing of a slave's ear with an awl. In Ex. 21.5–6 and Deut. 15.16–17, this action formalized the voluntary rejection of manumission by a Hebrew slave after six years and a transition to chattel slavery. The provision which allowed a Hebrew servant to forego freedom and voluntarily enter perpetual servitude out of affection for his master appears fundamentally inconsistent with the abolition of Jewish chattel slavery elsewhere in the Pentateuch and has no parallel in either Ancient Near Eastern or Greek law collections. But Ancient Near Eastern texts recorded several forms of slave insignia that involved facial markings for easy identification of their slave status. Slave insignia helped to prevent runaways and were often inflicted as a degrading form of punishment after an attempted escape (Hurowitz 1992: 47–77). Mutilation of an ear by cutting it off or piercing it was used as a severe form of punishment for both slaves and non-slaves (LH 205, 282, MAL A 40, 44; cf. Paul 1970: 51; Hurowitz 1992: 64–5). In the biblical statute, the mutilation of a slave's ear with an awl, a disfigurement originally intended to mark a slave for easy recognition by the authorities as a troublesome runaway, still served as a form of slave insignia and functioned to keep the slave in servitude, but the punitive aspects of piercing the ear were lost. Instead, the mutilation of a slave's ear with an awl was now interpreted as a voluntary sign of love and almost filial devotion for his master by a Hebrew who desired to cast aside Jewish ideals of freedom and enter a life of slavery, together with his descendants, in perpetuity. The primary purpose for the creation of slave insignia to prevent runaways disappeared, because this measure would be completely unnecessary for an individual in voluntary servitude with no intention or history of running away. The piercing of the ear thus makes no sense as it appears in the biblical statute and is best taken as a maladaptation of an antiquarian Ancient Near Eastern custom by an author from a later period who either misunderstood or intentionally revised the original purpose and social context of slave mutilation.

Biblical, Ancient Near Eastern and Greek law collections shared a common view of chattel slaves as property whose corporal punishment resulting in injury or death were matters of relative legal insignificance and usually resulted only in financial compensation of some kind. The biblical laws appear most humanitarian in their redress of permanent injuries by the freeing of the slave. Both biblical and

Greek laws, unlike those found in the Ancient Near East, allowed for asylum for the slave mistreated by his master. Biblical laws, like Greek laws, and unlike the Ancient Near Eastern law collections, were also concerned with the marital rights of slaves (cf. Chirichigno 1993: 254–5).

8. Social legislation

Biblical law

Social support of the financially distressed is a prominent concern of many Pentateuchal texts. The biblical text frequently called for the protection of strangers, widows and orphans, societal classes without legal protections and vulnerable to abuse by the powerful (Ex. 22.21–24; 23.9; Lev. 19.33–34; Deut. 5.14; 10.18; 14.29; 16.11, 24; 24.15, 17, 19–21; 26.11–13; 27.19; Ps. 82.2–3; Job 24.3; Jer. 7.6; 22.3; Ezek. 22.7, 9; Zech. 7.10; Mal. 3.5). However, the Pentateuch made only moral appeals and called upon Yahweh to avenge wrongdoing (Ex. 22.22–24; Deut. 10.18; 24.15; cf. Mal. 3.5), without making specific provisions for care of strangers, widows and orphans[220] or penalties for their abuse. Less specific attention was paid to the financial dependence and physical care of aged parents, but laws protecting parents from verbal and physical abuse demonstrate some awareness of the problems of the aged.[221]

The poor constituted another vulnerable class, one particularly susceptible to economic exploitation by creditors and employers (Deut. 24.14–23; 28.38–44; Prov. 14.31; 22.7; Job 24.4; Zech. 7.10; Mal. 3.5). One law containing elements of social compassion called for day laborers to receive the pay by the end of the day (Deut. 24.14–15; cf. Mal. 3.5). Although all Israelites were pictured as land owners, a slide into poverty was possible through a poor harvest, subsistence loans secured by landholdings and loan default.[222] Although the return of land in the year of release legislatively prevented a state of permanent debt slavery (Lev. 25.10–17, 23–34; Deut. 15.1–6), in the short term poverty was a social and political reality. Under Pentateuchal law, the landless "poor" were treated as a distinct class, exempted from severe financial obligations, allowed less expensive sacrifices and supported by both the collection of an agricultural tax for their relief and by enjoined acts of private charity. The kinship group constituted the first and primary source of support for the poor.[223]

The distress and vulnerability of the injured and infirm, especially the deaf and the blind, was also a subject of ethical concern (Lev. 19.14; Deut. 27.18), but not legislative protection.

One final class of the financially distressed was the Levite who, lacking ancestral lands, theoretically had no steady source of income, but had to make do on temple offerings, tithes and charity (cf. Berman 2008: 67). However, the Pentateuch assigned them a number of cities, which included both houses and agricultural lands within their suburbs (Lev. 25.32–34; Josh. 21.1–42), undermining their alleged total impoverishment as pictured in other texts.

Besides enjoining private charity, especially within the kinship group, the Pentateuch contained several statutes designed to relieve the plight of the poor and vulnerable. One such law allowed the stranger, the fatherless and the widow to glean the corners of the field after a harvest (Deut. 24.19–22), gathering unharvested grain, olives and grapes. Another called for an agricultural tithe to be consumed at the place where God would place his name and shared with the Levites within the gates (Deut. 14.22–27). Every three years, this tithe would be stored up within the city gates and given in its entirety to the Levite, the stranger, the fatherless and the widow (Deut. 14.28–29; 26.12–15; cf. Berman 2008: 95). Festival laws provided that Levites, widows, orphans and strangers should be brought to the place Yahweh placed his name to participate in yearly festivities (Deut. 16.11, 14).

Ancient Near Eastern law

Humanitarian concerns are absent from the law collections, with certain isolated exceptions. In the prologues and epilogues, the king was portrayed as the protector of the widow, the orphan and the defenseless,[224] although this was seldom manifested in the laws themselves. Repayment of farm loans for seed grain was waived when storm or drought destroyed a grain harvest (LH 48). An impoverished man who sufficiently recovered financially could redeem his house (LE 39) and any slave girl who had borne him children (LH 119; cf. Westbrook 1991: 115; Westbrook 2009b: 148–50).

The primary vehicle for social relief in the Ancient Near East was *misarum* edicts and *andurarum* edicts, royal proclamations of "righteousness" and "freedom" from the Old Babylonian period that typically took place in the king's first year, but could also be enacted at different points later in his reign as emergency relief measures to provide economic relief to the lower classes and reduce social unrest.[225] These social enactments typically included the remission of overdue taxes, suspension of conscriptions into the military or forced labor corvée, the voiding of private grain and silver interest loans, freeing of debt slaves and (by implication) return of mortgaged lands to their owners (Westbrook 1991: 45–6; Weinfeld 1995: 89–91, 167; Westbrook 2009b: 151–5). Such measures of social relief were of limited duration and limited geographical application, presumably to those regions hardest hit by economic hardship. The liberation of debt slaves after three years of labor at LH 117–18 must be interpreted as an excerpt from a *misarum* decree of Hammurabi that functioned as a temporary measure of economic relief for those in debt slavery in the year the edict was proclaimed, not as a legislative measure intended to hold force throughout Hammurabi's reign.[226]

Greek law

In the Athenian legal system, special care was taken to provide legal safeguards and to some extent to provide for the financial needs of those who did not possess the usual protections of the household. Recognized protected classes included widows, fatherless orphans and heiresses, aged or infirm parents and the disabled.[227] Because all Athenian men were liable for military duty in the citizen army, the assurance that a soldier's family would be provided for in the event of injury or death was an important aspect of battlefield morale. In times of war, and especially after disastrous defeats, Athens sometimes exceptionally provided special funds for the maintenance of orphaned children of fallen soldiers (Thucydides, *Peioponnesian War* 2.46.1; Aristotle, *Politics* 2.1268a). Disabled citizens, especially injured veterans, could receive an allowance from the state after they underwent a scrutiny to verify their inability to provide for themselves.[228] Normally, however, care for financially distressed individuals fell to their immediate relatives. The office of Archon, one of the three highest positions in Athenian government, oversaw the rights of widows, orphans, heiresses and parents. This ordinarily meant ensuring that widows, fatherless male and female minors and infirm parents were appointed guardians, normally the next of kin: a male parent who reached the age of sixty usually entrusted himself and his finances to his eldest son, who became the new head of the household. Guardians managed the estate of the individuals under their care and provided for their upkeep out of the income so generated (if any). The custodial relationship of a guardian to those under his charge was prone to abuses, especially of a financial nature. There was often competition among relatives over obtaining custody of a wealthy minor or widow. At Athens, the Archon would hear cases where someone was accused of abusing a widow, orphan or aged parent or mismanaging that person's assets. Such cases were heard by the Archon at the Prytany, which we might today refer to as "family court." Any Athenian who witnessed physical or other mistreatment of such protected individuals could bring a suit before the Archon on their behalf, because these people were often not in a legal or practical position to do so themselves.[229]

Resident foreigners *(metics)* and visiting strangers came under the jurisdiction of another of the three chief Athenian officials, the Polemarch or war-commander, who in peacetime also had the duty of overseeing lawsuits on behalf of foreigners whose protection under the law was in most respect equal to that of Athenians (Aristotle, *Athenian Constitution* 58.2–3). Because resident aliens must have a sponsor and be enrolled in the *deme* or political district of his residence, such foreigners were usually (and perhaps always) represented at court by their designated sponsor (Rhodes 1993: 497).

Athenian law also contained important provisions safeguarding the rights of the impoverished. The poorest of the four assessed economic classes of Athenian citizens was the *thetes* class. The *thetes* were, effectively, those who did not own an estate to provide them with a reliable source of income from farming. Prior to Solon's reforms of ca. 594 BCE, "the poor were in slavery to the rich" and had no share in Athenian political life (Aristotle, *Athenian Constitution* 2; Plutarch, *Solon* 13.6; cf. Stanton 1990: 34–6). Solon provided direct relief to the poor by canceling all current debts, a measure that also returned mortgaged farmlands to their owners.[230] Under the reforms of Solon, the *thetes* were also granted full legal and political rights as citizens, including a voice in the Assembly and the right to sit as jurors at trial (Aristotle, *Athenian Constitution* 9.1). The most important of Solon's reforms was the prohibition of loans secured by the person of the debtor (Aristotle, *Athenian Constitution* 6.1; 9.1; 10.1; 12.4; Plutarch, *Solon* 15.2; cf. Stanton 1990: 54–8, 61–3, 78–9). Previously, a small farmer who had to borrow from the wealthy for seed money could lose his land and fall into slavery, together with his wife and family, as a result of a single crop failure caused by drought or pest. Solon's reforms permanently outlawed debt slavery and the loss of ancestral estates at Athens, putting a limit on the disastrous effects of impoverishment. This guaranteed that Athenians and their families could never be enslaved as a result of transient financial misfortune and thereby permanently disenfranchised as citizens.

In many new colonies and in the ideal state described by Plato's *Laws,* all citizens were landowners. The land was to provide a minimum subsistence for a household, to be supplemented by trade. Plato considered the land allotment to be the minimum poverty level for citizens (explicitly at Plato, *Laws* 5.744d-e). In Plato's system, and in some surviving laws from Greek city-states, land was not to be sold or to pass out of a family's possession.[231] To be landless was virtually synonymous with being impoverished, and the continued possession of the ancestral landholding thus prevented complete destitution. The inalienability of land in Plato's *Laws* thus represented a significant strengthening of Solon's measures against debt slavery by guaranteeing that every household remained in possession of its allotted ancestral lands into perpetuity.[232]

Another feature of Athenian law that benefited the poorest citizens was the tax system. In the imperial period, Athens was supported mainly by taxes levied on its overseas possessions. Domestic taxation usually took the form of a tithe on agricultural produce, which affected only landowners, not the *thetes* class.[233] Juror pay, which increased from one obol to three obols a day during the course of the fifth century BCE (Aristotle, *Athenian Constitution* 41.3; 62.2), allowed the poorest citizens to participate in government.[234] Private charity was encouraged.[235] Finally, one may note the popular social aspect of Athenian festivals, at which even the poorest could participate in banquets, sacrifices and the enjoyment of athletic events, theater, song and other public festivities that they normally could not afford.[236]

Comparisons and conclusions

Biblical, Ancient Near Eastern and Greek legal writings all exhibited a common concern for those who had fallen into a position of economic distress and legal vulnerability, especially widows, orphans and those who had lost their lands and sold themselves into debt slavery. Whereas addressing the problems of widows and orphans was considered a simple matter of righteous rule, alleviating the problems of the impoverished had a more practical aspect, because those who had fallen on hard times posed a constant threat of social unrest. Options for addressing the problems of the distressed took one of three forms: special decrees intended to resolve an immediate crisis, social legislation intended to provide a permanent solution to social ills and appeals to charity.

The phenomenon of debt slavery was common to many lands in the ancient Mediterranean. Inscriptional and literary sources from both the Ancient Near East and the Greek world document many examples of proclamations of liberation and debt relief, especially at the outset of a king's reign (Weinfeld 1995: 9–11, 75–96). These edicts were intended to demonstrate the character of the ruler as benefactor and to win the support of the impoverished masses (Weinfeld 1995: 10–11), but were only retrospective and thus of temporary effectiveness. The *misarum* and *andurarum* edicts of the Old Babylonian period illustrate this approach. A legislative approach to the problem of debt slavery was found in both Greek and biblical legal writings. The reforms of Solon outlawed loans secured by the person of the debtor, eliminating debt slavery in Attica. Land allotments for all citizens and land inalienability as a cure for poverty is common to biblical law, Plato's *Laws,* and some Greek city-states, but not Athens. The biblical law codes allowed for the possibility of debt slavery, but limited to a maximum of six years of servitude under relatively mild, humane working conditions. This statute appears to have drawn on LH 117–18, which mandated the release of debt slaves after three years of servitude, but misunderstood this law as a piece of universal social legislation meant to have effect throughout Hammurabi's reign instead of an excerpt from a liberation decree of strictly limited application for the year it was issued.

Although the prologues and epilogues of Ancient Near Eastern law collections depicted the king as benefactor of the widow and orphan, none of the laws in these collections can be construed as benefiting them or protecting their rights. Probably the king's beneficence toward the widow and orphan was limited to the *misarum* decrees of liberation from debt slavery, which is likely to have disproportionately affected families without an adult male head of household. Athens, on the other hand, had extensive social legislation that protected the legal rights of widows, orphans, aged parents, the disabled and foreign residents. Biblical laws recognized the legal and financial problems of widows, orphans and the poor, but sought to alleviate their difficulties neither by royal decrees nor through guardianship laws, but rather by appeals to charity and the granting of interest-free loans and other acts of generosity within kinship groups.

Additionally, Deuteronomic law – like Athenian law – laid out a schedule of public festivals as occasions of joy in which the poorest classes took part in banquets, sacrifices and general revelry.

9. Livestock laws

Biblical law

The Pentateuch had a number of laws relating to livestock, many of them found in the Covenant Code. The laws that dealt with "the goring ox" required that an ox that killed a man or woman must be stoned and not consumed (Ex. 21.28–29)[237] and its owner should also be stoned or pay blood money if he had been told the animal was dangerous but had failed to keep it penned up (Ex. 21.28–30). If an ox killed another animal, the live ox was to be sold and both the money and the dead ox divided between the two ranchers; or, if the owner knew the animal was dangerous, full restitution was required (Ex. 21.35–36; Lev. 24.18, 21). Theft of farm animals incurred a five-fold penalty if the animal was slain or a two-fold penalty if the animals were recovered (Ex. 21.1, 4). If a neighbor's farm animals fell into an open pit or cistern negligently left uncovered, full restitution was required, but the carcass was given to the owner of the pit (Ex. 21.33–34). If a farmer was in custody of a neighbor's animal – for instance, if a farmer rented a work animal – and the animal died or was injured or was stolen or strayed, various remedies applied depending on whether the animal was unsupervised and whether it was slain by a predator (Ex. 22.9–15). A farmer was expected to return a neighbor's stray animal or lost possessions, even if the two were feuding (Ex. 23.4; Deut. 22.1–3), and to assist an injured or fallen animal (Ex. 23.5; Deut. 22.4). An ox and an ass should not be yoked together (Deut. 22.10), and oxen should not be muzzled when treading corn (Deut. 25.4).

Ancient Near Eastern law

Rates for renting oxen and herd animals were strictly regulated (LH 241–3, 268–70), as were veterinary fees (LH 224–5). Various laws dealt with infractions by hired herdsmen (LH 57, 262–7). Other laws dealt with stray animals and the timeliness of their return.[238] Multiple restitution appears as the usual penalty for animal theft.[239] Injury or death of rented animals was extensively discussed in the Hammurabi Law Code.[240] The family of a free man or the owner of a slave killed by "the goring ox" would receive a monetary compensation if the owner knew the animal was dangerous and failed to fasten it up or bind its horns (LH 250–2; LE 55). The law did not require the animal to be killed. If an ox killed another ox, both the value of the living ox and the carcass of the dead one were divided between the two owners (LE 53–4).[241] Dangerous animals also included vicious dogs (LE 56–7). Although negligence was addressed in several cuneiform laws, the case of an animal falling into an uncovered pit does not appear.

Greek law

The case of a mule or other dangerous animal or inanimate object that killed a person was treated at Plato, *Laws* 9.873d-874a. The convicted animal was to be killed, and the offending animal's carcass or the convicted object cast beyond the territorial borders of the *polis*.[242] Both animals and inanimate objects such as axe-heads or javelins or a collapsed wall could be tried for murder in a special court at the Prytaneion presided over by the *Archon Basileus* and the four tribal kings *(phylobasileis)*.[243] One stated reason for the trial and penalty was the horror of the ghost at the continuing presence of the agent of its death; the practical benefits of being rid of a dangerous animal or object may have also been a consideration. Solon was said to have enacted a law whereby dangerous dogs had to be restrained with a wooden leash (Plutarch, *Solon* 24.3; cf. Xenophon, *Hellenica* 2.4.41). Property damage caused by animals was subsumed under Athenian damage laws.[244] Animal theft was subsumed under the broader theft statutes. Special laws for rental animals or for stray or fallen animals are not known, but Solon's agricultural zoning laws required that a ditch, grave, pit or well be placed a safe distance within the property lines (Plutarch, *Solon* 23.8; Justinian, *Digest of Roman Law* 10.1.13; cf. Phillips 2013: 290).

Comparisons and conclusions

The case of the goring ox in the Covenant Code famously and uncontroversially displays literary dependence on the Hammurabi Law Code, such as in considering the degree of negligence of the owner and in the awarding of monetary damages if the dangerousness of the animal could have been anticipated. Similarly, the Covenant Code's law regarding an animal that killed another animal uncontroversially displays literary dependence on the Laws of Eshnunna, in dividing both monies from the live ox and the carcass of the slain beast between the two animal owners.[245]

In other details, the Law on the Goring Ox in the Covenant Code contained striking departures from LH, such as in the separate determination of guilt for the homicidal animal and for the animal's punishment of being stoned and its polluted carcass left as unfit for human consumption, presumably to be consumed by animals at the stoning site outside the city.[246] These specific details have striking parallels in Athenian laws and in Plato's *Laws*. The Platonic law held that neither the animal nor its owner could be held culpable if the death took place in the course of the games (which were known among the Romans as gladiator contests). Otherwise, the owner and the animal were to undergo separate trials. If the owner was acquitted, blood-guilt still attached to the animal, which, if it went unpunished, would result in the ghost of the victim wreaking vengeance in the land of the living.[247] The condemned animal was considered a source of pollution for the city which could only be assuaged by the animal's execution outside the city limits; similarly, inanimate objects polluted by blood-guilt were cast outside the city limits.[248] Animal trials and executions were contemplated only in the Law of the Goring Ox in the Covenant Code and in Athenian law (Finkelstein 1981: 26–7, 58–9). Although there is no dispute that the biblical laws on dangerous animals display literary dependence on the older Ancient Near Eastern law collections, it is also apparent that these laws were updated with elements taken from Athenian legal tradition, most likely by way of Plato's *Laws*.[249]

10. Property crimes and agricultural law

Biblical law

Several biblical laws dealt with agricultural land and produce. These included provisions for restitution of damages caused by trespass, either by grazing animals in a neighbor's field or by causing a fire that consumed a neighbor's crops (Ex. 22.5–6); laws against changing property lines by moving boundary stones (Deut. 19.14; 27.17; cf. Hos. 5.10; Job 24.2; Prov. 22.28; 23.10); laws allowing sampling (but not harvesting) of produce from a neighbor's field (Deut. 23.24–25); laws allowing the gleaning of agricultural produce by the poor and the stranger (Lev. 19.9–10; 23.22; Deut. 20.19–22); land sabbath laws, which also contained provisions for the poor (Ex. 23.10–11; Lev. 25.1–7, 18–22); laws regarding firstfruits from new orchards (Lev. 19.23–25); and provisions against hybrid breeds or crops (Lev. 19.19; Deut. 22.9–11).

Ancient Near Eastern law

It was once thought that a Babylonian genre of inscriptions (*"kudurru"* monuments) that detailed property lines and landowner property rights granted in perpetuity by the king were Ancient Near Eastern examples of boundary stones (King 1912), but these large stone texts, found exclusively in temple archives, are now understood as records of land grants and property transfers.[250] Water rights disputes arising out of shared irrigation projects were mediated by judges (MAL B 17–18; MAL J 2–3; MAL O 5). Overstepping boundary lines by plowing or planting in a neighbor's field or moving a property line was a serious offense (LU 30; MAL B 12–13, 20; HL 166–9). Other violations of property rights included flooding a neighbor's property (LH 53–6; LU 31; SLHF 4.35–41; LNB 3), grazing animals in a neighbor's field (LH 57–8; LNB 2) or vineyard (HL 107) or starting a fire that spread to a neighbor's crops (HL 105–6).[251] Individuals who trespassed into a farmer's field or orchard were prosecuted as thieves (LL 9; LE 12). Ancient Near Eastern laws that permitted agricultural gleaning are unknown.

Theft laws itemized penalties for stealing bees or beehives (HL 91–2), seed grain (LH 253–5), grain harvest, either in the field or the silo (MAL B 4–5; HL 96–7), plants and vines (LH 253; HL 101–3, 108, 113) or agricultural equipment (LH 259–60; HL 121–31, 143–4). Diverting irrigation water (HL 109, 162) and cutting down a neighbor's trees also incurred penalties (LH 59; LL 10; HL 104).

The king set standard fixed rates for hire of agricultural workers (LH 257–8, 261; HL 158–9), purchase of farm animals (HL 178–81), rental of work animals (LH 241–3, 268–71; LL a; LE 3, 10; HL 151–2), rental of farm equipment (LH 271–2; LE 3, 9a; HL 157), fees for grain storage (LH 121) and the rent or purchase of agricultural land (LX q-s; SLHF 8.16–30).[252] Several laws dealt with nobility's land tenure rights (LH 27–41; HL 39–41) and with the execution with land lease agreements (LH 42–54, 60–5; LL 7–8; SLHF 8.16–43). Agricultural negligence laws dealt with failure to plant crops or orchards as agreed (LH 42–4, 65, 253–6; LU 32; LL 8; MAL B 19). Repayment of farm loans for seed grain was waived for any year in which either storm or drought destroyed a grain harvest (LH 48).

Greek law

Athenian laws on property and agriculture were addressed under their damage laws.[253] Compensation for damages was simple compensation if unintentional or double damages if intentional.[254] A section on agricultural laws began at Plato, *Laws* 8.842e-843a with a law against moving sacred boundary stones. Athenians were normally satisfied with natural boundary lines such as a fence, stone wall, ditch or natural feature. Where such natural boundaries were absent, or where property lines were disputed, boundary stones were set up, of which many have been found. Deities invoked for the protection of boundaries included Zeus, Apollo and Hermes.[255] Many were inscribed only with the word *horos* or "boundary."[256] Solon enacted various agricultural laws regarding zoning, water rights and other matters (Plutarch, *Solon* 23.5, 7–8; 24.3; Justinian, *Digest of Roman Law* 10.1.13). Agricultural laws found at Plato, *Laws* 8.843c-e also addressed trespass on a neighbor's pasturelands, stealing his bees or allowing a fire to spread to his neighbor's property. Although literary or inscriptional parallels are unknown, an Athenian prototype for these laws is likely (Chase 1933: 187). Plato discussed eating grapes or figs from another man's field at *Laws* 8.844d-845d. The law found there allowed a foreigner to sample choice grapes or figs as a "gift of hospitality," but a citizen who did so would be fined, and a slave beaten; lesser quality fruit could be eaten on the spot, but not carried away.

Comparisons and conclusions

The laws against trespass in Ex. 22.4–5 (grazing and fires) have parallels in the Laws of Hammurabi (grazing), Hittite Laws (fires and grazing, in reverse order from Ex. 22.4–5) and Plato's *Laws* (grazing, bees and fires). The closest parallel to the law in Exodus appears to be Plato's *Laws*,[257] the only substantial difference being an additional provision regarding the theft of bees. The biblical law allowing passers-by to eat produce from a field, which has no Ancient Near Eastern parallel, stands relatively close to the provision in Plato's *Laws*.[258] The law on moving boundary stones has no Ancient Near Eastern parallel, but a strong parallel in Plato's *Laws* (as noted at Eusebius, *Preparation for the Gospel* 12.38; cf. Wajdenbaum 2011: 199–200). This parallel is reinforced by the common discovery of boundary stones in Attica and the apparent absence of archaeological parallels in ancient Mesopotamia or ancient Israel and Judah. To my knowledge, the earliest Judean boundary stones so far discovered are thirteen boundary stones found at Tel Gezer, written in Hebrew and Greek, dating to no earlier than the

Hasmonean Era, suggesting that the use of boundary stones in Judah was a Hellenistic Era development taken over from the Greeks.[259]

11. Commercial law

Biblical law

The Pentateuch contained a variety of explicit and implicit laws about commercial transactions. Both legal and narrative passages took for granted routine categories of contracts, such as purchases, animal rentals and work agreements. Except for writs of divorce and (in Jeremiah) land sales, written documents were not contemplated: instead, various biblical passages recorded the use of observing witnesses, often elders in the gate, whose memory of contract agreements sufficed to enforce them (Willis 2001: 298). One key statute was the requirement for speedy fulfillment of promises secured by oath (Deut. 23.21), a category which included both vows to Yahweh and contracts secured by an oath to Yahweh. The master of a household, whether the patriarch or a divorced or widowed woman (Num. 30.9), was always competent to enter into such a contract. A daughter or wife could enter into a contract, subject to the father or husband's approval; if such vows were not annulled within a day by the male master of the house, they were allowed to stand (Num. 30.1–15). Animals vowed to Yahweh could be redeemed with suitable compensation (Lev. 27.1–8, 11–23).

Humanitarian interests underpinned several commercial laws regarding the poor. Day laborers were entitled to speedy payment (Deut. 24.14–15). Interest loans were allowed to foreigners but not to Israelites (Ex. 22.5; Lev. 25.35–37; Deut. 23.19–20; cf. Ps. 15.5; Ezek. 22.12).[260] Pledges taken as guarantees for loans were not to include a millstone (Deut. 24.6), and if garments were taken as a pledge, they were to be returned before sundown (Ex. 22.26–27; Deut. 24.12–13). It was unlawful to enter a man's house to obtain a pledge (Deut. 24.10–11).

The Pentateuch also presumed governmental standards on weights and measures to establish fair trade. The standard monetary unit was the temple shekel (Ex. 30.13, 24; Lev. 27.3; Num. 3.47, 50; 7.13–86; a royal shekel was mentioned at 2 Sam. 14.26). Several passages specified standard exchange rates between different units of measurement.[261] An omer of barley was legislated to cost fifty shekels of silver (Lev. 27.16; Num. 18.16). Consumer protection laws included requirements to have accurate balances and weights – the possession of unequal weights was considered evidence of intent to cheat (Lev. 19.35–36; Deut. 25.13–16; cf. Prov. 11.1; Mic. 6.11).[262] Assessors were sometimes employed to value livestock, houses or land (Lev. 27.2–25).

Ancient Near Eastern law

Laws collections, court records and private financial documents addressed a wide variety of commercial transactions that included purchases, animal rentals, work agreements, loans and commercial ventures. Exact parallels with biblical commercial laws are few. Possession of goods without a purchase contract or observing witnesses was considered evidence of theft (LH 7, 9–13; LE 40). Sometimes an oath was used to supplement documents that had been called into question (LH 106).

Royal price rates have already been discussed earlier in connection with livestock and agriculture. The palace also exerted systematic control over all other major aspects of the economy.[263] Various laws governed trade ventures and business partnerships (LH 100–7). Rates of exchange were established by royal edict (LU prologue [A 3.135–4.149; C 1.11–21]; LH prologue [3.45–4.7]; cf. LH gap x, 108 in which exchange rates featured). Laws regulated loans (LE 19–20) and debt collection (LH 113–19, 151). Merchants were penalized for using different weights when weighing silver for loans and for loan payments (LH gap x). Interest rates were fixed for silver loans (LH gap t; LE 18, 20–1; LX n), grain loans (LH gap t-u; LX m) and loans by innkeepers (LH 111; LX l). No laws prohibited lending at interest to distressed classes. Merchants were forbidden to accept payments from slaves or advance credit to sons who had not yet inherited (LE 15–16).

Prices were fixed for the full range of agricultural, raw and finished products (LE 1–2, 41; HL 178–86). Fixed prices for specific trades included physicians' fees (LH 215–23; LX g-i), veterinary fees (LH 224–5), builders' fees and penalties (LH 228–33; HL 145), shipwrights (LH 234–5), rental fees for all different kinds of boats (LH 275–7; SLHF 5.37–44), boatman fees and penalties (LH 236–40; LE 4–6; LL 5; SLHF 4.42–5.44; SLEx 3; MAL M 1–2), wages for unskilled or day laborers (LH 273; LE 11; HL 150, 177), wages for instructors (HL 200b), wages for various categories of artisans (LH 274; LE 14; HL 160–1) and prices to purchase an artisan's apprentice (HL 176).

Other laws dealt with professional negligence by physicians (LH 218), builders (LH 232–3), shipwrights (LH 235), sailors (LH 236–8, 240; LE 5; LL 5; SLEx 3'; SLHF 4.42–5.11; LE 5; MAL M 1) and guards (LE 60). Punishment for professional negligence consisted of replaced products or compensation for losses (LH 232–3, 325; SLEx 3'; SLHF 4.42–5.11; 5.21–26), fines (LH 236–8), disfigurement (LH 218) or death (LE 60), depending on the perceived seriousness of the infraction and the social class of the victim.

Greek law

Greek laws and surviving public and private records document commercial transactions.[264] Athenian court cases typically relied on witnesses rather than documents until the early fourth century BCE, which saw an expanding use of public archives for records of economic transactions. In Plato's time, security deposits for commercial transactions were witnessed and recorded in writing (Plato, *Laws* 12.953e–954a). Penalties accrued for work contracts that were not fulfilled on schedule (Plato, *Laws* 11.921c-d).

Interest loans were considered unjust, because they led to debt slavery and the seizing of landholdings of the poor by the wealthy class (Aristotle, *Nicomachian Ethics* 5.1133a; Aristotle, *Politics* 1.1258b; Plato, *Laws* 5.742c; cf. Berman 2008: 97). At being appointed Athens' lawgiver, Solon famously canceled debts in 594 BCE and created a law that loans could not be secured with the person of the borrower, thereby abolishing debt slavery in Attica (Aristotle, *Athenian Constitution* 6.1). Both interest loans and loans secured by other items were otherwise allowed under Athenian law (Phillips 2013: 371–6). Pledges of pawned items for security on small loans are known at Athens, but not very well documented (Harrison 1968: 1.260–62; MacDowell 1978: 142–3). A provision at Plato, *Laws* 5.742b advised that repayment of either principal or interest on loans was strictly unenforceable. These laws all implicitly or explicitly dealt with loans between fellow-citizens; Athens had no law against interest loans to foreigners.

Athens had various laws and institutions aimed at consumer protection. Official weights and measures, first established under Solon's reforms in 594/593 BCE,[265] were enforced by the Controllers of Measures *(metronomoi),* who ensured the use of just weights.[266] Honest trade in the Agora was enforced by the Market Administrators *(agoranomoi),* who ensured that products were not adulterated and that each merchant adhered to a single price for their goods on any given day (Plato, *Laws* 8.849e; 11.916d, 917e, 919d-920c; cf. Morrow 1993: 144, 183–4). Special legislative attention was aimed at ensuring that Athenians had adequate food supplies and low food prices, because Athens was dependent on food imports for its large population.[267] The city's food supply was on the agenda of the regular monthly meeting of the Assembly at Athens.[268] The import of grain was subject to careful oversight by harbor magistrates and brought to Athens (Aristotle, *Athenian Constitution* 51.4). Municipal magistrates called the Guardians of the Grain *(sitophylakes),* selected by lot from among the citizens, made sure that corn, barley and wheat were sold in the market at a fair price, in proportion to costs at import, whether in the form of raw grain, ground meal or baked loaves of standard size (Aristotle, *Athenian Constitution* 43.4; Lysias, *Against the Grain Dealers* 16). In 374/373 BCE the Assembly began to set prices for barley and wheat imported from certain Athenian-held grain producing islands.[269]

Comparisons and conclusions

Similar areas were covered under contract and commercial laws in the Pentateuchal, Ancient Near Eastern and Athenian legal traditions. The competency of male heads of households, widows and divorcees to enter contracts under biblical law may show Athenian influence.

The government established standards for weights, measures and money (whether coinage or weights of precious metals) in all three systems. Honest weights were required in the marketplace. In the Ancient Near East, the king exercised far-reaching control over the economy by aggressively setting wages and prices for all sorts of services and commodities. This differed from both the biblical and Athenian societies, where the main interest of selective price controls appears to have been to ensure the availability of food supplies, primarily grain, for the citizenry.[270] It is possible that the legislation of barley prices at Lev. 27.16 and Num. 18.16 was influenced by the control of grain prices by the Athenian assembly starting in 374/373 BCE. It may be relevant to note that the Ptolemies held a monopoly on grain exports and set prices on grain and other Egyptian commodities.[271]

Humanitarian concerns for the poor were found throughout the Pentateuchal laws, including in the commercial laws. Such concerns are not reflected in any of the Ancient Near Eastern law collections, but were instead alleviated by sporadic royal edict. The poor of Attica, comprising the *thetes* class explicitly identified through the economic assessment, received various protections under Athenian law. The law of Solon that ended debt slavery by ending Athenian interest loans to fellow-Athenians parallels the Pentateuchal law against interest loans to fellow-Israelites.

12. Military law

Biblical law

Military laws in the Pentateuch appeared both explicitly within the Deuteronomic law code (notably Deut. 20) and implicitly within narratives (notably Num. 31). The creation of a citizen army, enrolled as soldiers at age twenty, organized by tribe and under the command of tribal generals, was extensively discussed in Chapter 2 §§ 2–3. The king had no military role in Pentateuchal laws governing warfare, which was to be conducted by the national leader, tribal generals, priests and citizen officers. The conscription and enrollment of troops was extensively described in Numbers. Statutory exemptions from military service were provided for those who had built a new house, planted a new vineyard or taken a bride (Deut. 20.5–7); a duration of one year was specified for the man with a new wife (Deut. 24.5). Cowardice also provided a basis for exemption from active duty because of its possible demoralizing effect on fellow-soldiers (Deut. 20.8). The manner of conducting a war was extensively addressed: religious guidance under priests (Num. 10.1–9), prophet (Num. 27.21), and the ark (Num. 10.35–36; cf. 1 Sam. 4.3–11); the disposition of the war camp and marching order by tribal units (Num. 2.1–34; 10.14–28); issues of sanitation in the camps (Deut. 23.10–15); the use of military trumpets and trumpets of assembly (Num. 10.1–10); officer exhortations to the troops before battle (Deut. 20.1–4); laws of siege warfare (Deut. 20.19–20); enslavement of fallen cities (Deut. 20.10–13); genocide against select enemies (Ex. 23.23–25, 32–33; Num. 14.40–45; 31.13–16; Deut. 7.1–5; 20.16–18; 25.17–19; Josh. 11.12–20) except for young virgins (Num. 31.17–18); purification from corpse impurity after battle (Num. 31.19–20); the collection and distribution of war booty from battles against both nearby enemies (Num. 31.9–12, 25–47) and those far away (Deut. 20.14–15),[272] with purification by fire of metallic objects (Num. 31.21–24); and the rights of the rejected war-bride (Deut. 21.10–14). Peace treaties with the nations occupying the Promised Land were strictly forbidden (Ex. 23.32; 34.12, 15; Deut. 7.2; 20.16–18); nego-tiation of terms of surrender for nations farther off could be dictated by field commanders or the princes of the people (Deut. 20.10–11, 15; Josh. 9.3–27) with some degree of involvement from the full assembly, to whom the princes were accountable (Josh. 9.6–7, 15–18).

Ancient Near Eastern law

Neither Babylonian nor Assyrian law collections contained statutes dealing with conscription or soldiers' military service. In the time of Hammurabi, land grants involved supplying a set number of men to serve in public work projects or as sol-diers for the army, mainly taken from the slave and lower classes, and assembled and assigned duties by levy officers.[273] The king's role as military commander and protector of his people appeared prominently in the epilogue to the Hammurabi Law Code. Duties and privileges of levy officers were detailed in LH 26–41. Desertion was seemingly a significant problem (MAL B 3; HL 40). Desertion was punishable by death (LH 26, 33). Harboring a fugitive from the levy was punish-able by death (LH 16). The Hammurabi Law Code was otherwise silent with respect to military matters. Temples and some land owners and cities were granted exemptions from levies for military service and public works, as documented in land charters and in letters (Hermann and Johns 1904: 204, 325–6). Middle Assyr-ian conscription of farm workers as soldiers created a limited campaign season between the spring planting and fall harvest. The collection of war booty and Assyrian practices of besieging and razing cities and relocating populations were not reflected in law collections but are known from royal annals. No limitations were placed on Babylonian or Assyrian royal powers to make treaties and peace agreements.

Greek law

The citizen hoplite army of Athens, its enrollment procedures and military train-ing (the *ephebate*), its tribal organization and command structure, was discussed in Chapter 2 §§ 2–3. Athenian law allowed an exemption from military duty during the *ephebate* if a soldier-in-training was appointed to a hereditary priest-hood or became the *kurios* of a new household, either by marrying a heiress *(epikleros),* inheriting an estate, or coming of age in a household administered by a widow (Aristotle, *Athenian Constitution* 42.5; Lacey 1968: 141, 197 n. 65; Rhodes 1993: 509). Athenians could be tried for evading military service, deser-tion, cowardice or throwing away their shield in battle.[274] Such trials took place in a military court at Athens that was presided over by generals and had a jury composed of fellow soldiers.[275] Officers themselves were subject to an audit of both their finances and their military performance on return from the field (Hamel 1998: 126–30). War booty might help finance the military campaign, go directly to the troops if they had inadequate financial support, or be sent back to Athens (often with a tithe to the temple gods as thanks for success in battle), but in any case came under review in the audit process (Hamel 1998: 44–8). Captives were often put into the slave market (Xenophon, *Hellenica* 6.2.36; Diodorus Siculus, *Library* 12.5).

The conduct of warfare was subject to the discretion of the generals, but key military decisions required approval by the Assembly at Athens. The use of prophets by generals in the field has been treated elsewhere (see Chapter 2 §10). Cities that resisted and required a siege to reduce were often razed[276] and their male population exterminated.[277] Generals lacked the authority to conclude peace treaties or alliances. They sometimes negotiated terms of surrender in the field, but the agreements required ratification by the Assembly at Athens to take force (Hamel 1998: 40–4).

Comparisons and conclusions

The lack of a military role for the king in Pentateuchal law contrasts with the king as leader of the army at war in both the Ancient Near East and in the historiography of the biblical monarchy. The citizen army described in both the narratives and legal passages of Exodus–Joshua corresponds closely to the Athenian model.[278] The notion of military practices being governed or limited by law is characteristically Greek. The involvement of the national Assembly in negotiating peace treaties in wartime in Josh. 9 suggests a commitment to democratic practices similar to that found at Athens but unheard of in the Ancient Near East. The Deuteronomistic exemption from military duties for a soldier with a new house, vineyard or wife appears to have been modeled on the statutorial exemption from military training for an Athenian soldier who newly became head of a household through marriage or inheriting an estate.

13. Treason laws

Biblical law

Both Pentateuchal narratives and law collections addressed a category of public crimes in which the victim was society as a whole rather than an individual member of society. Crimes against the social order included both political crimes and crimes against religion. Both political and religious crimes were put on a parity as forms of treason. Treason could take the form of speech, conspiracy or public action. Where Pentateuchal treason laws specified a penalty, the penalty was always death, and often took the form of stoning by the community.

Political crimes included seditious speech, conspiracy and rebellion. Restrictions on speech against public leaders were explicit at Ex. 22.28, where it was paired with restrictions on religious speech: "You shall not revile the gods, nor curse the ruler of the people."[279] In a narrative sequel found at Lev. 24.10–16, cursing God carried a death penalty by stoning. The same penalty may be presumed for cursing the princes of the people.[280] A second restriction on political speech was the statute against spreading a false report (Ex. 23.1), a public crime with serious consequences.[281] In Pentateuchal narratives, Moses represented the authorized leader of the nation as well as God's prophet. Rebellion against Moses was a capital crime, although he typically interceded on the people's behalf even when they merited death.[282]

The interactions between Moses and the children of Israel illustrated the mechanics of political rebellion and the basic shape of treason laws as the Pentateuchal authors conceived them. The Pentateuch recounted several incidents of rebellion during the wilderness wanderings of the children of Israel. The children of Israel that Moses led out of Egypt vocalized complaints against Moses due to thirst or hunger at Marah ("rebellion"), the wilderness of Zin, and at Rephidim (Ex. 15.23–24; 16.1–12; 17.1–4); at the last location, they were ready to stone Moses (Ex. 17.4). After Sinai, they again complained against Moses about hunger or thirst at the spring of Meribah (Num. 20.1–13; cf. 27.14) and the way of Hor (Num. 21.4–7). But the most serious episode was in the wilderness of Paran, at the return of the spies sent to the Promised Land, when seditious talk led to an outright rebellion against Moses. When the spies gave their formal report to Moses, Aaron and the full assembly of the children of Israel (Num. 13.26), Caleb encouraged the people to enter and conquer the land, but the other spies gave an "evil report" (Num. 13.32; 14.36–37) that claimed the inhabitants were giants and too great to overcome (Num. 13.31–33). This false report not only discouraged the children of Israel (cf. Deut. 1.26–28)[283] but caused them to complain against Moses, to rebel against his leadership (cf. Deut. 9.23–24), and to seditiously set about appointing a new captain to lead them back to Egypt instead of Moses (Num. 14.1–5). When Joshua and Caleb addressed the assembly to try to reverse the course of the rebellion, they were nearly stoned (Num. 14.6–10). As a result of this sedition, God condemned the entire generation of warriors to die in the wilderness, excepting Caleb and Joshua (Num. 14.22–39). Among all the wilderness episodes, this one best illustrates the treasonous nature of seditiously spreading a false report – especially by misleading the assembly – that could sow discontent, spread cowardice and panic in the ranks, undermine morale among the troops and, ultimately, cause mutiny and rebellion. With an assembly that was composed of citizen soldiers, the crime of making a false report had elements of both political and potentially military treason, especially as affecting military decisions as in the episode in Num. 13–14.

The conception of treason as national rebellion found in Exodus–Numbers was echoed in the introduction and epilogue to Deuteronomy. Failure to obey the divine commandments as a nation was portrayed as rebellion, a form of treason the children of Israel had been guilty of in the past (Deut. 1.26, 43; 9.7, 23–24; 31.27) and would be in the future (Deut. 31.27, 29). In Dtn (the collection of laws in Deut. 12–26), political treason laws are mostly absent, except in the constitutional sub-document (Deut. 16.18–18.22). The authors of Deuteronomy displayed little concern for treasonous political conspiracies against officials, who were, after all, appointed by the citizenry themselves. Deuteronomy nowhere referred to offenses against the office of kingship, although the history of the monarchy contained numerous anecdotes regarding the suppression of rebellion and conspiracy against the king (2 Sam. 15–18; 1 Kgs 12.16–19; 15.27–29; 16.9–11, 16, 20). Nor did Deuteronomy contain treason laws regarding opposition to the other magistrates, except for the "Prophet like Moses" (Deut. 18.18–19). Rather, the overriding concern of Deuteronomy was the rule of law. Deuteronomy contained several instructions for the magistrates to perform their duty lawfully, concentrated in the constitutional sub-document: the judges were not to respect persons or take a bribe (Deut. 16.19); various restrictions were placed on the future office of kingship, foremost of which was to observe all the instructions found in the law (Deut. 17.18–20); the Prophet like Moses that God would raise – a literary reference to Joshua, except at Deut. 34.10–12 – must be obeyed absolutely (Deut. 18.18–19; cf. Deut. 34.9; Josh. 1.16–18), but a prophet who spoke lawlessly, under his own authority, was to be executed (Deut. 18.20–22).

All the treason laws in Deuteronomy of a political character, and representative examples of those of a religious character, are found in the constitutional sub-document. Judges were enjoined to reject bribes, but no statutory penalty for corruption was specified (Deut. 16.18–20).[284] Treason in the form of apostasy carried a death penalty (Deut. 16.21–17.7; 18.9–14; cf. 13.1–18). The first novel political crime specified in Deuteronomy was the lawless rejection of a ruling by the central court (Deut. 17.8–13), which carried a death penalty. The Torah of the King enjoined kings to obey the law, but contained no treason law for rebellion against the office of king or for kingly misconduct (Deut. 17.14–20). Qualifications and rights for the Levitical priests were listed (Deut. 18.1–8). God would raise up for the people a Prophet like Moses as a leader who (in contrast to the king) must be unconditionally obeyed (Deut. 18.15–19); it is evident that rebellion against this Prophet constituted treason. Yet the people must test those who claimed to be prophets, and unlawful prophecy was a form of treason that carried a death penalty (Deut. 18.20–22; cf. 13.1–5).

Biblical statutes combined political crimes and crimes against religion into a unified body of law against treason. Forbidden speech included both cursing the gods and cursing rulers at Ex. 22.28. The constitutional sub-document at Deut. 16.18–18.22 treated both political offenses and apostasy as forms of treason that carried the death penalty. The laws against apostasy in Deut. 13 contained political terminology relating to rebellion (Deut. 13.5, discussed later). Political and religious offenses were expressly compared at 1 Sam. 15.23: "For rebellion is as the sin of witchcraft." Both types of crimes, political and religious, constituted a dire threat to the social order by treacherous forces from within the nation.[285]

Impious acts considered worthy of the death penalty included cursing parents (Ex. 21.17), cursing the gods (Ex. 23.28; Lev. 24.15–16), sorcery, divination and witchcraft (Ex. 22.18; Lev. 19.26, 31; 20.6–7, 27; Deut. 18.9–12) and, most important, worshipping of other gods (Ex. 20.3; 34.14; Deut. 5.7, etc.). Specific banned practices included setting up groves, images or sacrificial altars to other gods. The penalty for crimes of impiety, when specified, was stoning by the community (Lev. 20.2, 27; 24.13–14; Deut. 13.6–10; 17.2–5; Josh. 7.25).[286] Unlike the homicide law, in which only the perpetrator, and not his family, was to be punished, the penalty for apostasy could extend to the entire family and the livestock of the accused (Josh. 7.24–25) or to their entire city (Deut. 13.13–16).

Pentateuchal passages containing judicial procedures for public crimes are concentrated in Deut. 13 and 17 in conjunction with the investigation and prosecution of apostasy.[287] Deut. 13 was concerned with conspiracies to introduce a foreign cult instigated by a prophet (Deut. 13.1–5), an individual (Deut. 13.6–11) or an influential faction within a city (Deut. 13.12–18), whereas Deut. 17.2–7 was concerned, not with conspiracies, but solely with the individual who secretly worshipped other gods. Regarding prophets and visionaries (Deut. 13.1–5; 18.20–22), Deuteronomy contained no discussion of witnesses or investigation, because the prophets and visionaries' statements were in the public arena. What little that was said procedurally had to do with criteria for their conviction and execution: if a prophet spoke in the name of other gods (Deut. 18.20), or offered a sign or wonder or prediction that failed to come to pass (Deut. 18.22), or even if it came to pass but he advocated serving other gods (Deut. 13.2), there was sufficient cause for execution for having "counseled rebellion" against God (Deut. 13.5).[288] The subversive introduction of foreign cults by individuals or groups of citizens involved more detailed procedural matters, because these criminals conducted their activities in secret (Deut. 13.6, 8). Anyone who had been approached with an enticement to worship other gods, whether by brother, offspring, wife or closest friend (Deut. 13.6), should not listen to them, but had the obligation to either immediately execute the offender (Deut. 13.8)[289] or to act as informer and bring the crime to the attention of the magistrates (Deut. 13.8, 12 [implied]; 17.4).[290] The magistrates were required to conduct a thorough investigation to verify the truth of the charges (Deut. 13.4; 17.4). A public trial before the entire assembly is implied in the instance of a single offender (Deut. 17.7). At least two accusing witnesses were required at trial for a conviction (Deut. 17.6). The witnesses were required to be the first to stone the condemned, followed by all the people (Deut. 13.9; 17.7). If an entire city had turned to other gods, it was to be utterly destroyed (Deut. 13.15–16).

Ancient Near Eastern law

In Ancient Near Eastern law collections, laws dealing with political treason were almost non-existent. Rejecting judicial decisions from a king or magistrate was punished by beheading (HL 173). The inheritance of a young man who spoke treason or fled the territory would be determined by the king (MAL B 3). Individuals who met at a tavern to talk conspiracy were to be promptly denounced to the authorities or else the tavern keeper was to be executed (LH 109). Harboring a military deserter was a capital offense (LH 16). Palace officials were required to report on any individual who flirted with the royal harem (MAPD 8, 19, 21). Palace officials who cursed the king or swore by the name of either the king or a god were severely punished (MAPD 10–11, 17).[291] But although the law collections contained few regulations on political matters, extensive provisions regarding treason appeared in Hittite, Aramean and Neo-Assyrian vassal treaties. These dealt at length with the types of speech and activities considered treasonous, requirements for reporting treasonous conspiracies to the authorities, how such allegations were to be investigated, and how treason was to be dealt with. Although vassal treaties were publicly read and approved (so Weinfeld 1972: 101), they were primarily aimed at the ruling class of the subject territory or nation. Their extensive provisions that required prompt denouncement of conspiracies to the authorities, even if the traitors were fathers, sons, wives or other relatives, applied mainly to the royal family and governors of the vassal states, because only the ruling class had the capacity or motivation to marshal resources for a rebellion. Sedition, once detected, was brutally repressed by putting entire cities to the sword, if necessary. Some of the language in vassal treaties, especially the Vassal Treaties of Esarhaddon (VTE) of 672 BCE, has been compared with language found in Deut. 13, although the latter dealt with apostasy, not political rebellion (Weinfeld 1972: 91–101).

Laws against apostasy or sacrifices to other gods are found nowhere in the Ancient Near Eastern law collections. Blasphemous cursing by a palace woman was a capital offense (MAPD 10), but blasphemy and temple theft were elsewhere punished by a beating (MAL N 1–2) or left up to the institutions of the temple (MAL A 1). Sorcery, on the other hand, which was often directed against the king and consequently considered a serious public danger, required an investigation by the royal authorities and was typically punished by execution (MAL A 47; HL 44, 111; *Telepinu Edict* 50; cf. Westbrook 2009e). Persons accused of sorcery were subjected to the River Ordeal; if they didn't drown in the ordeal, their accuser was executed instead (LH 2). A witch caught performing magic acts intended to harm a private person's property was fined three times the damage or loss she inflicted; but if the sorcery was conducted against the residence, it was considered a capital offense (LNB 7) comparable to attempted homicide.

Greek law

Athenian law carefully defined a legal category of crimes against the *polis* and the procedures for their reporting, investigation, trial and punishment.[292] Both political and religious crimes were covered together under the law of treason *(prodosia)*, also known as the law of impeachment.[293] Public offenses included in this law consisted of treason, conspiracy to overthrow the democracy or constitution, bribery of a public official, misleading the Assembly and impiety *(asebia)*.[294] Such crimes were prosecuted under the procedure called *eisangelia* ("reporting") whereby any citizen could report treasonous or sacrilegious activity to the magistrates, who were in turn required to conduct a full investigation and to assign a prosecutor to the case, which was tried before the full Assembly.[295]

The most serious categories of crimes against the *polis* were those of treason and attempting to overthrow the constitution. The earliest law against overthrowing democracy was attributed to Solon (Andocides, *On the Mysteries* 95). Athens had several dark periods in its history during which the constitution and democratic rule were overthrown in favor of either tyranny or violent oligarchy.[296] Under the oligarchic revolution of 411 BCE and the rule by the Council of Four Hundred, members of the opposing party were exiled from Athens or executed by judicial murder. At the overthrow of the Council of Four Hundred in 410/409 BCE, the Assembly passed the Law of Demophantos that required all Athenians, assembled by tribe and *deme,* to swear with oaths over unblemished sacrifices to kill anyone who attempted to overthrow the restored democratic constitution (Arnaoutoglou 1998: 74–5; Rhodes 2007: 17; J. Shear 2007). Those who slew a would-be tyrant were held judicially blameless, as in the older law from Solon's time (Andocides, *On the Mysteries* 95). Indeed, blessings were pronounced on those who upheld the Law of Demophantos, and curses against those who didn't, not only on the individuals themselves but also on their descendants.[297] Gratitude and honors were showered on those who assassinated would-be tyrants; the assassins were elevated as public heroes in the cult of the tyrannicides.[298] The Assembly granted full citizenship to the assassins of Phynichos by the Assembly in 409 BCE (Lysias, *Against Agoratus* 72; cf. Fornara 1983: 183–5).

The provisions of the Law of Demophantos were strengthened in the Law Against Tyranny of 336 BCE, passed by the Assembly in the aftermath of the military defeat of the Athenians by Philip II of Macedon. The Law Against Tyranny affirmed that anyone who conspired to overthrow democracy in Athens or establish a tyranny could be slain on the spot with impunity by any citizen as an instance of justifiable homicide. Both the would-be tyrant and his descendants would be declared *atimia,* without civic rights, and have all their goods confiscated. The Law Against Tyranny specifically extended these sanctions to conspiracy in deliberations by the Council of the Areopagus.[299]

Athenians also considered misleading the Assembly a crime tantamount to treason and punishable by death.[300] Although this crime could apply to any citizen who made false statements before the Assembly, it especially applied to an ambassador or herald who inaccurately reported to the Athenians from another state, whether ally or enemy, or failed to accurately convey a message from the Athenians to a foreign power.[301] Such persons were naturally suspected of acting in the interests of a foreign power or being in their pay.

Bribery of a magistrate was also included under Athenian treason laws.[302] The legal definition of bribery *(doradokia)* was the acceptance of a gift *(doron)* "to the harm of the people or one of the citizens in any way" (Demosthenes, *Against Meidias* 113). Athenian law allowed for seven different legal procedures for filing charges of bribery, depending on the type of bribery and the seriousness of its consequences to the *polis*.[303] The penalty for bribery was either a tenfold fine,[304] *atimia* and exile (Demosthenes, *Against Meidias* 113; Dinarchus, *Against Demosthenes* 60; Diodorus Siculus, *Library* 17.108) or death (Isocrates, *On the Peace* 50; Aeschines, *Against Timarchus* 86–7; cf. Plato, *Laws* 12.955c-d). Judicial bribery called for the death penalty (Aeschines, *Against Timarchus* 86; Isocrates, *On the Peace* 50; Aristotle, *Athenian Constitution* 27.5). Bribery of a magistrate uncovered at an audit theoretically could warrant a death sentence, but generally was punished by fine, because no deaths are recorded in such cases.[305] Bribery that involved high treason, on the other hand, always resulted in exile (if tried *in absentia*) or execution (cf. Plato, *Laws* 12.955c-d). The majority of executions took place under the procedure of *eisangelia* and involved generals, ambassadors or public speakers.[306] The law against bribery made the office of diplomat especially perilous for Athenians, because gift-giving was a normal expression of royal hospitality toward visiting diplomats in foreign lands to which they might be sent, but accepting such gifts left the ambassador vulnerable to prosecution by his enemies on his return to Athens.[307]

The final category of crimes against the *polis* was impiety or sacrilege.[308] Several individuals were prosecuted in the fifth and fourth centuries BCE at Athens under charges of sacrilege (Ostwald 1986: 528–41; Morrow 1993: 471–2; Phillips 2013: 445–7; Josephus, Apion 2.262–68). These included the astronomer Anaxagoras of Clazomenae, whose cosmological theories sought a natural explanation for the universe and the celestial bodies;[309] a prophetess from Lemnos named Theoris and her twin sons who were condemned and executed for sorcery;[310] a priestess named Ninus who was executed for introducing a new religion with foreign gods into Athens;[311] the impiety trial of Theogenes, whose wife was accused of improperly serving as priestess at a festival of Dionysius in Athens (Demosthenes, *Against Neaera* 78–83); the impiety trial of Phryne, a courtesan who was accused of introducing a novel god and assembling an illegal religious group;[312] the trials in connection with the profaning of the Eleusian Mysteries in 415 BCE, discussed extensively later; and the prosecution of several prominent philosophers for impiety, including Socrates, who was forced to drink hemlock in 399 BCE;[313] Theophrastus, the famous successor to Aristotle at Athens;[314] and Demetrius of Phalerum (Athenaeus, *The Philosophers' Banquet* 12.542e-f; cf. O'Sullivan 1997: 139–42; O'Sullivan 2009: 211). The legal basis for the prosecution of impiety appears to have been the Decree of Diopeithes of ca. 438 BCE, the only known law against impiety at Athens, a vague law that called for prosecuting those persons "who did not acknowledge divine matters or teach doctrines about the heavenly bodies."[315] This law appears to have been directed in part against natural philosophers of the sixth and fifth centuries BCE who held that the sun, moon and stars were not divinities, as held in Greek popular religion, but objects whose properties could be studied as natural objects by studying the laws of motion.[316]

To some extent, Plato's *Laws* fills in the gaps in our knowledge about the prosecution of impiety at Athens (so Morrow 1993: 475), but also contained some provisions unique to his view of impiety as a societal danger. In line with Athenian laws, Plato specified severe penalties against setting up private shrines, sacrifices or unauthorized cults (*Laws* 10.909d-910c).[317] Plato's law against unauthorized cults appears to have been consistent with Athenian laws, but his law against all forms of magic contrasts with Athenian law, which contained no provisions against magic.[318] Plato's *Laws* also outlawed all forms of popular magical incantations, spells, potions and poisons (*Laws* 11.932e-933e).[319] Plato discounted most expressions of magic as childish expressions of naïve superstition that could be corrected through education, but condemned as dangerous any notion that the wicked could buy the gods' favor or forgiveness for unjust deeds with propitiations, sacrifices, prayers or incantations. Plato considered both views that he deemed atheistic and the establishment of any private or unauthorized religious cult in competition to those sanctioned by the *polis* to be matters of utmost seriousness that threatened the virtue of the city and must consequently be punished with death.

The most famous Athenian case of sacrilege was the profaning of the Eleusian Mysteries and the mutilation of the statues of Hermes in 415 BCE.[320] The accusations centered on members of a private political club who secretly met in their members' homes. One of the prominent oligarchs by the name of Alcibiades was accused of illegally presiding over the sacred rites of the Eleusian mysteries – or a parody thereof – in his private residence, having sacrilegiously donned the sacred garb of the *hierophant* or Eleusian priest and performed the mysterious rites that could only legally be conducted at the sacred temple of Demeter in Eleusis. When this sacrilegious deed was discovered, the city was in an uproar, especially because this offense against the gods took place at a time when Athens was undertaking a war against Sicily, and because Alcibiades was one of the three generals in command of the expedition. If this was not bad enough, members of his political club had also carried out a plot to mutilate all the statues of Hermes, the god of messengers, found throughout Athens. Private citizens brought accusations of impiety against Alcibiades and his associates before both the Assembly and the Council.[321] A panel of magistrates was immediately appointed to investigate the charges (Andocides, *On the Mysteries* 36, 40; cf. Plutarch, *Alcibiades* 18.4). Huge rewards and immunity from prosecution were offered to informers who could unmask the plotters.[322] A total of six informants eventually came forward, including the oligarch Andocides, one of the participants.[323] Most of those accused immediately fled Athens, whereas those who were caught or chose to remain were imprisoned (Andocides, *On the Mysteries* 45–8; Lysias, *Against Andocides* 23; Thucydides, *Peloponnesian War* 6.53.2; Plutarch, *Alcibiades* 20.3; 21.1–2), and many of these were tried and executed.[324] Trials took place before the full Assembly (Andocides, *On the Mysteries* 17). Those who fled, thereby admitting their guilt (Andocides, *On the Mysteries* 49), were tried and convicted *in absentia* (Andocides, *On the Mysteries* 13; Thucydides, *Peloponnesian War* 6.61.7; Diodorus Siculus, *Library* 13.5.4), and a huge reward offered for any who would capture and execute them.[325] All those convicted, whether in Athens or having fled abroad, were publicly cursed, their citizenship revoked and their property forfeit. The names of those convicted and their properties were listed on inscriptions (the "Attic Stelai") displayed at the Eleusinion near the Agora of Athens, major fragments of which were discovered in excavations in late 1930s.[326] The public filing of charges before the Assembly and Council, the impaneling of magistrates to investigate the charges and the subsequent trials by the full Athenian Assembly conformed to the usual procedures of *eisangelia* under Athenian law (MacDowell 1978: 199; Ostwald 1986: 533–6).

Comparisons and conclusions

The biblical treason laws are in close conformity with the treason laws of Athens, but sharply conflict with those of the Ancient Near East. The unity of political treason and impiety laws in both biblical and Greek legal systems is striking, whereas in the Ancient Near East treason was conceived of solely in the form of conspiracy against the king.

Other than severe penalties for witchcraft, which are common to biblical, Ancient Near Eastern and Greek law collections alike, the only form of impiety that appeared in the cuneiform tradition was blasphemy. Broad statutes against all forms of black magic and malicious pharmacology were absent from both Ancient Near Eastern and Athenian law, but were common to Plato's *Laws* and Pentateuchal laws.[327] Provisions against cursing either the gods or the king in MAPD 10–11, 17 are comparable to those found in Ex. 22.28 and 1 Kgs 21.10, 13, but were restricted to the palace, where disrespect for the national gods was a matter of some seriousness. In the Greek world, cursing the gods was frowned upon, but freedom of speech and artistic expression allowed irreverence toward the gods to a greater degree than the biblical laws permitted. The ancient Mesopotamian powers were accommodating to foreign gods and local cults. Neither Ancient Near Eastern law collections nor vassal treaties included worshipping other gods as either impious or treasonous.

The biblical text, in common with Attic law, held both sacrilege and conspiracy to overthrow the laws and constitution as acts of treason punishable by death. False report was considered a criminal matter in the Covenant Code and false report to the Assembly appears as an element of treasonous rebellion in the Sojourn narratives that led to a death sentence for the wilderness generation, but did not appear as an explicit element of treason statutes. Although bribery was condemned in biblical law collections, including in the constitutional sub-document in Deuteronomy, bribery did not appear as an element of treason in either statutes or narratives and did not carry a death sentence.[328] Although the Primary History contained polemics against tyranny (1 Sam. 8.11–18; 1 Kgs 12.1–19; 21.1–16), there was nothing close to the Athenian Law Against Tyranny that encouraged tyrannicide as a form of justifiable homicide. Although the biblical and Athenian conceptions of treason were close in spirit, it thus does not appear that the biblical treason laws were directly informed by Athenian statutes. It appears likely that the biblical authors became acquainted with Athenian notions about treason through the filter of Plato's *Laws,* in which the categories of treason corresponded more closely to those found in biblical law.[329]

It remains to consider whether Deut. 13, which dealt with the crime of trying to establish a false religion, was based on the Vassal Treaties of Esarhaddon (VTE), as commonly held, or drew on legislation against impiety found at Athens and in Plato's *Laws*. One obvious consideration is the fact that VTE was not directed against impiety by the establishment of an unsanctioned religious cult – a topic that appeared nowhere in Ancient Near Eastern treaties or law collections – but aimed exclusively to prevent and punish political rebellion. Conversely, capital punishment for impiety figured prominently as a key provision in Greek treason laws, both in Plato, *Laws* 10.909d–910d, which extensively discussed the crime of establishing a private religious cult, and at Athens, where the fear of foreign cults led to several executions in the fourth century BCE (Morrow 1993: 431–2, 494).

It has nevertheless been proposed that language found in the purely political VTE was transferred to the religious realm in Deut. 13, an argument based on alleged weighty verbal and topical parallels in the two texts. Under this theory, Assyrian language of political treason and rebellion in VTE was subversively adapted by the biblical authors, who applied this same language to rebellion against Yahweh as king.[330] The first of these proposed parallels was the appearance of the prophet as a dangerous figure in both Deut. 13 and VTE. Deut. 13.1–5 stated that if a prophet or dreamer of dreams arose and promised signs and wonders, the prophet should be executed, even if these signs came to pass, if he publicly called for the worship of another god. VTE 116–17, on the other hand, said that if anyone spoke rebellion against the crown prince Ashurbanipal, including any of several classes of prophet, the vassal should not listen to these treasonous words, but report them to the king. The main point in common was treasonous words spoken by a prophet (Weinfeld 1972: 97–8). But VTE said nothing about dreams, omens or portents, although these phenomena were all common to the biblical, Ancient Near Eastern and Greek worlds.[331] VTE did not single out the Assyrian prophetic figures for execution. Indeed, the assumption in VTE was not that the prophetic figures themselves were the instigators of rebellion, but that they had issued oracles that sanctioned the real instigators, Ashurbanipal's political rivals for the succession to Assyrian rule. A better parallel for Deut. 13.1–5 is Plato, *Laws* 10.909d-910d, which called for the execution of anyone who incited others to privately worship gods not sanctioned in the official cult. Plato, *Laws* 10.908d warned that such traitors might even seek to persuade and enchant followers by means of magical feats, in parallel to the signs and wonders performed at Deut. 13.1–2. Plato, *Laws* 10.908d explicitly labeled these instigator "prophets" *(manteis),* and enchanting acts of magic were associated with street-prophets at Plato, *Laws* 11.933a and elsewhere.[332] At Deut. 13.4–5, the prophet who introduced a new religion was said to deserve execution because he "spoke rebellion," which has been taken as a verbal clue that Deut. 13 was taken over from the political sphere and reapplied to a new, religious context.[333] But under Athenian law, establishing a new religion contrary to those sanctioned by the *polis* was an act expressly punishable under treason laws, and Plato, *Laws* 10.908d also stressed the danger to the *polis* posed by such an act. Deut. 13.5 did not apply political language in a novel way to religious crimes, but simply carried over such language as conventionally used in Athenian law.

The unit that followed, Deut. 13.6–11, dealt with secret conspiracies to worship another god. Magicians in Classical Greece were often accused of privately initiating their clients in the Mysteries.[334] The secrecy involved in both Deut. 13.6, 8 and Plato, *Laws* 10.909b-c are suggestive of mystery cults conducted in a private residence. Verbal parallels with VTE were adduced for Deut. 13.6, 8:

> If you listen to or conceal any word . . . from the mouth of your brothers, your sons, your daughters . . .
>
> (VTE 115–16)

> If anyone secretly entices you – even if it is your brother, your father's son or your mother's son, or your own son or daughter, or the wife you embrace, or your most intimate friend – saying, "Let us go and worship other gods" . . . you must not yield to or heed any such persons . . . and do not shield them.
>
> (Deut. 13.6, 8)[335]

But VTE exhaustively cataloged over twenty different potential sources of treasonous speech, including the relatives of Ashurbanipal, his palace officials, governors, prophets, foreign enemies, lesser officials, commoners, and relatives and advisors of the vassal himself (VTE 73–82, 108–22). None of these others – not even prophets! – were mentioned at Deut. 13.6, although three of those mentioned in Deut. 13.6 were absent from VTE, rendering the overlap much less impressive (Crouch 2014: 81–7). The presence of wives and closest friends in the list of intimates at Deut. 13.6 and their absence from VTE appears significant, because wives, blood relations and close friends figured prominently as informers in the impiety trials of 415 BCE.[336] The invitation by relatives and bosom friends to participate in secret religious rites in Deut. 13.6 is, indeed, directly evocative of the profanation of the Eleusian mysteries in 415 BCE, which took place in a political club who met as a secret brotherhood in private homes in Athens.[337] Such secret oligarchic political clubs were seen to be both a political and a religious threat, hotbeds of conspiracy and treason aimed at the overthrow of Athenian democracy (Thucydides, *Peloponnesian War* 6.27.2–28.2; 53.3; 60.1; 61.1–3; Andocides, *On the Mysteries* 36, 100; Plutarch, *Alcibiades*

21.1; Diodorus Siculus, *Library* 13.2.3–4; Plato, *Laws* 1.636b) as well as promoting drunken excess and religious irreverence (Thucydides, *Peloponnesian War* 6.28.1–2; Plutarch, *Alcibiades* 18.4; 19.1; cf. McGlew 1999: 36). The language of Plato, *Laws* 10.910a-b, which called for the execution of anyone who established a private religious shrine in the home, was written with the memory of events of 415 BCE in mind.

Finally, one may note the judicial procedure at Deut. 13.6–11 in parallel with Greek treason laws and in contrast with VTE. The rebels and traitors in VTE were either to be seized and executed by local authorities or, failing that, to report directly to Ashurbanipal, who would seize and execute or militarily defeat the rebels himself, assisted by the vassal's troops. In Deut. 13.8–9, the private citizen who witnessed the enticement to another god was encouraged either to himself execute the apostate[338] or to inform the authorities, who would initiate an investigation (cf. Deut. 17.4) and trial before the Assembly (Deut. 13.9; 17.7) followed by a public execution. This closely corresponds to the Athenian procedure of justified homicide of traitors and perpetrators of impiety[339] and the procedure of denouncement, investigation and trial before the Assembly under Athenian *eisangelia*. Plato's *Laws* also specified these same procedures for cases of treason.[340] The case for Deut. 13 having been modeled on VTE, subversively transferring the language of political rebellion to the religious realm, thus fails to stand close scrutiny.[341] Instead, Deut. 13 may be understood to reflect treason laws against impiety at Athens and in Plato's *Laws*.

14. Sacred law

Biblical law

Laws dealing with sacred matters are found throughout Exodus–Deuteronomy. Some of these appeared in law collections that were either dedicated to sacred laws, such as the Priestly Laws (P), or combined sacred and civil laws, such as the Covenant Code,[342] the Holiness Code (H) and the Deuteronomic Law Collection (Dtn). Other sacred laws were mentioned within narrative passages that sometimes provided an etiological explanation for the laws, especially festival laws. Topics addressed in biblical sacred law included the sacred space of the temple (Lev. 19.30; Deut. 12.5–21, 26–27); temple and priestly land-holdings and other property (Lev. 27; Num. 35.1–5); altar and temple (tabernacle) design, construction and dedication ceremonies (Ex. 20.24–26; 25–27; 30.1–30; 35–36; 38; 40, Lev. 9; Num. 7);[343] cultic furniture and utensils (Ex. 31, 37; Num. 8.1–4); sacred calendar, festivals and festival laws (Ex. 12–13; 23.14–19; 34; Lev. 16; 23; Num. 9.1–14; 28.16–31; 29; Deut. 16.1–17); sacred priestly personnel and responsibilities (Num. 1.47–53; 3.5–41; 4; 6; 8.5–26); priestly vestments and priestly investiture ceremonies (Ex. 28–29, 39; Lev. 8); sacrificial laws (Lev. 1–7; 17.1–9; 19.5–8; 22.17–30; 24.1–9; Num. 5.5–10; 15.1–29; 28–29; Deut. 17.1); sacred recipes (Ex. 30.31–38; Lev. 6.20–21), priestly portions, including sacrifices, firstfruits, firstborn and tithes (Ex. 13.1–2; 22.29–31; Lev. 7.31–35; 10.12–15; Num. 18; Deut. 15.9–23; 26.1–11), purity laws for priests (Lev. 10.8–11; 21–22) and for the public (Ex. 19.14–15; Lev. 11; Num. 5.1–4), including dietary laws (Ex. 22.31; Lev. 11.1–31, 41–47; 17.10–14; 20.5–6; Deut. 12.22–25; 14.3–21), contagion and hygiene (Lev. 13–15; Deut. 24.8–9), corpse impurity (Lev. 11.32–40; 17.15–16; Num. 19) and childbirth (Lev. 12). It is difficult to decide whether to categorize funeral regulations (Lev. 19.27–28; 21.1–6, 10–12; Deut. 14.1–2) as sacred laws or laws on public decorum.

The Priestly Laws did not concern themselves with criminal matters, nor were they formulated as *mishpatim* or judgments. Even when dealing with the religious consequences of social infractions, priestly law dealt exclusively with those purifications, scheduled sacrifices and voluntary individual sacrifices designed to relieve religious anxieties over public or private wrongdoings, not the levying of criminal penalties.[344]

Ancient Near Eastern law

A variety of Hittite, Egyptian and Akkadian texts deal with various ritual matters,[345] including the purification and construction of temples, temple furniture and statues; daily temple rituals;[346] priestly ordinations, responsibilities and punishments for infractions; sacrificial procedures; festival calendars; magic rituals and incantations; and funerary rituals. As a rule, apotropaic and prophylactic magic played a larger role in Ancient Near Eastern ritual texts than biblical literature, where magical rites were generally condemned. The esoteric magical and ritual procedures found in these religious texts were intended for use by technical experts and temple personnel. An aura of secrecy attached to these books, which sometimes featured curses against those who revealed their contents to the uninitiated, that is, the general public.[347]

Greek law

The category of Greek sacred laws and decrees is well represented in inscriptions throughout the Greek world from the start of the sixth century BCE on, and which Athenians also recorded in literary texts of ca. 400 BCE of which a few fragments have been preserved in quotations by later writers (Jacoby 1949: 16, 41, 44, 49–50). These laws dealt with such matters as temple foundations and boundaries; cultic rituals; purity and purification rules; sacred equipment and priestly dress; instructions for sacrifices; recipes for sacrificial meals, libations and temple incense; asylum laws; selection rules and tenure for priests; priestly portions and pay; oracle consultation fees; state sanctioned festivals, sacrificial schedules and other calendrical matters; and proper conduct during festivals (Rhodes and Osborne 2003: 298–311, 494–505; Parker 2004: 58–64; Lupu 2005; Robertson 2010).

Some sacred laws originated in decrees by Greek *boules* and assemblies and enforced by the *polis*. These dealt with public aspects of worship in the *polis*, including such matters as festivals to be included in the public calendar; the selection of priests from the citizens of the *polis;* priestly sacrificial fees; penalties for violating the sacred temple space *(temenos);* and laws governing funerals and public mourning. These written sacred laws and decrees were virtually indistinguishable from the civic laws of the *polis* with respect to either their formal proposal and ratification by the official legislative bodies of the city-state or their enforcement by the courts (Parker 2004: 58–61; cf. Fornara 1983: 88–9). A different category of sacred law dealt with customary sacred rituals, especially purification laws and procedures. The authority for these laws, which were sometimes broadly described as "unwritten laws" or "ancestral laws" *(patria nomima),* were based on long-standing custom (Plato, *Laws* 7.793a-b) and phrased as directions from a god ("Apollo decreed that . . . ") rather than from the state. Although penalties for infractions were commonly specified, they involved purification of a shrine or person or the voluntary offering of a sacrifice and were not enforced like laws originating from the civil bodies; instead, it was assumed that those participating in sacred rites freely complied with the regulations and would comply with the penalties from inadvertent trespasses out of a sense of religious anxiety.[348] Classical scholars sometimes describe these laws that originated out of long-standing unwritten religious custom as "private laws," as opposed to the "public laws" created and enforced by the *polis*. The phrase "sacred laws" found in Greek literature and inscriptions appears to have referred primarily to this category of ancestral religious laws. The oral transmission and interpretation of unwritten sacred laws in Attica, especially those dealing with purification rituals, was the special province of Exegetes of the *genos* Eumolpidae.[349] These "unwritten laws" were committed to writing in the fourth century BCE.[350]

Comparisons and conclusions

The systematic publication of sacred laws in the Pentateuch does not conform to the practices in the Ancient Near East, where religious texts contained closely guarded esoteric secrets for priestly eyes only. In the Greek world, such secrecy was associated with certain private cults that the Greeks called the Mysteries *(musteria),* such as the Pythagorean and Orphic mysteries, the Eleusian mysteries of Kore and Demeter and the Mithraic mysteries. These mystery religions possessed restricted membership and their secrets were disclosed only to the initiates. By contrast, the entire citizen body was enjoined to participate in the public cult and its festivals. Many sacred regulations, especially those enacted by Greek political bodies, were displayed on public inscriptions. Although the interpretation of "unwritten" or "ancestral" sacred laws was reserved for the Exegetes, in the early fourth century BCE even these traditionally oral regulations were systematically put into written form. The public character of sacred law in all the biblical law collections is comparable to Greek sacred laws, especially those governing official public cults sanctioned by the *polis*. The combining of civil and cultic regulations in the Covenant Code, Leviticus (H) and Deuteronomy (Dtn)[351] closely resembles Greek legislation. Indeed, in ca. 594 BCE the legislator Solon famously enacted and published both civil laws governing Athens and sacred laws governing the Athenian festival and sacrificial calendar (Gagarin 1986: 70; Knoppers and Harvey 2007: 110).

The biblical publication of sacred law, often published alongside civic statutes within the same Pentateuchal law collections, thus appears to reflect Greek practices regarding the public dissemination of religious legislation. That is not to say that the biblical sacred laws and festivals originated in the Hellenistic Era or did not incorporate authentic older, "ancestral" Jewish and Samaritan religious traditions. Sabbath, Passover and the Days of Unleavened Bread, for instance, are all attested in papyri or ostraca from Elephantine ca. 400 BCE, although certain features of these religious days appear to have developed later, perhaps as late as ca. 270 BCE and the creation of the Pentateuch.[352] It is possible that the *tamid* or daily sacrifices of Ex. 29.38–42 and Num. 28.3–8 reflects an older Ancient Near Eastern practice, because most Greek temples were open only on certain days and did not hold a daily sacrificial service (Lupu 2005: 74). In may be questioned whether the smaller temple at Jerusalem, with its limited financial resources, could have sustained a daily sacrifice during the Persian and early Hellenistic Eras, but the huge amount of animal bones discovered by archaeologists below the sanctuary on Mount Gerizim suggests the possibility of *tamid* sacrifices in the northern temple. One cannot completely discount Greek influence on the biblical statute, however, because Plato, *Laws* 8.828a-b required temple sacrifices to be performed on every day of the year.

15. Ethical law

Biblical law

Pentateuchal laws with ethical content appear to form a distinct genre, typified by the Ten Commandments (Ex. 20.1–17; Deut. 5.6–22).[353] Together, the Ten Commandments encapsulated the covenantal obligations of the citizens of the nation organized under Moses (Ex. 34.10, 27–28). The Commandments or *debirim* ("words") each took the form of a short second-person instruction or exhortation that can be interpreted as a law, with affinities to the apodictic laws of the Covenant Code. Unlike the *mishpatim* of Ex. 21–23, however, none of the Ten Commandments included a penalty or statutory consequence, although the first five had rhetorical additions (motive clauses) that were intended to persuade the hearer of the benefits of obedience. The short, memorable format of the Ten Commandments appears ideal for teaching and for memorization, and Pentateuchal passages indicate that it was used for both purposes (Ex. 24.12; Deut. 6.6–9; 11.18–20).

It is possible to understand the Ten Commandments as ethical laws, especially in light of the similar second-person format of Pentateuchal commands with undoubtedly ethical content, such as the famous commands to "Love God" (Deut. 6.5) and "Love your neighbor" (Lev. 19.18).[354] As such, the Ten Commandments provide a basis for a sort of moral education. The Ten Commandments contain significant overlap with themes expressed in Proverbs.[355] The Proverbs, too, are mostly in the form of short memorable second-person instructions, exhortations or commands. A key difference between the moral exhortations found in Proverbs and in the Ten Commandments is that the former consisted of instructions from a human father for his son, while the latter were divine words whose audience was the entire citizen body. One can identify the audience of the Ten Commandments specifically as the male heads of household, as especially evidenced by the seventh and tenth commandments.

Ancient Near Eastern law

The Ten Commandments contain some ethical injunctions that also carried criminal penalties, such as the commandments against murder, theft, adultery and bearing false witness in court. These matters also appear in the law collections of the Ancient Near East, but in a casuistic format that specified the crime and its penalty. The law collections did not directly address those under the rule of the king in second person, like the Commandments, nor did second-person wisdom texts circulate in the name of the kings associated with law collections. Mesopotamian "wisdom literature" consisted mainly of esoteric magical and cultic texts. Ethical precepts that resembled those found in the biblical book of Proverbs appear in *Counsels of Wisdom* and in *The Instructions of Shuruppak*.[356] The latter text contained purported words of wisdom from the antediluvian king Shuruppak, from the city of the same name, to his son Ziusudra, the Sumerian flood hero. These instructions mostly dealt with extremely prosaic matters, such as what kind of donkey to buy and who to associate with, but they also contained several striking parallels to the Ten Commandments. These parallels included appeals to listen to his parents and exhortations not to utter strong curses, quarrel, boast or lie, murder, steal, commit rape, marry a prostitute, or be alone with another man's wife, primarily because all these ill-advised activities could damage one's reputation in the city. Although these words of advice found in *The Instructions of Shuruppak* were in second-person voice, they mostly appeared in an informal conversational tone within topical passages of around three lines, rather than as one-line commands that carried divine authority. Additionally, these practical words of advice dealt with the social rather than the divine sphere and included no exhortations to piety.

Greek law

A key objective of Greek education was to instill virtue or excellence of character in the citizens of the *polis*.[357] An important category of ethical instructions among the Greeks was the maxim, a short *gnomic* statement, typically phrased in second-person singular voice that contained advice on proper conduct in the form of a commandment such as "Honor the gods," "Honor your father and your mother," "Seek wisdom," or "Help your friends."[358] A venerated collection of such sayings, the Commandments of the Seven Sages, was inscribed on a wall of the temple at Delphi. Although the sayings were anonymous, later writers attributed them to various wise men of the past. Copies of these sayings were used in primary school, where their brief format was conducive to memorization by young students and their high ethical content was perceived as valuable in instilling citizen virtues in the young.

Ethical instructions were also a prominent feature in Plato's *Laws*. Plato held that the legislators of the *polis* should not only formulate enforceable civic statutes in the form of commandments with prescribed penalties, but also record ethical advice to shape the character and behavior of the citizenry, especially the youth. This category of law was not to be enforced with civic penalties, but rather by praise or censure from public officials, elders, parents and other authority figures (cf. Rinella 2010: 223–4).

Comparisons and conclusions

The moral prescriptions found in the biblical law collections, especially in the Decalogue, have some affinities to the wisdom literature of the Ancient Near East – as well as the biblical book of Proverbs – in which a father gave moral and practical advice to his son by enjoining him to good behavior through direct parental commands. But such fatherly instructions differ significantly from the Decalogue in at least three respects: the divine sanction of the Decalogue; the conception of the Decalogue, not as wise advice, but as legislation; and the audience of the Decalogue, which was addressed, not to sons, but to the heads of households in the citizen body as a whole. The ethical precepts of the legislator in Plato's *Laws* were similar in spirit to the Decalogue, but typically appeared as advice within the context of persuasive speeches on an ethical topic rather than as pithy unadorned commandments. The Decalogue appears, instead, to have been modeled on the Commandments of the Seven Sages. The inscribing of these latter commandments on the walls of the temple at Delphi gave them an aura of divine authority, and the commandments included a call to honor the gods. Their attribution to the wise legislators of the past gave these commandments a quasi-legal authority, not as enforceable statutes with criminal or civil penalties, but as ethical principles of Greek society that were thought to underlie Greek law codes and define ideal citizen conduct. Finally, the Commandments of the Seven Sages were addressed to the citizen body as a whole, and specifically to adult males, the same receptive audience as the Decalogue.

Whereas some of the Ten Commandments were unique to the biblical text, others had an affinity, to a greater or lesser degree, to the Commandments of the Seven Sages. The most striking parallels from the maxims on the temple at Delphi, likely indicative of direct literary dependence, were the command-ments to "Honor the Gods"[359] and "Honor your Mother and Father."[360] Other commandments advised against oaths, murder, theft, adultery and the unjust acquisition of goods, but the formulations were not identical to those found in the Decalogue.[361]

One biblical commandment in particular stands out as distinctively Greek in spirit. The tenth commandment was the only one that addressed the inner psychological state of mind or passions rather than an objective behavior: "Do not covet." In a sense, this commandment was rendered unnecessary by the biblical statutes against debt slavery, which provided a legal mechanism that forestalled the permanent acquisition of a neighbor's ancestral lands or of their persons as slaves. But the tenth commandment was aimed at the very impulse of greed and acquisition as a source of social injustice. The wrong that it sought to eradicate was neither theft nor adultery, but rather the cre-ation of an oligarchy in which a wealthy class enriched itself by unjustly acquiring the lands of their neighbors and reducing them to debt slavery (cf. Mic. 2.1–2), creating a society stratified by wealth in which oligarchs owned and oppressed the poor. The tenth commandment drew a direct relationship between the oligarchic passion to acquire and the impoverishment, enslave-ment and disenfranchisement of their neighbors. The passion to acquire (under several synonyms, of which the most common was *pleonexia*) was also identi-fied as the root cause of the evils of oligarchy in the writings of Plato, Aristotle and other Greek theorists.[362] The identification of the passion to acquire as a primary cause of social evils illustrates the intersection of ethics and politics in both biblical and Athenian thought. By contrast, a central aim of Ancient Near Eastern law collections was to enforce the rights of the wealthy ruling class on the commoners and slaves.

16. Conclusions

Until recently, comparative legal studies have presumed an exclusively Ancient Near East background to the biblical laws and have focused on a handful of proposed literary dependencies with LH, LE and MAL A, mostly appearing in the Covenant Code. But it may be questioned whether the biblical law collec-tions are expressive of Ancient Near Eastern culture or legal philosophy. The great empires of the Ancient Near East such as Babylonia and Assyria were administered for the benefit of the king and the ruling class who possessed the greatest concentration of wealth and power. Wealth and other economic benefits poured into the empires of Babylonia and Assyria from subjugated territories through conquest, taxation and tribute, enslavement, conscription, forced labor and trade. The expansion of empire and the exploitation of con-quered or tributary regions were effected by military force and the terroristic suppression of all opposition or rebellion. Who can forget the carved reliefs with scenes of siege, conquest, the impalement of those who had resisted, the endless lines of prisoners being led into captivity. On the domestic scene, the enrichment of the king and nobility was similarly effected through the taxation, conscription and forced labor of members of the exploited class of commoners as well as bustling economic activity regulated by the government and its bureaucracy. The law collections of the Ancient Near East reflect this same world. In their prologues and epilogues, these laws were propagandistically portrayed as an expression of just rule by a king concerned with establishing righteousness and stability throughout his realm, but instead often appear to document an unjust enforcement of the rights of the ruling class over the exploited classes of commoners and slaves. Crimes were stratified according to the social classes of the perpetrator and victim with the most severe penalties exacted against the slave or commoner who committed a crime against the wealthy nobility. Any act of criminal mischief that disrupted the social order was met with brutal punishment that included the death penalty for property crimes like petty theft, the routine use of mutilation and corporal punishment on the lower classes, the endorsement of beatings and disfigurement of slaves and wives, and the extreme application of *lex talionis* such as the execution of a son (LH 229–30) or the rape of a wife (MAL A 55) in retaliation for crimes that affected corresponding members of another man's family. Such gruesome punishments, especially prominent in Assyrian law, but also found in earlier and later Babylonian law collections, were intended to terrorize the population into total submission and crush any tendency toward criminal misbehavior or rebellion against the social order. The law collections, by which the king claimed to have righteously established justice and domestic stability throughout the land for the benefit of his subjects, were in fact an expression of social control and royal might. A measure of the severity of economic exploitation of members of the lower class, who often fell from freedom into debt slavery as the result of exorbitant interest loans from the ruling class, was the necessity for periodic edicts of liberation and justice that the king was compelled to issue in order to alleviate the economic distress of the commoners and quell social unrest.

Biblical law codes nowhere partake of this Ancient Near Eastern vision of a law system as an expression of either idealized royal virtue or of terroristic royal might. Unlike the law collections of the Ancient Near East, the king was not the originator of biblical laws, nor was he portrayed as a benefactor of the widow, orphan or the people as a whole. Indeed, the king was entirely absent from the Pentateuch except in Deut. 17, in which he was assigned no administrative roles and denied the accoutrements of power such as harem, chariots and wealth. Nor does one see a ruling class. All Israelite citizens were free and equal, all were landowners (except for itinerant Levites) and offices (including that of king) were available to all. The raw brutality that characterized Ancient Near Eastern laws, with their impalements, amputations and capital punishment of innocent family members, was also largely absent. True, capital punishment was legislated for not only homicide and treason, but also impiety, sabbath violation, sexual crimes and adultery, but there was no capital punishment for property crimes as in the Ancient Near East. The application of *lex talionis* and corporal punishment seems half-hearted in comparison with Ancient Near Eastern laws, in which *lex talionis* was invoked in order to justify retaliation against innocent family members[363] or the terroristic infliction of mutilation on those who injured someone of superior social class.[364] The biblical text does not relish in cataloging such retaliatory inflictions of disabling injuries and death, and one gains the overall impression that *lex talionis* appeared in the Pentateuch as a literary artifact from the distant past.

One can identify several areas where biblical law collections likely reflected local customs dating from before the Hellenistic Era. First, there appears to have been a conservative preservation of traditional Ancient Near Eastern institutions associated with marriage, such as polygamy and bride-price. Second, there appears to have been a continuation of agricultural festivals from earlier times, on evidence of the *Elephantine Papyri,* but these festivals were significantly updated to reflect the foundation story of Exodus–Joshua authored in ca. 270 BCE (see Chapter 5 §2). Third, one may presume, in the absence of evidence to the contrary, that the priestly sacrificial procedures found in Exodus and Leviticus reflected older customs associated with practices in the temples at Jerusalem or Mount Gerizim.[365] Fourth, the civil laws contain scattered instances of literary dependence on Ancient Near Eastern law collections.

Antiquarian reflections of Old Babylonian or Assyrian legal traditions appear in all the biblical law collections but are most concentrated in the Covenant Code: the Law of the Goring Ox, injuries to a pregnant woman, *lex talionis,* the limited servitude of debt slaves and the mutilation of a slave's ear. These occasional echoes of Ancient Near Eastern laws and customs are best understood as the cultural legacy of the Assyrian and Babylonian educated elites who came to live in the Assyrian province of Samerina after 720 BCE.[366] In at least one instance (the mutilation of a slave's ear), the biblical authors misunderstood or altered the intent of the original law, suggesting that the statute did not reflect contemporary practices in force at the time the law was later added to the biblical text.

The Pentateuchal law collections evoke an entirely different time and a different culture from the Ancient Near East, one in which the land was divided among all the citizens, who were brothers with an equal share in their own government; in which a single law applied to all, from the poor to the king, not one law for the ruling class and one for the serf; in which both the laws and the justice system were in the hands of the citizens, not the king; in which obedience to the law was secured, not by terroristic threats, but appeal to citizen values such as love of freedom, shared ancestral traditions, piety and social conscience; a world, in short, that was foreign to the Ancient Near East until the arrival of democratic egalitarian Greek values in the Hellenistic Era. Several biblical legal genres were encountered throughout the Greek world, but absent in the Ancient

Near East, including constitutional law (discussed in Chapter 2), military law, publicly enacted and displayed sacred law and divinely sanctioned ethical "law" in the form of commandments given by ancient legislators.[367] Many specific aspects of biblical laws display obvious Greek influence: the mythology of the spilled blood calling for vengeance, a theme found in Greek myth, poetry and tragedy; the impurity that attached to bloodshed – whether avenged or unavenged – that caused plagues on the land, unless properly cleansed by ritual purifications administered by religious experts; spontaneous community outrage expressed by stoning; the flight of a suppliant for safety to a sacred altar or temple; exile for homicide, a theme found in many Greek plays and ancient legends as well as formally implemented in law; the careful legal management of inheritances to guarantee that ancestral lands remained within the kinship group and tribe;[368] and the notion of equal land allotments and land inviolability as a cure for poverty (Aristotle, *Politics* 2.1266a-1267a; 6.1319a; Plato, *Laws* 5.744c-e). All these features of biblical law, also found in various places in the Greek world, point to the predominantly Greek cultural background of the Pentateuchal law collections.

A number of biblical laws contain features that were not merely broadly Greek, but specific to Athens. Striking examples pertaining to homicide laws include the prosecution and execution of dangerous animals, found only in biblical and Athenian laws; the permissibility of slaying a night thief; the penalty of exile for unintentional homicide; and the role of the blood avenger in the legal prosecution or permitted extra-legal execution of an accused murderer. The prominent legal role of the same circles of close kinsmen in inheritance, marriage of orphaned heiresses and blood vengeance of homicide appears to demonstrate the biblical legislators' detailed knowledge of Athenian law. The combining of sacrilege and political subversion in biblical and Athenian treason laws lacks a parallel in the Ancient Near East or seemingly in other Greek city-states.[369] The same categories of exemptions appeared for military duty in Deuteronomy and military training at Athens. The biblical commandment against seeking to acquire the lands and persons of fellow-citizens appears to reflect an opposition to the creation of an oligarchy through the untrammeled passion to acquire that is commonly encountered in Athenian literature. Biblical laws against interest loans and permanent debt slavery were also similar in spirit to Attic laws against oligarchs enslaving less wealthy fellow-Athenians through defaults on interest loans.

Most of the aforementioned features of Greek and Athenian laws also appeared in Plato's *Laws*. Jewish access to Plato's *Laws,* the only ancient Greek text that programmatically detailed how to construct a constitution and law code, provides a simple mechanism whereby biblical legislators were exposed to many Greek and Athenian laws. The use of Plato's *Laws* by the biblical authors is also indicated by several laws found in both Plato's *Laws* and the Pentateuch that are otherwise unique. Plato was the first to introduce a legal distinction between premeditated and unpremeditated murder, as also found in the Covenant Code. Plato also introduced psychological factors – what we call "state of mind" – as crucial to evaluating the seriousness of assault and homicide cases. Plato's *Laws* contained the only known instance outside the Pentateuch of stoning as a sanctioned, legislated mode of execution. The biblical categories of treason appear to more closely correspond to Plato's *Laws* than Athenian treason laws, which also listed bribery and false report to the Assembly as capital crimes. The biblical laws on the division of the land into equal lots and the inalienability of citizen landholdings as a cure for poverty also resembled legal provisions in Plato's *Laws* but not in Athens. The Pentateuch's laws against magic appear to reflect Plato's *Laws*. The laws against establishing a private cult in Deut. 13 and Plato's *Laws* display close affinities, especially in the role of the false prophet as instigator. Other minor biblical laws that arguably drew on Plato's *Laws* included the provisions against grazing or setting fires in a neighbor's field, the law on moving boundary stones and the laws on gleaning. These points of comparison indicate direct literary dependence of Pentateuchal law on Plato's *Laws*. Although the exposure of Jewish legislators to Plato's *Laws* conveniently explains most features of Greek law present in the Pentateuch, a few features not encountered in Plato's *Laws* show that Jewish reading of Greek political and legal writings was not limited to Plato's *Laws*.

Various parallels between biblical and Greek laws have been noted in comparative studies of the past, including those regarding levirate marriage, blood avengers, exile in homicide cases and many others. Such parallels were commonly held to reflect a wider Eastern Mediterranean culture that hypothetically existed in the pre-Hellenistic period and that included shared legal traditions, premised on the assumption that the biblical legal traditions significantly predated Alexander's conquests. But it is improper to assume that Greek influences on biblical laws must have been either ancient or indirect. Given that the first definitive evidence for Pentateuchal writings appeared in the Hellenistic Era, legal comparative studies should take both Ancient Near East and Greek legal traditions fully into account and contemplate the possibility of direct legal influences on the biblical law collections. The striking parallels between biblical and Athenian laws noted earlier remove the need to hypothesize a diffuse Eastern Mediterranean legal tradition in pre-Hellenistic times, and instead indicate a direct acquaintance with Athenian law. This does not appear conceivable prior to Alexander's conquests in the east in 332–325 BCE and even in the Hellenistic Era is best understood as reflecting Jewish access to Athenian political and legal writings, a possibility affirmed by the many parallels with Plato's *Laws*. This in turn points to Jewish access to the texts housed in the Great Library of Alexandria after ca. 290 BCE. The tradition that put visiting Jewish legal experts at Alexandria in ca. 270 BCE at the invitation of Ptolemy II Philadelphus for the purpose of adding a text on Jewish laws to the holdings of the Great Library provides a historical context for the confluence of Jewish and Greek cultures that stimulated the creation of the Pentateuchal law collections.

Notes

1 Wright 2009: 103 took Deut. 4.6–8 to imply that Israel knew other law collections, which Wright assumed could only have been from the Ancient Near East.

2 Livy, *History of Rome* 3.31–34. According to this tradition, an official embassy of three ambassadors was sent from Rome to Athens "to copy out the celebrated laws of Solon and to become acquainted with the institutions, customs and laws of the other states of Greece." On their return to Rome, the ambassadors played a prominent role in drafting the famous *Twelve Tablets,* Rome's ancient law code.

3 See note 91 on the law of night theft. Justinian, *Digest of Roman Law* 10.1.13; 47.22.4, citing the *Commentary on the Twelve Tablets* by Gaius, mentioned statutes regarding land boundaries and on associations that drew on Solon's laws; Cicero, *On Laws* 2.23, 25 noted the Roman law on funeral expenses was taken almost word for word from Solon's laws.

4 Members of Plato's Academy were often consulted abroad by those fashioning laws and constitutions (Morrow 1993: 8–9), and it is apparent that they were well versed in political and legal systems throughout the Greek world. Universities such as Plato's Academy and Aristotle's Lyceum at Athens and the Museum later established at Alexandria provided gathering places for establishing international networks of high level intellectual social contacts. Comparative studies in constitutions and laws are known to have been topics of keen interest in such circles of ruling class elites.

5 In Plato's *Laws,* the panel of ten Cretan legislators charged with establishing a constitution and laws for a new colony in Cretan Magnesia were authorized to incorporate useful laws taken from other nations (3.702c; cf. 6.751e). At Plato, *Laws* 1.625a–642e, the dialogue opened with an extensive comparison of the aims and basic features of Spartan, Cretan and Athenian laws. The Athenian stranger who was the protagonist in Plato's *Laws* claimed to have investigated the laws on nearly every nation (1.639d-e). After the establishment of the colony had been completed, additional minor laws were later to be enacted taken from the law codes of other nations (12.957a-b).

6 Plato, *Laws* 12.951a-952d, 961a. On their return to Crete, the foreign travelers were encouraged to tell the young how superior their laws and customs were to those of other nations (*Laws* 12.951a; cf. Deut. 4.6–8). Many legendary or revered Greek lawgivers were said to have conducted extensive international travels prior to creating the law codes for which they were famous. These included Solon (Herodotus, *Histories* 1.30.1–3), Thales (Diogenes Laertius, *Lives of Eminent Philosophers* 1.29–32) and Lycurgus (Plutarch, *Lycurgus* 4.1–3). Although such traditions often lacked a firm historical basis, they attest to later perceptions of the legislative value of travel and study abroad.

7 Theophrastus wrote *On Laws* comprising twenty-four books, as well as several other shorter texts on laws and legislators. See Fortenbaugh et al. 1992: 1.445, 449; cf. Cicero, *On Ends* 5.11.

8 For a convenient collection of all extant Athenian laws (excluding constitutional and procedural laws) from both inscriptional and literary sources, with commentary, see Phillips 2013.

9 By contrast, Sparta had a law forbidding written laws, resulting in an almost total absence of inscriptional evidence on Lacedaemonian law; cf. Tigerstadt 1965: 1.24–25; Crawford and Whitehead 1983: 35.

10 Herodotus, Thucydides, the Atthidographers and many other historians included legal content relevant to their narratives. Some legal content is recoverable from the poetry of Solon, the great Athenian legislator of the early sixth century BCE. Contemporary legal developments were often the topic of parody in Athenian Comedy. See Chapter 5 for a discussion of the presentation of legal traditions within Greek narratives, also

a feature of biblical narratives, but entirely absent from Ancient Near Eastern legal sources.

11 Plato's texts on politics included *The Republic, The Stateman* and *Laws*.

12 Aristotle's political writings included *Of Justice, Of the Statesman, On Kingship, Extracts from Plato's Laws, Extracts from the Republic, Politics*, "a course of lectures on Politics like that of Theophrastus," *On Laws* (in four books) and "Constitutions of 158 Cities," of which only the *Athenian Constitution* has survived substantially intact. See Diogenes Laertius, *Lives of Eminent Philosophers* 5.21–27.

13 Political writings by Theophrastus, the most famous of Aristotle's students, included *On the Education of a King, On Laws* (in 24 books), *Epitome of Laws, Of Kingship, Of Legislators, Of Politics* and *Of the Best Constitution*. "We have learned from Aristotle about the customs, procedures, (and) systems of almost all political societies not only of Greece but also of the non-Greek world, (and) from Theophrastus about their laws" (Cicero, *On Ends* 5.11). The fragments of Theophrastus' writings were collected and discussed in Fortenbaugh et al. 1992. Fragments from *On Laws* are found at Fortenbaugh et al. 1992: 1.483–89.

14 Demetrius of Phalerum, who studied under Theophrastus, was the most prolific of the Peripatetic philosophers. After ruling Athens for ten years, Demetrius went into exile, winding up in Alexandria, where he advised Ptolemy I Soter and oversaw the acquisition of books for the Great Library. His political writings included *On Legislation at Athens, On the Constitution of Athens, On Statemanship, On Politics, On Laws, On Rhetoric* and *On Military Matters*. See Diogenes Laertius, *Lives of Eminent Philosophers* 5.80. The fragments of Demetrius' writings were collected and discussed in Fortenbaugh and Schütrumpf 2000.

15 Cicero, *On Laws* 3.13–14 listed several students of Plato and Aristotle who wrote on political matters.

16 Among Greek papyrus fragments found in Egypt, those from Plato's writings are numerically surpassed only by Homer's and include virtually all of the dialogues, including multiple fragments of *Republic* and *Laws*. See Pack 1967, with updated information in the online CEDOPAL searchable database Mertens-Pack 3. The arrangement of Plato into triads was made in ca. 200 BCE at the Great Library by Aristophanes of Byzantium (Diogenes Laertius, *Lives of Eminent Philosophers* 3.61).

17 Proposed biblical parallels with Plato's *Republic* and *Statesman* found in Wajdenbaum 2011 are not compelling. A good case for the use of Plato's *Timaeus* in Gen. 1–2 is made at Niesiolowski-Spanò 2007; Wajdenbaum 2011:92–6.

18 The description of Pentateuchal law will be synchronistic, with no attempt either to harmonize or identify diachronic developments in topics that appear in several locations. If these variations are due to differences in opinion among contemporary individuals or groups who contributed to the writing of the Pentateuch, as seems likely, this undermines the methodological validity of a diachronic analysis.

19 Texts and abbreviations are taken from Roth 1997. Additionally, I abbreviate Hittite Laws as HL. The description of Ancient Near Eastern laws will also be synchronistic, with no systematic attempt either to identify differences among Babylonian, Assyrian and Hittite laws or to trace diachronic developments in the laws (although Hittite laws appear in several redactions and note differing legal practices "in former times").

20 Insolent defiance of law *(yazid)* was mentioned at Ex. 21.14; Deut. 17.12–13; 18.20, 22; Isa. 13.11.

21 Forethought *(be-'ormah)* was elsewhere used with the sense of prudence (Prov. 1.4; 8.5, 12) or craftiness and guile (Josh. 9.4).

22 Lying in wait *(sadah)* was mentioned at Gen. 10.9; 25.27–28; 27.3, 5, 7, 33; Ex. 21.14; Lev. 17.13; 1 Sam. 24.11; Lam. 4.18. For a discussion of terms in Ex. 21.14, see Salzberger 1915: 291.

23 The case in Ex. 21.13 presumed animosity between the two parties, as indicated by the phrase, "but God delivered him into his hand," showing that this was an instance of intentional homicide. What distinguished this case was the lack of premeditation, as indicated by the phrase, "and if a man lie not in wait." The Covenant Code thus allowed flight to an asylum or place of voluntary exile in the case of unpremeditated murder.

24 Barmash incorrectly combined unpremeditated homicide and accidental homicide into one category, unintentional homicide. See Barmash 2005: 116–25. Her distinction between intentional (premeditated) homicide and unintentional homicide oversimplified matters, because Ex. 21.13 envisioned homicide that was intentional and malicious but not premeditated.

25 Cf. Barmash 2005: 120–3. Barmash correctly noted that witnesses were considered legally essential to determine the malice of the murderer toward his victim either in the past (Deut. 19) or at the time of the incident (Num. 35). Eyewitnesses were also required to identify the type of murder weapon and reconstruct the circumstances of the killing.

26 According to Katz 1993: 169–71, the animal could not be eaten because of its blood guilt, which rendered it unsuitable for sacrifice.

27 See Barmash 2005: 20–7 on the biblical blood avenger.

28 Six Levitical cities of refuge were mandated at Num. 35.6, 14–15, three on each side of the Jordan. Three cities of refuge east of the Jordan were specified at Deut. 4.41–43 and Josh. 20.8. Three in Canaan were mandated at Deut. 19.1–2, 7 and specified at Josh. 20.7. If other territories were added, provision was made for the addition of three more cities of refuge to ensure all slayers ease of access to a place of asylum (Deut. 19.8–10). The Deuteronomic cities of refuge had no Levitical association.

29 See Willis 2001: 89–144 for a discussion of biblical homicide, asylum and city elders, especially in the statute at Deut. 19.1–13. An attempt to trace the evolution of the biblical cities of refuge was made at Rofe 1986. Rofe noted the use of Jerusalem's temple as a place of asylum at Neh. 6.10–13 and also noted Jerusalem's official designation by Demetrius as an asylum city for debtors at 1 Macc. 10.31, 43.

30 See Weinfeld 1995: 123 for a discussion of altar refuge at Ex. 21.13–14; 1 Kgs 1.50–53; 2.28–29.

31 The historical and literary relationship between altar asylum law of Ex. 21.13–14 and the regulations regarding cities of refuge in Num. 35, Deut. 19 and Josh. 20 are much debated. The former appears conceptually related to the narrative traditions about seeking political asylum at local sanctuaries found at 1 Kgs 1.50–53; 2.28–34 (Adonijah and Joab) and Neh. 6.10–13; cf. Greenburg 1959: 126. Barmash emphasized that the episodes involving sanctuary asylum in Kings were for political offenders, not murderers, and were thus not directly relevant to the evolution of the cities of refuge (Barmash 2005: 8, 72–93). According to Weinfeld 1995: 123–4, there is no need to postulate a diachronic development of refuge by grasping an altar, seeking asylum in a temple or seeking asylum in a temple city, because comparative examples from Greece and the Ancient Near East (discussed extensively in Weinfeld 1995: 97–132) show the three forms of asylum often existed simultaneously. The cities of refuge in Deut. 19.1–13 have stripped the Covenant Code's altar asylum law and the Levitical cities of refuge in Num. 25 of any cultic associations; cf. Stackert 2006: 23–49, especially 41–5.

32 Willis (2001: 128) found a significant difference in the role of the slayer's city assembly in trying the case in the "priestly" sources (Num. 35.12; Josh. 20.6) and the role of

the city elders in fetching the convicted murder at Deut. 19.11–12. The point cannot be pressed, because it is not completely clear whether the elders in Deut. 19.12 were acting in a judicial (trial) capacity or in an executive capacity.

33 This provision likely dates to a period in which the high priest held a significant position in Jewish civil life. According to Greenburg 1959: 130, the death of the high priest may have satisfied the biblical requirement that blood purify blood (Gen. 9.5–6; cf. Num. 35.33). Greenburg cited Ex. 28.38 on the expiatory value of the high priest's life. Barmash 2005: 102–3) also cited Lev. 4.13–21 to support the same thesis.

34 See above on the blood avenger of the victim's kinsmen. Unavenged blood "cried out" for vengeance to God (Gen. 4.10; Isa. 26.21; Ezek. 24.7–8; Job 16.18). Discussions of Deut. 21.1–9 appear at Willis 2001: 145–62; Wells 2004: 56–9.

35 The formulaic legal justification of purging evil from the land is found at Deut. 13.5; 17.7, 12; 19.13; 21.9, 21; 22.21–22, 24; 24.7; cf. Willis 2001: 309.

36 The formula, "All Israel shall hear and fear," is found at Deut. 13.11; 17.13; 21.21; cf. Willis 2001: 182–3.

37 Num. 35.33–34; Deut. 19.10, 13; 21.9; Jer. 26.15. See especially the discussion of pollution and homicide at Barmash 2005: 94–106.

38 See Deut. 21.9 on the removal of blood guilt; the Levitical priests supervised the ritual aspects of the procedure (Deut. 21.5).

39 Ex. 21.28–29, 32 (the goring ox and almost certainly its owner); Lev. 20.2, 27 (idolaters and wizards); 24.14, 16, 23 (blasphemers); Num. 15.35–36 (sabbath violator); Deut. 13.9–10 (apostates); 17.5–7 (apostates); 21.21 (rebellious son); 22.21, 24 (nonvirgin daughters, adulterers and adulteresses); Josh. 7.25 (Achan). Gen. 38.24 exceptionally contemplated the execution of Tamar as an adulteress by burning; at Josh. 7.25, Achan and his family were first stoned and then burned.

40 Barmash (2005: 27–8, 44) took LH 1 to imply that any individual – not necessarily a relative – could bring an accusation of homicide against another.

41 See Barmash 2005: 132–4 on intentionality and the class of the victim as factors in prosecution.

42 Barmash 2005: 160 noted the application of *lex talionis* in the death of slave at LL f; LE 23, 55, 57.

43 LU prologue, "I eliminated enmity, violence, and cries for justice" (A 4.16–170, C 2.40–51); LL prologue, "to establish justice in the land, to eliminate cries for justice, to eradicate enmity and armed violence" (1.20–27); LH prologue, "to make justice prevail in the land, to abolish the wicked and the evil, to prevent the strong from oppressing the weak" (1.27–49; 4.14–24).

44 Athenian laws on homicide were collected at Phillips 2013: 44–84. Homicide courts were listed at Aristotle, *Athenian Constitution* 57; Demosthenes, *Against Aristocrates* 65–80; cf. Aristotle, *Politics* 4.1300b. The *Archon Basileus* was in charge of assigning homicide cases to the proper court (Aristotle, *Athenian Constitution* 57.4). Evidence for the jurisdiction and procedure for each of these courts were discussed in MacDowell 1963. Homicide laws were found at Plato, *Laws* 9.865a–874d.

45 Demosthenes, *Against Aristocrates* 22, 67–8; Aristotle, *Athenian Constitution* 57.3; cf. Plato, *Laws* 9.871b–872b. Intentional homicide was discussed at MacDowell 1963: 39–47, 90–100; Loomis 1972; Gagarin 1981: 31–7.

46 Only in the case of parricide was exile not an option (Pollux, *Onomasticon* 8.117; Plato, *Laws* 9.869a-b; cf. Chase 1933: 173).

47 Demosthenes, *Against Aristocrates* 72; cf. MacDowell 1963: 58–9; MacDowell 1978: 120. Laws on involuntary homicide appear at Plato, *Laws* 8.831a; 9.865a–866d, 869c-e. Drakon's homicide law ca. 621/0 BCE was the oldest known Athenian law whose text has been substantially preserved. It was retained by Solon (Plutarch, *Solon* 17) and revised and republished in 409/408 BCE. Drakon's homicide law distinguished

between intentional and involuntary homicide. See Meiggs and Lewis 1969: 264–7; Gagarin 1981; Stanton 1990: 27–31, 33.

48 Aristotle, *Athenian Constitution* 57.4; Demosthenes, *Against Aristocrates* 76; Pausanias, *Guide to Greece* 6.11.6, 9; cf. Plato, *Laws* 9.874a-b; MacDowell 1963: 85–9. The prosecution of the unknown slayer had the positive effect of putting into the judicial record the exoneration of those who might otherwise be suspected or pursued for vengeance by the victim's relatives.

49 Aristotle, *Athenian Constitution* 57.4; cf. Plato, *Laws* 9.873d-e. In Plato, the relatives prosecuted the animal, which, if convicted, was executed and cast outside the territorial borders. This procedure substantially reflected Athenian procedures; cf. Chase 1933: 177. Animal trials at the Prytaneion were also discussed at Finkelstein 1981: 58–9; Katz 1993: 171–7.

50 Aristotle, *Athenian Constitution* 57.4; Demosthenes, *Against Aristocrates* 55, 76; Aeschines, *Against Ctesiphon* 244: Pausanias, *Guide to Greece* 1.28.10; Pollux, *Onomasticon* 8.120; cf. Plato, *Laws* 9.873e-874a.

51 According to Plato, *Laws* 9.865d-e, the spirits of the victims of violence would be upset at the continued presence of the agent of their death.

52 Demosthenes, *Against Theocrines* 28–9; cf. MacDowell 1963: 9–10, 110. It was allowed in some Greek city-states on evidence of Theophrastus, *On Laws* book 16, which defined *hypophonia* as the money given because of a homicide to the relatives of the victim, so that they would not prosecute; cf. Fortenbaugh et al. 1992: 1.489.

53 Plato, *Laws* 9.871b, 872e-873a. See also Parker 1983: 257–80; Hagedorn 2003: 544–6 on bloodshed as pollution in ancient Greece.

54 See the discussion at MacDowell 1963: 141–50; cf. Plato, *Laws* 9.854e-855a, which emphasized the benefit of public punishment as an example to others.

55 Aristotle, *Athenian Constitution* 57.2–4; Demosthenes, *Against Macartatus* 57; Demosthenes, *Against Evergus and Mnesibulus* 72; Plato, *Laws* 9.871c; cf. MacDowell 1963: 34. The *Archon Basileus* assigned the homicide case to the proper court and presided over the trial (Aristotle, *Athenian Constitution* 57.4; cf. 56.6; 57.2).

56 The oldest known incident involving Greek right of temple asylum was the flight of Kylon and his co-conspirators to the Temple of Athena in the attempted revolt of 632 BCE (Herodotus, *Histories* 5.70–72; Thucydides, *Peloponnesian War* 1.126; Plutarch, *Solon* 12.1–9; cf. Weinfeld 1995: 121; Phillips 2013: 47–52). The supporters of Kylon were stoned outside the sacred precincts when the archons tricked them into leaving with promises of a fair trial; those responsible for this outrage were tried, convicted of sacrilege, and exiled from Athens under "the Kylonian curse."

57 On procedural matters, see generally Naiden 2004.

58 The right of self-exile from Attica to escape execution from the kinsmen avengers already appeared in the homicide law of Drakon; cf. Gagarin 1981: 58–62, 164–8. See Andocides, *On the Mysteries* 3, 49 on the self-incriminatory implications of flight into exile.

59 Forms of execution were discussed at Allen 2000: 200–1. Herodotus, *Histories* 7 33; 9.120, 122 described execution by hanging from a wooden plank.

60 Stoning was discussed at Pease 1907; Rosivach 1987; Allen 2000: 142–5, 205, 206, 213. References to community stoning in Greek tragedy were discussed at Hagedorn 2004: 130–1. Pease's article was especially useful in its comprehensive survey of Greek and Roman historical references to stoning. Stoning typically took place when a crowd became outraged at an act of treason, sacrilege or extreme immorality. The most historically secure incident of stoning was the famous execution of the traitor Lycides and his family in 479 BCE as described at Herodotus, *Histories* 9.5; Lycurgus, *Against Leokrates* 1.122; Demosthenes, *On the Crown* 104.

61 Demosthenes, *Against Macartatus* 57–8, 62, 65. See also Isaeus, *Menecles* 25 on funeral obligations as part of the duties of a child or successor to an estate.

62 Morrow 1993: 492; M. Hall 1996: 82–3; Allen 2000: 217–24. Plato, *Laws* 12.958d-960b laid out extensive rules for funerals and burials, and allowed for disposal of bodies without burial in the case of "parricides, temple-robbers and other such criminals"; cf. 9.854d-855a, 872c-873c.

63 Except for slaves, class status was not a factor in biblical homicide laws; cf. Paul 1970: 40, 76–7; Barmash 2005: 175.

64 See discussion at Barmash 2005: 106–8. The evidence is ambiguous on whether bloodshed was viewed as causing defilement in Mesopotamia; the cuneiform evidence suggests that the problem posed by spilled blood extended only to the parties directly involved (the perpetrator and the victim's family), never to the entire country in which the murder took place. This contrasts with the biblical picture in which unavenged innocent blood defiled the entire city or country (Num. 35.33–34; Deut. 19.10, 13; 21.9; Jer. 26.15; cf. Barmash 2005: 108, 115).

65 "It is questionable whether blood vengeance is found at all in the Mesopotamian corpora." Paul 1970: 63 n. 4; cf. Barmash 2005: 27–31.

66 Barmash 2005: 36–44, 49. As Barmash noted, the king maintained complete control of the judicial process, with no mandated judicial role for kinsmen of the victim and with "no specter of blood vengeance" interfering with the state's judicial investigation or prosecution.

67 Paul 1970: 78–9; cf. Finkelstein 1981: 26, 57–8; Malul 1990: 148–52; Katz 1993: 163–4. Malul noted that the punishment of the ox has no Mesopotamian parallel and should be considered a later development.

68 "If a mule or any other animal murder anyone, except when they do it when taking part in a public competition, the relatives shall prosecute the slayer for murder, and so many of the land-stewards as are appointed by the relatives shall decide the case, and the convicted beast they shall kill and cast out beyond the borders of the country" (Plato, *Laws* 9.873d-e).

69 Biblical and Greek pollution by shed blood was compared at Hagedorn 2003: 543.

70 Van Seters 2003: 106–8 incorrectly took Ex. 21.13 to refer to unintentional homicide and on this basis made comparisons to Ancient Near Eastern laws (LH 206–7).

71 Cf. Wright 2009: 5. The law also appeared in Plato, *Laws* 9.874b, as noted at Eusebius, *Preparation for the Gospel* 12.41. In LE 12–13, trespass into a field or building by day carried a fine of ten shekels, whereas the same offenses carried a death penalty if undertaken at night, but these legal penalties were imposed by the authorities, not by the property owner in an act of self-help. This law thus does not contemplate the slaying of a night thief as an instance of justifiable homicide; cf. Paul 1970: 86–7.

72 For the possible rejection of the biblical supplicant, see Ex. 21.13–14; Num. 35.24; Deut. 19.12; Josh. 20.4; cf. Weinfeld 1995: 124. For the possible rejection of the Greek supplicant, see Demosthenes, *Against Timocrates* 51–2; cf. Naiden 2004: 74–5.

73 The parallels between biblical asylum and asylums in temples and temple cities in the Greek and Hellenistic world were noted at Rofe 1986: 220; cf. Westbrook 1991: 164.

74 A number of parallels between biblical homicide laws and those found in Plato's *Laws* were cataloged at Eusebius, *Preparation for the Gospel* 12.41 (Ex. 22.2 cf. Plato, *Laws* 9.874b), 42 (Ex. 21.28–32 cf. Plato, *Laws* 9.873e), 13.21 (Ex. 21.12, 22–26 cf. Plato, *Laws* 9.867c-d, 868a-d, 869b, 871a, 877c), as noted in Wajdenbaum 2011:161–3.

75 "And all the magistrates, acting on behalf of the whole State, shall take each a stone and cast it on the head of the corpse, and thus make atonement for the whole State; and after this they shall carry the corpse to the borders of the land and cast it out unburied, according to law" (Plato, *Laws* 9.873b-c; cf. Wajdenbaum 2011: 160).

76 The two laws about a woman being embroiled in a fight were connected by Van Seters 2003: 113–14.

77 MAL A 21, 50–2 also called for various additional brutal punishments, invoking the principle of a life for a life. See generally Paul 1970: 71–4, on Ancient Near Eastern laws on assault resulting in miscarriage.

78 Athenian laws on wounding, battery and hubris were collected at Phillips 2013: 85–101. See especially 2013: 85–7 for the legal criteria that distinguished the types of assault.

79 Demosthenes, *Against Conon* 18; Lysias, *On an Intentional Wounding* 5–9. Typical weapons used in intentional assault included a knife or sword, a rock or a cudgel, although one famous case involved a broken piece of pottery; cf. Phillips 2013: 85.

80 Surviving excerpts of the law on *hubris*, such as Demosthenes, *Against Meidias* 47, do not legally define the term. According to Aristotle, *Rhetoric* 1.1378b, "A man who commits *hubris* also exhibits contempt; for *hubris* is doing and saying things that involve shame for the victim . . . The cause of pleasure for those who commit *hubris* is their belief that, by doing others ill, they themselves excel more; this is why the young and the rich are perpetrators of hubris: they think they excel by committing *hubris*. Dishonor is an element of *hubris*, and he who dishonors exhibits contempt." According to Photius, *Lexicon* s. v. *hubris*, "*Hubris* is battery accompanied by humiliation and spite; battery is blows alone."

81 See Rinella 2010: 32–4 for frequent incidents of *hubris* perpetrated by disorderly intoxicated revelers on innocent citizens during the *komos* or riotous procession home that typically concluded *symposia*.

82 Plato, *Laws* 9.874e. Athenian law did not appear to take the emotional state into account in the prosecution and adjudication of either homicide or assault.

83 For the Roman law of *lex talionis* attributed to the Locrians (that is, to Zaleucus of Locri), see Demosthenes, *Against Timocrates* 140–1; the law was attributed Charondas of Catana at Diodorus Siculus, *Library* 12.17.4–5; cf. Gagarin 1986: 66.

84 The assessment of damages for injuries at Plato, *Laws* 9.878b-d, 879b did not exactly correspond to Athenian laws, but awarded additional damages depending on aggravating factors such as criminal intent and the severity and shamefulness of the injuries; cf. Chase 1933: 179.

85 Plato, *Laws* 9.878c-d. It is not known whether this reflected Athenian practices.

86 For *lex talionis* in the biblical text compared with Ancient Near Eastern law, see Barmash 2005: 154–77; Greek and Roman references to *lex talionis* were also considered at Mühl 1933: 8, 18, 34, 45–51, 99–100.

87 Parental assault received the death penalty at Lysias, *Against Agoratus* 91; disenfranchisement and exile at Xenophon, *Memorabilia* 2.2.13; Diogenes Laertius, *Lives of Eminent Philosophers* 1.55; according to Plato, *Laws* 9.878e-879a, 881d; 11.932a-d, no penalty was too severe, including death preceded by corporal punishment. Cf. Chase 1933: 147 and n. 7.

88 An itemized list formalized with a contract and witnesses were required when goods were entrusted to a neighbor, or no claim of theft could be made (LH 122–24).

89 Inflating the value of pledged items was also a crime (MAL C 10–11).

90 Athenian laws on theft were collected at Phillips 2013: 332–69. Athenian Laws and procedures on theft were extensively surveyed at Demosthenes, *Against Timocrates* 103–5, 112–15, 120–21, 129, 146.

91 MacDowell 1978: 114; Plato, *Laws* 9.874b-c. The Athenian law that permitted the slaying of a night-thief was attributed to Solon (Demosthenes, *Against Timocrates* 113). An identical Roman law (*Twelve Tablets* 2.4; 8.3, 12) appears to reflect Roman knowledge of Athenian legal traditions; Livy, *History of Rome* 3.31–34 said a Roman

delegation visited Greek cities, including Athens, prior to framing their constitution and laws ca. 450 BCE. *Twelve Tablets* 8.13 held that a thief could not be legally slain by day unless they possessed a weapon and resisted arrest.

92 Dinarchus, *Against Demosthenes* 60; Demosthenes, *Against Timocrates* 114; Plato, *Laws* 9.857a-b; cf. Chase 1933: 166–67; Wajdenbaum 2011: 163. An incorrigible thief was liable for execution (Plato, *Laws* 12.941c-942a).

93 Isaeus, *Philectemon* 39–42; Aristophanes, *Clouds* 497–99 and scholion; Plato, *Laws* 12.954a; cf. Chase 1933: 168; Phillips 2013: 334, 341–42. An identical Roman law (Twelve Tables 8.15) may represent another instance of Athenian influence.

94 The fact is emphasized, in contrast to Ancient Near Eastern law, at Greenburg 1959: 129.

95 Eusebius, *Preparation for the Gospel* 12.40 compared the biblical laws on theft at Ex. 22.1, 4 with Plato, *Laws* 9.857a.

96 For biblical marriage customs, see Westbrook 1991: 10–4.

97 See Westbrook 1991: 145–64 for dowries in the Hebrew Bible and the Ancient Near East.

98 The harems of David and Solomon (2 Sam. 15.16; 16.20–22; 20.3; 1 Kgs 11.3) – and possibly Gideon (Judg. 8.30–31), although he was said to have rejected the kingship – were for royal prestige and should not be considered typical or normative examples of biblical polygamy.

99 The reason for this statute is unclear. See Westbrook 1986. Westbrook suggested that the husband's initial discovery of some (unspecified, probably sexual) "indecency" as grounds for divorce allowed him to keep the dowry and later remarry her at a reduced price. Yet the statute made no mention of financial arrangements, but instead emphasized matters of "defilement" and "abomination," suggesting other concerns. Westbrook noted that both Abraham and David took back wives after they had been with another man (1986: 392).

100 See Westbrook 1991: 17–20; Hagedorn 2004: 200–39 on biblical inheritance laws. Hagedorn took into account both Greek and Ancient Near Eastern parallels. According to Hagedorn 2004: 207, there are both biblical and Ancient Near Eastern precedents for the father choosing which son to consider his firstborn.

101 Judicial aspects were discussed at Willis 2001: 163–85. The law was understood as an expression of broad Mediterranean values of family honor at Hagedorn 2004: 224–38, where abundant Greek literary parallels on respect for elders and parents were cited, including several passages from Plato's *Laws*.

102 See Westbrook 1991: 157–64 on biblical inheritance.

103 The perpetuation of the family name was considered essential: "Go in to your brother's wife and perform the duty of a brother-in-law to her; raise up offspring for your brother" (Gen. 38.8); "Why should the name of our father be taken away from his clan, because he had no sons?" (Num. 27.4); "The firstborn whom she bears shall succeed to the name of the deceased brother, so that his name will not be blotted out of Israel . . . to perpetuate his brother's name in Israel" (Deut. 25.6–7); "To maintain the dead man's name on his inheritance" (Ruth 4.5, 10); cf. Westbrook 1991: 73–7.

104 See Westbrook 1991: 69–89. As Westbrook noted (1991: 63–8), levirate marriage was part of the same legal system as kinship land redemption (discussed at 1991: 58–68) and was intended to keep lands within the extended family group.

105 For a comprehensive discussion of marriage that also took into account documentation outside the law collections, see Hermann and Johns 1904: 123–40. Related topics also discussed included divorce (1904: 141–5), widows' rights (1904: 146–8), adoptions (1904: 154–60) and inheritance (1904: 161–7).

106 If the father was dead, the obligation fell to the brothers to negotiate their sister's marriage (LL 23). A marriage without parental contracts and consent was not recognized

(LE 27). However, if a widow lived with a man for two years, she was recognized as his wife, even without a contract (MAL A 34–5).

107 If a father died before securing a wife for a minor son, the bride-price was to be taken out of the estate (LH 166).

108 The dowry was forfeited if there was misconduct by the wife (LH 141–2).

109 If the wife died before having a son, the dowry reverted back to the bride's father (LH 163–4; LNB 10–11).

110 See §6 immediately following.

111 If a husband did not have sexual relations with his wife, the marriage was annulled (LH 128).

112 If his primary wife had given him children, he was not allowed to take a second wife (LH 144).

113 If she bore her master children, she could not be sold as a slave, although she could be demoted from second wife to handmaiden (LH 146). If the sons were formally acknowledged by the master, they took a share in the inheritance. Otherwise, if the husband died, the handmaiden and her children were to be freed (LH 170–1).

114 A common condition of adoption was that the adoptive father teach the son or daughter a skill.

115 In LU 9–11, there was a sliding scale of divorce payments depending on whether this was a first wife, a widow, or a widow without a formal marriage contract (who received no divorce settlement). If the husband had children by the divorced wife, he was required to provide child support (LH 137). According to MAL A 37–8, husbands could send wives away empty handed, but if she was still living in her father's house, she could keep the bride gifts.

116 If a judge found her guilty of squandering the wealth of the household, her dowry was forfeit and she could be made to serve as a slave in her husband's household; and if she had utterly neglected or ruined and abandoned her husband, she could be drowned (LH 141–3).

117 If a husband had sons by more than one wife, each would inherit a share of their mother's dowry, but all would receive equal shares of their father's estate (LH 167, 173–4).

118 If a father gave his preferred son a gift of deeded land, he was to receive this prior to the equal division of the remainder of the estate (LH 165). If a husband gave his wife deeded property, she could give it to her favorite son if the other sons did not raise a legal challenge (LH 150).

119 If the father acknowledged sons by a maidservant during his lifetime, they would share in his inheritance; otherwise they would go free along with their mother (LH 170–1).

120 MAL A 30, 43 stated that if a betrothal contract had been negotiated and the prospective groom had either died or disappeared, his brother, or a son of at least ten years of age (presumably by another marriage) could take over the betrothal contract. The intent of this law appears to have been to prevent the bridal contract from being voided (and the marriage gifts returned). HL 193 stated that if a married man died, his brother "shall take his widow as wife," and if he in turn died, his father or uncle, successively. The thrust of this law was that the obligations of taking care of the widow were inherited by the near kinsmen of the deceased. Neither law was predicated on the failure of the marriage to produce a son to act as a man's heir and to perpetuate his name, as in the biblical levirate law; cf. Westbrook 1991: 87–9; Willis 2001: 244–5.

121 Examples included chariot races in which the losing suitor would die, and by which Pelops won Hippodameia from her father Oenomaus (Apollodorus, *Epitome* 2.7; Apollonius of Rhodes, *Argonautica* 1.752–58; Pindar, *Olympian Odes* 1.87) and Idas won Marpessus from her father Evenus (Hyginus, *Fabula* 242; Apollodorus, *Library*

1.7.8; Plutarch, *Parallel Stories* 40); footraces in which the losing suitor would die, by which Melanion won Atalanta through a ploy (Hyginus, *Fabula* 185; Apollodorus, *Library* 3.9.2); the defeat of a sea monster, by which Perseus won Andromeda from her father Cepheus (Apollodorus, *Library* 2.4.3; Hyginus, *Fabula* 64; Ovid, *Metamorphoses* 4.663–752); the defeat of the Minotaur, by which Theseus won Ariadne the daughter of Minos (Plutarch, *Theseus* 29; Apollodorus, *Epitome* 1.8); and the defeat of the River-God Achelous, by which Herakles won Deianeira daughter of Oeneus (Ovid, *Metamorphoses* 9.1–100; Apollodorus, *Library* 1.8.1).

122 Athenian laws on marriage were collected at Phillips 2013: 137–73. See also Harrison 1968: 1.1–60 on Athenian marriage laws and customs.

123 No contemporary evidence exists for polygamy at Athens in the Classical period. Some later literary references that raise the possibility of Athenian polygamy were discussed and dismissed at Harrison 1968: 1.15–17; MacDowell 1978: 90. But see Crawford and Whitehead 1983: 598 on the polygamy of Philip II, the father of Alexander the Great.

124 According to Demosthenes, *Against Macartatus* 18 and Demosthenes, *Against Stephanus* 2.18, a maiden was betrothed by her father, brother or guardian *(kurios)*; cf. Arnaoutoglou 1998: 16–17.

125 For dowries at Athens, see Harrison 1968: 1.45–60; Lacey 1968: 47, 109–10; Brulé 2003: 122–3.

126 See Phillips 2013: 160–1 on charitable third party dowries.

127 Cf. Andocides, *On the Mysteries* 119. Dillon and Garland 2010: 412 recorded a decree for Athens to provide dowries for the daughters of fallen Thasian heroes.

128 Plato, *Laws* 5.742c; 6.774c-d; cf. Morrow 1993: 121. Plato may have here imitated an earlier law of Solon (but not implemented in later times) that outlawed dowries in order to end marriages for the purpose of financial gain (Plutarch, *Solon* 20.4).

129 Diogenes Laertius, *Lives of Eminent Philosophers* 2.26; cf. Lacey 1968: 105, 113; Brulé 2003: 141. Socrates was said to have taken advantage of this provision.

130 Athenian laws on inheritance were collected at Phillips 2013: 216–75.

131 Lacey 1968: 88; MacDowell 1978: 99–101. Prior to Solon, no wills were made and estates remained within the family. Solon allowed a man without a son to designate a friend as adoptive son and heir in his will (Plutarch, *Solon* 21.2). Athenian adoption of adults was common in order to put an estate under their care, since its object was to benefit the household and preserve the family name, not benefit a minor child, as is typical today. A will could provide for the division of an estate among sons or the gift of a small amount to a bastard son, but a man could not bequeath properties by will to whomever he pleased until after the Classical Era. Most wills were written, but Athenian law also allowed for an oral will with witnesses; cf. Phillips 2013: 259.

132 Chase 1933: 140–2; cf. MacDowell 1978: 101. Plato introduced an innovative law at *Laws* 11.923c-d (possibly modeled on a similar law from Sparta) whereby a single son was designated by his father to inherit the entire ancestral estate, preserving a fixed number of citizens with the means for self-support. Other sons were sent out in colonizing expeditions to other lands.

133 According to Dionysius of Halicarnassus, *Roman Antiquities* 2.26, Solon allowed a father to disinherit a son who was persistently disobedient or undutiful, but there are no known instances of disinheritance from Athens. Plato, *Laws* 11.928d-929c allowed disinheritance, accompanied by loss of citizenship, after a hearing by a family council; cf. Chase 1933: 147.

134 Lacey 1968: 116–17. See also Harrison 1968: 1.38–45 on death or divorce and unmarried women at Athens.

135 The primary and secondary evidence is extensively discussed in Harrison 1968: 1.97–121; MacDowell 1978: 93–9; Cudjoe 2000.

136 See Aristotle, *Athenian Constitution* 56.6–7 and Demosthenes, *Against Lacritus* 47–48; Demosthenes, *Against Macartatus* 18, 20, 22, 75 on the office and duties of the Archon. See Phillips 2013: 205–15 for Athenian laws on *kakosis* (maltreatment), which included sub-categories on maltreatment of parents, orphans and *epikleroi* (heiresses).

137 Plato gave considerable space to the problems of orphans and others who required guardians (Plato, *Laws* 6.766c-d; 10.909c-d; 11.922a-b, 923d-924c, 926d-928c). His legislation differed from that of Athens primarily by giving the oversight of guardianships to the *nomophylakes* or Guardians of the Laws, who replaced the Archons (including the Eponymous Archon) in his legal system.

138 Athenian laws on intestate succession and *epikleroi* were collected at Phillips 2013: 230–48.

139 The sequence of relatives is found at Isaeus, *Aristarchus* 4–5; Isaeus, *Pyrrhus* 71–4; Isaeus, *Hagnias* 1–2; Andocides, *On the Mysteries* 117–19; Demosthenes, *Against Macartatus* 51; cf. Phillips 2013: 218–19, 243–4.

140 Demosthenes, *Against Macartatus* 51, which noted that illegitimate offspring were excluded from the kinship circle for purposes of inheritance since the archonship of Eucleides (403 BCE).

141 A full explanation of Athenian inheritance laws, especially as it applied to the *epikleros,* appeared in Demosthenes, *Against Macartatus* 51, 54, 61, 75 and Isaeus, *Apollodorus* 20; cf. Plutarch, *Solon* 20.3; Harrison 1968: 1.9–12; Lacey 1968: 139–43. Similar rules of inheritance are found in the *Gortyn Law Collection;* cf. Arnaoutoglou 1998: 3–5. Heiresses at Gortyn and Sparta were known as *patrouchoi.* Literary references imply the existence of parallel practices regarding inheritance at Sparta (Herodotus, *Histories* 5.39; 6.57; 7.239).

142 Pollux, *Onomasticon* 3.33; cf. Phillips 2013: 138, 243. Inheritance of an intestate estate also required a lawsuit to prove relatedness; cf. Phillips 2013: 232.

143 In Plato, *Laws* 11.924d-925c, if no near kinsman was available, the heiress could marry any man of her choice – not necessarily within her tribe – in consultation with her guardians, so long as he was a citizen.

144 Plutarch, *Solon* 20.2–3; cf. Brulé 2003: 160. These provisions were aimed to prevent a man marrying an heiress in name only in order to gain control of her estate and to guarantee that an *epikleros* had offspring to perpetuate the family name.

145 Only rarely in Classical Greece did the father of the groom pay a bride-price, although this practice is attested for the Archaic Era in Homer's writings; cf. Harrison 1968: 1.5 n. 3.

146 Solon attempted to abolish dowries (Plutarch, *Solon* 20.4). Dowries were also outlawed at Plato, *Laws* 5.742c; 6.774c-d, cf. Chase 1933: 145.

147 The usual situation envisioned in the biblical text was for a husband to have a second wife (Gen. 25.1; 29.23–30; Deut. 21.15–17; 1 Sam. 1.2). References to multiple wives are found only at Judg. 8.30–31; 1 Kgs 11.1–3. See 2 Sam. 15.16; 16.20–22; 20.3 on David's ten concubines.

148 The kinship group was called *anchisteia* in Greek law and *mishpachah* in the biblical text.

149 In both Demosthenes, *Against Macartatus* 54 and Ruth 4.5–6, 10, if the closest relative declined to marry the heiress, the responsibility fell to the next in line within the kinship group.

150 See Chapter 2 note 131.

151 Num. 36.1–8. It is possible that the lack of an explicit provision covering this circumstance in Athenian law suggested the legal anecdote in Num. 36. Although Athenian law did not address the situation of an *epikleros* who had no close kinsmen within the *anchisteia* group to marry, Athenian inheritance law indicated that the estate would go

to the closest relative on the father's side (Demosthenes, *Against Macartatus* 51). The virtual identity of Athenian laws on inheritance and on the *epiklerate* suggests that an *epikleros* might have been required to marry the closest relative on the father's side, who would certainly be within the father's tribe or *phyle* as in the biblical statute.

152 Athenian law considered the case of a man who had no offspring but was survived by a pregnant widow (e.g. Aristotle, *Athenian Constitution* 49.7), but seemingly did not envision the possibility of a man with no offspring whose widow was not with child. It seems apparent that the man's estate would have been inherited by his next of kin, but no Athenian law that sheds light on the status of the widow has been preserved. In the biblical law, this situation is resolved by giving the widow the legal status of heiress or *epikleros*.

153 Gen. 21.14; 38.13–18; Josh. 2.1–21; 6.22–23, 25 (Rahab the harlot). Deut. 23.18 forbade a female or male prostitute's fee from being accepted in the temple, which seems to point to an uneasy toleration for this profession; cf. van der Toorn 1989. Prov. 2.16–19; 5.3–5; 7.5–27; 23.27–28, in which a son was advised to resist the charms and wiles of the prostitute, also acknowledged the profession. At Hos. 1.2, the prophet was told to take a prostitute for a wife.

154 Lev. 19.29; Deut. 23.17–18; Josh. 2.1–21. Implicit in the Deuteronomic law was a threat of disenfranchisement (revocation of citizenry) for either female or male prostitutes. Priests were forbidden from marrying a prostitute (Lev. 21.7, 14) and it was a capital crime for a priest's daughter to enter prostitution (Lev. 21.9), indicating a special level of purity. The *nokriah* or "strange woman" was a foreigner (1 Kgs 11.1; Prov. 5.20; 7.5; 23.27).

155 The terms "prostitute" *(zanah)* and "holy one" *(qadesh* or *qedeshah)* were used in parallel in Gen. 38.15, 21–22, 24; Deut. 23.17–18; Hos. 4.14, leading to an inference that the *qedeshah* was a sacred prostitute. The notion of sacred prostitution as a widespread phenomenon in the Ancient Near East was once uncontroversial, strengthening the proposition that biblical texts spoke of sacred prostitution, an argument that prominently appeared in Astour 1966: 185–96. But evidence that the Ancient Near Eastern cultic figure known as *qadistu* engaged in sacred prostitution is now considered lacking. It seems certain that the biblical *qadesh* or *qedeshah* was some sort of cultic figure, based on 1 Kgs 14.24; 15.12; 22.47; 2 Kgs 23.7, in which such figures were situated in Jerusalem's temple. But no biblical passage definitively represents a "holy one" engaged in sexual activities (prostitution), raising the possibility that they represented some other category of cult official, although this requires discounting the significance of the terms *zanah* and *qedeshah* appearing in parallel in biblical texts; cf. Fisher 1976: 225–36. On balance, the biblical tradition does appear to assert the existence of sacred prostitutes, though not beyond all doubt, and without supporting parallels taken from Ancient Near Eastern practices.

156 Although Lev. 18.18 prohibited taking two sisters as wives, Jacob married Rachel and Leah, the two daughters of Laban (Gen. 29–31).

157 See Hagedorn 2004: 240–77 on rape and adultery in Deut. 22.13–29, including a discussion of Greek parallels. Hagedorn emphasized the element of offended family honor as essential to understanding these laws in both biblical and Greek cultures, but largely overlooked the overriding concern of ensuring the legitimacy of offspring and potential heirs.

158 Prov. 6.32–35 contained advice that an angry husband would refuse a bribe, indicating that the offended party could choose payment rather than seek a death penalty, in contradiction to the Pentateuchal statute; cf. Westbrook 2009d: 248.

159 In a story found in 2 Sam. 13.1–39, Amnon the son of David lured and raped his virgin half-sister Tamar. When Absalom avenged Tamar and had Amnon slain, it was considered murder and Absalom had to flee into exile. A story with similar themes was

found in Gen. 34.1–31, where Dinah was seduced by a Shechem the son of Hamor and a marriage agreement was subsequently negotiated, but Simeon and Levi instead slew all the Shechemites.

160 This law was discussed at Willis 2001: 187–233 and Hagedorn 2004: 240–54, respectively drawing on Ancient Near Eastern and Greek parallels.

161 For secondary wives, see LL 24, 28; LNB 8; for concubines, see MAL A 40–41; for prostitutes, see LL 27, 30; MAL A 40, 49, 52; cf. §2.

162 Although Greek writers mistakenly claimed that Ancient Near Eastern (Babylonian) temples housed sacred prostitutes (Herodotus, *Histories* 1.199; Strabo, *Geography* 16.1.20), this is not supported by a reading of cuneiform sources; cf. Westenholz 1989.

163 If the son was betrothed but not married to the maiden, there was a financial penalty only, and the girl was allowed to marry whoever she pleased (LH 156).

164 Marriage contracts have been found that stipulated being thrown from a high place or killed by sword as a penalty for the bride's infidelity (Hermann and Johns 1904: 118).

165 In MAL A, an unproved accusation was punished with a heavy fine, a beating and a month's hard labor in service to the king. If it was just a husband's jealousy with no suspicion falling on a lover, the wife could be exonerated by a simple oath (LH 131).

166 See Willis 2001: 187–233 on the biblical bride accusation law with Ancient Near Eastern parallels.

167 See Westbrook 2009d: 275–83 on premarital sex.

168 See MacDowell 1978: 89; Sealey 1984 on concubines.

169 Demosthenes, *Against Neaera* 122 is often cited: "We have *hetaerae* (mistresses) for pleasure, *pallakae* (concubines) to care for our daily body's needs and *gynaekes* (wives) to bear us legitimate children and to be faithful guardians of our households." According to Athenaeus, *The Philosophers' Banquet* 12.572b, the relationship with a *hetaira* could be platonic, but other literary references show it was typically sexual. See discussion at Brulé 2003: 188–99.

170 See Dillon and Garland 2010: 433–9 for inscriptional and literary references to prostitution in Athens and the Greek world.

171 Athenian interest in regulating sexual relations was primarily restricted to preserving a wife's marital fidelity for the purpose of engendering legitimate sons to act as citizens. Other than adultery – that is to say, sleeping with another man's betrothed or wife – extramarital sexual activities of all sorts were tolerated for men, including frequenting prostitutes.

172 Athenian laws on pandering and prostitution were collected at Phillips 2013: 116–24. Prostitution had prices set by the state (Aristotle, *Athenian Constitution* 50.1–2; Hypereides, *In Defense of Euxenippus* 3) and was taxed (Aeschines, *Against Timarchus* 119).

173 Aeschines, *Against Timarchus* 13–15; Plutarch, *Solon* 23.1–2. The penalty for pimping or pandering a free boy or girl was death (Dinarchus, *Against Demosthenes* 23).

174 Aeschines, *Against Timarchus* 21; MacDowell 1978: 126; Arnaoutoglou 1998: 66.

175 See the survey of Greek and Roman literature mentioning temple prostitutes found at MacLachlan 1992; *contra* Budin 2008. Temple prostitution associated with Aphrodite is attested for Corinth, Cyprus and various ports of the western Mediterranean. Temple prostitution unrelated to Aphrodite worship is less certainly linked with various locales in Asia Minor.

176 Unwritten sacred laws were invoked against incestuous acts at Plato, *Laws* 8.838a-b.

177 Plato's *Laws* 8.838b; Plato, *Republic* 5.461b; Xenophon, *Memorabilia* 4.4.20; Euripides, *Andromeda* 173; cf. Harrison 1968: 1.22. Plato, *Laws* 8.838b listed Oedipus, Thyestes, Macareus and figures punished by the gods for incestuous relations in contemporary Greek tragedy.

178 Aristotle, *Politics* 7.1331a. See also the Macedonian inscription at Arnaoutoglou 1998: 117–23, which segregated the boys from older athletes and which also disallowed drunken or insane individuals from stripping at the gymnasium. Students were always supervised by the *gymnasiarch* or his assistants.

179 See note 174.

180 Plato, *Laws* 1.636b-e; 8.835d-842a; cf. Chase 1933: 183. Yet Plato, *Republic* 5.468b-c said that heroes in battle should have their pick of any maiden or youth they chose. Further, Plato, *Laws* 8.841c-e acknowledged that both adultery and homosexual relations were inevitable, given the difficulty of resisting such passions. Plato therefore gave a "second law" that such forbidden relations should at least be conducted discreetly, at the risk of public censure.

181 Athenian laws on sexual offenses were collected at Phillips 2013: 102–23. The primary concern in adultery laws at Athens was that infidelity by the wife or betrothed might introduce a bastard into the line of succession. See Lysias, *On the Murder of Eratosthenes* 33; cf. Harrison 1968: 1.32; Lacey 1968: 113; and *contra* Hagedorn 2004: 260–7, who considered the issue to primarily one of family honor, although this may have been a secondary consideration. Note that according to Plutarch, *Lycurgus* 15.10, there was no such thing as adultery in Sparta, because of fundamental differences from Athens in their political and marital institutions; cf. Lacey 1968: 264.

182 Harrison 1968: 1.32 n. 5 noted that although male marital infidelity was allowed, the husband was legally obligated to cohabit with his wife. Plato's exclusion of heterosexual sexual relations by a man outside of marriage applied only to relations with noble and freeborn women (Plato, *Laws* 8.841d); sexual relations with servant girls and foreign women, including prostitutes, were seemingly permitted though discouraged, and Plato conceded that adulterous affairs were inevitable, but should be conducted discreetly (Plato, *Laws* 8.840c-842a).

183 Slave girls and prostitutes were expressly exempted in Athenian laws regarding adultery according to Demosthenes, *Against Neaera* 67.

184 The exemption for the justified slaying of an adulterer was found in Drakon's homicide law and retained in Solon's laws. See Demosthenes, *Against Aristocrates* 53; Lysias, *On the Murder of Eratosthenes* 32, 47; Plutarch, *Solon* 23.1; cf. Harrison 1968: 1.13; Lacey 1968: 69, 130. Slaying an adulterer caught in the act entailed a certain amount of legal risk unless there were corroborating witnesses, as illustrated by Lysias, *On the Murder of Eratosthenes* 6–10, where the relatives of the adulterer accused the husband of premeditated homicide and entrapment. In Plato, *Laws* 9.874c, slaying a man caught *in flagrante* was deemed justifiable homicide only in the instance of forcible rape. Contrary to contemporary Athenian practices, adultery was treated as a relatively minor offense in *Laws*.

185 Harrison 1968: 1.33; Phillips 2013: 106–7. Acts of humiliation perpetrated on a seducer *(moichos)* were not subject to prosecution under Athenian *hubris* laws. For monetary payments as a penalty for adultery, see Lysias, *On the Murder of Eratosthenes* 25; Demosthenes, *Against Neaera* 64.

186 Euripides, *Trojan Women* 1030–2, 1039–41. A fragment of Aristotle quoted a law from Tenedos whereby the adulteress could not be slain unless the adulterer was as well; cf. Hagedorn 2004: 263.

187 "[Solon] does not permit the woman with whom a seducer is caught to adorn herself or attend public sacred rites, in order that she not mingle with and corrupt blameless women. And if she does attend or adorn herself, he commands anyone who encounters her to tear her clothing, remove her adornment, and beat her, with the restriction that he does not kill or maim her. Thereby Solon inflicts dishonor upon such a woman and makes her life unlivable." Aeschines, *Against Timarchus* 183; cf. Demosthenes, *Against Neaera* 87.

188 According to Plutarch, *Solon* 23.1, the adulterer could be killed, but a rapist was only fined. For a discussion of rape laws, see Harrison 1968: 1.32–36.

189 See the ancient passages and modern discussions cited at Hagedorn 2004: 261, 265. Gortyn's laws were explicit in situating the crime of adultery inside the home of the husband or a close relative; cf. 2004: 258, 268.

190 See Hagedorn 2004: 255–9; Dillon and Garland 2010: 403 for laws on rape and adultery at Gortyn, where a sliding scale of monetary penalties was specified according to the status of both the perpetrator and the victim. Neither rape nor adultery were capital matters at Gortyn.

191 Demosthenes, *Against Neaera* 71 provides the only direct evidence for such negotiations in Classical Athens, owing to the settlement of this case by legal arbitration.

192 The Athenian law regarding the case of the seduced virgin has not been discovered in inscriptions or contemporary oratory. Evidence for settlement of cases involving a violated virgin mainly comes from later literary sources, where the seducer was legally required to marry the seduced virgin, but this evidence is not decisive regarding earlier periods. See Scafuro 2004: 193–231 for sexual crimes in Greek and Roman law, and 232–78 for the resolution of such cases in New Comedy, especially 241–3, which lists passages that claimed a seducer or rapist was legally compelled to marry the victim. The seduced virgin was not treated in Plato's *Laws*.

193 Assistance to poorer Athenian citizens in the form of dowries for their daughters (Demosthenes, *Against Neaera* 113; Lysias, *On the Property of Aristophanes* 59) was likely aimed at keeping them from a life of prostitution, and most female prostitutes in Athens were either foreigners or slaves. Nevertheless, it appears certain that some female prostitutes in Athens were free citizens (Demosthenes, *Against Androtion* 61; Demosthenes, *Against Neaera* 36). At Plutarch, *Solon* 23.1–2, a law attributed to Solon stated, "No man is allowed to sell a daughter or a sister, unless he finds that she is no longer a virgin." This law, which seemingly conflicted with Solon's abolishing all slavery of Athenians, was convincingly argued to refer to selling a maiden's sexual favors at Glazebrook 2006. Both disgraced adulteresses and non-virgins were stripped of the usual citizen protections and vulnerable to being driven into prostitution either by necessity or by their relations.

194 See Hagedorn 2004: 267–76, on comparisons of rape and adultery in the Greek, Ancient Near Eastern and biblical worlds.

195 See Chirichigno 1993: 145–85 on biblical laws dealing with chattel slavery and debt slavery.

196 After successively considering the manumission laws in Exodus, Deuteronomy and Leviticus, Chirichigno proposed that the six year release applied only to the debt slavery of dependent members of a household, whereas the jubilee year represented a higher degree of insolvency that involved the debt slavery of the head of household and the loss of ancestral lands (Chirichigno 1993: 352). His harmonizing of the manumission and land redemption laws does not appear to have explicit support in the texts.

197 Cf. Matthews 1994: 132–4. According to Matthews, the sale of a daughter was a way for a father to obtain her marriage without a dowry.

198 It is debated whether this statute referred to chattel slaves or debt slaves (Chirichigno 1993: 149–85).

199 Chirichigno 1993: 30–54; Matthews 1994: 121–4; Westbrook 2009c: 172–81. Repudiating one's parents resulted in enslavement (SLEx 4'), and the palace official who failed to report a craftsman flirting with a member of the harem was disfigured and had his sons enslaved (MAPD 5). A judge could reduce a wife who financially ruined her husband to a slave in his household (LH 141).

200 Chirichigno 1993: 49 classified Ancient Near Eastern society into free individuals who owned the means of production, such as priests, officials, nobility, merchants and land-owning families; the semi-free who worked in temples or the palace; debt slaves who had hope of redemption; and chattel slaves.

201 See Chirichigno 1993: 55–100 on laws relating to debt slavery in Mesopotamia; 1993: 127 on the typical sequence of loans and defaults ending in slavery.

202 Westbrook 2009c: 181–97. Westbrook also discussed freedom from famine slavery after the conditions of famine were over (cf. HL 172).

203 As noted at Berman 2008: 104–7, Mesopotamian measures of social relief were "not enshrined in law but effected by royal decree."

204 For *misarum* edicts incorporated into Ancient Near Eastern law collections, see Finkelstein 1961: 100–4; Yaron 1969: 121–6, 292–4; cf. Weinfeld 1995: 29–30 on references in *misarum* edicts in the prologue and epilogue of LH. LH 117 is best understood as a scribal excerpt from one of Hammurabi's *misarum* edicts that was intended only for those currently in servitude at the time the edict was published. LH 117 contains several features that are directly comparable to *Ammisaduqu Edict* 20–1, as discussed at Chirichigno 1993: 87–91, strengthening the likelihood that LH 117 quoted from a *misarum* decree of Hammurabi. Unfortunately the text of such decrees have not come down to us, but Hammurabi is known to have issued *misarum* edicts in the first, twelfth, twentieth and thirtieth years of his reign (Chirichigno 1993: 86 n. 2), and LH 117 could have been abstracted from any one of these.

205 This is clear from *Ammisaduqu Edict* 20–1; cf. Finkelstein 1961: 101.

206 See Westbrook 2009c: 204–14, on the treatment of slaves in the Ancient Near East.

207 See Dillon and Garland 2010: 325–53 for ancient sources on slavery in the Greek world. Imported slaves usually originated as war-captives, although piracy could result in the enslavement of seized individuals who were ransomed by relatives. In some Greek states, the invasion of territory in antiquity and subjugation of the local population led to the creation of a slave class. The most famous examples of this type were the Helot slave class that originated with the Spartan conquest of Lakonia and Messenia in Greece and the subjugated barbarian Mariandynoi of Herakleia in Asia Minor; cf. Crawford and Whitehead 1983: 295.

208 The poorest economic class, the *thetes,* is thought to have formed a special class of tenant farmers known in archaic times as the *pelatai* (clients) or *hektemoroi* (sixth-partners), who paid their oligarchic creditors one-sixth of the produce of lands they had once owned; cf. *Athenian Constitution* 2, 10; Plutarch, *Solon* 13.2; Rhodes 1993: 90–1, 153.

209 One aspect of the canceling of debts was the return of lands to tenant farmers of the *hektemoroi* class who had been the original owners of the small land parcels before falling into debt to the wealthy oligarchs. This appears to have been alluded to in Solon's poems in which he claimed that he "took away the boundary-stones *(horoi)* planted everywhere" and "freed the Earth" (Plutarch, *Solon* 15.5); *horoi* recorded liens on mortgaged lands.

210 As Aristotle phrased it, Solon, by abolishing debt slavery, "liberated the people, both immediately and for all time" (*Athenian Constitution* 6.1).

211 See generally Rosivach 1999. Plato, *Republic* 5.469c articulated the ideal that Greeks should neither enslave fellow-Greeks nor raze their cities. See Aristotle, *Politics* 1.1253b-1255b on the Greek notion of the *barbaroi* as "slaves by nature."

212 Herodotus (*Histories* 8.144) defined Greeks as possessing common ancestry, language, religious practices and customs, but identification of specific groups as Greek often served as a rhetorical strategy in connection with international political debate. See, for instance, the essays in Malkin 2001.

213 See Rosivach 1999: 131–2 for a catalog of thirty-seven Greek cities whose populations were enslaved by the Athenians in the Classical Era. In many instances, when a
Greek city resisted and was conquered, all its men of military age were killed and the
women and children taken as slaves. Because they no longer belonged to an *oikos,*
the Greek ancestry of these slaves was effectively erased (1999: 140–1). Starting with
Philip of Macedon, Greek men from conquered cities were also sold as slaves (1999:
133–5).

214 Lysias, *Against Agoratus* 67; cf. Dillon and Garland 2010: 325. Legal protections for
slaves under Athenian law were summarized at Phillips 2013: 24.

215 See Scafuro 2004: 400–9 for remedies for enslavement and kidnapping in ancient
Athens and Rome. Although all three remedies were theoretically available, only *apagoge* is attested in legal cases. The laws regarding freeing of slaves at Plato, *Laws*
11.914e-915a generally accord with Athenian practices.

216 The offspring of a free woman with a slave also remained the possession of the slave's
master. The driving concern in Plato's *Laws* appears to have been to prevent the offspring of slaves acquiring citizen rights in the *polis.*

217 Plutarch, *Theseus* 36; cf. MacDowell 1978: 81; Naiden 2004: 73. The Sanctuary of
Demeter at Andania was another traditional refuge for slaves (Naiden 2004: 79). In
Egypt, the Temple of Herakles was an asylum for escaped slaves (Herodotus, *Histo-
ries* 2.13; cf. Weinfeld 1995: 122).

218 Cf. Eusebius, *Preparation for the Gospel* 12.37, in which the Mosaic law against
enslaving fellow-Hebrews was compared with the principle that Greeks should not
enslave Greeks at Plato, *Republic* 5.469c.

219 Contrasts between biblical and Ancient Near Eastern debt release and manumission
were discussed at Berman 2008: 101–7. The Ancient Near Eastern model of "righteousness and justice" as a royal responsibility to be implemented by means of sporadic royal decrees that gave limited relief in times of economic crisis is reflected
in the biblical Prophets but not the Pentateuch. See Weinfeld 1995: 45–96 on the
association of "righteousness and justice" by means of royal decrees of liberation and
economic relief in the Ancient Near East and in the depiction of Messianic (Davidic)
kingship in the Prophets.

220 At Deut. 14.29; 26.12–13, provisions were made to set aside the tithe every third year
for the care of destitute widows, orphans and strangers; and at Deut. 16.11, 14 for
their share in holy festivities. Deut. 24.17 proscribed taking a widow's garments as a
pledge. The Covenant Code contained no such social legislation.

221 Ex. 21.17; Lev. 20.9; Deut. 27.16. The oppression of (aged) parents was condemned
at Jer. 7.6.

222 Mic. 2.1–2 condemned those who coveted a man's ancestral fields and houses and
schemed to seize them.

223 Lev. 25.25, 29, 35–49; Deut. 15.7–11. The kinsman redeemer also figured prominently in Ruth 2.20; 3.9, 12–13; 4.1–10, 14. The book novelized the plight of the
widow and poor and the role of the charitable kinsman in their relief.

224 LU prologue (A 4.162–68; C 2.30–39); LH epilogue (47.59–78). For a discussion of
conception of social justice as protection of the weak, see Fensham 1991: 176–92;
Weinfeld 1995: 7–11; Westbrook 2009b: 143–60.

225 Westbrook 1991: 44–8; Weinfeld 1995: 75–96; Berman 2008: 104–7. *Misarum*
decrees are known to have been proclaimed in Rim-Sin of Larsa's years 26, 35 and
41, Hammurabi's years 1, 12, 20 and 33, Ammi-ditana's years 1 and 20, and Ammisaduqa's years 1 and 10 (Westbrook 1991: 45). The most extensively preserved *misarum* edict was that of Ammisaduqa.

226 See Chirichigno 1993: 89–90 on the limited duration and geographical scope of
the Ammisaduqu Edict. Given that Chirichigno saw LH 117 as a by-product of

Hammurabi's *misarum* edicts (1993: 60, 194) and recognized extensive parallels with the one-time *misarum* edict of Hammurabi's successor, Ammisaduqu (1993: 87–91), it is difficult to accept Chirichigno's unsupported claims that LH 117 stipulated the "periodic" release of debt slaves or that it was "meant to be administered throughout Babylonia" (Chirichigno 1993: 87, 89, 90, 99).

227 See Plato, *Laws* 9.881d; 11.932a-d; 927b-e, 928b-c on legislation related to widows, orphans and strangers. See Plato, *Laws* 11.929d-e on the mentally infirm.

228 Pisistratos enacted the law that provided for the public support of men disabled in war (Plutarch, *Solon* 31.3; cf. Stanton 1990: 109–10). For the scrutiny of the disabled, see Aristotle, *Athenian Constitution* 49.4.

229 The power of any citizen to initiate a legal action on behalf of any fellow-citizen was one of Solon's most important reforms (Aristotle, *Athenian Constitution* 9.1), one which especially benefitted minors, the infirm, and others with a tenuous legal or financial status.

230 Aristotle, *Athenian Constitution* 13; Plutarch, *Solon* 19.1–5; cf. Stanton 1990: 87–91. Greek acts of debt relief *(philanthropia)* often took place at the outset of a reign. Debt relief measures at Sparta at the outset of a new king's reign (Herodotus, *Histories* 6.59) were said to have been politically motivated (Plutarch, *Agis and Cleomenes* 7.7). Canceling debts and redistributing property, though a relief to the poorer citizens and a popular proposal among demagogues, were considered dangerous and socially disruptive by most Greek political theorists (cf. Plato, *Laws* 3.684d-e). See generally Weinfeld 1995: 145–9; Berman 2008: 98–9.

231 Plato, *Laws* 5.740a-741c. The laws at Locri and on the island of Leucas prevented the sale of family estates except under extreme circumstances proven before a court of law; cf. Aristotle, *Politics* 2.1266b. Forfeiture of citizenship and property for crimes such as treason or impiety formed an exception to such laws.

232 A redistribution of land to make all Athenian citizens equal landowners was contemplated at the time of Solon's reforms. But Solon rejected this proposed measure and steered a middle ground between the interests of the landless *thetes* class who called for this reform and the wealthy oligarchs. The compromise Solon effected by cancellation of all existing debts quelled the social unrest that had put Athens into its constitutional crisis, but neither group was happy with his reforms; cf. Plutarch, *Solon* 15.1–2; 16.1–4.

233 On the 10% (or possibly 5%) tax on agriculture initiated by Pisistratus, see Aristotle, *Athenian Constitution* 16.4; Herodotus, *Histories* 1.64.1; Thucydides, *Peloponnesian War* 6.54.5; cf. Stanton 1990: 106–9.

234 See Aristotle, *Politics* 6.1320a-b on revenues distributed among the poor and payment by the rich for the poor to attend public assemblies.

235 "Share the load of the unfortunate" (Sosiades, *The Commandments of the Seven Sages* 135).

236 "The people, realizing that it is impossible for each of the poor to offer sacrifices, hold banquets, set up shrines and govern a great and beautiful city, have discovered a way of having sacrifices, shrines, festivals and sacrifices. So the city sacrifices numerous victims at public expense, but it is the people who banquet and who are allocated the victims." Pseudo-Xenophon, *Athenian Constitution* 2.9; cf. Plato, *Laws* 2.653d. In ca. 360 BCE, a law proposed by Eubolos established (or perhaps expanded) the Theoric Fund (the *theorikon*) to allow poorer Athenians to attend the City Dionysia and pay the fee to attend theater performances; cf. Nightingale 2004: 50–1. For festival attendance as a communal expression of Athenian democratic values, see Monoson 2000: 88–110.

237 Cf. Gen. 9.5–6, where the execution was the penalty for bloodshed, whether the perpetrator was man or beast.

238 If the owner of a stray animal was unknown, the finder delivered the animal to the village elders or the king's palace for safekeeping or could be charged as a thief (HL 71). Officials who kept impounded stray animals or escaped slaves for over a month could be charged by the palace as a thief (LE 50). A stray ox that was found feeding in a neighbor's corral was not considered stolen (HL 66). A farmer could hitch up a stray ox to the plow until nightfall before returning it (HL 79). If a rented ox strayed and was not found, the renter had to replace it (SLEx 10').

239 LH 8; SLHF 3.13–15; MAL C 5–6, 8; MAL F 1; HL 57–70, 81–5, 119–20; cf. Paul 1970: 85–6. Corporal punishment as a penalty for animal theft appeared at MAL F 2. For the unauthorized sale of pledged animals, see MAL C 4. For the theft of livestock feed, see LH 253–54. Slain animals found on a neighbor's property were presumed stolen unless the neighbor had informed the owner (HL 72, 86).

240 LH 244–9, 263, 266–7; LL 33–8; LOx 1–9; SLEx 9'–10'; SLHF 6.11–36; LE 53; HL 43, 74–8, 80; cf. Paul 1970: 92–6. Compensation was given for slain herd, hunting or guard dogs, unless it could be proven that they had eaten the neighbor's lard (HL 87–90).

241 The literature on the goring ox is extensive. See Paul 1970: 78–85; Finkelstein 1981: 1–89; Malul 1990: 114–16, 134, 147–8; Van Seters 2003: 120–1; Wright 2009: 40–1.

242 No prosecution took place for a death that occurred during a public competition, in which the participants accepted the risks, or for a death by a lightning bolt. See Chase 1933: 177 on the influence of Athenian law on the trial of animals and lifeless objects in Plato's *Laws*.

243 Demosthenes, *Against Aristocrates* 76; Aeschines, *Against Ctesiphon* 244: Aristotle, *Athenian Constitution* 57.4; Pollux, *Onomasticon* 8.120. See also MacDowell 1963: 85–9; MacDowell 1978: 117–18; Finkelstein 1981: 58–9; Katz 1993: 155–78.

244 Solon's law on damage caused by animals was found at Plutarch, *Solon* 24.3. Compensation for property damage caused by animals was found at Plato, *Laws* 11.936e.

245 Evidence for a direct literary dependence of Ex. 21.28–32 on LH 250–2 and LE 53–5 was discussed at Yaron 1969: 193; Paul 1970: 78–85; Finkelstein 1981: 19–20; Malul 1990: 114–16, 134, 147–8; Van Seters 2003: 121–2; Wright 2009: 40–1; .

246 Paul 1970: 28–32; Finkelstein 1981: 26, 57–8; Malul 1990: 118, 148–52; Katz 1993: 163–4. According to Paul 1970: 169–71, the guilt attached to the homicidal animal rendered it unfit for sacrifice and thus unsuitable for human consumption. Note the stoning of animals that strayed onto the holy mount at Ex. 19.12–13. The identical penalty of stoning applied against the goring ox suggests that this crime involved a comparable (though less literal) transgression of a divine boundary.

247 The ancient myth of the vengeful spirit was invoked at Plato, *Laws* 9.865d-e, 870d-e.

248 The idea in Athenian law that blood-guilt could attach to an inanimate object, such as an axe, a javelin, a fallen beam or a statue, has legal affinities to the statute at Deut. 22.8, where parapets or balustrades for houses were mandated so that someone would not fall to the death and blood-guilt attach to the house.

249 The punishment of the ox was considered a later legal development at Malul 1990: 148–52. A comparison between the Law of the Goring Ox and Plato, *Laws* 9.873d was already made at Eusebius, *Preparation for the Gospel* 12.42. The stoning of the ox in the Covenant Code arguably echoes Plato's *Laws*. Although neither Athenian law nor Plato's *Laws* specified stoning as the method of execution for the condemned animal, stoning by the community was the form of capital penalty specified at Plato, *Laws* 9.873b-c; cf. note 60 on stoning in the Greek world.

250 Slanski 2000, 2003. Egyptian surveyors set up new boundary stones on a yearly basis after the inundation of the Nile (cf. Herodotus, *Histories* 2.109; Strabo, *Geography* 17.1.3) and Egyptian literature contained several references to the crime of moving

these boundary stones. See Lyons 1926: 242–4; Berger 1934. But the agricultural context in Egypt was markedly different from the biblical lands and it is difficult to see an otherwise-isolated Egyptian influence in the Deuteronomic provisions on boundary stones.

251 See Paul 1970: 87–8, 104 for illegal grazing and setting fires. Penalties for accidental fires that affected structures appear at HL 98–100. Encroaching on a neighbor's property with building structures, wells and brick-making operations incurred financial penalties, beatings and forced labor for the king (MAL B 10, 14–15).

252 The procedure for buying land involved public announcements in the city of the buyer's intention to purchase the parcel, in case it had existing liens (MAL B 6). LNB 5 dealt with proxy purchases without a contract that authorized the agent to act as the buyer's agent.

253 Athenian laws on property damage were collected at Phillips 2013: 286–331.

254 Phillips 2013: 286–7. The prosecutor assessed his own damages and proposed a figure for the judges.

255 The deity invoked at Plato, *Laws* 8.842e was "Zeus the God of Boundaries." Some boundary stone inscriptions contained curses against those who removed them. One interesting Attic inscription recorded the involvement of the *Archon Basileus*, the Kerykes and the Eumolpidae in resolving a boundary dispute for a sacred *temenos* in 352/351 BCE that arose out of claims that the boundary stones had been moved (Rhodes and Osborne 2003: 273–81, especially line 74). The later Romans had boundary laws similar to the Greeks and even had a sacred festival dedicated to their god of boundaries (cf. Ovid, *Fasti* 2.60). See Plutarch, *Numa* 16.1; Dionysius of Halicarnassus, *Roman Antiquities* 2.74 on one who was slain for having moved the stones sacred to Jupiter Terminus.

256 Tillyard 1904. A territorial boundary stone inscription was quoted at Plutarch, *Theseus* 25: "This is not Peloponnesus, but Ionia; This is not Ionia but Peloponnesus." Boundary stones *(horoi)* were the norm in Attica prior to the third century BCE, because mortgages not publicly recorded. They became less common after it became customary to register deeds, mortgages and land transfers in the Athenian public archives. See Posner 1972: 93, 110.

257 The legal parallel was noted in Eusebius, *Preparation for the Gospel* 12.38; cf. Wajdenbaum 2011: 163.

258 Cf. Wajdenbaum 2011: 203–4. Eusebius (*Preparation for the Gospel* 13.21) considered the biblical law more magnanimous, because a slave who ate premium grapes or fig was liable to a beating in *Laws*.

259 Reich 1990. The discovery of a twelfth boundary stone at Tel Gezer was discussed at Reich and Greenhut 2002. Press releases from summer of 2012 announced a thirteenth such stone.

260 Interest and borrowing was discussed at Berman 2008: 96–8.

261 An ephah was ten omers (Ex. 16.36). A shekel was twenty gerahs (Ex. 30.13; Lev. 27.25, Num. 3.47).

262 The use of scales was mentioned at Isa. 40.12; Job 31.6. Monetary sums in biblical texts were usually specified by metal and weight (Gen. 23.16; 43.21; Jer. 32.9). Whether some narratives anachronistically referred to coinage need not be discussed here.

263 For a discussion of economic matters that also brings in other cuneiform textual evidence, see Hermann and Johns 1904: 227–49 (sales contracts), 250–61 (loans), 262–70 (pledges and loan guarantees, such as silver, persons, land and houses) and 271–4 (fixed wage rates).

264 Athenian laws on contracts and commerce were collected at Phillips 2013: 370–406. Athenian law recognized and enforced "voluntary obligations" (discussed at Aristotle,

Nicomachian Ethics 5.1131a) or contracts, which included sales, hires, loans, pledges and business partnerships.

265 Aristotle, *Athenian Constitution* 10.1–2; cf. Rhodes 1993: 152. Solon alleviated debts and interest rates by means of increasing the measures and the value of money (Plutarch, *Solon* 15.2–5, drawing on Androtion; cf. Stanton 1990: 63–4, no. 37).

266 Aristotle, *Athenian Constitution* 51; cf. MacDowell 1978: 158. Ten *metronomoi* were appointed by lot, five for the marketplace in Athens and five for the harbor at Piraeus.

267 Xenophon, *Hellenica* 6.1.11; Demosthenes, *On the Crown* 87; Demosthenes, *Against Leptines* 30. Except for olive oil, it was illegal to export any agricultural product from Attica (Plutarch, *Solon* 24).

268 Importers *(emporoi)* brought grain shipments to Piraeus, the port controlled by Athens: it was a capital offense to ship grain to any harbor or to transport it elsewhere than Athens (Demosthenes, *Against Timocrates* 136; Demosthenes, *Against Phormio* 37, Demosthenes, *Against Lacritus* 50–4; Demosthenes, *Against Dionysidorus* 5–6, 10–11). The overseers *(epimeletai)* of the import market at Piraeus ensured that at least two thirds of the offloaded grain was sold immediately to the grain buyers *(sitopoloi)* instead of being stored for later sale at a higher price (Aristotle, *Athenian Constitution* 51.4).

269 The law with detailed commentary is found in Stroud 1998. In 388 BCE, a scandal arose when importers and grain buyers were accused of having colluded with the Guardians of the Grain to hoard grain supplies and artificially elevate prices during a grain shortage. This led to a capital case in 386 BCE whose details are known primarily through the forensic speech preserved in Lysias, *Against the Grain Dealers*. A detailed discussion of the case is found at Figueira 1986. These events may have played into the decision by the Assembly in 374/373 BCE to determine prices for publicly acquired grain themselves. In 329/328 BCE the Assembly set up similar rules for the sale of excess grain entering Eleusis.

270 This is explicit in the legislation on grain harvests at Plato, *Laws* 8.848a.

271 Cleomenes of Naucratis, the nomarch of the Arabian district under Alexander the Great, and builder of Alexandria, first established the grain monopoly, and was tried for buying up Egyptian grain and fixing the sale price for export to Athens (cf. Demosthenes, *Against Dionysodorus* 7–10; Pseudo-Aristotle, *Economics* 2.33). The first Ptolemies inherited and perpetuated control of the grain trade, establishing a system whereby the agricultural "corn-tax" on harvested grain was immediately collected in royal storehouses *(thesauroi)* from which the corn-collectors *(sitologoi)* sent them by canal-boats to Alexandria for sale and export or for redistribution in Egypt as rations.

272 A conflicting law of spoil attributed to David is found at 1 Sam. 30.21–25.

273 Hermann and Johns 1904: 78, 173, 201–7. Land owners were also assessed for military expenses. Under the Hittites, land tenure also required providing soldiers for the military and other royal obligations (HL 39–42, 46–56, 112).

274 Similar provisions were also found in the lengthy section on military law at Plato, *Laws* 12.942b-945b.

275 Lysias, *Against Alcibiades* 1.5; 2.1–4; Andocides, *On the Mysteries* 74; Hamel 1998: 63. See Plato, *Laws* 12.943a-d on military courts, desertion and cowardice.

276 The Greek city of Mytilene was almost annihilated (Thucydides, *Peloponnesian War* 3.28.1; 3.36–48; 3.49.2); cf. Hamel 1998: 54. For the razing of Olynthus, Porthmos, Thebes and other cities by Philip of Macedon, see Connor 1985: 98 and note 50.

277 For examples, which were especially common in Macedonian military campaigns, see Chapter 5 note 72.

278 Hagedorn 2004: 172–99 categorized the citizen army and command structure of Deuteronomy as "hoplite warfare" and compared it with that found in the Greek world. He

noted Greek parallels to "fear in battle as a danger to one's fellow warrior" (Euripides, *The Madness of Herakles* 189–94; cf. Deut. 20.8) and to the exhortation speech before battle (Thucydides, *Peloponnesian War* 4.126.1; cf. Deut. 20.1–4).

279 This law was invoked at 1 Kgs 21.10, 13, where false witnesses testified that "Naboth blasphemed God and the king."

280 Cursing one's parents also carried a death penalty (Ex. 21.17). This crime was also a serious offense against the social order and, indeed, one's parents stood very close to God as worthy of honor as a giver of life (cf. Ex. 20.12). At Deut. 21.18–22, the rebellious son was to be executed at the city gates by stoning.

281 This is historically illustrated at 2 Macc. 5.5, where a false report about the death of Antiochus IV Epiphanes in Egypt in 169 BCE led to a Judean revolt, with disastrous consequences for the Jews.

282 The intercession of Moses with God to save the children of Israel was a recurring theme that masked the death penalty deserved by the rebels in the wilderness. When Joshua later took over command of the children of Israel as the "Prophet like Moses," it became a capital crime to rebel against his command as it was with Moses (Josh. 1.17–18). Korah's rebellion (Num. 16–17) represents one episode where the death penalty against rebels was fully exacted.

283 See Isa. 23.5; Jer. 49.23–24 on the demoralizing effect of evil tidings.

284 Although honest judges who refused a gift were praised (Ex. 18.21; Deut. 10.17–18; 16.19; 1 Sam. 12.3; Ps. 15.5; Isa. 33.15) and judges who took gifts were condemned (Ex. 23.6–8; 1 Sam. 8.3; Ps. 26.6–10; Prov. 17.23; Job 36.17–19; Amos 5.12; Isa. 1.23; Ezek. 22.12), the Hebrew Bible contained no statutory penalty for judges or other officials who took bribes nor did biblical narratives include stories in which corrupt judges were punished, although some passages advocated bribery in various social situations (Prov. 17.8; 18.16; 21.14). This ambivalence toward bribery and lack of criminal penalties for bribery is remarkable in light of the acknowledgment of the role of bribery in judicial murders (Ex. 23.6–8; 1 Kgs 21.8–14; Ps. 26.6–10; Ezek. 22.12). See the comprehensive discussion of bribery in the biblical text at Noonan 1984: 14–30. Instead of blaming miscarriages of justice on judicial corruption and bribe-taking, biblical legal passages focus exclusively on the culpability of false witnesses (Ex. 20.16; Deut. 5.20; 19.15–21; 1 Kgs 21.8–14).

285 Capital crimes in Deuteronomy were surveyed and analyzed at Stulman 1990. Stulman concluded that Deuteronomy was exclusively concerned with threats to the social order by dangerous groups and individuals within the national borders that he called "indigenous outsiders," whose positions of influence potentially allowed them to incite the people into anomalous or heterodox behaviors (1990: 632).

286 The ones casting the stones were identified as the people of the land (Lev. 20.2), the congregation (Lev. 24.14; Num. 35–36), all the people (Deut. 13.9–10; 17.7), the men of the city (Deut. 21.21; 22.21) or all Israel (Josh. 7.25). The stoning was to be initiated by the accusing witnesses (Deut. 13.9; 17.7). Stoning of Joshua and Caleb by the congregation was narrowly averted at Num. 14.10.

287 See Levinson 1998: 98–143 for a discussion of theories on the nature of the literary relationship between the apostasy laws in Deut. 13 and 17.

288 Weinfeld 1972: 99 noted that identical language was used at VTE 502 to describe political subversion. The same phrase was used at Jer. 28.16; 29.32 as a stock phrase to condemn Jeremiah's enemies the prophets Hananiah b. Azur and Shemaiah the Nehelemite.

289 "Neither shall your eye pity him, neither shall you spare him." This language is always directly associated with an act of violence, especially in a judicial setting, where it often attached to the execution of a death sentence; cf. Deut. 7.16; 13.8; 19.13, 21; 25.12; Isa. 13.18; Jer. 13.14; 21.7.

290 For the use of informers in biblical judicial proceedings, see Westbrook 1991: 10; Wells 2004: 92.

291 Other forms of forbidden speech included insolence by a slave (LU 25) and blasphemies or disgraceful talk by a man's wife or daughter (MAL A 2).

292 Athenian laws on treason, subversion, bribery and deceiving the people were collected at Phillips 2013: 463–508.

293 Harrison 1968: 2.53–54. The version of the law of impeachment found at Hypereides, *Against Athenogenes* 8 and Hypereides, *In Defense of Euxenippus* 7–8 was written between 330 and 324 BCE.

294 MacDowell 1978: 184; cf. Plato, *Laws* 9.856b-857a, which listed the three categories of individuals chargeable with treason as "the traitor, the temple-robber, and the man who wrecks the State laws by violence." The remarkable joining of sacrilege and treason under the same Athenian law, subject to the same penalty of death, received comment at Xenophon, *Hellenica* 1.7.22 and Thucydides, *Peloponnesian War* 1.138; cf. Chase 1933: 166; Harrison 1968: 2.59; MacDowell 1978: 176 (which noted the legal unity of sacrilege and treason in Plato's *Laws*).

295 For a discussion of *eisangelia*, see Harrison 1968: 2.50–59; Rhodes 1972: 162–70; MacDowell 1978: 183–6; Morrow 1993: 264–70.

296 Pisistratos posed as the champion of the masses and with their initial support established sole rule as tyrant from 605 to 527 BCE. His policies of imperial expansion led to a period of unprecedented wealth in Athens and he was mostly popular in his time, but subsequent rule by his warring sons was unpopular and their overthrow in 510 BCE led to the democratic reforms of Kleisthenes. After democratic control of Athens during the Peloponnesian War led to disastrous military defeats, the oligarchic revolution of 411 BCE claimed to restore competent leadership to Athens, but led to a huge bloodletting of the opposition in quasi-judicial and extra-judicial executions. Democracy was again restored, but defeat by the Spartans in 404 BCE led to a return to oligarchic rule in the form of the Thirty Tyrants. Their democratic overthrow led to a renewed hatred of tyranny and the restoration of the constitution and laws of Solon that formed the basis for Athenian government in the time of Plato and Aristotle.

297 Andocides, *On the Mysteries* 96–8, where the Law of Demophantos is quoted in full.

298 See Podlecki 1966: 129–41; Monoson 2000: 21–50; Dillon and Garland 2010: 119–21. See also Aristotle, *Politics* 2.1267a on the great honor bestowed on tyrannicides.

299 The text may be found at Arnaoutoglou 1998: 75–6.

300 MacDowell 1978: 139. Euxenippus was tried for accepting bribes to make a false report to the Assembly in the 320s BCE (Hypereides, *In Defense of Euxenippus* 3).

301 Cf. Plato, *Laws* 12.941a-b, and also 12.955b-c, which called for the death penalty for any citizen who entered into private negotiations for peace or war with a foreign power.

302 The connection between bribery and treason was explicit at Demosthenes, *On the False Embassy* 268. Treason cases that involved bribery included Ergocles in 389 BCE, Thrasybulus in 388 BCE, and the losing generals of the battle of Embata in 356 BCE.

303 Bribery prosecution procedures included four types of public lawsuits *(graphai)* covering bribing a witness, bribing a jury, and bribery in general; *eisangelia* for impeaching a serving magistrate; the *euthyna* or audit at the end of a magistrate's term; and the *apophasis* procedure introduced in the 340s BCE for the investigation by the Council of the Areopagus of charges of treason or public corruption. See Taylor 2001b. A useful survey of bribery accusations, acquittals and convictions appeared in Taylor 2001a.

304 The penalty against a magistrate convicted at audit of bribery was either ten times the amount of the bribe or death (Aristotle, *Athenian Constitution* 54.2; Dinarchus,

Against Demosthenes 60; Dinarchus, *Against Aristogiton* 17; Hypereides, *Against Demosthenes* 24). Plato, *Laws* 6.767e called for a minimum penalty of twice the bribe to be levied against a corrupt judge.

305 The Oath of the Archons recorded at Aristotle, *Athenian Constitution* 55.5 specified the dedication of a golden statue if a magistrate did not perform his duties justly in accordance with the laws or if he accepted a bribe.

306 Several bribery trials of generals took place in the fifth century BCE. Trials and executions of ambassadors and public speakers became common after 411 BCE.

307 Taylor 2001a listed eight Athenian ambassadors who were executed for accepting bribes in the fourth century BCE. The accepting of gifts by a servant of the State seemingly warranted prosecution only if the returning ambassador adopted positions viewed as undermining Athens' best interests (Hypereides, *In Defense of Lycrophon* 24–5; Isocrates, *On the Peace* 50).

308 Athenian laws on impiety were collected at Phillips 2013: 407–62.

309 Anaxagoras, who was the first to propose that the moon was a rock that shone with light reflected from the fiery rock of the sun (Plato, *Cratylus* 409a), was prosecuted at Athens for impiety for his teachings on astronomy and left Athens in ca. 435–430 BCE (Plutarch, *Perikles* 32.1; Plutarch, *Nicias* 23.3; Diogenes Laertius, *Lives of Eminent Philosophers* 2.12–14; Plato, *Apology* 18b, 26d-e; Josephus, Apion 2.265–67; see generally Curd 2007). Plato praised Anaxagoras as a wise man of the past (*Hippias Major* 281c; cf. Plato, *Phaedrus* 269e). Nevertheless Plato asserted that the sun and planets were divinities (Plato, *Laws* 7.821b; 10.886a, d-e, 889b-c; Plato, *Cratylus* 397c-d; Plato, *Timaeus* 38c-40d) and said that the study of heavenly bodies as mere physical objects was subject to prosecution as an impious expression of atheism (cf. Plato, *Apology* 26d; Xenophon, *Memorabilia* 4.7.4–7).

310 "Theoris was a prophetess, who was found guilty of impiety and put to death, as Philokhorus writes in (book) six." Philokhorus F60=Harpokration, *Lexicon* s. v. Theoris; cf. Demosthenes, *Against Aristogiton* 1 79–80 (where she was called a *pharmakis* or sorceress); Plutarch, *Demosthenes* 14.6; Dickie 2001: 50–1, 80–1; Harding 2008: 165–6; Rinella 2010: 183. This trial likely took place between ca. 357 and 322 BCE, the probable limits of the sixth book by Philokhorus.

311 Demosthenes, *On the False Embassy* 281 and scholiast (who identified the convicted priestess as Ninos); Demosthenes, *Against Boetus* 2.9; Josephus, Apion 2.267; Dickie 2001: 52–3; Rinella 2010: 184.

312 Plutarch, *Lives of the Ten Orators* 849e; Harpocration s. v. Isodaites; cf. Phillips 2013: 456–8. See Dickie 2001: 81–5 on the common correlation of prostitution and sorcery in ancient literary references.

313 Diogenes Laertius, *Lives of Eminent Philosophers* 2.40. For discussions of the trial of Socrates, see Stone 1988; Colaiaco 2001; Waterfield 2009; Phillips 2013: 437–43. Socrates was accused of not recognizing the gods that the state recognized, for introducing new divinities, and corrupting the youth. Plato and Xenophon each wrote a book titled *Apology* that detailed the legal defense of Socrates.

314 Diogenes Laertius, *Lives of Eminent Philosophers* 5.37; cf. O'Sullivan 2009: 209–10. Not much is known about the prosecution of Theophrastus for impiety. O'Sullivan suggests the charges may have been undermining the worship of the Twelve Gods at Athens (1997: 136–9).

315 Plutarch, *Perikles* 32.1. The law against impiety in Plato's *Laws* appears to have been based on the Decree of Diopeithes; cf. Morrow 1993: 475; Saunders 1996: 92.

316 It is likely that the Decree of Diopeithes was directed against the astronomical theories of Anaxagoras of Clazomenae (according to Plutarch, *Perikles* 32.1, "[Diopeithes] was attempting to place suspicion on Perikles through Anaxagoras") and resulted immediately in his impiety trial, which is to be dated in either 437 or 431 BCE

according to the most commonly accepted arguments, with the weight of evidence favoring 437 BCE. See Mansfeld 1979, 1980.

317 See generally Chase 1933: 151; Morrow 1993: 430–3; Saunders 1996.

318 Dickie 2001: 50; Rinella 2010: 174–5, 182–3. Dickie (2001: 18–46) discussed the formation of the notion of magic and magicians among the Greeks after the time of Homer (whose writings did not contain such ideas) but before the second half of the fifth century BCE, when Greeks referred to magicians under several names *(goes, magus, epodos, pharmakeus)*.

319 See also Plato, *Republic* 9.584a; 10.602d; Plato, *Sophist* 234c-235b. Plato's views on magic were discussed at Dickie 2001: 44–5, 60, 63–4.

320 The principal sources for these events are Thucydides, *Peloponnesian War* 6.27–29, 53, 601; Plutarch, *Alcibiades* 1821; Andocides, *On the Mysteries*. A legal discussion of the affair of Andocides is found at Phillips 2013: 421–37.

321 Andocides, *On the Mysteries* 11, 27, 37. For the impeachment of Alcibiades in the Assembly by Thessalus the son of Cimon for profaning the Mysteries, see Plutarch, *Alcibiades* 19.2, with the text of the impeachment at 22.3. Diocleides brought an impeachment before the Council for those who defaced the statues of Hermes. The list of those he denounced (who were eventually acquitted) is found at Andocides, *On the Mysteries* 47, and included many kinsmen and associates of Andocides.

322 Andocides, *On the Mysteries* 15, 27, 34, 40, 42; Lysias, *Against Andocides* 23; Thucydides, *Peloponnesian War* 6.27.2; Plutarch, *Alcibiades* 21.3; Diodorus Siculus, *Library* 13.2.3. For the decree at Thasos that established a reward for informers against conspiracies, see Meiggs and Lewis 1969: 252–5; Arnaoutoglou 1998: 86–7.

323 Andocides, *On the Mysteries* 12-17, 34, 37, 40, 43, 51–2, 61, 63–66; Andocides, *On His Return* 6–7; Lysias, *Against Andocides* 23; Plutarch, *Alcibiades* 19.1; 20.4–5; 21.1, 3–4; Thucydides, *Peloponnesian War* 6.60.2–4; Diodorus Siculus, *Library* 13.2.4. Informers included the slave Andomachus, the alien Teucer, Agariste the wife of Alcmaeonides, the slave Lydus, Diocleides, who subsequently retracted his testimony and was executed and Andocides, whose testimony was supplemented by that of his slaves, whom he allowed to be interrogated under torture to bolster his credibility as a witness (Andocides, *On the Mysteries* 64; Plutarch, *Alcibiades* 21.4). The impiety prosecution of the prophetess Theoris was also initiated by an informer, her maid; cf. Demosthenes, *Against Aristogiton* 1 80; Dickie 2001: 51; Rinella 2010: 183.

324 Andocides, *On the Mysteries* 13, 15–16, 34–5, 44, 49, 52, 66–7; Thucydides, *Peloponnesian War* 6.60.4; 61.6–7; Plutarch, *Alcibiades* 21.4. Alcibiades and several of his soldiers were summoned back from Sicily to stand trial, but escaped when the ship transporting them laid over in Thurii (Thucydides, *Peloponnesian War* 6.53; 6.61.6–7; Plutarch, *Alcibiades* 21.5; Diodorus Siculus, *Library* 13.5.2–3).

325 See Thucydides, *Peloponnesian War* 6.60.4; Philochorus, *FGrH* 328 F134=Scholiast to Aristophanes, *The Birds* 766; cf. Fornara 1983: 170–1. A reward had also been offered in 415 BCE for anyone who killed Diagoras of Melos, the convicted atheist who had fled into exile; cf. Lysias, *Against Andocides* 17–18; Aristophanes, *The Birds* 1072–3; Diodorus Siculus, *Library* 13.6.7; Josephus, Apion 2.266.

326 Pollux, *Onomasticon* 10.96–97; Philochorus, *FGrH* 328 F134; Athenaeus, *The Philosophers' Banquet* 11.476e; Plutarch, *Alcibiades* 22.4, 33.3, Andocides, *On the Mysteries* 51. For the fragments, see Pritchett 1953.

327 Similar provisions on magic in Deut. 18.9–14 and Plato, *Laws* 11.933c-e were noted at Wajdenbaum 2011: 197. Black magic (sorcery) by amateurs was considered harmful and illegal in the Ancient Near East, but white magic was allowed (cf. Westbrook 2009e: 289–90). Magic was an important component of both Ancient Near Eastern religious rituals and the Greek mystery religions. Negative connotations of magic

and the idea of magicians as a distinct social class are absent in Homer's writings and appear to have emerged Greece as late as the fifth century BCE (cf. Dickie 2001: 18–46). Dickie (2001: 21–2) noted that categories of Greek magic were compared with those found in Deut. 18.9–14. Plato and some others appear to have conceived of magic as a means of coercing the gods (cf. Dickie 2001: 25), usually by chants, rituals, special prayers and bribes (sacrifices). Plato sought to exclude this form of magic from both public and private religion (the mysteries). The only two examples of magicians prosecuted in Classical Greece (namely Theoris and Ninos) were charged under Athenian impiety laws under suspicion that they acted as priestesses in private religious ceremonies that initiated clients into foreign mysteries (Dickie 2001: 49–54; Rinella 2010: 183–4).

328 See Hagedorn 2004: 123–5 for a comparison of biblical and Greek statutes on bribery; 2004: 136–7 compared provisions against bribery at Deut. 17.2–7 and Plato, *Laws* 10.907d-e.

329 Plato, *Laws* gave a procedure that corresponded to Athenian *eisangelia*, in which citizens informed the magistrates (5.730d; cf. 7.808e-809a), who then conducted an investigation (10.907d-e), following which offenses against the state were tried by the Assembly (6.767e-768a); cf. Morrow 1993: 488. Plato, *Laws* 9.864d listed treason laws as dealing with "those who plunder the gods and with traitors, and also with those who wreck the laws with intent to overthrow the existing constitution." Bribery of a magistrate appeared separately at Plato, *Laws* 6.767e; false report by an ambassador at Plato, *Laws* 12.941e. Plato's *Laws* contained no exemption for tyrannicide in its laws on justified homicide.

330 The scholarly theory that Deut. 13 and 28 contained subversive appropriations of Assyrian language and ideology was examined and systematically rebutted in Crouch 2014.

331 Cf. Weinfeld 1972: 98, notes 2–3, where Weinfeld brought in references to dream interpretation, omens and portents in other Assyrian texts to bolster the purported parallel with VTE.

332 Cf. Morrow 1993: 430–1. See Dickie 2001: 63–4 on prophets as magicians in Plato's writings. The execution of Theoris the "prophetess" was discussed in note 310. In the Pentateuch, a figure who performed signs and wonders and publicly called for worship of a new god was labeled a prophet: Moses himself, who utilized signs and wonders to persuade the children of Israel to worship a new god, Yahweh (Ex. 4.1–9, 17, 28–31), was precisely such a figure.

333 Cf. Weinfeld 1972: 99, where it was noted that the expression דכר סדה is cognate with *dabab serrāte* at VTE 502. The parallel is not very striking, because the expression for seditious speech is common in both languages (cf. Jer. 28.16; 29.32).

334 Dickie 2001: 29, 35 n. 63, 39, 41, 52–3 (discussing the prosecution of Ninus), 64, 73; Rinella 2010: 181–4. Heraclitus of Ephesus (ca. 535–475 BCE) appears to have described initiation into the mysteries as one of the main activities of magicians (Dickie 2001: 27–9).

335 Weinfeld 1972: 98–9. All biblical quotations are from the *NRSV*.

336 Andocides, *On the Mysteries* 16 (Agariste, wife of Alcmaeonides), 63–4 (Andocides, close friend with many of the accused; cf. Lysias, *Against Andocides* 51). Andocides was accused of informing against his father and other kinsmen (Andocides, *On the Mysteries* 19–20, 22, 52–3, 67; Lysias, *Against Andocides* 23; Plutarch, *Lives of the Ten Orators* 834e; Tzetzes, *Chiliades* 6.367–75), although he denied this charge (Lysias, *Against Andocides* 23; Andocides, *On the Mysteries* 52–3, 67). The prophetess Theoris was accused of impiety and executed along with her twin sons (Demosthenes, *Against Aristogiton* 1 79–80), to whom she taught magic, probably through magic books; cf. Dickie 2001: 81.

337 Thucydides, *Peloponnesian War* 6.28.1; Andocides, *On the Mysteries* 11–12, 16–17, 47, 64; Plutarch, *Alcibiades* 22.3; Diodorus Siculus, *Library* 13.2.3; 5.1. The members of these political brotherhoods *(hetaireiai)* were sworn to secrecy with oaths that bound them more closely than kinsmen (Lysias, *Against Eratosthenes* 47, 67, 77; Thucydides, *Peloponnesian War* 3.82.4–6). The terms *hetaireia* (brotherhood) and *sunomosia* (conspiracy) were used interchangeably in ancient sources such as Thucydides. See generally Calhoun 1913: 4–9, 34–9; McGlew 1999. Initiates in the Eleusian mysteries also called each other brothers (Plutarch, *Epistles* 334e-335b). This language of "brotherhood" may have played into the biblical command that required informers to come forward against even close friends and brothers (Deut. 13.6).

338 In order to strengthen the procedural parallels with VTE, Weinfield (*Deuteronomy and the Deuteronomist School*, 94–6) emended Deut. 13.8 from "you shall kill him" (MT) to "you shall deliver him up" (LXX). But the preceding text in Deut. 13.8, "neither shall your eye pity him, neither shall you spare him," clearly contemplates killing the perpetrator.

339 The perpetrators of the sacrileges of 415 BCE could be killed with impunity, and indeed with a reward of one talent. See note 325. According to Lysias, *Against Andocides* 54, one guilty of impiety could either be immediately executed without trial or arrested and tried "for the sake of the populace, so that other people would listen and watch and be more prudent"; cf. Phillips 2013: 430.

340 For Athenian *eisangelia,* see note 295. Plato's *Laws* frequently noted the importance of informers (5.730d; 7.808e-809a). Plato, *Laws* 10.910c required that the establishment of a private cult should be reported to the magistrates for investigation. The Guardians of the Laws would determine whether the crime was serious enough to bring capital charges (10.910d). Plato, *Laws* 6.767e-768b specified that all crimes against the *polis* should receive a trial before the entire populace, which is to say, the Assembly.

341 We need not consider the parallel cited at Weinfeld 1972: 99 between the destruction of the city by the sword in Deut. 13.12–18 (for impiety) and in the *Sefire Treaty* 3.12–13 (for rebellion), other than to note that this verbal commonplace – the destruction of a city by the sword – did not appear in VTE.

342 The Covenant Code of Ex. 20.22–23.19 contained a "distinctive blending of legal, moral and cultic prescriptions" (Paul 1970: 34).

343 The tabernacle construction in Exodus and the temple construction in 1 Kgs 6–8 display features of either common authorship or literary dependence.

344 Wrongdoings alleviated by trespass offerings included not coming forward as a witness to the improper invoking of God's name, either in cursing or in an oath that was not fulfilled (Lev. 5.1–2), or by stealing items by force or guile or failing to return a found item (Lev. 6.2–6). Making amends for these latter infractions involved voluntarily restoring the goods to the owner, plus 20%. This was not a criminal penalty imposed in a judicial setting, but a private voluntary action by the one making the offering to relieve a guilty conscience. The attempt to illuminate the sacred laws in Lev. 5.1–6 by seeking parallels from Neo-Babylonian criminal legal traditions at Wells 2004: 73–82 fails to grasp the difference between sacred and civil laws and consequently appears misguided.

345 See especially the description and discussion of key ritual texts in Sparks 2005: 144–215.

346 The daily sacrifices at Uruk (*ANET*³ 338–9) bear comparison to the daily *tamid* of Ex. 29.38–42; Num. 28.3–8.

347 The contents of these Akkadian ritual texts "are not even disclosed to the laity, but are revealed only to the priests" (Paul 1970: 9).

348 See Parker 1983 on sacred law and the alleviation of religious anxieties.

349 See the discussion of the Exegetes in Chapter 2 §10.

350 Jacoby, 1949: 16, 41, 44, 49–50; cf. Plato, *Laws* 7.793a-d on recording unwritten laws.

351 Paul (1970: 34) commented on the "distinctive blending of legal, moral and cultic prescriptions" in the Covenant Code (Ex. 20.22–23.19), Leviticus and Deuteronomy.

352 Although references to the sabbath have been found in both ostraca and papyri at Elephantine, it was associated with neither a cessation of work (on evidence of *TAD* D7.16.1–5, where business was conducted as usual by Jews on the sabbath) nor the creation or foundation myths of Ex. 20.11; Deut. 5.15. Neither the Passover (in ostraca *TAD* D7.6.9–10; D7.24.5) nor the Days of Unleavened Bread (in *TAD* A4.1) were associated with the biblical Exodus story of ca. 270 BCE: see Chapter 5 §2.

353 Several Pentateuchal passages have close affinities with a single Commandment, such as laws about monolatry (Ex. 34.14), graven images (Ex. 34.17; Lev. 19.4; 26.1; Num. 33.52; Deut. 12.3; 27.15), swearing (Lev. 19.12), sabbath(s) (Ex. 31.13–17; 34.21; 35.2–3; Lev. 26.2; cf. Num. 15.32–36), parents (Ex. 21.17; Lev. 19.32; 20.9–10; Deut. 27.16), adultery (Lev. 20.9–10), theft (Lev. 19.11) and lying (Lev. 19.11).

354 Other passages in the same format and containing strong ethical content include Ex. 23.3, 6; Deut. 10.19; 16.19; 18.13, and a remarkable series of moral exhortations against mistreating one's neighbor at Lev. 19.13–18.

355 Prov. 1.8–9; 6.20 (hear the instructions of one's mother and father); 1.10–14 (don't join sinners to kill and rob the innocent); 6.24–35 (don't commit adultery with a neighbor's wife).

356 Lambert 1996: 1. For "Counsels of Wisdom," see 1996: 99–106. For "The Instructions of Shuruppak," see 1996: 92–5; Alster 1974.

357 Plato, *Republic* 2.376d-3.412b; 4.423e-424a; 7.521c-540c; Plato, *Laws* 1.643d-644a; 2.653a-c, 659b-c, e; Aristotle, *Politics* 2.1263b; 3.1288a-b; 5.1310a; 8.1337a; cf. Berman 2008: 170–1. According to Aristotle, *Rhetoric* 1.1359b, ethics was a branch of political science.

358 Maxims were discussed at Gagarin 1986: 53–5.

359 Sosiades, *The Commandments of the Seven Sages* 1 ("Follow God"), 3 ("Worship the Gods"). Although the Greeks were known to curse or mock the gods (cf. Dionysius of Halicarnassus, *Roman Antiquities* 2.18–20), the Pythagoreans taught reverence in speech toward the gods, heroes, parents and other benefactors (Porphyry of Tyre, *Life of Pythagoras* 38) and had a law against blasphemy close to that of the Jews (Josephus, Apion 1.164–65).

360 Sosiades, *The Commandments of the Seven Sages*, 4 ("Respect your Parents"), 126 ("Respect an Elder"), 131 ("Crown your Ancestors"). Greeks placed honoring one's parents as a sacred duty close to honoring the gods (Plato, *Laws* 4.717b-d; 11.930e-932a), and maltreatment of parents in any form was prosecuted with utmost severity (Aristotle, *Athenian Constitution* 56.6; Demosthenes, *Against Timocrates* 60; Lysias, *Against Agoratus* 91; Plato, *Laws* 10.885a; 11.932a-d; cf. Chase 1933: 180). The commandment to honor one's parents was compared with Plato, *Laws* 11.931e at Eusebius, *Preparation for the Gospel* 12.36.

361 Some commandments advised against using oaths (Sosiades, *The Commandments of the Seven Sages* 19, 69); cf. the Platonic provision against invoking the names of the gods in commercial transactions (*Laws* 11.916e-917b). Other parallels to the Decalogue appear at Sosiades, *The Commandments of the Seven Sages* 51 ("Shun Murder"), 34 ("Shun what Belongs to Others"), 117 ("Acquire Wealth Justly"), 46 ("Fear Deceit"). The version found in the inscription at Miletopolis also listed an additional commandment, "Testify what is Right" (Oikonomides 1987: 76).

362 For the passion to acquire and its negative effects, see Plato, *Republic* 2.359c, 373e; 3.393e; Plato, *Laws* 8.831c; 9.870a-c. For its association with the rise of

oligarchies, see Plato, *Republic* 7.538a; 8.550d, 553b-c. The topic is extensively discussed in Balot 2001. Athenian orators also commented on covetousness, cf. Demosthenes, *Against Callicles* 1: "Really, men of Athens, there is nothing more difficult than encountering a wicked and covetous neighbor . . . lusting after [your] property."

363 In LH 229–30, if a building collapse resulted in the death of the owner's son, the builder's son was slain. In MAL A 55, if a man raped another man's virgin daughter, the perpetrator's wife was to be raped. Deut. 24.16 specified that a father should not be executed for a son's crime, or vice versa. Although it is possible that this statute was intended to limit revenge killings (cf. its application in the context of blood feud at 2 Kgs 14.6), it may have instead (or additionally) aimed to curtail an application of *talionis* or symmetrical justice to the perpetrator himself (cf. Jer. 31.29–30; Ezek. 18.2–4, 19–20, where the statute is invoked as a general principle of justice with no thought of blood feud).

364 In LH 196–201, the principle of *talionis* was only invoked for injuries in which the victim was a member of the ruling class. When the victim was of a lesser class, a monetary penalty was specified.

365 The thousands of bones of animals sacrificed in the temple on Mount Gerizim established in ca. 450 BCE included sheep, goats, cattle and doves, consistent with Levitical prescriptions, but not other animals local to the area. See Magen 2007: 162. This suggests that the sacrificial rules found in Lev. 1–7 reflect cultic practices going back at least to the Persian period.

366 Samaria was converted into an Assyrian province in 720 BCE and received an influx of deportees from Arabia in 716 BCE and from Babylonia in the aftermath of Sargon II's defeat of Merodach-baladan II in campaigns of 710–709 BCE. See Na'aman and Zadok 1988; Zertal 2003; cf. 2 Kgs 17.24, 30–31. Assyrian provincial administrators and transplanted Babylonian ruling class elites must have represented a significant component of the educated upper class of Samerina, especially after the deportation of 27,780 conquered troops and native ruling class elites from Samaria to Assyria and Media in 716 BCE. Judah was never converted into an Assyrian province. The Assyrian and Babylonian component of the population of Samerina are a far more plausible conduit for the import of cuneiform legal traditions to the region than either hypothetical Assyrian-trained scribes from Judah in 740–640 BCE (Wright 2009: 91–120, 346–64) or later diaspora Jews (Van Seters 2003: 173–4).

367 The Commandments of the Seven Sages were a common heritage of the Greek world as a whole, published at the temple of Delphi and attributed to wise legislators from many different ancient Greek city-states.

368 Legal features similar to biblical levirate and Athenian *epiklerate* marriage rules were also found in the Great Code of Gortyn, Crete; cf. Hagedorn 2004: 221–2.

369 See notes 293 and 294.

Bibliography

Allen, Danielle S., *The World of Prometheus: The Politics of Punishing in Democratic Athens*. Princeton, NJ: Princeton University Press, 2000.

Alster, Bendt, *The Instructions of Suruppak*. Copenhagen Studies in Assyriology 10. Copenhagen: Akademisk Forlag: 1974.

Arnaoutoglou, Ilias, *Ancient Greek Laws: A Sourcebook*. New York: Routledge, 1998.

Astour, Michael C., "Tamar the Hierodule: An Essay in the Method of Vestigal Motifs," *JBL* 85 (1966): 185–96.

Balot, Ryan K., *Greed and Injustice in Classical Athens*. Princeton: Princeton University Press, 2001.

Barmash, Pamela, *Homicide in the Biblical World*. Cambridge: Cambridge University Press, 2005.

Berger, Suzanne, "A Note on Some Scenes of Land-Measurement," *JEA* 20 (1934): 54–6.

Berman, Joshua A., *Created Equal: How the Bible Broke with Ancient Political Thought*. Oxford: Oxford University Press, 2008.

Blum, R., *Kallimachos: The Alexandrian Library and the Origins of Bibliography*. Translated by H. Wellisch. Madison, WI: University of Wisconsin Press, 1991.

Brulé, Pierre, *Women of Ancient Greece*. Translated by Antonia Nevill. Edinburgh: Edinburgh University Press, 2003.

Budin, Stephanie Lynn, *The Myth of Sacred Prostitution in Antiquity*. Cambridge: Cambridge University Press, 2008.

Calhoun, George, *Athenian Clubs in Politics and Litigation*. Austin: University of Texas Bulletin, 1913.

Chase, Alston Hurd, "The Influence of Athenian Institutions on the Laws of Plato," *HSCP* 44 (1933): 131–92.

Chirichigno, Gregory C., *Debt-Slavery in Israel and the Ancient Near East*. JSOTSup 141. Sheffield: Sheffield Academic Press, 1993.

Colaiaco, James A., *Socrates Against Athens: Philosophy on Trial*. New York and London: Routledge, 2001.

Connor, W. R., "The Razing of the House in Greek Society," *TAPA* 115 (1985): 79–102.

Crawford, Michael H. and David Whitehead, *Archaic and Classical Greece: A Selection of Ancient Sources in Translation*. Cambridge: Cambridge University Press, 1983.

Crouch, C. L., *Israel and the Assyrians: Deuteronomy, the Succession Treaty of Esargaddon, and the Nature of Subversion*. SBL Ancient Near East Monographs 8. Atlanta: SBL Press, 2014.

Cudjoe, Richard V., *The Social and Legal Position of Widows and Orphans in Classical Athens*. Dissertation. Glasgow: University of Glasgow, 2000.

Curd, Patricia, *Anaxagoras of Clazomenae, Fragments and Testimonia: A Text and Translation with Notes and Essays*. Toronto: University of Toronto Press, 2007.

Dickie, Matthew W., *Magic and Magicians in the Greco-Roman World*. London: Routledge, 2001.

Dillon, Matthew and Lynda Garland, *Ancient Greece: Social and Historical Documents from Ancient Times to the Death of Alexander the Great*. New York: Routledge, 2010.

Fensham, Charles, "Widow, Orphan, and the Poor in Ancient Near East Legal and Wisdom Literature." Pages 176–92 in Frederick C. Greenspahn (ed.), *Essential Papers on Israel and the Ancient Near East*. New York: New York University, 1991.

Figueira, Thomas J., "*Sitopolai* and *Sitophylakes* in Lysias' 'Against the Grain Dealers:' Governmental Intervention in the Athenian Economy," *Phoenix* 40 (1986): 149–71.

Finkelstein, J. J., "Ammisaduqa's Edict and the Babylonian 'Law Codes'," *JCS* 3 (1961): 91–104.

———, "The Ox that Gored," *TAPhS* 71 (1981): 1–89.

Fisher, Eugene J., "Cultic Prostitution in the Ancient Near East? A Reassessment," *Biblical Theology Bulletin* 6 (1976): 225–36.

Fletcher, Judith, "Horkos in the *Oresteia*." Pages 102–13 in Alan H. Sommerstein and J. Fletcher (eds.), *Horkos: The Oath in Greek Society*. Exeter: Bristol Phoenix Press, 2007.

Fornara, Charles W. (ed.), *Archaic Times to the End of the Peloponnesian War*. Cambridge: Cambridge University Press, 1983.

Fortenbaugh, William W., Pamela M. Huby, Robert W. Sharples and Dimitri Gutas (eds.), *Theophrastus of Eresus: Sources for his Life, Writings, Thought and Influence*. 2 vols. Leiden: E .J. Brill, 1992.

Fortenbaugh, William W. and Eckart Schütrumpf (eds.), *Demetrius of Phalerum: Text, Translation, and Discussion*. New Brunswick, NJ: Transaction Publishers, 2000.

Gagarin, Michael, *Drakon and Early Athenian Homicide Law*. New Haven, CT: Yale University Press, 1981.

———, *Early Greek Law*. Berkeley: University of California Press, 1986.

Glazebrook, Allison, "Prostituting Female Kin (Plut. *Sol.* 23.1–2)," *Dike* 8 (2006): 33–54.

Greenburg, Moshe, "The Biblical Conception of Asylum," *JBL* 78 (1959): 125–32.

Hagedorn, Anselm C., "Deut. 17, 8–13: Procedure for Cases of Pollution?" *ZAW* 115 (2003): 538–56.

———, *Between Moses and Plato: Individual and Society in Deuteronomy and Ancient Greek Law*. Göttingen: Vandenhoeck & Ruprecht, 2004.

Hall, Margaretha Debrunner, "Even Dogs Have Erinyes: Sanctions in Athenian Practice and Thinking." Pages 73–89 in L. Foxhall and A.D.E. Lewis (eds.), *Greek Law in Its Political Setting: Justifications Not Justice*. Oxford: Clarendon Press, 1996.

Hamel, Debra, *Athenian Generals: Military Authority in the Classical Period*. Leiden: E. J. Brill, 1998.

Harding, Philip, *The Story of Athens: The Fragments of the Local Chronicles of Athens*. London: Routledge, 2008.

Harrison, A.R.W., *The Law of Athens*. 2 vols. Oxford: Clarendon Press, 1968.

Hermann, Claude and Walter Johns, *Babylonian and Assyrian Laws, Contracts and Letters*. New York: Charles Scribner's Sons, 1904.

Huffmon, Herbert B., "A Company of Prophets: Mari, Assyria, Israel." Pages 47–70 in Martti Nissinen (ed.), *Prophecy in Its Ancient Near East Context: Mesopotamian, Biblical and Arabian Perspectives*. SBLSymp 13. Atlanta, GA: Society of Biblical Literature, 2000.

Hurowitz, Victor, "His Master Shall Pierce His Ear with an Awl (Exodus 21.6): Marking Slaves in the Bible in Light of Akkadian Sources," *PAAJR* 58 (1992): 47–77.

Jacoby, Felix, *Atthis: The Local Chronicles of Ancient Athens*. Oxford: Clarendon Press, 1949.

Katz, Marilyn A., "Buphonia and Goring Ox: Homicide, Animal Sacrifice and Judicial Process." Pages 155–78 in R.M. Rosen and J. Farrell (eds.), *Nomodeiktes: Greek Studies in Honor of Martin Ostwald*. Ann Arbor, MI: University of Michigan Press, 1993.

King, L. W., *Babylonian Boundary-Stones and Memorial-Tablets in the British Museum*. London: Oxford University Press, 1912.

Knoppers, Gary N. and Paul B. Harvey Jr., "The Pentateuch in Ancient Mediterranean Context: The Publication of Local Lawcodes." Pages 105–41 in Gary N. Knoppers and Bernard M. Levinson (eds.), *Pentateuch as Torah: New Models for Understanding Its Promulgation and Acceptance*. Winona Lake, IN: Eisenbrauns, 2007.

Kooij, Arie van der, "The Septuagint of the Pentateuch and Ptolemaic Rule." Pages 289–300 in Gary N. Knoppers and Bernard M. Levinson (eds.), *Pentateuch as Torch: New Models for Understanding Its Promulgation and Acceptance*. Winona Lake, IN: Eisenbrauns, 2007.

Lacey, W.K., *The Family in Classical Greece*. Ithaca, NY: Cornell University Press, 1968.

Lambert, W.G., *Babylonian Wisdom Literature*. Oxford: Oxford University Press, 1996.

Levinson, Bernard M., *Deuteronomy and the Hermeneutics of Legal Innovation*. Oxford: Oxford University Press, 1998.

Loomis, W.T., "The Nature of Premeditation in Athenian Homicide Law," *JHS* 92 (1972): 86–95.

Lupu, Eran, *Greek Sacred Law: A Collection of New Documents*. Religions in the Graeco-Roman World 152. Leiden: E.J. Brill, 2005.

Lyons, Henry, "Two Notes on Land-Measurement in Egypt," *JEA* 12 (1926): 242–4.

MacDowell, Douglas Maurice, *Athenian Homicide Law in the Age of the Orators*. Manchester: Manchester University Press, 1963.

———, *The Law in Classical Athens*. Ithaca, NY: Cornell University Press, 1978.

———, "The Oikos in Athenian Law," *CQ* 39 (1989): 10–21.

MacLachlan, Bonnie, "Sacred Prostitution and Aphrodite," *Studies in Religion/Sciences Religieuses* 21 (1992): 145–62.

Magen, Yitzhak, "The Dating of the First Phase of the Samaritan Temple on Mt Gerizim in Light of Archaeological Evidence." Pages 157–212 in Oded Lipschits, Gary N. Knoppers and Rainer Albertz (eds.), *Judah and the Judeans in the Fourth Century BCE*. Winona Lake, IN: Eisenbrauns, 2007.

Malkin, Irad (ed.), *Ancient Perceptions of Greek Ethnicity*. Center for Hellenic Studies Colloquia 5. Harvard: Harvard University Press, 2001.

Malul, Meir, *The Comparative Method in Ancient Near Eastern and Biblical Legal Studies*. *AOAT* 227. Neukirchener: Verlag Butzon & Bercker Kevelaer, 1990.

Mansfeld, J., "The Chronology of Anaxagoras' Athenian Period and the Date of His Trial," *Mnemosyne* 32 (1979): 39–69.

———, "The Chronology of Anaxagoras' Athenian Period and the Date of His Trial. Part II. The Plot against Pericles and His Associates," *Mnemosyne* 33 (1980): 17–95.

Matthews, Victor H., "The Anthropology of Slavery in the Covenant Code." Pages 119–35 in Bernard M. Levinson (ed.), *Theory and Method in Biblical and Cuneiform Law*. JSOTSup 181. Sheffield: Sheffield Academic Press, 1994.

McGlew, James F., "Politics on the Margins: The Athenian 'Hetaereaia' in 415 BCE," *Historia* 48 (1999): 1–22.

McLoughlin, Bonnie, "Epinician Swearing." Pages 91–101 in Alan H. Sommerstein and J. Fletcher (eds.), *Horkos: The Oath in Greek Society*. Exeter: Bristol Phoenix Press, 2007.

Meiggs, Russell and David Lewis (eds.), *A Selection of Greek Historical Inscriptions to the End of the Fifth Century BC*. Oxford: Clarendon Press, 1969.

Monoson, S. Sara, *Plato's Democratic Entanglements: Athenian Politics and the Practice of Philosophy*. Princeton: Princeton University Press, 2000.

Morrow, Glenn Raymond, *Plato's Cretan City: A Historical Interpretation of the Laws*. Princeton: Princeton University Press, 1993.

Mühl, Max, *Untersuchungen zue Altorientalischen und Althellischen Gesetzebung*. Leipzig: Dieterich'sche Verlagsbuchhandlung, 1933.

Na'aman, Nadav and Ran Zadok, "Sargon II's Deportations to Israel and Philistia (716–708 BC)," *JCS* 40 (1988): 36–46.

Naiden, F. S., "Supplication and the Law." Pages 71–91 in Edward M. Harris and Lene Rubenstein (eds.), *The Law and the Courts in Ancient Greece*. London: Duckworth, 2004.

Niesiolowski-Spanò, Lukasz, "Primeval History in the Persian Period?" *SJOT* 21 (2007): 106–26.

Nightingale, Andrea Wilson, *Spectacles of Truth in Classical Greek Philosophy: Theoria in Its Cultural Context*. Cambridge: Cambridge University Press, 2004.

Noonan, Jr., John T., *Bribes: The Intellectual History of a Moral Idea*. Berkeley: University of California Press, 1984.

Oikonomides, A. N., "Records of 'The Commandments of the Seven Wise Men' in the 3rd Century BC," *The Classical Bulletin* 63 (1987): 67–76.

Ostwald, Martin, *From Popular Sovereignty to Sovereignty of Law: Law, Society, and Politics in Fifth Century Athens*. Berkeley: University of California Press, 1986.

O'Sullivan, Lara, "Athenian Impiety Trials in the Late Fourth Century BC," *CQ* 47 (1997): 136–52.

———, *The Regime of Demetrius of Phalerum in Athens, 317–307 BCE: A Philosopher in Politics*. Leiden: E. J. Brill, 2009.

Pack, R. A., *The Greek and Latin Literary Texts from Greco-Roman Egypt*. Ann Arbor, MI: The University of Michigan Press, 1967.

Parke, H. W. and D. E. W. Wormell, *The Delphic Oracle*. 2 vols. Oxford: Blackwell, 1956.

Parker, Robert, *Miasma: Pollution and Purification in Early Greek Religion*. Oxford: Clarendon Press, 1983.

———, "What Are Sacred Laws?" Pages 57–70 in Edward M. Harris and Lene Rubenstein (eds.), *The Law and the Courts in Ancient Greece*. London: Duckworth, 2004.

Parpola, Simo, *Assyrian Prophecies*. SAA 9. Helsinki: Helsinki University Press, 1997.

Paul, Shalom M., *Studies in the Book of the Covenant in the Light of Cuneiform and Biblical Law*. VTSup 18. Leiden: E. J. Brill, 1970.

Pease, Arthur Stanley, "Notes on Stoning among the Greeks and Romans," *TAPhA* 38 (1907): 5–18.

Phillips, David, *The Law of Ancient Athens*. Ann Arbor, MI: University of Michigan Press, 2013.

Podlecki, Anthony J., "The Political Significance of the Athenian 'Tyrannicide'-Cult," *Historia* 15 (1966): 129–41.

Posner, Ernst, *Archives in the Ancient World*. Cambridge: Harvard University Press, 1972.

Pritchett, Kendrick W., "The Attic Stelai, Part I," *Hesperia* 22 (1953): 225–99.

Reich, Ronnie, "The 'Boundary of Gezer' Inscriptions Again," *IEJ* 40 (1990): 44–6.

Reich, Ronnie and Zvi Greenhut, "Another 'Boundary of Gezer' Inscription Found Recently," *IEJ* 52 (2002): 58–63.

Rhodes, Peter John, *The Athenian Boule*. Oxford: Clarendon Press, 1972.

———, *A Commentary on the Aristotelian Athenaeion Politeia*. Oxford: Clarendon Press, 1993.

———, "Oaths in Political Life." Pages 11–25 in Alan H. Sommerstein and J. Fletcher (eds.), *Horkos: The Oath in Greek Society*. Exeter: Bristol Phoenix Press, 2007.

Rhodes, Peter John, and Robin Osborne, *Greek Historical Inscriptions 404–323 BC*. Oxford: Oxford University Press, 2003.

Rinella, Michael A., *Pharmakon: Plato, Drug Culture, and Identity in Ancient Athens*. New York: Lexington Books, 2010.

Robertson, Noel, *Religion and Reconciliation in Greek Cities: The Sacred Laws of Selinus and Cyrene*. New York: Oxford University Press, 2010.

Rofe, Alexander, "The *History of the Cities of Refuge* in Biblical Law." Pages 205–39 in Sara Japhet (ed.), *Studies in Bible*. Scripta Hierosolymitana 31. Jerusalem: Magnes Press, 1986.

Rosivach, Vincent J., "Execution by Stoning in Athens," *Classical Antiquity* 6 (1987): 232–48.

———, "Enslaving '*Barbaroi*' and the Athenian Ideology of Slavery," *Historia* 48 (1999): 129–57.

Roth, Martha T., "'She Will Die by an Iron Dagger': Adultery and Neo-Babylonian Marriage," *Journal of the Economic and Social History of the Orient* 31 (1988): 196–206.

———, *Law Collections from Mesopotamia and Asia Minor*. WAWSBL 6. Atlanta, GA: Scholars Press, 1997.

Salzberger, Mayer, "The Ancient Hebrew Law of Homicide II," *JQR* 5 (1915): 289–344.

Saunders, Trevor J., "Plato on the Treatment of Heretics." Pages 91–100 in L. Foxhall and A.D.E. Lewis (eds.), *Greek Law in Its Political Setting: Justifications Not Justice*. Oxford: Clarendon Press, 1996.

Scafuro, Adele C., *The Forensic Stage: Settling Disputes in Graeco-Roman New Comedy*. Cambridge: Cambridge University Press, 2004.

Sealey, R., "On Lawful Concubinage in Athens," *Classical Antiquity* 3 (1984): 111–33.

Shear, Julia L., "The Oath of Demophantos and the Politics of Athenian Identity." Pages 148–60 in Alan H. Sommerstein and J. Fletcher (eds.), *Horkos: The Oath in Greek Society*. Exeter: Bristol Phoenix Press, 2007.

Slanski, Kathryn E., "Classification, Historiography and Monumental Authority: The Babylonian Entitlement 'narûs (kudurrus)'," *JCS* 52 (2000): 95–114.

———, *The Babylonian Entitlement narûs (kudurrus): A Study in Their Form and Function*. ASORB 9. Boston: American Schools of Oriental Research, 2003.

Sparks, Kenton L., *Ancient Texts for the Study of the Hebrew Bible: A Guide to the Background Literature*. Peabody, MA: Hendrickson, 2005.

Stackert, Jeffrey, "Why Does Deuteronomy Legislate Cities of Refuge? Asylum in the Covenant Collection (Exodus 21:12–14) and Deuteronomy (19.1–13)," *JBL* 125 (2006): 23–49.

Stanton, G.R., *Athenian Politics: c. 800–500 BC: A Sourcebook*. London: Routledge, 1990.

Stone, I.F., *The Trial of Socrates*. Boston, MA: Little, Brown and Company, 1988.

Stroud, Ronald S., "The Athenian Grain Tax Law of 374/3 BC," *Hesperia, Supplements* 29 (1998): 1–140.

Stulman, Louis, "Encroachment in Deuteronomy: An Analysis of the Social World of the D Code," *JBL* 109 (1990): 613–32.

Taylor, Claire, "Bribery in Athenian Politics Part I: Accusations, Allegations, and Slander," *GR* 48 (2001a): 53–66.

———, "Bribery in Athenian Politics Part II: Ancient Reactions and Perceptions," *GR* 48 (2001b): 154–72.

Tigerstadt, E. N., *The Legend of Sparta in Classical Antiquity*. 3 vols. Stockholm: Almquist & Wiksell, 1965, 1974, 1978.

Tillyard, H.J.W., "Boundary and Mortgage Stones from Attica," *The Annual of the British School at Athens* 11 (1904): 63–71.

van der Toorn, Karel, "Female Prostitution in Payment of Vows in Ancient Israel," *JBL* 108 (1989): 193–205.

Van Seters, John, *A Law Book for the Diaspora: Revision in the Study of the Covenant Code*. Oxford: Oxford University Press, 2003.

Wajdenbaum, Philippe, *Argonauts of the Desert: Structural Analysis of the Hebrew Bible*. London: Equinox Publishing, 2011.

Waterfield, Robin, *Why Socrates Died: Dispelling the Myths*. New York: W. W. Norton & Company, 2009.

Weinfeld, Moshe, *Deuteronomy and the Deuteronomistic School*. Winona Lake, IN: Eisenbrauns, 1972.

———, *Social Justice in Ancient Israel and in the Ancient Near East*. Minneapolis: Fortress Press, 1995.

Wells, Bruce, *The Law of Testimony in the Pentateuchal Codes*. Beiheft zur Zeitschrift für Altorientalische und Biblische Rechtsgeschichte 4. Wiesbaden: Harrassowitz Verlag, 2004.

West, M. L., *The East Face of Helicon: West Asiatic Elements in Greek Poetry and Myth*. Oxford: Oxford University Press, 1997.

Westbrook, Raymond, "The Prohibition on Restoration of Marriage in Deuteronomy 24.1–4." Pages 387–405 in Sara Japhet (ed.), *Studies in Bible*. Scripta Hierosolymitana 31. Jerusalem: Magnes Press, 1986.

———, *Property and the Family in Biblical Law*. JSOTSup 113. Sheffield: Sheffield Academic Press, 1991.

———, "The Nature and Origin of the Twelve Tablets." Pages 21–71 in Bruce Wells and F. Rachel Magdalene (eds.), *Law From the Tigris to the Tiber: The Writings of Raymond Westbrook*. Winona Lake, IN: Eisenbrauns, 2009a.

———, "Social Justice in the Ancient Near East." Pages 143–60 in Bruce Wells and F. Rachel Magdalene (eds.), *Law from the Tigris to the Tiber: The Writings of Raymond Westbrook*. Winona Lake, IN: Eisenbrauns, 2009b.

———, "Slave and Master in Ancient Near Eastern Law." Pages 161–216 in Bruce Wells and F. Rachel Magdalene (eds.), *Law From the Tigris to the Tiber: The Writings of Raymond Westbrook*. Winona Lake, IN: Eisenbrauns, 2009c.

———, "Adultery in Ancient Near Eastern Law." Pages 245–87 in Bruce Wells and F. Rachel Magdalene (eds.), *Law From the Tigris to the Tiber: The Writings of Raymond Westbrook*. Winona Lake, IN: Eisenbrauns, 2009d.

———, "Witchcraft and the Law in the Ancient Near East." Pages 289–300 in Bruce Wells and F. Rachel Magdalene (eds.), *Law from the Tigris to the Tiber: The Writings of Raymond Westbrook*. Winona Lake, IN: Eisenbrauns, 2009e.

Westenholz, Joan Goodnick, "Tamar, Qĕdēšā, Qadištu, and Sacred Prostitution in Mesopotamia," *HTR* 82 (1989): 245–65.

Willis, T. M., *The Elders of the City: A Study of the Elders-Laws in Deuteronomy*. Atlanta, GA: Society of Biblical Literature, 2001.

Wright, David P., *Inventing God's Law: How the Covenant Code Used and Revised the Laws of Hammurabi*. Oxford: Oxford University Press, 2009.

Yaron, R., *The Laws of Eshnunna*. Jerusalem: Magnes Press, 1969.

Zertal, Adam, "The Province of Samaria (Assyrian Samerina) in the Late Iron Age (Iron Age III)." Pages 377–412 in O. Lipschits and J. Blenkinsopp (eds.), *Judah and the Judeans in the Neo-Babylonian Period*. Winona Lake, IN: Eisenbrauns, 2003.

4

GREEK AND ANCIENT NEAR EASTERN LAW COLLECTIONS

The reasons for creating and publishing a law collection, the forms in which individual laws were presented, the structure of the law collection as a whole and the authority that law collections possessed differed considerably in the Ancient Near Eastern and Greek worlds. It was once held as certain that biblical legal content drew directly on Ancient Near Eastern law collections (notably the Hammurabi Law Code) and the Vassal Treaty of Esarhaddon (VTE). It was therefore taken for granted that the biblical law collections, including the Covenant Code, the Decalogue and the Deuteronomic Law Code, must somehow correspond to these assumed Ancient Near Eastern antecedents in terms of purpose, form, authority and presentation. In the previous two chapters, however, evidence was presented that the implicit and explicit constitutional content found in Pentateuchal law collections have no counterpart in the Ancient Near East, but instead reflect the Greek genre of constitutional law (Chapter 2), and that individual laws from all the Pentateuchal law collections frequently reflected legal provisions found in Greek or Athenian laws or in Plato's *Laws* of ca. 350 BCE (Chapter 3). This calls into question the weight traditionally accorded to Babylonian and Assyrian comparative materials and suggests that Greek law collections might provide more compelling models for those found in the Pentateuch. The current chapter reevaluates the cultural background of the literary genres and legal concepts found in the biblical law collections by comparing the structures, aims and authority of the Pentateuchal law collections against those found in both the Ancient Near Eastern and Greek worlds.

1. Ancient Near East law collections

Several categories of Ancient Near Eastern documents with legal content exist. One category was the legal contract, such as a purchase, lease, loan or marriage contract, in which two parties formally entered into a legally binding agreement. A second category was the scribal case record or case notes of legal proceedings, which typically listed the nature of the case and the judicial decision. A third category was the royal edict, a published document that carried legal force. Perhaps the most important of these were the *misarum* decrees, most commonly issued at the start of a king's reign, in which the king decreed certain immediate measures for social relief, such as release from debt, the freeing of prisoners, and manumission of debt slaves. A fourth category was the law collection that listed various civil and criminal infractions and the penalties they incurred. Unlike the other types of legal documents just mentioned, the law collection was not grounded in day-to-day practicalities of legal proceedings and the bureaucratic administration of justice, but was instead theoretical and literary in character. This genre of document is most relevant to the current discussion, because some laws that appeared in Ancient Near Eastern law collections have biblical parallels and because it is commonly held that biblical law collections such as the Covenant Code and the Deuteronomic Law Code were modeled on Ancient Near Eastern law collections. Ancient Near Eastern law collections important for comparative purposes include the following:[1]

Laws of Ur-Nammu (LU)	Ur	ca. 2100 BCE
Laws of Lipit-Ishtar (LL)	Isin	ca. 1930 BCE
Laws of Eshnunna (LE)	Eshnunna	ca. 1770 BCE
Laws of Hammurabi (LH)	Babylon	ca. 1750 BCE
Hittite Laws (HL)	Anatolia	ca. 1650 to 1180 BCE
Middle Assyrian Laws (MAL)	Assur	ca. 1075 BCE
Neo-Babylonian Laws (LNB)	Sippar	ca. 700 BCE

One may also mention in passing Egyptian Pharaonic decrees which were stored in the House of Life (the Egyptian term for libraries attached to various temples). Many of these texts suffered destruction during the reign of the Persian conqueror Cambyses (525 BCE). Darius I subsequently sponsored the collection of Egyptian laws into eight volumes in 518–502 BCE. The character of the laws published under Darius is a matter of considerable debate.[2] These laws survived into the Hellenistic period and likely formed a partial basis for the description of Egyptian laws by Hecataeus of Abdera.[3] Because it is widely agreed that these laws are unrelated to the Pentateuchal law collections, they will not be further discussed here.

Ancient Near Eastern law collections that contained laws with direct biblical parallels include LE, LH and MAL A (see Chapter 3). The most famous and best preserved of these legal corpora was the Hammurabi Law Code, which contained certain laws that were also found in the MAL and in the Pentateuch, including the famous *lex talionis,* "an eye for an eye and a tooth for a tooth." All the law collections of the Ancient Near East known from inscriptional and cuneiform sources, whether Hittite, Babylonian or Assyrian, appear to have originated under royal sponsorship. The Old Babylonian law collections, which included LE and LH, appear to have followed a common pattern: a prologue that praised the righteous king who created the law code and the gods who inspired him with wisdom and righteousness;[4] the main body, which contained a series of laws that listed various crimes, the class status of both the perpetrator and victim and the prescribed penalty; and an epilogue that promised blessings on later kings who preserved the inscription and curses on the person and realm of any king who defaced the inscription.[5] It is generally accepted that these codes did not have prescriptive force, because cuneiform records of judicial rulings never cited law codes for their authority and sometimes conflicted with the penalties that the inscribed law codes recorded (Eckart 1994: 160; Roth 1997: 5; Westbrook 2009b: 36 and the literature cited there). These law collections in their published form appear to have served primarily as royal apologia to praise the righteousness of a particular ruler's reign.[6]

The judicial machinery of ancient Mesopotamia had three components: the king, the royal officers and judges who acted as his agents and the elders and village assemblies who administered justice on a local level. Ancient Near Eastern courts often consisted of local respected town elders or judicial assembly meetings called by the elders (see generally Jacobson 1946: 159–72; Jacobson 1957: 91–104). Their decisions were based, not on written law codes, but on their own sense of fairness,[7] together with traditional or unwritten customary law that reflected local community values. Such local courts tried cases of lesser importance and came under the supervision or oversight of governmental officials. More serious cases were referred to royal judges. Capital cases often came before the king. Judicial decisions were recorded by scribes and became a source of raw material for scribal legal theory. A legal literature is thought to have arisen in scribal circles that collected lists of legal infractions and their typical judicial remedies.[8] These lists of judicial precedents did not carry legal force, but did accurately reflect traditional judicial values and tendencies and may have effectively become an informal source of Ancient Near Eastern law. Such descriptive collections of case law, when incorporated into inscribed royal law collections, served to illustrate the righteousness and justice that characterized a king's reign, but did not reflect prescriptive laws disseminated to the public or enforced by the judicial machinery (LeFebvre 2006: 8–18).

This is not to say that the Ancient Near East did not possess any form of positive law. Royal *misarum* decrees formed an important source of law that was actively enforced by the king's officials, as shown by references in legal case records (Finkelstein 1961: 101, 103). Royal edicts aimed at curbing social ills or judicial abuses represented a king's personal commitment to establishing justice and righteousness within his realm (Weinfeld 1995: 9, 45–56, 75–96). Such royal edicts lasted only as long as the king's reign: no mechanism existed for perpetuating a king's righteous decrees beyond the king's own lifetime. Indeed, *misarum*-act provisions were characteristically temporary measures intended to solve an economic emergency and were not intended to be in force throughout the king's reign (Finkelstein 1961: 101; Westbrook 1991: 47). The subject matter of case law and *misarum* decrees did not overlap,[9] and positive royal authority attached only to the latter (Paul 1970: 5). The positive law represented by *misarum* decrees was thus of an extraordinary type that did not usually apply to mundane court cases. Nevertheless, because *misarum* decrees illustrated the king's positive concern for just rule, they were well suited for inclusion in inscribed law collections.[10] Select excerpts from such decrees, such as wage and price measures or decrees for the relief of debt slavery, were incorporated into inscribed royal law collections such as LE and LH along with case law traditions.[11] Legal documents that cited such authoritative royal measures did not cite the law collections, however, but rather the *misarum* decrees themselves (Finkelstein 1961: 103; Westbrook 2009c: 84–8).

Law collections thus do not represent prescriptive royal legislation to be enforced by the judicial machinery, but a retrospective descriptive survey of just royal measures and informal judicial norms[12] that illustrated the righteousness of the king's rule. In addition to the law collection itself, the royal inscription incorporated a prologue and epilogue, written in poetic form,[13] that suitably extolled the righteousness, justice and divine favor of the king and called for the preservation of the royal stele as an eternal testament to the king's virtue. The creation of the stele containing the Hammurabi Law Code at the end of that king's reign is illustrative of its character as a memorial, like other inscriptions describing a king's mighty deeds, rather than as a body of prescriptive legislation.

2. Comparison with biblical law collections

Under the traditional view that the Pentateuch was authored prior to the dawn of the Hellenistic Era, it once appeared self-evident that the biblical law collections could only have been influenced by Ancient Near Eastern prototypes. As a result, comparative studies on biblical laws, with a few exceptions, focused on cuneiform parallels and neglected the substantial differences between biblical and Ancient Near Eastern law collections. Yet it is easy to see that the biblical law collections differed radically from their Ancient Near Eastern counterparts in virtually all fundamental respects.[14]

Source

Although the creation of lists of infractions and penalties was performed by scribes, the publication of Ancient Near Eastern law collections took place under royal initiative. The laws so published were always attributed to the king (Paul 1970: 8). Biblical law collections claimed a divine origin, mediated by Yahweh's prophet Moses, not royal authorship as in Ancient Near Eastern law collections (Paul 1970: 7, 37, 100; Berman 2008: 59). Pentateuchal laws not only were not published at royal initiative, but also they envisioned a nation with no king, or, under a future change of constitution, a king stripped of virtually all the executive powers universally associated with Ancient Near Eastern monarchs. The pervasive anti-monarchic content of the Pentateuchal law collections appears inconsistent with the otherwise universal Ancient Near Eastern conception of the royal origin of law.

Purpose

Ancient Near Eastern law collections were intended as royal apologia to advertise the king's establishment of righteousness and justice throughout the lands he ruled (Westbrook 2009a: 7), much as other stelae commemorated his military victories, building activities and other mighty deeds. Such propagandistic features were entirely absent from the biblical law collections (Westbrook 2009a: 6). Although the biblical laws were said to be more righteous than that of other nations (Deut. 4.6–8), there was no claim that Moses was a superlatively wise or righteous man, even in his capacity as lawgiver.[15]

Framing structure

Ancient Near Eastern law collections from the Old Babylonian Period were often framed by prologue (LU, LL and LH) and epilogue (LL and LH). The royal prologue dealt extensively with the king's piety and praiseworthy reign, especially as evidenced by his authorship of laws that benefited the land and its peoples. The royal epilogue was also intended to enhance the king's reputation, not only by further dwelling on the positive features of his reign, but also through a section that contained blessings and curses. Standard clauses blessed future rulers who preserved the royal stele and cursed those who would dare to destroy or deface it or replace the royal name with their own. These measures were intended to preserve the stele as an eternal monument to the greatness of the king.[16] None of the biblical law codes were framed by propagandistic royal prologue or epilogue.[17] Blessings and curses attached to biblical law collections served an entirely different purpose. These were pronounced, not on some future ruler who might preserve or deface the law collection and royal monument, but on the people called upon to obey the divine laws the collection contained.

Legal content

Ancient Near Eastern law collections were entirely unconcerned with either private ethics or religious infractions, but were instead exclusively occupied with corrective judicial law that recorded penalties incurred for various crimes and misbehaviors, often organized by the social classes of the perpetrator and victim. Biblical laws contained many legal topics not found in Ancient Near Eastern law collections, such as constitutional law, military law, sacred law and ethical law.[18] The biblical law collections also contained many moral exhortations that enjoined the citizens to act justly and charitably toward their neighbors, advice that placed the locus of righteousness among the citizenry, not in the person of the king as in Ancient Near Eastern monuments and propaganda. Additionally, biblical law collections did not aim at the enforcement of class structure (Paul 1970: 40).

Legal form

The provisions found in Ancient Near Eastern law collections almost exclusively appeared in the casuistic format that is intrinsic to judicial law, in which the infraction *(protasis)* and penalty *(apodosis)* are both predictable elements.[19] Apodictic laws, which took the form of a simple command, were commonly encountered in biblical law, but were almost entirely absent from Ancient Near Eastern law collections.[20] The motive clause, which either explained the purpose of a law or exhorted the citizen to obey it, was a feature found in all the biblical law collections as well as in biblical narratives with legal content, but was entirely absent from Ancient Near Eastern law collections.[21]

In addition to the essential features of Ancient Near Eastern laws which were radically different in biblical laws (source, purpose, framing structure, legal content, legal forms), there were several features found in biblical law that were absent in law collections from the Ancient Near East:

Divine promulgation

As noted earlier, the biblical law collections were presented as a divine law code, both authored and enforced by the deity (Paul 1970: 36), whose name was often invoked within not only the narrative context but also motive clauses attached to individual laws.

Historical contextualization

The biblical law collections were portrayed as the ancestral laws of the Israelites, written down by their founder Moses, and presented within a foundation story of their liberation, migration, conquests and settlement in a new land. This foundation story was frequently invoked within introductory speeches to the laws as well as motive clauses attached to individual laws. The sense of history was strengthened by *ex eventu* prophecies that linked the downfall of the later nations of Israel and Judah to their desertion of the ancestral laws. The linking of the law code to the foundation and subsequent historical fortunes of the nation lacks a parallel in Ancient Near Eastern legal or historical traditions.[22]

Recitation

The oral presentation of the biblical law collections before an assembly of the nation was said to have taken place both at the initial promulgation of these laws (Ex. 24.3–4, 7–8; Deut. 1–26; Josh. 8.30–35; cf. Berman 2008: 43) and periodically thereafter (Deut. 31.10–13). A public reading of the laws was not envisioned for any of the law collections of the Ancient Near East (Paul 1970: 38). Nor were priestly and cultic laws publicly disseminated in the Ancient Near East, in contrast with the publication and recitation of biblical sacred laws (Paul 1970: 9, 38).

Ratification

The collective ratification and adoption of the laws by the nation in public rituals associated with covenant sacrifices (Ex. 24.1–8) and a formal oath of obedience by the assembled people (Deut. 27, 29; Josh. 8.3–35) was central to the presentation of the biblical law collections but has no parallel in connection with the laws of the Ancient Near East.

Covenant blessings and curses

The public ratification of the biblical laws involved a covenant ceremony at which the people promised to obey the laws in perpetuity, with divine blessings on the people and the land in return for their compliance and curses that the deity would rain down on them and their descendants if they disobeyed. These elements of a covenant with the nation and its people, enforced by the deity, are missing in the presentation of Ancient Near Eastern law collections (Weinfeld 1972: 149), which neither enjoined the people to obedience nor promised any consequences for disobedience other than civil or criminal penalties on individual lawbreakers.

Educational utility

The biblical law collections were presented in the form of the "teachings" or Torah of Moses, wherein he reminded the assembled Israelites of their history, of their debt of gratitude and loyalty to the deity that liberated them from slavery, of the regulations they were expected to obey, the blessings of obedience and the consequences of disobedience (cf. Paul 1970: 39). The people were expected to learn the laws, take them to heart and obey them. The Decalogue, in particular, was written for easy memorization and recitation (Carr 2005: 137). Education in the nation's history, culture and laws formed an integral part of the authorized national festivals. There is no evidence that the Ancient Near Eastern law collections were used for the purposes of enculturation or education, except within a narrow scribal setting.

Prescriptive force

The biblical law collections carried authority as prescriptive law, unlike the Ancient Near Eastern law collections, which were descriptive only. The authority of the biblical laws was reinforced by the claims of divine authorship, the pervasive exhortations to obedience they contained, the binding oaths associated with their public ratification, the promised blessings for obedience and threatened curses for disobedience, and the historical narratives in which the consequences of obedience and disobedience played out as a recurrent theme in connection with Yahweh's actions for or against his people in history.

Programmatic implementation

Ancient Near Eastern law was essentially retrospective (Finkelstein 1961: 101; Westbrook 1991: 49–50; Chirichigno 1993: 59). The publication of law collections looked back on a king's reign and described the just legal decisions that marked his rule as righteous. These law collections stood as literal monuments to the greatness of a king. Once published, their purpose was served. By contrast, biblical law collections were forward-looking and programmatic, crafted as literary tools to be used to educate, enculturate and mold the character of the citizen body.

In summary, biblical law collections did not possess the basic features characteristic of Ancient Near Eastern law collections such as royal authorship, apologetic purpose, standard framing structure and limited legal forms and genres. Conversely, Ancient Near Eastern law collections did not share the basic features of biblical law collections such as their divine authority, prescriptive force, programmatic aims, public recitation, educational utility or role in defining the nation's sense of history, culture and ethics. Given these fundamental differences, it does not seem reasonable to maintain that biblical law collections were based on those of the Ancient Near East or influenced by them to a significant degree.

3. Ancient Near Eastern vassal treaties

A key feature of the presentation of biblical law collections was that the people's oath to obey these laws constituted a covenant that bound the nation to Yahweh. This posed a serious difficulty to explain against an Ancient Near Eastern cultural background, because such binding oaths were not associated with the cuneiform law collections. An alternative proposal sought to explain the biblical covenant by comparison with Hittite or Assyrian vassal treaties. Under this model, the biblical relationship between Yahweh and his people was that of a sovereign king and his vassals, where the biblical law collections represented stipulations within a vassal treaty. Support for this theory was sought primarily in claimed structural parallels between the biblical presentation of laws or covenant ceremonies (the Decalogue, Deuteronomy, Josh. 24) and Ancient Near Eastern vassal treaties, bolstered by claimed literary dependence of biblical legal texts on the Vassal Treaty of Esarhaddon of 672 BCE. In chart form, the claimed structural parallels were as follows:

	Hittites	*VTE*	*Biblical*
Preamble identifying parties	yes	yes	Deut. 4.44–45
Historical prologue	yes	no	Ex. 20.2; Deut. 5–11; Josh. 24.2–13
Stipulations	yes	yes	Deut. 12–26; Ex. 20.3–17; Josh. 24.14
Deposit in temple	yes	no	Deut. 10.1–5
Divine and cosmic witnesses	yes	yes	Deut. 30.19; cf. Isa. 1.2
Blessings of obedience	yes	no	Deut. 28.1–14
Curses of disobedience	yes	yes	Deut. 28.15–68
Periodic public readings	yes	no	Deut. 31.10, 13
Literary dependence	no	yes	Deut. 13, 28

The case for biblical adaptation of features from Hittite vassal treaties lies primarily in structural parallels as argued by in Mendenhall 1954. Hittite vassal treaties have a greater number of claimed features in common with the biblical text, including a historical prologue, blessings for obedience, periodic public reading of the vassal treaty and deposit of a copy of the vassal treaty in the temple. However, it has been questioned whether the deposit of a copy of a Hittite vassal treaty in the temple constitutes a valid parallel to the deposit of the Ten Commandments (Deut. 10.1–5; 1 Kgs 8.9), the Book of the Covenant (perhaps Ex. 25.16, 21; 40.20–21) or the book of Deuteronomy (Deut. 31.9) in the ark of the covenant, because the ark was not initially located in a temple in biblical narratives, but in a portable shrine.[23] Furthermore, it is difficult to view the Hittite Empire of ca. 1450–1200 BCE as part of the same historical stream as the biblical authors, even as early as the monarchic period. For these reasons, the case for Hittite treaty forms as a prototype for biblical covenants has largely been abandoned in recent decades.[24]

Alternatively, although a strong case may be made for the dissemination of a version of VTE to Judah under king Manasseh,[25] when Judah was subservient to Esarhaddon, and although Deut. 28 contains parallels to the curses section of VTE, most of the structural parallels between the biblical text and Hittite vassal treaties do not exist with VTE. For instance, VTE lacked a historical prologue and contained only curses but no blessings.[26]

More important to the current discussion, biblical law codes have significant differences with both Hittite and Assyrian vassal treaties.

Literary form

Although a comparison has been made between vassal treaties and the Decalogue or vassal treaties and Deuteronomy, neither the Decalogue nor Deuteronomy conforms to the conventions of a treaty. The Decalogue was written as second person commands, which corresponds to the grammatical voice of stipulations in a vassal treaty, but lacks any recognizable elements of a treaty's prologue or epilogue, such as historical introduction or blessings and curses.[27] Additionally, only the first three commandments resemble the demands of loyalty that a sovereign placed on his vassals.[28] Deuteronomy, on the other hand, was written in the form of an oration, not a treaty (Weinfeld 1972: 10).

Contractual parties

The Vassal Treaties of Esarhaddon were all between two kings, namely Esarhaddon, king of Assyria, and kings of various vassal states. Seventeen of eighteen Hittite vassal treaties were also between two kings. Only one exceptional Hittite vassal treaty was between the Hittite overlord and a subordinate people, with no named vassal king.[29] In no instance was there a vassal treaty in which one of the parties was a deity. Even under the hypothesis that the biblical covenants somehow reflected a vassal treaty between Yahweh as king and an obedient sub-ordinate, one would expect the second party to have been a king, such as king Josiah, under whose reign Deuteronomy was composed and introduced under this theory. But there is no hint of a king as a covenant party in the biblical text.

Stipulations

The stipulations in a vassal treaty dealt strictly with enforcing the political loyalty of a vassal king to his overlord, with the vassal swearing opposition to all conspiracies or attempts at rebellion and swearing unyielding support for the king's dynasty and named successor (cf. Wiseman 1958: 23–5; Weinfeld 1972: 94). In no instance did a vassal treaty involve obedience to a body of adopted laws. A hybrid genre that included both treaty and legal features, as hypothesized for the biblical text,[30] was unknown in the Ancient Near East. Weinfeld argued that the impiety laws of Deut. 13, which condemned the setting up of a new religious cult as a form of treason, preserved vassal treaty language from VTE that originally applied to political rebellion (Weinfeld 1972: 91–100), but as shown earlier (Chapter 3 §13), Deut. 13 was not based on VTE but on impiety laws found at Athens and in Plato's *Laws*.

Curses

The case for dependence of the biblical law collections on the genre of Ancient Near Eastern vassal treaties thus rests primarily on similar curse language employed in VTE and Deut. 28 (Wiseman 1958: 26 n. 201; Weinfeld 1972: 116–29). And the curses are indeed sufficiently striking in form that some sort of literary dependence appears likely. But the Pentateuchal use of language originally taken from the Assyrians appears to have been restricted to these curses. Neither VTE nor Ancient Near Eastern law collections of any period associated the language of curses with disobedience to laws, nor did the curse language of Deut. 28 contain any literary overlap with the laws presented in Deut. 12–26. A direct link thus does not exist between the repertoire of curses found in VTE and Deut. 28 with Dtn or with any other law collection, either biblical or Assyrian. Furthermore, similar curse language appeared at the end of many types of Assyrian inscriptions (Wiseman 1958: 27–8; Weinfeld 1972: 61–2) and was found in many other biblical contexts with no legislative or treaty associations whatever, such as in Deuteronomistic prophecies in Jeremiah, in Job and even in curse language with Assyrian affinities found in the account of the destruction of Sodom and Gomorrah in Genesis.[31] This shows a distant Assyrian background to the generic vocabulary of imprecation employed in a variety of biblical contexts, but indicates that the use of such imprecatory language does not point to an original context that involved vassal treaties (so Crouch 2014: 54–78). Literary parallels between VTE and Deut. 28 thus do not indicate that Deuteronomy represents a modified form of vassal treaty, but only that Deut. 28 drew on a tradition of curse language with Assyrian roots (Crouch 2014: 108–17).

In summary, it is difficult to understand the biblical law collections as stipulations in a modified vassal treaty between Yahweh and the people of Israel. The parallels with Ancient Near Eastern vassal treaties such as VTE have been overstated and the differences are striking. The association of the biblical law collections with covenant rituals does not appear to derive from the Ancient Near East.

4. Greek law collections

By now it should be evident that neither Ancient Near Eastern law collections nor vassal treaties provide convincing comparisons for biblical law collections, but differ markedly in such fundamental aspects as the sources and purpose of law, basic categories of law, the prescriptive force of law and the public recitation and ratification of law. It is legitimate to consider whether ancient Greek law provides a better match on such fundamental matters.[32]

Greek law collections

Many ancient law collections from the ancient Greek world have been preserved, to a greater or lesser extent, either in inscriptional form uncovered in archaeological excavations or through quotation in literary texts from antiquity. Many Greek city-states were said to have received their law codes during the Age of Lawgivers (ca. 650–510 BCE).[33] Extensive portions of the Great Code of Gortyn (ca. 450 BCE), inscribed on the walls of the Temple of Temple of Apollo Pythia, were unearthed at Gortyn, Crete. Most of these laws were corrective laws phrased in casuistic form on topics such as slavery, rape, adultery, divorce and inheritance.[34] Spartan laws attributed to Lycurgus, known as *Rhetra,* were intentionally not recorded in fixed inscriptions (Xenophon, *Lacedemonian Constitution* 13.1), but many of the *Rhetra* have been preserved in literary sources, notably at Xenophon, *Lacedemonian Constitution* 6.1–2; 13.1–6. Ancient Roman laws of ca. 450 BCE, which were said to have been modeled on those of Greece (Livy, *History of Rome* 3.31–34), and which have affinities with several laws known to have been authored by Solon, were famously inscribed on the *Twelve Tablets* publicly displayed at Rome. These tablets have not survived to the present, but the *Twelve Tablets* were extensively quoted (with variations) in surviving literary sources. These also predominantly took the form of casuistic laws and dealt with such topics as theft, debtors, marriage, inheritance, assault and judicial procedures.[35] Athenian laws were inscribed and put on display at various locations around the city, the most important collection being those found at the Royal Stoa.[36] Some of these laws have been recovered by archaeologists, including an inscription from 404 BCE that quoted most of Drakon's famous homicide law of ca. 620 BCE. Many other Athenian laws have been preserved in literary sources, often quoted in full in Athenian legal orations. Athenian substantive laws predominantly appeared in casuistic format (Phillips 2013: ix). Other inscriptions that dealt with a wide variety of legal matters, including constitutional, sacred and civic laws, have been discovered at sites throughout the Greek world, from the Archaic Era to the Hellenistic and Roman Eras. One important quasi-legal inscription known as the Commandments of the Seven Sages was found on the walls of the temple of Delphi (sixth century BCE), a set of ethical maxims in apodictic form reproduced or excerpted in inscriptions and many literary texts from later times. Finally, one may note Plato's *Laws,* which contained a complete constitution and law collection written in casuistic and apodictic forms, and uniquely also containing supplementary material in the form of legal introductions as well as motive clauses attached to individual laws.

Legal forms and content

As noted earlier, Greek law included a wide range of genres that corresponded to biblical legal categories: constitutional law, sacred law, civic regulations, judicial law and ethical law. Constitutional laws, which defined the magistracies of the *polis* and their qualifications, methods of selection and responsibilities, were primarily descriptive and procedural. This genre closely corresponds to Deut. 16.18–18.22, a sub-document of Dtn that dealt primarily with constitutional matters. Sacred laws were largely procedural; for religious infractions, they also specified ritual remedies or penalties such as sacrifices which, although voluntary, served to alleviate religious anxieties. Civic law dealt with citizen responsibilities, ranging from simple apodictic commands to more extensive procedural directives, such as when and how to report for military duty. Greek laws that dealt with corrective justice described judicial procedures and specified criminal and civic infractions and their penalties.[37] These laws contained the same range of legal forms encountered in the biblical text: casuistic law that listed infractions and penalties, apodictic commands and (in Plato's *Laws*) explanatory motive clauses. Ethical laws took the form of brief maxims that were phrased in the form of commands, but did not have prescriptive force. They essentially defined the things that an ethical person should do, such as honoring their parents or the gods and doing justice by their friends and fellow-citizens. This wide range of legal subject matter was common to biblical and Greek legislation, but does not correspond to Ancient Near Eastern law collections, which dealt exclusively with judicial corrective law, only rarely mentioned incidental matters of procedure[38] and contained no constitutional, sacred or ethical law.

Forms of legislation

Five categories of legislation were recognized in the Greek world. The first was the maxim, commandments by ancient legislators that enjoined ethical behavior, but which carried no prescriptive weight as enforceable law (Gagarin 1986: 53–5). The second was unwritten law, also called ancestral law, which usually included or subsumed the category of sacred law. In Sparta, uniquely, all law was unwritten law (Xenophon, *Lacedemonian Constitution* 13.1). Unwritten or ancestral law typically carried legal force in a law court, but in 404 BCE the Athenians enacted legislation that proclaimed that only written laws were enforceable and that magistrates and judges should never rely on unwritten law. This resulted in a new initiative to accomplish the systematic written codification of Athenian law: even traditional unwritten sacred law was actively recorded in written form starting in ca. 400 BCE. A third category was written law. In sixth and fifth century BCE Athens, unwritten, customary laws were referred to as *nomoi*, whereas laws enacted by a legislator or ruler were referred to as *thesmoi* (Ostwald 1969: 12–40; Rhodes 1993: 177). But by ca. 400 BCE, *nomoi* came to denote written legislation enacted and ratified by the *polis* (Ostwald 1969: 57; Thomas 1996: 16–19). By this time, written law in Athens had come to be seen as a visible expression of democracy and a protection against injustice (Euripides, *Suppliants* 433; Aristotle, *Politics* 2.1270b; 3.1286a, 1287b; cf. Thomas 1996: 17). A fourth category of legislation was constitutional law, which dealt with the administration of the *polis*. A fifth category was the *psephema* or decree, enacted by the council or assembly to address matters of an immediate character, such as declarations of war, ratifications of treaties, allocation of funds and granting of honors to individuals. In 403 BCE, legislation was passed in Athens that made it a crime to propose or enact a decree that contravened either the constitution or written law (Andocides, *On the Mysteries* 85, 87, 89). The preeminent authority given to the Athenian constitution and body of written laws in ca. 400 BCE represented a revolution in the notion of law. For the first time, government was made fully subject to the rule of law.[39] This elevated conception of law was unknown to the Ancient Near East, where all authority was invested in the person of the king (Levinson 2001: 532). Among the Greeks, even kings were subject to law (Aristotle, *Politics* 4.1292a) – including at Athens, where an office of *Archon Basileus* or king existed alongside the other magistracies – whereas the arbitrary wielding of power by a single person not subject to law was known by another name, tyranny. The Torah of the King (Deut. 17.14–20) also allowed an office of king subject to law.[40] The idea of a nation under the rule of sovereign law was thus common to both the biblical and Athenian legal systems, but was entirely alien to the Ancient Near East.

Sources

In the Greek world, constitutions and laws came from one of three sources. Several Greek states claimed divine authorship for their laws: Minos was said to have received the laws of Crete from Zeus at the Cave of Zeus on Mount Idas (Plato, *Minos* 318c; Plato's *Laws* 1.624a-b, 625b, 632d; Strabo, *Geography* 10.4.19); Lycurgus of Sparta received his laws from Apollo at the temple of Delphi (Plutarch, *Lycurgus* 1.1–3; 5.3; 6.2; 13.6; Plato, *Laws* 1.624a, 632d, 634d; Xenophon, *Lacedemonian Constitution* 8.5; Strabo, *Geography* 10.4.19); the laws of Zaleucus of Locri were revealed to him by Athena in a dream (Scholiast on Pindar, *Olympian Odes* 10.17; Clement of Alexandria, *Miscellanies* 1.170.3; cf. Mühl 1933: 85; Gagarin 1986: 58); Plato claimed that the laws of primordial Athens were revealed by the goddess Athena (Plato, *Timaeus* 23d, 24b-d) and that the laws of mythical Atlantis were revealed to its first kings by Poseidon (Plato, *Critias* 119c-120a; cf. Morrow 1993: 582; Hagedorn 2004: 74). The divine inspiration or authority of laws were reinforced by their inscription on temple walls (cf. Thomas 1996: 31), such as the Great Code of Gortyn on the temple of Apollo Pythia (Hagedorn 2004: 69, 79) or the Commandments of the Seven Sages on the temple of Apollo at Delphi (Morrow 1993: 410). Human legislators often journeyed to oracles to gain divine approval for the laws they crafted. The oracle at Delphi gave its sanction to the laws of Lycurgus (Plutarch, *Lycurgus* 1.1–3; 5.3; 6.2; 13.6; Xenophon, *Lacedemonian Constitution* 8.5; Strabo, *Geography* 10.4.19), to the sacred laws of Cyrene (Callimachus, *Hymn to Apollo*, 5; *Cyrene Foundation Inscription*, line 1; cf. Weinfeld 1993: 36) and to other law codes.

Founders of colonies were a second source of laws. The expedition leader or *oikist*, usually assigned this role by an oracle of Apollo, was expected to provide a constitution and system of laws for the colony he established.[41] Many Greek city-states viewed a famous legendary or historical figure believed or known to have authored their ancestral constitution and laws as founder of their *polis*, even when that foundation was not a colonization (Hagedorn 2004: 84). Sparta had already been in existence for a long time when its constitution and laws were established by the legendary lawgiver Lycurgus, and Athens was viewed as having been refounded when it received a new constitution and laws from Solon (ca. 594 BCE) and again later under Kleisthenes (ca. 508 BCE). The foundational laws of Drakon, Solon and Kleisthenes were considered "ancestral laws" *(patrios politeia)* by both warring oligarchic and democratic political parties during the turmoil of 410–404 BCE (Andocides, *On the Mysteries* 83; Jacoby 1949: 43; MacDowell 1978: 43; Ostwald 1986: 416, 514; Rhodes 1993: 376, 434, 440). Whether the laws were authored by gods or by legendary founders or historical refounders of the *polis*, the antiquity of ancestral laws enhanced their prestige and authority.[42] Ancestral laws, especially those revealed or authored by the gods, were often considered immutable.[43]

A third source of legislation encountered in the Greek world was a specially convened panel of *nomothetai* or legislators. In legendary and historical accounts of foundations down to the early Classical period, the laws were crafted by a single legislator, but starting in the fifth century BCE, it became increasingly common for the mother city or *metropolis* to assign a small panel of legislators to the task (Diodorus Siculus, *Library* 12.10.4–5 [Thurii]; Livy, *History of Rome* 3.34 [Rome]; Plato, *Laws* 3.702c [Magnesia]). In 410 BCE, a panel of legislators was assigned the job of drafting a new constitution and laws based on those of Solon, but after six years its task was still incomplete (Lysias, *Against Nicomachus* 2–6; Andocides, *On the Mysteries* 83–4; cf. MacDowell 1978: 46–8; Ostwald 1986: 372, 415, 511; Rhodes 1991; 1993: 373–74, 441). An extraordinary panel of 500 *nomothetai* was convened at Athens in 404 BCE, after the overthrow of the Thirty Tyrants, to restore the ancestral constitution and laws of Athens that had been authored by Solon and Kleisthenes.[44] Their task of researching and publishing the ancestral laws took them all of 404–400 BCE (Ostwald 1986: 511–23; Rhodes 1993: 416, 441–2). Subsequent Athenian law called for a panel of *nomotheiai* to be selected by lot each year to review Athenian written laws, identify possible omissions or internal inconsistencies, and propose revisions consistent with existing legislation (Rhodes 1985; Ostwald 1986: 520; Ostwald 1993: 523). The proposed revisions were published near the statues of the Eponymous Heroes for public viewing and these revisions – or possibly the entire body of Athenian laws (Andocides, *On the Mysteries* 83; cf. Ostwald 1986: 515) – were read before the Assembly of Athenian citizens for ratification, with debate and votes on each proposed change (Demosthenes, *Against Timocrates* 20–3; cf. Nightingale 1999: 109).

Sources of law in the Greek world thus included the gods, founder figures and appointed panels of legislators. The figure of king is notable in its absence, with certain rare exceptions where the role of king and founder figure coincided.[45] The creation of the biblical law collections as described in the Pentateuch closely followed Greek patterns. The biblical laws were considered to be of divine – not royal – authorship. The figure of Moses was portrayed as a typically Greek colonizing expedition leader, founder and lawgiver, both in the *Aegyptiaca* by Hecataeus of Abdera (ca. 315 BCE) and later in the biblical account. The representation of the Torah as the *patrios nomima* of the Jews[46] gave it an air of authority that derived from its purported antiquity.[47] The journey by Moses to Mount Sinai to receive the divine laws has ample Greek precedent (see Chapter 5 §2). Although the Seventy Elders who also made the trek to Mount Sinai (Ex. 24.1, 9) were not given an explicit legislative role, this group appears to have alluded to the *gerousia* of seventy(-two) elders who played a prominent role in recreating the ancient ancestral laws of the Jews at Alexandria in ca. 270 BCE (see Chapter 2 §7). The reading of the biblical law collections before the full assembly for ratification (Ex. 24.3; Deut. 27.26; *The Letter of Aristeas* 308–11), which has no parallel in Ancient Near Eastern legal tradition, is consistent with prosaic Greek legislative practices.

Oaths and rituals

In a Greek city-state with features of democratic self-rule like Athens during most of the Classical Era, the constitution and laws were understood as a written expression of the social contract that bound together the citizens of the *polis* and gave each of them a share in the government.[48] This social contract often took explicit form on various occasions in which the citizens swore an oath, often accompanied by ritual sacrifices,[49] in conjunction with the execution of his public duties as a member of the *polis*. Every citizen took an oath to defend the *polis* at his induction into the citizen body and military at age twenty (Lycurgus, *Against Leokrates* 1.76–82; Meiggs and Lewis 1969: 89–94; Fornara 1983: 56, 70–3; Gruen 1993: 345–6; Rhodes and Osborne 2003: 440–9; Hagedorn 2004: 76 n. 237; Rhodes 2007: 20). Other oaths were sworn by members of each session of the Assembly;[50] jury members had their own oath (Mirhady 2007: 48–59; Sommerstein 2007: 4); those elected to the Council had another oath.[51] Swearing to uphold the constitution and laws of the *polis* was one aspect of many of these oaths. Public rituals at which the entire citizen body swore to uphold the constitution and laws were reported in conjunction with major constitutional and legal reforms. Perhaps the most elaborate literary description of the ceremonies associated with the adoption of a new constitution and laws was the one Plato reported when Poseidon gave his laws to the first kings of Atlantis. This ceremony, which involved the slaughter of sacrificial animals, oaths to uphold the laws of Atlantis and the inscribing of sacred laws on pillars, has been compared to both the covenant ceremonies in Exodus and inscribed laws in Deuteronomy (Plato, *Critias* 119c-120b; Ex. 24.3–8; Deut. 27.2–8; cf. Hagedorn 2004: 74–5; Wajdenbaum 2011: 164–5). Blessings on Atlantis were promised so long as it upheld the divine laws, but curses should she ever depart from them;[52] indeed, when the Atlantians of a later generation unjustly undertook wars of aggression on the peoples of the Mediterranean, the gods punished Atlantis by sending earthquakes that caused the island kingdom to sink beneath the ocean (Plato, *Critias* 108e, 121b; Plato, *Timaeus* 25c-d). But oaths were not restricted to mythical tales. After the great legislator Solon introduced a new constitution and laws for Athens in ca. 594 BCE, the citizens assembled and swore amid public sacrifices to obey the laws for at least ten years (some sources say a hundred years) without modifying them (Herodotus, *Histories* 1.29; Plutarch, *Solon* 16.5; 25.1–3, 6; Aristotle, *Athenian Constitution* 7–8; cf. Stanton 1990: 39–40, 83–5; Rhodes 1993: 130, 135; Rhodes 2007: 15–16). At the overthrow of the Thirty Tyrants and the restoration of a democratic constitution and ancestral laws in 404 BCE, the peoples of Athens assembled by tribe in the Agora and swore, amid sacrificial ceremonies, not only to uphold the restored constitution but to slay on the spot any who conspired to overthrow the constitution or establish a tyranny – the famous Oath of Demophantos.[53] In both the Greek and biblical worlds,[54] the adoption of a constitution and laws thus represented a critical event in the history of the nation, one associated with the gathering of the citizen body, the conducting of public sacrifices and ceremonies and the administering of oaths of obedience on all those assembled.

Programmatic reform

At Athens, the introduction of a new constitution and laws under Solon in ca. 594 BCE, under Kleisthenes in ca. 508 BCE, and under the democratic reformers of 404 BCE were in each case prompted by social and constitutional crises which the reforms were designed to resolve. The planned effect of these constitutional and legal reforms was nothing less than the refounding of the nation, a change in its basic character and an elevation of the rights of its citizens. The introduction of a law code was thus not retrospective, like in the Ancient Near East, but forward-looking and programmatic. The constitution and laws of the biblical and Greek world had comparable roles in reforming and shaping the fundamental character of the nation, not aggrandizing the past rule of a king.[55]

Publication

An important aspect of law in the Greek world (except in Sparta) was its publication in written form, which added to its authority and gave access to their laws to the citizenry of the *polis*. Inscriptions with constitutional and prescriptive legal content are found throughout the Greek world. Solon's reforms of ca. 594 BCE resulted in a body of laws that were recorded for public viewing at Athens.[56] Legal research by the panel of *nomothetai* in 410–404 BCE resulted in a definitive body of restored ancestral laws that were published on the walls of the Royal Stoa.[57] Copies of laws were stored in the Metroön. Proposed laws or laws published for temporary display appeared on plastered stones (Demosthenes, *Against Timocrates* 23; Lysias, *For the Soldier* 6; cf. Rhodes 1993: 555; Rhodes and Osborne 2003: 27–37; Hagedorn 2004: 72–6). Several authors have compared the Athenian publication of laws on plastered surfaces with the biblical provision at Deut. 27.1–8 (cf. Josh. 8.30–35) that called for the Mosaic laws to be recorded on plastered stones on Mount Ebal (Hagedorn 2004: 72, 76; Knoppers and Harvey 2007: 139 n. 145). Oral publication by periodic public reading of laws was also common to biblical provisions and Athenian historical practices.[58]

Educational utility

The aim of education at Athens was to impart those skills and values that would be useful to students, not to learn a trade, but to take their place as citizens in the *polis*. Such virtues as courage, wisdom, justice and temperance were qualities valued in citizens in their capacity as soldiers, jurors and magistrates. Although the law defined proper behavior, encouraging just behavior and meting out punishments for injustice, Athenian educators and philosophers did not view the laws themselves as a vehicle of education – like the Torah or teachings of Moses – with one exception, namely in Plato's *Laws,* where Plato introduced new legal forms designed to educate the citizens and foster virtuous thought and behavior.

From the earlier discussion, it should be apparent that the biblical law collections closely resembled those of the Greeks in terms of their divine authorship or authority, their introduction by a founder figure, their prescriptive force and programmatic aims and the oaths, sacrifices and other public rituals associated with their introduction. The ratification of law by an assembly and their publication for viewing by the citizenry reflect practices at Athens and other Greek city-states. Certain aspects of the biblical law collections such as the synthesis of law and education appear specifically indebted to Plato's *Laws*. None of these features of biblical and Greek laws are associated with Ancient Near Eastern law collections.[59]

5. Pentateuchal law collections

The previous section showed the fundamental consistency between the biblical law collections as a whole and Greek legal traditions. In the current section, Greek literary parallels to individual biblical law collections will be considered.

The Covenant Code

Unlike Ancient Near Eastern law collections, the Covenant Code (Ex. 20.19–23.19) contained both civil and sacred laws (Paul 1970: 34). Greek political bodies legislated both civil laws and laws relating to the festival calendar and official religious cults of the *polis*.[60] The Covenant Code resembled Greek law collections in this respect. As discussed in Chapter 3, the Covenant Code also contained several legal provisions that appear to display literary dependence on Plato's *Laws*. Although it is not possible to find systematic correspondence in the structures of the Covenant Code and Plato's *Laws,* it may be significant that the main body of laws at Ex. 21.12–22.15 appear to be arranged for the most part in descending order of severity, starting with homicide and assault, much like Plato's *Laws*, and in contrast to the somewhat random arrangement of laws in Ancient Near Eastern collections.[61]

The priestly code

Sacred laws were the exclusive subject matter of Ex. 35–40 and Lev. 1–16. The content of these priestly laws correspond with topics found in Greek sacred law (see Chapter 3 §14). Although sacred laws associated with mystery cults were closely guarded secrets, the Greeks often published sacred laws associated with the civic cults, either in inscriptional or written form.[62] The publication of biblical sacred laws corresponds to Greek practices, but appears inconsistent with practices in the Ancient Near East, where cultic laws were closely guarded secrets of the temples and their priests.

The Holiness Code

The mixture of civic and sacred law in the Holiness Code (Lev. 17–26), like that found in the Covenant Code and the Deuteronomic Law Code, appears to correspond to Greek rather than Ancient Near Eastern practices.

The Deuteronomic Law Code

The book of Deuteronomy presents a collection of laws and constitutional provisions in the form of a fictional speech by Moses in the plain of Moab, just prior to the Israelites entering the Promised Land. This sophisticated composition is an example of what the Greeks called *logographia* or speech-writing. Greek training in rhetoric included both oral presentation and written composition, with prose writing techniques based on principles taken from the art of public speaking.[63] Biblical literature, especially that traditionally classified as Deuteronomistic, contained significant rhetorical content.[64] The book of Deuteronomy contained extensive use of rhetorical argument to persuade the listener of the benefits of obeying the statutes presented (see generally Watts 1999, especially pp. 32, 129–30). This included a lengthy introduction to the law collection as a whole (Deut. 1–11), a hortatory (parenetic) address that was intended to put the listener in a receptive frame of mind to heed the Mosaic laws. Shorter exhortations were interspersed throughout the main collection of laws in Deut. 12–26 (Dtn). Motive clauses attached to individual laws attempted to persuade the citizens to obey the laws, either by explaining the reason for the law or by making an appeal to obedience in the form of either positive incentives for compliance or threats for disobedience.[65] Although legal introductions, exhortations and motive clauses are also found attached to other Pentateuchal laws, they predominate in Deuteronomy.[66] Both parenetic hortatory addresses and motive clauses are entirely absent from Ancient Near Eastern law collections[67] and have often been claimed as unique biblical innovations.[68] This claim to biblical originality appears inaccurate, however, because the same combination of legislation and persuasive rhetoric appeared prominently in Plato's *Laws* of ca. 350 BCE.

A prominent characteristic of Deuteronomy was its presentation of law as education. The word for law used most often in Deuteronomy was *torah* or teaching; the Mosaic discourse in the plain of Moab was described as the teachings of Moses (Deut. 1.5; 4.8, 44; 17.18–19; 27.3, 8, 26; 28.58, 61; 29.21, 29; 30.10; 31.9, 11–12, 24, 26; 32.46). The Deuteronomic law was not merely a constitution and body of legislation to govern the tribes of Israel in the land they were about to conquer, but an educational text to shape their character and behaviors as citizens and as worshippers of Yahweh. The entire text of Deuteronomy was to be read every seven years at the festival of Succoth for the education and enculturation of the entire citizen body, including men, women, children and even the strangers who were resident in the land (Deut. 31.9–13). This text was also to be published in its entirety on plastered stones so that all the people could read it, and excerpts were to be posted at the threshold of every house and worn on the hand and forehead as a constant reminder and a ready reference (Deut. 6.8–9; 11.18–21). The law was to be inculcated in the mind and soul of every citizen, written on their hearts (cf. Carr 2005: 135–6). The leader of the children of Israel was to meditate on it day and night (Josh. 1.8), and should the people ever choose rulership under a king, his primary duty was to personally make a copy of the laws under priestly supervision and to study it every day (Deut. 17.19). A copy of the law was to be laid up in the ark of the testimony where it would someday serve as dire witness to the wicked last kings that their coming inevitable destruction was due to the people's disobedience to the Mosaic laws.[69] Even this had educational as well as rhetorical value, because it interpreted the history of the Jews in light of their fidelity to the ancestral laws.[70] While Ancient Near Eastern law collections were sometimes publicly displayed to provide evidence for the righteousness and justice of a king's rule, they were never promoted as educational tools for the people nor celebrated and disseminated within a festival context. The idea of legislation as education was also not found in the Greek and Roman world, with the exception of Plato's *Laws* and later writings that interacted with that seminal text. Plato innovated the idea that the lawgiver should both create a set of laws for the *polis* and educate the citizenry in the benefits of obedience (see especially Jaeger 1943: 3.213–16). Plato contrasted the usual method of presenting law codes as a series of commands and penalties, which he described as tyrannical prescriptions, with his innovative methods of combining laws with education and persuasion that sought to secure voluntary compliance to the laws, whenever possible (Plato, *Republic* 3.389c; 5.459c; 6.489c; 8.564b-c; Plato, *Statesman* 293a-b; Plato, *Laws* 3.684c; 4.719e-720e; 9.857c-e). The Deuteronomic notion of law as *torah* appears directly indebted to Plato's *Laws*. Outside the legal system of the Jews and Samaritans, the innovative Platonic approach that combined legislation with teaching was never implemented in any real world setting, and was criticized as utterly impractical by Posidonius of Apamea, among others, but was theoretically endorsed by the Roman authors Seneca and Cicero (Seneca, *Letters* 94.38 [which commented on Posidonius]; Cicero, *On Laws* 1.15; 2.14–16).

Plato's entire body of writing displayed ongoing concerns with rhetoric and education, especially as tools for promoting virtue, both within individuals and politically within the *polis* as a whole. In Plato's *Laws,* his final dialogue, which represented the culmination of his thinking on the intersection of philosophy and politics, Plato advocated a new type of political system in which education, rhetoric and legislation would be combined to create a body of citizens who had been enculturated and conditioned from birth toward obedience of the laws. In this text he laid out his plans for the innovative use of persuasive argument by the colony's legislators in the presentation of both the law collection as a whole and – selectively – of individual laws or groups of laws. Plato's program for combining legislation and persuasion began with the lawgiver crafting a persuasive *prooem* or prologue to the laws as a whole in order to make the citizens pliant and not hostile to the laws that would soon govern their conduct (Plato, *Laws* 4.719e-720a). Smaller blocks of laws should also have their own *prooimia,* as appropriate, and even individual laws should contain carefully crafted persuasive content (Plato, *Laws* 4.718b-723d; cf. Morrow 1993: 553–5). Plato insisted that every legislator who wished to be effective must master the art of skillfully combining the usual commands and penalties of the law with persuasive explanations (which Plato designated as *paramuthia* or "exhortations"), in order that the citizens would understand the benefits of complying with the laws the legislators had crafted.[71] Plato described his innovative legislative technique for attaching persuasions to individual laws as writing a double law, in contrast to the usual single law that he disparaged as a format appropriate for tyrants, who utilized only threats without any effort at persuasion or education.[72] A single law would consist of a simple apodictic command ("a man shall marry between the ages of thirty and thirty-five years old" in his example) followed by a casuistic command ("if he fails to do so, he shall be punished by both a monetary fine and by degradation, the fine being of such and such amount, and the degradation of such and such a kind") (Plato, *Laws* 4.721a-b). A double law would interpose between the two a persuasive and educational explanation of the law, which might include its basic rationale, its divine background or holy character, the benefits of compliance and the negative effects of disobedience, both for the citizen himself and for the *polis* as a whole, and by so combining threats and persuasion achieve greater compliance to the law than by using threats alone (Plato, *Laws* 4.721b-d). A more explicit definition, explanation and example of the motive clause (as biblical scholars call it) can scarcely be imagined.[73] This blending of persuasive rhetoric, education and legislation was a Platonic innovation and was encountered nowhere in antiquity (Annas 2010: 75) outside of Plato's *Laws,* the Pentateuch and occasional later literary texts that explicitly endorsed the innovative legislative approach found in Plato's *Laws* such as Cicero's *On Laws* of ca. 50 BCE.[74] Given the striking correspondence between the biblical use of parenetic introductions and motive clauses and the persuasive *prooimia* or *paramuthia* first advocated in Plato's *Laws,*[75] there can be little doubt regarding the influence of Plato's *Laws* on the text of Deuteronomy.[76]

In fact, the book of Deuteronomy appears to have been written in direct accordance with legislative strategies and instructions found in Plato's *Laws*. This is brought out, not only by the strikingly similar synthesis of law, education and rhetoric, by the use of legal *prooimia* and *paramuthia,* and by the similar constitutional and legislative provisions discussed in Chapter 2 and 3, but by structural and narrative features found in Deuteronomy that appear directly indebted to Plato's *Laws*. Broadly speaking, both were written versions of oral presentations (Watts 1999: 29–31; Nightingale 1993: 288). The two pieces had a similar fictional setting, just prior to the setting up of a new colony. Both Moses and the fictional protagonists of Plato's *Laws* were legislators who were presenting a new law code for this new colony. Both texts included both constitution and laws.[77] Plato's *Laws* was an esoteric, behind-the-scenes manual for creating this constitution and laws, but contained explicit directions for an exoteric, public presentation of the laws to the general citizenry that strikingly corresponds to the book of Deuteronomy. When the colonists were newly arrived at the land, the legislator was to gather them together and address them (Plato, *Laws* 4.715e). Before presenting the laws, he was first to deliver a lengthy prelude or *prooem* in which he would emphasize the divine character of the state they were about to establish (4.716a); the divine vengeance that would be visited on lawbreakers (4.716a-b); the necessity to live nobly in accordance with divine will (4.716c-d), to engage in constant sacrifice, prayer and communion with the gods (4.716e-717a), to honor the ancient gods, their ancestors and their parents (4.717a-e); and the divine blessings on the *polis* about to be founded that would be secure by the noble and pious conduct of the citizens (4.718a-b). After these preliminaries, and other introductory ethical exhortations designed to make the gathered colonists docile and receptive (4.718c-d), the legislator would then begin to present the constitution and legislation itself, intermixed by suitable *prooimia* and *paramuthia* to individual laws (4.718b-c). Plato's *Laws* contained many major and minor sections designed to be directly incorporated into the legislator's speech to the colonists.[78] Clearly, the legislator's envisioned address to the colonists in Plato's *Laws* corresponds in great detail to Moses' speech and legislation in Deut. 1–26. Both law collections incorporated persuasive introductions and motive clauses attached to individual laws, features effectively unique to biblical law and Plato's *Laws*.[79] Both texts referred to themselves as supremely valuable for educational purposes[80] and both envisioned legal readings at public festivals where all citizens were present, including women and children (Deut. 31.9–13; Plato, *Laws* 3.664d; 7.811d-e, 812e-813a; 10.887d). Both books contained unusual self-references to the book as though already written: Moses referred several times to the completed book of Deuteronomy, much like Plato referred to *Laws* as a finished text.[81] The end of both books contained praise for the legislator as a figure who would be revered by later generations.[82] These parallels are sufficiently unique to the two texts under discussion to indicate that Deuteronomy sought to imitate Plato's *Laws,* insofar as this was possible within the constraints of Deuteronomy's fictional ancient narrative setting.

The Decalogue

The Decalogue constitutes a distinct category of law collection that lays out the fundamentals of societal ethics in a set of ten commandments, brief admonitions whose form consists of a simple apodictic directive, sometimes preceded or followed by a motive clause (Sonsino 1980: 86–7). Stripped of these secondary additions, the Decalogue is reduced to a set of ten very simple ethical maxims (ten "words" or "sayings") that appear intended to shape both the outward behavior and inner conscience of those addressed. The brevity of the commandments appears to have made them ideal for memorization and for oral recitation (Carr 2005: 137). Their educational significance is highlighted by the instructions to the children of Israel to wear these commandments in phylacteries on their foreheads, post them on their doorposts and inculcate them as part of the education of their children (Ex. 13.9, 16; Deut. 6.8–9; 11.18, 20; Prov. 6.21; 7.3; cf. Carr 2005: 135).

The Decalogue has no direct parallel in Ancient Near Eastern literature[83] but closely corresponds to the Commandments of the Seven Sages famous in the Greek world.[84] These commandments consisted of a collection of ethical maxims that tradition attributed to the Seven Sages of archaic Greece.[85] Each commandment consisted of a brief ethical maxim in a standard apodictic format, such as: Follow God, Obey the Law, Honor Your Parents, Know Yourself, Despise a Slanderer, Guard Friendship, and so forth. The Commandments of the Seven Sages appeared on an inscription located in the temple of Pythian Apollo at Delphi, home to the famous Delphic oracle.[86] This Delphic inscription dated to 514 BCE at the latest, because, according to Plato, it was used for educational purposes during the time of the Pisistratids.[87] The popular attribution of these commandments to the Seven Sages of antiquity gave these ethical maxims an informal legal stature, because the Seven Sages were all famous lawgivers.[88] The prominent display of the Commandments of the Seven Sages in the most revered of all Greek temples gave these wise commandments an aura of divine sanction, much like the tablet inscribed with the Ten Commandments said to reside in the ark of the covenant within the Jewish temple (Ex. 25.16; 40.20; Deut. 10.5; 1 Kgs 8.9). The Commandments of the Seven Sages was commonly used as a school text[89] and found a widespread distribution, not only in the Greek world, but also, as a result of Alexander's conquests, in the Hellenized east.[90] The Jewish and Greek commandments possessed identical apodictic form, divine association with a famous temple, purported authorship by famous legislators of the distant past, widespread use as an educational text to instill citizen ethics and even some shared content,[91] all pointing to their belonging to the same Greek literary genre.[92] Jewish exposure to the Commandments of the Seven Sages certainly could have taken place at the Great Library of Alexandria,[93] if not earlier.[94]

6. Conclusions

The current chapter compared Ancient Near Eastern, Greek and biblical law collections with respect to their sources, aims, structure, prescriptive force and the categories of laws they contained. In the Ancient Near East, the king was said to be the author of laws, and the laws were cataloged, published and displayed on monuments for the purpose of royal self-aggrandizement. Law collections dealt exclusively with corrective justice, that is, the listing of criminal and civil infractions and their punishment. Law collections retrospectively recorded general judicial practices under a king's reign, as found in scribal collections, but lacked prescriptive force, contained no references to public readings, ritual ceremonies or oaths whereby the people swore to obey the laws and did not represent a form of social contract binding on either the king or the people. Prescriptive force attached only to decrees, which were enforced by royal power, and which were of a fundamentally different character than the judicial law collections, despite occasional quotes from decrees that scribes inserted into law collections. Vassal treaties were also discussed earlier. Although these imposed loyalty of a subject ruler and were enforced by oaths and dire curses, they contained no legal content. Traditional attempts to force a relationship between the biblical law collections and Ancient Near Eastern law collections and treaties do not appear convincing.

By contrast, biblical and Greek law collections shared many essential features, including claims of divine authorship or inspiration, the initial introduction by a revered founder figure, the respect accorded to the ancient ancestral constitution and laws, the prescriptive force of law, authorization by an assembly, oaths and rituals associated with their adoption by the citizen body, public recitation and use as a programmatic force of social reform. Several Pentateuchal law collections had special affinities with categories of Greek law. The constitutional subdocument found at Deut. 16.18–18.22 is without precedent in the entire Ancient

Near East, but has ample precedent in many Greek constitutional inscriptions and written texts. The mixture of civil and sacred law in biblical law collections was also common in the Greek world, which also allowed for the publication of most sacred laws, except those associated with the mysteries. The Decalogue shows close affinities with the Commandments of the Seven Sages, whereas the book of Deuteronomy shows clear signs of having been directly modeled on Plato's *Laws*. The use of law as education and the pervasive use of rhetoric and persuasion in prologues and motive clauses, especially pronounced in Deuteronomy but also found in other Pentateuchal law collections, also shows direct influence from Plato's *Laws*. These systematic parallels demonstrate pervasive influence of Greek law on the biblical law collections.

This is not to claim that there is no legacy of Ancient Near Eastern law in the Pentateuch. As discussed in Chapter 3, the biblical law collections contained distant literary echoes from LH and LE in the Law of the Goring Ox, MAL A in the law on assault of a pregnant woman, and LH in the invocation of *lex talionis* as a legal principle. Biblical laws also conservatively preserved ancient customs relating to marriage, such as polygamy and bride-price. Curse language in the Hebrew Bible, including the curses found in Deut. 28, preserved formulaic Assyrian curse language found in VTE, as discussed in §3. But taken as a whole, the biblical law collections are a much later product of the Greek world. This is evidenced by the many common constitutional features (Chapter 2), many instances of laws found in the Greek world and especially at Athens (Chapter 3) and in the fundamentally Greek conception of the biblical laws as a whole (the current chapter). Additionally, there are several lines of evidence that point to Plato's *Laws* as having exerted a decisive influence on the formulation of the biblical legal system. All available evidence appears to point to the biblical laws as a product of Jewish reading of Greek legal and political writing in the Hellenistic Era, supplemented by the incorporation of literary artifacts of Ancient Near Eastern law and curse language from the distant past.

Notes

1 Transcription and translations of these texts may be found in Roth 1997. Roth's book also includes two student exercises, Laws about Rented Oxen (LOx) and Middle Assyrian Palace Decrees (MAPD). Although these texts contain legal content, they are not of direct comparative value for biblical law collections.

2 Redford (2001: 135–59) argued that the collection of laws sponsored by Darius represents longstanding customs or traditional practices rather than a legal code in the sense of a binding body of laws. Redford's reconstruction of the likely contents of this law collection was based primarily on his analysis of papyrological discoveries with legal content. He discounted the description of Egyptian law by Hecataeus of Abdera in Diodorus Siculus, *Library* 1.69–95 because it contained certain Hellenistic notions such as Egyptian laws as legislation presented by famous Egyptian lawgivers of the past (Redford 2001: 135–8). Yet Hecataeus of Abdera claimed to have consulted Egyptian priests knowledgeable on their laws and customs and had access to an eight-volume work on Egyptian laws housed in the House of Life (Diodorus Siculus, *Library* 1.75.5), which

was arguably the set of laws compiled earlier under Darius (cf. Gmirkin 2006: 252 n. 77). The testimony of Hecataeus of Abdera on Egyptian law thus becomes extremely important as a possible ancient witness to the laws collected under Darius.

3 The description of Egyptian customs by Hecataeus of Abdera appeared at Diodorus Siculus, *Library* 1.69–95, included Egyptian legislation (1.70–82) and famous legislators (1.94–95). Although the list of lawgivers in 1.94–95 was likely imaginatively reconstructed by Hecataeus of Abdera based on his inquiries into Egyptian history rather than taken from an Egyptian source (except for the last two, Amasis and Darius, who were mentioned in the introduction to the Darius law collection preserved in the Demotic Chronicle), the categories of law that appear in 1.94–95 are consistent with laws detailed in 1.70–82, suggesting that both came from the same source, namely the eight-volume work on Egyptian law in the House of Life (1.75.5) as summarized by the Egyptian priests Hecataeus consulted. Contradictions between 1.94–95 and 1.45–68 regarding laws introduced by various kings indicate that Hecataeus did not draw on these eight volumes on Egyptian law in writing the earlier section on the deeds of the Egyptian kings.

4 Law collections with a prologue included LU, LL and LH.

5 Law collections with an epilogue included LL and LH. Blessings on later rulers who preserved the stelae are found at LL 21.36–48; LH 48.59–94. Curses for damaging the stela or substituting a different name appeared at LL 21.49–22.52; LX rev. 3.9'–20'; LH 49.18–44. Additional curses appeared at LH 49.45–51.91. Similar curses appeared on Mesopotamian stelae with a variety of genres, including treaty and memorial inscriptions.

6 "Their primary purpose was to lay before the public, posterity, future kings, and, above all, the gods, evidence of the king's execution of his divinely ordained mandate to have been 'the Faithful Shepherd' and *šar mēšarum*" or just ruler. Paul 1970: 25; cf. Finkelstein 1961: 103; Eckart 1994: 161; LeFebvre 2006: 11–12. It has also been suggested that law collections had secondary functions as legal reference works or didactic tools for the training of judges (cf. Westbrook 2009a: 9–14), but direct evidence on such matters is lacking and the inscriptions themselves do not indicate that this formed part of the original royal intent.

7 As pointed out at Paul 1970: 5–6, there was no Mesopotamian word for "law"; judicial decisions were guided instead by the notions of *kittum* (truth and right) and *misarum* (equity and justice).

8 Westbrook 2009a: 7–9. Mesopotamian law collections are often compared with scientific omen literature, which consisted of scribal lists of omens and their interpretations written in casuistic format, with *protasis* and *apodosis* ("if X then Y"), like Mesopotamian case law; cf. Westbrook 2009d: 30. The scribes themselves are thought to have become a source of new legal traditions by envisioning additional theoretical legal infractions and extrapolating their appropriate judicial penalties in order to deal exhaustively with legal topics.

9 Royal edicts dealt with only three types of reforms: retrospective cancellation of debts, reorganization of the royal administration and fixing of prices (Westbrook 1991: 45–6; Westbrook 2009d: 25). Royal edicts virtually ignored areas addressed in law codes (Westbrook 2009c: 89–90). In contrast to the casuistic format that dominates Mesopotamian law collections, royal edicts were written in apodictic format as a series of direct commands (Westbrook 2009d: 111–12).

10 See especially Finkelstein 1961: 100–4 on the relationship of *mīsarum* decrees and the Old Babylonian law collections.

11 Cf. Finkelstein 1961: 103; M. Roth 1997: 6–7. In LE, royal wage and price regulations were incorporated into the prologue (LE 1–4, 7–8, 10–11, 14); in LH they appeared in the main collection of laws (LH 178–85, 268–77). In LH 178–85 they retained their

original prescriptive apodictic format, but at LH 268–77 the price regulations were clumsily rephrased in casuistic format (cf. Westbrook 2009d: 112). LH gap u expressly stated that grain and silver interest rates were established by royal edict. "He (the merchant) shall take grain and silver in accordance with the royal edict."

12 "CH is not even prescriptive; it is descriptive. It is essentially a record of the common law . . . together with the occasional intervention of administrative measures" (Westbrook 2009b: 36).

13 Paul 1970: 12. It has been suggested that the poetic prologue and epilogue were of different scribal authorship than the law collection that they framed. Prologues and epilogues were extensively discussed at 1970: 11–26.

14 See Paul 1970: 36–40 for a survey of distinct features in biblical law.

15 The absence of an incipient personality cult that glorified the person of Moses is reinforced by his lack of faith at Num. 20.11–12. The mystery of place of final interment removed any possibility of establishing a hero cult that honored Moses, because such cults were usually centered at the burial site of the hero.

16 Similar clauses routinely appeared on stelae and reliefs that commemorated the military victories and other achievements of Mesopotamian kings.

17 The problems of finding prologue and epilogue in biblical law codes was discussed at Paul 1970: 27–42. Paul identified Deut. 1–11 as a prologue to the laws of Dtn at Deut. 12.1–26.15, and Deut. 26.15–31.30 as an epilogue, but was not able to establish a convincing parallel with prologue and epilogues in Ancient Near Eastern law collections. Attempts to impose a structure of prologue–law collection–epilogue on the Covenant Code analogous to that found in LH were made at Paul 1970: 35–6, 101 and Van Seters 2003: 56–7, 67–81, but both appear artificial and unconvincing. See Westbrook 2009a: 6 for a critique of Paul's claim to have identified a prologue and epilogue frame structure for the Covenant Code and Deuteronomy.

18 "These three realms [civil, moral and religious obligations], which in extra-biblical societies would be incorporated respectively in law collections, wisdom literature, and priestly handbooks, are here combined into one body of prescriptions" (Paul 1970: 37).

19 Comparative studies once saw great significance in the casuistic format that was common to Ancient Near Eastern and biblical judicial law; cf. Alt 1966: 103–71; Westbrook 2009d: 110–14. But the casuistic format was also found in the *Great Law Code* of Gortyn, Crete (ca. 450 BCE), the *Twelve Tablets* of Rome (ca. 450 BCE), Drakon's homicide law at Athens (ca. 620 BCE) and various other Greek and Athenian judicial laws. The casuistic framing of corrective judicial laws was explicitly discussed at Plato, *Laws* 4.720e–721b.

20 A few instances of apodictic formulations in Hittite and Assyrian sources were collected by Weinfeld 1973.

21 See note 67.

22 The integration of the Covenant Code with its narrative framework was extensively discussed at Van Seters 2003: 47–67.

23 The ark was eventually placed in Solomon's temple according to 1 Kgs 8.6–9.

24 The case for biblical knowledge of Hittite treaty forms was revived at Berman 2008: 29–40; Berman 2011.

25 Manasseh was listed (and pictured) as a tributary to Esarhaddon in 674 BCE at *ANET*[3] 291.

26 Weinfeld 1972: 68. Berman (2008: 185 n. 77) noted that VTE also lacked provisions for periodic public readings.

27 Ex. 20.2 and Deut. 5.6 introduced Yahweh as having brought the Israelites out of Egypt. This is the closest approach to a historical prologue to the Ten Commandments. Yet this same fact frequently appears in motive clauses to Pentateuchal laws for which no vassal treaty form has been claimed; cf. Sonsino 1980: 86–7.

28 According to Weinfeld 1972: 157, only the first three commandments contain vassal terminology.

29 Berman 2008: 40, 186 n. 88. The unusual aspects of CTH 133 ("Treaty between Arnuwanda I of Hatti and the Men of Ismerika"), which included the lack of either a historical prologue that was standard for Hittite vassal treaties or stipulation of benefits to the people of Ismerika, has led some to doubt whether this text should be considered a vassal treaty; cf. Altman 2003: 741; Altman 2004: 478.

30 Weinfeld 1972: 148, 150, 157. As Weinfeld noted, vassal treaties belonged to the category of international law, which was distinct from domestic law as found in the biblical text (1972: 156). There is also no question that the Hittites and Assyrians viewed treaty stipulations as prescriptive and enforceable, unlike the laws found in Hittite and Assyrian law collections, which were descriptive, retrospective and unenforced.

31 Passages where Weinfeld found echoes of Assyrian treaty curse language included Gen. 19.13–14, 20–25, 29; Judg. 9.45; Job 18.8–21; Isa. 34.9; Jer. 17.6; Zeph. 2.8–10; cf. Weinfeld 1972: 110–14. According to Weinfeld (1972: 111), "We may legitimately assume that the overthrow of Sodom and Gomorrah was conceived as the classic punishment of breach of covenant with the Deity. . . and that the Deity was conceived as employing the conventional means of punishing treaty violators." Weinfeld's reading of a vassal treaty between Yahweh and the cities of Sodom and Gomorrah into Gen. 19 seems unwarranted (although in a 1994 regional SBL presentation, "The Historical Context of Genesis 14," I suggested that the legend of the destruction of Sodom and Gomorrah and other cities near the Dead Sea may have originated with the fall of the cities in this region to Sennacherib in 701 BCE as corroborated by LMLK stamps in destruction layers at En-Gedi, Qumran and other nearby sites). Rather, Gen. 19 attests to biblical curse language that originally may have been taken from Assyrian sources about threatened or historical actions against rebellious cities, whether found in vassal treaties similar to VTE or in Assyrian campaign narratives, but which survived as stock imprecation of universal applicability.

32 Broad comparisons of biblical law collections and written laws in the Greek world suggestive of a common cultural background were made at Hagedorn 2004: 62–89; Knoppers and Harvey 2007: 105–44; cf. Berman 2008: 214 n. 104. These authors all shared an assumption that the biblical law collections were promulgated in the Persian Era or earlier.

33 Crawford and Whitehead 1983: 132. Greek traditions claimed that the earliest written laws were those authored by Zaleucus of Locri (ca. 662 BCE). Fragments of written laws from Dreros have been dated to ca. 650 BCE. Inscriptional origins of Greek written laws were discussed in detail in Gagarin 1986: 81–97.

34 For the text, see Willetts 1967: 39–50; Meiggs and Lewis 1969: 94–9. The Gortyn Law Code and biblical laws were compared at Hagedorn 2004: 64–71; Knoppers and Harvey 2007: 111–14.

35 The *Twelve Tablets* were discussed at Knoppers and Harvey 2007: 114–18; Westbrook 2009b: 21–71.

36 Comparisons of biblical and Athenian written laws were made at Knoppers and Harvey 2007: 108–11 and Berman 2008: 130–3, with an emphasis on the constitution and laws introduced by Solon in ca. 594 BCE.

37 Early Greek laws contained predominantly procedural rather than substantive laws (cf. Gagarin 1986: 72–80). Many biblical civil laws also contained procedural content (e.g. Ex. 21.6; Lev. 25.47–54; Num. 5.11–31; 27.8–11; 35.10–30; Deut. 13.9, 12–15; 14.28–29; 15.1–4, 12–14, 17; 17.2–12; 19.1–13, 15–19; 20.5–13; 21.1–23; 22.13–21; 23.24–25; 25.1–3, 5–10).

38 Gagarin 1986: 72. As Gagarin noted (1986: 128), Ancient Near Eastern law collections contained almost no procedure, and in the Hammurabi Law Code procedural elements

appear only in LH 1–5. Legal topics for which Ancient Near Eastern laws mention procedures included false witnesses (LH 1, 3–4), use of the River Ordeal for cases of suspected sorcery or infidelity (LH 2; LU 13–14; MAL A 24), reporting lost animals (HL 71), joint irrigation operations (MAL A 17) and the acquisition of a field or house (MAL B 6). A key concern in this procedural content was enforcing the jurisdiction of the royal instruments of justice over matters affecting state security and social stability (HL 111, 173a; MAL A 47). Some laws specified whether a case was under local or royal jurisdiction, the latter commonly including capital murder cases or cases involving suspected witchcraft.

39 The definitive discussion of how this came about was Ostwald 1986. Although Plato claimed in *Phaedrus* and *Statesman* that leadership by an expert statesman was better than written law, Plato later claimed in *Laws* 3.680a-681d, 700a that written law (properly integrated with educational and persuasive legal introductions) was supreme, and that people should become willing slaves to the law; cf. Morrow 1993: 85, 229, 546; Nightingale 1999: 107.

40 Berman 2008: 62–3. Berman noted that the king's subservience to the law "essentially places him on a par with the common citizen."

41 See Chapter 5 §2. According to one theory, lawgiving in the Mediterranean world arose, or was at least promoted, by colonization and the need to establish order in new city-states; cf. Knoppers and Harvey 2007: 121–2.

42 Demosthenes, *Against Timocrates* 139–41; Plutarch, *Lycurgus* 29.6; Xenophon, *Lacedemonian Constitution* 15.1; Thucydides, *Peloponnesian War* 1.18.1; cf. Szegedy-Maszak 1978: 201, 208–9; Hagedorn 2004: 83–5.

43 Demosthenes, *Against Timocrates* 139–41; Plutarch, *Lycurgus* 29.1–32; Plutarch, *Solon* 25.1–3, 6; cf. Hagedorn 2004: 83–5. New constitutions and law codes, such as those Solon established for Athens in ca. 594 BCE, often contained a clause, to which all the founding generation swore, that the laws would remain unchanged for a fixed period (Aristotle, *Athenian Constitution* 11; Herodotus, *Histories* 1.29.2; cf. Rhodes 1993: 135) or, like Deut. 4.2, in perpetuity (for Brea, Cyrene and Naupaktos, see Graham 1964: 60–1; for Drakon's law, see Demosthenes, *Against Aristocrates* 62; cf. Gagarin 1981: 23). Plato, *Laws* 6.772b-d; 12.957a-b took a different approach, allowing minor changes and adjustments in the laws for the first ten years, after which the laws would become effectively immutable.

44 Andocides, *On the Mysteries* 81–9; cf. MacDowell 1978: 47; Crawford and Whitehead 1983: 566; Ostwald 1986: 513. The initiative was known as the Teisamenus Decree, after one of the 500 *nomothetai*.

45 See Herodotus, *Histories* 4.153–61 on king Battus as founder of Cyrene and the fortunes of his dynasty.

46 The legendary giving of the law in Mosaic times gave the Torah an authority as ancestral law that would have been understood in the Greek world. The prophetic condemnation of Israel and the Jews frequently portrayed them as having rejected the laws given to their fathers. The description of the Torah as *patrios nomima* was explicit at Josephus, Ant. 12.303, 382; cf. 280.

47 See Chapter 3 for a discussion of isolated laws with Ancient Near Eastern legal content preserved in the Pentateuchal law collections, mainly in the Covenant Code. These exhibit the antiquarian legal interests of some of the legislators of ca. 270 BCE. The integration of these ancient laws with newly composed laws drawing on Greek legal traditions was important to give the law collections an air of hoary antiquity.

48 Hagedorn 2004: 75. The notion of social contract was explicit at Plato, *Crito* 13–14; Plato, *Republic* 2.369a-b; Plato, *Statesman* 276e; Demosthenes, *Against Leptines* 36–7; cf. Klosko 2006: 34, 69, 204–5. Under Athenian self-rule, all citizens voted in the Assembly, served on juries, defended the country as soldiers in the military and took

their turn in the Council, whose members were selected by lot from the citizen body. The ideal citizen was one who knew both how to rule and how to be ruled (Aristotle, *Politics* 1.1252a; 3.1277a-b, 1279a, 1283b, 1287a; 7.1332b-1333a; Plato, *Laws* 1.643e).

49 Oaths were commonly strengthened by curses and sacrifices (McLoughlin 2007: 91; Sommerstein 2007: 2), not only in the Greek world but also in the Ancient Near East (Bachvarova 2007: 179–80). Greek oaths were accompanied by *horkion* or oath-sacrifices, which invoked Horkos and the Erinyes as oath-gods, agents of vengeance who enforced oaths (Hesiod, *Theogony* 219–24; cf. Fletcher 2007: 105, 107–12; McLoughlin 2007: 97).

50 According to Aristophanes, *Thesmophoriazusae* 331–71 (discussed at Sommerstein 2007: 6), the Assembly opened with a ceremony in which the herald recited a series of curses, which the members of the Assembly would repeat in antiphonal responses (cf. Deut. 27.11–26; Josh. 8.33–34).

51 For the Bouleutic Oath, see Aristotle, *Athenian Constitution* 55.5. The full text of the Bouleutic Oath was reconstructed at Rhodes 1972: 194–9.

52 Plato, *Critias,* 119e-120a, 120e. Blessings and curses on future generations were also found in inscriptions at Teos (Meiggs and Lewis 1969: 62–6; Arnaoutoglou 1998: 84–5), Erythrae (Meiggs and Lewis 1969: 89–94; Fornara 1983: 70–3), possibly Naupaktos (the Pappadkis Bronze, quoted at Hagedorn 2004: 79 n. 258), Cyrene (Graham 1964: 226; Meiggs and Lewis 1969: 5–9; Weinfeld 1993: 28–9); and in connection with the First Sacred War (Aeschines, *Against Ctesiphon* 107–13; cf. Weinfeld 1993: 29–31).

53 J. Shear 2007: 149–50, 153; cf. Rhodes 2007: 17. As noted at Sommerstein 2007: 5, the Oath of Demophantos had enduring force even for those not yet born.

54 Ex. 24.1–18; Lev. 26.3–13; Deut. 27.15–26; 29.1–2, 10–12; Josh. 8.30–35.

55 Westbrook (2009d: 28) compared biblical and Greek prescriptive laws, which he considered contemporary seventh century BCE phenomena; cf. LeFebvre 2006: 143–5.

56 Plutarch, *Solon* 25.1–2; Aristotle, *Athenian Constitution* 7.1; Demosthenes, *Against Aristocrates* 28; Lysias, *Against Nicomachus* 17–18, 20–1; Plato, *Statesman* 298d; Pausanias, *Guide to Greece* 1.18.3. For a discussion of the literary and archaeological evidence for these laws, see Robertson 1986.

57 Lysias, *Against Nicomachus* 2–5; Andocides, *On the Mysteries* 82–5; cf. Ostwald 1986: 416–17. Drakon's homicide law of ca. 620 BCE was among those reenacted and put on public display in 409/408 BCE in an inscription discovered at Athens.

58 For biblical public readings of the law, see Deut. 31.10–12; Josh. 8.32–35; 2 Kgs 23.1–3; Neh. 7.72–8.18; cf. Watts 1999: 15–24; Berman 2008: 114–15. Greek public readings of the laws currently in force took place yearly at special sessions of the Assembly, along with proposed revisions (Demosthenes, *Against Timocrates* 20–3, unless this referred only to the proposed revisions; cf. Nightingale 1999: 109), supplementing the publication of these laws on display at the Royal Stoa and other locations in Athens.

59 Gagarin 1986: 128–9, 132–3, 144. In past scholarship, biblical laws were widely assumed to have a pre-Hellenistic, scribal Ancient Near Eastern background (e.g. Knoppers and Harvey 2007: 134, 139–41; Berman 2008: 166–7), sometimes resulting in anachronistic assertions of biblical legal developments that were prior to or contemporary with comparable Greek phenomena (Berman 2008: 138, 166–7; Westbrook 2009d: 28). It was also commonly asserted that biblical laws gradually gained respect and authority over time and only in the Hellenistic Era attained prescriptive legal force comparable to Greek law (see Fitzpatrick-McKinley 1999: 21, 96–108; LeFebvre 2006: 30–182 and the literature discussed there). In many such discussions, it is apparent that an Ancient Near East legal model has been imposed on Hellenistic material.

60 Parker 2004: 58–61. In ca. 594 BCE the legislator Solon famously enacted and published both civil laws governing Athens and sacred laws governing the Athenian festival and sacrificial calendar; cf. Jacoby 1949: 23. The Athenian Assembly had one session each year devoted to sacred laws; cf. Aristotle, *Athenian Constitution* 43.6.

61 Although neither Plato's *Laws* nor the Covenant Code in their entirety rigorously adhere to this arrangement of laws, this appears to be the organizing principle in major parts of both. Attempts to interpret the structure and sequence of the Covenant Code laws as based on the Laws of Hammurabi by Wright (2009: 29–90) and Van Seters (*A Law Book for the Diaspora*, 96–9, 125) cannot be viewed as successful.

62 For sacred inscriptions, see Lupu 2005. Surviving fragments of *Exegetica* and *Patria*, literary works on sacred laws, were discussed at Jacoby 1949: 16, 41, 44, 49–50.

63 The use of speech-writing techniques was especially prominent in Thucydides, *Peloponnesian War*. The school of tragic historiography that arose in the mid-fourth century BCE was based on the speech-writing techniques taught by the rhetorician Isocrates. Aristotle's *Rhetoric*, which took into account Isocrates' writings, frequently touched on prose writing.

64 Aspects of rhetoric and oratory – including political oratory – in Deuteronomic literature was extensively discussed in Weinfeld 1972: 10–58, 171–8. Weinfeld attempted to explain such oratorical features against a hypothetical Ancient Near Eastern background as having emanated from wisdom circles who acted as royal advisors during the monarchic period (1972: 51–8, 161–71, 177–8). The existence of royal advisors skilled in oratory during the biblical period is an exceedingly precarious scholarly construct. A less problematic explanation for oratorical elements in Deuteronomistic literature may be found in the well-documented education in rhetoric in those destined for political life in the Greek world and in the Hellenistic east.

65 The seminal work on motive clauses was Gemser 1953. Motive clauses invoked reasons for the law, or for obedience to the law, that included the practical (Deut. 20.19), ethical (Deut. 24.6), religious (Lev. 17.4), and historical (Ex. 23.14). Common historical themes were the deliverance from slavery in Egypt and the giving of the Promised Land to the Israelites, coupled with the warning that they would be taken from the land if they failed to obey.

66 Motive clauses and parenetic passages throughout the Pentateuch law collections were cataloged, analyzed and numerically compared in Sonsino 1980.

67 The most thorough arguments for the existence of a few motive clauses in Ancient Near Eastern law collections were made in Sonsino 1980. Sonsino incorporated and built upon arguments from a few other scholars that he listed at 1980: 154. Sonsino claimed to have found motive clauses in LH 7, 9–11, 13, 29, 47, 78, 107, 136–7, 146, 162–3, 171, 178, 194, 232, and MAL A 23–4, 29, 36, 45, 49. However, not a single instance from the cuneiform sources that Sonsino or his predecessors proposed either gave a motive for the law in question or an incentive for observing it, as required under Gemser's definition of a motive clause. In all instances, the proposed motive clause instead gave a reason for the verdict or the disposition of the case, such as a failure of one side to provide adequate witnesses or documentation (LH 7, 9–11, 13), circumstantial evidence pointing to innocence or guilt (MAL A 23–4), a determination of which party possessed legal rights to an inheritance or a disputed property (LH 162–3, 171, 178; MAL A 29, 49), a determination of whether one or both parties had lived up to the terms of a contract (LH 45–7, 78, 194, 232; MAL A 36), a determination that one party had voluntarily forfeited certain rights (LH 107, 136; MAL A 45) or an identification of special legal obligations that affected the disposition of the case (LH 29, 137, 146). Such explanatory clauses aimed at clarifying the forensic evidentiary standards required for a judicial ruling, whether acquittal or conviction and penalty, also appeared in Pentateuchal law collections, where secondary literature usually refers to

them under the misnomer "explanatory motive clauses." As Sonsino commented, "It is noteworthy that, unlike biblical laws, no cuneiform law is ever motivated by reference to a historic event, a promise of well-being or, for that matter, a divine will. In fact, the deity is completely silent" (1980: 174; cf. Janzen 1994: 81 n. 12). It follows that the motive clause, as defined by Gemser, is indeed absent from Ancient Near Eastern law. Although both types of subordinate clauses have similar grammatical structure, it is best to terminologically distinguish the persuasive motive clause found in biblical law collections from the evidentiary clause common to biblical, Ancient Near Eastern and other ancient law collections. The evidentiary clause justified a legal ruling proceeding from the law, whereas the motive clause contained an extra-legal rhetorical justification for the law itself or for citizen obedience to it.

68 "In absolutely none of these law books or code collections can one single instance of motive clauses be discovered. The motive clause is clearly and definitely a peculiarity of Israel's or Old Testament Law." Gemser 1953: 52; cf. Janzen 1994: 61; Berman 2008: 115.

69 Deut. 31.19–27. In an obvious sequel at 2 Kgs 22.1–17, the copy of the Deuteronomic law purportedly discovered during the reign of Josiah served as a witness to the impending fall of wicked Jerusalem.

70 The fall and exile was seen as an educational opportunity for the enculturation of the Jews regarding their past at Deut. 29.20–28; 31.16–21. The meditation on the past failures caused by disobedience was balanced by the offering of redemption and renewed favor under conditions of repentance and a new commitment to obedience to the ancestral laws (Deut. 30.1–10).

71 Plato, *Laws* 4.721a-722a, 723c-d. The *prooimia* and *paramuthia* were functionally equivalent in Plato's *Laws,* both containing persuasive content to motivate citizen obedience to a law or law. But *prooimia* always took the form of a prefatory passage, while *paramuthia* might appear within the statement of the law itself.

72 Plato, *Laws* 4.721b-e. At Plato, *Laws* 4.719e-720e, Plato compared this novel legislative technique to the dispensation of cures by the best physicians, whose prescriptions were accompanied by education and persuasion designed to make the patient voluntarily comply with the course of treatment.

73 Wajdenbaum (2011: 54–5) mentioned the use of legal preambles advocated in Plato's *Laws,* but incorrectly correlated these with biblical narratives that illustrated or introduced laws, such as the story of the daughters of Zelophehad in Num. 27, 36.

74 According to Cicero, *On Laws* 1.15; 2.14, Cicero based his works on Plato's *Laws,* which he admired greatly. Cicero *On Laws* 2.14–16 used introductions explicitly styled on Plato's legislative approach.

75 In the description of Moses' legislative technique at Philo, *Life of Moses* 2.49–51, Philo praised Moses' avoidance of the usual tyrannical commands and punishments without encouragement *(paramuthia)* in favor of persuasion through prefaces *(prooimia),* exhortations and inducements; cf. Annas 2010: 80. It is evident that Philo here drew on terminology from Plato's *Laws* to describe Mosaic legislation in Platonic terms, and accurately so.

76 Parallels between Deuteronomy and Plato's *Laws* were discussed in Kaiser 2000: 60–79; cf. Hagedorn 2004: 36–7. Kaiser found the educational value attached to the laws, their divine authority, and the presentation of a law code within a fictional setting in both texts noteworthy. Because he favored a date for Deuteronomy either contemporary with or earlier than Plato's *Laws,* he did not consider the possibility of direct literary dependence of Deuteronomy on *Laws,* but hypothesized, based on these striking parallels, that the Ancient Near Eastern and Greek worlds must have had much closer intellectual contacts far earlier than commonly supposed. The evidence for an influence of Plato's *Laws* on Deuteronomy appears undeniable, but the historical obstacles

to understanding a relationship between these two texts in the time Kaiser proposed appears insurmountable. All these difficulties disappear on the hypothesis that this influence took place in the Hellenistic Era, when Plato's *Laws* could easily have been available to the authors of Deuteronomy.

77 Plato, *Laws* 6.751a-768e detailed constitutional features of the new colony; cf. the constitutional sub-document at Deut. 16.18–18.22. Plato, *Laws* 6.771a–12.960c dealt with specific laws.

78 The citizens were directly addressed by the lawgiver at Plato, *Laws* 4.715e-718a; 5.726a-734e, 741a-e; 6.772e-773e; 7.823d-824a; 9.854b-c; 10.888a-d, 899d-900c, 903b-e; 11.916d-917b, 923a-c; cf. Nightingale 1993: 287–8.

79 Plato proclaimed that mixing persuasion and laws to make law a form of instruction was his unique innovation (*Laws* 4.722e); cf. Morrow 1993: 555–6. Seneca, *Letters* 94.38 said that Posidonius found Plato's use of legislative introductions absurd, but Seneca found some merit to the idea, as did Cicero, who made use of preambles for religious laws he proposed at *On Laws* 2.14–16; cf. Asmis 2008: 25–6, 29.

80 The educational value of the laws was pervasive in Deuteronomy. The laws are indeed described as *torah* or teachings at Deut. 1.5; 4.8, 44; 17.18–19; 27.3, 8, 26; 28.58, 61; 29.21, 29; 30.10; 31.9, 11–12, 24, 26; 32.46. For Plato's *Laws* as an educational text, see 7.811c-813e; 9.858c-859a; 12.957d. The entirety of Plato, *Laws* 7.788a-824c was devoted to educational concerns. Eusebius, *Preparation for the Gospel* 12.17 compared the prominence of education in Plato's writings and in Deuteronomy. Josephus, Apion 2.257 claimed that Plato copied his educational system from Moses.

81 Deut. 1.5; 4.8, 44; 17.18–19; 27.3, 8, 26; 28.58, 61; 29.20–21; 30.10; 31.9, 11, 24, 26; cf. Plato, *Laws* 5.734e; 7.811d-e; 12.957c-d; cf. 9.858c-e. References to the "book of the law" are limited to Deuteronomistic writings (Deut. 28.61; 29.20; 30.10; Josh. 1.8; 8.31, 34; 23.36; 1 Kgs 2.3; 2 Kgs 14.6; 22.8, 11; 23.24–25).

82 Deut. 34.10–12; Plato, *Laws* 12.969a-b. In both instances, this was a brief anticipatory piece of *epideictic* or "display" rhetoric, a category of speech that honored a citizen, often at a funeral.

83 Egyptian and Mesopotamian wisdom literature conveyed ethical advice from fathers to sons, but lacked both the brevity and moral authority of the Decalogue. See Chapter 3 §14.

84 The most authoritative surviving list, consisting of 147 ethical maxims, was that of Sosiades, *Commandments of the Seven Sages,* preserved in its entirety at Stobaeus, *Anthology* 3.1.173. For the Greek text, see Wachsmuth and Hense 1894: 3.125–29; Greek text with a provisional English translation and now-standard numbering is found at Oikonomides 1987: 74–5.

85 See Gagarin 1986: 53–5 on the genre of maxims. Gagarin noted that the conciseness of maxims made them suitable for memorization and oral repetition.

86 Doubts whether the list preserved by Sosiades was actually inscribed at the Temple of Delphi were laid to rest by the discovery of the inscribed base of a third century BCE stele that originally contained the commandments of the sages "copied carefully" by Klearchos, the famous pupil of Aristotle, found during excavations of a Greco-Bactrian city in Afghanistan. See Robert 1968. The five sayings preserved on the statue base of the *Inscriptio Bactriana* agreed with the last five sayings from Sosiades. Third century BCE papyrus fragments of the Commandments of the Seven Sages were later published at Oikonomides 1980. Another version was found on an inscription from a gymnasium at Miletus. The sayings from these various sources include eighteen commandments not found in the list from Sosiades.

87 Plato, *Hipparchus* 228c-229a; cf. Oikonomides 1987: 68 n. 8. According to Demetrius of Phalerum (quoted at Diogenes Laertius, *Lives of Famous Philosophers* 1.22), these seven first became known as "the wise men" in the archonship of Damasias (582 BCE). A copy of Demetrius of Phalerum's *Sayings of the Seven Sages* was preserved at Stobaeus, *Anthology* 3.1.172.

88 According to later traditions, it was in their capacity as the wisest men of their times that they were consulted as legislators. The list of Seven Sages found at Plato, *Protagoras* 343a-c consisted of Thales of Miletus, Pittacus of Mytilene, Bias of Priene, Solon of Athens, Cleobus of Lindus, Myson of Chenaem and Chilon of Sparta. Various figures of antiquity – eighteen altogether – appear in other lists of the Seven Sages given by other ancient writers, such as Demetrius of Phalerum, Ephoros, and others: only the legislators Solon, Thales and Pittacus were common to all such lists. Assignment of authorship for specific sayings also varied greatly. The archaic commandments inscribed in Delphi's temple were anonymous, and attribution of these proverbial sayings to wise figures from antiquity was a matter of considerable informed speculation by later scholars, who matched the content of the commandments with traditions about famed ancient legislators (and in some instances preserved writings).

89 See note 87. The copy found in the gymnasium at Miletus was also evidently of educational value for the young men taught there.

90 Klearchos of Soli, the pupil of Aristotle, evidently accompanied Alexander the Great during his conquests when he left a copy of the "wise commandments of men of old" on the famous stele in Greek Bactria. The *Inscriptio Bactriana* says Klearchos carefully copied the prized commandments at the Pythian temple and "brought them here in the shrine of Kineas [the city hero-founder] to shine far around it."

91 As noted in Chapter 3 §14, the Commandments of the Seven Sages – as listed by Sosiades – included such sayings as Worship the Gods (2), Respect Your Parents (4), Do Not Use an Oath (19), Shun what Belongs to Others (34), and Shun Murder (51).

92 A direct comparison between the Ten Commandments and the commandments from the Delphic inscription was made by Oikonomides 1987: 73. Oikonomides opined that the latter "express a higher concept and a more realistic vision of ethical law."

93 Demetrius of Phalerum, who was brought to Alexandria as Ptolemy I Soter's advisor and appears to have played a role in the creation of the Great Library, wrote a text on the Commandments of the Seven Sages (Diogenes Laertius, *Lives of Famous Philosophers* 1.22).

94 "Copies traveled to every corner of the Greek world and far outside it after the conquests of Alexander the Great" (Oikonomides 1987: 73). Some children from ruling class families may have received a Hellenistic education in the period ca. 325–270 BCE and may have been exposed to the Commandments of the Seven Sages as a school text. Such members of the educated elite may have included some who became Jewish senators and were brought to Alexandria in ca. 270 BCE to provide the Great Library with a copy of the Jewish legislation. It is interesting that Klearchus of Soli, the student of Aristotle who brought a copy of the Commandments of the Seven Sages with him to the east, knew about the Jews from Jerusalem and Judea and recorded a (fictional) encounter between Aristotle and a Greek-speaking Jew residing in Asia Minor, quoted in Josephus, Apion 1.175–82. (See Bar-Kochva 2010: 40–89 for a careful assessment of this passage from Klearchus.) Both Klearchus and his contemporary Megasthenes knew about the Jews and purported Jewish wisdom in the generation after Aristotle. It seems possible that the Jews were also exposed to Greek wisdom during this same period, especially in light of the active Hellenization of the east under Alexander and his successors. The *Inscriptio Bactriana* seems to indicate that the Commandments of the Seven Sages were disseminated as part of this process.

Bibliography

Alt, Albrecht, "The Origins of Israelite Law." Pages 103–71 in *Essays on Old Testament History and Religion*. Translated by R. A. Wilson. Garden City, NY: Anchor, 1966.

Altman, Amnon, "Rethinking the Hittite System of Subordinate Countries from the Legal Point of View," *JAOS* 123 (2003): 741–56.

————, *The Historical Prologues of the Hittite Treaties*. Ramat Gan, Israel: Bar-Ilan University Press, 2004.

Annas, Julia, "Virtue and Law in Plato." Pages 71–91 in Christopher Bobonich (ed.), *Plato's Laws: A Critical Guide*. Cambridge: Cambridge University Press, 2010.

Arnaoutoglou, Ilias, *Ancient Greek Laws: A Sourcebook*. New York: Routledge, 1998.

Asmis, Elizabeth, "Cicero on Natural Law and the Laws of the State," *Classical Antiquity* 1 (2008): 1–33.

Bachvarova, Mary R., "Oath and Allusion in Alcaeus Fr. 129." Pages 179–88 in Sommerstein, Alan H. and J. Fletcher (eds.), *Horkos: The Oath in Greek Society*. Exeter: Bristol Phoenix Press, 2007.

Bar-Kochva, Bezalel, *The Image of the Jews in Greek Literature*. Berkeley: University of California Press, 2010.

Berman, Joshua A., *Created Equal: How the Bible Broke with Ancient Political Thought*. Oxford: Oxford University Press, 2008.

————, "CTH 133 and the Hittite Provenance of Deuteronomy 13," *JBL* 130 (2011): 25–44.

Carr, David, *Writing on the Tablets of the Heart: Origins of Scripture and Literature*. New York: Oxford, 2005.

Chirichigno, Gregory C., *Debt-Slavery in Israel and the Ancient Near East*. JSOTSup 141. Sheffield: Sheffield Academic Press, 1993.

Crawford, Michael H. and David Whitehead, *Archaic and Classical Greece: A Selection of Ancient Sources in Translation*. Cambridge: Cambridge University Press, 1983.

Crouch, C. L., *Israel and the Assyrians: Deuteronomy, the Succession Treaty of Esargaddon, and the Nature of Subversion*. SBL Ancient Near East Monographs 8. Atlanta: SBL Press, 2014.

Eckart, Otto, "Aspects of Legal Reform and Reformulations in Ancient Cuneiform and Israelite Law." Pages 160–96 in Bernard M. Levinson (ed.), *Theory and Method in Biblical and Cuneiform Law*. JSOTSup 181. Sheffield: Sheffield Academic Press, 1994.

Finkelstein, J. J., "Ammisaduqa's Edict and the Babylonian 'Law Codes'," *JCS* 3 (1961): 91–104.

Fitzpatrick-McKinley, Anne, *The Transformation of Torah from Scribal Advice to Law*. JSOTSup 287. Sheffield: Sheffield Academic Press, 1999.

Fletcher, Judith, "Horkos in the *Oresteia*." Pages 102–13 in Alan H. Sommerstein and J. Fletcher (eds.), *Horkos: The Oath in Greek Society*. Exeter: Bristol Phoenix Press, 2007.

Fornara, Charles W. (ed.), *Archaic Times to the End of the Peloponnesian War*. Cambridge: Cambridge University Press, 1983.

Gagarin, Michael, *Drakon and Early Athenian Homicide Law*. New Haven, CT: Yale University Press, 1981.

————, *Early Greek Law*. Berkeley: University of California Press, 1986.

Gemser, Berend, "The Importance of Motive Clauses in Old Testament Law," VTSup 1 (1953): 50–66.

Gmirkin, Russell E., *Berossus and Genesis, Manetho and Exodus: Hellenistic Histories and the Date of the Pentateuch*. Library of the Hebrew Bible/Old Testament Studies 433. Copenhagen International Series 15. New York: T & T Clark, 2006.

Graham, A. J., *Colony and Mother City in Ancient Greece*. New York: Barnes and Noble, 1964.

Gruen, Erich S., "The Polis in the Hellenistic World." Pages 339–54 in R. M. Rosen and J. Farrell (eds.), *Nomodeiktes: Greek Studies in Honor of Martin Ostwald*. Ann Arbor, MI: University of Michigan Press, 1993.

Hagedorn, Anselm C., *Between Moses and Plato: Individual and Society in Deuteronomy and Ancient Greek Law*. Göttingen: Vandenhoeck & Ruprecht, 2004.

Jacobson, T., "Primitive Democracy in Ancient Mesopotamia," *JNES* 2 (1946): 159–72.

———, "Early Political Developments in Mesopotamian Assemblies," *ZA* 52 (1957): 91–104.

Jacoby, Felix, *Atthis: The Local Chronicles of Ancient Athens*. Oxford: Clarendon Press, 1949.

Jaeger, Werner, *Paideia: The Ideals of Greek Culture*. Translated by Gilbert Highet. 3 vols. New York: Oxford University Press, 1943.

Janzen, Waldemar, *Old Testment Ethics: A Paradigmatic Approach*. Louisville, KY: Westminster/John Know Press, 1994.

Kaiser, Otto, "Das Deuteronomium und Platons Nomoi: Einladung zu einem Vergleich." Pages 60–79 in H. Spieckermann and R. G. Kratz (eds.), *Liebe und Gebot: Studien zum Deuteronomium*. Forschungen zur Religion und Literatur des Alten und Neuen Testaments 190. Göttingen: Vandenhoeck & Ruprecht, 2000.

Klosko, George, *The Development of Plato's Political Theory*. Oxford: Oxford University Press, 2006.

Knoppers, Gary N. and Paul B. Harvey Jr., "The Pentateuch in Ancient Mediterranean Context: The Publication of Local Lawcodes." Pages 105–41 in Gary N. Knoppers and Bernard M. Levinson (eds.), *Pentateuch as Torah: New Models for Understanding Its Promulgation and Acceptance*. Winona Lake, IN: Eisenbrauns, 2007.

LeFebvre, Michael, *Collections, Codes and Torah: The Re-Characterization of Israel's Written Laws*. New York: T & T Clark, 2006.

Levinson, Bernard M., "The Reconceptualization of Kingship in Deuteronomy and the Deuteronomic History's Transformation of Torah," *VT* 51 (2001): 511–34.

Lupu, Eran, *Greek Sacred Law: A Collection of New Documents*. Religions in the Graeco-Roman World 152. Leiden: E. J. Brill, 2005.

MacDowell, Douglas Maurice, *The Law in Classical Athens*. Ithaca, NY: Cornell University Press, 1978.

McLoughlin, Bonnie, "Epinician Swearing." Pages 91–101 in Alan H. Sommerstein and J. Fletcher (eds.), *Horkos: The Oath in Greek Society*. Exeter: Bristol Phoenix Press, 2007.

Meiggs, Russell and David Lewis (eds.), *A Selection of Greek Historical Inscriptions to the End of the Fifth Century BC*. Oxford: Clarendon Press, 1969.

Mendenhall, George E., "Covenant Forms in Israelite Tradition," *BA* 17 (1954): 50–76.

Mirhady, David C., "The Dikasts' Oath and the Question of Fact." Pages 48–59 in Alan H. Sommerstein and J. Fletcher (eds.), *Horkos: The Oath in Greek Society*. Exeter: Bristol Phoenix Press, 2007.

Morrow, Glenn Raymond, *Plato's Cretan City: A Historical Interpretation of the Laws*. Princeton: Princeton University Press, 1993.

Mühl, Max, *Untersuchungen zue Altorientalischen und Althellischen Gesetzebung*. Leipzig: Dieterich'sche Verlagsbuchhandlung, 1933.

Nightingale, Andrea Wilson, "Writing/Reading a Sacred Text: A Literary Interpretation of Plato's *Laws*," *Classical Philology* 88 (1993): 279–300.

———, "Plato's Lawcode in Context: Rule by Written Law in Athens and Magnesia," *CQ* 49 (1999): 100–22.

Oikonomides, A. N., "The Lost Delphic Inscription with the Commandments of the Seven and P. Univ. Athen 2782," *Zeitschrift für Papyrologie und Epigraphik* 37 (1980): 179–83.

————, "Records of 'The Commandments of the Seven Wise Men' in the 3rd Century BC," *The Classical Bulletin* 63 (1987): 67–76.

Ostwald, Martin, *Nomos and the Beginnings of the Athenian Democracy*. Oxford: Clarendon Press, 1969.

————, *From Popular Sovereignty to Sovereignty of Law: Law, Society, and Politics in Fifth Century Athens*. Berkeley: University of California Press, 1986.

Parker, Robert, "What Are Sacred Laws?" Pages 57–70 in Edward M. Harris and Lene Rubenstein (eds.), *The Law and the Courts in Ancient Greece*. London: Duckworth, 2004.

Paul, Shalom M., *Studies in the Book of the Covenant in the Light of Cuneiform and Biblical Law*. VTSup 18. Leiden: E. J. Brill, 1970.

Phillips, David, *The Law of Ancient Athens*. Ann Arbor, MI: University of Michigan Press, 2013.

Redford, Donald B., "The So-Called 'Codification' of Egyptian Law under Darius I." Pages 135–59 in James W. Watts (ed.), *Persia and Torah: The Theory of Imperial Authorization of the Pentateuch*. SBLSymp 17. Atlanta, GA: Society of Biblical Literature, 2001.

Rhodes, Peter John, *The Athenian Boule*. Oxford: Clarendon Press, 1972.

————, "Nomothesia in Fourth-Century Athens," *CQ* 35 (1985): 55–60.

————, "The Athenian Code of Laws, 410–399 BC," *JHS* 111 (1991): 87–100.

————, *A Commentary on the Aristotelian Athenaeion Politeia*. Oxford: Clarendon Press, 1993.

————, "Oaths in Political Life." Pages 11–25 in Alan H. Sommerstein and J. Fletcher (eds.), *Horkos: The Oath in Greek Society*. Exeter: Bristol Phoenix Press, 2007.

Rhodes, Peter John and David M. Lewis, *The Decrees of the Greek States*. Oxford: Clarendon Press, 1997.

Rhodes, Peter John and Robin Osborne, *Greek Historical Inscriptions 404–323 BC*. Oxford: Oxford University Press, 2003.

Robert, Louis, "De Delphes à l'Oxus: Inscriptions Grecques Nouvelles de la Bactriane," *Comptes Rendus de l'Académie des Inscriptions* 112 (1968): 442–54.

Robertson, Noel, "Solon's Axones and Kyrbeis and the Sixth-Century Background," *Historia* 35 (1986): 147–76.

Roth, Martha T., *Law Collections from Mesopotamia and Asia Minor*. WAWSBL 6. Atlanta, GA: Scholars Press, 1997.

Shear, Julia L., "The Oath of Demophantos and the Politics of Athenian Identity." Pages 148–60 in Alan H. Sommerstein and J. Fletcher (eds.), *Horkos: The Oath in Greek Society*. Exeter: Bristol Phoenix Press, 2007.

Sommerstein, Alan H., "Introduction." Pages 1–10 in Alan H. Sommerstein and J. Fletcher (eds.), *Horkos: The Oath in Greek Society*. Exeter: Bristol Phoenix Press, 2007.

Sonsino, Rifat, *Motive Clauses in Hebrew Law: Biblical Forms and Near Eastern Parallels*. SBLDS 45. Chico, CA: Scholars Press, 1980.

Stanton, G. R., *Athenian Politics: c. 800–500 BC: A Sourcebook*. London: Routledge, 1990.

Szegedy-Maszak, Andrew, "Legends of Greek Lawgivers," *GRBS* 19 (1978): 199–209.

Thomas, Rosalind, "Written in Stone? Liberty, Equality, Orality, and the Codification of Law." Pages 9–31 in L. Foxhall and A.D.E. Lewis (eds.), *Greek Law in Its Political Setting: Justifications Not Justice*. Oxford: Clarendon Press, 1996.

Van Seters, John, *A Law Book for the Diaspora: Revision in the Study of the Covenant Code*. Oxford: Oxford University Press, 2003.

Wachsmuth, Curt and Otto Hense (eds.), *Stobei Anthologium*. 3 vols. Berlin: Weidmann, 1894.

Wajdenbaum, Philippe, *Argonauts of the Desert: Structural Analysis of the Hebrew Bible*. London: Equinox Publishing, 2011.

Watts, James M., *Reading Law: The Rhetorical Shaping of the Pentateuch*. Sheffield: Sheffield Academic Press, 1999.

Weinfeld, Moshe, *Deuteronomy and the Deuteronomistic School*. Winona Lake, IN: Eisenbrauns, 1972.

———, "The Origin of the Apodictic Law: An Overlooked Source," *VT* 23 (1973): 63–75.

———, *The Promise of the Land: The Inheritance of the Land of Canaan by the Israelites*. Berkeley: University of California Press, 1993.

———, *Social Justice in Ancient Israel and in the Ancient Near East*. Minneapolis: Fortress Press, 1995.

Westbrook, Raymond, *Property and the Family in Biblical Law*. JSOTSup 113. Sheffield: Sheffield Academic Press, 1991.

———, "Biblical and Cuneiform Law Codes." Pages 3–20 in Bruce Wells and F. Rachel Magdalene (eds.), *Law from the Tigris to the Tiber: The Writings of Raymond Westbrook*. Winona Lake, IN: Eisenbrauns, 2009a.

———, "The Nature and Origin of the Twelve Tablets." Pages 21–71 in Bruce Wells and F. Rachel Magdalene (eds.), *Law from the Tigris to the Tiber: The Writings of Raymond Westbrook*. Winona Lake, IN: Eisenbrauns, 2009b.

———, "Cuneiform Law Codes and the Origins of Legislation." Pages 73–95 in Bruce Wells and F. Rachel Magdalene (eds.), *Law from the Tigris to the Tiber: The Writings of Raymond Westbrook*. Winona Lake, IN: Eisenbrauns, 2009c.

———, "What is the Covenant Code?" Pages 97–118 in Bruce Wells and F. Rachel Magdalene (eds.), *Law from the Tigris to the Tiber: The Writings of Raymond Westbrook*. Winona Lake, IN: Eisenbrauns, 2009d.

Willetts, R. F., *The Law Code of Gortyn*. Berlin: Walter de Gruyter, 1967.

Wiseman, D. J., "The Vassal-Treaties of Esarhaddon," *Iraq* 20 (1958): 1–99.

Wright, David P., *Inventing God's Law: How the Covenant Code Used and Revised the Laws of Hammurabi*. Oxford: Oxford University Press, 2009.

5

GREEK AND BIBLICAL LEGAL NARRATIVES

In the previous chapters parallels were considered between the Pentateuch's constitutional features, laws and aspects of the law collections as a whole and features of Ancient Near Eastern and Greek legal traditions. The current chapter examines the Pentateuchal legal tradition within its larger narrative context. In Pentateuchal legal accounts, the presentation of the laws of Moses took place in a series of episodes within a historiographical narrative purporting to recount the migration of the Israelites from Egypt to the Promised Land under the leadership of Moses.[1] The detailed narrative context for Mosaic law has no precedent in the Ancient Near East, where the only surrounding legal framework for law collections, when they exist – namely the royal prologue and epilogue attached to some of the law collections of the Old Babylonian period – are entirely lacking in narrative elements or historical context, but are restricted to general descriptions praising the justice, righteousness and divine favor of the king. Because Ancient Near Eastern law collections possess no narrative context, there is no need to consider Mesopotamian parallels in discussing the Pentateuchal legal narratives.[2] Instead, the current chapter will examine the many literary parallels that exist between the Pentateuchal legal narratives and Greek literature that featured laws and lawgivers, especially stories about expedition leaders who created constitutions and law codes for the colonies their founded in a new land that provide direct parallels to the foundation story in Exodus–Joshua.

1. Greek legal narratives

The topics of constitution and law pervaded Greek thought and writing. The possession of a constitution and laws were integral to the self-conception of Greeks as members of a *polis* and participants in its government. The origins of the legal tradition of the *polis* was thus a basic part of Greek heritage, and there was a great interest in lawgivers and the creation of law codes throughout the Greek world that found frequent expression in both prose and poetic literature.[3] The educated elite who produced the major works of Greek literature were often statesmen or other prominent figures in Greek public life[4] who were consciously concerned with political matters.[5] It is not surprising, then, that constitutions, laws and lawgivers appeared frequently in the writings of Greek historians and philosophers. Legal content often appeared within a narrative framework in Greek prose as in biblical writings. This mixture of narrative and law appeared in a variety of Greek genres, including the following.

Historical narratives

Constitutional and legal matters relating to Athens commonly appeared in the writings of historians such as Herodotus and Thucydides. Thucydides incidentally mentioned the legendary origin of Athenian constitutional institutions with Theseus. Both mentioned the constitution and laws of the great lawgiver Solon (ca. 594 BCE), the reorganization of the Athenian state by the constitution of Kleisthenes (508 BCE), and the various *stateis* or revolts that affected Athenian laws and constitution in the fifth century BCE. For both authors, Greek political history was not just an account of the Greek leaders and their doings – in contrast to Ancient Near Eastern historiography, which is mostly a recitation of the mighty deeds of kings – but the story of the vicissitudes of the government, constitution and laws of the *polis*.

Panegyric

The Athenian constitution and laws appeared prominently as subject matter in Athenian panegyrics, a form of elevated speech that celebrated the history of Athens, usually presented in the form of a funeral oration by a prominent politician at the yearly festival that honored fallen Athenian soldiers.[6] Standard elements in such speeches often included an account of the mythical origins of Athens, an idealized patriotic survey of its military history and its courage at war on behalf of Greek freedoms[7] and a description of its superior constitution, laws and way of life.[8] The discussion of the Athenian constitution and laws might appear in connection either with the mythical or legendary past[9] or the historical present.[10]

Origin stories

Greek stories about autochthonous peoples who had lived in a region from earliest times could include traditions about the ancestral laws and constitution along with other charter myths about national civic and religious institutions. Such stories served a rhetorical function by bolstering the political agenda of those telling the story, who sought to link their favored form of government with revered ancestral traditions.[11]

Foundation stories

The Greek genre *ktisis* or foundation story frequently contained constitutional and legal content in a narrative setting. The founding of a new city involved the creation of its various civil and religious institutions, including the framing of a constitution and law code by the *oikist* or founder. As a consequence, foundation stories often noted the ancestral laws inaugurated at the colony's establishment. The story of the migration of the Israelites to the Promised Land under the leadership of Moses, and his creation of a constitution and laws for the new nation, closely conformed to the conventions of the Greek foundation story. A foundation story of the Jewish nation written by a Greek historian might have read much as the present text of Exodus–Joshua.

Indeed, it so happens that we possess a detailed Greek account of Jewish origins that predates the Pentateuch by almost a half century and illustrates just how closely the Pentateuchal foundation story conformed to Greek literary conventions. The account of the origins of the Jewish nation in the *Aegyptiaca* of Hecataeus of Abdera (ca. 320–315 BCE),[12] although entirely independent of the Pentateuchal account, provides a concrete example of Jewish origins within a Greek foundation story:[13] the personal qualities of Moses, the *oikist;* his leading a band of colonists out of Egypt to take possession of the land later called Judea; the foundation of Jerusalem and its temple by Moses; his institution of sacred laws and fashioning of political institutions and laws; his division of the people into twelve tribes; his appointment of qualified magistrates to act as priests, judges and Guardians of the Laws; his provisions for military training; his allotment of conquered lands into equal shares (except for the priestly magistrates, who would receive a double share); the inalienability of the land so divided to prevent the wealthy from buying up the land and creating an impoverished underclass. This remarkable fictional Greek foundation story about the Jews is striking both for its close correspondence in outline with the Pentateuchal narrative and for its disagreement in detail that demonstrates its complete literary independence from biblical account.[14] The common features of the Pentateuchal and Hecataean narratives are entirely attributable to their conformity to the standard features of Greek foundation stories. Significantly for the present discussion, one *topos* shared by the two accounts was the establishment of a constitution and laws by the founder within a narrative context.

Ethnographies

The ethnography was a distinctively Greek genre that gave a full description of a particular *ethnos* or nation. Standard elements of an ethnography included a geographical description of a land and an account of its people's origins, history and customs, although not every ethnography necessarily included all these literary units. A nation's customs included its laws: indeed, the same word *nomos* could designate either custom or law. Herodotus' *Histories* incorporated ethnographies of many nations around the Mediterranean, containing information Herodotus picked up during his broad travels.[15] His ethnography of Egypt mentioned several distinctive or curious Egyptian customs, but nowhere referred to a formal Egyptian body of law (Herodotus, *Histories* 2.35–37, 80). The most highly developed and influential example of ethnography was arguably the *Aegyptiaca* of Hecataeus of Abdera (ca. 315 BCE), which gave an extensive account of the Egyptian gods, ancient origins, geography, flora and fauna, political history (from its earliest kings to Darius), laws and customs and a list of its most famous lawgivers. The legal content in the *Aegyptiaca* was highly influenced by Greek notions of law, but are of intrinsic interest, especially in connection with biblical law collections that displayed similar influences. Legal topics found in the *Aegyptiaca* – many of which also appeared in Pentateuchal law – included laws regarding incest (Diodorus Siculus, *Library* 1.27.1); laws governing the conduct of kings (1.70–72);[16] distribution of land among the warrior, priestly and agrarian classes (1.73–74); the administration of justice (1.75–76); criminal laws governing perjury (1.77.1–5), murder (1.77.6–10) and parricide (1.77.7–8); military law and laws on treason (1.78.1–3);[17] commercial laws regarding contracts and loans (1.79);[18] theft and lost articles (1.80.1–2); marriage laws (1.80.3–6); ethical and textual education (1.81); medical practices dictated by law (1.82); sacred animals (1.83–90); funeral customs (1.91–93); and prominent lawgivers and the legal innovations that Hecataeus dubiously attributed to each (1.94–95).[19] The *Aegyptiaca* also included an imaginative account of the origins of the Jewish nation as an Egyptian colony. This Greek foundation story, which owed nothing to the biblical narrative,[20] stated that Moses had led a colonizing expedition from Egypt to the land later known as Judea, which was then uninhabited, and established the city of Jerusalem and its temple, conquered nearby territories, and authored the constitution and ancestral laws of the Jews. Hecataeus of Abdera's *Aegyptiaca* was written in Egypt under the patronage of Ptolemy Lagus (later Ptolemy I Soter) in order to educate him about the realm over which he had become ruler, and this text undoubtedly also served as an important text in the education of his son, Ptolemy II Philadelphus, to prepare the latter for kingship (cf. Gmirkin 2006: 252). The story about Moses as the author of the legislation of the Jews in the foundation story found in the *Aegyptiaca* appears to have provided the stimulus for the project to acquire a copy of the Jewish laws for the Great Library.[21] The biblical authors may have first become acquainted with the foundation story in the *Aegyptiaca* at the time of the request from Alexandria for a copy of their legislation. It may have been through a reading of the *Aegyptiaca* that the Jews came to appreciate the character and scope of the literary project that had been requested of them and the full possibilities of integrating historical narrative and legislation within a single literary work. The biblical story echoes the foundation story in the *Aegyptiaca* in key respects.[22] Hecataeus of Abdera's great ethnographic work on Egypt spawned a number of other apologetic ethnographies in the Hellenistic east that competed with his account of Egypt's past greatness. These included the *Aegyptiaca* of Manetho (ca. 285 BCE), the *Babyloniaca* of Berossus (ca. 278 BCE), the *Indica* of Megasthenes (after 278 BCE) and what we might call the *Judaica* of the Jews (ca. 270 BCE), that is, the Primary History of the Jews comprising the biblical books of Genesis–Kings. Of all the previously mentioned ethnographies listed, only the *Aegyptiaca* of Hecataeus and the *Judaica* of the Jews integrated into one work both the history of the nation from its earliest times and a full account of the nation's constitution and laws.

Biographies

The biography of famous persons was a popular literary genre among both Greeks and Romans.[23] Virtually every prominent political figure in Greek antiquity was the subject of one or more biographies. To the extent that Greek politicians were involved in lawmaking, their biographies typically listed the laws for which they were famous. Perhaps the most famous of Greek authors of political biography was the historian and essayist Plutarch (ca. 46–120 CE), who wrote fifty biographies that have survived in part or in full. Although Plutarch's interests were primarily biographical, both legal and constitutional content appeared in his essays on the lives of Theseus, Lycurgus, Solon, Romulus and Numa, to mention only a few. Plutarch's discussion of legal topics within a biographical narrative is comparable to the mixture of biographical and legal elements in the biblical accounts of Moses and Joshua.[24]

Constitutional histories

The constitutional history was a genre invented by Aristotle in conjunction with his research and philosophical writings on the nature of government. Aristotle and his students investigated and described 158 Greek and barbarian constitutions from city-states throughout the Mediterranean. Although fragments of several of these works survive in the form of quotations by later authors, Aristotle's *Athenian Constitution* is the only one that has survived to modern times relatively intact. In this important text, Aristotle (or his students) first gave a narrative account of the constitutional history of Athens, from legendary times down to his present day (ca. 325 BCE), providing a historical background to each of eleven changes in form *(metastatis)* that the constitution underwent. The text concluded with a systematic account of the current Athenian constitution of ca. 325 BCE, apparently taken from official records (Aristotle, *Athenian Constitution* 42–68; cf. Rhodes 1993: 30–7). The genre of constitutional history that Aristotle created was a composite form that combined pure narrative dealing with legal and political topics with what amounted to a constitutional law collection.

Philosophical dialogues

Another distinctive Greek literary genre was the philosophical dialogue, Plato's favorite literary form, but also used by other Greek philosophers like Aristotle (in works mainly lost). The Platonic dialogue was effectively a prose adaptation of Greek drama, a sort of prose play in which the main characters were philosophers and public figures who discussed various topics and provided a fictional vehicle for many of Plato's own ideas, especially in Plato's later works.[25] Plato's favorite character was Socrates, his former teacher, who appeared in all of Plato's dialogues except for the last one, Plato's *Laws.* Two dialogues with expressly legal content were *The Republic* and *The Statesman,* about the qualities of ideal government and rulership, respectively. Plato's *Laws* took the form of a dialogue that took place between a Cretan, Klinias, charged with framing a constitution and laws for a new colony of Magnesia, and his two traveling companions, a Spartan, Megillos, and the anonymous Athenian Stranger, who laid out the constitution and laws he considered ideal for the colony. The fictional narrative outlining of the system of government in *Laws* shares many features with the presentation of Mosaic laws in Deuteronomy (see Chapter 4 §5).

In summary, the discussion of constitutions, laws, lawgivers and other legal subject matter appeared within a narrative context in several genres of Greek literature, fictional and non-fictional, poetry and prose, but nowhere within narrative texts of the Ancient Near East. Greek foundation stories provide the closest correspondence with the Pentateuchal narratives that introduce the Mosaic laws and merit a detailed comparative analysis.

2. Foundation stories

Comparisons with Greek literature show that the biblical account of the Israelite Exodus and Sojourn under Moses and Conquest under Joshua follow the familiar pattern of the Greek foundation story.[26] This genre of narrative, unknown in the Ancient Near East (as noted at Weinfeld 1993: 1; Malkin 2015: 20), was extremely popular in the Hellenistic world.[27] The current section contains detailed discussion of standard literary features of Greek foundation stories and corresponding elements in the story of Moses leading the children of Israel to the Promised Land.

Greek foundation stories might take place in mythical times (when men and gods coexisted long before the flood of Deucalion),[28] legendary times (the age of heroes, approximately ending in the Trojan War)[29] or archaic and historical times.[30] Direct encounters between gods and men were restricted to mythical and legendary times; in archaic and historical times, the gods were consulted in temples and oracle sites. Rarely was an entire foundation story set in legendary times. More often, ancestral land promises were given in a legendary setting, with the actual foundation having taken place later in archaic or historical times.

Ancestral land promises were an important feature in many Greek foundation stories, providing a charter myth that legitimized the later conquest and settlement of the territory in question.[31] Usually the ancestor was a hero famous for his world travels in legendary times, such as Herakles or Aeneas or the members of the Argonaut expedition. In most cases, the hero's travels took him through the territory later to be colonized by his descendants. During this earlier visit, the hero was typically given the land as a gift by Apollo or one of the other Greek gods.[32] The hero's travels continued and he settled (or died) elsewhere, but his divine rights to the land were passed down to his offspring. A gap of several generations might exist between the ancestral land promises and the colonization of the land by his descendants.[33] The most famous example of this literary *topos* was the adventures of Herakles, in which the gods gave the hero the rights to rule various locales in his travels around the Mediterranean. The legendary Dorian invasion of the Peloponnese and the Cyclades was legitimized as the Return of the Heraklids (discussed at Tigerstadt 1965: 1.28–36); the Spartans who ruled the Peloponnese used the travels of Herakles to justify their establishment of other colonies throughout the Mediterranean.[34] The colonization of Cyrene in North Africa provides another example. According to a tradition recorded by Pindar and by Apollonius of Rhodes, when the Argonauts landed on the Libyan coast in the course of their travels, a son of Poseidon presented Euphemus, the Minyan, a clod of Libyan soil, symbolizing rulership rights over the land, as a guest-gift. This was passed down through the generations until it was inherited by Battus, the founder of Cyrene in Libya.[35] The case of Aeneas, who traveled the Mediterranean after the conclusion of the Trojan War, was exceptional, in that he never visited the Promised Land of Latium. Instead, he received a prophecy at Troy that his descendants would one day found a city that would rule the world – namely, Rome (Homer, *Iliad* 20.307; Virgil, *Aeneid* 3.97–98). Weinfeld compared the ancestral promises made to Abraham, Isaac and Jacob with those made to Herakles (Weinfeld 1993: 2 n. 1; cf. Malkin 2015: 24) and to Aeneas.[36] The patriarchal period formed a prehistory to the foundation of the Israelite nation under Moses and Joshua in the same way as Greek stories about ancient heroes and eponymous ancestors formed a historical backdrop and charter myth for later migrations and conquests. The conquest and settlement of the Promised Land was portrayed as a return of the Israelites to the ancient ancestral lands after the familiar pattern of the Return of the Heraklids and other Greek charter myths.

The foundation story proper typically included an explanation of the circumstances leading up to the launching of an expedition of colonization to a new land. According to the typical sequence of events, negative circumstances at home, such as overpopulation,[37] famine,[38] plague,[39] natural disaster,[40] economic subjection,[41] *stasis*,[42] exile,[43] defeat at war,[44] or escape from impending conquest[45] and enslavement[46] prompted a decision to found a new colony. In the Jewish foundation story by Hecataeus of Abdera in ca. 315 BCE, overpopulation was the reason why the Egyptians sent colonists to settle Babylon, Argos, Colchis and Judea (Diodorus Siculus, *Library* 1.28.1–3 [colonization accounts]; 29.5 [reason for colonies]). In Manetho's story of ca. 285 BCE, Jerusalem and Judea were first settled by the Hyksos, foreign kings who had enslaved Egypt, who were eventually expelled by the Egyptians because of a plague caused by their impious foreign practices (Josephus, Apion 1.75–91, 228–51; cf. Gmirkin 2006: 170–213). In the biblical Exodus story of ca. 270 BCE, Manetho's story was turned on its head: plagues fell on the impious Egyptians for enslaving the children of Israel and to convince Pharaoh to release them so they could worship Yahweh in the wilderness (cf. Gmirkin 2006: 187–91, 212–13). The Exodus as an escape from slavery was in keeping with Hellenistic foundation story motifs and was a central recurring theme in biblical accounts. Egyptian enslavement of its populace and the use of slave labor for the creation of Egyptian monuments such as the pyramids were also proverbial (Herodotus, *Histories* 2.124; Aristotle, *Politics* 5.1313b). The miraculous deliverance of the children of Israel was a narrative element unique to the biblical story, without a parallel in Greek foundation stories, mythical or historical, but the departure of the Israelites to seek freedom in a new land is otherwise fully in line with Greek accounts.

A key episode in the Exodus narrative was Yahweh's selection of Moses as liberator and expedition leader of the Jews. This scene took place when Moses was in exile from the land of Egypt, when Moses stumbled upon the sacred site of Yahweh's oracle in the wilderness of Sinai.[47] Moses was told by Yahweh that he would lead the Israelites out of Egypt to a new land, and that Aaron would assist him. This came to Moses as a complete surprise, but he reluctantly undertook this important mission, despite personal misgivings.

The divine appointment of Moses as expedition leader in the biblical narrative followed the normal conventions of Greek foundation stories. A consultation at an oracle – most commonly the oracle of Apollo at Delphi[48] – identified the *oikist* or expedition leader for the band of colonists.[49] The *oikist* acted as expedition commander, military commander, religious authority and lawgiver for the new city-state.[50] A common literary and historical motif was the surprise of the *oikist* at being designated expedition commander.[51] The Delphic oracle often provided landmarks or a travel itinerary to guide the colonists in their travels[52] and signs to later identify appropriate places for the location of the colony's main *polis* and for the establishment of sanctuaries (cf. Plutarch, *Moralia* 407f–408a; Parke and Wormell 1956: 1.49–50, 53, 60, 67–73; Malkin 1987: 2–3, 5). Sometimes expeditions were accompanied by a prophet or *mantis* who assisted the *oikist* throughout the foundation process.[53]

In the biblical narrative, the children of Israel were led out of Egypt as armies and were portrayed in Numbers as an armed troop that marched in formation, always at the ready for battle (Ex. 6.26; 7.4; 12.17, 41, 51; cf. Num. 10.14–28). Moses acted as their general, although it was Yahweh who delivered the victory, both by leading the Israelites out of Egypt "with a mighty hand" and in subsequent battles against the Amalekites, Amorites and Midianites along the way (cf. Ex. 17.8–16; Num. 21.21–35; 31.1–12). The description of those in the Exodus as an army or host anticipated the Conquest story, when Joshua would serve as Yahweh's general instead of Moses. Throughout both Exodus and Conquest narratives, women, children and herds were under protection of the troops. The status of the non-soldiers was entirely secondary: it was the men of the army who were numbered (Num. 1.4–46; 26.2–51), and it is these same soldiers who were counted as the generation who perished in the wilderness (Num. 15.29; 32.11; Deut. 2.14–16; Josh. 5.4, 6). Exodus–Joshua was, throughout, the story of an army on the move, departing one land to conquer another. In this the biblical narrative also conforms to the conventions of Greek foundation stories. Greek colonization expeditions often set out in warships and were effectively armies on the move.[54] It was in his capacity as the patron god of migrations and colonies that Apollo was consulted in his temple at Delphi, where he was known both as "Apollo Archegetes, the god of foundations" (cf. Malkin 1994: 145) and as Agetor, "leader of the host."[55]

In the biblical narrative, the first major destination of the Israelites was Mount Sinai, which functioned as a sacred oracle where Yahweh could be consulted. The return to Sinai in Exodus set the stage for the famous theophany scene, where Moses ascended the mountain of Yahweh's presence and there received the divine laws. Several Greek foundation stories featured the *oikist* revisiting the oracle at Delphi to consult the deity about important matters.[56] This return to Delphi often involved leaving the expedition on its own for an extended period comparable to Moses' forty days and nights on the mountain. Moses' role as lawgiver was in perfect keeping with a Greek foundation story. A key role of the *oikist* in both legendary and historical Greek foundations was to craft laws and constitution for the new settlement. The Greek tendency was to attribute the most ancient laws to a single legendary, semi-legendary or archaic lawgiver of great repute, such as Minos, Theseus, Lycurgus or Solon (see generally Szegedy-Maszak 1978: 199–209; cf. Hagedorn 2004: 83–5). Some of these ancient codes were given added prestige by a tradition wherein the lawgiver received his laws or constitution direct from a god.[57] In historical times, procedures existed whereby draft law codes could be submitted to an oracle and receive the divine sanction of a deity such as Apollo at Delphi.[58] The Greek world possessed a variety of oracular procedures for communicating with a god, and the divine communication of inspiration for ancient Greek laws are best visualized as having taken place through these channels.[59] By contrast with Greek traditions, in the biblical narrative Moses received his laws in a face-to-face encounter with Yahweh at Sinai, amid fearful thunderings, smoke and fire.

At Sinai, Moses oversaw the construction of the wilderness tabernacle and its furniture, which not merely served as a mobile cult center but actually housed the deity, who traveled with the children of Israel in their wilderness trek. Moses acted as religious authority over the expedition, speaking for Yahweh and regulating cultic practices of the Israelites in their travels. Similarly, the *oikist* acted as religious authority and spokesman of Apollo both during the expedition itself and after the settlement in the new territory (Malkin 1987: 5). Greek colonizing expeditions involved not only the migration of the group of colonists, but also the transfer of its deity[60] and his cult, symbolized by the sacred fire that was used for sacrificial offerings *en route*.[61] Apollo's oracle at Delphi provided a travel itinerary and signs by which the location of the new settlement and its sanctuary could be recognized (Plutarch, *Moralia* 407f-408a); perhaps in consequence of this, Apollo was sometimes said to have led the colonists to their new land (see Malkin 1994: 147, on Apollo guiding Battus to Cyrene).

In the biblical narrative, the Israelites, on approaching the Promised Land, sent spies in advance to reconnoiter the land. The Israelite expedition stalled on receiving the daunting report of the forces they would have to conquer and the children of Israel were condemned to sojourn forty years in the wilderness, until that entire generation of soldiers had perished in its entirety. Greek foundation stories occasionally also featured a preliminary expedition to reconnoiter the land.[62] In legendary accounts set in ancient times, the migration could take many years, and the actual settlement might occur a generation or more after the initial expedition set out.[63] Colonizing expeditions that took place in historical times were also known to have suffered setbacks[64] and delays of years or decades.[65] Colonists sometimes attempted to return to their original land, both for reasons of nostalgic attachment and for difficulties in establishing a prosperous settlement.[66]

Both the biblical narrative and Greek foundation stories prominently featured the establishment of the ancestral constitution and political institutions. At the conclusion of the forty years in the wilderness, the book of Deuteronomy detailed a second giving of the law in the plain of Moab. This second set of Mosaic law described the institutions and laws that were to apply after the children of Israel had settled into the Promised Land. These laws were ratified by solemn oath by all the people with attached blessings and curses. Provisions were made for their publication and display in the new land. When Joshua led the host across the Jordan, he made haste to construct an undressed stone altar, inscribe the laws on plastered stone, reenact the covenant with blessings and curses and in every other respect implement the Mosaic laws for the land.

In both Greek foundation stories and in the biblical narrative, the ancestral constitution and laws were framed by the lawgiver who led the colonizing expedition to the new territory. In this respect, the figure of Moses precisely fulfilled the responsibilities of an *oikist*.[67] Like Moses, the Greek founder-figure formally established a constitution for the new nation[68] that defined its political, religious and military institutions, its class structure and social organization, how the land would be allotted, the legal rights and responsibilities of the citizenry and other laws governing the new nation. The constitution was ratified by the people, often with accompanying oaths and sacrifices.[69] The foundation decree, constitution or laws were often published, inscribed on stone for view by all.[70]

The Israelite arrival to the Promised Land was a return to the ancestral homeland of the patriarchs Abraham, Isaac and Jacob, much like the Return of the Heraklids in Greek tradition. In both cases the return was accomplished by a divinely mandated conquest of the native populations. The stories of the partial conquest of the Promised Land under Joshua naturally have its parallel in Greek foundation stories. In both biblical and Greek narratives the land was a gift from the deity, and its conquest by the colonizing forces was not only permitted, but also required. In successful colonizations, the original inhabitants of the land were typically conquered and enslaved[71] or displaced,[72] an action sometimes justified by some moral pretext that became part of the foundation legend.[73] In his capacity as military commander, the *oikist* was usually accorded the status of hero.[74] But rarely were the new colonists welcomed;[75] and resistance sometimes forced Greek colonists to change or abandon their plans.[76] Failure to conquer the lands given to colonists by oracle of Apollo was a matter of enduring reproach among the Greeks, much as the failure to conquer the entirety of the Promised Land was criticized in the book of Judges.[77]

Besides conquering territory for the colonists, the duties of the *oikist*[78] included determining a location for the main city; defining sacred precincts, raising temples and altars and establishing festivals and other cultic institutions;[79] dividing up the land among the tribes and allotting land parcels of equal value to the expedition participants.[80] Extensive parallels between the activities of Joshua during conquest and settlement phases and accounts of Greek colonizations have been thoroughly explored by Weinfeld (Weinfeld 1993: 22–51).

The foundation of the colony reached completion with the death of the founder figure.[81] The memory of the founder was important to later generations, who typically set up a founder's cult in his honor at the site of his tomb,[82] which was usually found in a place of honor in the *agora* for colonies established in historical times: in cases of cities that claimed a foundation by some famous or eponymous hero in legendary times, the location of the founder's tomb was sometimes unknown.[83] The location of the tomb of the lawgiver Moses was unknown, but those of his successor Joshua, along with his chief priest Eleazar,[84] were prominently mentioned at Josh. 24.30, 33, suggesting a special honor for the tombs of the founders.[85]

The *oikist* cult typically involved an annual festival in which the ancestral colonization under the leadership of the *oikist* was commemorated (Malkin 1987: 11, 189–204). Perhaps the best known of these was the annual Dorian festival called Karneia,[86] which commemorated the successive foundations of Sparta, Thera and Cyrene. The Karneia was originally an agricultural festival in honor of Karnus, an ancient ram-god who came to be identified with Apollo (Parke and Wormell 1956: 1.56). Apollo Karneios was Apollo in his role as the leader of migrations, like a ram leads a herd (Malkin 1994: 150, 153): he led the legendary Dorian migration to Sparta, the Spartan colonization of the island of Thera, and the Theran colonization of Cyrene.[87] The Karneia lasted nine days, from the seventh to the fifteenth day of the autumnal month Karnios. The Karneia involved the sacrifice of a ram (Theocritus, *Idylls* 5.82–83; cf. Malkin 1994: 153). It prominently included the reenactment of a military expedition, with troops arranged by tribes and phratries dwelling in a military camp in special tents or canopies.[88] Public festivities included a weapons dance and a procession with model ships that recalled the Dorian "Return of the Herakleidai" (Malkin 1994: 151, 155). Many features of the Karneia are highly reminiscent of the biblical Passover and eight day Festival of Unleavened Bread. Both originated as agricultural festivals that prominently featured the sacrifice of sheep.[89] Both were later transformed into important national festivals that reenacted a migration or colonization expedition.[90] The Exodus narrative described the outset of an expedition of colonization. The Passover festival, in its reinvention as a commemoration of this event, dramatized the story of Israelite origins in the same way that the Karneia dramatized the story of Spartan origins. As such, the Passover festival illustrates the influence of Greek foundation stories and associated festival traditions to which the Jews had been exposed in the early Hellenistic Era.

As can be seen from the earlier comparisons, the biblical narratives about the patriarchal promises and the later Exodus, Sojourn and Conquest form a connected unity that closely conforms to the Greek literary genre of *ktisis* or foundation story.[91] As with many foundation stories, the biblical account has its own distinctive features. Although some Greek colonizing expeditions began as an escape from slavery, and although some Greek lawgivers claimed divine inspiration, both the biblical Exodus and the giving of the law at Sinai were accompanied by divine signs and wonders not typical of Greek accounts. The authors of Deuteronomy appear to have been keenly aware of these innovations in Israel's foundation story. Deut. 4.32–34 claimed that one could make inquiries and not find another nation to the ends of the earth and the dawn of time that had heard the voice of God speaking directly out of the fire (an allusion to the Sinai theophany of Ex. 19–20, 24) or was taken by signs, wonders and a mighty hand from out of the midst of another nation (cf. Ex. 34.10). This statement displays consciousness of a literary genre dealing with the origins of nations – namely the foundation story, which was known only in the Greek world – and that the Israelite foundation story was unique in Yahweh's direct role as deliverer and lawgiver.

3. A constitutional history

Although the Greek foundation story narrated the circumstances surrounding the creation of a city-state's ancestral constitution and laws, the constitutional history, a prose genre invented by Aristotle to facilitate research in political science, traced each change in a nation's form of government *(metastasis)* from the most ancient times to the present. Although Aristotle brought this literary form to perfection, certain passages on the origins and evolution of government by Thucydides and by Plato may be considered literary precursors to Aristotle's *Constitutions*. The biblical narratives of Genesis–Kings also contained elements of a constitutional history that traced the changes in the form of government from the patriarchal period through the fall of the monarchies of Israel and Judah. The biblical discussion of changes in constitution and the relative merits of forms of government, unprecedented in Ancient Near Eastern literature, appear close in spirit and substance to Greek texts on these same topics. A comparison of Ancient Near Eastern and Greek theories of the origins of government provides a useful starting point for understanding the intellectual context of biblical narratives on government.

In Mesopotamian traditions, there was no question of an evolution of governmental institutions: kingship was present from the beginning, part of the gifts of civilization revealed by the gods to the first generation of humankind. This is fully illustrated by the *Babyloniaca* of Berossus, in which unenlightened humanity as originally created was no better than the animals. Then the gods sent Oannes, an *apkallu,* to teach humankind the arts of civilization, including the establishment of kings and cities (Berossus *FGrH* 680 F1b). In Berossus and the late Babylonian sources he used, the ten generations before the flood were each ruled by a famous king from a prominent Mesopotamian city (Berossus *FGrH* 680 F3b, discussed at Gmirkin 2006: 107–8). After the flood destroyed almost all of humankind, the institution of kingship was immediately restored among the survivors (Berossus *FGrH* 680 FF 3b, 4b, 5a).

Although Genesis–Kings was patterned on Berossus' *Babyloniaca,* it rejected the theory of origins of government found there. Kingship was entirely absent in the primordial world, but first originated in Babylonia under Nimrod after the flood. The chosen people first lived under patriarchal rule, and then under a tribal constitutional democracy instituted by the founder Moses. Only many years later did a change in constitution create a monarchy, which in the space of a single generation degenerated into a state of tyranny. For the biblical narrators, kingship brought not benefits, but oppression and, ultimately, the downfall of the Jewish nation and people.

Among the Greeks, there was a variety of choices of possible forms of government, of which monarchy and its "perversion" into tyranny represented only two. This allowed the same sort of theoretical and practical reflection on the merits and drawbacks of governmental forms seen in the biblical narratives (most explicitly at Deut. 17 and 1 Sam. 8). As a result, Greeks were keenly aware of the alternative constitutional forms at their disposal and present through the different stages of the histories of their cities and to what extent each type of constitution benefited or harmed those under its rule. Whereas Mesopotamian literature had no notion of the people choosing their own form of government, Greek theories on the origin of government were constructed around democratic notions of self-organization and self-determination.

Our main intact documents dealing with the evolution of government among the Greeks are Thucydides' *History of the Peloponnesian War* (ca. 410 BCE), Plato's *Laws* (ca. 350 BCE), Aristotle's *Politics* (ca. 330 BCE) and Aristotle's *Constitution of Athens* (ca. 325 BCE). Of these, only Plato's *Laws* connected the origins of government with the Greek flood tradition. According to Plato's model, "the world of men has often been destroyed by floods, plagues, and many other things," with only a few survivors, the latest such catastrophe being the famous Deluge – presumably that of Deucalion of Thessaly, but perhaps a reference to the earlier flood under Ogygus. In the aftermath of such destruction, earlier states and constitutions were lost to Greek memory,[92] and the survivors, perhaps a few herdsmen in the mountaintops, would have had to start out fresh.[93] Plato traced a hypothetical subsequent course of political evolution in the post-flood world through four stages of social complexity: individual families or households under patriarchal rule; villages governed under traditional, ancestral laws; city-states with constitutions; and leagues among city-states (Plato, *Laws* 3.677a-683b; cf. Morrow 1993: 61–2). Although Plato idealized the ancient, primordial Athenian government, he saw later historical constitutions and laws as a degeneration from the aristocracy and timocracy of distant antiquity to the oligarchies, democracies and tyrannies of recent Athenian history.[94]

Although Aristotle did not introduce Greek flood traditions into his analysis of the origins of government, he posited a similar scheme which saw an evolution from autocratic households under patriarchal law to successively larger forms of government through the unification of families into clans or villages and villages into city-states.[95] The biblical scheme adhered to this same basic organic evolutionary outline: the patriarchal period with households under the authority of the family head (see Gen. 18.19; 23.6 for authority vested in the family patriarch); the growth of clans, villages and tribes; and the creation of a nation of twelve constituent tribes with lawgiver, constitution and laws.

A concern with *metastasis* or change in constitutional form in the government of the Israelites is explicit and prominent in Deut. 17.14–15 and 1 Sam. 8.5–22. The former envisioned a time when the democratic institutions Moses created for Israel would be disturbed by the introduction of kingship; the latter gave the rise of the monarchy in Israel a concrete narrative setting. In the interim period between the times of Moses and Saul, the tribes of Israel were ruled by a series of judges *(shotrim)*, tribal magistrates whose powers appear to have been local, but who assumed wider powers of military command over troops from multiple tribes when required by extraordinary circumstances. The autonomous tribes sometimes came into conflict with each other, as in the case of the prosecution of a war against Ephraim at Judg. 12.1–6 or against Benjamin at Judg. 19–21. A full centralization of political power took place only under David with the establishment of the monarchy and the creation of its capital city, Jerusalem. This interim phase was comparable to the early history of Attica, when the countryside consisted of a multiplicity of walled villages, each operating with its own autonomy except when facing a common threat.[96] The four Ionian tribes, each divided into three *trittyes,* occupied twelve principal cities.[97] These were said to have been first joined together under a single constitution and government by Theseus, who established a single central democratic assembly and council hall in a new city he called Athens (Thucydides, *Peloponnesian War* 2.15.2; Plutarch, *Theseus* 24.1–4). The unification of Attica in a single pan-Athenian state was celebrated in a yearly festival, the Panathenaea. However, the reform under Theseus formed a contrast to the change of constitution in the time of Samuel: Theseus offered, and the people accepted, a reduction in powers for the *basileus* or king and an increase in democratic citizen participation.[98]

The introduction of kingship to Israel was portrayed in both a positive and negative light in the biblical narrative.[99] Three distinct forms of kingship were envisioned in the Primary History. The first was elective kingship subject to law, the form provisionally endorsed by the Torah of the King (Deut. 17.14–20), subject to certain caveats and limitations aimed to prevent the exercise of office in a tyrannical or oligarchic manner. The second was the heroic kingship of David, in which the office of king included military, judicial and religious powers not envisioned in the Torah of the king, and in which the office was hereditary, not elective. The third was the degeneration of kingship into luxury and tyranny as predicted by Samuel and as found in the narratives about Solomon and in the northern kingdom (see especially 1 Kgs 21.1–14 [Ahab]). These categories of kingship were all found in the discussion of monarchy at Aristotle, *Politics* 3.1284b–85b, which distinguished among hereditary and elective kingships, kingships subject to law and those resembling tyrannies and kingships with limited and unlimited powers. Aristotle noted that kingship in the heroic age was often bestowed on an outstanding individual for the benefits he conferred on society, such as military leadership or acquisition of territory, and passed on to his descendants. The biblical rise of David to power followed this positive model. But both Plato and Aristotle, like the biblical Samuel, described a devolution of kingship from a rulership of excellence to a tyranny of oppressive rule intended to benefit only the ruler and his associates, who lived lives of luxury at the expense of the people.[100] The biblical discussion of the transformation from the Mosaic governmental institutions to that of hereditary monarchy appears to be informed at every point by Greek notions of kingship and tyranny, especially as discussed by philosophers at Athens.

4. Conclusions

In the Ancient Near East, law collections such as the Law Code of Hammurabi were published as part of royal memorial inscriptions that lacked any form of story content. As a result, the narrative context of biblical laws has received scant attention in comparative studies of the past. But Greek literature abounds with examples of constitutional and legal topics discussed within prose narratives that provide rich and compelling parallels to biblical legal narratives.

The Primary History, a narrative that covered events from primordial times to the fall of the kingdom of Judah, has close structural parallels to Hellenistic national histories such as the *Babyloniaca* of Berossus and the *Aegyptiaca* of Manetho. Within this national history, the Primary History incorporated a history of constitutional changes that has close affinities to Greek materials. The organic evolution of biblical social and legal institutions was entirely in line with models taken from Greek political philosophy. The postdiluvian setting of the patriarchal period dominated by the rise of autocratic ancestral households and clans shows the closest affinity with the discussion of the origins of government in Plato's *Laws* 3.[101] The formal rise of the Israelite nation is presented within the narrative context of a formulaic Greek foundation story, with the introduction of a democratic constitution and laws by the *oikist* Moses. The Primary History also shows a characteristic Greek concern for subsequent *metastasis* or change in constitutional form with the introduction of a hereditary monarchy. The discussion of the transformation of kingship into tyranny in Samuel's speech could have come from the pages of Plato's *Republic* or Aristotle's *Politics*. Biblical constitutional and legal topics consistently received a thoroughly Greek presentation, including incorporation within narrative contexts, that is best explained by Jewish exposure to Greek literature and political philosophy in the early Hellenistic period.

Notes

1   Several narrative episodes featured well-integrated legal content: the initiation of the sacred Passover laws on the occasion of the Exodus, the Sinai theophany, the wilderness institution of sacred laws associated with the mobile sacrificial cult of the

tabernacle, the military and citizen registration procedures of the host of the Israelites in the wilderness, the new law created by judicial decisions of cases brought before Moses during the Sojourn, the Mosaic legal orations prior to the entry into the land and the formal publication and ratification of the laws at Mount Ebal at the outset of the Conquest under Joshua. Legal content presented in Ezra–Nehemiah was also fully integrated into the narrative context.

2 The integration of the Covenant Code with its narrative context was extensively discussed at Van Seters 2003: 47–56. Although he attempted to demonstrate an exclusively Ancient Near Eastern background of the Covenant Code – he emphasized both general parallels with Mesopotamian legal traditions and direct literary contacts with LH and LE law collections – Van Seters did not discuss the lack of literary parallels of the surrounding Covenant Code narratives with the Mesopotamian legal prototypes he adduces. The same may be said for Wright 2009, although Wright considered the Covenant Code in isolation from its narrative context.

3 The fragments of poetry written by Solon, the great Athenian lawgiver, extensively treated the political situation he was called to mediate and the legal reforms he initiated; cf. Aristotle, *Athenian Constitution* 12.4; Plutarch, *Solon* 2.3–4; 14.5–6; 18.4. For the text and translation of the fragments of Solon's poems, see Linforth 1919: 103–248. According to one tradition, Solon created a version of his laws in poetic verse (Plutarch, *Solon* 2.4). A more "low-brow" instance of legal content in Greek poetry was the Athenian drinking song quoted at Athenaeus, *The Philosophers' Banquet* 15.695a-b, which celebrated the overthrow of the Thirty Tyrants and the restoration of Athenian democracy and *isonomia* (equality under the law); cf. Stanton 1990: 115–18. Themes involving legality and justice also appeared in Greek tragedies, such as the great *Prometheus Bound* by Aeschylus, in which the scathing criticisms of Zeus by chained and unjustly punished Prometheus constituted a bold commentary on the injustice of contemporary tyranny.

4 Thucydides, for example, was an Athenian general; Demetrius of Phalerum was both a philosopher and the tyrant of Athens; Plato was consulted by kings on constitutional matters; and Aristotle was famously the teacher of Alexander the Great.

5 The philosophers Plato and Aristotle both wrote extensively on politics; many of their students went on to become statesmen of note.

6 The most authoritative and comprehensive treatment of the funeral oration was Loraux 1986. Athenian political leaders constructed and interpreted the nation's past for the benefit of the populace by means of these emotion-filled and patriotic orations. Loraux observed that ordinary Athenian citizens were educated in their nation's past through such public panegyric speeches, not by reading history books.

7 Plato, *Menexenus* contained an exaggerated panegyric that satirized the genre in high-flown language, deftly glossing over Athenian military defeats and injustices. *Menexenus* is thought to have drawn upon the funeral oration of Perikles in Thucydides; cf. Kahn 1963; Coventry 1989: 1–15.

8 The most famous panegyric was the funeral oration of Perikles as found at Thucydides, *Peloponnesian War* 2.35–46, which praised the Athenian constitution and laws at 2.37. Similar praise for the Athenian constitution and laws appeared in panegyrics authored by the famous rhetorician Isocrates (*Panegyricus* 39–40; *Panathenaicus* 114, 119–51).

9 The account of the just laws and mighty military deeds of the primordial Athenians in Plato, *Timaeus* 20d-e, 23c, e, 24d-25c was patterned on the genre of panegyric; cf. Morgan 1998: 101, 106–7. In Isocrates, *Panathenaicus* 129, a mixed constitution with democratic elements was said to have been introduced in legendary times by Theseus; cf. Aristotle, *Athenian Constitution* 41.2.

10 In Perikles' funeral oration, the current constitution and laws were praised with no mention of their date or circumstances of origin. The orations of Isocrates took note of

both the legendary features of the Athenian constitution and more recent constitutions whose features were either praised – such as those of Solon and Kleisthenes – or necessitated by political and international circumstances.

11 In Plato, *Timaeus,* the earliest Athenian constitution and laws were said to have been given to the original autochthonous inhabitants of the land by the goddess Athena (*Timaeus* 23d, 24b-d). The laws, which Plato claimed were the greatest ever known (*Timaeus* 23c-d), by coincidence corresponded exactly to the system of government in Plato's *Republic* (Plato, *Timaeus,* 17c-18c, 25e; Plato, *Critias* 110c-d).

12 See Gmirkin 2006: 66–7 on the date of *Aegyptiaca* of Hecataeus of Abdera, written in Alexandria under the patronage of Ptolemy I Soter in ca. 320–315 BCE.

13 See Gmirkin 2006: 38–67 for the isolation of the authentic fragments of the Hecataean foundation story from the passage at Diodorus Siculus, *Library* 40.3.1–8, which Diodorus lifted from an account of Pompey's wars by Theophanes of Mytilene (62 BCE). The reconstructed Hecataean foundation story was quoted in full at Gmirkin 2006: 63.

14 See the detailed analysis of the Hecataean foundation story at Gmirkin 2006: 44–66. Each and every point of similarity is completely explicable as a standard feature of Greek foundation stories, whereas the striking dissimilarities rule out any acquaintance with the Pentateuchal account.

15 Aristotle (*Rhetoric* 1.1360a) noted the usefulness of travel writings for legislators, because such essays often contained descriptions of foreign laws and customs.

16 According to Hecataeus, Egyptian kings were not autocrats but were subject to written laws (Diodorus Siculus, *Library* 1.70.1–2; 71.1; 96.5–6), surrounded by educated priestly servants and advisors who counseled them on virtue and read to them from the sacred books (1.70.2–9), resulting in a stable, felicitous and long-lasting government (1.71.5). This material did not accurately portray the pharaohs or his ministrants, and was strongly influenced by Greek notions of monarchy subject to law, but the parallels to Deut. 17.18–20 in the Torah of the King are obvious.

17 Military law in the *Aegyptiaca,* like Athenian and Pentateuchal military law, dealt mainly with the issues of desertion and cowardice; cf. Chapter 3 §12.

18 These commercial laws were attributed to Bocchoris (Diodorus Siculus, *Library* 1.79.1; 94.5).

19 The majority of biblical laws were attributed to Moses. David was said to have originated the military law regarding the division of booty (1 Sam. 30.21–25); at Diodorus Siculus, *Library* 1.94.4, military laws were attributed to Sesostris. As is well known, the catalog of lawgivers found in the *Aegyptiaca* was not of Egyptian origin, but was created by Hecataeus of Abdera (or perhaps a later source used by Diodorus, according to the arguments given at Murray 1970: 149 n. 1), who imposed the characteristic Greek notion of famous lawgivers from the past on Egyptian materials that mostly lacked such traditions (although the reverse of the Demotic Chronicle mentioned Darius in connection with the collection and publication of Egyptian laws in 518–503 BCE).

20 See Gmirkin 2006: 34–66 on the Hecataean story of Judea's colonization by Egypt as a stereotypical Greek foundation story that contained no narrative elements dependent on the biblical account and many incompatible details. Its fictional character is illustrated by other invented foundation stories found in the *Aegyptiaca* in which Hecataeus of Abdera narrated the purported Egyptian foundation of Babylon by Belus (Diodorus Siculus, *Library* 1.28.1), the foundation of the Colchians by the Pontus (Black Sea) during the course of a military expedition that Sesostris led throughout Asia (1.28.2; 55.4–5), the Egyptian foundation of Argos by Danaus (1.28.2) and that many Athenian customs and some of their ancient kings came from Egypt (1.28.4–29.5). Hecataeus also claimed that Herakles and Dionysius were Egyptians and that many of the Greek gods and customs came from Egypt (1.15.6–9; 17.3–5; 23.1–25.1).

21 Cf. *The Letter of Aristeas* 31, which mentioned Hecataeus of Abdera in connection with the Ptolemaic request for a copy of the laws of the Jews.

22 Story elements taken over from Hecataeus of Abdera included the role of Moses as expedition leader and ancestral lawgiver (see §2), the organization of the Jews into twelve tribes (Diodorus Siculus, *Library* 40.3.3) and the inalienability of Jewish land allotments (40.3.7). Corrections to the account by Hecataeus included the Jewish claim to Mesopotamian rather than Egyptian ancestry and the rejection of the claim that the Jewish custom of circumcision was of Egyptian origin. Gen. 17.9–14 explained the custom of circumcision, not as a custom taken over from Egypt, as in Herodotus, *Histories* 2.104 and Hecataeus' *Aegyptiaca* (at Diodorus Siculus, *Library* 1.28.2–3), but as a distinctive sign of the special relationship between Elohim and the descendants of Abraham.

23 Greek biography had its origins in the fifth and fourth centuries BCE. Panegyrics such as Isocrates, *Evagoras* (ca. 370 BCE) and Xenophon, *Agesilaus* (after 360 BCE) were precursors to biographies *per se* such as Xenophon's *The Education of Cyrus*. Biography became the special province of Peripetic philosophy starting with Aristoxenus, the student of Aristotle, who wrote Lives of Socrates, Pythagoras and others. See generally Stuart 1928; Momigliano 1993.

24 Exodus–Deuteronomy incorporated a biography of the lawgiver Moses that included accounts of his birth (Ex. 2.1–4), upbringing (Ex. 2.5–10), marriage (Ex. 2.15–22; Num. 12.1), his adult life and notable accomplishments (Exodus–Numbers), orations (Deuteronomy) and death (Deut. 34). Joshua mainly appeared as assistant and successor to the expedition leader and lawgiver Moses. Incidental legal elements include his publication of Mosaic law and administration of the oaths of the *polity* at Shechem (Josh. 8.30–35) and the legal oration at Josh. 24.1–28.

25 Scholars on Plato have debated the extent to which Plato's early dialogues portrayed Plato's own thinking or that of his teacher Socrates; it is likely the two largely overlapped at the beginning of Plato's development as a philosopher.

26 See especially Weinfeld 1988, 1993; Malkin 2015. Foundation stories were inexplicably omitted in the analysis of Greek historiography at Van Seters 1983: 8–54.

27 Plato, *Hippias Major* 285d stated that Greeks were "very fond of hearing the genealogies of heroes and the foundation of cities in ancient times." This literary genre, called *ktisis* or "foundation," appeared across a spectrum of factuality from pure legend about ancient foundations to factual accounts by historians such as Ephorus and Thucydides about more recent Archaic and Classical Era foundations. Foundation stories set in historical times almost always described an expedition sponsored by a mother city to establish a new *polis* abroad. These colonizing expeditions, when details are found in our sources, were typically of definite date and point of origin, and led by a named leader sometimes known from contemporary history (e.g. Thucydides, *Peloponnesian War* 6.3–5; 7.57), although some late colonization stories also have added mythical embellishments. See generally J. Hall 2008: 2.383–426. For colonies whose historical founder was unknown, an eponymous founder was often invented; cf. Malkin 1985; 1994: 134–6. Foundation stories set in legendary times (sometimes termed the "age of origins") often dealt with large scale regional migrations, such as those of the Dorians or Ionians, led by an eponymous ancestor or an ancient hero. Israel's settling of the Promised Land more closely resembles legendary than historical Hellenistic foundation stories.

28 For instance, in Plato's writings, the foundation of Athens by Hephaestus and Athena, set long before the flood of Deucalion (*Timaeus* 22a-24d; *Critias* 109a-112e) and the mythical kingdom of Atlantis established by Poseidon (Plato, *Timaeus* 25a-d; *Critias* 113b-120d). Other Greek writers also set the autochthonous origins of the Athenians in the time of Hephaestus and Athena. Erechtheus, the "earthborn king of Athens"

(Homer, *Iliad* 2.546–29), was the offspring of Athena and worshipped at Athens in the Erechtheum, a temple associated with Poseidon, Athena and "Erechtheus the Earth-born" located in the Acropolis (Herodotus, *Histories* 8.55; Homer, *Odyssey* 7.81; cf. Papachatzis 1989).

29 The foundation of Thebes by Cadmus the Phoenician at the direction of the oracle of Apollo at Delphi took place several generations before the Trojan War (Apollodorus, *Library* 3.4.1; Ovid, *Metamorphoses* 3.3–137). The foundation of Scheria by the Phaeacians took place under the leadership of Nausithous the son of Poseidon a generation before the time of Odysseus (Homer, *Odyssey* 6.4–10).

30 Foundation stories from historical times (the Classical Era) were more likely to have written documentation, whereas foundation stories from earlier archaic times were more often based on local oral traditions, sometimes preserved in association with the founders cult for that city.

31 According to Weinfeld (1993: 19), "The genre of foundation stories consists of two parts: the first part describes the migration of the ancestor, and the second describes the settlement." The two phases were discussed at 1993: 19–21. This generalization does not universally hold true, because charter myths with ancestral land promises are sometimes lacking for historical foundations in the classical period, when consultation of the oracle at Delphi provided an alternative means of legitimizing colonial territorial conquests.

32 Malkin 1987: 23. "Sometimes we hear of a colony as a 'gift' of Apollo to the *oikist*. In this respect the foundation oracles are similar to the biblical notion of the 'promised land'" (1987: 6; cf. 28, 48–9). The land was described as a gift from Yahweh at Deut. 19.1–3, 8–10.

33 Weinfeld 1993: 6–9. Weinfeld compared the 430 years that intervened between the Abrahamic promises and the conquest of the Promised Land to the 333 years between the promises to Aeneas and the birth of his descendants Romulus and Remus, the founders of Rome (1993: 6).

34 Spartan foundation myths were the special topic of Malkin 1994. The Dorians and the Return of the Herakleidai were discussed at Malkin 1994: 15–45. The Spartan poet Tyrtaeus famously wrote that "Zeus himself . . . has given this land to the Herakleidai" (Malkin 1994: 3, 19).

35 Pindar, *Pythian Odes* 4.1–24, 35–39; Apollonius of Rhodes, *Argonautica* 4.1547–63; 1731–64; see discussion at Parke and Wormell 1956: 1.77. The motif of the gift of a clod of earth to symbolize sovereignty rights was also seen in the foundation stories for both Miletus and the land of the Aenianes; cf. 1956: 58, 62–3. Spartan charter myths for Libyan colonization were discussed at Malkin 1994: 169–91.

36 Weinfeld 1993: 1–21. Weinfeld compared the Abrahamic promises that prompted his emigration from Mesopotamia to Canaan with the similar destiny prophesied for the legendary Trojan hero Aeneas at the outset of his travels: much as the descendants of Aeneas would someday found Rome (Homer, *Iliad* 20.307; Virgil, *Aeneid* 3.97–98), so Abraham's descendants would become a great nation and rule many peoples (Gen. 12.3; 17.5; 27.29).

37 Overpopulation was the historical impetus for Athenian establishment of colonies (Thucydides, *Peloponnesian War* 1.2.5–6; Plato, *Laws* 4.707e, 708b; 5.740e). At Diodorus Siculus, *Library* 1.29.5, in a passage thought to draw on the *Aegyptiaca* of the Hellenistic historian Hecataeus of Abdera, this was also the reason given for Egyptian colonies abroad. According to Herodotus, *Histories* 4.151.1, Cyrene was founded ca. 630 BCE to relieve famine in Thera caused by overpopulation. See generally Gwynn 1918.

38 Famine was given as the reason for sending colonists to settle Rhegion in southern Italy (Strabo, *Geography* 6.1.6; Diodorus Siculus, *Library* 8.22.2); Tyrrhenia, the home of

the Etruscans (Herodotus, *Histories* 1.94); Cyrene, after a seven year drought in Thera (Herodotus, *Histories* 4.153, 156); Syracuse (Plutarch, *Moralia* 773a-b); Rhodes and Knossos, by the so-called Famine-Dorians (Hesychios, s. v. *Limodorieis*). Crop-failure and migration were linked at Lycurgus, *Against Leokrates* 83. See also Camp 1979: 405–10.

39 A divine plague *(loimos)* of drought and pestilence at Corinth prompted the exile of the founders of Syracuse (Diodorus Siculus, *Library* 8.10.1–3). Pestilence prompted the Boeotians to found Herakleia Pontus (Justin, *Epitome* 16.3.4–7).

40 Malkin 1987 noted that natural disasters and resulting food shortages were often interpreted as signs of divine wrath, for which the Delphic oracle often advised colonization expeditions as a cure and relief.

41 See Homer, *Odyssey* 6.4–10 (cf. Apollonius of Rhodes, *Argonautica* 4.539–50) on the plundering of the Phaeacians of Hyperia by the legendary Cyclopes and their liberation and resettlement in Scheria under the leadership of Nausithous. Weinfeld (1993: 23) described the raids on the Phaeacians by their aggressive neighbors as "enslavement" and compared their plight to the biblical slavery in Egypt, but Homer appears to have seen the Cyclopes as lawless pirates rather than political or economic overlords.

42 Plato, *Laws* 4.708b-c. According to Thucydides, *Peloponnesian War* 1.2.5–6, Athens was a refuge for powerful men "driven out of their own communities by war or *stasis*." Such men sometimes led or participated in colonization expeditions. An expelled faction founded Tarentum according to Aristotle, *Politics* 5.1306b. Dorieus, who led a failed colonization expedition to Libya and Sicily, was a member of Spartan royalty who was implicated in an unsuccessful *stasis* or revolt (Herodotus *Histories* 5.42.2). Taras was said to have been founded by the Partheniai (or "virgin-born," that is, illegitimate sons of unmarried Spartan women during the nineteen years of the First Messenian War), a disaffected faction from Sparta (Strabo, *Geography* 6.3.2–3; Crawford and Whitehead 1983: 99; Fornara 1983: 11–12; Malkin 1994: 47; Dillon and Garland 2010: 17).

43 A common motif of foundation stories set in legendary times was the establishment of a colony by a hero such as Herakles exiled from his home for unintentional homicide (Parke and Wormell 1956: 1.54, 59; Malkin 1994: 42). The Bacchides who led the historical Corinthian foundation of Syracuse (733 BCE) were also said to have been exiled for blood guilt (Diodorus Siculus, *Library* 8.10.1–3; scholiast on Apollonius of Rhodes, *Argonautica* 4.1212; cf. Malkin 1994: 41). The Locrian colony of 673 BCE was slandered in later times as having been founded by (fugitive) slaves, thieves and criminals (Polybius, *Histories* 12.5–16).

44 Fugitive Messenians looking for a place to settle joined the colonizing expedition to Rhegion as a result of their defeat by the Spartans in the First Messenian War (Strabo, *Geography* 6.1.6; cf. Crawford and Whitehead 1983:96–8; Malkin 1994: 32–3). Timoleon of Sicily famously gave refugees from the great wars land to resettle (Plutarch, *Timoleon* 35). Miletans fleeing Cimmerian conquest of Asia Minor refounded Sinope (Pseudo-Skymnos, *Geographical Description* 986–97; Dillon and Garland 2010: 14). Teians fleeing the Persian conquest of Asia Minor by Harpagos founded Abdera in Thrace (Herodotus, *Histories* 1.168.1; cf. Malkin 1994: 54).

45 After consulting the Delphic Oracle, Athens was evacuated in 481 BCE in the face of conquest by the Persians (Herodotus, *Histories* 7.139–44; 8.40, 51–53). The Athenians seriously entertained permanent resettlement in another land (Herodotus, *Histories* 8.143). The episode was thoroughly discussed at Bowden 2005: 100–8. See further note 46.

46 In the Greek world, military defeat often resulted in the enslavement of some or all of the defeated party. Colonization undertaken in order to escape from imminent military defeat thus avoided the fate of slavery. The Ionians of Phocaia, threatened with

conquest by the Persians, debated whether to set off in an expedition to establish a colony in Sardinia where they would be "free of slavery and prosperous" (Herodotus, *Histories* 1.169–70). The Teians who fled the Persian general Harpagos to found Abdera were said to be "the only Ionians who abandoned their native lands because they were unable to endure slavery" (Herodotus, *Histories* 1.168); but the Phocaians also famously fled Persian conquest and enslavement, abandoning their city *en masse* in warships to relocate west, eventually founding Massalia (Marseilles) (Herodotus, *Histories* 1.164–65). The Spartans of Laconia completely enslaved subjugated populations, most famously the slave class Helot populations of Lakonia and Messenia (Thucydides, *Peloponnesian War* 1.101; cf. Crawford and Whitehead 1983: 295). The Messenians who fled the Spartans in the First Messenian War thereby avoided enslavement. The Partheniai who left Sparta to colonize Taras after an unsuccessful *stasis* at the conclusion of the Second Messenian War were said to have been allied with the Helots or slave class according to a tradition found at Strabo, *Geography* 6.3.2. A revolt of Messenian Helots, who were besieged on Mount Ithome by the Spartans for ten years, was concluded in ca. 460 BCE when the Spartans let them depart the Peloponnesus unmolested with their wives and children with the understanding they never return. The Athenians subsequently resettled them at Naupaktos (Thucydides, *Peloponnesian War* 1.103).

47 In the biblical narrative, communications with Yahweh took place at Sinai, which effectively served as Yahweh's oracle before the construction of the wilderness tabernacle.

48 Apollo was consulted in his capacity as the god of colonies and migrations. Many colonies claimed Apollo as their founder; cf. Graham 1964: 26. Colonization oracles at the temple of Apollo at Delphi were discussed at Parke and Wormell 1956: 1.49–81; Fontenrose 1978: 137–44; Malkin 1994: 17–29.

49 The term *oikist* comes from the Greek work *oikos* which means household. The colony was called an *apoikia*, a "new home" for the members of the expedition.

50 "The *oikist* . . . embodied in his person the functions of the king, the priest, the lawgiver and the military leader" (Malkin 1987: 5; cf. 88–91). The *oikist* in his capacity of exegete or expounder on sacred matters (Malkin 1987: 3, 88–9) has an obvious biblical parallel in Moses. The *oikist* was extensively discussed at Graham 1964: 29–40. According to Graham, "in the earlier colonies the *oikists* seem to have been all-responsible, even monarchic," but were less all-powerful in later Athenian colonies with democratic constitutions. The *oikist* for earlier colonies tended to act with full independence, whereas *oikists* sent by later tyrants to establish dependent colonies maintained close ties with their *metropolis* or mother city, and the *oikist* of the imperial colonies of the fifth century BCE did not even establish residence in the new settlement.

51 A common feature of the Delphic designation of the *oikist* was his surprise at being divinely appointed as colony leader (Parke and Wormell 1956: 1.50, 74–5; Malkin 1987: 6–7, 27–8; cf. Ex. 3.1–11). Typically the individual whom Apollo designated as *oikist* had visited Delphi to consult the oracle on some entirely unrelated matter when he received the divine instruction to act as expedition leader. Classical scholars assume such scenes were often staged in historical times to conform to expected conventions. Battus, the historical founder of Cyrene in Libya, famously visited Delphi to inquire how to cure his stammer when the oracle designated him as leader of the Theran colonizing expedition (Pausanias, *Guide to Greece* 10.15.5–6; Diodorus Siculus, *Library* 8.29; Scholiast to Pindar, *Pythian Odes* 4; cf. Herodotus, *Histories* 4.150). Wajdenbaum (2011: 150–2) compared the stammer of Battus with that of Moses in the biblical account. Moses' stammer could conceivably have been modeled on that of Battus, as Wajdembaum suggests, on the hypothesis that the biblical authors were familiar with the famous story of Cyrene's foundation, either from Herodotus or some later source. Callimachus, who created the catalog for the Great Library of Alexandria, claimed

that Battus was his ancestor (Strabo, *Geography* 17.3.21). Jewish troops had been settled in Cyrene under Ptolemy I Soter (a settlement date of ca. 312 BCE was argued at Applebaum 1979: 130–8) and may have somehow been a conduit by which other Jews became acquainted with some elements of Greek traditions.

52 According to Herodotus, *Histories* 4.150, for seven years the men of Thera disregarded instructions from the Delphic oracle to found a colony in Libya, "since they were quite ignorant where Libya was, and were not so venturesome as to send out a colony in the dark." The oracle was frequently consulted for directions to the colonization site. Examples of landmarks and itineraries were given at Parke and Wormell 1956: 1.53, 60, 65, 67–70, 72.

53 Malkin 1987: 2, 8, 92–113; Malkin 2015: 31–3. Weinfeld (1993: 27) compared Joshua and Eleazar at Josh. 24.30–33 to Battus the founder of Cyrene and Onymastos the seer who accompanied him (mentioned in the *Sacred Laws of Cyrene* 22–3; cf. Rhodes and Osborne 2003: 495).

54 This especially applied to colonies established by populations fleeing war, or by armies stranded in a foreign land, such as the failed expedition into Asia under the command of Xenophon to put Cyrus the Younger on the throne; cf. Xenophon, *Anabasis* 5.6.15–20, 27–31. Colonies established by force typically had a military character. Leucippus, for instance, the Magnesian *oikist*, was instructed to set out for the Pamphylia, "leading the kindred folk of the Magnesians under arms" (Parke and Wormell 1956: 1.53).

55 "At Argos, Apollo Karneios is called Zeus Agetor, because he too was the leader of an army" (Theopompos, *FGrH* 115 F357; cf. Malkin 1994: 150). The Karneia, a celebration of Apollo as the god of Dorian (Spartan) migrations and colonizations, emphasized military deeds and included a ceremonial weapon dance (1994: 155).

56 Examples of expedition leaders who returned to Delphi in the midst of their travels for further instructions from the oracle included Battus of Cyrene (Herodotus, *Histories* 4.156–57), Myscellus, the founder of Croton (as discussed at Parke and Wormell 1956: 1.69–70), the Magnesians who resided at Crete for eighty years, at the direction of the Delphic oracle, until instructed by the oracle to found a colony in Asia Minor (1956: 1.52–53) and the colonists who founded Ephesus (as discussed at 1956: 1.60).

57 Szegedy-Maszak 1978: 204–5. The shepherd Zaleucus was said to have been given the laws by Athena in a dream (Scholiast *ad* Pindar, *Olympian Odes* 10.17; according to Clement of Alexandria, *Miscellanies* 1.170.3, this was found in Aristotle's *Locrian Constitution*). According to Ephoros, quoted at Strabo, *Geography* 10.4.19, Rhadamanthys and Minos of Crete claimed that they received their law codes for mankind from Zeus; cf. Plato, *Laws* 1.624a. At Plato, *Critias* 119c-e, the Atlantian laws were given direct by Poseidon. Plutarch said that Minos, Zaleucus, Zoroaster, Numa and Lycurgus all claimed to have conversations with a god, thinking this would promote acceptance of their law codes (Plutarch, *Numa* 4.6–8; Plutarch, *Lycurgus and Numa* 1; cf. Polybius 10.2.8–12; Cicero, *On the Nature of the Gods* 3.91; Dionysius of Halicarnassus, *Roman Antiquities* 2.61). Tradition was divided whether Lycurgus brought his laws and constitution from Crete or obtained them from the priestess at the Delphic oracle (Herodotus, *Histories* 1.65; Plato, *Laws* 1.624a; Plutarch, *Lycurgus* 1.1–3; 5.3; 6.1; 29.2–4; Diodorus Siculus, *Library* 7.12). According to Parke and Wormell 1956: 1.85–92, the association of the Lycurgan reforms and the oracle at Delphi, unknown to Herodotus, may have originated in a pamphlet on the Spartan Constitution by King Pausanias after his exile from Sparta in 395 BCE. Diodorus Siculus, *Library* 1.94.1–2 cataloged traditions in which laws from various nations were attributed to divine authorship, including the laws of the Jews which "Moyses" credited to the god Iao. Diodorus suggested that the reasons for ascribing the laws to a god were either the perception of the laws as marvelous or the increased likelihood that the populace would obey the laws if they believed they had a divine origin (Diodorus Siculus, *Library* 1.94.1–2; cf. Josephus, Apion 2.162, with similar language).

58 According to Parke and Wormell 1956: 1.90–91, a draft of the laws or constitution was brought to Delphi, where the priestess would communicate Apollo's approval. *The Sacred Laws of Cyrene* were attributed to Apollo, presumably as a result of this formal procedure. Parke and Wormell argued that the Spartan constitution, traditionally attributed to the legendary lawgiver Lycurgus, may have received sanction from the Delphic oracle when it was created ca. 600 BCE shortly after the Messenian revolt. The posting of laws – including civil laws – in the temples of Greece illustrates their divine sanction; cf. Hagedorn 2004: 79–81. According to one tradition, the lawgiver Solon received an oracle from Pytho (Plutarch, *Solon* 14.4).

59 For instance, Lycurgus received the Spartan constitution from the oracle of Delphic Apollo; Athena communicated laws to Zaleucus in a dream, perhaps through a ritual of incubation; Rhadamanthys and Minos received the Cretan laws at "the cave of Zeus," presumably the location of a sacred oracle. At Plato, *Laws* 1.625a-b, the Athenian Stranger and his two road companions were headed to the "cave and temple of Zeus" on mount Idas, where Klinias was presumably headed to consult the oracle about laws for the planned Cretan colony that was the subject of the dialogue. Kaiser (2000: 78–9) compared the trek of the three legislators to the cave of Zeus in Plato's *Laws* to Moses' climb of Mount Sinai to receive the laws of Yahweh.

60 See Weinfeld 1993: 11–14 on the transfer of the ancestral gods. Weinfeld noted the transfer of the Trojan gods to Latium as a recurrent motif in various retellings of the Aeneid foundation legend and compared the theft of the Trojan sacra to the theft of the teraphim by Rachel at Gen. 31.19, 34.

61 See Parke and Wormell 1956: 1.49; Malkin 1987: 9, 114–34 on the transfer of the sacred sacrificial fire in Greek colonial expeditions. The transfer of cultic apparatus (the wilderness tabernacle) and sacred fire (see especially Lev. 9.24; 10.1–2; Num. 16.35; cf. the legend at 2 Macc. 1.19–2.7, where Nehemiah transferred the sacred fire to the Second Temple) figured in the wilderness period. The deity was literally transported from Sinai to the Promised Land in the wilderness tabernacle, his mobile dwelling place (Ex. 13.21–22; 29.42–44; 40.34–38; Num. 9.15–23; Josh. 22.19).

62 Herodotus, *Histories* 4.151–53 recounts the preliminary Theran reconnoitering expeditions to the Libyan coast preparatory to the main colonization.

63 Colonizations that spanned several generations were commonly associated with migrations in legendary times, such as the Dorian conquest of the Peloponnese, which involved various setbacks and delays (Parke and Wormell 1956: 1.55–56). Weinfeld (1993: 2–8) discussed the example of Virgil's *Aeneid*, in which several generations intervened between the departure of Aeneas from Troy and the settling of Rome by his descendants. This scheme appears to have been necessitated in order to accommodate the participation of Aeneas in the Trojan War and Latin legends of the foundation of Rome by Romulus 400 years later. Although *The Aeneid* was written by a Latin author, it conformed to the well-known Greek genre of foundation story and drew on earlier Greek traditions about Aeneas.

64 See, for instance, the initial unsuccessful attempts by the Dorians from Megara to settle in Sicily reported at Thucydides, *Peloponnesian War* 6.4.1. The attempts by the Spartan Dorieus to establish a colony in Libya in ca. 514–512 BCE notoriously ended in failure when his forces were expelled by a coalition of Carthaginians and Libyan Makai, and Dorieus later perished during a subsequent attempt to conquer territory in Sicily (Herodotus *Histories* 5.42.2–45.1; cf. Malkin 1994: 192–218). The establishment of a Greek colony at Plataia was also initially unsuccessful (Plutarch, *Timoleon* 22–5).

65 The Theran colonization of Cyrene was initially delayed seven years before setting out under the leadership of Battus (Herodotus, *Histories* 4.150–51); then dwelled first on the island of Platea for two years and then at the coastal site of Azirus for six more years before finally founding Cyrene (4.156–58). The Thessalian colonization of Magnesia

in Asia Minor took place in stages over several decades, with a lay-over of eighty years in Crete (cf. Parke and Wormell 1956: 1.52–53). See Herodotus, *Histories* 1.164–67 on the wanderings of the Phocaians.

66 An oracle from Delphi instructed the Magnesian exiles residing in Crete that they should not return to Thessaly as they desired, but should instead colonize the mountains above the Pamphylian Gulf (Parke and Wormell 1956: 1.52–53). *The Cyrene Foundation Decree* (Meiggs and Lewis 1969: 5–9) contained a clause allowing colonists to return as full citizens to their properties in Thera only after five years of unremitting hardship. The initially impoverished colonists of Libya under the leadership of Battus attempted to return to Thera after only two years, but were repelled and forced to set out for Libya a second time (Herodotus, *Histories* 4.156). The Phocaians who sailed *en masse* from Ionian Phocaia rather than be enslaved by the Persians swore never to return to their home city, but some broke their oath and returned (Herodotus, *Histories* 1.165). Compare the nostalgia of the biblical wilderness generation for Egypt and attempt to return there (Ex. 16.2–3; Num. 11.5, 18, 20; 14.2–4; 21.5).

67 At Josephus, Ant. 2.180, Moses was described as a *nomothetes* or lawgiver, and at Ant. 4.194, 196, 302, "Moses gave the Israelites not only laws but also a constitution, thus making the Jewish state comparable to the Greek city-states"; cf. Feldman 1993: 321. In colonies of later imperial Athens, the *oikist* appears to have been almost exclusively concerned with crafting a constitution and laws. Athens sent a panel of *oikists* that included the *mantis* Lampon to its new colony of Thurii in Italy in ca. 434 BCE to fashion a democratic constitution and divide the land among the ten tribes (Diodorus Siculus, *Library* 12.11.2; 35.1–2; cf. Fornara 1983: 123–4). It is known that Lampon did not even establish a residence at Thurii, but returned immediately to Athens. Another telling example was Timoleon of Sicily, who gave refugees from the great wars land and helped craft their constitutions. Despite not having led a colonizing expedition, Timoleon was considered the *oikist* of the communities he thereby helped established (Plutarch, *Timoleon* 35).

68 Licht 1980: 98–128 (Hebrew) compared to the creation of a new nation in Deuteronomy and in historical and legendary Greek foundation stories. Licht took Deut. 27.9 ("Today you have become the people of the Lord your God") as an announcement of the establishment of the Israelite nation; cf. Weinfeld 1993: 3.

69 The *Cyrene Foundation Decree* contained explicit instructions for the gathering of all men, women and children to swear to the provisions of the decree, with blessings and curses that would attach to them and their descendants depending on their faithfulness to the agreement; cf. Graham 1964: 27–8, 226; Weinfeld 1993: 29. Similar blessings and curses appeared on the Pappadakis bronze, possibly from Naupaktos; cf. Hagedorn 2004: 79 n. 258. The notion of blessings and curses on a city contingent on their justice was already present in ca. 600 BCE in Hesiod, *Works and Days* 224–48.

70 Cf. Weinfeld 1993: 36–40. Foundation decrees for Cyrene, Naupaktos and Brea have survived relatively intact, and are found, with extensive discussion, at Meiggs and Lewis 1969: no. 5 (Cyrene, pp. 5–9), no. 20 (Naupaktos, pp. 35–40), no. 49 (Brea, pp. 128–33); Graham 1964: 225–9 (text), 40–68 (discussion). A fragment of the foundation decree for Black Corcyra was discussed at 1964: 58–9. The *Brea Foundation Decree* made explicit provisions for its inscription and display on a stele to be located on the acropolis; cf. 1964: 63, 229.

71 Gwynn 1918: 108. The Spartans were famous for having subjugated and reduced to slavery the pre-existing Greek populations of Lakonia and Messene, who became an oppressed slave class known as the Helots (Strabo, *Geography* 6.3.2; 8.4.10; 5.4; Thucydides, *Peloponnesian War* 1.101; cf. Crawford and Whitehead 1983: 295). The Delphic oracle did not typically direct the conquerors to enslave local populations. The oracle quoted at Diodorus Siculus, *Library* 8.21.3 was unusual in having instructed

the Spartan colonists of Satyrion and Taras to "be a plague to the Iapygians" (cf. Malkin 1987: 48–9; Malkin 1994: 9, 33, 115–42). Neleus, the legendary Ionian (Athenian) founder of Miletus, was told to "drive out the wicked Karians" (Parke and Wormell 1956: 2.122; Malkin 1994: 51. Such oracles "create the impression of a divinely justified and inspired war, with the god personally at the side of the founder" (Malkin 1987: 51–2). The barbarian Mariandynoi of Herakleia, a Greek foundation on the southern Black Sea coast, were said to have voluntarily surrendered themselves as slaves to the more capable and intelligent Herakleots, according to a tradition from Posidonius quoted at Athenaeus, *The Philosophers' Banquet* 6.263d.

72 See Dionysius of Halicarnassus, *Roman Antiquities* 19.2 on the barbarians displaced from Rhegion by the colonists from Chalcis. See Diodorus Siculus, *Library* 8.21.3; Strabo, *Geography* 6.3.2–3 and Justin, *Epitome* 2.4 on the expulsion of the earlier inhabitants from Taras. See Weinfeld 1993: 76–98 on the terminology and traditions regarding the "expulsion, dispossession or extermination" of the Canaanites by the conquering Israelites. Greeks and Macedonians sometimes practiced extermination of defeated cities, such as when the Athenians killed all the Melian men and enslaved the women and children (Thucydides, *Peloponnesian War* 5.84–116), when Philip of Macedon razed the cities of Phocis, Olynthus and Porthmos (Demosthenes, *On the Crown* 39, 65, 71, 182) or when Alexander the Great destroyed various cities during his conquests (Arrian, *Anabasis* 1.4.5; 23.6; 4.23.5; 5.24.8). See Connor 1985: 79–102 on the razing *(kataskaphe)* of the houses of tyrants, traitors, murderers and the impious, and the razing of entire cities for acts of rebellion or impiety.

73 Malkin 1987: 2, 6, 90. Colonization was often described as a return of the Heraklids, the Argonauts, or those who had fought at Troy. Such "charter myths" legitimized the seizure of land from their current inhabitants. Malkin noted that old myths, such as the exploits of Herakles or of Argonauts, were sometimes attached to the sites of new colonies. "This association could be used to justify, or validate, a claim on a particular site." The reassurances of the *oikist* of the divine sanction for acts of conquest and land seizure served to remove the fear of divine wrath for criminal acts falling on the colonists.

74 Malkin 1987: 51. The founder's tomb was sometimes labeled a *heroon* or hero's tomb.

75 Malkin 1994: 115–52 on native hostility to colonists. For initial Libyan cooperation with the Thera colonists at Cyrene, see Herodotus, *Histories* 4.158. Arganthonius, king of Tartessos in Iberia, invited the Phocaeans to settle there (Herodotus, *Histories* 1.163). Aristotle's *Massaliot Constitution* recorded the hospitable reception of the colonist Euxenos of Phocaia by the king of Massalia (quoted at Athenaeus, *The Philosophers' Banquet* 13.576a-b; cf. Herodotus, *Histories* 1.163; Gwynn 1918: 107–8). Hyblon, a Sicel king, gave the Megarians land and guided them to it (Thucydides, *Peloponnesian War* 6.4.1).

76 Malkin 1987: 11. A notable example was Timesius of Klazomene, who failed in his attempt to found Abdera in ca. 650 BCE when the warlike Thracians expelled the colonists. A second colonization of Abdera by the Teians succeeded in ca. 545 BCE; cf. Herodotus, *Histories* 1.168; Parke and Wormell 1956: 1.61; Malkin 1987: 54–6. Dorieus of Sparta, after expulsion from Libya, attempted to settle his forces in Sicily (Herodotus, *Histories* 5.42.2–45.1). The Cumaeans were expelled from Zankle by the Samians and other Ionians (Thucydides, *Peloponnesian War* 6.4.5). Greeks were twice expelled from Sybaris in Italy (Diodorus Siculus, *Library* 12.9–10). The oracle of Delphi denied requests to colonize Sikyon (Diodorus Siculus, *Library* 8.21.3) and Arcadia (Herodotus, *Histories* 1.66.1) because of the strong military resistance the colonists would have encountered (cf. Malkin 1987: 48–9).

77 See Judg. 1.17–2.5. The most famous Greek example was Dorieus, of Spartan royal lineage, who failed in repeated attempts to colonize North Africa as directed by the

Delphic oracle. "Prophecies and oracles kept reminding the Spartans what was expected of them: colonization at Lake Tritonis, in the 'precinct of Zeus Ammon' (=Libya). Paradoxically, the recurrence of this unrealized prophecy underlies its importance as an authentic expression of Spartan ambitions." Malkin 1994: 143.

78 The legendary activities of the founder Nausithous at Homer, *Odyssey* 6.8–10 are considered typical: "[He] settled them in Scheria . . . drew a wall around the city, and built houses, and made temples to the gods, and divided up the corn-lands"; cf. Crawford and Whitehead 1983: 62; Dillon and Garland 2010: 5.

79 Cf. Parke and Wormell 1956: 1.49; Malkin 1987: 89, 135–88. These functions were distributed between Moses and Joshua (Weinfeld 1993: 36–40, 46–51); the wilderness tabernacle functioned as a mobile cult center prior to the construction of the Solomonic temple according to biblical narratives.

80 Malkin 2015: 29–31. Weinfeld (1993: 22–3) noted the "surprising similarity" between procedures for founding a settlement and allotting land in Plato, *Laws* 5.745b-c and the book of Joshua. For the selection of ten men from each tribe to act as *geonomoi* for the purpose of dividing the land in the *Brea Foundation Decree* 6–8, see Graham 1964: 59, 228; Weinfeld 1993: 35–6. For allotment of lands during colonization, see also Aristotle, *Politics* 6.1319a.

81 Malkin 1987: 28. Note the closing of the book of Moses with the death of Moses and of the book of Joshua with the death of Joshua.

82 E.g. Thucydides, *Peloponnesian War* 5.11.1; Herodotus, *Histories* 6.38.1. The cult of the *oikist* was extensively discussed in Malkin 1987: 11, 189–266. Malkin dated the origin of the *oikist* cult to the eighth century BCE, at the beginning of the Greek colonization movement, based on inscriptional, archaeological and literary evidence. Weinfeld (1993: 14–15, 32–4) compared the importance of founders' tombs to the Greeks with the emphasis on the tombs of Abraham, Jacob and Joseph in Genesis. He noted the parallel between the transfer of the bones of Jacob and Joseph from Israel to their ancestral tombs in Canaan with the legendary transfer of the bones of Aeneas to Latinium, Theseus to Athens, and Orestes to Sparta (cf. Plutarch, *Theseus* 36; Herodotus, *Histories* 1.67–68; Parke and Wormell 1956: 1.96; Malkin 1987: 81; Malkin 1994: 26–31).

83 Greek colonists sometimes consulted the oracle at Delphi for signs to locate the "secret burial place of heroes" in order to determine the ideal location for their settlement (Plutarch, *Moralia* 407f-408a; Malkin 1987: 6, 33). According to Sophocles, *Oedipus at Colonus* 1518–34, the bones of Oedipus were hidden in a spot known only to the Athenian line of kings.

84 Both Battus, founder of Cyrene, and Onymastos, the "seer" from Delphi who accompanied him, were honored with tombs in the *agora* of Cyrene, according to *The Sacred Laws of Cyrene* 21–5; cf. Parker 1983: 336–8. Weinfeld (1993: 27) compared these to the tombs of Joshua and Eleazar.

85 Weinfeld (1993: 14–15, 32–4, 39) understood the mention in Joshua as indicating a special care for the tombs of the founders. Jewish eponymous ancestors, ancient heroes and their burial places were celebrated in the biblical text. Note the ancestral tomb of Abraham and Jacob at Hebron at Gen. 23.1–20; 25.9–10; 49.29–32 – or at Shechem according to Gen. 33.19 – and the tomb of Joseph at Shechem in Gen. 50.5. The mention of the unknown location of Moses' tomb suggests a special interest in the tombs of the founders.

86 The cult of Apollo Karneios and the Karneia as a foundation commemorative festival were extensively discussed at Malkin 1994: 143–58.

87 The successive foundations of Sparta, Thera and Cyrene by Apollo Karneia were recounted in Callimachus, *Hymn to Apollo*. Pindar, *Pythian Odes* 5 emphasized the foundation of Cyrene. See discussion at Malkin 1994: 143–7.

88 Athenaeus, *The Philosophers' Banquet* 4.141e, citing the Book 1 of the Trojan Array by Demetrius of Skepsis. The canopies or skiathes (σκιάδες) are reminiscent of the Succoth or temporary dwellings of the Jewish autumnal Feast of Tabernacles.

89 The original character of Passover and Days of Unleavened Bread as a spring harvest festival has long been recognized. Only at some later stage were they transformed into a commemoration of the Exodus (cf. Wellhausen 1965: 87–8). An association with the Exodus was entirely lacking in the so-called "Passover letter" (*TAD* A4.1) from Elephantine. Indeed, the Elephantine papyri and ostraca, although they contained references to Passover, Festival of Unleavened Bread and Sabbath, lacked any features of these observances that suggest acquaintance with the biblical narrative tradition in Exodus. See Gmirkin 2006: 30–1; Kratz 2007: 84–6.

90 For the Passover as commemorating the Exodus, see Ex. 12.1–28; 13.3–10; Deut. 16.1–12. The festival involved a dramatic or theatrical reenactment of the Exodus in which all family members participated (Ex. 12.3–11, 26–27; 13.3–4). As a ritualized commemoration of the Israelite departure from Egypt, intended for celebration after possessing the land (Ex. 13.3–9), Passover implicitly anticipated the expedition of migration, conquest and colonization as a whole, and indeed the children of Israel were said to have celebrated Passover immediately after entering the Promised Land (Josh. 5.10–11).

91 The tradition history approach of Rolf Rendtorff and the European school hypothesized the independent formation of the various units composing the narratives of Genesis–Joshua, which were thought to have been unified only at the last stage of redaction; cf. Rendtorff 1990. But these narrative units (aside from the primordial history in Genesis 1–11) may now be seen as essential story elements within a typical foundation story: the ancestral land promises, the departure or exodus, the wanderings, the receiving of the law, the conquest and settlement of the land. The individual units are best understood as having been composed with overall narrative scheme in mind. The explanation of these units as expected components of a foundation story appears to weigh decisively against the redaction critical model.

92 Plato, *Timaeus* 20e, 22b-23c; Plato, *Critias* 109d-110a; Plato, *Laws* 3.677a-e, 702a; cf. Aristotle, *Politics* 2.1269a. But the Egyptians, whose land was never destroyed by floods, preserved records from these ancient times, 9,000 years before Plato's present (Plato, *Timaeus* 21e-22a, 22e-23a, 27b).

93 Plato, *Laws* 3.676a-677b. According to the Atthidographers, probably starting with Hellanikos of Lesbos, the first Athenian king was Kekrops; cf. Harding 2008: 20–2; Thucydides, *Peloponnesian War* 2.15.1. Kekrops was an approximate contemporary of Deucalion, who fled Thessaly after the Deluge to take refuge in Athens according to some traditions.

94 Plato, *Republic* 8.544c-569c; 9.576d-e; cf. Bury 1951: 86–8; Morrow 1993: 119. Aristotle, *Politics* 5.1316a-b contained a critique of Plato's theories on degeneration of government. This theory was given a mythical setting in Plato's *Critias,* where the degeneration of the kingdom of Atlantis into wickedness led to its ultimate destruction by the gods, a pattern similar to that found in Genesis–Kings (cf. Wajdenbaum 2011: 274–5).

95 Aristotle, *Politics* 1.1252b-1253a. According to Aristotle, "the most natural form of the village appears to be that of a colony from the family," or blood relatives, ruled by the eldest family member. The village was thus approximately equivalent to the extended family or clan.

96 "Under Cecrops and the first kings, down to the reign of Theseus, Attica had always consisted of a number of independent townships, each with its own town hall and magistrates. Except in times of danger the king at Athens was not consulted; in ordinary seasons they carried on their government and settled their affairs without his interference; sometimes even they waged war against him." Thucydides, *Peloponnesian War* 2.15.1–2; cf. 2.16.1.

97 According to the Atthidographer Philokhoros, a division into twelve communities was originated by Cecrops, the first king of Attica (Strabo, *Geography* 9.1.20; cf. Harding 2008: 21).

98 Plutarch, *Theseus* 24.1–4; Isocrates, *Panathenaicus* 129; Aristotle, *Athenian Constitution* 41.2. The mythical figure of Theseus is thought to have been recast as the champion of Athenian democracy in the sixth or fifth century BCE by Kleisthenes or Pisistratos. See generally Walker 1995. Wajdenbaum (2011: 241–2) compared Samuel's speech at 1 Sam. 8.11–18 with Theseus' speech against tyranny at Euripides, *The Suppliants* 430–60.

99 It is evident that Samuel–Kings is a composite text whose authors included both pro- and anti-monarchists. A positive view of the monarchy of Judah underlies the depiction of the kings of Judah from David to Hezekiah (the "era of David"), whereas a uniformly negative view appears in the monarchy of Israel (the "era of Jeroboam"). The earliest portrayal of the kings of Judah from Manasseh to Zedekiah (the "era of Manasseh") was uniformly negative in the books of Kings, Zephaniah, Jeremiah and Ezekiel. The original negative portrayal of Josiah in 2 Kgs 22–23 was revised and supplemented with a positive depiction of Josiah as reformer, as I argued in a 2011 presentation at an annual meeting of the Society of Biblical Literature, San Francisco, titled, "The Deuteronomistic History: a Hellenistic Era Composition in Two Redactions." I assigned 2 Kgs 21.1–22.1; 22.3–10, 12–17; 23.26–25.26 to the earlier DtrM or Manasseh redaction, and restricted the later DtrJ or Josiah redaction to 2 Kgs 22.2, 11, 18–20; 23.1–25. As so assigned, DtrJ materials display consistent literary dependence on DtrM, whereas DtrM shows none on DtrJ, demonstrating the chronological priority of DtrM. It is also apparent that 2 Kgs 22.2 originally contained a negative formula that described Josiah as wicked like his forefathers, a formula also found at 2 Kgs 21.20; 23.32, 37; 24.9, 19.

100 Aristotle, *Politics* 5.1310b-1311a, 1313a-1315b; Plato, *Republic* 9.576d-580a; cf. Balot 2001: 53–4. The description of the luxurious state at Plato, *Republic* 2.372e-373c has points of contact with 1 Sam. 8.10–18; note especially the need for "confectioners and cooks" in both.

101 This comparison was already found at Eusebius, *Preparation for the Gospel* 12.15; cf. Wajdenbaum 2011: 53, 106.

Bibliography

Applebaum, Shimon, *Jews and Greeks in Ancient Cyrene*. Leiden: E.J. Brill, 1979.

Balot, Ryan K., *Greed and Injustice in Classical Athens*. Princeton: Princeton University Press, 2001.

Bowden, Hugh, *Classical Athens and the Delphic Oracle*. Cambridge: Cambridge University Press, 2005.

Bury, R.G., "Plato and History," *CQ* 1 (1951): 86–93.

Camp, John McK. II, "A Drought in the Late Eighth Century BC," *Hesperia* 48 (1979): 397–411.

Connor, W.R., "The Razing of the House in Greek Society," *TAPA* 115 (1985): 79–102.

Coventry, Lucinda, "Philosophy and Rhetoric in the *Menexenus*," *JHS* 109 (1989): 1–15.

Crawford, Michael H. and David Whitehead, *Archaic and Classical Greece: A Selection of Ancient Sources in Translation*. Cambridge: Cambridge University Press, 1983.

Dillon, Matthew and Lynda Garland, *Ancient Greece: Social and Historical Documents from Ancient Times to the Death of Alexander the Great*. New York: Routledge, 2010.

Feldman, Louis H., "Josephus' Portrait of Moses: Part Three," *JQR* 83 (1993): 301–3.

Fontenrose, Joseph, *The Delphic Oracle: Its Responses and Operations with a Catalog of Responses*. Berkeley: University of California Press, 1978.

Fornara, Charles W. (ed.), *Archaic Times to the End of the Peloponnesian War*. Cambridge: Cambridge University Press, 1983.

Gmirkin, Russell E., *Berossus and Genesis, Manetho and Exodus: Hellenistic Histories and the Date of the Pentateuch*. Library of the Hebrew Bible/Old Testament Studies 433. Copenhagen International Series 15. New York: T & T Clark, 2006.

Graham, A. J., *Colony and Mother City in Ancient Greece*. New York: Barnes and Noble, 1964.

Gwynn, Aubrey, "The Character of Greek Colonization," *JHS* 38 (1918): 88–123.

Hagedorn, Anselm C., *Between Moses and Plato: Individual and Society in Deuteronomy and Ancient Greek Law*. Göttingen: Vandenhoeck & Ruprecht, 2004.

Hall, Jonathan M., "Foundation Stories." Pages 383–426 in volume 2 of Gocha R. Tsetskhladze (ed.), *Greek Colonisation: An Account of Greek Colonies and Other Settlements Overseas*. 2 vols. Leiden: E. J. Brill, 2008.

Harding, Philip, *The Story of Athens: The Fragments of the Local Chronicles of Athens*. London: Routledge, 2008.

Kahn, Charles H., "Plato's Funeral Oration: The Motive of the *Menexenus*," *Classical Philology* 58 (1963): 220–34.

Kaiser, Otto, "Das Deuteronomium und Platons Nomoi: Einladung zu einem Vergleich." Pages 60–79 in H. Spieckermann and R.G. Kratz (eds.), *Liebe und Gebot: Studien zum Deuteronomium*. Forschungen zur Religion und Literatur des Alten und Neuen Testaments 190. Göttingen: Vandenhoeck & Ruprecht, 2000.

Kratz, Reinhard G., "Temple and Torah: Reflections on the Legal Status of the Pentateuch between Elephantine and Qumran." Pages 77–104 in Gary N. Knoppers and Bernard M. Levinson (eds.), *Pentateuch as Torah: New Models for Understanding Its Promulgation and Acceptance*. Winona Lake, IN: Eisenbrauns, 2007.

Licht, Jacob, "The Biblical Claim of Establishment," *Shnaton* 4 (1980): 98–128 (Hebrew).

Linforth, Ivan M., *Solon the Athenian*. Berkeley: University of California Press, 1919.

Loraux, Nicole, *The Invention of Athens: The Funeral Oration in the Classical City*. Translated by Alan Sheridan. Cambridge, MA: MIT Press, 1986.

Malkin, Irad, "What's in a Name? The Eponymous Founders of Greek Colonies," *Athenaeum* 63 (1985): 115–30.

———, *Religion and Colonization in Ancient Greece*. Leiden: E. J. Brill, 1987.

———, *Myth and Territory in the Spartan Mediterranean*, Cambridge: Cambridge University Press, 1994.

———, "Foreign Founders: Greeks and Hebrews." Pages 20–40 in Naoíse Mac Sweeney (ed.), *Foundation Myths in Ancient Societies: Dialogues and Discourses*. Philadelphia: University of Pennsylvania Press, 2015.

Meiggs, Russell and David Lewis (eds.), *A Selection of Greek Historical Inscriptions to the End of the Fifth Century BC*. Oxford: Clarendon Press, 1969.

Momigliano, Arnaldo, *Development of Greek Biography*. Cambridge, MA: Harvard University Press, 1993.

Morgan, Kathryn A., "Designer History: Plato's Atlantis Story and Fourth-Century Ideology," *JHS* 118 (1998): 101–18.

Morrow, Glenn Raymond, *Plato's Cretan City: A Historical Interpretation of the Laws*. Princeton: Princeton University Press, 1993.

Murray, Oswyn, "Hecataeus of Abdera and Pharaonic Kingship," *JEA* 56 (1970): 141–71.

Papachatzis, Nicolaos, "The Cult of Erechtheus and Athena on the Acropolis of Athens," *Kernos* 2 (1989): 175–85.

Parke, H. W. and D.E.W. Wormell, *The Delphic Oracle*. 2 vols. Oxford: Blackwell, 1956.

Parker, Robert, *Miasma: Pollution and Purification in Early Greek Religion*. Oxford: Clarendon Press, 1983.

Rendtorff, Rolf, *The Problem of the Process of Transmission in the Pentateuch*. Translated by John J. Scullion. JSOTSup 89. Sheffield: Sheffield Academic Press, 1990.

Rhodes, Peter John, *A Commentary on the Aristotelian Athenaeion Politeia*. Oxford: Clarendon Press, 1993.

Rhodes, Peter John and Robin Osborne, *Greek Historical Inscriptions 404–323 BC*. Oxford: Oxford University Press, 2003.

Stanton, G. R., *Athenian Politics: c. 800–500 BC: A Sourcebook*. London: Routledge, 1990.

Stuart, Duane Reed, *Epochs of Greek and Roman Biography*. Berkeley: University of California Press, 1928.

Szegedy-Maszak, Andrew, "Legends of Greek Lawgivers," *GRBS* 19 (1978): 199–209.

Tigerstadt, E. N., *The Legend of Sparta in Classical Antiquity*. 3 vols. Stockholm: Almquist & Wiksell, 1965, 1974, 1978.

Van Seters, John, *In Search of History: Historiography in the Ancient World and the Origins of Biblical History*. New Haven, CT: Yale University Press, 1983.

———, *A Law Book for the Diaspora: Revision in the Study of the Covenant Code*. Oxford: Oxford University Press, 2003.

Wajdenbaum, Philippe, *Argonauts of the Desert: Structural Analysis of the Hebrew Bible*. London: Equinox Publishing, 2011.

Walker, Henry J., *Theseus and Athens*. New York: Oxford University Press, 1995.

Weinfeld, Moshe, "The Pattern of the Israelite Settlement in Canaan." Pages 270–83 in John Adney Emerton (ed.), *Congress Volume: Jerusalem*. SVT 40. Leiden: E.J. Brill, 1988.

———, *The Promise of the Land: The Inheritance of the Land of Canaan by the Israelites*. Berkeley: University of California Press, 1993.

Wellhausen, Julius, *Prolegomena to the History of Ancient Israel*. Translated by J. Black and A. Menzies. Repr. Cleveland: World Publishing, 1965.

Wright, David P., *Inventing God's Law: How the Covenant Code Used and Revised the Laws of Hammurabi*. Oxford: Oxford University Press, 2009.

6

THE CREATION OF
THE HEBREW BIBLE

The current study laid out substantial new arguments for viewing the Primary History of Genesis–Kings as a Hellenistic Era composition that displays considerable influences from the Greek world: its structural form as a nationalistic history, patterned on such works as the *Aegyptiaca* of Manetho (ca. 285 BCE) and the *Babyloniaca* of Berossus (278 BCE); its integration of elements from discussions of constitutional history taken from Plato and perhaps Aristotle; its incorporation of the Greek genre of the foundation story in its narratives about the patriarchal promises, the Exodus, wilderness wanderings and conquest of the Promised Land; its characteristically Greek integration of narrative and legal content; its Greek constitutional and legal content; and its Greek conception of law as prescriptive, educational and useful for instilling citizen virtues. The new understanding of the Primary History as a composition of ca. 270 BCE, substantially indebted to Greek legal and historiographical literature and containing only a few genuinely archaic legal and historical elements, stands in sharp contrast to the rival model of Genesis–Kings as an ancient and essentially Near Eastern composition that faithfully described Jewish traditions rooted in near-contemporary memories of the monarchic period. Rather than a reflection of authentic ancient Jewish memories, the earliest historiographical writings represent a learned construction of Jewish antiquity by means of antiquarian research in both Greek and Jewish sources, and the embedded legal content represents Hellenistic Era efforts to construct a Jewish constitutional and legal system informed not only by local Jewish legal traditions but also by extensive research in Greek legal literature.

Greek influences on the biblical text discussed in earlier chapters include the substantial use of Plato's *Laws*. It is apparent that this particular philosophical text exerted a profound influence on the political thinking, educational philosophy and literary activities of the biblical authors. This is illustrated most decisively in the book of Deuteronomy, which was written according to directions laid out in Plato's *Laws* as a speech to the gathered colonists of the nation about to be founded, recounting their laws suitably framed by hortatory introductions and other educational and rhetorical content. This shows the very direct impact of Plato's *Laws* on the creation of the Torah by the biblical authors. Significantly, the literary program envisioned in Plato's *Laws* was not limited to the creation and promulgation of a divine constitution and laws as the foundational document of the new nation. Plato also envisioned a second phase of literary activity, the ambitious, historically unprecedented creation of a national literature with approved texts, both new and old, to be used in the education and indoctrination of the citizens of the *polis* in the proper values of virtue and justice as laid out in Plato's *Laws*. This chapter will argue that the Hebrew Bible was first assembled as an authoritative national literature in ca. 270 BCE or shortly thereafter following the detailed instructions recorded in Plato's *Laws*.

1. Authorized literature in Plato's *Laws*

Plato was first and foremost an educator whose Academy trained its students in advanced studies advantageous to prepare them for leadership roles in politics (Morrow 1993: 5). Plato's writings display a progression of thought regarding education, rhetoric and the character of good government. Rhetoric, or the art of persuasion, was a skill vital to the functioning of a democracy such as Athens, but was often used to the detriment of the *polis* in Plato's view. Plato's early works contained penetrating critiques of the amoral character of political rhetoric as taught in competing Athenian schools run by Sophists such as Protagoras and Gorgias.[1] Plato described rhetoric as a form of *psychogogy* or education of the soul in which the soul could be swayed to either virtue or vice by the persuasive powers of speech.[2] Plato considered both rhetoric and poetry forms of magical enchantments designed to cast spells over their listeners.[3] Through Socrates, Plato's teacher and the hero of Plato's early dialogues, Plato argued that education should seek to cultivate, not rhetoric and sophistry, but the art of true reason, in order for the student to attain a deep philosophical knowledge of the nature of virtue. But Plato held out the possibility of developing a new art of rhetoric informed by philosophy that might be used to educate the soul in a positive way to the benefit of the *polis* (a theme he took up in his later writings). Plato held that the art of politics required the statesman to be an educator who not only commanded and ruled the people, but also taught them excellence (*arete* or virtue).[4] According to Plato, proper statecraft therefore required the study of individual and civic ethics, which could be achieved only through a deep knowledge of philosophy. Indeed, Plato held that philosophers were the only true statesmen and that the philosopher, prophet, social critic and educator Socrates, although he held no public office, was the only statesman of his day worthy of that name.[5] Plato upheld Socrates as a man of true wisdom and virtue, in contrast to the rhetors who dominated the contemporary political and educational scene. Yet Plato also portrayed Socrates as a master of rhetoric and as a magician who was able to enchant his audiences as skillful as any orator in his day (see generally Gellrich 1994), but with an aim to instill virtue in the souls of the citizenry.

In Plato's middle works, and especially in the *Republic* of ca. 360 BCE, Plato developed the role of the state as an educational instrument.[6] In his philosophical study of the soul and the forces that shaped it, Plato had carefully considered the rhetorical persuasive effect, not only of public speech, but also of every aspect of both public and private life, including the myths that the populace were exposed to through literature and public performances. In Athens, the purpose of education was to create model citizens for the *polis* (Aristotle, *Politics* 2.1263b; 3.1288a-b; 5.1310a; 8.1337a; Plato, *Republic* 4.423e-424a; Plato, *Laws* 1.643d-644b; 7.809c) – not vocational training, which was looked down upon as demeaning[7] – and for Plato, this meant that the state should inculcate ethical values by establishing and enforcing standards of private and public education aimed at promoting virtue in the citizenry. Plato believed that many aspects of Athenian education and culture had a negative effect on the souls of its citizens, especially the impressionable young, and threatened the health of the *polis*. Plato therefore advocated the careful regulation of not only speech and conduct, but also music, art, dance, theater, literature and even nursery rhymes and the games that children were allowed to play. A new form of government was required to eliminate the negative persuasive effects of literature by censoring literature in all its forms, starting by getting rid of the works of Homer and Hesiod and by banishing all the poets.[8] In Plato's *Republic,* he envisioned the *polis* organized into three classes, corresponding to the three types of souls.[9] At the lowest level were the ordinary citizens, the agriculturalists and craftsmen, with souls of iron and bronze (Plato, *Republic* 2.369c-371e; 3.415a). Above them was the class of professional soldiers, the silver-souled Auxiliaries, whose desire to achieve honor through acts of courage made them the ideal watchdogs to protect the state from both revolution and invasion (Plato, *Republic* 2.374a-376b; 3.412b-417b). Highest of all was the aristocratic ruling class, called Guardians, with souls of gold, an educated elite of philosopher-kings who would act as rulers and watch over the souls of the citizenry (Plato, *Republic* 5.473c-d, 474b-c; 6.484a-487a, 501e-502a, 503b; 7.540a-c). While the Craftsmen received no formal education and the Auxiliaries received an education that emphasized military training such as found at Sparta and in the *gymnasia* of Athens,[10] only the Guardians received a higher education in philosophy, for only these were endowed with the divine facility of reason *(nous)* required to attain and comprehend philosophical truth.[11] Lacking reason, the two lesser classes possessed only opinions, the shadows or imitation of truth,[12] which must be carefully shaped and regulated by the Guardians through rhetoric and myths (Plato, *Phaedrus* 273d-e; Plato, *Statesman* 303e-304d; Plato, *Gorgias* 504d; Plato, *Republic* 3.389d; 4.429d; 6.484a-c; 7.522a-b; 9.590c-d; 10.604d; Kauffman 1994: 112; Klosko 2006: 116, 170). Plato acknowledged that the notion of three types of souls was itself a myth and a fiction,[13] but one useful for the population to believe so that they would entrust the government to the guardianship of the auxiliaries and philosopher-kings.[14] In order to facilitate the adoption of this myth, Plato proposed that the Guardians, after obtaining power in Athens, should expel everyone over the age of ten from Athens to live in the countryside, and that the philosopher-kings should personally undertake the nurture and education of the new generation of children in the city.[15] By seizing control of education and only allowing the young to be exposed to the approved myths, Plato believed that the *polis* could be wholly brought over to the new way of life within a generation or two (Plato, *Republic* 3.415c).

In Plato's last works, he fully integrated the use of rhetoric into his system of state-sponsored education.[16] In Plato's *Laws,* of ca. 350 BCE, his final work, he extended his educational program to include the constitution and laws of the *polis* and proposed the novel idea of legislation as an educational instrument. According to Plato, the effective legislator must be a philosopher, an educator, and an absolute master of rhetoric (Jaeger 1943: 3.213–16; Morrow 1953: 242). The book that described the law code (namely Plato's *Laws* itself) must not only lay out the constitution and laws for the *polis,* but also persuade the citizenry to adopt and obey them. According to Plato's reasoning, laws should not function as an arbitrary, tyrannical set of rules enforced by naked coercion, but should be written in such a way as to promote voluntary compliance.[17] Legislation must always accordingly be accompanied by ethical persuasion, within a carefully crafted rhetorical framework not only for the laws as a whole, but also for each law individually.[18] Obedience to the law should be accomplished using every means of persuasion available, including poetry (Clark 2003: 147–9), music (Clark 2003: 117–46), myth[19] and magic.[20] In Plato's *Laws,* Plato now adopted a system of universal compulsory education (broadly modeled on the Spartan system of compulsory education[21]) in which the citizens would be constantly exposed from cradle to grave to ethical influences tailored to their age and intellectual development.[22] The youth, who were impetuous and especially susceptible to dangerous, irreligious new ideas, required intensive shaping of beliefs and character (see Clark 2003: 89–103 on the education of the young in Plato's *Laws*). The general education would not be philosophical but aimed instead at instilling civic virtue and obedience.[23] Insofar as the citizens were receptive to moral instruction, they were to be influenced toward inner virtue and voluntary compliance through ethical praise or condemnation by their elders and by education by the book of the law, which was to function as the foundational educational document for the *polis* (Plato, *Laws* 7.811c-d; 9.858e; cf. Nightingale 1999: 102). Those lacking an inner goodness were to be compelled to acquire the outward semblance of virtue by obedience to the law, through persuasion by threats and compulsion that were also found in the book of the law (Plato, *Laws* 4.718b). Citizens who committed crimes were carefully evaluated for their potential for rehabilitation by imprisonment and retraining.[24] As a last resort, serious or recalcitrant offenders convicted of certain crimes that undermined society, such as impiety, and who were deemed incapable of reeducation, were to be put to death (Plato, *Laws* 9.862e-863a; 10.908e-909a), a harsh measure necessary to preserve the virtue of the *polis.*[25] In Plato's *Laws,* education and persuasion were thus the primary tools of government, although the threat of force always lurked in the background.

In Plato's *Laws,* Plato introduced his novel theories on government, education and literature in the form of a dialogue among three aged men on a trek up Mount Idas in Crete to visit the Cave of Zeus, where legendary King Minos received the ancient divine Cretan laws. The three learned men were Klinias of

Crete who, as it turned out, was charged with writing a constitution and laws for a new colony to be established in Magnesia, a district in Crete; Megillus of Sparta, a land with a reputation for good laws *(eunomia)*[26] and for citizen obedience to the laws and rulers (Herodotus, *Histories* 7.104, 228; Xenophon, *Memorabilia* 4.4.15; cf. Tigerstadt 1965: 1.166; Morrow 1993: 49–50) such that the Spartan system of government had continued unchanged for over 400 years since its establishment by the legendary founder Lycurgus, the savior of Sparta;[27] and the anonymous Athenian Stranger, who had studied the laws and practices of many nations, a stand-in for Plato. The topic of their discussion was how to establish a new nation with an ideal constitution, laws and other civic and religious institutions that would be a model of civic justice and virtue that would last forever.[28] Although the various institutions that Plato proposed through the philosophically-minded Athenian Stranger were inherently political in nature, enforced by the laws and magistrates of the *polis,* his whole scheme of government was infused with theology to such a degree that it has often been described as a theocracy.[29] Plato called the novel form of "divine government" (Plato, *Laws* 12.965c) he had invented *Nous,*[30] after "the god who is the true ruler of rational men."[31] Plato's *Laws* presented arguments that political stability and internal harmony could be achieved only by systematically programming the beliefs and emotions of the citizenry through a strict control of literature and education designed to promote piety and obedience to the colony's divine laws. The rulership and spiritual protection of the colony would be entrusted to a *gerousia* of leading priests and educators, steeped in theology, philosophy and international law, who would oversee the beliefs of the citizenry.[32] At the end of the dialogue, the Athenian Stranger was pressed into service by his two new friends to help oversee the creation of the colony of the Magnesians according to the inspired program he had persuasively laid out.

Plato's key strategy for persuading the colonists to adopt the new system of government he proposed and to remain loyal to them down through time was to invest these laws and institutions with an aura of antiquarianism. Plato thought it essential to persuade the population that their new laws were divine (Plato, *Laws* 1.624a, 634d-e; 2.663b-d; 6.762e; 10.887b-c, 907c; 12.969b) and had been observed by the nation unchangingly from time immemorial (Plato, *Laws* 7.793b-c, 798a-b; Plato, *Timaeus* 23d, 24b-d). In a crucial passage, Plato stated,

> If there exist laws under which men have been reared up and which (by the blessing of Heaven) have remained unaltered for many centuries, so that there exists no recollection or report of their ever having been different from what they now are, then the whole soul is forbidden by reverence and fear to alter any of the things established of old. By hook or by crook, then, the lawgiver must devise a means whereby this shall be true of his State.
>
> Plato, *Laws* 7.798a-b

Plato's *Laws* contained many examples of suggested mechanisms whereby the new laws and institutions of the *polis* might convincingly be portrayed as ancient and divine. One major problem Plato sought to overcome was the lack of any ethnic or historical connection between the colonists, who had been brought in from locations scattered throughout Sparta and Crete, and the land of Magnesia or its customs. Although the district of Magnesia was presently deserted, and had been for some time,[33] the new colonists were encouraged to believe that they were the returned descendants of the ancient Magnesians, and that the new colony was a divinely established restoration of the ancient nation.[34] In a similar vein, Plato sought to preserve or revive any local gods with ancient connections to the region of Magnesia.[35] A connection between the gods and the land was to be forged by diligent inquiry into local customs. Plato considered it essential that the state without exception should recognize all ancient local oracles and altars and temples to the gods, spirits and heroes, whether sanctioned by a major oracle such as Delphi or by ancient inspired local traditions (Plato, *Laws* 5.738c-d). All ancient hereditary priesthoods associated with ancient local sites were to be recognized and consulted on cultic matters (see Plato, *Laws* 6.759b on the preservation of hereditary priesthoods). The written laws for the new colony would include a body of conservative sacred laws that specified the appropriate festivals, sacrifices and other rites, in accordance with both the Delphic oracle and ancient local practices (Plato, *Laws* 8.828a-c; cf. 3.681a-c). Ancient traditional songs and dances were incorporated into the corpus of works approved for public performance by the "legislators of the arts" (Plato, *Laws* 7.802a-b). The systematic collection and recording of oral traditions consistent with the writings of the lawgiver facilitated the construction of a body of ancient myths about the land, its gods, sanctuaries and local heroes.[36] Despite the introduction of *Nous,* the new god of the intellectual ruling class,[37] the theocratic government envisioned in Plato's *Laws* not only tolerated the popular religion of the ordinary citizens, but also championed it through the enforcement of impiety laws that severely penalized the establishment of competing religious cults, even in a private setting (Plato, *Laws* 10.907d-910d). By all these means, the new laws and religious conceptions of the *polis* were given the appearance, not of radical innovation, but of conservatism of revered ancient laws and traditions.[38]

Plato's program of creating a mythic past in which the divine laws of the nation had been established in distant antiquity faced an obvious practical difficulty, namely the living memory of the new colonists. Plato fully recognized this problem and sought to overcome it by devising strategies to erase the nation's memory of any other way of life, like erasing a tablet and starting with a clean slate.[39] In order to erase the cultural memories of the past and replace them with new memories, the rulers would exercise complete control over the nation's education, literature, public speech and cultural contacts with other nations. A key part of the educational program found in both Plato's *Republic* and *Laws* was the strict control of literature. Plato was highly critical of the literature typically used in Athenian primary schools which, although it excelled as poetry, contained material that Plato deemed unsuitable to impressionable minds. Plato found fault with various passages in the classics that undermined the fundamental virtues of justice, wisdom, temperance and courage by depicting the gods as unjust, quarrelsome, deceptive or dissolute, or some of the heroes of the epics as intemperate, ruled by ungovernable impulses and emotions, or fearful of death. Plato advocated editing out extensive passages that contained offensive content in the writings of Homer, Hesiod and other Greek poets (Plato, *Republic* 2.376d-398b; Plato, *Laws* 9.858e) or banning these works altogether.[40] Only approved myths about the gods would be allowed in nursery songs, childhood stories, education or public festivals and speeches. In similar fashion, only approved stories about the mythic past that supported the antiquity and divinity of the nation's laws and way of life would be allowed. Plato's program of censorship encompassed all the arts, with detailed specifications of what constituted permissible poetry, prose, drama, comedy, music, dance, song and prayer.[41] Plato found educational, rhetorical and moral content in all the arts and deemed every public performance an educational and rhetorical opportunity for the rulers to instill the proper citizen virtues in the gathered populace. In Plato's *Laws,* poets were no longer to be banned altogether as in the *Republic,* but could compose sacred hymns (Plato, *Laws* 7.799e-801d; cf. Plato, *Republic* 10.607a), poems that accompanied awards of merit for service to the *polis,*[42] uplifting funeral orations for noble individuals[43] and poetic versions of beneficial myths,[44] subject to proper oversight and approval.[45] Prose compositions were also regulated, because of their potential historical, rhetorical and ethical content. Greek *logoi* of Plato's day, such as panegyrics and histories, borrowed heavily from the enchanting language and rhythms of poetry[46] and from the dramatic techniques and moralizing content of Greek tragedy,[47] calculated to move the emotions and shape the character and opinions of listeners and reading audiences.[48] Prose *logoi* thus also posed a danger to public morals and required strict supervision (Plato, *Laws* 7.810c). Control over literature and speech extended both to the school system, in which only approved subjects and texts were allowed,[49] and speeches and performances at festivals and other public occasions (Plato, *Laws* 7.817a-d; 8.829c-e; 11.934e-936b; 12.957d). Another potential source of danger to the *polis* was knowledge of novel foreign customs acquired by contacts with foreigners.[50] Following the Spartan example of cultural self-isolation, foreign travel would be regulated[51] and the conduct of foreign visitors strictly controlled.[52] By insulating the nation from foreign contacts and by carefully shaping the people's understanding of their own cultural history, an illusion was deliberately fostered that the citizenry had lived under their utopian government and system of laws since the dawn of time (Plato, *Laws* 7.793b-c, 798a-b; cf. Klosko 2006: 225). For Plato as a social engineer, a system of censorship and universal compulsory education by which the state could maintain control of theology, of literature, of the arts, of all forms of public discourse knowledge about the world and of the nation's past was considered essential to allow the effective indoctrination, enculturization and social control of all members of the ideal city-state he envisioned.

In Plato's *Laws,* the system of education and state regulation of literature consisted of three institutional elements: the Minister of Education, an important magistrate charged with supervising the educational system as a whole; a panel of *nomophylakes,* or Guardians of the Laws, who played a prominent role, in association with the temple priestesses and priests, in approving, censoring or rejecting literature; and the education officers who supervised both schools and public events. The Ministers of Education (past and present) and the ten senior Guardians of the Laws were members of the Nocturnal Council, the supreme ruling body of the *polis,* underscoring the importance of education in Plato's theocratic system (Plato, *Laws* 12.951d-e). The Minister of Education, an office invented by Plato,[53] was the most important of all the state's magistrates. He was to be selected by secret ballot from among the Guardians of the Laws as the most excellent citizen of the *polis,* and must additionally be a father of legitimate children (Plato, *Laws* 6.765d-766b; cf. 7.811d). The Guardians of the Laws were elected officials of at least fifty years of age who were in charge of policing all aspects of public morality.[54] For the first ten years of the colony, the Guardians of the Laws would act as secondary lawgivers, authorized to make minor adjustments in the law code, as needed, in line with the legislative aims laid out in Plato's *Laws,* in consultation with the original lawgiver, if he was still alive, and drawing on the laws of other nations (Plato, *Laws* 6.770a-b, 772a-d; 12.951c, 952b; cf. Nightingale 1993a: 297–8). After the first ten years, the laws became effectively fixed[55] and the duties of the Guardians of the Laws were restricted to preserving and enforcing the existing law code. It was essential that the Guardians of the Laws understood not only the letter of the law, but also its philosophical aims, namely the establishment of virtue and the betterment of the soul.[56] This necessarily involved intensive higher training in philosophy, including science (Plato, *Laws* 7.809a, 818a; 12.965a, 966b-968b; cf. Morrow 1993: 337), very much along the lines of the higher education given the Guardian class of philosopher-kings in the *Republic.*[57] Such higher education required a thorough familiarity with the key philosophical and educational text written by the supreme legislator, namely Plato's *Laws* itself. Because the establishment and preservation of a proper constitution and laws for the *polis* was a divine undertaking, the Guardians of the Laws were required to have thoroughly mastered theology, an important topic covered in detail in Plato's *Laws.*[58] Their deep understanding of law, virtue and theology qualified the Guardians of the Laws to act, under the direction of the Minister of Education, as "legislators of the arts."[59] In their capacity as "legislators of the arts," the Guardians of the Laws reviewed and approved the literature and music permitted in the *polis,* including public prayers and hymns, tasks which they performed in consultation with the priestesses and priests of the *polis.*[60] Only the canon of literature and songs approved by the Guardians of the Laws, priestesses and priests could be publicly performed or used as educational texts (Plato, *Laws* 7.799b, 801c-802b, 809b; cf. Morrow 1993: 354–5). The superintendents of schools and the officials who presided over festivals (which featured literary, artistic and musical competitions, in accordance with Greek custom) were responsible for enforcing the

257

restrictions imposed by the Guardians of the Laws in their role as "legislators over the arts" (Plato, *Laws* 6.764c-765a). The competitions supervised by the Guardians of the Laws and the festival officials provided a mechanism whereby new artistic works could be added to the open canon of approved literature and music.

The most important text for Plato's ideal state was the book of the law (by which Plato meant his treatise, *Laws*).[61] The law book was the primary educational document, not only for the populace, who were to learn and obey its statutes (Plato, *Laws* 7.811c-e), and for the judicial magistrates, who were to study and enforce the laws (Plato, *Laws* 12.957c-d), but for the Guardians of the Laws, who were to be steeped in the legal system's aims and deep philosophical underpinnings (Plato, *Laws* 7.811c-d; 12.966b-968a). Of all literary compositions, read or heard, in poetry or prose, the discourse on the *Laws* was considered the most virtuous and most suitable for educational purposes (Plato, *Laws* 7.811c-d; 9.858e). In order to enhance its authority, the book was cloaked in an aura of divinity[62] and – so far as possible for a new composition – antiquity (see especially Plato, Laws 7.793b-c, 798a-b; cf. Clark 2003: 123, 144 n. 2), as a sacred foundational document (Plato, *Laws* 7.811c-d; 9.858e) that possessed a status in the *polis* close to scripture,[63] whose importance was reinforced through public recitation.[64] The authority of the constitution and legal code laid out in Plato's *Laws* was absolute.[65] Criticizing or questioning of these laws was strictly forbidden, because they were of divine origin.[66] Many lawgivers in Greek antiquity were credited with divine inspiration,[67] and Plato, both as inspired lawmaker[68] and philosopher, counted himself as one of these "divine men."[69] Although Plato's *Laws* was a prose composition (Plato, *Laws* 7.810b, 811e; cf. Meyer 2011: 398), and thus lacked true artistic merit, Plato claimed that the legislation it contained represented a novel form of divinely inspired poetry (Plato, *Laws* 4.719c; 7.811c-d, 817b-d) and conceived of himself as a poet of the highest order,[70] the type of poet who composed plays on serious topics (that is, tragedies).[71] Plato described the constitution found in *Laws* as an artistic imitation of the divine polis,[72] the finest form of drama, the "truest tragedy," a dramatic composition suitable for public performance, the equal of any Greek tragedy.[73] Tragedy as a literary form, if properly executed, was a form of "noble lie" or fictional account about the distant past[74] in which the poet immersed the audience in an imagined recreation of famous episodes from Greek myth or legend,[75] one that could convey positive truths, if constructed according to the theological and ethical standards Plato laid down.[76] Tragedy thus conveyed cultural memories in the form of dramatic reenactment, something Plato also sought to do in the form of government he had created in *Laws*. Unlike the usual play, which was performed once on a stage with actors imitating famous characters from the distant past and reciting their speeches memorized from a script, in Plato's imagined theocratic state the entire population would be actors[77] who would constantly imitate life under the rule of the gods in the idyllic mythical Age of Kronus[78] according to the divine script laid out in Plato's *Laws*.[79] Within this archaist theocratic state, Plato's *Laws* would function as an inspired text with divine authority, like scripture (Plato, *Laws* 7.811c-d; 9.858e; cf. 1993a: 289;

Nightingale 1999: 102; Monoson 2000: 228). The inspired and authoritative status of Plato's *Laws* reinforced the sacred character of this divine national theater acted out in the real world.

As "legislators of the arts," the Guardians of the Laws were charged with actively undertaking a systematic review of all written literature, whether poetry or prose, to seek out other literary works that agreed with the *Laws* (Plato, Laws 2.664a; 7.811c-e; cf. 9.858c-d; 12.957c-e; Morrow 1993: 339–40; Nightingale 1999: 102). Approval of the other texts for inclusion in the national library was conditional on these texts' conformity to Plato's *Laws*, which was to serve as the paradigm for all other literary works, whether prose discourse or poetry (Plato, *Laws* 9.858c-859a), and for all speech, whether public or private (Plato, *Laws* 7.811c-e; 8.829c-e; 12.957d). All writings submitted to the Guardians of the Laws for approval were to be judged according to the criterion of consistency with the writings of the lawgiver (Plato, *Laws* 7.811c-d), and accepted, censored, revised or rejected accordingly (Plato, *Laws* 7.802b-c). By this means, the literature and arts of the *polis* would achieve a homogenous content in conformity with the laws and ethics of the founding legislator and the divine charter myth of the nation.[80] Oral compositions and discourses compatible with the writings of the supreme legislator were also to be sought out and written down. Wisdom literature, containing ethical advice, was singled out as particularly valuable for shaping the character of the young.[81] All these "approved" texts should then be used as educational materials by the teachers, who were to be compelled to learn and praise them or else to be expelled as instructors.[82] All "rejected" texts were excluded from being read or performed, either publicly or privately, because of their positive deleterious effects. Similarly, only "approved" topics could be taught as part of the school curriculum.[83] The criterion for composition and approval of literature was not necessarily what was true, but what would be the most beneficial to the state, if it were believed.[84]

Nor was the literary activity of the censors restricted to the written word or existing oral traditions. Contemporary theater and other performing arts also required strict regulation, because of their potential moral influence on the audience.[85] Although Plato's city would sponsor international literary competitions featuring tragedies – that is, serious dramatic performances – the only works that would be permitted would contain an elevated ethical content equal to the constitution described in Plato's *Laws*, which was considered the truest and most beautiful tragic drama, one that elevated the souls of audiences during public readings (Plato, *Laws* 7.817a-c; 9.858c-859a). Although only approved works could be read or performed, either publicly or privately (Plato, *Laws* 11.936a), such public literary competitions of screened works allowed new texts to be admitted into the national body of ethical literature.[86]

As "legislators of the arts," the Guardians of the Laws were also required to conduct a systematic review of all the musical compositions of the ancients, including traditional hymns to the gods of varying types,[87] which were then to be approved, rejected, or revised according to the ethical and educational standards laid out in Plato's *Laws,* with a similar procedure for traditional dances.[88] The editing of ancient songs was to be carried out in consultation with poets and musicians, in order to capitalize on their poetic gifts and expertise, "without, however, trusting to their tastes or their wishes."[89] New poetic and musical compositions were also to be commissioned, as required, for performance in the *polis.* The beauty and emotional power of music would stimulate an appetite for new hymns, which would be produced in great variety on positive themes within Plato's guidelines (Plato, *Laws* 2.665c; 7.798d; 11.936c). Prominent among the subjects for such compositions was the law itself.[90] Prayers recited at the daily public sacrifices were also composed by poets at the request and under the strict supervision of the Guardians of the Laws (Plato, *Laws* 2.656c; 4.719b; 7.799e-801d; cf. Plato, *Republic* 10.607a). Such prayers not only served key ritual purposes, but also exposed the attendees to theology and ethics, promoting public virtue.

After this body of songs, dances and public prayers had been revised and approved by the Guardians of the Laws, it was to be formally consecrated and assigned for performance[91] at appropriate annual feasts that the gods had established to give men cheer and rest from their labors.[92] The hymns and dances were to be fixed for all times as a special category of sacred law.[93] Any performer in the choristry who uttered a note or moved a limb outside this canon of sacred songs was liable for expulsion from the festival and prosecution for impiety by the Guardians of the Laws, the priestesses and the priests (Plato, *Laws* 7.799a-800a). The body of songs, stories and other discourses were to be performed before the entire community on all public occasions in order to inspire virtue in the citizens, especially in the impressionable youth, whose malleable souls could be persuaded of anything (Plato, *Laws* 2.653b, 659d-e, 663e, 664a-c; 8.840b-c; cf. Welton 1996: 214). Plato's writings, especially the *Republic* and *Laws,* gave great attention to the educational and magical aspects of oral presentation, of song, of dance and of theatrical performance. Plato well understood the magical, mood altering power of music, as well as the medicinal benefits of music, chants and dances, which effected a sort of rhythmic or kinetic education (Plato, *Laws* 2.653e-656c, 672e-673e; 7.790b-791b, 798d, 812b-c, 814e-816e; Plato, *Republic* 3.399e-402a, 411a-412b). The chanting of songs at public festivals was specially designed to exert a magical influence on the minds of the young through the feelings of pleasure that music stimulated,[94] but also intended to enchant the adults,[95] who were also loosened up into a convivial and suggestible state by liberal drink and song.[96] The laws and their persuasive preludes, which often contained elements of myth,[97] were to be included among the festival songs and chants.[98] The recitation of entertaining and engaging stories, myths and noble histories, by which the listeners acquired a knowledge of their cultural past, was also designed to enchant those attending public events.[99] All the citizens, from school age and older, were required to participate in the choristry. At festivals, performances of sacred songs took place in three stages[100] – first the children's choir, then those sung by performers under thirty, then those between thirty and sixty – followed by myths *(muthoi)* and inspired speeches *(logoi)* with noble ethical content that were recited by elders aged sixty and older no longer capable of song.[101] In this manner, the entire citizenry would constantly be enchanting themselves[102] by means of the approved body of myths, songs and literature,[103] not only in the schools but also on all public occasions, that would educate them in their national traditions[104] and persuade them to virtue as laid out in the laws (Morrow 1993: 242).

Plato's *Laws* thus laid out an audacious plan whereby a new nation could be founded with a new system of government and laws, yet its citizenry persuaded that the system was both ancient and divine. In order to erase the oral traditions of the colonists and replace them with the new national mythos, Plato thought it essential to exert complete control over the nation's education, literature and contacts with the outside world, enchanting the population through constant exposure to the new body of approved myths. By these means the citizenry who grew up in this system would come to understand themselves as descendants of the original inhabitants of the land and their laws as ancient and divine. These deep connections with the past, once securely planted in the nation's consciousness, and reinforced by its literature, would create a fierce attachment to the laws and new way of life that would last through all time, or so Plato hoped.[105] Plato's program of political innovation dressed up as conservatism was not carried out anywhere in the Greek world in his own time, and in later ages was often dismissed as impractical (so Posidonius of Apamea [Seneca, *Letters* 94.38]) and utopian,[106] although it had its champions.[107] But the extensive use of Plato's *Laws* in the Torah and the close correspondence of the Hebrew Bible to the national literature that Plato envisioned suggests the possibility that Hellenistic Era Judea was politically reorganized along Platonic lines (cf. Wajdenbaum 2011: 55), the only such implementation of Plato's theories on theocratic government to be carried out in antiquity.

2. The Hebrew Bible and Plato's *Laws*

By all accounts, the national and religious life of the Jews underwent a remarkable transformation in the early Hellenistic Era. The system of government changed from rule by a provincial governor in the Persian Era to a theocracy or hierocracy sometime after the conquests of Alexander the Great,[108] with a high priest presiding over a *gerousia* of seventy elders (see Chapter 2 §7). A new system of education was put in place, starting in the third century BCE in Egypt, and later spreading to Palestine, in the synagogue or house of prayer.[109] A new monotheism was put in place, superimposed on the old polytheism of El, Yahweh and other ancient Canaanite gods.[110] The Torah, as I have argued elsewhere, was written as late as ca. 270 BCE by Jewish and Samaritan ruling class elites who carried out this task using sources found in Alexandria's Great Library (Gmirkin 2006: 81–8, 240–56). The Jewish festivals were reimagined in line with the Torah's new Mosaic foundation story (see Chapter 5 §2). It is evident that the Hebrew Bible, the only historical example of an approved national literature in antiquity, also began to take shape around this time, because almost every text in this literary collection drew on the new Torah traditions. All these facts point to a transformation of Jewish national life in the early Hellenistic Era, one that greatly resembled the institutions and way of life described in Plato's *Laws*. The current section will address the literary aspects of that transformation, namely the creation of the Torah and the Hebrew Bible in comparison with the literary program laid out in Plato's *Laws*.

Plato's *Laws* contained detailed instructions for the legislators and founders of a new nation to create a constitution, law collection and authorized national literature. The first step in Plato's political and literary program was to draft an authoritative version of the constitution and laws to serve as the central, foundational document in the planned national literature. From Chapter 2–5, it appears certain that the biblical authors were profoundly influenced by Plato's *Laws* when they created the Pentateuch.[111] Direct influence of Plato's *Laws* was especially prominent in the book of Deuteronomy, which appears to have directly followed the instructions found in Plato's *Laws* for the founding legislator's persuasive presentation of a constitution and inspired laws to the gathered colonists at the establishment of a new nation-state. These laws closely conform to Plato's innovative conception of legislation as instruction, and in the rhetorical devices used in the Torah, otherwise unique to Plato, such as hortatory introductions that prefaced the legislation and persuasive motive clauses attached to individual laws. The primary aim of the Torah was to lay out a constitutional and legislative framework for the nation, suitably presented in a persuasive format that would encourage its adoption by the citizenry. A second objective was to give these laws an aura of antiquity, divine authority and unchangeability in line with Greek notions of revered ancestral laws so as to link obedience to the law with deep-seated notions of piety and tradition.[112] A third goal was to create a charter myth for those divine laws in the dramatic narrative form of a foundation story that forged a powerful sense of national identity in those who adopted this literary narrative as their own historical past as descendants of the ancient children of Israel. The refounding of the Jewish nation in the early Hellenistic Era, with new civic and religious institutions and a new constitution and laws, was thus successfully portrayed as a new edition of the ancient writings of Moses, the divine legislator, educator and founder of the ancient Jewish nation, in line with the Platonic legislative agenda.[113]

A prominent legislative and literary strategy found in Plato's *Laws,* designed to give the new government an aura of divinity and respectable antiquity, was to link the new system of laws, wherever possible, to existing ancient and revered local religious institutions. This strategy appears to have been systematically implemented in the Pentateuch. Although the Torah legislation projected a vision of monotheism, or at least monolatry, the new supreme god of the Pentateuch, portrayed as the one and only god of the ancient Jews and Samaritans,[114] combined a veritable pantheon of ancient Canaanite deities into a single universal god, the creator of the universe. The Pentateuch's newfound monotheism thus sought to incorporate and assimilate the ancient traditional polytheism of the region. Plato had recommended that the organizers of the state research and recognize the sacred status of local religious sites such as ancient temples, altars and oracles. In seeming conformity with this Platonic strategy, stories in Genesis featured a multiplicity of sacred locations – including several sites revered by the Samaritans – where the patriarchs saw visions; built altars to Yahweh, El Shaddai, El Elyon and others; performed sacrifices; and called on the deity's name.[115] Similarly, the books of Deuteronomy and Joshua gave special recognition to the sacred status of various prominent Samaritan locales, namely Gerizim, Ebal and Shechem (Deut. 11.27–29; 27.4, 11–13; Josh. 8.30–35; 24.1–28). Plato also recommended recognizing the traditional rights of existing priestly families,[116] something that the Pentateuchal authors did in singling out the Aaronid priesthood and the broader category of Levitical priests as possessing special privileges in administering the cult of Yahweh.[117] Plato reinforced the continuity of religious practices by granting the priests and priestesses, in conjunction with the prophets and exegetes, the authority to establish the calendar of religious festivals and related cultic matters, their decisions to be affirmed by the Delphic Oracle (Plato, *Laws* 6.759c-d; 8.828a; Plato, *Republic* 4.427b-c). The priestly origin of the sacrificial laws in Leviticus and substantial portions of festival laws elsewhere in the Pentateuch is universally acknowledged and it seems likely that these sacred laws reflected long-standing cultic practices.[118] The Pentateuch thus created numerous links between the new monotheistic religion of the Jews and Samaritans and the ancient gods, cultic sites, religious laws and priesthoods of the land. The Pentateuch also sought to incorporate ancient legal traditions into the new, mostly Greek Mosaic law code. These old laws from Babylonia and Assyria, best understood as reflecting Mesopotamian cuneiform legal traditions imported to Assyrian Samerina and still preserved among the Samaritans of the early Hellenistic Era,[119] further enhanced the aura of seeming antiquity of the legislation drafted in ca. 270 BCE. A prominent though implicit theme of the Pentateuch was that the Jews and Samaritans for whom the Torah was written were the returned, repentant, now-obedient descendants of the ancient children of Israel.

The Pentateuch thus employed a number of strategies that sought to forge a link between the new laws of the refounded Jewish and Samaritan nations and the religious institutions and traditions of their forefathers, much as Plato advocated. But although the Pentateuch appeared to endorse traditional gods and cultic institutions, some of which were associated with the polytheistic "Canaanite" pantheon, the Pentateuch also sought to reform them. The older gods of the land were consolidated into a single new deity who closely resembled the one eternal, supreme creator god of Plato's writings.[120] The reinvented god of the biblical text was not, however, the abstract philosopher's god, *Nous*, a new god for worship by the ruling elite. Instead, the biblical authors directly identified this supreme deity with Yahweh, a local god traditionally worshipped in Judea and Samaria, who was newly conceived in elevated terms as (in the words of Josephus) "One, uncreated and immutable to all eternity; in beauty surpassing all mortal thought, made known to us by His power, although the nature of his real being passes knowledge."[121] This supreme god was portrayed, like Plato's *Nous*, as the creator of the *kosmos*, of life, and of humankind, a supremely ethical being who was the source of all good,[122] who both cared for and watched over humanity (Hesiod, *Works and*

Days 121–6, 252–5; Plato, *Symposium* 209a,c-d; cf. Josephus, Apion 2.180). This elevated conception of God was not entirely consistent with the old traditional religious practices of the land. The Pentateuch, like Plato's *Laws,* accordingly sought to suppress the more superstitious long-standing elements of popular religion that fell under the general rubric of magic.[123] The temple cult, although tolerated as an important traditional expression of popular piety, was itself somewhat disvalued as an expression of public virtue. The book of Deuteronomy, in which Platonic influences are most prominently expressed, concerned itself almost exclusively with civic laws, in contrast to the priestly legislation of Exodus–Numbers that was mostly concerned with cultic matters. A consistent Platonic theme running throughout the prophets (especially the so-called pre-exilic prophets) was that God wanted justice, not the endless stream of sacrifices offered by the temple cult, and rejected the prayers and sacrifices of the wicked.[124] Under the new philosophical conception of religious life promulgated by the Torah and Hebrew Bible, the aim of religion was not to bribe or coerce the gods by sacrifices and magic, either public or private, but to promote piety, justice, wisdom, virtue and universal belief in a supreme righteous god, identified with the local god of the land, known as El or Yahweh. Much like Plato's *Laws* both adopted and reformed traditional Greek religion, the Hebrew Bible thus also sought to radically reform the ancient Jewish and Samaritan religious traditions that it portrayed itself as conserving.

In Plato's *Laws,* the primary task of the lawgivers was the creation of a constitution and laws with accompanying persuasive rhetoric as the foundational text for the nation they were about to establish, but the legislative program did not end there. Plato envisioned a second, critically important phase of legislation in which the Guardians of the Laws would act as "legislators of the arts" to create an authorized national literature consistent with the ethical, educational and theological values that Plato's *Laws* espoused. The resulting body of national literature described in Plato's *Laws* strikingly resembles the Hebrew Bible, the national literature of the Jews.[125] Whereas the first phase of legislation corresponds closely with the creation of the Torah by Jewish and Samaritan educated elites at Alexandria in ca. 270 BCE, the second phase corresponds to the larger literary project that took place at Jerusalem in the years immediately following and resulted in the creation of the Hebrew Bible (in its initial form), a diverse collection of sacred documents of central importance to the religious, political and cultural life of the Jews as a people and a nation. Like the approved texts in Plato's *Laws,* the Hebrew Bible comprised a restricted literary collection that was central to an ambitious educational program with both oral and written dimensions that sought to inculcate ethical values on a national scale to create an obedient, compliant citizenry.[126] Indeed, Plato's *Laws* provides the only example in antiquity of an ethical or national literature comparable to the Hebrew Bible. One may therefore reasonably propose that the biblical authors not only found in Plato's *Laws* a blueprint for the creation of a persuasive legal code, but a mandate and program for the creation of an authoritative national literature intended to supplement and bolster the laws of the Torah.

The most important text within the Hebrew Bible was the Torah, whose stories and ethics permeate virtually the entirety of the Hebrew Bible. The Former Prophets (Joshua–Kings), which continued the story of the nation established by Moses down to the fall of the kingdoms of Samaria and Judah, contained a running ethical commentary on the persons and events in the account of Israel's past[127] and attributed the downfall of the ancient monarchies to their lack of fidelity to the divine Mosaic laws.[128] The Latter Prophets, given pseudonymous attributions of authorship by divinely inspired seers from legendary times, continued in the same rhetorical vein, containing prominent ethical, legal and narrative content that drew extensively on the Primary History and especially on the Torah tradition. The Writings included Psalms, Proverbs and other miscellaneous texts. The importance that Plato's *Laws* placed on creating a body of sacred songs with ethical and theological content appropriate for public performances was mirrored by the high ethical tone of the Psalms, a collection of consecrated hymns whose performance by the temple choristry on public occasions appears to have constituted an important element in the national life of the Jews and which prominently featured explicit legal themes,[129] retellings of the foundation myths of the children of Israel[130] and other high ethical content consistent with the Torah's educational agenda (see Wenham 2012 on ethics in the Psalms). The Hebrew Bible as a universal national literature also included a number of literary works with little or no theological content. Proverbs contained ethical maxims, attributed to Solomon and other venerable ancient sages, appropriate for the education of the young.[131] For those in the flower of life, the erotic poetry of the Song of Songs contained a celebration of love of the highest literary value.[132] The book of Job, which dramatized the Platonic theme of God's providence toward the righteous in this life,[133] took the written form of classic Greek tragedy, a genre Plato expressly envisioned within the national literature assembled by the "legislators of the arts" in Plato's *Laws*.[134] It is quite possible that Job was performed on stage at a Jewish literary competition, not unlike those found in the Greek world.[135] Ecclesiastes contained deep philosophical ruminations appropriate for the aged.[136] The creators of the Hebrew Bible thus succeeded in creating a collection of approved works that spanned the entire range of poetic and prose literature, including whatever literary creations were consistent with the spirit of the Torah, regardless of genre. There seems little doubt that the Hebrew Bible represents the construction of an approved Jewish literature according to the literary agenda laid out in Plato's *Laws,* the only other text in antiquity that envisioned the creation of such an all-encompassing approved national literature.

Not only is the range of literary genres found in the Hebrew Bible comparable to the national literature envisioned in Plato's *Laws,* but also the range of authors. In Plato's *Laws,* oversight for the creation of a national literature was assigned to the Guardians of the Laws in their capacity as "legislators of the arts." These in turn enlisted the assistance of a wide variety of specialists: expert legislators versed in international legal studies for the creation of the constitution and civil laws; priestesses, priests, prophets and exegetes as experts on holy matters for the creation of a body of sacred laws; poets, storytellers and musicians for the creation of myths, songs, dances and prayers; composers of orations and authors of edifying prose discourses. A similar collaboration among authorial groups representing diverse social classes appears evident in the creation of the Pentateuch, a composite text whose authorship included contributions from storytellers, priests, poets and legislators of both Samaritan and Judean backgrounds.[137] Diversity of authorship is seen in the rest of the Hebrew Bible as a whole, with the caveat that literary contributions reflecting Samaritan perspectives are largely absent or overwritten by a Jerusalem-centric point of view in texts outside the Torah (Davies 1998: 120–1). Poets, musicians, historians, storytellers and skilled Deuteronomistic orators all contributed to the creation of the Former Prophets (Joshua–Kings). The Latter Prophets incorporated material from poets, musicians and composers of prose rhetoric.[138] The contribution of poets and musicians are evident in the Psalms, whereas the Writings included additional works of pure poetry (Song of Songs), drama (Job), proverbial wisdom (Proverbs[139]), and philosophy (Ecclesiastes). The creation of the Hebrew Bible, like the creation of the national literature in Plato's *Laws,* thus entailed literary contributions from virtually every segment of the educated elite, resulting in a book collection that contained a broad range of literary genres.[140]

Significantly, the literary processes that gave rise to the Hebrew Bible according to conventional models of biblical criticism appear to mirror the literary activities conducted under the authority of the Guardians of the Laws in their capacity as "legislators of the arts." Plato's *Laws* contained instructions for the systematic collection and review of older hymns and literary texts, and even the recording of oral compositions by the "legislators of the arts," preserving whatever was found to have value; the editing, revision and reworking of these older literary compositions to bring them in line with the ethical and legal content of the writings of the legislator; and the soliciting and approval of new texts that conformed to the spirit of the foundational legal documents, a process that culminated in the creation of a national collection of approved literary works with a consistent ethical, legal and theological outlook. Similarly, biblical criticism has viewed the Hebrew Bible as the end result of recording oral traditions, preserving and transmitting literary works from the past, and revising and supplementing these texts, although this process has traditionally been assumed to have taken place organically – almost accidentally – over a span of centuries within a Jewish scribal environment.[141] Such an extended time frame for the creation of the Hebrew Bible does not appear intrinsic to the literary activities involved, because Plato's *Laws* laid out a program for such literary activities to take place in service of the creation of a national literature in a relatively brief time span – arguably a decade or less – through the concerted and closely coordinated efforts of the educated ruling elite. The Hebrew Bible was thus not the result of lengthy organic developments over centuries of time within a scribal community, as often imagined. Instead, this creation of a canon of approved national texts was the result of a purposeful literary agenda carried out by the aristocratic Jewish ruling class of ca. 270 BCE and possessed from its inception both political and sacred authority as the ancestral laws and literature of the Jews. Like the national literature envisioned by Plato, the Hebrew Bible was an open canon, with worthy new compositions added from time to time, until the closing of the canon in the first or second centuries BCE. Although the incorporation of older antiquarian texts and traditions into the Hebrew Bible points to a conscious effort to systematically collect and preserve written and oral materials from the past that had survived into the Hellenistic Era, pervasive references to the Mosaic traditions found throughout the Hebrew Bible demonstrate a concern to subordinate these same texts and traditions to the legal and ethical agenda of the Pentateuch. This effort to create a universal collection of Jewish literature, and yet subordinate this literature to the legal, ethical and narrative content of the Torah, well explains the mix of antiquarian book collecting, editorial revision and new composition found in the Hebrew Bible, literary activities all anticipated in Plato's *Laws*.

The Hebrew Bible may thus be understood as a national literature created with the aims and by the procedures found in Plato's *Laws*. In the educational systems associated with both the Hebrew Bible and Plato's *Laws,* students were required to memorize the writings of the lawgiver (Plato, *Laws* 7.810e-811e; Deut. 6.6, 21–25; 11.18–21; cf. Carr 2005: 134–42). Both literatures included a constructed historical past that supported an understanding of the laws as ancient and divine, but otherwise contained little by way of factual content. Instead, both literatures emphasized ethical, theological and rhetorical content that sought to shape the character, behavior and emotions of its audience, what Plato called *psychogogy* or the education of the soul, a form of education repudiated by Aristotle and little studied in modern educational theory, but carefully worked out in great detail in Plato's writings, especially in Plato's *Laws,* where the national literature played a prominent role in the shaping of the consciousness and character of the nation. The Hebrew Bible as a whole can best be understood as a literature intended for the education of the soul, utilizing all the tools in the Platonic psychogogic arsenal: poetry, myth and song, theology and prayers, pageant and spectacle, theater, drink and dance and persuasive rhetoric that appealed to the patriotic, praised the noble and exalted and condemned the wicked and disobedient, who were threatened with punishments in this life and terrors in the next. All these agents of emotional influence are present, to one degree or another, in the texts of the Hebrew Bible. Although mythic, poetic, hymnic, theological and rhetorical content in the Hebrew Bible are widely recognized and discussed in biblical criticism, the emotional and irrational power of such materials and their educational utility for shaping the psyche have largely escaped scholarly notice, largely because of the divorce of education and the irrational as incompatible notions in the Aristotelian tradition inherited by modern western academic institutions. But once the notion of education is broadened to include the shaping of emotions and impulses, the Hebrew Bible is easily recognized as the same sort of literature for the education of the soul that Plato envisioned.

To fully appreciate the biblical educational system, however, it is not sufficient to discuss the rational and irrational aspects of the Hebrew Bible as a set of written texts. The educational program laid out in the Hebrew Bible also included many occasions, both public and private, in which teaching took the form of oral recitation, song and dramatic performance. The Hebrew Bible's written materials often took the form of scripts to be read, songs to be sung or dramas to be performed, often in a festival setting. Both textual literacy and oral recitation were important aspects of the biblical system of education, which began with daily instructions in civic values within a family setting. The citizens were pictured as immersed in spiritual and educational influences, with written excerpts of the law posted on their doorposts and carried on their persons (Deut. 6.8–9; 11.18–21; cf. Ex. 13.9, 16), fathers reciting the law daily to their children for purposes of memorization (Deut. 6.7, 20–25; 11.19), meditating on the law day and night (Deut. 6.7; 11.19; 17.18–19; Josh. 1.8) and writing it on their hearts (Deut. 11.18; 30.11–14; cf. Carr 2005: 135–8).

In Plato's *Laws,* the major vehicle for citizen education was immersion in a stream of festivals and public religious events to overwhelm the senses and emotions with music, songs, rhythmic chants, dance, poetry, recitation of myths, theater, panegyric speeches, pageantry and spectacle, wine, banquetry, celebrations, sacrifices, prayers and the contemplation of the divine. The elevated emotional atmosphere and the conscious cultivation of both sensual and intellectual pleasures encouraged receptivity to the ethical, legal, theological, cultural and historical educational content of these festivals as communicated through songs, myths and discourse. So, likewise, the system of universal education found in the Hebrew Bible prominently featured mandatory attendance at festivals. Whereas Plato's *Laws* conceived of its citizenry having leisure time every day for the attendance of public religious ceremonies and the contemplation of the divine, in biblical legislation only the seventh day was expressly set aside for holy purposes as a day of rest.[142] Although the Jews and Samaritans used a week of seven days in pre-Hellenistic times,[143] it appears on evidence of inscriptional finds at Elephantine that the sabbath was not yet observed as a day of rest as late as ca. 400 BCE.[144] Indeed, there is no compelling extra-biblical evidence for sabbath observance as a day of rest prior to the creation of the Pentateuch in the third century BCE.[145] The biblical text did not specify the leisure activities for the weekly sabbath, other than to keep it holy, but according to later Hellenistic and Roman Era sources, Jews traditionally observed this day by gathering together for prayer and Torah discussions at synagogues (Josephus, Apion 2.175; cf. Ant. 16.43; Philo, *On the Creation* 128). The biblical texts also legislated festivals as occasions at which education in the laws and the foundation stories and charter myth took place on a national scale in a joyful celebratory climate filled with banquetry, drink, the recitation of dramatic stories in both public and family settings, music, song, dance, sacrifices and prayers. Those who attended were not mere spectators, but rather, like participants in Greek national and sacred festivals, active participants in choral and dramatic performances that intensified the educational value through the performers experiencing the materials in their persons. A joyful sense of community and national cohesion was promoted among those who sang, danced and performed together.[146]

The spring Passover festival, as reinvented in the Pentateuch,[147] was celebrated in a family setting as a dramatic reenactment of the Exodus experience, with all family members participating as actors, following the script laid out in Ex. 13.3–16. As a set feature of the Passover meal, children asked about the significance of the holiday and fathers responded by recounting the events surrounding the divine deliverance of the ancient children of Israel from slavery in Egypt. The feast of Succoth also had elements of dramatic performance, using the book of Deuteronomy as a script.[148] Legislation at Deut. 31.9–11 required that the speech Moses addressed to the children of Israel was recited in full every seven years at the feast of Succoth, educating the Jews and Samaritans as to their national heritage and their present-day civic and religious responsibilities. This public reading of the book of Deuteronomy amounted to a stylized reenactment of the Mosaic recitation of the divine laws to the children of Israel and the establishment of the Jews and Samaritans as a nation in ancient times.[149] In both Jewish and Samaritan communities, the participants in these festivals were encouraged to identify with this divinely established nation and to adopt the Mosaic foundation story and Mosaic laws as their own (Watts 1999: 121–9). Under the biblical system of education, instruction was not based exclusively on texts or confined to a school setting, but instead educated all members of society, in both intimate family settings in which fathers were enlisted as instructors for their children (Ex. 13.8, 14–16; Deut. 6.7, 20–25; 11.19) and in public national gatherings, in which the audience included men, women, children and resident aliens (Deut. 31.9–13).

One can now begin to understand the full scope of the reorganization – one might say reinvention – of Jewish national life undertaken by the legislators of ca. 270 BCE, following the ambitious program laid out in Plato's *Laws*. Their task began only with the creation of a new constitution and law collection, written with persuasive features as Plato's *Laws* dictated, and narrated within a charter myth that described the nation's ancient, divine origins. Additionally, as "legislators of the arts," they oversaw the creation and approval of a national literature centered on the book of the law, but encompassing every literary genre, designed to give the nation's foundation myths the apparent factual force of history and to promote the nation's laws and ethical values through songs, stories and discourses directed at both the rational and the irrational, in order to shape the mind, emotions and impulses of every citizen, young and old. The legislators also established a new system of universal education to disseminate the laws and national myths to the citizenry by means of both the written texts of the approved national literature and by the oral and dramatic presentation of these same laws and myths through a new festival system designed to reinforce their national heritage in a heightened atmosphere of pageantry and celebration that involved all the senses and emotions. The creation of all these new national institutions – the establishment of new laws, approved literature and reinvented festivals – constituted a refounding of the Jewish nation along the lines laid out in Plato's *Laws,* with careful attention to imbuing the citizenry by every means possible with fierce loyalty to their laws, their land and their mythic past.

3. The afterlife of the Hebrew Bible

In the early Hellenistic Era, the Jewish and Samaritan peoples came under a new set of laws, a new form of government and (for the Jews) a new national literature. The recent origin of the Torah and Hebrew Bible was deliberately obscured by the ruling class elites who wrote, collected, edited and approved this ancient literary collection. Internal biblical claims of antiquity alleged that this literature, along with the new law code it contained, was both ancient and divine, authored by the national founder-figure Moses, his successor Joshua and other legendary figures of the biblical past. These claims came to be widely accepted at face value within a few short generations, as the Mosaic Torah was recognized as containing the ancestral laws of both Jewish and Samaritan peoples, and the Hebrew Bible was promulgated as the authentic ancient literature of the Jewish nation.

Yet the evidence laid out in the earlier chapters indicates that these laws and texts were not, as a whole, as ancient as they were portrayed. Instead, it now appears that the Mosaic law collections were created in large part as the result of legislative research conducted at the Great Library of Alexandria and were especially indebted to Plato's *Laws*. The creation of the Pentateuch at Alexandria by Jewish and Samaritan legislators and writers appears to have been part of an initiative approved by the Jewish senate (or "Seventy") to refound the nation with new laws, a new literature and a new past, in line with the legislative strategies found in Plato's *Laws*. In the subsequent creation of the Hebrew Bible, the Jews of Jerusalem played a dominant role, but following the same Platonic literary agenda earlier set in motion in Alexandria.

The creation of the Torah at Alexandria and the Hebrew Bible subsequently at Jerusalem following the literary program laid out in Plato's *Laws* is not directly attested in historical traditions about the early Hellenistic Era. Memories of the authorship of the Pentateuch by the Septuagint scholars at Alexandria were erased in later times, or rather transformed into a tradition in which this team of legislators and writers was portrayed as mere translators of long-existing Mosaic laws and traditions. The recent Hellenistic Era date and Platonic inspiration of the theocratic government, the laws, the literature and the educational system of the reinvented Jewish nation were rendered invisible by the founders of the novel system of government in line with the strategies outlined in Plato's *Laws* itself, which called for the legislators to use any device available to persuade the citizenry that the nation's laws and ways of life had remained unchanged for centuries since having been divinely revealed to their distant forefathers. The presentation of the Torah as the traditional laws of the ancestral generation necessitated the rejection of any connection with Greek literary or legislative traditions, despite the creation of the Torah at the leading center of Greek learning, Alexandria.

Nevertheless, despite the internal claims in the Torah and Hebrew Bible to have drawn exclusively on ancient local Judean and Samarian traditions, the close connection between Mosaic writings and Greek philosophy was a recurrent theme in classical antiquity. Jewish, Christian and "pagan" authors alike more-or-less independently rediscovered the extensive and striking commonalities between Plato and the Hebrew Bible. It is remarkable how often scholars in the Hellenistic and Roman eras were compelled to comment on the striking parallels between the Hebrew Bible and Greek literature, especially Plato's dialogues. Comparisons between Platonic philosophy and biblical teachings were made by Jewish intellectuals such as Aristobulus (fl. ca. 150 BCE),[150] Philo of Alexandria (20 BCE–50 CE),[151] and Flavius Josephus (37–ca. 100 CE); Church Fathers such as Justin Martyr (ca. 150 BCE),[152] Clement of Alexandria (ca. 150–215 CE),[153] Eusebius of Caesarea (263–339 CE),[154] and Augustine (354–430 CE);[155] and even Gentile writers such as the Neo-Pythagorean philosopher Numenius of Apamea (second century CE).[156] Virtually every scholar in antiquity who was proficient in both Platonic and Mosaic writings agreed that there was a direct relationship between the two. This chorus of voices was also united on the nature of that relationship: that Plato must have been exposed to the ancient writings of Moses. The logic by which Greek knowledge of Jewish literature was demonstrated was straightforward. The argument was: the biblical texts claimed an antiquity greater than the earliest Greek writings; therefore the biblical texts in fact predated the earliest Greek writings; therefore similarities between biblical and Greek writings must be due to Greek literature borrowing from that of the ancient Jews; and Plato, in particular, must have drawn on Mosaic writings, given the profound agreement between the two. It is only in the last two decades that it has gradually dawned on the world of biblical scholarship that the relationship between the two literatures might actually be the reverse: that Plato and many other Greek writers may have been temporally antecedent to and the inspiration for the Torah and much of the Hebrew Bible.

Several of the arguments for the direct indebtedness of the Torah and the Hebrew Bible to Plato's *Laws* made in the present volume were already anticipated in classical antiquity. Eusebius discussed many specific legal parallels between the legislation and educational system in Mosaic writings and in Plato's *Republic* and *Laws*. In Apion 2.145–295, Josephus drew many parallels between the Jewish constitution and system of government in Plato's *Laws*.[157] Josephus' description of Jewish antiquity was virtually identical to the mythic past that Plato said the legislators should construct: the Jews were an exceedingly ancient people referred to by Berossus, Manetho and many other historians (Apion 1.1–320; cf. 2.1); Moses was the most ancient legislator known, having lived centuries before the earliest Greek lawgivers such as like Lycurgus or Solon (2.154–55);[158] the laws he gave to the ancient Jews were divinely inspired (2.160, 184, 221); Moses demonstrated his excellence as a lawgiver by persuading his own and all subsequent generations to revere God and obey his laws; and the excellence of the Jewish nation was shown by their having observed the laws, unchanged down through the centuries (2.153, 156, 182–83). In Josephus' day, the Jews were still subject to the novel system of government

Moses had instituted, for which Josephus coined the neologism "theocracy."[159] Although formally described as rule by God, the theocracy of Josephus was actually administered by priests who conducted the business of government (2.181–87) and acted as judges and Guardians of the Laws (2.193–94). All actions, thoughts and speech of the Jewish people were constantly guided by God (2.160), religion (2.171) and the divine laws (2.183). Mosaic laws governed all aspects of life (2.173–74).[160] The Jews were the most law-abiding people on earth (2.150, 220), exceeding even the Spartans in this respect,[161] with an unrivalled attachment to their ancestral laws (2.190–91, 212, 218–19, 228, 232–35). The laws formed the basis for the Jewish educational system. Children were both habituated to ethics and verbally educated in the laws from the first dawning of intelligence within them (2.171–73, 178, 204).[162] All citizens met once a week – an allusion to the synagogue – for prayer and instruction in the laws (2.175). All Jews shared the same universal beliefs (2.179) grounded in the Jewish national literature (1.42, 128, 154, 160, 218), a sacred body of literature (1.1, 54, 127, 216–17; 2.45) that embodied Jewish legal and ethical traditions. The Jews allowed no statements against God or providence, such as sometimes encountered among the Greeks (2.180), but held that God both cared for and watched over humanity (2.180).[163] Josephus agreed with the negative assessment of Plato on poets such as Homer, painters and others who promoted erroneous conceptions of god (2.250–54). No such negative portrayals of God could be found among the Jews. The monotheistic Jewish conception of God was sublime (2.167), having been first introduced by Moses and adhered to by the Jewish people for ages (2.222). Since distant antiquity, the Jews had observed their divinely ordained ancestral laws and customs without ever changing them (2.153, 182), in large part because of the wise policy of cultural self-isolation or *amixia*. This cultural self-isolation was an important feature of Jewish national life (1.60–61, 68; 2.210, 229, 257)[164] and was to be admired greatly, because it had preserved their way of life unchanged for 2,000 years since it was originally instituted by Moses (2.226). It was sometimes wrongly interpreted by foreigners as an expression of xenophobia *(misoxenia)* (Diodorus Siculus, *Library* 40.3.4; Josephus, Apion 2.309) or even misanthropy.[165] Josephus acknowledged Jewish cultural self-isolation, but pointed out that laws preserving cultural isolation were praised among the Spartans (Apion 2.225, 259–60, 273)[166] and even to some extent among the Athenians (2.262–68, listing famous impiety trials at Athens). Josephus argued that the Jews were not misanthropic, but on the contrary philanthropic, welcoming all foreigners into their nation who voluntarily adopted Jewish practices as their own.[167]

Any educated Greek or Roman conversant with Plato's *Laws* could not have helped but observe that Josephus described the Jewish way of life in Platonic terms. At several points Josephus made the comparison explicit (cf. Wajdenbaum 2011: 65–6). Josephus noted that the sublime Jewish conception of God was directly comparable to the supreme god described by Greek philosophers such as Pythagoras, Anaxagoras, Plato and the Stoics (2.167–68). It is apparent that

Josephus here alluded to the god *Nous* (Anaxagoras, Plato, the Stoics) or *Logos* (Pythagoras, the Stoics), the divine intelligence that ruled the universe. Josephus claimed this proved that Plato and the other Greek philosophers obtained their elevated concept of God from the Jews, because Moses predated Plato by many centuries, as was universally acknowledged (2.156, 168, 281). The Jewish system of divine laws instituted by Moses, Josephus claimed, was not only one of the world's most ancient, long predating the earliest Greek legislators (2.156), but also was the model for Greek philosophers, especially for Plato and his laws (2.168, 223–24, 257, 281). Additionally, Plato imitated Moses on both the universal study of law by all citizens and on *amixia* (2.257). Where Plato's system differed from the Jews, it was due to the superiority of the Jewish constitution and way of life. For instance, the cultural self-isolation of the Jews was not like the brutish practice of *xenelasia* or expulsions by the Spartans, which was rightly despised by Plato and other Greek philosophers (2.255–56).[168] Jewish *amixia* was even more liberal than the moderate cultural self-isolation recommended by Plato, which allowed for closely monitored secret contacts between ruling class educated elites for the purpose of exchanging information on laws and education (Plato, *Laws* 12.949e-950a; cf. Josephus, Apion 2.257–59). Instead, the philanthropic Jewish implementation of cultural isolation allowed the acceptance of foreigners into Jewish society, conditioned on their observation of Jewish laws (Apion 2.123, 209–10, 261).[169] Josephus also argued that the elevated Jewish conception of a benevolent monotheistic deity was superior to that of the Greek philosophers, and Plato in particular. Whereas Plato's beautiful conception of god was not shared with the masses, but reserved only for philosophers, the Jewish worship of the supreme god was universal (2.169). Josephus compared the Jewish way of life to an initiation into the mysteries conducted on a national scale (2.188–89; cf. Philo, *On the Contemplative Life* 25), where all citizens were inducted into the highest knowledge of the divine. Finally, Josephus claimed that the Jewish constitution was more successful than any established by the Greeks. The divine laws and theocratic government of the Jews achieved what was criticized in Plato as utopian and impractical (Apion 2.220–25). In ca. 90 CE, Josephus could claim that the Jews, although deprived of their wealth and their cities (2.277), still possessed the most noble and most successful form of constitution and laws ever known, one that had lasted unchanged for "two thousand years" (2.226; cf. 2.156, 221) without any innovation (1.42; 2.153, 169, 182–85, 226; cf. Deut. 4.2), longer than those of the Spartans or any other Greeks (2.225), a law code that was virtually immortal (2.277, 229–80), to which the Jews of his time still continued in unwavering obedience (2.150, 220–21, 226, 232–35). Josephus claimed that the Mosaic constitution, if judged by "the test of time," must be viewed as not only the oldest body of legislation, but also the most successful (2.279–80).

In Apion 2.145–295, Josephus presented two fundamental arguments with respect to the relationship of the Mosaic constitution and Plato's *Laws*. The first argument was that the Jewish laws and national way of life closely resembled and sometimes even exceeded Plato's conception of the ideal *polis*. Even allowing for the fact that Josephus tailored his utopian presentation of the Jewish way of life to an educated Greek and Roman audience familiar with Plato's *Laws,* the comparisons Josephus drew appear substantial and compelling. Having argued for the existence of a relationship between Plato's *Laws* and the system of Jewish government, Josephus presented his second argument, that the Jewish way of life had been established 2,000 years earlier, in the time of Moses, long prior to Plato's era, and thus must necessarily have influenced Plato's writings as well as those of other Greek philosophers. This second argument was dubiously based on a naive acceptance of the mythic past as laid out in the biblical text. Although one may accept the existence of a genuine connection between the provisions in the Torah and Plato's *Laws,* much as Josephus and other ancient writers inferred from their knowledge of both, it now appears evident that the Mosaic writings were informed by those of Plato and not the reverse.

It seems certain that by the early second century BCE the Jewish nation had come to accept the biblical writings as an ancient literature authored by their ancestors. The attachment of the Jews as a religion and as a people to their literature was and is extraordinary. No other nation in antiquity was so thoroughly defined by its literature. In later times, the Jews would come to be known as "the people of the book,"[170] an apt description, because to an extraordinary degree the Jews derived their distinctive culture, religion, ethics, laws, historical traditions and sense of ethnic identity from their treasured national literature. Remarkably, the Jewish people, religion, literature and way of life long outlived even the disastrous fall of the Jewish nation and its temple in 66–70 CE.[171] Although one must challenge both the exaggerated antiquity of the Jewish laws and the direction of influence between Moses and Plato as claimed by Josephus, the historical persistence of Jewish laws and literature after the time of Josephus matches and exceeds even Josephus' extravagant claims. If judged by "the test of time" (2.279–80), the sacred biblical texts can be understood as perhaps the world's most successful experiment in social engineering, having created not one but two *ethnoi* – the Samaritans and the Jews – that have successfully persisted for over 2,000 years with an undiminished loyalty to their respective foundational national literatures, much as Plato predicted. The Torah and the Hebrew Bible, understood as ancient literary implementations of the program found in Plato's *Laws,* demonstrate how extraordinarily successful Plato's legislative and literary strategies for nation-building were when applied in the real world.

Notes

1 The earliest Platonic dialogues, which typically featured encounters between Socrates – Plato's teacher – and various celebrated figures in Athens, are widely agreed to have been *Apology, Crito, Laches, Lysis, Charmides, Euthyphro, Hippias Minor, Hippias Major, Protagoras, Gorgias* and *Ion,* although *Gorgias* is sometimes assigned to Plato's middle period. For a discussion of Plato's early dialogues, see Jaeger 1943: 2.107–59; Klosko 2006: 31–62. It has been debated whether the views found in these

early dialogues more accurately represent those of the character Socrates or the author Plato, which did not necessarily coincide. Extracting information on Plato's views is complicated by the fact that Plato's compositions were not straight discourses, such as written by other philosophers such as Aristotle, but dialogues, essentially plays written in prose on a philosophical topic. Additionally, the character of Socrates was occasionally given to sarcastic playfulness, requiring critical evaluation of whether the views he expressed were serious or tongue-in-cheek. My description of Plato's views will not take such fine points of Platonic studies into consideration, but generally summarize consensus views on Plato, referring the interested reader to the relevant secondary literature as appropriate.

2 At *Gorgias* 452e, Plato described rhetoric as "the ability to persuade by words jurors in the law-court, councilors in the council, assemblymen in the assembly, and anyone in any other meeting that is political." Plato, *Phaedrus* 261a-b redefined rhetoric as "an art which leads the soul by means of words, not only in the law courts, but in private companies as well." The term *psychogogia* carried connotations of beguiling or enchanting the soul. Aristotle (*Rhetoric* 1.1355b) later defined rhetoric more precisely as the art of analyzing the means of persuasion appropriate to an audience.

3 See, generally, de Romilly 1975. For poetry as enchantment, see Isocrates, *Evagoras* 10; Plato, *Ion* 535a-e; Plato, *Republic* 10.598d, 602d. For rhetoric as enchantment, see Gorgias, *Encomium on Helen* and Plato, *Protagoras* 315a; *Phaedrus* 261a; *Euthydemus* 289e-290a; cf. Gellrich 1994: 276–9. For the most part, Plato rejected magic, enchantments and other arts of sorcery (Plato, *Republic* 2.364b-365a; Plato, *Laws* 10.909b; 11.932e-933e; Morrow 1953: 238–9), although Plato also acknowledged the curative effect of chants on a troubled soul (*Phaedo* 77d-78a; *Charmides* 156d-157c; *Euthydemus* 289e-290a; cf. Brisson 1998: 78–81).

4 See Plato, *Gorgias* 503d-504a on the statesman as a craftsman of souls; cf. Klosko 2006: 115. Jaeger 1943: 2.154 considered "Socratic *paideia* [education] as equivalent to the art of politics" in Plato's early dialogues.

5 See Jaeger 1943: 2.126–59 on the educator as statesman and Socrates as the one true statesman.

6 Jaeger 1943: 3.216. It is generally agreed that Plato's middle works, in which he developed his own distinctive philosophical ideas, including his theory of forms, consisted of *Meno, Phaedo, Republic, Symposium, Phaedrus, Euthydemus, Menexenus, Cratylus* (and perhaps *Gorgias*). Discussion of these dialogues may be found at Jaeger 1943: 2.160–372; 3.182–96; Klosko 2006: 63–192.

7 Herodotus, *Histories* 2.164–67; Aristotle, *Politics* 3.1278a; Plato, *Laws* 1.644a. Athens relied on foreign residents *(metics)* and slaves for its craftsmen. Pursuit of a craft was considered unworthy of an Athenian, although the *thetes* or members of the landless class were commonly employed as farm workers.

8 For Homer's use in Greek schools to instill virtue, see Plato, *Protagoras* 326a; Xenophon, *Symposium* 3.5; cf. Carr 2005: 100–1. For philosophers and poets as rivals in moral education, see Monoson 2000: 220. For Plato's criticism and censorship of poetry and myth, see *Republic* 2.376d-398b; the complete abolition of imitative poetry was advocated at 10.595a-608b. Plato allowed for the possibility that poets might selectively be recalled from exile if they could demonstrate that their poetry was useful for the *polis* (10.607c; cf. 3.398a). The only forms of poetry that Plato retained were hymns to the gods and praises of famous men (10.607a).

9 Plato, *Republic* 3.414b-415d; 4.434a-b; cf. Klosko 2006: 70–1. The myth that Plato created was based on a well-known earlier myth that Athenians were autochthonous or "earthborn" (Isocrates, *Panegyricus* 24–25; Isocrates , *Panathenaicus* 124; cf. Plato, *Timaeus* 23d-e; Plato, *Critias* 109d; Plato, *Laws* 2.663d-e). In Plato's version, the Athenians sprang from the earth with souls that contained an admixture of valuable metals.

10 See Plato, *Republic* 2.376d-3.412b on the lower education of the Auxiliaries, which included letters, music and physical training.

11 See Plato, *Republic* 7.521c-540c on the advanced studies of the Guardians, which included both philosophy and practical arts necessary for statesmanship and military command; cf. Gellrich 1994: 283; Klosko 2006: 102–4. Plato's later dialogues also claimed that those Plato considered fit members of the ruling class possessed an exceptional divine intellect (Plato, *Timaeus* 51e; Plato, *Laws* 7.818a; cf. Brisson 1998: 95). The advanced philosophical training of the philosopher-kings made them the only individuals qualified to rule the populace. Because Plato expected philosophers by nature to prefer to stay away from public life and devote themselves to higher studies, he held that they should be compelled to rule (*Republic* 6.499b-c; 7.519c-521b).

12 See Plato, *Republic* 3.413a-c; 5.467d-480a; Plato, *Meno* 97a-98a; Plato, *Timaeus* 51d-52a for the distinction between knowledge attained by reason and changeable belief or opinion *(doxa)* that was conditioned by irrational influences such as persuasion, passion, pleasure and fear. See Plato, *Republic* 3.392d-398a on imitation *(mimesis)*, which was used in the arts (as well as in rhetoric) as a substitute for true knowledge.

13 Plato called this myth a "noble lie" (*Republic* 3.414b) and an "audacious fiction" (3.414d; cf. 3.415d), one which Plato conceded would never be believed by the first generation, but might be accepted by their sons, grandsons and descendants. See Plato's similar later comments on the usefulness of the myth of autochthony at *Laws* 2.663d-e.

14 Plato, *Republic* 3.414b, 415d. Although citizens and especially poets were forbidden from lying, the rulers were not only permitted but also expected to lie, both to foreign powers, as a necessary aspect of diplomacy, and to the citizens for the public good (2.382c-e; 3.389b-d; 5.459c-d; cf. Kauffman 1994: 114). Lies about the gods were forbidden, but it was permitted to make up false stories about ancient times that served the public good, because the truth about antiquity was impossible to know (Plato, *Republic* 2.382a-e). Plato continued to elaborate on his ideas of beneficial deceit in later dialogues (cf. Plato, *Laws* 2.664a). For Plato's distinction between harmful lies, such as often found in Greek poetry, and beneficial lies constructed to convey a philosophical truth or to promote ethical behavior and shape public beliefs, see Plato, *Republic* 2.376e-377a; Plato, *Protagoras* 320b-c; cf. Belfiore 1985; Brisson 1998: 91, 113.

15 Plato, *Republic* 7.540e-541b; cf. 3.415d. This solution was likely inspired by the Spartan system of education, in which all male children were taken from their parents at age seven to enter "boot camp" and begin their military training, which continued until their graduation into the citizen warrior class at age twenty-one; cf. Morrow 1993: 52–3.

16 Plato's late works consisted of *Parmenides, Theaetetus, Sophist, Statesman, Timaeus, Critias, Philebus* and *Laws*. Discussion of these dialogues may be found at Jaeger 1943: 3.213–62; Klosko 2006: 193–262.

17 For Plato's criticism of legislation in the form of tyrannical commands, see Plato, *Laws* 4.719c-d, 720a, c-d, 722e; 9.857e, 859a, 880e; cf. Morrow 1953: 243; Nightingale 1999: 117. Plato instead advocated combining coercion with persuasion (*Laws* 2.660a, 661c; 4.718b, 720e, 722b-c; 6.753a). The ideal was for both rulers and citizenry to be persuaded to voluntarily submit to the laws as a form of willing slavery (*Laws* 3.698a-c; 699c-d, 700a, 701b-c, 4.715b-d; cf. Nightingale 1993a: 299; Annas 2010: 72–3, 76).

18 Plato, *Laws* 5.741a; 6.773e; 7.823d; 9.854a-c, 857e, 880a; 10.885b, 899d; cf. Nightingale 1993a: 291–2, 295; Annas 2010: 88. As discussed in Chapter 4 §5, this Platonic innovation was implemented in the homiletic format of the Deuteronomic law code, which contained both a comprehensive rhetorical introduction addressed to the citizen populace in Deut. 1–11 and motive clauses or persuasive comments attached to individual laws, features with no precedent in Ancient Near Eastern law collections.

19 "I believe that we have to find a form of myth to charm them into agreement" (Plato, *Laws* 10.903a-b). Plato's use of myth for persuasion was discussed at Kauffman 1994:

108, 112; Brisson 1998: 75–86. Plato's *Laws* contains fourteen instances of myths, many appearing in legislative preludes or *paramuthia;* cf. Plato, *Laws* 11.927c, which explained *paramuthia* as "a myth *(muthos)* which precedes the law." Plato was not above using the gods to scare the citizens into obedience (Klosko 2006: 248), and invoked myths about the afterlife several times in preludes to the laws, such as judgment in Hades (Plato, *Laws* 9.870d-e, 881a; 10.904c-905c; 12.959b) or the vengeance of the Furies (4.716a, 717d; 9.872e-873a) or the troubled ghosts of murder victims (9.872c-e). In these myths, which were adapted from the Orphic mysteries, the immortal soul would either ascend to a new abode in the Islands of the Blessed or descend to suffer the fiery torments of Tartarus, depending on whether one had led a life of virtue and obedience to the divine laws of the *polis*. See Plato, *Laws* 5.727d; 9.870d-e, 872e-873a; Plato, *Gorgias* 523a; Plato, *Phaedo* 114d; Plato, *Republic* 2.363c-e; 10.614b-621d; cf. Morrow 1993: 455. Plato labeled these stories about the afterlife myths, that is, traditions that were not capable of verification (*Laws* 9.872e; cf. Brisson 1998: 9–11). He acknowledged that the truth of such claims about a divine judgment in the afterlife could not be proven, but that it was important to encourage the citizens of the *polis* to accept them anyway, in order to encourage obedience to the laws (Plato, *Laws* 2.663b-c; cf. 10.907c). Although the Hebrew Bible had no systematic exposition on the soul or the afterlife, preludes to the laws sometimes nevertheless invoked myths regarding divine judgment or the wrath of slain murder victims similar to those found in Plato's *Laws*.

20 Morrow 1993: 238; Clark 2003: 28–49; Rinella 2010: 243–8. Magical enchantments *(epodai)* were condemned as part of sorcerers' arts at Plato, *Laws* 10.906b, 909b; 11.933a-d (cf. *Euthydemus* 289e; *Republic* 2.364b; 4.426b; *Symposium* 202e), but were endorsed as an effective means of education and persuasion for the citizenry (and especially the young) at Plato, *Laws* 2.659e, 664b, 665c, 666c, 671a; 6.773d; 7.812c; 8.837e; 10.887d, 903b; 12.944b.

21 Plato's system of universal state-imposed education was modeled on that found in Sparta, where children not of the Helot or slave class were taken from families and entered into a strict regimen of compulsory education and training starting at age seven years aimed at creating a courageous military class (Herodotus, *Histories* 7.104; Xenophon, *Lacedemonian Constitution* 2.2–11; Plutarch, *Lycurgus* 16.1–6; Aristotle, *Politics* 4.1294b; 7.1324b; 8.1337a). Sparta and Crete were the only nations in the Classical Greek world that legislated on child-rearing and education (Aristotle, *Nicomachian Ethics* 10.1180a; Aristotle, *Politics* 8.1337a). For Spartan influences in general in Plato's *Laws,* see Plato, *Laws* 1.630d-e; 3.691d-692a; 8.836b; Plato, *Republic* 10.599d; Plato, *Phaedrus* 258b-c; Plato, *Epistles* 8.354b; cf. Tigerstadt 1965: 1.255–56; Morrow 1993: 40–62. For Spartan influences in the area of education, see Plato, *Protagoras* 342a-344b; cf. Morrow 1993: 52–4, 298–301. Aristotle also advocated universal compulsory education for citizens (*Politics* 8.1337a).

22 See Plato, *Laws* 7.788a-824c on Plato's compulsory educational system. "The youthful mind will be persuaded of anything, if one only takes the trouble to persuade it" (Plato, *Laws* 2.663e). Plato defined education for the young as training the soul to virtue, which would lead to the proper pursuits in later life (1.643d-644a). This could be achieved at the earliest ages by training the emotions and charming the young through pleasant songs and myths (2.659d-e; 10.903b); as an adult, true virtue would be achieved through rational consent, for those who possessed the requisite intellectual abilities (2.653a-c).

23 Nightingale 1993a: 300. Philosophy was reserved for a smaller elite capable of comprehending higher truths (cf. Plato, *Laws* 7.817e-818e; Plato, *Statesman* 292e, 297b, 300e; Plato, *Republic* 6.494a).

24 Plato, *Laws* 9.862c; 10.908e. Plato considered this system to exhibit mercy toward those who had sinned through ignorance that could be corrected by reeducation (9.863c-d).

One major Platonic innovation was to propose a special prison for the indefinite incarceration of certain classes of criminals until they were successfully reeducated by the Nocturnal Council and allowed reentry into society (10.907e-908a, 908e-909a).

25 A favorite simile for rulership in Plato's writings was that of a physician whose efforts to preserve the life of a patient might call for extreme and unpleasant measures, for which the best physicians attempted to gain the voluntary compliance of the patient by education and persuasion, when possible; cf. Plato, *Republic* 3.389c; 5.459c; 6.489c; 8.564b-c; Plato, *Statesman* 293a-b; Plato, *Laws* 3.684c; 4.720c-d; 9.857c-e; cf. de Romilly 1975: 20–1; Clark 2003: 71–88. Exile, permanent expulsion or execution of citizens deemed dangerous were described as a sort of catharsis or curative purging that purified the *polis* from unhealthy elements (Plato, *Laws* 5.735d-736e; cf. Plato, *Republic* 3.399e; 6.496b; 8.560a, e; Plato, *Gorgias* 466c, 468d; Plato, *Protagoras* 325b). For death as the appropriate treatment for those whose dangerous opinions could not otherwise be cured, see Plato, *Laws* 5.735e; 9.854e, 862e-867a; 12.957e-958a.

26 Diodorus Siculus, *Library* 7.12.1 claimed that the Pythia at the temple of Delphi hailed the Spartan legislator Lycurgus as a god (cf. Herodotus, *Histories* 1.65) and promised to grant him *eunomia* greater than all other kingdoms. For Sparta as a paradigm of *eunomia*, see Tigerstadt 1965: 1.71, 73–74, 113–14, 211. In contrast with Spartan *eunomia*, Athens was seen as a model of equality under the law *(isonomia)* and democracy.

27 Thucydides, *Peloponnesian War* 1.18.1. For Lycurgus as savior *(soteros)*, see Plato, *Symposium* 209d; Plato, *Laws* 3.691e-692a; cf. Morrow 1993: 45. See Tigerstadt 1965: 1.70–78, on the legend of Lycurgus and his reforms of Spartan institutions.

28 Plato, *Laws* 12.960b. The governments most admired in the Greek world were those that had survived without change to their constitutions or laws the longest, such as Sparta and Egypt, which by this criterion were considered exceptionally well-run states. Whereas Greek advocates of democracy emphasized individual freedom and happiness, Greek aristocrats (including Plato) tended to measure the success of a constitution and laws by their ability to create long-range political stability. Sparta's mixed constitution and its system of unwritten laws were widely admired for having gone unchanged for over 400 years since their institution by Lycurgus (Thucydides, *Peloponnesian War* 1.18.1; Xenophon, *Lacedemonian Constitution* 10.8; 15.1). Egypt did not have a constitution *per se,* but Egypt was considered the most ancient civilization (Aristotle, *Politics* 7.1329b), and Egypt's system of government had persisted unchanged for 10,000 years (Plato, *Laws* 2.656d-657a; 7.797a-d, 799a-b; cf. Klosko 2006: 250). The Athenian rhetorician Isocrates claimed that the Athenian form of government had been in existence for a thousand years before Solon (Isocrates, *Panathenaicus* 148) and that the Spartans copied their mixed constitution from Athens (Isocrates, *Panathenaicus* 153–5), although alternate traditions claimed that Lycurgus borrowed some of his laws from Crete (Plutarch, *Lycurgus* 4.1–2) or Egypt (Diodorus Siculus, *Library* 1.96.2–3).

29 Bury 1934: 1.xiv; Solmsen 1942: 163; Klosko 2006: 249–50; Annas 2010: 89. "In the *Laws* the City becomes once more the property of the gods" (Solmsen 1942: 169).

30 The fifth century BCE astronomer and natural philosopher Anaxagoras, an older contemporary of Socrates, had been the first to introduce *Nous* or Mind as the divine intelligence that had set the universe into motion and steered the creation of the *kosmos*. It is difficult to ascertain from the surviving fragments of the book written by Anaxagoras whether he viewed *Nous* as a true divinity or as a quality of intelligence that ran throughout the universe (Curd 2007: 192–205), but for Plato it appears that *Nous* was the original, supreme deity, more ancient than the *kosmos* it had fashioned (Plato, *Laws* 10.892a-c, 893a, 896b-d, 899c-d; 12.966d-e, 967b; Plato, *Timaeus* 28c, 34b-c) or the other, lesser gods worshipped by the Greeks (Plato, *Timaeus* 40d-41a). See Hackforth 1936 and Menn 1995 for *Nous* as a divine entity Plato's writings.

31 Plato, *Laws* 4.712e-713a; cf. Morrow 1953: 244. Plato's use of *Nous* to describe a government under divine law had the same sense as the term theocracy that Josephus later coined to describe the form of government established by Moses (Apion 2.165). Following scholarly conventions, I use lower-case *nous* to designate the faculty of reason that is present in every thinking creature and upper-case *Nous* to designate the divine intelligence that ordered and governs the *kosmos*.

32 Plato called this *gerousia* the Nocturnal Council, because it met nightly at the city's Acropolis to oversee the business of the state (Plato, *Laws* 10.908a; 12.951d). Its members consisted of the current and past high priests, the current and past Minister of Education, and the ten senior Guardians of the Laws, who also had important educational duties in the *polis* (12.951d-e). The Nocturnal Council engaged in ongoing research into the laws and educational practices of other nations (12.951d-952c). Executive duties of the Nocturnal Council included confining to house arrest (12.952c-d), imprisoning and reeducating (10.887d, 888a-d, 908e-909d), corporal punishment (10.890c), exile (10.890c) or, failing these measures, executing those who sought to disrupt the beliefs of the *polis* (10.890b-c, 908e-909a). Offenders included *theoroi* who had visited a foreign land and on their return did not praise the colony as having superior laws and political institutions (12.950e-951a, 951c, 952b-d); anyone who secretly established an unapproved cult in a private residence (10.908e-909d); and anyone, especially youth exposed to the theories of natural science (10.886d-e), who did not acknowledge the existence of the gods and their active benevolence toward humanity (10.887d, 888a-d, 903a).

33 According to Plato's *Laws,* the site of the new colony had once been occupied by the ancient Magnesians (Plato, *Laws* 4.704a-c), evidently the Magnesians of Thessaly who other sources said had resided in Crete for a time before emigrating to found Magnesia-on-the-Manaender in Asia Minor (Strabo, *Geography* 14.1.11, 40; cf. Parke and Wormell 1956: 1.52–3; Morrow 1993: 31). Their emigration to Asia Minor had left the district of Magnesia in Crete effectively uninhabited.

34 Although there was clearly no ethnic or historical connection between the ancient Magnesians of Crete and the new colonists of Plato's *Laws,* Plato nevertheless addressed or referred to the citizens of his new *polis* as Magnesians (Plato, *Laws* 8.848d; 9.860e; 11.919d; 12.946b, 969a), instructed the founders to establish cults honoring the gods of the ancient Magnesians (8.848c), and suggested that the *polis* be given the old name Magnesia (4.704a-b). Plato claimed that the ancient Magnesia was being restored and refounded by god (11.919d), by whom the nation of Magnesia was being saved (12.946b). It is fully apparent that Plato intended for the new *polis* of Magnesia to be perceived by its citizens as a revival of the former city-state of the same name, conserving all its ancient religious institutions and divine laws. In the speech to be recited at the yearly appointment of the high priest and his two associates dedicated as first fruits offered to Apollo and Helios (Plato, *Laws* 12.946b-c), Plato went so far as to invoke an "ancient law" of Magnesia for the institution he was clearly only now inventing.

35 Plato, *Laws* 8.848c: "If there exist any local deities of the Magnetes or any shrines of other ancient gods whose memory is still preserved, we shall pay to them the same worship as did the men of old."

36 See Plato, *Laws* 10.886c-d on revered archaic prose and poetic accounts of the origin of the gods and the world, which should be used despite Plato's reservations about their factuality. See Plato, *Laws* 5.738c on authoritative ancient sayings *(palaioi logoi)* about local sacred sites, whether in the form of an ancient vision or some other inspired utterance, which were to be given the same weight of authority as a consultation of the oracle at Delphi. The lawgiver was instructed to assign to each of the twelve tribal districts an ancient god, spirit or hero (5.738c-d, 745c-d; 6.771b-d; cf. 8.828b-c), presumably on the basis of local traditions linking them to specific locales, as in the eponymous heroes of Athens.

37 Plato believed that only those endowed with superior reason had the capacity to attain true knowledge of the god *Nous* through advanced training in philosophy. Plato described philosophy as an enchanting initiation into the mysteries (Armstrong 2004), in which those inducted into the knowledge of the divine lived in a state of bliss, as though communing with the gods in the Islands of the Blessed (cf. Plato, *Republic* 7.519c, 540b; Plato, *Phaedo* 82b, 114b-c), a common feature of mystery religions. The one-on-one relation between the sponsoring member of the Nocturnal Council and his protégé was somewhat similar to that between a mystagogue and an initiate or *mystai* in the Eleusian Mysteries of Athens. See Plato, *Laws* 12.961b, 968c-e on the secret nomination and screening of young candidates for the Nocturnal Council.

38 Similarly, the overthrow of the Thirty Tyrants in 404 BCE claimed to restore the ancestral laws devised by Solon and Kleisthenes; cf. Chapter 4 §4.

39 Plato, *Republic* 6.501a-b; cf. Plato, *Laws* 7.798a-b, where Plato said that the *polis* should preserve "no recollection or report of ever having been different from what they are now." The words "recollection" *(mneme)* and "report" *(akon)* referred respectively to memory (especially as conveyed by stories) and oral tradition. See Plato, *Republic* 3.392a; Plato, *Protagoras* 320c; Brisson 1998: x–xi, 7, 13–39 on memories ("recollections") transmitted from old to young in myth. For *akon* or "report" used as a synonym for oral tradition, see Thucydides, *Peloponnesian War* 1.23.3. *Mneme* was the name of one of the nine Muses, the muse of memory. Plato's notion of erasing the national memory in order to effect a rebirth of the nation appears to have been influenced by his adoption of Orphic notions of reincarnation. Prior to a rebirth into another life, a soul must first drink from the waters of forgetfulness (the River of Lethe), so that there would not be confusing memories of previous lives (Plato, *Republic* 10.621a-c).

40 Plato, *Republic* 10.595a-608b. For the need to legislate or constrain poets, see also Plato, *Laws* 2.660a, e, 661c; 7.801c, 817b-c; 12.941b-c.

41 Many elements of the program of censorship at Plato, *Laws* 2.656c, 660a; 4.719b and implicit in 7.788a-824c were already found in Plato, *Republic* 2.376d-398b; cf. Chase 1933: 183–4; Kauffman 1994: 114.

42 Awards of merit *(arete)* were given as public recognition for outstanding military service (Plato, *Laws* 11.921e; 12.943c-d) or for outstanding conformity to the written laws of the *polis* (11.922a; 12.952c). Such awards were presented at festivals, accompanied by a laudatory poem (8.829c).

43 Aristotle, *Rhetoric* 1.1358b, 1366a-1368a discussed the genre of rhetoric called *epideictic*, which was utilized in funeral orations and in speeches associated with the awarding of honors. *Epideictic* speeches given annually at Athens to honor recently fallen war heroes became an occasion to survey the glories of Athenian history and are thought to have shaped how Athenian citizens came to view their past. In his early dialogues, Plato criticized the genre of *epideictic*, as discussed in Nightingale 1993b. Plato allowed for the use of *epideictic* to influence citizen behavior in Plato, *Republic* 6.492a-c; 10.607a; Plato, *Laws* 2.663b-c; 4.711b-c; 5.730b-c; 7.801e-802a, 822d-823a; 8.829e-e. In Plato's *Laws*, the Guardians of the Laws were enjoined to either praise or condemn figures in accordance with their service to the *polis* and its laws. This praise or condemnation of citizen conduct was applied to conformity to both formal written laws and legally unenforceable "unwritten" ethical precepts in order to promote noble character by public honors or to use peer pressure and public humiliation to shame the blameworthy (4.711b-c; 5.730b-c; 7.807e-808a; 8.829c-e). All surviving examples of *epideictic* speeches fall into the category of public praise, not blame (cf. Roundtree 2001); *epideictic* as a speech of public condemnation *(psogos)*, a notion found mainly in Plato's *Laws* but mentioned as a (theoretical) category of *epideictic* at Aristotle, *Rhetoric* 1.1366a-1386a, may have been a Platonic innovation.

44 Plato, *Republic* 2.382c-d; Plato, *Timaeus* 21c-d, 26e (where Plato expressed his wish that the myth of Atlantis should be converted to a poetic format to be chanted at the Lesser Panathenaeia); Plato, *Critias* 113a; Plato, *Laws* 2.663e-664a. For the poet as myth-maker, see Plato, *Phaedo* 60b-61b; Plato, *Republic* 2.379a; cf. Brisson 1998: 33, 36, 40, 44–5.

45 Censorship of storytellers was explicitly enjoined at Plato, *Republic* 2.377b-c (cf. 3.401b), where censors would review and either approve *(egkriteon)* or reject *(apo-criteon)* the myths storytellers created. Approved myths would form a list *(egkrithen-tes)* of myths that nurses and mothers would be compelled to recite to their children to beneficially shape their souls. In Plato's *Laws* a similar process, with similar vocabulary, was applied to the approval or rejection of musical and poetic compositions (7.802b), comedic works (11.936a) and topics of study in schools (7.820d; 12.952a). (Potential members of the ruling class were also subject to severe tests of character and either approved or rejected at *Republic* 3.413d, 414a; 6.503a.) Later, under the librarian and grammarian Aristophanes of Byzantium (cf. ca. 200–180 BCE), the Great Library of Alexandria created lists *(egkrithentes)* of exemplary orators, playwrights and other writers of the past whose works were recommended for study in school; the Romans later created similar lists of classics *(classici)*. But these lists of texts approved for their excellence, which have sometimes been compared with the biblical canons, were based on a positive literary appraisal rather than an ethical criterion or evaluation of content, and had no corresponding mirror list of rejected works comparable to the censored myths of Plato.

46 See de Romilly 1975: 3–22 on the use of spell-binding rhythms and poetic excess by the famous sophist Gorgias, a contemporary of Socrates, who likened the effects of properly delivered rhetoric on audiences to magical incantations. As Romilly noted (1975: 25–39), Plato criticized the dangerous power of rhetoric, which could be used irresponsibly to persuade the people to any position a skilled orator desired. Although Plato rejected the use of rhetoric by the sophists who did not grasp the nature of virtue, in his later dialogues he held that philosophers in positions of power could legitimately use rhetoric to shape the character and behaviors of the populace.

47 For "tragic" Greek history with moralizing content starting in the fourth century BCE among the students of the rhetorician Isocrates, see Ullman 1942; Walbank 1960.

48 Plato, *Laws* 2.664d, 667d, 671a (in which the stories and speeches of the old enchanted the young); Plato, *Menexenus* 525a-c (which compared the rhetorical effects of pan-egyrics on Athenian history with the initiation into the mysteries).

49 Plato, *Laws* 7.817e-822c; 12.952a. Plato saw special dangers in exposing young minds to astronomy and philosophy (Plato, *Republic* 6.497e-498c; 7.537d-539d; Plato, *Laws* 7.819a, 820e-822a), especially the natural philosophy of the astronomer Anaxagoras, whose scientific theories claimed that the universe took form through natural processes and that the sun, moon, planets and stars were material objects rather than visible deities (10.886d-e, 889a-c.). Plato thought it better that students not be taught astronomy or science at all than to be exposed to it in the atheistic form that Anaxagoras presented it, where chance and material forces shaped and governed the universe (7.819a, 821a; cf. 10.886a, d-e); but Plato said that an introductory instruction in astronomy was acceptable for middle schools, provided that the celestial bodies were described as gods (7.821b-822c; 10.886a-e, 887e, 899a-b; cf. 7.817e).

50 The dangers of travel and cultural intermixture were discussed at Plato, *Laws* 12.949e-951e. A conscious program of cultural isolation, modeled on that of Sparta, helped to ensure that outside information and knowledge of other customs would not foster dissatisfaction and a desire for change. Plato consciously designed his laws limiting cultural contacts with peoples from other nations so as not to be as crudely hostile to foreigners as those of Sparta (*Laws* 12.950a-b; cf. Plutarch, *Lycurgus* 27.3–4 on the

Spartan Aliens Expulsion Act). Unlike Sparta's xenophobic laws that had given their country an evil reputation, Plato allowed delegations to travel abroad to Greek festivals and similar reciprocal visits from foreigners, but regulated in such a manner as to prevent positive views of foreign cultures to infiltrate the *polis*.

51 Plato, *Laws* 12.950d-951a. No private travels were allowed for any purpose and emissaries who traveled abroad on missions of state (other than war) has to be at least forty years old. Such travelers included heralds, members of civic *theoria* to consult the oracles of Zeus or Apollo or participate in the sacrifices and international athletic competitions of Greek festivals, and theoric missions undertaken by select citizens to research foreign laws and customs. On their return from foreign travels, ambassadors were required to tell the young how superior their laws and political institutions were to those of other nations (cf. Deut. 4.6–8).

52 Plato, *Laws* 12.952d-953e. Foreign merchants who visited the *polis* to deliver their wares were received by the harbor and market officials, who minimized their contacts with the public and prevented them from introducing innovations of any kind. Visitors to the city's festivals and music competitions were lodged in the temple and supervised by priests until their departure. Foreign emissaries on public business were housed and supervised by the generals. *Theoroi* visiting the *polis* for the purpose of acquiring wisdom were housed by the wisest and most virtuous citizens such as the Minister of Education, with whom they were allowed to exchange information (see note 53).

53 There existed no Athenian parallel for Plato's Minister of Education, although such an office may have existed at Sparta. See Morrow 1993: 324–5.

54 See Morrow 1993: 195–215 on the Guardians of the Laws in Plato's *Laws*. See Plato, *Laws* 6.752d-e, 755a-b; 7.802b on the qualifications for the Guardians of the Laws. According to Xenophon, *On Household Management* 9.14, "'well ordered cities' are not content only to pass good laws, but also appoint *nomophylakes* as overseers to commend the law-abiding and chastise the law-breakers"; cf. Cicero, *On Laws* 3.46. Many Greek states had a panel of Guardians of the Laws to ensure that both magistrates and private citizens observed the laws of the *polis*. See further Chapter 2 §9. See also O'Sullivan 2009: 72–89 for the important role the *nomophylakes* or Guardians of the Laws played in regulating public conduct in Athens under Demetrius of Phalerum in 317–307 BCE.

55 An extraordinary procedure allowed a change in the law code only if unanimously agreed upon by all the magistrates, the general assembly of citizens and the divine oracles (Plato, *Laws* 6.772c-d).

56 Plato, *Laws* 7.811c-d; 12.966b; cf. 1.630e-631a. For law as the embodiment of virtue and the means for instilling it in the citizen body in Plato's *Laws*, see Annas 2010: 71–91. Laws and habituation since youth were the main means of inculcating virtue (Plato, *Laws* 1.643d-e; 2.659d-e; cf. Aristotle, *Nicomachian Ethics* 10.1180a; Aristotle, *Politics* 7.1332b). The aim of child-rearing, education and legislation in Plato's *Laws* was the establishment of virtue in the citizenry (Plato, *Laws* 1.630b-e; 3.688a-b; 4.705e-706a; 6.770b-771a; 9.853b-c; 12.963a); and making the citizens happy by rendering them virtuous (1.631b-632d; 4.718a-b; 8.828d-829b). A central tenet of Plato's public theology was that virtue and justice always resulted in a happy life, and that the poets should be compelled to say so (*Republic* 3.392a-c; *Laws* 2.662b-c; 3.660e). Plato recognized that this was a fiction, because it was possible an unjust life might be happiest (Plato, *Laws* 2.663d-e; cf. Clark 2003: 144), but a fiction beneficial to the state for citizens to believe because it would promote obedience and virtue (*Laws* 2.662b-663c). Plato therefore proposed that the youth and ordinary citizens be taught that the gods rewarded virtue and punish wickedness, if not in this life then in the afterlife, in order to promote virtue and obedience in the *polis* (*Laws* 2.662c-d, 664b-c), although bringing in the gods made this an unverifiable appeal to myth (Nightingale 1993a: 296).

57 The Guardians of the Laws *(nomophylakes)* were effectively identical with the Guardians *(phylakes)* or philosopher-kings of the *Republic,* except that in the aristocratic
form of government described in the *Republic* they represented a formal ruling class.

58 Plato, *Laws* 12.966c-968a. Theology ("the study of God") was a Platonic neologism
that first appeared at Plato, *Republic* 2.379a. The Roman author Varro distinguished
among three forms of theological discourse: mythical theology, concerning the origins of the gods; natural theology, dealing with philosophical analysis of the nature of
god; and civil theology, concerning public rites and religious observances (*Human and
Divine Antiquities,* as summarized in Augustine, *The City of God* 4.27, 32; 6.5).

59 References to the Guardians of the Laws as legislators were found at Plato, *Laws*
6.770a-e, 772a-c; 7.801d; 8.828b, 835a, 843e, 846b-c; 9.855c-d; 12.957a, 968c. These
legislative duties included regulating the arts; cf. Nightingale 1999: 102. Although the
phrase "legislators of the arts" does not appear in Plato's *Laws,* it appears frequently in
secondary literature as a convenient way of referring to the Guardians of the Laws in
their capacity as regulators of literature, theater, music and dance. Among the Greeks,
all these arts were under the control and inspiration of the Muses, who were mentioned
frequently in Plato's *Laws* in connection with the "legislators of the arts."

60 The primary responsibility for approving the content of the sacred hymns and prayers
fell to the Guardians of the Laws in their capacity as "legislators of the arts" (Plato,
Laws 11.936a specified the Minister of Education), but these were authorized to bring
in poets and musicians to help with editing and revision (7.802b).

61 Plato explicitly designated "these discourses" (that is, *Laws*) as the writings of the
lawgiver that should be used as the foundational legal, literary and educational text for
the planned colony at Cretan Magnesia (Plato, *Laws* 7.811d-e; 12.957c-d; cf. 9.858c-e).
This striking literary self-reference has exact literary parallels in Deuteronomy, in
which Moses stated that "this book" was to be copied for the education of the king
(Deut. 17.18–19) and to be publicly read at festivals (Deut. 31.9–12), along with other
Deuteronomic references to the Torah that Moses spoke and recorded (Deut. 1.5; 4.8,
44; 27.3, 8, 26; 28.58, 61; 29.20–21; 30.10; 31.24, 26).

62 Plato, *Laws* 1.624a, 634d-e; 2.663b-d; 6.762e; 10.887b-c, 907c; 12.969b; cf. Nightingale 1993a: 284–5, 299; Klosko 2006: 248–50; Annas 2010: 89. The citizens "are
required by law to believe not only that the gods exist and are good, but that the laws
are the product of divine *nous*" (Nightingale 1999: 121).

63 "Here the lawcode is conceived as a distinct genre of writing which is not only elevated
above all other modes of discourse but is accorded an almost scriptural status" (Nightingale 1999: 102; cf. Nightingale 1993a: 289).

64 See Plato, *Laws* 7.811a, c-e; 9.854c on the laws and their preludes being memorized
(instead of poetry) and chanted at festivals; cf. 2.664b-d.

65 See Nightingale 1993a: 284–5. "The utterances of the Athenian-as-lawgiver are
invested with an authority that is divine. Throughout the text, the lawgiver occupies a
privileged center of speech that preempts all criticism." Nightingale 1993a: 299.

66 Plato, *Laws* 1.634d-e; cf. Nightingale 1993a: 293; Clark 2003: 8. "Public opinion has
an amazing power, when nobody ever attempts to breathe a word contrary to the lawcode." Plato, *Laws* 8.838c-d; Nightingale 1993a: 290–3. The unquestioned authority
of the law in Plato's *Laws* appears to mirror attitudes among the Spartans, who were
greatly devoted to their laws (Herodotus, *Histories* 7.104; Xenophon, *Lacedemonian
Constitution* 8.1, 3; cf. Morrow 1993: 49–50), where none were allowed to question the
laws in public, although the old were permitted frank discussions when no youth were
present (cf. Plato, *Laws* 1.625b).

67 Lists of legislators who claimed to have received their laws from a deity appeared at
Diodorus Siculus, *Library* 1.94.1–2; Strabo, *Geography* 16.2.38; Plutarch, *Numa* 4.1.
Strabo, *Geography* 16.2.39 listed legislators who claimed to be prophets. For Lycurgus

the Spartan lawgiver as part god, as declared by the Delphic oracle, see Herodotus, *Histories* 1.65; Diodorus Siculus, *Library* 7.12.1; Plutarch, *Lycurgus* 5.3; cf. Plato, *Laws* 3.691e, where Plato described Lycurgus as having human nature blended with the divine. Spartan traditions said their laws were given to Lycurgus as divine oracles from Apollo (Herodotus, *Histories* 1.15; Plato, *Laws* 1.624a, 632d, 634d; Xenophon, *Lacedemonian Constitution* 8.1–3, 5; Plutarch, *Lycurgus* 1.1–3; 5.3; 6.2; 13.6; 29.1–4; Strabo, *Geography* 10.4.19; 16.2.38; cf. Plato, *Laws* 3.696a-c; Tigerstadt 1965: 1.51–61). For the inspiration and divine ancestry of Minos and Rhadamanthys, see Plato, *Minos* 318c, 319c-e; Plato's *Laws* 1.624a-b, 625b, 630b,d, 632d, 634d; 12.948b; Strabo, *Geography* 10.4.8, 19; 16.2.38; cf. Tigerstadt 1965: 1.211. Plato believed that divinely inspired men existed in every nation and should be sought out and consulted for their ideas on laws and education (Plato, *Laws* 12.951b-c, 952b).

68 According to Plato, God was guiding the course of their conversation on legal matters (*Laws* 3.702b-c; 4.722c-d; 7.811c; 12.968b; cf. 4.712b; 11.921c). For a discussion of the breath (inspiration) of the gods in Plato's writings, see Büttner 2011: 114.

69 The Greeks, including Plato, allowed for the divination of exceptional men as spirits after their death (Plato, *Cratylus* 397b, 398b-c). The members of the Guardian class who died protecting the *polis,* and other good men, were to be so divinized: "We will inquire of Apollo, then, how and with what distinction we are to bury men of more than human, of divine qualities, and . . . we will bestow on their graves the tendance and worship paid to spirits divine" (Plato, *Republic* 5.469a-b). Similarly, the philosopher-kings, after departing to the Islands of the Blessed, were to be accorded a cult and sacrifices either as divinities or as divine or godlike men, in accordance with the instructions of the Pythian oracle (Plato, *Republic* 7.540b-c). At Plato, *Laws* 12.947b-e, the elaborate funeral attended by priests and the sanctified tomb of the *Euthynoi* or priestly auditors are indicative of their recognition as divine spirits after death. After Plato's death, he was seemingly viewed as a divine spirit by his immediate followers, as illustrated by the epitaphs that called him divine (Diogenes Laertius, *Lives of Eminent Philosophers* 3.43–44, discussed in Notopoulos 1942). *Plato's Funeral Feast* by Speusippus, Plato's nephew and his successor as leader of the Academy, contained a supporting story about Plato's semi-divine birth (Diogenes Laertius, *Lives of Eminent Philosophers* 3.2).

70 This claim recurs in Plato's writings. See Gaiser 1984: 103–23; Büttner 2011: 128–9. According to Diogenes Laertius, *Lives of Eminent Philosophers* 3.5, Plato had written lyric poems and tragedies as a youth, but burned them and turned to the pursuit of philosophy after listening to Socrates.

71 See Aristotle, *Poetics* 6.1449b on the definition of tragedy as a literary genre among the Greeks, essentially a play written in poetic meter on a serious or noble topic for public performance, which typically hinged on the divine consequences of a character flaw or an error in conduct. Aristotle was unable to fit Plato's Socratic dialogues into any of the normal literary categories (6.1447b), because it was written in a play-like format, but in prose.

72 Plato, *Laws* 4.713b, e; cf. Plato, *Republic* 5.472e; 6.500e-501c (where Plato claimed that the artist who created a constitution must imitate the divine city).

73 Plato, *Laws* 7.817a-b; cf. 9.858c-859a. Elsewhere Plato claimed philosophy was the highest form of music (*Phaedo* 61a; cf. *Phaedrus* 248d).

74 Plato, *Republic* 2.382c-d distinguished useful lies about the past that contained an element of truth from wicked lies about the past that said bad or harmful things about the gods and heroes.

75 See Aristotle, *Poetics* 6.1449b-1462b on tragedy. Only rarely was the subject matter of tragedy taken from recent history such as the Persian Wars. In contrast to tragedy, Greek comedy typically made fun of contemporary figures.

76 See Plato, *Republic* 2.382c-d; 3.389b-d, 414b-415d; 5.459c-d on the permitted construction of useful lies and myths.

77 Like actors in a tragedy, the citizens were to imitate noble life in the mythical city under divine rule (Plato, *Laws* 2.659d-660a, 669b-c; 4.713a-b,e; 7.817b-d). Choral performances at festivals constituted a type of acting (2.655d; 7.798d) in which all citizens were required to take part (2.653c-654a), and were the primary form of education in Plato's polity (2.653c-654a, 672c-673b), because of choral participation's ability to influence the soul (2.659a-660a, 673a). See generally Meyer 2011: 398–401.

78 The Age of Kronus was the first of Hesiod's five Ages of Men, when humans coexisted with the gods and lived a life of leisure, free from toil or sorrow (Hesiod, *Works and Days* 109–20). Hesiod's myth was politicized by Plato in several of his dialogues in which the golden race became a model for the divine philosophical ruling class of the *polis* who ruled over a virtuous, obedient citizenry modeled on Hesiod's second child-like silver race (Plato, *Republic* 3.415a-c; 5.468e-469a; 8.546e-547a; Plato, *Statesman* 268e-272d; *Laws* 4.713b-e; cf. Dillon 1992). The imagery of humanity as contented herds of tame sheep, oxen or goats tended by the divine rulers in the Age of Kronus was used by Plato in *Statesman* 271e-272b, 275a-b and *Laws* 4.713c-e; 6.766a.

79 See generally Meyer 2011. It was the quality of imitation (*mimesis*) that qualified the polity in Plato's *Laws* as a tragic play (Meyer 2011: 392). "The best run cities, he says, are imitations of the mythical city ruled by divine wisdom," acted out by obeying the divine laws (Meyer 2011: 394, citing Plato, *Laws* 4.713a-b, 713e-714a).

80 Plato, *Laws* 2.664a; cf. 7.816d. The lawgiver "must devise all possible means to ensure that the whole of the community constantly, so long as they live, use exactly the same language, so far as possible, about these matters, alike in their songs *(odais),* their tales *(muthois),* and their discourses *(logois).*"

81 Plato, *Laws* 7.822d-823a; cf. Nightingale 1993a: 288. Plato, *Laws* 5.726a-734d contains a lengthy ethical prelude for the laws. The lawgiver was expected not only to pass enforceable laws but also discourse on virtuous behavior in order to render the citizens docile and obedient to the laws of the *polis.*

82 Plato, *Laws* 7.811d-812a. Plato's exclusive aim in the creation of a national canon of literature appears to have been the regulation of ethical, theological and mythological content. Plato did not specifically address the question of exemplar texts and accurate letter-perfect copying of texts, which appears to have been a literary concern that arose only after the time of Plato, especially among textual critics at Alexandria.

83 Plato, *Laws* 7.811b-c. Philosophy and advanced astronomy were among topics to be excluded from elementary and middle school education.

84 Plato, *Laws* 2.663d-664a. Plato's comprehensive program of rhetorical as a means of social control was extensively discussed in Kauffman 1994: 101–16. See also Plato, *Republic* 2.382c-d; 3.389b-d, 414b-415d; 5.459c-d, on the necessity and advantage of beneficial lies for shaping the conduct and character of the citizens of the state. Plato is thought to have been influenced by Spartan political philosophy, in which calculated deception was cultivated as a skill useful both in dealing with foreign powers (Herodotus, *Histories* 9.54.1; Euripides, *Andromache* 451–2; Aristophanes, *Lysistrata* 1233–5; Thucydides, *Peloponnesian War* 2.39.2; cf. Plato, *Republic* 2.382c) and its own citizenry, especially the Helot slave class (Plutarch, *Lycurgus* 28.1–7; cf. Plato, *Republic* 5.459c-d). Spartan deception was discussed at Hesk 2000: 27–33.

85 Serious drama, once approved, could be rehearsed and publicly performed. In Athens, comedic plays typically contained scathing social criticism of contemporary figures. Socrates was the subject – one might say victim – of *The Clouds* by Aristophanes (cf. Plato, *Apology* 18a-e, especially 18c). In Plato's *Laws,* the study of comedy was permitted, because drama could not be taught without its opposite, but could not be performed or even rehearsed by citizens of the *polis* because of what Plato viewed as its

detrimental moral effects. Comedy was limited to improvised performances by slaves or foreigners, which the citizens of the *polis* were to ignore as frivolous (Plato, *Laws* 7.816e-817a). Innocent jests about fellow-citizens in songs written by approved poets were permitted, after first being reviewed by the Guardians of the Laws, but if rejected as malicious were subject to prosecution, whether the songs were performed in public or in private (Plato, *Laws* 11.935e-936b).

86 Plato, *Laws* 7.817a-d. The national literature that Plato envisioned thus represented an open canon, that is, a restricted list of approved texts, but with a mechanism for admitting new works.

87 Plato, *Laws* 7.799a-b, 809b; 9.866c. See Harvey 1955: 157–75 for a discussion of the different forms of songs, such as "the hymn, the dirge, the paean, the diathramb and the nome" mentioned at Plato, *Laws* 3.700a-b. In this passage of *Laws,* Plato described hymns as "prayers directed to the gods."

88 Plato, *Laws* 7.802a-c. Plato condemned the artistic license found in almost every nation, with the alleged exception of Egypt, where – Plato claimed – the temples posted official lists of consecrated musical forms, dances and standard forms of artistic representation; artists and musicians were strictly forbidden to introduce any innovation outside these purported lists (Plato, *Laws* 2.656c-657a; cf. 7.799a-b). No such Egyptian regulations or approved lists for the arts are thought to have existed; cf. Morrow 1993: 355.

89 Plato, *Laws* 7.802b. Plato laid out three laws with respect to psalms and prayers composed by poets (*Laws* 7.800e-801d). First, such sacred compositions should always be auspicious or *euphemous* (not blasphemous, according to Plato's notions of blasphemy). Second, they should be appropriate to the occasion and sacred offerings at which they would be read. This provision sanctioned the festivals of the twelve Olympian gods whose worship Plato allowed alongside his universal supreme god *Nous*. Third, because poets lacked formal philosophical training in ethics and might consequently request a bad thing from the gods (such as forgiveness for evildoing), all their compositions must first be reviewed and approved by the Guardians of the Laws, before being shown or read even to another private citizen. This last provision guaranteed that the content of the psalms and prayers to the older gods conformed to the new theological reforms Plato imposed on the civic religion of the *polis*. The net effect of these laws was to conservatively support the old religious traditions, but in a revised form according to Plato's higher theological standards.

90 Plato, *Laws* 7.812a-e; cf. Brisson 1998: xxvi–xxvii. According to Plutarch, *Solon* 2.3–4, Solon published his laws in Homeric hexameter, and Plato, *Timaeus* 20d-21d referred to Solon's poems having been sung at artistic competitions. Plato was likely indebted to the Spartans for the idea of setting the laws to music for public recital and for the education of school children; cf. Plutarch, *Lycurgus* 4.1–2; Morrow 1993: 340.

91 For the regulated performance of songs and dances at fixed festivals, see Plato, *Laws* 7.799a-b; cf. 7.809b, 816c-d. See *Laws* 2.656c on the potential for music and dance to instill either virtue or depravity, highlighting the need for their strict regulation in order to protect the citizens, especially the young.

92 Plato, *Laws* 2.653d. Festivities were ordained by Plato as a pleasant reward to show the citizens the benefits of living a virtuous life (Plato, *Laws* 2.664b-c; 8.828d-829a). Leisure time was to be devoted to theology, sacrifice and the divine (Plato, *Laws* 7.803d-e). Plato, *Laws* 8.828a-c mandated the establishment of 365 feasts throughout the year so that the people would be constantly involved in prayers and sacrifices; cf. Pseudo-Xenophon, *Athenian Constitution* 2.9 on frequent Athenian festivals.

93 Using a pun on the word *nomos,* which could mean a law, a chant or a tune, Plato claimed that the consecration of authorized hymns was an act of legislation. See Plato, *Laws* 7.799e ("Let the strange fact be granted, we say, that our hymns are now made into *nomes*"); cf. 7.800a, which prescribed penalties for violating the sacred tunes, "just as in violation of any other *nome* (law)."

94 Plato, *Laws* 2.659e, 664a-b, 665c, 666c, 671a; 6.773d; 7.812c; 8.837e, 840b-c; 10.887d, 903b-d; 12.944b; cf. Gellrich 1994: 283; Klosko 2006: 224. Children were also entertained by the visual spectacle of public festivals, making them especially receptive to positive influences (Plato, *Laws* 10.887d).

95 Morrow 1953: 239–40. See Brisson 1998: xxviii, on the "trance-like state" induced by the communal performance of poetry and rituals.

96 Plato, *Laws* 1.645d-650b. See 1.645d-646a on wine's effects of increasing pleasure and passion and decreasing the intellect in the old, making them like children. See 2.665b-666d on Dionysian festival drinking parties for those of age fifty and over to loosen up their inhibitions, induce them to sing and speak with greater freedom and make them more suggestible. See Rinella 2010: 3–72 on the routine addition of a wide variety of psychotropic substances to wines in antiquity, including those used in *symposia* or drinking parties, and Plato's attempt to reform and adapt drinking parties for educational and political purposes.

97 Plato, *Laws* 6.771c, 773b; 7.790c, 812a; 8.841c. Plato referred to preludes as either *prooimia* or – punning on the word *muthos* – as *paramuthia* (Plato, *Laws* 6.773e; 9.880a; 10.885b; cf. Nightingale 1993a: 295; Brisson 1998: 132).

98 For the festival recitation of the laws and their preludes, see Plato, *Laws* 7.811b-812e; 9.854c; cf. Morrow 1953: 241; Welton 1996: 215; Nightingale 1999: 104. See also note 90. Morrow (1993: 43–4) noted an annual public reading at Spartan of a treatise on their laws by Dicaearchus, a student of Aristotle (Suidas, s. v. *Dicaearchus*).

99 See Plato, *Laws* 10.903a-b on enchantment via myths. For myth as the medium by which elders transmitted traditions to youth, see Plato, *Republic* 3.392a; Plato, *Protagoras* 320c; cf. Brisson 1998: 11, 62–5, 78. For the childlike pleasure induced by the recitation of myths, see Plato, *Protagoras* 320b-c; Plato, *Statesman* 268d-e; cf. Brisson 1998: 83–4, 113.

100 Plato here imitated Spartan practices; cf. Plutarch, *Lycurgus* 21.2.

101 Plato, *Laws* 2.664b-d. Plato, *Protagoras* 320b-c described both discourse *(logoi)* and myth as valid teaching tool (cf. *Phaedo* 61b; Brisson 1998: 113–15). Myths were frequently quoted or created in Plato's dialogues as a tool for easily inducing belief, whereas philosophical *logoi* transformed such beliefs into knowledge. Besides myths recited by the seniors, primarily for the benefit of the young, the elders also gave *logoi* on unspecified subjects. The noble topics of festival orations may have included recitation of eloquent ethical preludes to the laws (such as found at 5.726a-734d), panegyrics on noble figures from the past (Plato, *Laws* 2.660a, 664b; 7.801d-e; cf. Plato, *Republic* 10.607a; Plato, *Protagoras* 325d-326a) and elevated, rhetorically colored discourses on national history such as that found in Plato's *Menexenus*. According to Plato, *Charmides* 157a-c, noble words were a type of *epode* or enchantment. Prose *logoi* composed by Athenian orators were filled with persuasive rhetoric aimed at enchanting and stirring their audiences and the festival *logoi* of Plato's *Laws* were clearly intended to have such persuasive, enchanting content rather than the reasoned philosophical arguments that Plato reserved for schools of higher education.

102 For self-enchantment, see Plato, *Laws* 2.665c; 8.835e; Plato, *Phaedo* 114d; cf. Clark 2003: 144; Klosko 2006: 224.

103 Plato, *Laws* 2.659d-e, 664b-d, 665c, 666c, 671a, 672d-673a; 7.812c; 8.839b-c; 10.903a. For the notion of an approved list of myths appropriate for children to be exposed to during child-rearing *(trophos)* in nursery rhymes and mothers' songs, see Plato, *Republic* 2.377b-3.398b, especially 2.377c, 383c; Plato, *Laws* 8.839b-c; cf. Brisson 1998: 56–7. Approved myths were also selected for later schooling (explicitly at Plato, *Republic* 2.377b-3.398b). For the topics covered in a formal classroom setting, see Plato, *Laws* 7.804d, 809a-810c, 817e-818e, 819a-822c; for the selection of texts for classroom education, see Plato, *Laws* 7.810b-c, e, 811a-b, 811d-812a. For

restrictions on myths performed in songs and plays for adult audiences at festivals, see Plato, *Laws* 8.829c-e. For the recommended use of some myths known to be false but beneficial to believe, see Plato, *Republic* 3.414b-415d; Plato, *Laws* 2.663b-d; 664a; 10.886c-d.

104 For the recitation of Athenian history in a festival setting as the primary means by which Athenian citizens acquired a knowledge of their past, see Loraux 1986: 132–71; Morgan 1998: 107–8. For the idealized character of that history, see Loraux 1986: 263–327. At Plato, *Menexenus* 525a-c, Socrates commented on the enchanting power of such historical recitations on their Athenian audiences, like the euphoria that clung to initiates in the mysteries: "Every time I listen fascinated I am exalted and imagine myself to have become all at once taller and nobler . . . It is scarcely on the fourth or fifth day that I recover myself and remember that I really am here on earth, whereas till then I almost imagined myself to be living in the Islands of the Blessed – so expert are our orators."

105 According to Plato, the founding of a nation was a game of chance in which success required both careful strategy and luck. See Plato, *Laws* 12.968e-969a; cf. 3.685a; 6.769a. For a survey of play and games in Plato's *Laws,* including legislation as an "old man's game," see A. Jacobson 1999: 769–88. See Plato, *Laws* 6.769a on the "game of reason."

106 Although in this text he was only establishing a divine nation "by words" (Plato, *Laws* 3.702c-e) in a sort of a "myth" (2.664b-d; 6.752a; 7.812a) or "dream" (12.969b), Plato believed it possible for the utopian theocracy he had imagined to be implemented someday in reality (Plato, *Laws* 12.969b; cf. Plato, *Republic* 2.369c; 5.450d, 473c; 6.502a-b; 7.534d, 540d-541b). Plato's later critics accused him of constructing utopias in both *Republic* and *Laws* (Aristotle, *Politics* 2.1260a-1266a; Polybius, *Histories* 6.47.7–10; Cicero, *On the Republic* 2.21–22), but both texts claimed that the systems of government was achievable; cf. Klosko 2006: 183–91. The distinction between an as-yet unrealized, theoretical possibility (as in Plato's *Republic* and *Laws*) and an unrealizable utopia was discussed at Zuolo 2012: 39–60.

107 Cicero's book *On Laws* was essentially a Roman version of Plato's *Laws* (1.15; 2.14–16) that pictured a new Roman political system based on new persuasive laws but which conserved the revered ancient Roman religious institutions.

108 See Chapter 2, note 267.

109 See the collection of articles in Urman and Virgil 1998. The first evidence for synagogues *(proseuchai)* comes from Egypt in inscriptions dated to the reign of Ptolemy III Euergetes (246–221 BCE); cf. Griffiths 1998. In Palestine, synagogues are first known from archaeological excavations and literary references from the Roman Era. Known as the "house of assembly" *(bet kneset, sunagoge),* "house of prayer" *(bet tefilah, proseuche)* and perhaps "house of study" *(bet midrash).* The synagogue was a place of prayer (as indicated by the name) and for Torah instruction (Josephus, Apion 2.175; Philo, *Life of Moses* 2.215–16; Acts 15.21). However, van der Kooij (2007: 294) noted the lack of decisive evidence for Torah readings in Alexandrian synagogues in the third century BCE.

110 For elements of older local deities and cultic practices in the authorized religion of the biblical text and in Iron I and II archaeological remains from the territories of biblical Judah and Samaria, see Cross 1973; Smith 1990, 2001; Miller 2000; Dever 2008. In Stern 1982, it was argued that archaeological remains showed a transition from polytheism to monotheism in Judea and Samaria during the Persian Era. However, Stern's methods and conclusions were systematically challenged in the collection of articles in Frevel et al. 2014. The Elephantine papyri appear to document a Jewish acceptance of polytheism as late as ca. 400 BCE. The emergence of monotheism among the Jews

and Samaritans cannot securely be dated prior to the early Hellenistic Era and the creation of the Pentateuch.

111 See Wajdenbaum 2011: 51–62, 87–91 for Wajdenbaum's views on the influence of Plato's *Laws* on how the biblical text was written, which have many points of contacts with my reconstruction below.

112 Cf. Wajdenbaum 2011: 54: "I believe that the biblical writer read the *Laws* and followed Plato's advice: he had to rewrite myths in order for the people to accept the laws as divine."

113 Although Plato's *Laws* promised eternal fame to any legislator who followed his bold legislative plans (12.969a-b), Plato also said it was essential that the legislators contrive to portray the laws as having been observed for untold centuries (7.798a-b), a goal that would seemingly require the legislators to obscure their role to future generations. The incompatible objectives of legislative fame and anonymity was historically achieved for the Seventy of ca. 270 BCE, who were credited with the Septuagint and honored at Alexandria by subsequent generations as inspired prophets and legislators on a par with the seventy elders at Mount Sinai (Philo, *Life of Moses* 2.41–42), but in the role of translators, not authors.

114 See Deut. 4.35, 39; 6.4; 2 Sam. 7.22; 2 Kgs 19.15, 19; Ps. 86.10 on Yahweh as the "one" or only god (cf. Smith 2001: 152–3). This new elevated conception of God contrasts with Ex. 20.3 and Deut. 5.7 which, although demanding cultic exclusivity, famously acknowledged the existence of a plurality of gods.

115 Shechem: Gen. 12.7–8; 33.18–20. Bethel: Gen. 12.8; 13.3–4; 28.11–19; 35.1–3. 6–7. 9–15. Salem: Gen. 14.18–20. Hebron: Gen. 13.18. Beer-Sheba: Gen. 22.33; 26.23–25, 29. Jehovah-Jireh: Gen. 22.13–14. Mahanaim: Gen. 32.1–2.

116 Plato, *Laws* 6.759a-b. Other priesthoods were to be fulfilled by lots (6.759c) or election (12.945e-946c).

117 Priestly families whose rights were emphasized in later sources included the Zadokites of the book of Ezekiel and the Oniads of the early Hellenistic Era in Josephus and 1 and 2 Maccabees. The exact nature of the relationship of the Aaronids, Zadokites, Oniads and the courses of priestly clans listed in 2 Chronicles (which included the Hasmonean family of Jehoiarib) is a matter of ongoing scholarly debate.

118 See Chapter 3 note 365 on the correspondence between sacrificial animals listed in Leviticus and sacrificial remains found on Mount Gerizim, which appears to indicate the conservative character of priestly cultic regulations recorded in the Pentateuch as reflecting practices prior to 270 BCE.

119 See Chapter 3 note 366 on Assyrian and deported Babylonian residents in the Assyrian province of Samerina.

120 Josephus portrayed the god of the Jews as directly comparable to the supreme god described by Greek philosophers such as Pythagoras and Plato. This close similarity, Josephus claimed, proved that Plato obtained his elevated concept of God from the Jews (Apion 2.168), because Moses predated Plato by many centuries, as was universally acknowledged (2.156; cf. Chapter 1 note 10). Wajdenbaum (2011: 85–6) also saw the influence of Greek philosophy on biblical monotheism.

121 Josephus, Apion 2.167. Greek and Roman authors also commented on the elevated Jewish conception of God. Tacitus, *Histories* 5.5: "The Jews have a purely mental conception of the deity, as one in essence . . . They believe that Being to be supreme and eternal, neither capable of representation, nor of decay." Diodorus Siculus, *Library* 40.2.4: "But he [Moses] had no images whatever of the gods made for them, being of the opinion that God is not of human form; rather the Heaven that surrounds the earth is alone divine, and rules the universe." This last quote, echoed by Posidonius at Strabo, *Geography* 16.2.35, may have derived from the foundation story of the Jews found in Hecataeus of Abdera (ca. 315 BCE), which in turn drew heavily on

Plato's *Laws*. Greek philosophical thought generally rejected the anthropomorphic depictions of God found in Greek literature and civic religion.

122 For Plato's equation of God and goodness, see Menn 1992.

123 The Hebrew Bible, like Plato's *Laws*, legislated against all forms of magic such as sorcery, necromancy, magical pharmacology and spells (Ex. 22.18; Lev. 19.26, 31; 20.6–7, 27; Deut. 18.9–12).

124 Criticism of the sacrificial cult in the Prophets appeared Isa. 1.10–15; 58.3–6; Jer. 7.21–22; 8.8; Hos. 2.11; 6.6; Amos 2.8; 5.25; Mic. 6.6–8. The thesis that God rejects the offerings of the wicked also appeared at Gen. 4.7; Deut. 10.16–18; 1 Sam. 15.22–23; Prov. 15.8; Ps. 40.6; Eccl. 5.1. Plato's theological arguments against the effectiveness of prayers and sacrifices by the wicked appeared at *Republic* 2.364b-365a, 365e-366a; 3.390d-e; Plato, *Laws* 4.716b-717a; 10.885b-d, 888c, 905d-907b, 908e, 909b, 910b. See also Plato, *Euthyphro, passim,* where Socrates was said to have come into conflict with Euthyphro, an Athenian prophet and religious expert, on the nature of holiness, piety and the gods, questioning whether the gods needed the prayers and sacrifices by which Athenians sought to placate and bribe them.

125 For the Hebrew Bible as a national literature, see Josephus, Apion 1.42, 128, 154, 160, 218. For the Hebrew Bible as sacred literature, see Josephus, Apion 1.1, 54, 127, 216–17; 2.45; cf. Barclay 2007: lvii. For other nations such as the Egyptians and Babylonians with sacred texts, see Josephus, Apion 1.105, 116, 228.

126 See Carr 2005: 111–38 on the educational value of the Torah. See Carr 2005: 143–56 on the educational value of the Prophets, Psalms and other biblical texts. See van der Toorn 2007: 236–51 and the literature cited there for comparisons between libraries catalogs, school curriculums and the canon of the Hebrew Bible as collections of texts. Van der Toorn concluded that neither libraries nor school curriculums provide a compelling antecedent to the Hebrew Bible.

127 See note 47.

128 As Wajdenbaum pointed out (2011: 27, 55, 73, 165, 274–5), a similar pattern was seen in the downfall of Atlantis in Plato, *Critias* 119e-121c as divine punishment for breaking their founders' oaths to observe the laws down through time. Wajdenbaum's claim that Genesis–Kings was a unitary composition modeled on the *Critias* (2011:73), however, does not take into account clear differences between the favorable treatment of the ancestors of the Samaritans in Genesis–Joshua and their negative treatment in favor of the ancestors of the Jews in Samuel–Kings.

129 Wenham 2012: 86–8, 100–38. See especially Ps. 119, which is a celebration of the Torah's laws.

130 Ps. 44.1–3; 66.6; 68.7–8, 17; 78; 81.9–10; 105; 106; 114; 135.4–12; 136.10–22. "The plagues of Egypt are mentioned, as are the exodus, wilderness wanderings, and the conquest of Canaan, but the lawgiving is noticeable by its absence" (Wenham 2012: 98).

131 Compare the biblical concern for shaping children's character with topics found in Plato's *Laws* such as ethical training, enforced by praise or blame (see note 43), exhortations to virtue at (5.726a-734d) and the ethical advice from the lawgiver such as a parent might give children (7.822d-823a; 9.858a-859a).

132 The Song of Songs was written in a pastoral setting strongly reminiscent of the bucolic or pastoral style of poetry originated by Theocritus of Syracuse, the court poet of Ptolemy II Philadelphus in the 270s BCE. Many scholars have noted the affinities between Song of Songs and the *Idylls* of Theocritus, including subject matter, style, voice (especially with respect to the assertiveness of female sexuality) and striking instances of shared imagery. A very thorough comparison of Theocritus and Song of Songs appeared at Burton 2005: 180–205. Bloch and Bloch 1995: 24 n. 20 compared imagery at Song 1.5 and *Idylls* 10.26–27, Song 1.9 and *Idylls* 18.30–31, Song 2.15 and *Idylls* 1.48–49; 5.112–13. See Burton 2005: 180, n. 1 for earlier scholarship that

dated Song of Songs to the early Hellenistic Era based on its links with the poetry of Theocritus. A Hellenistic Era date and influence from Alexandrian poetry, especially Theocritus, is widely accepted.

133 One of the central tenets of Plato's theology, dramatized in Job, was that the righteous were happy and the wicked miserable, notwithstanding the apparent contrary evidence of empirical experience. See Plato, *Republic* 3.392a-c; *Laws* 2.661c, 662b, 663d-e; 3.660e. Note also Plato, *Republic* 3.412b-414b, which called for the testing of the Guardian class to see if they could sustain their beliefs in the face of argument, pain or grief and emotions, seemingly reflected in the testing of Job.

134 Interesting literary and thematic parallels exist between Job and the Prometheus cycle of plays by Aeschylus in the fifth century BCE. Cf. Pope 1973: xxx–xxxi. In *Prometheus Bound,* the protagonist was chained at Mount Caucasus in a situation reminiscent of Job in his distress. Conversations between Prometheus and various visitors centered on the tyranny of Zeus. Prometheus was eventually restored to freedom and favor and (it is thought) the reputation of Zeus was restored as the embodiment of justice in *Prometheus Unbound.* The resolution of Job's philosophical dilemma by the appearance of God in a storm has been compared to the *deus ex machina* of Greek tragedy, especially in the plays of Euripides. The use of dramatic devices from Euripides in the book of Job was first argued in Kallen 1918: 25–6, (*deus ex machina* and Euripides), 28 (Euripidean prologue).

135 For Jewish stage performances, compare the plays produced by Ezekiel the Tragedian, "the poet of Jewish tragedies" (Clement of Alexandria, *Miscellanies* 1.23), whose dramatization of the Exodus in a work titled *Exagoge* was preserved at Eusebius, *Preparation for the Gospels* 9.28–29. Ezekiel the Tragedian, who was manifestly familiar with Greek tragedy, is thought to have written in Alexandria, with the evidence favoring a date under Ptolemy III Euergetes in the late third century BCE (cf. R. Robertson 1983: 2.803–4).

136 The theme of aging is prominent at Eccl. 12.1–7, among other passages. Ecclesiastes appears to have interacted with Stoic and Epicurean Greek philosophy. See Bartholomew 2009: 54–8 for secondary literature and extensive discussion on possible Greek philosophical influences and Hellenistic Era date. The philosophical content of Ecclesiastes cannot be directly identified with any one of the Greek schools of philosophy, but the interaction with Greek theories of reason and natural observation seems apparent.

137 Favorable references to Gerizim and other important Samaritan locales in Genesis–Joshua were discussed in Kratz 2007; Nihan 2007.

138 The extensive poetic and rhetorical content of the Prophets needs no comment. For psalms incorporated into the Prophets, see Gerstenberger 2003: 72–89. Inspired songs attributed to Orpheus and Musaeus that the Greeks viewed as prophetic suggest that the Greeks did not draw a sharp distinction between song and prophecy. See Plato, *Phaedrus* 244e-245a, 265a, *Ion* 534c on the divine inspiration of poets, songwriters and prophets. The *chresmodoi*, whom Plato considered divinely inspired (see *Apology* 22c; *Meno* 99c; *Ion* 534c), possessed characteristics of all three.

139 The book of Proverbs appears to have included both collections of traditional wisdom literature and new compositions. Jews continued to write in this genre long into the second and first centuries BCE, as illustrated by Sirach and various wisdom texts among the Dead Sea Scrolls (the Sapiential Texts such as 4Q411–412, 4Q419,4Q425–426) and the Apocrypha (such as Testaments attributed to Abraham, Isaac, Jacob, the Twelve Patriarchs, Moses and others).

140 See P. Davies 1998: 89–151 on the various canons or sub-collections within the Hebrew Bible, including (in his terminology) the Mosaic Canon, the Prophets, the Canons of David and Solomon, the Musical Canon and the Solomon and Wisdom

Canon. One may hypothesize, on the basis of the literary program outlined in Plato's *Laws,* the separate collection and editing of these various "canons" by specialists enlisted from the educated elites of Jewish society such as poets, musicians, storytellers and so forth, who operated under government mandate subject to the oversight and approval of Jewish "legislators of the arts."

141 For a recently presented case for gradual canonization, see van der Toorn 2007: 235–6, 252–63.

142 See Plato, *Laws* 2.667e; 4.716d; 7.803c-e, 815c-d on the role of play and leisure time dedicated to the joyful worship of the gods in Plato's theocracy. Aristotle, *Politics* 7.1329a claimed that leisure time was necessary for citizens both to exercise their political duties and to cultivate the qualities of excellence. For Plato, citizens were to occupy their leisure activities in contemplating how to best live a life pleasing to the gods (Plato, *Laws* 7.803d-e).

143 Zerubavel 1985: 1–11. The astrological week of seven days used by the Greeks and Romans appears to have originated in Alexandria and came into usage only in the first century BCE according to most scholars, the major relevant literary source being Dio Cassius, *Roman History* 37.18.

144 See Chapter 3 note 352. Although a day described as the sabbath *(yom sbh)* was known to the Jews and Samaritans who resided in the military colony at Elephantine in ca. 400 BCE, it apparently did not feature the suspension of work activities, because one ostraca *(TAD* D7.16.1–5) specified that a boat carrying vegetables was to be met and off-loaded on the sabbath; cf. Porten 1969: 116.

145 According to Josephus, Ant. 12.4–6 and Apion 1.209–11, the city of Jerusalem fell to Ptolemy I Lagus without resistance during one of his campaigns through Syria in ca. 320–300 BCE because of Jewish laws against bearing arms on the sabbath. However, the major source Josephus named in both passages, namely, the historian Agatharchides of Cnidus (ca. 150 BCE), is not thought to have given accurate testimony on this episode, because his source on the campaign appears to have made no mention of the Jewish sabbath (see the extensive discussion at Bar-Kochva 2010: 280–305). A second, unnamed source on this episode (Josephus, Ant. 12.4) appears to have been Pseudo-Hecataeus (ca. 105–95 BCE), who in my opinion can be conclusively identified as Josephus' primary source for fictionalized events under Alexander and Ptolemy I in Ant. 11.297–12.10.

146 See Monoson 2000: 88–110 on the democratic character of Greek festivals, in which citizens participated in songs and in choruses for performances of plays much as they participated in juries or the assembly.

147 In ca. 400 BCE, the annual agricultural festivals of Passover and the Days of Unleavened Bread had seemingly not yet become occasions for the recitation of the foundation story of the Jewish nation *(TAD* A4.1); cf. Porten 2003: 70–2. The transformation of the sabbath day as a holy day of leisure and the biblical festivals into occasions of education and national enculturation appear to have been Pentateuchal innovations.

148 Carr (2005: 139–40) compared public readings of the Deuteronomic laws mandated at Deut. 31 with readings at pan-Hellenic recitation of Homeric poetry, and also noted the oral recitation of the scroll commanded at Josh. 1.7–8. Public readings of the law also appeared at Neh. 8.7, 9, 11, 13.

149 Cf. Carr 2005: 139, where this reading of the nation's laws was interpreted as a reenactment of the Horeb theophany.

150 Aristobulus wrote two works around 150 BCE, namely *The Letter of Aristeas* and *Commentaries on the Law of Moses.* (See Gmirkin 2006: 76–81, on the date and authorship of *The Letter of Aristeas.) The Letter of Aristeas* purported to describe circumstances surrounding the official delegation of seventy-two learned elders invited to Alexandria under Ptolemy II Philadelphus to create an exemplary text of the Jewish

laws in Greek (the Septuagint translation) for inclusion in the Great Library. In the *Commentaries on the Law of Moses,* written as a sequel to *The Letter of Aristeas,* a delegation of elders returned to Alexandria in response to an earlier invitation (*The Letter of Aristeas* 318, 321) to explain to the king the inner meaning of the Pentateuch. Aristobulus did not consider the possibility that the Pentateuch was both written and subsequently translated at Alexandria. The role of the Seventy as authors was consequently obscured, and the Pentateuch portrayed as an ancient text known to the earliest Greek writers and philosophers, including "Pythagoras, Socrates and Plato, who with great care follow [Moses] in all respects" (*Commentaries,* quoted at Eusebius, *Preparation for the Gospel* 13.13.4)).

151 Philo's writings synthesized the philosophical tenets of Middle Platonism with Jewish literature and teachings. It is interesting that Philo recorded a yearly festival at Alexandria in which the seventy elders responsible creating for the Septuagint translation of the Pentateuch were celebrated as inspired prophets and legislators on a par with the seventy elders who received the divine law at Mount Sinai (Philo, *Life Of Moses* 2.41–42). Greek "plagiarism" of Mosaic writings was asserted at Philo, *Special Laws* 4.10.61; *Who is the Heir of Divine Things?* 213–14; *Questions and Answers on Genesis* 3.5; 4.152; cf. Runia 1986: 528–9; Droge 1989: 47–8.

152 *ANF* 1.187=Justin Martyr, *First Apology* 49. Justin argued that Plato did not mention Moses out of fear of execution for impiety, like his teacher Socrates. *ANF* 1.282–83=Justin Martyr, *Against the Greeks* 25.

153 Clement, a Platonist like Philo, claimed that Plato was "aided in legislation by the books of Moses" (*ANF* 2.338=Clement of Alexandria, *Miscellanies* 1.25). Clement emphasized the antiquity of Moses (*ANF* 2.316–17, 324–25, 332=Clement of Alexandria, *Miscellanies* 1.15, 21) and claimed that the Greeks plagiarized the Jews (*ANF* 2.446, 465–76=Clement of Alexandria, *Miscellanies* 5.1, 14).

154 Eusebius noted the influence of Jewish philosophy and law on Plato's writings. Parallels with Plato's *Laws* were singled out at *Preparation for the Gospel* 12.4–5, 36–42, 47. Eusebius claimed that Plato was inspired by God as a sort of prophet to the Gentiles as part of a divine plan to prepare the Greeks to be receptive to the Christian gospel (11.1; 12.15; 13.12).

155 Like Eusebius, Augustine believed that Plato's teachings closely approximated the truth (Augustine, *City of God,* Book 8).

156 Numenius of Apamea, the second century CE Neo-Pythagorean "pagan" philosopher, famously asserted, "What is Plato but Moses writing in Attic?" (Clement of Alexandria, *Miscellanies* 1.150.4; Eusebius, *Preparation for the Gospel* 9.6).

157 Josephus alludes to Plato's *Laws* several times in his discussion of Jewish laws in Apion 2.145–295. See Barclay 2007: xxvi and literature cited there.

158 See Chapter 5 §2 on the divine legislation of Moses in the context of his activities as *oikist* of the nation within the foundation story of Exodus–Joshua. The parallels between the activities of Moses and Lycurgus of Sparta as *oikists* and legislators of their respective nations are especially striking, especially in the recounting of the Mosaic foundation story in Josephus *Antiquities of the Jews;* cf. Feldman 2005: 209–42, reprinted in Feldman 2006: 523–56. Feldman felt convinced that there was a literary relationship between the account of Moses in Josephus and the Lycurgan reforms in Plutarch's *Lycurgus,* but was unable to uncover that Josephus read or utilized Plutarch's writings or that Plutarch had read Josephus (Feldman 2006: 547–54), nor could he identify a common source behind the two authors (Feldman 2006: 554–6). Feldman did not consider the possibility that the portrait of Moses as an *oikist* and legislator along the lines of Lycurgus was not merely a late innovation by Josephus that aimed to adapt the biblical account to an audience familiar with Greek traditions, but

that the earlier biblical account of Moses was itself profoundly influenced by Greek literature.

159 The term "theocracy" that Josephus invented at Apion 2.165 is directly comparable to the term *"Nous"* by which Plato described the new form of government he had invented in *Laws*. Plato introduced *Nous* as his a novel form of government directly after briefly discussing the other traditional forms, such as democracy, oligarchy, aristocracy and monarchy (*Laws* 4.712c-e). Josephus, Apion 2.164–65 did the same before introducing the term theocracy, seemingly modeling his discourse here on Plato's *Laws,* which Josephus alludes to several times in his discussion of Jewish laws in Apion 2.145–295.

160 See also Josephus, Ant. 4.261; cf. Feldman 2006: 542–3. Plato also held that the laws should govern all aspects of life, although some of these laws, such as those regarding childrearing, were of an advisory rather than a compulsory character. Probably following the Spartan model, Plato held that citizens should follow a regimen or program that governed their actions at every hour of the day (*Laws* 7.807e). For the influence of Plato's *Laws* on the Talmud, especially on the idea of legislating every detail of life, see Hadas 1958: 11–13.

161 Feldman (2006: 545) compared Spartan and Jewish obedience to laws.

162 Compare Plato, *Laws* 1.643d-e; 2.659d-e on habituation and education in the laws as the two means of developing virtue. Compare Plato, Laws 10.887d-e on the use of enchantments, such as mothers' songs and stories that taught young children to believe in the gods and conditioned their emotions prior to the development of reason.

163 The language Josephus used recalls Plato's theology, which consisted of four propositions about the gods: (1) that the gods existed, (2) that the gods were virtuous and admirable in all respects, (3) that they cared for humanity, and (4) that the gods could not be bribed or coerced by sacrifices, prayers or magic (Plato, *Republic* 2.379a-383c; Plato, *Laws* 10.885b-907d).

164 Cf. 1 Macc. 1.11–15; 2 Macc. 4.11; Diodorus Siculus, *Library* 34/35.1.1–3; 40.3.4; Josephus, Ant. 13.247 . For biblical injunctions against intermarriage with foreigners, see Num. 25.1–9; Deut. 7.3–4; 23.3–6; against adoption of abominable foreign teachings, see Lev. 18.24–30; Deut. 12.29–31; 18.9–14; 20.18; against participation in foreign cults, see Ex. 22.20; 23.24, 32–38; Lev. 20.2–6; Deut. 6.14; 11.16; 28.14; 29.17–18; 31.16; for erasing foreign populations, see Ex. 23.23, 28; 34.11, 24; Num. 31.7–18; Deut. 7.1–32, 23–25; 20.10–17 (except for Edomites and Egyptians; cf. Deut. 23.7–8); for destroying foreign cult sites, see Ex. 23.24; Deut. 7.5, 25–26; 12.2–3.

165 Diodorus Siculus, *Library* 34/35.1.1–4; Tacitus, *Histories* 5.5; Josephus, Apion 2.89, 91–96, 121–22, 148. At Diodorus Siculus, *Library* 40.3.4 misanthropy was softened to *apanthropy.*

166 In classical antiquity, only three nations were famous for their culturally isolationist policies, namely Egypt, Sparta and Judea. Egyptian hostility to strangers, which ended during the reign of Psammetichus I (664–610 BCE) (Herodotus, *Histories* 2.152, 154; Diodorus Siculus, *Library* 1.67.9–10) was credited for preserving Egyptian religion and laws unchanged for 10,000 years (Plato, *Laws* 2.656d-657a; 7.797a-d, 799a-b; Aristotle, *Politics* 7.1329b; cf. Klosko 2006: 250). Sparta's long-lived constitution was thought to have survived for over 400 years without innovation in large part because of Spartan cultural self-isolation. For Spartan cultural self-isolation, see Herodotus, *Histories* 1.65; Plutarch, *Lycurgus* 27.6–7; Josephus, Apion 2.259–60, 273; cf. Tigerstadt 1965: 1.63; Figueira 2003: 47–8, 52–3. For Jewish cultural self-isolation, see Diodorus Siculus, *Library* 40.3.4; Tacitus, *Histories* 5.5; Josephus, Apion 2.210; cf. Feldman 1988: 207–10; Feldman 2006: 545–7.

167 For Jewish philanthropy as demonstrated by Jewish acceptance of proselytes who observed Jewish laws, see Josephus, Apion 209–10, 2.123, 261; cf. Feldman 2006: 545–7; Barclay 2007: lix, 315 n. 1038. For Jewish proselytism throughout the

Mediterranean world in Second Temple times swelling the numbers of those who identified themselves as Jews, see Sand 2009: 150–78.

168 Spartan law had strict travel restrictions and the Spartans were reported to have conducted periodic *xenelasia* or expulsions of foreigners (see generally Figueira 2003), sometimes beating them before driving them outside their borders (Aristophanes, *Birds* 1013). Such xenophobic Spartan practices were said to have been instituted by Lycurgus, their legendary lawgiver, in order to preserve their customs from corrupting foreign influences (Plutarch, *Lycurgus* 9.3–4; Plutarch, *Agis* 10.1–6; cf. Figueira 2003: 52–3). Although admired as effective in preventing the destabilizing introduction of foreign customs into the nation, Spartan implementation of laws against foreigners were also considered brutish, unsophisticated and unconducive to a positive international reputation (Plato, *Laws* 12.950a-b; Josephus, Apion 2.260; cf. Thucydides, *Peloponnesian War* 1.84.3).

169 Both the Pentateuch and later books of the Hebrew Bible envisioned a positive international reputation and the welcome reception of distinguished visitors from abroad. Theoric journeys of gentiles to Jerusalem to offer sacrifices and learn about the Torah were predicted at Isa. 2.2–3; 49.6; 60.3, 5, 11; Mic. 4.1–2; Zech. 8.22–23.

170 The phrase is first encountered in pre-Islamic poetry and in the Qur'an, where People of the Book *(Ahl al-Kitab)* and similar phrases referred to Jews and Christians collectively; cf. AlBayrak 2008. Later Jews adopted this outsider definition with pride, translating it into Hebrew as *am ha-sefer*.

171 Similar comments equally apply to the Samaritans, whose religion and literature (the Samaritan Torah) survived for 2,000 years after the destruction of the temple on Mount Gerizim in 128 BCE and Samaria in 107 BCE.

Bibliography

Albayrak, Ismail, "People of the Book in the Qur'ān," *Islamic Studies* 47 (2008): 301–25.

Annas, Julia, "Virtue and Law in Plato." Pages 71–91 in Christopher Bobonich (ed.), *Plato's Laws: A Critical Guide*. Cambridge: Cambridge University Press, 2010.

Armstrong, John M., "After the Ascent: Plato on Becoming Like God," *Oxford Studies in Ancient Philosophy* 26 (2004): 171–83.

Barclay, John M. G., *Flavius Josephus: Translation and Commentary, Volume 10: Against Apion*. Leiden: E. J. Brill, 2007.

Bar-Kochva, Bezalel, *The Image of the Jews in Greek Literature*. Berkeley: University of California Press, 2010.

Bartholomew, Craig G., *Ecclesiastes*. Baker Commentary 6 on the Old Testament Wisdom and Psalms. Grand Rapids, MI: Baker Academic, 2009.

Belfiore, Elizabeth, "'Lies Unlike the Truth': Plato on Hesiod, Theogony 27," *TAPA* 115 (1985): 47–57.

Bloch, Ariel and Chana Bloch, *The Song of Songs: A New Translation with an Introduction and Commentary*. Berkeley: University of California Press, 1995.

Brisson, Luc, *Plato the Myth-Maker*. Translated by Gerard Naddaf. Chicago: University of Chicago Press, 1998.

Burton, Joan B., "Themes of Female Desire and Self-Assertion in the Song of Songs and Hellenistic Poetry." Pages 180–205 in Anselm C. Hagedorn (ed.), *Perspectives on the Song of Songs*. Berlin: Walter de Gruyter, 2005.

Bury, R. G., *Plato: Laws*. Loeb Classic Library. 2 vols. Cambridge, MA: Harvard University Press, 1934.

Büttner, Stephan, "Inspiration and Inspired Poets in Plato's Dialogues." Pages 111–30 in Pierre Destrée and Fritz-Gregor Herrmann (eds.), *Plato and the Poets*. Leiden: E. J. Brill, 2011.

Carr, David, *Writing on the Tablets of the Heart: Origins of Scripture and Literature*. New York: Oxford, 2005.

Chase, Alston Hurd, "The Influence of Athenian Institutions on the Laws of Plato," *HSCP* 44 (1933): 131–92.

Clark, Randall Baldwin, *The Law Most Beautiful and Best: Medical Argument and Magical Rhetoric in Plato's Laws*. Plymouth, UK: Lexington Books, 2003.

Cross, Frank Moore, *Canaanite Myth and Hebrew Epic: Essays in the History of the Religion of Israel*. Cambridge, MA: Harvard University Press, 1973.

Curd, Patricia, *Anaxagoras of Clazomenae, Fragments and Testimonia: A Text and Translation with Notes and Essays*. Toronto: University of Toronto Press, 2007.

Davies, Philip R., *Scribes and Schools: The Canonization of the Hebrew Scriptures*. Louisville, KY: Westminster/John Knox Press, 1998.

Dever, William, *Did God Have a Wife? Archaeology and Folk Religion in Ancient Israel*. Grand Rapids, MI: Eerdmans, 2008.

Dillon, John, "Plato and the Golden Age," *Hermathena* 153 (1992): 21–36.

Droge, Arthur J., *Homer or Moses? Early Christian Interpretations of the History of Culture*. Hermeneutische Untersuchungen zur Theologie 26. Tübingen: Mohr, 1989.

Feldman, Louis H., "Pro-Jewish Intimations in Anti-Jewish Remarks Cited in Josephus' 'Against Apion'," *JQR* 78 (1988): 187–251.

———, "Parallel Lives of Two Lawgivers: Josephus' Moses and Plutarch's Lycurgus." Pages 209–43 in J. Edmondson, Steve Mason and James Rives (eds.), *Flavius Josephus and Flavian Rome*. Oxford: Oxford University Press, 2005.

———, *Judaism and Hellenism Reconsidered*. Leiden: E. J. Brill, 2006.

Figueira, Thomas J., "*Xenelasia* and Social Control in Classical Sparta," *CQ* 53 (2003): 44–74.

Frevel, Christian, Izak Cornelius and Katharina Pyschny (eds.), *A "Religious Revolution" in Yehûd?: The Material Culture of the Persian Period as a Test Case*. Göttingen: Vandenhoeck and Ruprecht, 2014.

Gaiser, Konrad, *Platone come Scrittore Filosofico: Saggi Sull'ermeneutica dei Dialoghi Platonici*. Naples: Bibliopolis, 1984.

Gellrich, Michelle, "Socratic Magic: Enchantment, Irony, and Persuasion in Plato's Dialogues," *Classical World* 87 (1994): 275–307.

Gerstenberger, Erhard, "Psalms in the Book of the Twelve: How Misplaced Are They?" Pages 72–89 in Paul L. Redditt and Aaron Schart (eds.), *Thematic Threads in the Book of the Twelve*. Berlin: Walter de Gruyter, 2003.

Gmirkin, Russell E., *Berossus and Genesis, Manetho and Exodus: Hellenistic Histories and the Date of the Pentateuch*. Library of the Hebrew Bible/Old Testament Studies 433. Copenhagen International Series 15. New York: T & T Clark, 2006.

Griffiths, J. Gwyn, "Egypt and the Rise of the Synagogue." Pages 3–16 in Dan Urman and Paul Virgil (eds.), *Ancient Synagogues: Historical Analysis and Archaeological Discovery*. Leiden: E. J. Brill, 1998.

Hackforth, R., "Plato's Theism," *CQ* 30 (1936): 4–9.

Hadas, Moses, "Plato in Hellenistic Fusion," *Journal of the History of Ideas* 19 (1958): 3–13.

Harvey, A. E., "The Classification of Greek Lyric Poetry," *CQ* 5 (1955): 157–75.

Hesk, Jon, *Deception and Democracy in Classical Athens*. Cambridge: Cambridge University Press, 2000.

Jacobson, Arthur J., "The Game of the Laws," *Political Theory* 27 (1999): 769–88.

Jaeger, Werner, *Paideia: The Ideals of Greek Culture*. Translated by Gilbert Highet. 3 vols. New York: Oxford University Press, 1943.

Kallen, Horace Meyer, *The Book of Job as a Greek Tragedy*. New York: Moffat, Yard and Company, 1918.

Kauffman, Charles, "The Axiological Foundations of Plato's Theory of Rhetoric." Pages 101–16 in Edward Schiappa (ed.), *Landmark Essays on Classical Greek Rhetoric*. David, CA: Hermagoras Press, 1994.

Klosko, George, *The Development of Plato's Political Theory*. Oxford: Oxford University Press, 2006.

Kooij, Arie van der, "The Septuagint of the Pentateuch and Ptolemaic Rule." Pages 289–300 in Gary N. Knoppers and Bernard M. Levinson (eds.), *Pentateuch as Torah: New Models for Understanding Its Promulgation and Acceptance*. Winona Lake, IN: Eisenbrauns, 2007.

Kratz, Reinhard G., "Temple and Torah: Reflections on the Legal Status of the Pentateuch between Elephantine and Qumran." Pages 77–104 in Gary N. Knoppers and Bernard M. Levinson (eds.), *Pentateuch as Torah: New Models for Understanding Its Promulgation and Acceptance*. Winona Lake, IN: Eisenbrauns, 2007.

Loraux, Nicole, *The Invention of Athens: The Funeral Oration in the Classical City*. Translated by Alan Sheridan. Cambridge, MA: MIT Press, 1986.

Menn, Stephen, "Aristotle and Plato on God as *Nous* and as the Good," *The Review of Metaphysics* 45 (1992): 543–73.

———, *Plato on God as Nous*. Carbondale, IL: Southern Illinois University Press, 1995.

Meyer, Susan Sauvé, "Legislation as a Tragedy: On Plato, *Laws* VII 817a-b." Pages 387–402 in Pierre Destrée and Fritz-Gregor Herrmann (eds.), *Plato and the Poets*. Mnemosune Supplements 328. Leiden: E. J. Brill, 2011.

Miller, Patrick D., *The Religion of Ancient Israel*. Louisville, KY: Westminster/John Knox Press, 2000.

Monoson, S. Sara, *Plato's Democratic Entanglements: Athenian Politics and the Practice of Philosophy*. Princeton: Princeton University Press, 2000.

Morgan, Kathryn A., "Designer History: Plato's Atlantis Story and Fourth-Century Ideology," *JHS* 118 (1998): 101–18.

Morrow, Glenn Raymond, "Plato's Conception of Persuasion," *The Philosophical Review* 62 (1953): 234–50.

———, *Plato's Cretan City: A Historical Interpretation of the Laws*. Princeton: Princeton University Press, 1993.

Nightingale, Andrea Wilson, "Writing/Reading a Sacred Text: A Literary Interpretation of Plato's *Laws*," *Classical Philology* 88 (1993a): 279–300.

———, "The Folly of Praise: Plato's Critique of Encomiastic Discourse in *Lysias* and *Symposium*," *CQ* 40 (1993b): 112–30.

———, "Plato's Lawcode in Context: Rule by Written Law in Athens and Magnesia," *CQ* 49 (1999): 100–22.

Nihan, Christophe, "The Torah between Samaria and Judah: Shechem and Gerizim in Deuteronomy and Joshua." Pages 187–224 in Gary N. Knoppers and Bernard M. Levinson (eds.), *Pentateuch as Torah: New Models for Understanding Its Promulgation and Acceptance*. Winona Lake, IN: Eisenbrauns, 2007.

Notopoulos, James A., "Plato's Epitaph," *AJP* 63 (1942): 272–93.

O'Sullivan, Lara, *The Regime of Demetrius of Phalerum in Athens, 317–307 BCE: A Philosopher in Politics*. Leiden: E. J. Brill, 2009.

Parke, H. W. and D.E.W. Wormell, *The Delphic Oracle*. 2 vols. Oxford: Blackwell, 1956.

Pope, Marvin H., *Job*. AB 15. Garden City, NY: Doubleday & Company, 1973.

Porten, Bezalel, "The Religion of the Jews of Elephantine in Light of the Hermopolis Papyri," *JNES* 28 (1969): 116–21.

———, "Elephantine and the Bible." Pages 51–84 in L. Schiffman (ed.), *Semitic Papyrology in Context: A Climate of Creativity: Papers from a New York University Conference Marking the Retirement of Baruch A. Levine*. Culture and History of the Ancient Near East 14. Leiden: E. J. Brill, 2003.

Rinella, Michael A., *Pharmakon: Plato, Drug Culture, and Identity in Ancient Athens*. New York: Lexington Books, 2010.

Robertson, R. G., "Ezekiel the Tragedian," *OTP* 2 (1983): 803–19.

Romilly, Jacqueline de, *Magic and Rhetoric in Ancient Greece*. Cambridge, MA: Harvard University Press, 1975.

Roundtree, Clarke, "The (Almost) Blameless Genre of Classical Greek Epideictic," *Rhetorica: A Journal of the History of Rhetoric* 19 (2001): 293–305.

Runia, David T., *Philo of Alexandria and the Timaeus of Plato*. Leiden: E. J. Brill, 1986.

Sand, Shlomo, *The Invention of the Jewish People*. Translated by Yael Lotan. New York: Verso Press, 2009.

Smith, Mark S., *The Early History of God: Yahweh and the Other Deities in Ancient Israel*. Grand Rapids, MI: Eerdmans, 1990.

———, *The Origins of Biblical Monotheism: Israel's Polytheistic Background and the Ugaritic Texts*. Oxford: Oxford University Press, 2001.

Solmsen, Friedrich, *Plato's Theology*. Cornell Studies in Classical Theology 27. Ithaca: Cornell University Press, 1942.

Stern, Ephraim, *Material Culture of the Land of the Bible in the Persian Period 538–332 BC*. Jerusalem: Israel Exploration Society, 1982.

Tigerstadt, E. N., *The Legend of Sparta in Classical Antiquity*. 3 vols. Stockholm: Almquist & Wiksell, 1965, 1974, 1978.

Toorn, Karel van der, *Scribal Culture and the Making of the Hebrew Bible*. Cambridge: Harvard University Press, 2007.

Ullman, B. L., "History and Tragedy," *TAPhA* 73 (1942): 25–53.

Urman, Dan and Paul Virgil (eds.), *Ancient Synagogues: Historical Analysis and Archaeological Discovery*. Leiden: E. J. Brill, 1998.

Wajdenbaum, Philippe, *Argonauts of the Desert: Structural Analysis of the Hebrew Bible*. London: Equinox Publishing, 2011.

Walbank, F. W., "History and Tragedy," *Historia* 9 (1960): 216–34.

Watts, James M., *Reading Law: The Rhetorical Shaping of the Pentateuch*. Sheffield: Sheffield Academic Press, 1999.

Welton, William A., "Incantations and Expectations in 'Laws' II," *Philosophy and Rhetoric* 29 (1996): 211–24.

Wenham, Gordon J., *Psalms as Torah: Reading Biblical Song Ethically*. Grand Rapids, MI: Baker Academic, 2012.

Zerubavel, Eviatar, *The Seven Day Circle: The History and Meaning of the Week*. Chicago: University of Chicago Press, 1985.

Zuolo, Federico, "Plato's Political Idealism and Utopia in the *Republic*, the *Laws* and the *Timaeus-Critias*." Pages 39–60 in Francisco L. Lisi (ed.), *Utopia, Ancient and Modern: Contributions to the History of a Political Dream*. Contributions to Classical Political Thought, 6. Sankt Augustin: Academia Verlag, 2012.

INDEX OF REFERENCES

INDEX OF AUTHORS

334

For Product Safety Concerns and Information please contact our EU
representative GPSR@taylorandfrancis.com
Taylor & Francis Verlag GmbH, Kaufingerstraße 24, 80331 München, Germany